IN WAR'S
DARK SHADOW

In War's Dark Shadow

The Russians Before the Great War

W. BRUCE LINCOLN

THE DIAL PRESS

NEW YORK

Published by
The Dial Press
1 Dag Hammarskjold Plaza
New York, New York 10017

Design by Paul Chevannes

Library of Congress Cataloging in Publication Data

Lincoln, W. Bruce.
In war's dark shadow.

Bibliography: p. 513
Includes index.
1. Soviet Union—History—Alexander III, 1881–1894.
2. Soviet Union—History—Nicholas II, 1894–1917.
3. Soviet Union—History—Revolution, 1917–1921—Causes.
I. Title.
DK240.L56 1983   947'.08   82–22152
ISBN 0–385–27409–2

For Pat

Contents

Foreword/*ix*

Acknowledgments/*xiii*

CHAPTER I.   1891: The Fateful Year/*3*

CHAPTER II.   In the Wake of Famine/*35*

CHAPTER III.   Russia's New Lords/*69*

CHAPTER IV.   Life in the Lower Depths/*103*

CHAPTER V.   The Few Who Dared/*135*

CHAPTER VI.   Defenders of the Old Order/*191*

CHAPTER VII.   "A Small Victorious War"/*227*

CHAPTER VIII.   1905: The Year of Turmoil/*273*

CHAPTER IX.   "What *We* Want Is a *Great Russia*!"/*313*

CHAPTER X.   "The Children of Russia's Dreadful
                Years"/*349*

CHAPTER XI.   The Last Days of Peace/*389*

CHAPTER XII.   The Drums of War/*421*

                Afterword/*439*

                Notes/*445*

                Works Cited/*513*

                Index/*543*

Foreword

THIS IS THE STORY OF THE RUSSIANS AS THEY ENTERED THE twentieth century. Within the all too finite limits of a single volume, it is an effort to explore the lives, thoughts, hopes, and dreams of the men and women who lived in the world's largest empire and to convey some sense of the tensions that tore at the fabric of their society on the eve of the Great War and the Revolution of 1917. Such an exploration will take us into remote areas of Russian life that remain virtually unknown in the West to all but those specialists who read and speak Russian. We shall have to recast a number of long-standing images that derive from that flood of widely read and too often believed reminiscences written by men and women who fled the Revolution, and we shall have to ask questions that sometimes are not even addressed in their accounts of life in their former homeland. What was it like to be a peasant in a land where almost every second person faced hunger each year? What was it like to be a factory worker? Or an industrialist? What was it like to be a Jew in a society that was the most anti-Semitic of any in modern times before the rise of Nazi Germany? And, what was it like to be a revolutionary at a time when any hope for revolution seemed utterly dim, and the passing years brought only failure? At the other end of the political spectrum, what was it like to be an aristocrat as the old order entered its final twilight? For there were a surprising number in Russia who, like Madame Ranevskaia in Chekhov's *Cherry Orchard*, stood helplessly by while the axes of upstarts felled the long-standing trees of tradition.

In War's Dark Shadow begins in the reign of Alexander III, when the Russian Empire was very backward in comparison with the West. The pace of life still moved at the speed of a horse-drawn cart at a time when railroads had tied the Western world together as never before. San Francisco stood less than a week's journey from New York, and Chicago scarcely a day's travel from New Orleans, but it still took many months to traverse the length or breadth of the Russian Empire. Only a tiny fraction of Russians lived in cities in those days, and most of the Tsar's subjects still lived in villages remote from the world of machines and technology that their nation was about to enter. To catch up with the West, Russia had to telescope her Industrial Revolution into about a third of the time it had taken in France or England. Great changes thus came at a dizzying pace upon people who were sadly unprepared to face them. Already unsure of their course, their steps became still more uncertain.

Even before August 1914, many thoughtful Russians were consumed by a sense of doom that made their lives very different from those lived by Frenchmen, Germans, Austrians, Englishmen, or, especially, Americans of the same era. To a great extent their forebodings were justified, for only one out of three of the men and women who heard Nicholas II declare war against Germany and Austria in 1914 would be alive or living in Russia half a decade later when Lenin announced the Bolsheviks' final victory.

Once the Great War came, Russia thus suffered more than any other nation. The reasons for that lay in the missed opportunities, miscalculations, and outright failures that had crowded into the twenty-five years before the war's coming. *In War's Dark Shadow,* finally, is the tale of those years.

The spelling of names in this volume may appear somewhat unfamiliar to readers who are accustomed to reading books that employ English counterparts for Russian names (Peter, Paul, Mary, Alexandra, Catherine, etc.) rather than proper transliterations such as Petr, Pavel, Maria, Aleksandra, and Ekaterina. Still, this is a book about Russia and the Russians, not one about England or the United States, and I therefore have avoided Anglicizing most Russian proper names. Readers should remember that the feminine form of family names in Russian usually ends in "a" or "aia," while the masculine form does not. Therefore, while Lenin's real last name was Ulianov, his sister's was Ulianova.

Generally, I have used Russian transliterations for all but the names of Emperors and such familiar places as Moscow and St. Petersburg (not Moskva and Sankt Peterburg), and a handful of people especially well known to Western readers. Therefore, such names as Diaghilev and Chaliapin appear as they have on countless opera and ballet programs during the past eighty years, not as Diagilev and Shaliapin, as they would if they were transliterated directly from the Russian.

All this being said, I confess to violating these principles on several occasions where there seemed good reason to do so. I have eliminated the Russian hard and soft signs from my transliterations (they are preserved for purists in the notes and the list of works cited, however). Thus, the name of the well-known late-nineteenth-century philosopher appears as Solovev, not Solov'ev. Further, I have

Anglicized the names of Russian Emperors but have preserved the Russian forms for the names of their wives. Readers thus will encounter the Empresses Aleksandra and Maria, not Alexandra and Mary. Finally, where transliterations have produced repeated vowels in the middle of a first name, I have eliminated them, with the result that the wife of Alexander III, for example, appears as Maria (not Mariia) Feodorovna. In the case of patronymics, however, such repetitions of vowels have been preserved since they are necessary for better pronunciation.

In the matter of dates, I again admit to a certain amount of caprice in an effort to balance clarity against historical precision. For events occurring in Russia, I have used the Julian calendar, in use in Russia from 1699 until 1918, while I have dated all Western European events according to the more modern Gregorian calendar that has long been used throughout Europe. Readers should remind themselves that, during the nineteenth century, the Julian (old style) calendar was twelve days behind the Gregorian (new style) one and remember that the gap widened by an additional day when the twentieth century began. I have broken the rule of Julian dates for Russian and Gregorian dates for Europe in the last chapter of this volume, however, in an effort to avoid adding further confusion to the complex events leading up to the outbreak of the Great War. Although historically more precise, it would not have added clarity to readers' understanding of the war's beginnings to be told that, on August 1, 1914, the Kaiser instructed his ambassador, Count Pourtalès, to declare war on Russia and that Pourtalès hastened to do so six hours later on July 19! In those few cases where it was necessary to mention both Gregorian and Julian dates, they are indicated as "o.s." (old style) and "n.s." (new style), or separated by a slash, as in July 19/August 1, 1914.

W. Bruce Lincoln
Sycamore, Illinois
Easter 1982

Acknowledgments

I AM INDEBTED TO MANY PEOPLE IN THIS COUNTRY AND IN THE Soviet Union, whose encouragement and support have helped me to write this book. To my good fortune, their names make a very long list and, for that and other obvious reasons, I cannot include them all here. Still, I must thank, at the very least, Stephen Cohen (Princeton University), Lee Congdon (James Madison University), Ralph Fisher (University of Illinois), Leopold Haimson (Columbia University), Daniel Orlovsky (Southern Methodist University), Alexander

Rabinowitch (Indiana University), Marc Raeff (Columbia University), Charles Timberlake (University of Missouri), Richard Wortman (Princeton University), and Petr Andreevich Zaionchkovskii (Moscow State University) for their counsel, encouragement, and support. With an infallible sense of good timing, Helen Barrett and Robert Gottlieb provided the proper measures of enthusiasm, reassurance, and encouragement whenever I felt overburdened by the tasks of research, writing, and rewriting, and Joyce Johnson at The Dial Press has continued her invaluable service as an editor par excellence.

Here at Northern Illinois University, it is more than a pleasant formality to express my gratitude to a number of friends and colleagues. George Gutsche, my colleague in Russian literature, has been a source of wise counsel and good humor, both of which I have appreciated more than probably was apparent on some occasions. Carroll Moody, my department chairman, has been generous in his efforts to juggle teaching schedules and other assignments in order to give me the time I needed to write. I am also indebted to James Norris, William Monat, Jon Miller, John LaTourette, and Dean Jaros, an unusual group of senior administrators here, who have supported my work on this book in a number of important ways. Finally, more than ritualistic thanks are due to Mary Livingston, Director of Northern Illinois University Press. An able editor who combines acute critical judgment with a rare generosity of spirit, she has offered many helpful comments about a manuscript destined from its beginning to be published elsewhere.

My wife Pat deserves a special paragraph of thanks in any acknowledgment of the help I have received in writing this book. Her good humor and good sense, not to mention her ability to put up with my persistent quirks and her willingness to read and reread the chapters that comprise this volume, have helped more than I can express here.

In times such as these, it is the rare scholar who enjoys the private means to pursue research halfway around the globe and at many points in between. I could not have done so had it not been for the generosity of foundations and research agencies. Thus, I am more than grateful when I mention the following, who have helped me to continue my research over the course of the past decade:

—The Academy of Sciences of the Soviet Union, Moscow and Leningrad, U.S.S.R.

—The American Council of Learned Societies, New York, New York

—The Fulbright-Hays Faculty Research Abroad Program, U. S. Department of Education, Washington, D. C.

—The Historical Institute, Warsaw University, Warsaw, Poland

—The Institute of History, Leningrad State University, Leningrad, U.S.S.R.

—The Institute of History, Moscow State University, Moscow, U.S.S.R.

—The International Research and Exchanges Board, New York, New York

—The John Simon Guggenheim Memorial Foundation, New York, New York

—The National Endowment for the Humanities, Washington, D. C.

—Northern Illinois University, DeKalb, Illinois

—The Russian and East European Center, University of Illinois at Urbana-Champaign, Urbana, Illinois

—The Russian Institute, Columbia University, New York, New York

Yet, even with the support of family, colleagues, and generous research foundations, a scholar cannot finish his work unless libraries and archives open their resources to him. In this respect, I have been more than fortunate. Archivists and librarians in the Soviet Union, Poland, England, and the United States have been generous in their help, and they remain the unsung heroes in the research saga that lies behind *In War's Dark Shadow*. Finally, I must acknowledge still

ACKNOWLEDGMENTS

a further debt to Rebecca Atack, Marianna Choldin, Laurence Miller, and June Pachuta, the stalwart keepers of a Slavic collection that now numbers more than a half-million volumes at the University of Illinois Library. For the dedication with which they have met my sometimes outrageous requests for assistance, I am especially grateful. Often on inexcusably short notice, they have obtained microfilms of rare Russian materials from almost every corner of the globe and have ferreted out priceless volumes from the most unlikely places. To them, and to many others in the United States, England, Poland, and the Soviet Union, I owe a special debt that formal thanks such as these cannot begin to repay.

IN WAR'S
DARK SHADOW

CHAPTER I
1891: The Fateful Year

Saturday, July 13, 1891, dawned warm and clear in St. Petersburg. It promised to be one of those brilliant, cloudless days that sometimes adorn Russia's great northern capital during the brief weeks around the summer solstice, when the magic of the famous "White Nights" floods the city with an aura that washes away the damp grayness that pervades it for so much of the year. At such times, Dostoevskii once wrote, St. Petersburg called to mind a young woman grown faded and worn before her time, "who sud-

3

denly and unexpectedly, in the space of a single brief instant, becomes inexplicably and marvelously beautiful."[1] These summer days stirred Petersburgers to the depths of their souls, warmed their bodies, and renewed their resolve to face the inevitable rigors of another harsh winter.

The sense of anticipation that gripped Russia's capital on this particular Saturday stemmed from more than just the promise of rare fine weather. Less than two days before, Admiral Gervais, commander of France's Baltic squadron, had sailed his flagship, the *Marengo*, into the harbor at the nearby Russian naval bastion of Kronstadt. "A fine French squadron has anchored off Kronstadt," St. Petersburg's leading daily had announced to its readers on Thursday evening. "Beginning tomorrow, they will be our guests and we must endeavor to give them the warmest of all possible welcomes."[2] For the first time in almost a century, French ships of war had come to Russia on a mission of peace. The implications of that event were immense, the prospects for the future of European diplomacy awesome, for the mere fact of Gervais's arrival proclaimed Russia's willingness to turn away from more than seven decades of rock-solid alliance with Central Europe's conservative monarchies.

Excitement gripped the city as the Emperor Alexander III, his councillors, the lords and ladies of the Court, and the city's lesser dignitaries prepared to welcome the emissaries of the revolutionary and republican order that all Romanovs had feared since the Paris mob had stormed the Bastille. The mayor of St. Petersburg proclaimed that Gervais's planned stay promised to be "far too brief" and vowed that his city and its citizens would welcome its guests "with arms flung wide."[3] For their part, the French proposed to do no less than their Russian hosts. Gervais's flotilla, one commentator wittily remarked, carried "an inexhaustible supply of bottles and casks" with which the Admiral intended to launch "such a cannonade of champagne corks against the walls of the Russian fortress that the hearts of the Russians, already half-open, must inevitably capitulate."[4] In the words of Paul de Laboulaye, France's retiring ambassador to St. Petersburg, the emissaries were determined to express "the profound respect which the entire French nation feels for His Majesty the Emperor Alexander III."[5] Within hours after the *Marengo* dropped anchor, Laboulaye entertained Grand Duke Aleksei Aleksandrovich, the Chief of Russia's Admiralty, along with his senior officers at a lavish banquet at France's newly acquired embassy, the Pashkov Palace.[6]

Ambassador Laboulaye's banquet was but a modest prelude to Saturday's grand events. Early that morning, the Imperial yacht *Tsarevna*, her blue hull shining brightly in the early morning sun, set sail from Peterhof, the Romanovs' great summer palace that lay across the gulf from Kronstadt. Alexander III, his Empress Maria Feodorovna, their children, the Empire's senior Grand Dukes, and a number of Russia's greatest lords and ladies stood proudly at the yacht's rail watching the French squadron come into view as the *Tsarevna* approached the foreboding dark stone mass of Kronstadt's fortifications. Some twenty Russian warships fired salvos in greeting at their approach. From the *Marengo*'s deck, Laboulaye saw the smoke from the ships' cannon rise in small puffs and quickly break apart. He remembered that it imparted a fairy-tale-like quality to the scene. The sound of the Russian guns had barely died away when Gervais's flagship shuddered from her own 101-gun salute to the approaching Autocrat of All the Russias and his suite. Within minutes after the *Tsarevna* drew alongside, Russia's towering and broad-shouldered Emperor, his brothers Aleksei and Vladimir, and his uncle Mikhail led the Imperial party aboard while the *Marengo*'s band played "Sambre-et-Meuse." Although rarely given to any display of emotion, Alexander found this greeting especially moving and asked that copies of the French military march be sent to the Russian Admiralty so that it could be played at other naval ceremonies.[7]

For several hours, the Imperial visitors inspected the *Marengo* and her sister ships, admired the modern technology incorporated into their design, and praised their armaments. Alexander then entertained Gervais and his senior officers aboard the *Derzhava*, where he toasted France's President Carnot and stood bareheaded while a Russian band played the "Marseillaise." "The figure of Alexander III standing at attention while the 'Marseillaise' was

5

played," wrote one historian, "will remain as symbolic in the annals of history as the words of Henri IV that 'Paris is well worth a Mass.' "[8] It was indeed an event without precedent. Never before had the anthem of revolution been played publicly in Russia. Never had anyone expected to see the most conservative of all nineteenth-century Romanovs stand with head bared from the moment its first stirring note was struck until its last chord resounded; even the French did not customarily pay their anthem so high a tribute.[9] To the delight of the French, the scene was repeated on several occasions as Gervais, his officers, and their crews were treated to enthusiastic receptions wherever they appeared.[10] Count Vladimir Lamsdorf, one of Foreign Minister Giers's closest associates, reported that the ritual became so popular that those Petersburgers who knew French only slightly began to call for the "Mitrailleuse" at public gatherings (confusing the French term for the machine guns that their Tsar's officers would use less than two decades later to disperse revolutionary crowds with the name of France's national anthem).[11] From beginning to end, it was a memorable fortnight. Even a Belgian diplomat's caustic remark that, had the Russian authorities permitted it, a Chinese squadron probably would have received an equally enthusiastic reception could not obscure the very obvious fact that European affairs had taken a momentous turn.[12] "One handshake between Tsar and Admiral," a French publicist later rejoiced, "restored the equilibrium of Europe" that had been put into jeopardy by the rise of a united Germany some two decades before.[13]

Such dramatic shifts in the affairs of modern states are never spontaneously conceived, and the new entente between France and Russia that began to emerge in the summer of 1891 was no exception. During the early days of his reign, Alexander III had taken few pains to conceal his convictions that France harbored "nothing but atheists and radicals"[14] and made no secret of his dislike for the diplomats and politicians of the Third Republic. Nonetheless, because his superiors at the Elysée Palace continued to seek a counterbalance to the threat they perceived in the awesome industrial and military might of Wilhelmian Germany, Laboulaye attempted to foster closer ties with Russia from the moment he took up his duties in St. Petersburg in the fall of 1886. He found powerful allies to speak on his behalf, and he used them well. The ardently nationalistic and deeply conservative Mikhail Katkov, who edited one of Russia's best-known newspapers, was one of his allies, and so was Konstantin Pobedonostsev, the Emperor's former tutor and trusted confidant.[15] Both had come to fear Germany's growing power almost as much as did the French, but their best efforts were slow to move Alexander, whose thoughts seemed to shift as ponderously as his great physical bulk. Slow to change his opinions, the Tsar was even slower to alter his loyalties. For a decade, he had held Russia to her traditional diplomatic course of alliance with Germany, the nation in Europe whose political principles seemed to coincide most closely with his own.[16]

But Alexander's dedication to an alliance with Germany was not shared by the men who rose to direct that nation's destiny after the great Bismarck left office. The men who took his place in the Foreign Office on Berlin's Wilhelmstrasse were confident that the Iron Chancellor's fears of a Franco-Russian alliance that might one day pose the fearsome specter of a two-front war for their nation were merely the worryings of an old man grown timorous with age. They insisted that greater simplicity and clarity of vision were needed if Germany was to escape an alliance system that had become far too complex and to gain the power to which her great industrial resources entitled her. Their nation's true destiny, they asserted, thus lay in close alliance with Austria and Italy at Russia's expense. There must be an end to what one of them called Bismarck's shameful policy of "groveling before Russia." Autocratic Russia had so little in common with the other states of Europe that she had little choice but to accept whatever crumbs Germany offered.[17]

This fateful combination of German arrogance and German miscalculation began to drive Alexander into the arms of France. Within two years of Kaiser Wilhelm II's accession in late 1888, Germany's impetuous and often ill-advised young ruler forced Bismarck into retirement and hastened to tie his nation's course more closely than ever to the declining fortunes of the Austrian Habsburgs. Convinced that the Tsar's contempt for republican principles would keep Russia from an alliance with France under almost any circumstances and anxious to prove himself the equal of even the most stalwart of autocrats, Germany's new Kaiser abandoned a number of diplomatic instruments that the wiser Bismarck had thought vital to his nation's defense. Especially at the urging of Friedrich von Holstein, whom diplomats at the Wilhelmstrasse called "the man with the hyena eyes,"[18] Wilhelm decided not to renew his empire's Reinsurance Treaty with Russia when it expired in the summer of 1890, thereby withdrawing Bismarck's guarantee that Russia would never have to face the combined armies of the Central Powers should her growing conflicts with Austria in the Balkans lead to war. Then, after renewing the Triple Alliance with Austria and Italy in June 1891, he announced the news by first telling the president of the German steamship company on whose ship he was sailing that weekend rather than informing the Russians through the appropriate diplomatic or private channels of an act they would regard as a grave threat to their nation's security.[19]

Alexander III could not bear such haughty affronts nor tolerate such contempt for Russia's interests for very long. He and his Foreign Minister Nikolai Giers continued to send warning signals to the Wilhelmstrasse throughout 1891 and 1892, but the Kaiser and his advisers refused to take seriously the *entente cordiale* that had begun to take shape at Kronstadt. In the words of Wilhelm's Secretary of State for Foreign Affairs Marschall von Bieberstein, it was a *"joujou"* —a mere bauble—and, even a decade later, Germany's newly appointed Chancellor Prince Bernhard von Bülow continued to insist that the interests of France and Russia were too divergent for even their military alliance to cause Germany serious concern.[20] Therefore, although Germany had no vital interests in the Balkans region, Wilhelm steadfastly and arrogantly continued to refuse Russia any assurance that he would not join with Austria should the Balkan conflicts between the Habsburgs and the Romanovs lead to war. At the same time, the French continued to press Alexander for a more substantial commitment to a mutual pact against the Central Powers.[21] Eventually he gave it, first in the form of a military convention signed between the Chief of Russia's General Staff, General Nikolai Obruchev, and the French General Boisdeffre in August 1892, and then by giving his personal and formal assent to their agreement on December 17, 1893.[22] For the first time since Alexander I had signed the Treaty of Tilsit with Napoleon in 1807, Russia was a military ally of France. In taking that step, Alexander III launched the diplomatic realignments in Europe that paved the way for the First World War.

From that moment, the French became entranced by a vision of what they called the "Russian steamroller"—waves of tsarist infantry that numbered in the millions—advancing westward across the fields and marshes of Poland and East Prussia into the heart of the Kaiser's domains. By 1914, they and the Russians had deluded themselves into the belief that the "Russian steamroller" was a weapon with which they could overwhelm Wilhelmian Germany. They could not have been more tragically mistaken. The overall effect of events that occurred in the fateful year 1891 and during the next two decades made it certain that their vision was hopelessly, fatally flawed.

If Alexander's turn toward France in the summer of 1891 altered Russia's relations with the West, his nation's policies in the Far East experienced an equally momentous shift. Like the Soviet Union today, far more of Alexander's domains lay in Asia than in Europe. Beginning at the ancient and much-eroded Ural Mountains, the source of the iron from which the Romanovs had cast their armies' weapons since the time of Peter the Great, the vast expanses of Asiatic Russia stretched to the Pacific Ocean and the Bering Strait, a distance greater than that which separates Chicago from London. Westerners of that era found it all but impossible to comprehend the vastness of the region in comparison with the world they knew because cartographers always had drawn it on such a reduced scale. To gain a clearer notion of its amazing expanse, the American scholar-journalist George Kennan told his readers in 1891, they should envision the region drawn to the scale used in England's famous Ordinance Survey maps, an undertaking that would require a sheet of paper nearly a half-mile in width. If opened, Kennan pointed out, such an imaginary atlas would cover the entire tip of Manhattan from Wall Street to the Battery.[23] So long and arduous was the journey across these Asiatic wilds, according to one often-repeated tale, that each of the six carefully chosen virgins who set out from Kamchatka to attend the coronation of the Empress Elizabeth in the 1740s gave birth twice to children fathered by their lusty Cossack escorts before they reached Moscow.[24]

Loosely termed Siberia, the region had been a rich source of furs even before the days of the first Romanovs, when intrepid trappers and hunters had pushed ever eastward toward the Pacific. Above all, the trappers had sought the elusive ermine and sable whose pelts could bring nearly their weight in gold in the capitals of Europe, but their greed for more common furs so depleted the population of lynx, fox, marten, and otter that the center of Russia's pelt-gathering activity was driven more than a thousand miles eastward in the brief span of twenty-five years, during the reign of Tsar Mikhail Feodorovich in the early seventeenth century.[25]

Furs were only the first of Siberia's vast store of natural treasures to be discovered by the Russians. Diamonds, rubies, and emeralds of great size and quantity were unearthed there, as were great veins of malachite, a semiprecious stone of rich, deep green hue in which jet black swirls formed fanciful designs. In Europe, malachite was used to create jewelry and small, elegant caskets. Wealthy Russians used it more lavishly to adorn the tops of gilded tables, chests, and desks, and from it the Romanovs' architects created huge columns of immense value to grace the interiors of the Winter Palace and St. Isaac's Cathedral. Yet malachite—and even diamonds, rubies, and emeralds—comprised only a small fraction of Siberia's total wealth. The region's mines yielded over a million ounces of gold each year and many times that quantity of silver. At one point, Siberian platinum seemed so plentiful that Nicholas I experimented with using it for coins in place of gold.

Amazingly, these great quantities of precious metals were extracted by the most primitive and wasteful means imaginable.

George Kennan was amazed at the inefficiency of the mines he saw in Siberia during the 1880s and reported that they could be made to produce far more than they did if only American ingenuity and know-how could be applied. He was equally amazed to find some two thousand tons of lead, a by-product of the silver smelting process, cast aside as waste at one of the many silver mines at Nerchinsk. The cost of shipping the lead would have been inordinate, in the absence of railroads.[26]

At the time of Kennan's journey, Russians were only beginning to become aware that Siberia also held locked in the permafrost beneath its surface vast hoards of other vital natural resources; even in 1900, the authors of the official *Guide to the Great Siberian Railway* candidly confessed that "the greater part of Siberia's mineral wealth is as yet lying waste, and is scarcely even known."[27] Iron, coal, zinc, manganese, copper, lead, chrome, oil, and natural gas headed a list that grew as each decade brought new explorations and new discoveries. Many of these mineral deposits could not be exploited until well into the twentieth century, but the mere fact of their discovery proclaimed to the world that Russia had within her borders the greatest treasure trove of natural resources on the face of the earth.

As if regretting her generosity in favoring Siberia with such vast stores of mineral wealth, Nature had endowed her with one of the harshest climates to be found anywhere on the globe's surface. During the long winter months, the winds rose to gale force, the thermometer fell below minus fifty degrees, and the snowfall could be measured in yards. Much of Siberia lay in latitudes well to the north of New York and Chicago, and great portions of its subsoil remained permanently frozen. The entire continental United States could be placed into its center, never once touch its boundaries at any point, and still have 2.4 million square miles of space left over. Yet, in 1891, the city of Chicago boasted a greater population than did all of Siberia. When Alexander III had mounted the throne a decade before, there was not a single city in the entire region that could claim fifty thousand dwellers, and most of its land was uninhabited. Aside from its diamonds, emeralds, gold, silver, and platinum, all mined by convict labor, Siberia thus was rich only in potential when the first rails of the Trans-Siberian Railway were laid. As a sparsely settled wilderness of well over five million square miles, it continued to stand as a vast and inhospitable natural barrier between European Russia and the Pacific, the only coastline in the entire Empire that did not abut seas that were landlocked, nearly closed by narrow straits guarded by hostile nations, or frozen during much of the year.[28]

The problem and promise of Siberia posed complex dilemmas for Alexander III and his advisers. How could the region's natural wealth be tapped and its nearly endless expanses of wilderness traversed? How could the region be endowed with sufficient population to unlock its mineral wealth and unleash its incalculable stores of energy when the brutality of its winters and the brevity of its summers made it almost certain that native farmers could not hope to feed any significant increase in the region's nonrural population? In 1891, Alexander took the step that promised to resolve these dilemmas and, at the same time, gave a dramatic impetus to Russian expansion into the Far East. "This [is a] truly national task that I have undertaken," he wrote on March 17. That day, he signed the Imperial decree that announced the beginning of "the construction of a continuous railroad line across the whole of Siberia."[29]

The construction of the Trans-Siberian Railway was an undertaking whose dimensions exceeded any that modern man had yet attempted. More than a hundred tunnels, some as much as two miles in length, had to be hewn through solid rock. Men had to build countless bridges over rivers wider, deeper, and more violent than any known in the United States or Europe. They had to work in temperatures that fell to such extremes that laborers grew numb and fell from the scaffolding to certain death. Millions of trees had to be felled, and billions of cubic feet of earth transported, to hew a track through some five thousand miles of near-virgin wilderness. In all, the task demanded the labor of tens of thousands of men for more than a decade. Between 1891 and 1904, an average of thirty-five thousand workmen were needed every year, and sometimes the demand rose to twice that number. Siberia itself could supply only about one-quarter of this work force, and Russian officials and government contractors therefore had to draw upon many and diverse sources of manpower. In any given year, convicts and exiles made up over a third of the railroad's labor force. Almost one out of every five workers came from abroad. Some were recruited in Europe, especially in Italy, but, like the railroad construction gangs in the western United States, many were brought in from China. The rest, including most of the skilled workers, came from European Russia.[30]

Regardless of their origins, workmen on the Trans-Siberian Railway labored long hours under cruel conditions. Seventeen-hour days were commonplace during those summer months when the sun hardly slipped below the horizon, and there were some reports of construction gangs who wielded picks and shovels for twenty hours at a single stretch. Such backbreaking labor consumed well in excess of four thousand calories in a day, but most workers had far less than that to eat. One newspaper account written not long after work on the railroad began reported that many workers were fed with "putrid meat and bread that was so badly spoiled that even the local pigs would not eat it!" Another reporter wrote that "when the workers saw what went into their daily *shchi* [a sort of cabbage soup], they could not eat despite their hunger." Nor were such accounts simply naïve statements by reporters unaccustomed to the rough and primitive manner in which Russia's masses generally lived. "The food's so bad, you guys, that it makes you want to puke right off," one laborer was heard to tell some newcomers. "No kidding! While two-thirds of our men are eating, the rest are around the corner puking all over the place."[31] Such wretched rations cost these men almost a quarter of their daily pay, yet it barely sustained them in the heavy labor required to fell trees, move earth, lay track, build bridges, and dig tunnels. "This ain't construction," one group of workers lamented. "It's a struggle, a war to the death."[32]

Almost none of these laborers could hope for medical aid if they were sick or injured. On the average, there was one clinic bed for about every thousand workers. Along one seven-hundred-mile stretch of railroad, there were only two aid stations with in-patient facilities for eighty. In the region east of Lake Baikal, some thirty thousand workers, service personnel, and dependents had to share less than a hundred hospital beds, and, farther east, there were hundreds of miles that had no medical facilities at all. For more than a decade, tens of thousands of men bent their backs to the heaviest of labors, while they ate the poorest food and lived under the most primitive conditions, to lay mile after mile of track over some of the roughest, most tortuous terrain on the face of the earth.[33]

Once the Trans-Siberian was completed, cynical foreigners hastened to proclaim that it was nothing more than "rusty streaks of iron through the vastness of nothing to the extremities of nowhere."[34] Perhaps too confidently, they insisted that it was "impossible to expect the sudden economic development of Siberia or any fundamental change in the conditions of world trade as a consequence of the railroad's construction."[35] But there were others who proclaimed that "after the discovery of America and the construction of the Suez Canal, history has never recorded an undertaking with greater significance, or one with such profound direct and indirect consequences, than the construction of the Trans-Siberian railway."[36] Certainly, the latter view was more accurate, for the railroad's impact upon Siberia's development was dramatic and almost instantaneous. Emigrants from European Russia poured into its virgin lands during the decade after the first rails were laid; by 1902, almost a million and a half Russians lived there.[37] Within less than two decades, the railroad's eastern terminus at Vladivostok grew nearly tenfold to a population of 120,000, while such Siberian cities as Tomsk, Omsk, Barnaul, and Irkutsk grew apace. By 1914, the inhabitants of these five cities alone totaled more than half the number of Siberia's entire population before the railroad came.

But the impact of the Trans-Siberian Railway on the course of Russian and world affairs reached far beyond the important fact of great population movements. Sensitive to the shifting diplomatic and commercial balance in the world's more remote regions, one British commentator best summed up the railroad's momentous significance:

> Not only is this railroad becoming one of the greatest freight routes that the world has ever seen and radically undermining

England's maritime trade as a result [he wrote], but it has placed in Russia's hands a potential weapon, the force and significance of which still are difficult to determine. Siberia is far from being that barren plain, that cheerless region of exile, that Europeans usually picture in their thoughts. On the contrary, it is the richest of lands . . . the full industrial development of which can, in time, establish the base for a new industrial era. The main significance of the Trans-Siberian railroad, however . . . lies in the fact that it makes Russia a totally self-contained state, no longer dependent upon the Dardanelles or the Straits [for shipping goods and supplies from one end of the Empire to the other], and will give her an economic independence with which she can attain a degree of power such as no state has yet dreamed of.[38]

Alexander's historic decision to build the Trans-Siberian Railway also brought new problems to Russia. Perhaps most significant, Russia's greater access to her Far Eastern lands quickly led to bitter conflicts with Japan just when that nation's immensely successful program of modernization encouraged her to seek new footholds on the Asian continent. There were, of course, varied and complex reasons for Russian expansion in the Far East. Tsarist policy was animated by all those motives that impelled Western nations into the region in addition to a number of more unique visions in which Russian statesmen saw their nation as the emerging mistress of the entire Asian continent.[39] One factor, however, overshadowed all others in determining the tortuous course of Russo-Japanese relations after 1891. Without the Trans-Siberian Railway to transport large numbers of troops and supplies, however imperfectly that task might be accomplished, a large-scale conflict between Russia and Japan would have been impossible. Although the brutal conflict between Russia and Japan remained beyond the range of statesmen's vision when Alexander signed the Trans-Siberian Railway decree, the implications of his act were almost as awesome as were those of his turn toward France some four months later. There was remarkable foresight indeed in one French newspaper's statement that the construction of the Trans-Siberian Railway was "not only a national, but a dynastic" issue.[40]

Alexander's diplomatic shift to France and his decision to build the Trans-Siberian Railway were both very much connected to the surge of economic progress and industrial development his Empire had experienced throughout his reign, which Russia continued to sustain at the highest level in all of Europe until the outbreak of the Great War.[41] The 1880s brought nearly eight thousand kilometers of new railway lines to Russia and signaled the beginnings of a railroad boom that produced more than forty thousand kilometers of new track between 1891 and 1914. As in other nations, the construction of railroads in Russia spurred the development of heavy industries. During the last half of the 1880s alone, coal production rose by 50 percent, the output of iron and steel doubled, and oil production increased almost threefold.[42] Although Russia remained predominantly an agrarian nation, peasants began to swarm into her cities as the Empire's booming infant industries demanded more workers. Clearly the Industrial Revolution, which had begun in England a century before, was well under way in Russia by 1891.

In the face of such economic growth, Russians' thoughts turned quickly to natural resources and the need to develop new foreign markets for Russian goods. Because such markets obviously were not to be found in the more highly developed economies of Europe, it was only natural that Russian businessmen and government officials should turn to the Far East. To support their efforts, the Trans-Siberian Railway became a necessity. At the same time, conservative, economy-minded statesmen wanted to recoup the immense costs of building the railroad without delay and grew more aggressive in their search for new markets and new business for the railway. Among Alexander III's advisers, the brilliant and resourceful Sergei Witte especially wanted new trade, not new territory. The Russians "already have more [territory] than they could possibly develop in a hundred or two hundred years," he once reportedly told Britain's ambassador in a flash of candor that was remarkable for any statesman. What Russia needed to accomplish, he insisted, was "to bring out the wealth of the country, [and] foster trade, commerce, and industry."[43] Such goals demanded foreign peace, domestic stability, and immense amounts of money, and a continuing search for all three remained always in the forefront of Alexander III's concerns. With the exception of the infant Ivan VI, who was driven from the throne shortly after his first birthday in 1741, Alexander was the only autocrat in the course of the three centuries in which the Romanovs ruled Russia who did not embroil his people in a foreign war.

Russia's industrial development in the 1880s required vast sums of capital, much of which had to be found in money markets outside the Empire, and her successful quest for these much-needed billions was first due to the efforts of a humble priest's son, whose rapid rise as a captain of industry saw him become Alexander's Minister of Finance in 1887. Ivan Vyshnegradskii has been called an "aggressive and unrepentant conservative,"[44] whose personal financial interests were very much tied to the success of Russia's industrial surge. He is reported to have speculated shamelessly in a number of commercial and industrial ventures during his years in office and apparently had no qualms about using the privileged information he obtained as Minister of Finance to increase his personal fortune. Impressed by his minister's obvious talent and his seemingly uncanny ability to navigate the treacherous currents of Europe's money markets, Alexander took pains to look the other way. "Let him make ten millions, as long as he makes a hundred [million] for the government," he reportedly remarked when some of Vyshnegradskii's enemies reported his unsavory activities.[45]

Regardless of his speculations while in office, Vyshnegradskii's conservative fiscal policies and his fierce determination to increase Russia's gold reserves in order to introduce the gold standard won him particular support among the capital-rich bankers of Paris. So impressed were they by the Finance Minister's careful policies that French investors poured a deluge of capital into Russian stocks and bonds with very dramatic results. By 1900, an amazing one-fourth of all French foreign investment was in Russian industries, utilities, and railroads; the amount of French capital invested in Russia by 1914 was more than three times greater than all German, British, and Belgian investments combined.[46] The Romanovs' preference for autocratic governments, and their fear of revolution, had tied

Russia to Prussia and a united Germany for most of the nineteenth century. Extensive French investments now bound Russia even more closely to the Third Republic as the nineteenth century closed.

Attractive though they seemed to eager investors, Vyshnegradskii's policies had a dark and dangerous side that went unrecognized at first. Within five years, they produced unlooked-for and tragic results that added yet another dimension to the events that made 1891 such a fateful year in Russia's history. A central part of Vyshnegradskii's program to increase his nation's gold reserves was an effort to better her balance of trade. Unlike his counterparts in the more advanced nations of Europe, however, he had only one course of action open; Russia's infant industries produced little that was marketable in the West, and it was impossible to increase trade with the Far East before the Trans-Siberian Railway was built. Proclaiming in 1887 that "we may not eat enough, but we will export,"[47] Vyshnegradskii set out to increase the value of Russia's grain exports at a time when prices were plummeting on the world grain market. With amazing efficiency, he increased exports by a third and instituted the highest tariff in Europe to reduce imports. By 1890, Alexander's Finance Minister had turned the small budget deficit he had inherited into a massive surplus. It seemed he had found the magic key to solve Russia's economic difficulties that had eluded so many before him.[48]

Always coldly efficient, Vyshnegradskii had achieved his ends through the simple device of forcing Russia's peasants to sell more of their crops. He had done so by collecting taxes in the fall when domestic grain prices were the lowest and, at the same time, raising the already excessive excise taxes on the tobacco and vodka that peasants consumed in large quantities.[49] The Empire's balance of trade quickly improved, its currency became more stable, and its nascent industries grew more attractive to foreign investors. Russia's peasants—those faceless millions who paid most of the taxes and spilled most of the blood in her wars—simply were expected to pay the price again. Not even Vyshnegradskii realized how very little they had left with which to pay. Even before his program began, one expert calculated, the average Russian consumed only a quarter as much food as his American counterpart.[50] By 1891, such undernourished peasants had nothing left to fall back upon should they encounter even moderate adversity.

Like so many catastrophes in the history of mankind, the first signals of impending famine in Russia came unnoticed and went unheeded. Only the most astute observer could have perceived them as they flickered through those tens of thousands of peasant villages that dotted the landscape of European Russia. Nonetheless, the telltale signs were there, and, just as Vyshnegradskii's program seemed certain of success at the close of the 1880s, a yellowish, coarse, breadlike substance, called *golodnyi khleb*—famine bread—by those unfortunates obliged to consume it, began to appear in unexpectedly large quantities on peasant tables throughout Russia's grain belt. It was a fatal signal, for the appearance of *golodnyi khleb* when there was no famine bore silent, ominous testimony to the fact that the Empire's long-suffering peasants had exhausted the very last of their meager reserves in a final pitiful effort to meet the demands of Vyshnegradskii's program. By the time government officials realized what was happening, the point of crisis was at hand. Even the slightest crop failure would bring disaster.

The trend that had brought large amounts of *golodnyi khleb* to peasant tables could not be reversed quickly, nor could it be accomplished without a dramatic shift in the government's policies. As Vyshnegradskii and his advisers knew all too well, grain reserves could be replenished only by lowering taxes so that the peasants once again could sell less. Then as now, however, bountiful harvests were a rarity in Russia, and several years might be needed to restore the balance. In the meantime, the fate of millions of peasants lay in the hands of Nature. To their great misfortune, Nature proved cruelly fickle during the winter of 1890–91. Unusually hard frosts struck Russia's central agricultural region and the grain-growing provinces along the Volga River, but almost no protective snow fell to guard the winter wheat and provide moisture when the spring thaws came. Spring and summer reversed the process and brought scorching heat. Still the rains did not come.[51] As Alexander signed the decree to begin work on the Trans-Siberian Railway and entertained Admiral

Gervais and his officers at Kronstadt, fears of drought must have gnawed at the back of his mind. There is some indication that Vyshnegradskii may have attempted to conceal the full truth from him, at least for a time. Certainly, he took pains to suppress a number of important warnings. "The most terrible specter of famine is advancing on Russia," one of his department directors warned him at the end of May. Vyshnegradskii reportedly took the report, placed it in a desk drawer, turned the key and placed it in his pocket. "Your notes will never come out of this drawer," he replied. "No one should know of this."[52]

Although Russian statesmen were traditionally reluctant to bring unpleasant tidings to their Emperors and Empresses, evidence of disaster in the Empire's grain fields mounted so rapidly during the summer of 1891 that it could be neither concealed nor ignored. Before the summer was half over, it was becoming appallingly certain that, even should the rain come, it would be too late. By midsummer, Russians no longer asked, "Will the harvest be poor?" The fearsome question had become, "How poor will the harvest be?" Even before Gervais's squadron arrived at Kronstadt, Alexander's Minister of Internal Affairs had begun to receive ominous reports from the provinces. The governor of Tambov warned that he probably would need almost two million rubles from the government to buy enough grain to see the people in his province through the winter. Already frightened and desperate, the governor of Nizhni-Novgorod, home of the Empire's greatest annual fair, simply telegraphed that his province needed a million rubles for famine relief immediately. So urgent and so obvious was his need that he did not think it necessary to supply documents to support his request.[53] Word of widespread drought and crop failure splashed across the pages of newspapers long accustomed to underreporting disasters. Not long afterward, the great novelist Tolstoi posed what he called "the terrible question" in the liberal *Russian Gazette*. "Would there be grain enough?" he asked.[54] In the provinces, officials had been asking that question all summer long; their superiors in St. Petersburg soon had to confront it. All of them feared to hear the answer.

Summer in St. Petersburg was traditionally a time when the high and mighty fled the city as the summer heat transformed its picturesque canals, always counted among its greatest charms by Russian novelists and foreign travelers, into stinking sewers. In addition, the city's water supply was so poor that, even as late as 1914, the compilers of Baedeker's *Russia* warned that, in St. Petersburg, *"unboiled water should on no account be drunk."*[55] These conditions posed health hazards during the summer months that knowledgeable folk with the means to do so sought to avoid, especially since cholera often appeared in the city's homes during the summer, sometimes reaching epidemic proportions.

St. Petersburg's laboring masses had no choice but to remain in the city, but the Imperial family, their Court, most senior statesmen, and even a large number of lesser officials, businessmen, writers, and artists all spent the fetid summer months in the country or along the Gulf of Finland where the air was clean and the water pure. Admiral Gervais's arrival had found Alexander III, the Empress Maria Feodorovna, and much of their Court at Peterhof, a huge summer palace on the Gulf of Finland with hundreds of rooms. In the vicinity, there were several thousand smaller *dachi* (summer houses) owned or rented by the residents of St. Petersburg. Throughout the summer of 1891, these *dachi* held men who had seen the ominous reports from the provinces that spring. While their families frolicked along the shore and arranged picnics in the region's many pine woods, these officials and statesmen worried about the crisis in Russia's countryside. They hoped beyond hope that it would not be there to confront them when they returned to the capital in the fall, but they knew that such hopes were in vain.

By the time Russia's senior officials and statesmen had returned to St. Petersburg at the beginning of October, they could no longer doubt that Russia was in the grip of the worst crop failure she had known in more than four decades. Nor could they doubt that the lives of millions hung upon the success of their effort to purchase hundreds of thousands of tons of grain and move it quickly into the hands of starving peasants. The cost, they already knew, would be immense. Despite his most diligent efforts to husband the government's resources, Minister of Internal Affairs Ivan Durnovo had been obliged to allocate more than 29 million rubles—almost four times the government's entire relief fund—for famine relief by early September. By October, he conceded that far more money would be required "to spare the population of the stricken region the distressing consequences of the disaster which has befallen them."[56] "All ministers are gripped by despair about the famine that is appearing in so many provinces [but] no one among them has yet any really clear plan about what course to follow," the chairman of the State Council's Department of Economy told the statesman Aleksandr Polovtsov.[57]

The question that Alexander and his councillors faced in the fall of 1891 was not whether Russians would die from hunger and famine-related diseases that winter, but how the number of deaths could be minimized. Even during normal times, Russian peasants lived a precarious existence, and many faced hunger (even starvation) by winter's end. According to a study undertaken by a country doctor about a decade after the famine had ended, abject poverty remained the rule for peasants throughout Russia's grain belt. Not surprisingly, meat was a rarity on their tables, but many also had to do without cabbage, cucumbers, eggs, and milk. Only one household in ten had enough grain to last from harvest to harvest; the remainder still needed to rely in part upon *golodnyi khleb* to eke out their dwindling supplies during the early days of spring.[58] Usually made from such hardy weeds as goosefoot, ground and mixed with increasingly smaller amounts of rye flour as supplies dwindled, famine bread did little but fill the stomachs of hungry peasants with indigestible roughage. "*Golodnyi khleb* reminds one more of earth or peat than of bread," wrote one medical expert. "When made [entirely] from goosefoot, it tends to fall apart," he continued. "Such bread has a moldy smell; it has a bitter, sour taste."[59] Although government doctors in the 1840s actually had recommended it as a viable bread substitute in times of famine, physicians and scientists in the 1890s were unanimous in condemning it as worthless, even dangerous. Bread baked from goosefoot quickly induced diarrhea, vomiting, and a variety of more serious gastrointestinal disorders. Over time, it produced serious protein deficiency. Nonetheless, peasants continued to prepare famine bread during the last weeks of 1891 because they had nothing else. When there was no more goosefoot left, they ate clay to deaden the pangs of hunger.[60] If government aid were to save them it could not be delayed for long.

In order to minimize deaths among starving peasants, immense quantities of grain grown in those distant provinces of southern Russia that had escaped the ravages of the drought would have to be diverted from the Empire's booming export grain trade. If that could be accomplished, the grain then had to be shipped to the provinces gripped by famine along a sparsely developed network of railroads that had not been designed for shipping great amounts of freight into Russia's interior.[61] It would have been difficult to accomplish either of these tasks under even the most favorable conditions. To undertake both in the space of a few months seemed almost impossible. Yet the consequences of failure were frightening. Alexander and his advisers realized that millions of Russians would die from hunger and disease if their effort failed.

Because Russia's leading statesmen had directed their energies toward increasing grain exports for a number of years, it proved awkward to shift the movement of grain traffic back toward the Empire's interior on a moment's notice. The difficulties of changing the flow of Russia's grain shipments increased dramatically when large numbers of those grain speculators who had flourished as a result of Vyshnegradskii's export policies learned that the harvest of 1891 would be poor throughout Europe. That single fact became a powerful magnet to draw Russia's grain beyond her borders as greedy speculators leaped at the opportunity to exploit shortages in Western Europe in return for French, German, and Austrian gold. Even though they knew that Russia would suffer a serious grain shortage in the fall, these unscrupulous men devoted themselves to profiting from the far more lucrative demand they found in Europe. During the first six months of the year, the volume of Russian grain exports rose accordingly.[62]

By early summer, Minister of Internal Affairs Durnovo realized that only a ban on all exports of rye, the staple of most peasant diets, could retain desperately needed grain in Russia. It was obviously necessary, but it meant the end of Vyshnegradskii's carefully planned program to strengthen Russia's standing in international economic circles. In a futile attempt to avoid the inevitable, Vyshnegradskii used his authority as Minister of Finance to postpone Durnovo's ban for two critical months while greedy speculators and exporters raced to ship still more grain abroad. Ship after ship steamed out of Odessa, Russia's great port on the Black Sea, their holds packed with grain destined for the markets of Europe. At the same time, so much grain was shipped across the western frontier during the weeks before the ban finally went into effect that even the superbly efficient German railroads needed more than a month to remove the huge mountains of rye left at Königsberg by grain dealers anxious to beat the deadline.[63]

All along the western frontier, sullen, hungry Russians watched as trainload after trainload of grain disappeared into Germany. Pushed beyond the limits of forbearance by the sight, the peasants rioted in protest, only to be crushed by truncheon-wielding Cossacks. When Vyshnegradskii finally allowed the ban to take effect in mid-August, Europeans had enough grain to see them through the winter; in European Russia 36 million peasants spread out over almost a million square miles were on the verge of starvation.

Nonetheless, despite the best efforts of grain speculators, Durnovo's ban kept enough grain within Russia's borders to feed her starving population. According to official estimates, which admittedly tended to inflate the available supply and understate potential need, there was perhaps as much as ten times more grain in Russia in December 1891 than was needed to save her population from starvation. The problem Alexander's advisers had to resolve was how to deliver it to those millions whose lives hinged upon it. Even if Nature was kind and the spring thaws did not come early, Russia's desperate planners had no more than three months' time in which to complete their task.[64] From long experience they knew that in March the Empire's villages would begin their month-long isolation from the outside world as spring thaws transformed the primitive, unpaved tracks that tied Russia's rural communities together into rivers of mud. Horses would stand bemired up to their knees, and even the lightest of wagons would sink to axle depth. Once the thaws began, communication between town and country in Russia would be cut and could not be restored until after the fields had dried. If the starving peasants had not received grain before then, many more would die, and the living would be unable to sow their fields. Should the planting season pass without the fall crop being sown, it went without saying that the famine would extend for another year.

The attention of Alexander III and his advisers thus shifted at the end of 1891 to the vital issue of transportation. Railroads held the key to moving immense quantities of grain, but Russian statesmen had little experience with modern transportation. Compared with the rest of Europe in 1891, Russia still had shockingly few railroads. Criss-crossed by hundreds of rail lines, almost no part of France, Germany, Belgium, or Great Britain lay much beyond the sight and sound of the great steam locomotives that were tying the continent together at speeds that would have seemed impossible to men who lived a generation before. Even Italy, whose industry was comparatively backward, could claim at least a mile of track for every fourteen square miles. Yet, despite her surge of growth in the 1880s, Russia lagged far behind these nations. Even without counting the vast and empty expanses of Siberia, the rest of the Empire boasted less than one mile of railroad for each 150 square miles of territory and most of that lay to the west and south of the famine region. At least three of the famine provinces still had no main rail lines within their boundaries in 1891, and all had far too little rolling stock at their disposal. There were exactly three heavily congested trunk lines from the grainfields of southern Russia and the northern Caucasus into the famine region, and over a million tons of grain had to be moved over them.[65]

Alexander III's only hope for success lay in finding someone forceful and expert enough to direct all of Russia's limited resources toward the task of moving grain. Thanks to the recommendations of Prince Vladimir Meshcherskii, editor of the ultraconservative *Citizen,* he found such a man in Colonel Alfred von Wendrich. On November 28, 1891, the Tsar gave von Wendrich full authority over

Russia's railroads. The situation turned out to be even worse than anyone in St. Petersburg had supposed; von Wendrich found even major rail lines clogged with huge grain shipments that moved nowhere. At just one southern station he visited a few weeks after his appointment, he found some eight hundred loaded boxcars sitting unattended on a siding. Hastily made inquiries revealed that they had been there for almost two months. Unhappily, that was far from being an isolated case. To everyone's relief, however, von Wendrich's success was nearly instantaneous and almost phenomenal. During the month after he assumed command of the railroads, he doubled the amount of grain shipped to the Empire's starving peasants. By February 1892, he and his deputies were moving over four hundred thousand tons a month, and the worst of the crisis was past. Fearing the rise of a dangerous and efficient rival, Russia's new Minister of Transport Sergei Witte relieved the Colonel of his duties in April with the brief statement that von Wendrich's efforts had made it possible "to terminate the extreme procedures necessitated by the extraordinary circumstances of the past winter."[66] Some years later, Witte characterized von Wendrich—uncharitably and untruthfully—as a man who was "limited, foolish, and well known for his direct insolence." Von Wendrich, he concluded, actually "created more confusion than he rendered help" in resolving the crisis posed by the famine.[67] It was a statement unworthy of a man of Witte's own great talent.

Von Wendrich was not alone in his efforts to feed the peasants during the famine of 1891: a variety of public and private endeavors joined in the largest relief operation anyone in Russia had ever seen. An average of almost six million peasants received some sort of assistance each month between September 1891 and August 1892, and, during April and May, that number almost doubled thanks to the grain shipped under von Wendrich's direction. But even such efforts as those could not spare many peasants from starvation and disease, and the leading expert on the famine has estimated that no less than four hundred thousand Russians died before the new crops were harvested in 1892. Nonetheless, the relief efforts of Alexander III and his ministers deserve at least a word of commendation.

Especially when compared to the better-known and much-vaunted British efforts at famine relief in India, the Russians' achievement was impressive for, despite British aid, death rates during the Indian famine of 1899–1900 (which was not as widespread as the one the Russians had faced a decade before) rose to fully ten times what they had been in Russia.[68] Yet the British efforts have been held up as models of famine relief, while those of Alexander's government were condemned as inept and deserving of indictment as a major cause for the resurgence of revolutionary sentiment in Russia's countryside at the century's end. The resurgence was there, but its causes lay in other factors connected with the famine's aftermath.

In spite of Alexander's efforts, misery among the poverty-stricken, always hungry peasants of Russia reached new depths during the winter of 1891–92. For even if many were spared starvation, almost all were desperately hungry. Although they were illiterate and inarticulate, they almost certainly understood that their suffering stemmed from Vyshnegradskii's oft-stated axiom that "we may not eat enough, but we will export." Such callous unconcern for their well-being must have engendered deep and enduring resentment, and it is remarkable that its outward expression was limited to a handful of scattered riots along Russia's western borders during the summer of 1891. Many contemporaries were amazed at the resignation with which Russia's peasants seemed to accept their bitter fate. In the face of tensions that would have sparked open rebellion among other peoples, the Empire remained calm.

The personality of Alexander III and the policies he had imposed on his Empire explain in part why Russia remained unruffled by political and social strife during the fateful months of 1891. Alexander was a man who possessed almost nothing in the way of intellectual curiosity. He knew his mind, what he should do, and what his policy ought to be. His political vision was unclouded by any of those conflicts that had marred his father's efforts to strike a balance between the anachronistic tenets of autocracy and the more complex precepts of economic progress and political modernization. "Very *clever* I do *not* think him, and his mind is an uncivilized one," England's outspoken Queen Victoria once had said of his grandfather Nicholas I,[69] and her estimate applied even more properly to Alexander III. As a Grand Duke, his tutors had imbued him with a rigid sense of morality, a deep awareness of right and wrong, that made it possible for him to perceive the world in uncomplicated terms of good and evil. Symbolically, he was a man of iron will and iron body, who endeavored to protect all of Russia and all Russians as he had shielded his wife and children when he had held up the collapsing roof of the Imperial dining car in a train wreck in 1888 to save them from being crushed beneath its weight. He saw his relationship to all Russians as an infinite extension of a father's to his children, in which he bore full responsibility for their behavior before society and before God.

Physically, Alexander's ponderous frame matched his stolid attitudes. "His body was huge and unwieldy, his movements clumsy, in part because of his almost morbid shyness," wrote one of his contemporaries. "It was as if all the forces of his being had flooded outward to the periphery, for the greater development of bones and muscles, and, as a consequence, had left a lack of passion and intellectualism at the center."[70] Alexander once said that he thought of himself as nothing more than "a conscientious regimental commander,"[71] and he ruled his family and Russia in just that manner. Very quickly, he became notorious for his blunt remarks and fearsome roughness. "Stop playing the Tsar," he once telegraphed when his brother Sergei took too much authority. When one of his ministers threatened to resign over a policy dispute, he seized him by the collar, shook him like a rag doll, and bellowed, "Shut up! When I choose to kick you out, you will hear about it in no uncertain terms!"[72] In his evaluations of advisers, foreign diplomats—and even the rulers they served—he made no effort to disguise his strongly held opinions. "What a herd of swine!" "What a beast!" were comments he wrote in the margins of reports sent by his ambassadors and ministers even though he knew that his words would circulate far beyond the confines of his study in the Winter Palace.[73] Indeed, he was as forthright in public as in private. There is a story that, when the Austrian ambassador once spoke at a state dinner of mobilizing two or three corps of the Austrian army against Russia in the Balkans, Alexander picked up a silver fork, bent it into a knot with apparent unconcern, and tossed it to the amazed diplomat with the calm remark, "That is what I am going to do with your two or three army corps."[74] Although the least schooled of any nineteenth-century Romanov Emperor in military affairs, he had a deep faith in Russia's ability to withstand the assault of all enemies at home and abroad. "We have just two allies in this world: our army and our navy" was one of his favorite comments when crises and turmoil confronted Russia.[75]

To his family and, indeed, to all of Russia, Alexander III stood as Tsar, Autocrat, and *Bogatyr*, that folk hero who loomed larger than life in the legends of olden times. He was not greatly loved by his people, but they held him in awe. Most certainly, he was more feared than revered, and the ardent young Russian revolutionaries he had driven into hiding or exile hated him with a deep and abiding passion. Those young terrorists, who had joined in one last desperate attempt to assassinate Alexander II, saw their dreams for a new Russia evaporate in an instant when his heir ascended the throne. "The terrible nightmare that has been oppressing the youth of Russia for the past decade has been lifted," they had proclaimed when the man known as the "Tsar-Liberator" fell before their crude homemade grenades in 1881. "Reaction must end in order to make way for the rebirth of Russia."[76] Firm, unyielding, and confident in his suppression of all dissent, Alexander III knew otherwise. For Russia's youthful revolutionaries the "nightmare" from which they sought release had, in fact, just begun. The only rebirth they and their comrades would witness was one of political reaction more severe than any Russians had known for many years.

From the moment he arose from his dead father's bedside, Alexander III's actions were calculated to show Russians that his would be a different sort of reign. Quickly, and with unhesitating sureness, he directed the police in their efforts to arrest his father's assassins. Within a fortnight, they were in prison. There could be no question of mercy for the four men and two women accused of tsaricide, and no doubt about their fate. Before their trial began, one of Alexander's closest advisers worried aloud that his Emperor might allow himself to be moved by the eloquent pleas for mercy that flowed from the pens of such prominent Russians as the philosopher Vladimir Solovev and the great novelist Count Lev Tolstoi. "Do not be alarmed," Alexander assured his worried councillor. "I can promise you that all six will be hanged."[77] Five of them were, and within less than a month after their arrests. Only the twenty-six-year-old Gesia Gelfmann was spared the death sentence. Because Russian law prohibited the execution of a pregnant woman regardless of her crime, Gelfmann's death sentence was commuted to lifelong imprisonment. This was Alexander's first warning that revolutionaries must expect to pay a high price for their dreams. Within a year, the revolutionary forces that had appeared so threatening in the late 1870s were in utter disarray. Their organizations had been destroyed, their leaders executed, imprisoned, exiled to Siberia, or forced to flee abroad. With just one exception—a hopelessly bungled assassination attempt in 1887 that involved Lenin's elder brother, Aleksandr Ulianov—Alexander III did not face the drawn weapons of terrorists during his reign.

Alexander III rode out to begin his rule over Russia "accompanied by a whole regiment of Don Cossacks galloping in attack formation, their red lances shining brightly in the last rays of a crimson March sunset."[78] That simple act—his first public one as Emperor—symbolized the barrier he deliberately erected between himself and his subjects. Unlike his father, he made no apologies for the gulf that separated him from his people. Indeed, he saw it as his task to rule over them, not reign with them. Perhaps more than any of his predecessors, including even Nicholas I, Alexander had firmly established political principles before he rose to the throne. He disliked Catholics, distrusted Protestants, and despised Jews with an all-pervasive passion. "He is a rotten, lousy Jew," he once remarked to explain why he had turned down a recommendation that a certain official be promoted to high office.[79] "We must not forget that it was the Jews who crucified our Lord and spilled his precious blood," he wrote at another point.[80] There was an obvious and crude bigotry in the Tsar that was unusual even in a world where neither sensitivity nor tolerance were counted as particular virtues.

Despite the primitive quality of Alexander's manner and attitudes, he possessed homely virtues that, in all fairness, need to be recalled. He never dissembled, spoke his mind with candor, and "always practiced what he preached," in the words of an admiring minister.[81] "Once given," his Minister of Finance wrote, "his word was as firm and solid as a mountain of stone."[82] Alexander's sense of duty was as pervasive as that of Nicholas I, the Romanov Emperor who had raised duty to the level of life's sanctioning principle. He was probably the first truly frugal member of a dynasty notorious for its extravagance, a sovereign, in Witte's words, who guarded every kopek as though it were his own.[83] Above all, he was one of the most diligent and dedicated autocrats ever to rule Russia. He took his duties seriously, actually read the mountains of reports his ministers and aides prepared for his attention, and commented dutifully (though often not very politely) in their margins.

From more than any other living source, Alexander III drew his political principles from Konstantin Pobedonostsev, a jurist who had become his favored mentor in the mid-1860s and in whom he placed his deepest confidence throughout his years as Russia's Emperor. Tall, balding, and thin, his cold, slightly myopic stare shielded by thin, wire-rimmed spectacles, Pobedonostsev was a man of rigid morality, uncompromising in his defense of conservative principles, who encouraged his sovereign's bigotry and prejudice. He insisted that "the most precious gift of a statesman is an ability to organize," followed by the qualities of "resolution in action, ability to seize the proper moment, [and] to embrace rapidly the details of all work without losing sight of its fundamental principles." "Fine observation of men and knowledge of character are indispensable," he added. A ruler must have a finely developed "knowledge of whom to trust, and experience [to teach him] that the best of men are not free from low instincts and interested motives."[84] As tutor and confidant, Pobedonostsev instilled these precepts in Alexander III. Above all, he tempered them with warnings about constitutional government, a phenomenon he cursed as "the greatest falsehood of our time." For him, democracy was "a fatal error" and parliament "one of the greatest illustrations of human delusion," "an institution serving for the satisfaction of the personal ambition, vanity, and self-interest of its members."[85] According to him, any constitution would be "a lie." On one occasion, he exclaimed: "God forbid that a true Russian shall see the day when this lie will become an accomplished fact" in Russia.[86] Alexander fully shared his mentor's view. On the issue of constitutional government, as on the question of any lesser political concessions to liberal Russian opinion, he would brook no compromises.

Alexander remained unyielding on all questions of social and political change throughout his reign. He hastened to replace the handful of progressives among his father's ministers with conservatives, with whom he set out to restore the full power of autocracy by attacking every one of the Great Reforms his father had instituted. His domestic programs were designed to impose political order and social stability upon Russia, and his foreign policy was directed toward much the same end. Above all, stability was an essential prerequisite for attracting the foreign investments that Russia's nascent industrial establishment required, and Alexander was determined to provide it. His regime thus was a time of outward harmony, much as his grandfather Nicholas I's had been. Order reigned supreme. Not even such a catastrophe as the great famine of 1891 could disturb the stability of Alexander III's Empire. The same would not be the case with his son Nicholas II, who was to succeed him unexpectedly soon. Alexander had faced the crises of 1891 with firm resolve and apparent robust health. Yet, on October 20, 1894, scarcely more than three years after he had entertained Admiral Gervais aboard the *Derzhava* in Kronstadt harbor, he was dead, the victim of nephritis at the age of forty-nine. His eldest son and successor was cast from a very different mold.

According to one member of his family, Nicholas II's first words as Russia's new Emperor were: "What am I going to do? . . . I am not prepared to be a Tsar. I never wanted to become one. I know nothing of the business of ruling. I have no idea of even how to talk to ministers."[87] It was indeed a very different beginning from the afternoon of March 1, 1881, when Alexander III, stern, tight-lipped, dry-eyed, and resolute, had strode from the Winter Palace to punish the murderers of his father.

For Nicholas II's weakness and ineptitude, Alexander III was himself not without blame. Unaware that his time on earth was destined to be so brief, he had not trained his heir in the art of ruling despite urgent pleadings from some of his most trusted councillors. In late 1891, he had named his son to chair a special committee on famine relief, and Nicholas had dutifully attended its meetings, although one would be hard pressed to find any evidence that he made much of an impact upon its discussions.[88] Aside from that one assignment, and the dutiful appearances he made at the State Council twice each week, Nicholas continued to do little except command his squadron in the Hussar Life Guards and pursue the ballerina Kschessinska with increasing ardor. By 1893, Minister of Finance Witte, among others, had become seriously concerned about Nicholas's lack of knowledge about governing the vast Empire he would someday inherit. Witte had therefore suggested that the Tsarevich be appointed Chairman of the Commission for the Construction of the Trans-Siberian Railway.

"What?" Alexander had reportedly demanded. "Tell me, are you acquainted with the Tsarevich?"

"How could Your Majesty think that I would not be acquainted with the Tsarevich?"

"But have you ever tried to discuss anything of real consequence with him?" Alexander persisted.

"No, Your Highness," Witte confessed. "I have never had the pleasure of having had such a conversation with the Tsarevich."

"Well, he's an absolute child," Alexander told his surprised minister. "His opinions are utterly childish. How could he possibly preside over such a committee?"[89]

Witte persisted in his urgings, nonetheless. As a consequence, Alexander appointed Nicholas to chair the Commission for the Construction of the Trans-Siberian Railway under the watchful eye of its vice president, the former Minister of Finance and veteran elder statesman Nikolai Bunge, who had been chosen in part for the guidance he could provide to Russia's heir apparent. It was a limited exposure to Russian affairs at best, and one that was far too brief, before Nicholas II was called to mount the throne scarcely more than a year later.

A mild-mannered young man of twenty-six, with large, soft, dark eyes and a neatly trimmed Vandyke beard, Nicholas II loved sports, playing with dogs, and gathering mushrooms in the forests around St. Petersburg. At the age of twenty-five, he still thought a game of hide-and-seek worthy of inclusion in his diary. Just three weeks before he inherited the throne, he set forth in that volume, to which he confided his innermost thoughts, a description of an afternoon during which he and his cousin pelted each other with pine cones and chestnuts.[90] He had none of his father's singleness of purpose. Nor was he blessed with his unshakable belief in the rightness of the course he had chosen. Alexander III had marched across history's stage, confident of his purpose and direction. Nicholas wandered fitfully and hesitantly, the victim of events and forces he could not hope to understand. For two of the most critical decades in their nation's history, Russians were condemned to follow him along a halting and uncertain course.

CHAPTER II
In the Wake of Famine

I N THE EMPIRE THAT NICHOLAS II INHERITED FROM HIS STERN father late in 1894, more than eight out of every ten men and women were peasants. Many of these had never set foot in a city; relatively few ever had seen a building that stood more than two stories high. Most of those who proclaimed Nicholas Tsar and Emperor eked out their lives in thousands of tiny hamlets buried deep in the remote countryside, where conditions were so primitive that every outsider who ventured into their midst was appalled. In humble cottages, which the Russians called *izby,* most of Nicholas's subjects were fated to be born, wed, raise their families, and die, all within a pitifully brief span. Among these millions of peasant folk, a woman was thought middle-aged at thirty-five. Once past forty, she was excused from weaving during the winter months because the task was thought beyond her strength. Many peasants died before they reached the age of fifty, and not one in twenty saw his sixtieth birthday.[1] Progress was so painfully slow in this world that a man and a woman could live out their entire lives without ever catching more than a glimpse of it.

Since time immemorial, these toiling men and women had labored to provide the raw material from which Russian autocrats had fashioned their nation's greatness. Peter the Great had relied upon their strength to win his victories over the armies of Sweden, and he had paid the price of Russia's entrance into the ranks of Europe's Great Powers with their blood. It was upon the bent backs and broken bones of these peasants' grandsons and granddaughters that Catherine the Great had lifted the Empire to still greater heights. Peasant hands built St. Petersburg, Russia's new Imperial capital that Peter the Great had founded as his Empire's "window on the West." Time and again, bayonets wielded by peasant soldiers who marched to their deaths in the tens of thousands against such awesome foes as Frederick the Great and Napoleon defended the Russian land from foreign enemies. While these peasant soldiers shed their blood for Russia's freedom, their families lived in bondage to noble lords who held life-and-death power over them.

The first steps to freedom for these peasant millions began only in 1861, and it came at such a high price that most who heard Alexander II announce their emancipation could not even hope to pay its full cost within the span of their lifetimes, for they had to redeem not only their lands but their very bodies from their former masters' yokes. Desperately poor, and victims of diseases that had all but disappeared in Europe, these peasants thus were expected to give Russia much and be satisfied with amazingly little. On the day of Nicholas II's accession, their vision of tomorrow held nothing beyond a repetition of the pain and toil of today.

Vital though they were to their nation's past, present, and future, the lives of the peasant masses remained largely unknown to educated Russians until almost the end of the nineteenth century. For the men and women who met in the salons of St. Petersburg and Moscow and produced Russia's art and letters, these were the "dark people"—the *narod*—rarely seen and greatly misunderstood. As in all modern slave-owning societies, most educated Russians preferred to think of their bonded countrymen in abstract and idealized terms. They envisioned peasant women working in humble, but always clean *izby*, their strong hands and dimpled white arms kneading dough, churning butter, or spinning flax, while their equally vigorous young husbands bent their backs to the tasks of cutting wood, reaping grain, or working in the smithy. In their imaginings, the lives of such rural folk were clean and pure, made healthy by the clean air and fresh food that lords and ladies enjoyed in such plenty during infrequent summer visits to their country estates. Such a life brought pleasure as a reward for toil in the mind's eye of those who envisioned it. Another common vision of rural life therefore emphasized its innocent pleasures and portrayed peasant lads and lasses, decked in their holiday best, singing and dancing in fresh-cut meadows or some similar pastoral setting.

So ingrained were these images in the minds of literate Russians that even Aleksandr Radishchev, the first writer to condemn serfdom as a crime against humanity, could not refrain from including such idealized portraits in his *Journey from St. Petersburg to Moscow*. Radishchev's peasant women had "cheeks glowing with good health," their teeth "whiter than the purest ivory." "See how the limbs of all my rustic beauties are round, firm, well-shaped, and unblemished," he exclaimed at one point, and hastened to draw an unflattering comparison with vain city women who sickened themselves with rich foods and tortured their bodies with laces, corsets, and shoes made only for fashion.[2] Radishchev's was an image very much reflected in the *Portrait of a Peasant Girl* that his contemporary Ivan Argunov painted in 1784, the first effort by any Russian to portray one of the "dark people" on canvas. Argunov's subject boasted a flawless face and perfect figure and was dressed in an elegance that would have allowed her to step into a masked ball in the greatest of St. Petersburg's palaces to play the part of a peasant maid. Such a combination of face, figure, and dress could, in fact, have been found only in a Petersburg drawing room; it was an ideal unattainable in any peasant village in the Empire.

Bodies wasted by chronic malnutrition and disease and lives equally wasted by poverty and ignorance had no place in such portrayals as Radishchev's and Argunov's. Nor were they reflected in the rare descriptions of peasant life that appeared in the fictional works of such Russian masters as Nikolai Karamzin and Aleksandr Pushkin in the first quarter of the nineteenth century.[3] The persistence of such sentimental and idealized images reflected educated Russians' ignorance of the appalling want in which most of their countrymen lived. Perhaps even more important, such comforting visions spared them from admitting that their society held millions of its own people in crushing bondage. Very few Russians ever thought of themselves as cruel or heartless masters. Even those who condemned serfdom's evils during the first fifty years of the nineteenth century almost always owned serfs themselves and tried to justify that glaring contradiction by references to their serfs' ignorance and their need for paternal guidance. Comforting images of rural idylls reassured them that their peasants could draw satisfaction from lives lived well in faithful service to benevolent masters and mistresses. It would have been too frightening to see every serf as a potential enemy whose heart overflowed with hatred for his oppressors and who might someday hold a dagger at the throat of master and mistress alike.

But the brutal conditions that had sparked great serf rebellions in the seventeenth and eighteenth centuries reflected more accurately the reality of life among Russia's peasants than did the idealized visions of educated Russians, and the fact that the nineteenth century saw no further great upheavals did not mean that conditions had grown better. The best evidence indicates that life became worse for Russia's peasants during these years.[4] Deep within St. Petersburg's chanceries, a handful of progressive young civil servants had begun to examine how peasants lived in order to learn what might be done to better their lives, but it would require many years of thankless effort before their labors bore fruit.[5] In the meantime, most noblemen, government officials, and educated Russians continued not to know how the Empire's peasants lived, how they thought, or what hopes they nourished deep within their hearts. Nor did they care.

Russia's peasants found their first literary portraitist in Ivan Turgenev, a wealthy nobleman from the province of Orël. Turgenev had seen serfs flogged, sent off to the army, forced to marry against their wishes, or sold away from their families. In a manner equaled by few literate Russians of his day, he understood the deep agony of serf life and saw how men and women deadened its pain through the opiate of supreme resignation. In 1852, when Harriet Beecher Stowe published *Uncle Tom's Cabin* in America, Turgenev assembled twenty-two sketches about peasant life and published them in a volume that bore the unpretentious and unrevealing title, *Notes of a Huntsman*.[6] His message was more muted, more subtly offered than Mrs. Stowe's, for it was neither in keeping with his literary style nor the rules of censorship to proclaim the injustices of serfdom in blatant tones. In any case, most educated Russians had come to admit that, *in theory,* serfdom should be abolished, although they could not agree that it should be abolished at that particular time.[7] *Notes of a Huntsman* reminded Russians that serfs were human in every sense of the word, as warmed by life and torn by tragedy as the lords and ladies who bought and sold them, rented them to factory owners, or gambled them away at cards.

For mid-nineteenth-century Russian lords, Turgenev's message was more than awkward. An official report condemned the author for "ridiculing the landowners, presenting them in a light derogatory to their honor and, in general, propagating opinions detrimental to the respect due to the nobility from other classes."[8] The Emperor ordered him to live in isolation on his estate for more than a year as punishment for his daring statement. But Turgenev had made his point and made it well. In 1861, less than a decade after *Notes of a Huntsman* appeared, and two years before Abraham Lincoln freed America's slaves, serfdom fell in Russia.

Alexander II's proclamation of Russia's Emancipation Acts did not immediately free all of Russia's peasants. Nor did it make the condition of the Empire's "dark people" better known or more clearly understood. A number of educated Russians now stressed the "historical" social, cultural, even political virtues that the "dark people" had preserved deep within their communities across the land.[9] Some thought that the principles of life in the peasant communes could bring socialism to Russia more quickly and more effectively than in the more industrialized nations of Europe. Aleksandr Herzen, a radical publicist who fled Russia to live out his life in European exile in 1847, was the first to make that claim,[10] but others soon followed energetically and even more insistently in his footsteps. Still utterly ignorant about the way in which Russia's peasants actually lived, radical young men and women began to insist that the peasant community could become the foundation for a new order in Russia. In a manifesto addressed "To the Younger Generation" in the summer of 1861, the young radical Mikhail Mikhailov proclaimed: "We are a people who have been slow to develop, and in this lies the key to our salvation. We should thank our lucky stars that we have not lived the life of Europe. . . . We do not want her proletariat, her aristocratic society, her system of government, and her Imperial power." The communal traditions of the Russian peasants, Mikhailov insisted, would enable Russia "to introduce a new foundation in history . . . and not to repeat the mistakes of Europe."[11] The sacred mission of thoughtful and thinking Russians, the older and wiser Petr Lavrov added a few years later, must be to educate these noble rural toilers.[12] To do so would help them to "develop a conscious socialist ideal out of their confused, collectivist strivings."[13]

Beginning in the summer of 1874, and throughout the next few years, scores of radical young Russians made their way into the Empire's distant villages to serve the people and to join with them. Untrained and unprepared, they went with great excitement. At the same time, apprehension, even fear, gripped their hearts. "For the first time in my life, I found myself face to face with village life, along with the *narod,*" recalled the future terrorist Vera Figner. "I confess that I was lonely, weak, and helpless in that peasant sea. Furthermore, I had no idea about how even to approach a person from the lower classes." Such moderate apprehension soon gave way to utter shock when these young radicals saw the conditions in which Russia's "dark people" lived their lives. "Until that point, I had never seen the true ugliness of peasant life at first hand," Figner confessed. "Under those horrible impressions that I drew from seeing the material side of the people's daily life, those three months [in the village] were for me a terrible experience."[14]

Even the best efforts of such dedicated idealists as Figner could not save the movement "to the people" from failure. Although the reasons are many and complex, the first and greatest obstacle was the vast cultural chasm that separated Russia's westernized, elite youth from her unlettered, superstitious, and suspicious *narod*. They shared no common ground and had no basis for communication. Nor could either group offer any practical solutions to the dilemmas the other faced, as Turgenev explained with dramatic sureness in a memorable passage in the novel *Smoke*. "Do you see this peasant overcoat?" Sozont Potugin exclaimed cynically toward the beginning of the novel. "All other idols are to be destroyed, so we shall put all our belief in this peasant overcoat. . . . You know, if I were a painter, I should paint the following scene: an educated man comes upon a peasant and bows low before him. 'Cure me, I beg you dear little peasant, little father mine,' he says. 'I am perishing from disease.' Then the peasant in his turn bows low before the educated man: 'Teach me, O little father, master mine,' he says. 'I am perishing from ignorance.' Well, of course," Potugin concluded, "neither one gets anywhere at all."[15]

The young radicals of the 1870s hoped to find within the *narod* some deeper truth that could become the foundation for a more just social and economic order in Russia. What they discovered were men and women who, like most others, allowed self-interest to direct their lives and were not very concerned about the well-being of their fellows. Wrote one agronomist who worked among the *narod* for many years, "Every peasant, if circumstances permit, will, in the most exemplary fashion, exploit every other."[16] On their side, the *narod* simply found it incomprehensible that educated young men and women would come into their villages without some sinister motive. Unwilling to admit that the peasant was, as the great novelist Maksim Gorkii later wrote, "a stern realist and a man of cunning,"[17] the student radicals tried to be more like their peasant idols rather than study their plight. "The position of a common laborer," wrote one idealistic youth, "is the best means for drawing closer to the *narod*."[18] That the peasants remained sullen and suspicious of their efforts only impelled Russia's radical youth to pursue them with greater passion. As the *narod* continued to refuse their ministrations, their faith waned. Guiltily they abandoned their infatuation and rededicated themselves to work among the proletariat of the Empire's cities.

The great famine of 1891 brought a new movement to the people. Hundreds of well-trained men and women went into the Russian countryside eager to do their part. Unlike the radical youths of the 1870s, the technicians of the 1890s often were skilled and able to offer real benefits to the people they hoped to serve. Their training in public health, agronomy, and education also made this new wave of educated Russians more inclined to subject rural life to scientific and scholarly scrutiny. They went to Russia's villages to deal with the specific problems of rural poverty and rural hunger, not to appropriate for their revolutionary cause the moral force of a nonexistent dream of peasant socialism. For such experts, Russia's countless villages, and the toiling men and women who had for so many generations suffered the scourges of poverty, famine, and disease, provided rich material for drafting blueprints for social action.

Already conditioned to think in terms of small deeds, not revolutionary transformations, these technicians and experts readily accepted positions offered by local government councils (the *zemstva*) and began to assemble accurate information about Russia's peasantry. Some of the most dramatic and revealing materials were compiled by those dedicated men and women who worked in *zemstva* public health services and, for the first time, saw Russian rural life in all its brutality and pathos. These showed even the most casual reader the immense distance that rural Russia had to travel before her farmers could even begin to aspire to the standard of living enjoyed by their British, French, and American brethren. From the evidence these technicians assembled, we can begin to construct a portrait of the daily lives of Russia's 79 million "dark people" as they entered the twentieth century.

Unlike those redoubtable and self-reliant American farm families who spread their log cabins and sod huts across the plains of North America during the nineteenth century, few of those who tilled Russia's fields lived in isolated homesteads or farmed their lands alone. According to information collected by officials in the Imperial Ministry of Internal Affairs, most Russian peasants lived in hamlets that sheltered between fifty and three hundred folk as the day of emancipation dawned. Only one village in twenty had fewer than ten dwellers, but even fewer could claim more than a thousand. Larger villages tended to be in the so-called Black Soil region of Russia—the lands that produced most of the grain consumed by the Russians themselves and the area most seriously affected by the great famine. Even there the settlements were not large. Only one in a hundred could boast of more than two thousand people living within its boundaries.[19] For centuries, Russians had lived in this manner. They had labored and died in the villages of their birth. Frequent marriages among close relatives caused them to suffer all the genetic disorders such unions inevitably produce over the course of several generations. Only during the last part of the nineteenth century had these folk begun to leave the land to make new lives in the cities where work could be found in the Empire's many new factories. Even so, most of them took pride in keeping firm roots in their native villages. Whenever times grew hard in the factory, they tried to return.

People, the places they inhabit, and the customs they cherish are always unique to some extent, and to generalize about any society is to invite retribution from those legions of experts who very properly can point to the many exceptions that defy every rule. Yet generalizations persist, and rightly so, because they can provide an overview of important social and political phenomena that would be incomprehensible to all but the dedicated scholar without such broader descriptions. Qualifications must apply to any description of a "typical" Russian peasant village, just as they pertain elsewhere, but any such re-creation can help to explain Russian peasant life at the beginning of this century more clearly.[20]

Travelers who entered the typical late-nineteenth-century peasant village in Russia's Black Soil region were struck by its disorder and dirt. Peasant *izby* stood crowded at its center, usually clustered along a single unpaved street that almost always was deeply scarred by ruts and potholes. Most *izby* were built of logs poorly fitted together, the large gaps between stuffed with a mixture of mud and straw. By the turn of the century, a few brick structures might have begun to replace some of these crude wooden ones in a "typical" village, especially if there were some sort of industry nearby where the peasants could earn extra money from part-time work. But such were relatively rare at the Great War's outbreak. Peasants who lived in them were thought by their neighbors to be people of means.

Fire was a particular hazard in Russian villages in the late nineteenth century. Most often, peasants roofed their buildings with crude thatch, not woven and neatly tied as in the case of those picturesque cottages for which southern England is famous, but simply constructed of brush and straw laid across crude frames at right angles to the ridgepole and held in place with cut saplings. The least spark could set dried thatch of this type ablaze in an instant, and, once the flames had taken hold, they leaped from one *izba* to another with frightening speed. At the turn of the century the government urged peasants to replace thatched roofs with tin and even offered it on easy credit terms to encourage its use. Yet peasants learned new ways slowly; unused to constructing proper supports for the heavier tin roofs, they built them so clumsily that the walls of their *izby* sometimes collapsed under the added weight.[21]

Most peasants went on as in olden times building their *izby* without chimneys in an effort to keep sparks away from flammable thatched roofs. Especially on a cold winter's day, smoke could be seen escaping from the buildings' interiors through slightly opened windows and around loosely fitting doors. Windows, however, were few, and glass still not the rule. Even at the end of the century, many windows were still covered with stretched and dried bulls' bladders or some other such translucent material that allowed only the faintest amount of light to penetrate into the *izba*'s murky, grimy interior at midday.

Whatever the materials of its construction, each *izba* stood in the midst of a small garden plot where peasants grew a few vegetables to vary their meager diet. Nearly every plot held some sort of crude shed and, if the family was a bit better off in comparison with its neighbors, there might also be a threshing shed, some sort of granary and, in rare cases, a bathhouse. More prosperous peasants fenced their plots with crude wattles. For poorer peasants in that part of Russia, wood was too precious to be squandered in such a manner. With rare exceptions, outbuildings were of the flimsiest sort, often with walls made of wicker and clay, and only those of the most well-to-do peasant families were solid enough to shield livestock from the winter's brutal cold. In winter, most peasant families brought their livestock into the *izba* itself.

Typical of peasants everywhere, families tended to be large, with several generations living under one roof in a single room that measured about twenty feet in width by twenty-five in length on the average. The floor was usually of dirt, packed hard by the passage of many feet over the decades. There were no comforts and few of the most basic necessities. Everything was crude, dark, and dismal. The only decorations might consist of a handful of crude prints and brightly colored postcards upon which peasants sometimes squandered a few extra kopeks when they visited the local market. At best cheap cartoon art, they provided the rare splash of color and evidence of the outside world to enter the peasants' gray and dreary daily lives.

Whether its inhabitants were rich or poor, the family members few or numerous, the interior of every *izba* shared two features. The corner farthest from the door was filled by a huge square oven, usually built of brick and clay, that rose to within a couple feet of the eaves. The oven warmed the interior, cooked the family's bread and other scant stores of food, and its flat top provided sleeping space for the elderly and the infirm. Because few *izby* had chimneys, smoke from the oven drifted into the interior and, over time, covered everything it touched with a coating of black, greasy soot. Diagonally from the oven, in the corner nearest the door, was the "place of honor" where the family hung the ikons toward which everyone bowed and murmured a brief prayer as they entered. St. Nicholas the Miracle-Worker was the religious image most commonly seen in peasant dwellings, although he was often found in the company of a cheap copy of any one of several miraculous ikons of the Holy Mother. Worn by age and darkened by smoke and dirt, these crude images were illuminated by the flickering light of a red-glass lamp that hung before them. In addition to a burning splinter or two, the ikon lamp—the *lampada*—often provided the only light in the *izba*'s interior. Only in the homes of prosperous peasants might a kerosene lantern be found, although these were rare even at the end of the century. One public health doctor found them in only one *izba* out of twelve as late as 1902.[22]

The furnishings of the remaining two corners of the typical *izba* in Russia's Black Soil region tended to vary more with the means of its inhabitants. One area was used by the family for eating and sleeping. Commonly, it was furnished only with a number of crude wooden benches upon which people sat and ate during the day and upon which everyone (with the exception of the sick and the elderly) slept at night. More prosperous families might boast of one large bed in addition, although beds were not common even at the turn of the century. Bedding most frequently was coarse ticking stuffed with straw that was none too clean. All of it was infested with vermin, as was everything else in the *izba*'s interior. Beetles were everywhere, although bedbugs and even cockroaches tended to diminish in numbers in the most impoverished households. "The bedbug is a natural aristocrat and requires a greater degree of comfort than can be found in the dwellings of the rural poor," one *zemstvo* doctor commented ruefully on the eve of the Revolution of 1905, while the peasants themselves had a saying that "those folks have become so poor that even the cockroaches have left!"[23] The *izba*'s remaining corner was called the "women's corner," and it was there that the peasant matriarch presided over her daughters, daughters-in-law, and, perhaps, a maiden aunt or unmarried sister, while they performed the household chores and prepared the family's meager meals.

All lived in crowded turmoil, especially during the long months of winter. Wrote one mid-century observer: "Together with the peasant in his hut during the winter live from ten to fifteen lambs with their mothers, two or three pigs with piglets, two or three calves, and sometimes a young colt."[24] The filth and stench were appalling. The excrement of people and animals alike usually was left in the courtyard or in the *izba*'s outer passageway where, according to one doctor's report, "it was devoured by the pigs, dogs, and chickens." There were some cases in which public health officials found entire villages without a single privy.[25] People destined to live out their lives under such conditions obviously did not enjoy the idyllic existence that sentimental and romantic authors had attributed to them in earlier days. Nor did they possess those cultural blessings and moral virtues imagined by the more radical intelligentsia.

The technological revolution that had transformed agriculture in the United States and Western Europe during the second half of the nineteenth century had passed by Russia's impoverished peasant villages almost without a trace. At the end of the century, Russia's peasants still tilled the soil with implements much like those their ancestors had used two or three centuries before. Crudely fashioned wooden plows, sometimes with two shares but usually with only one, were the rule, and their use was supplemented by harrows made with wooden teeth, often no more than sharpened stakes, that were tied to a primitive frame. Iron plows, which could cut so much more easily to turn deeper, more fertile, furrows in the grain belt's heavy black earth, and harrows with cast-iron teeth that could break up heavy clods of soil were rarely seen in Russia's Black Soil villages before the turn of the century; even by 1914, the best estimates are that only one household in ten owned one or the other.

Like the preparation of the land for planting, harvesting was done by hand. Reapers and threshers were almost unheard of among the peasants, and the primary implements for the harvest continued to be the sickle (wielded only by women) and the scythe (used only by men) as in the time of Ivan the Terrible. Threshing was done with chains or with primitive flails. Most peasants never had seen steam power used to ease the burden of their toil. From the moment the first furrow was turned in the spring until the last sheaf of grain was carried away in the fall, it was peasant hands and peasant backs that supplied the labor to produce Russia's grain. For the overwhelming majority of country folk whose rare extra rubles had to be spent to buy food as winter neared its end, thoughts of acquiring any sort of machine had to be relegated to the realm of the wildest fantasy. Only a handful of peasants—perhaps only one or two families in any village—could reasonably look forward to a time when such labor-saving implements might be theirs. The appearance of even a few prosperous peasants, however, indicated that a dramatic transformation was beginning in Russia's rural communities.

Far more than their counterparts a half-century earlier, travelers who passed through Russian villages in the 1890s observed very obvious economic gradations among peasant households. By that time, a few well-to-do peasants had begun to replace their log *izby* with ones built of brick, and the impression of solidity that these conveyed was reinforced by the better-built barns and outbuildings that surrounded them. The most obvious indicator of wealth, however, was the quantity of livestock in a peasant homestead. Milch cows and sheep were of less consequence; draft animals were the most critical measure of prosperity because their presence or absence dictated the quantity of land a peasant could plow during the growing season. Therefore, it was a matter of great concern to government agronomists that more than half of all peasant households owned only one draft animal and that, in some of the Black Soil provinces, as many as four out of ten had none at all.[26] Such poor peasants had to hire their more affluent neighbors to plow their fields at costs that could reach as high as one-half of the crop they harvested in the fall, condemning them to even greater poverty in the process.

Since most peasants could at best hope to grow only enough

grain to pay their taxes and feed their families until the next harvest, those who had to pay their neighbors to plow their fields reached the point of near-starvation long before winter's end. Many abandoned any effort to work their lands, left their use to other peasants, and worked as wage laborers. Some went to the cities.[27] Others fell into those rural proletarian ranks that moved about the Russian country-side in a never-ending quest for employment, their migrations to the great latifundia of southern Russia becoming an annual feature of rural life at the end of the century. Such men and women lived at the brink of starvation at all times in a world where farm hands earned a miserable wage of only twenty-four kopeks a day (twelve cents at the official exchange rate in 1900) except during the short weeks of harvest, when the pay doubled.[28]

The many peasants who struggled to eke out a living on the land, as well as that handful who had begun to prosper, usually lived and farmed within the broader framework of village communes that held title to most of the lands they tilled in Russia's Black Soil provinces. The commune also determined the quality, quantity, and location of the fields that every household worked. As the nineteenth century drew to a close, this became a vital issue because most families had too little land for their needs. For a variety of reasons related to the complex provisions of the Emancipation of 1861 and to the poverty of Russia's peasantry in general, it was extremely difficult for communes to purchase more land during the last third of the century. Peasants stood by helpless and bitter as their numbers increased by more than 50 percent during those years, while their communes were able to increase their holdings by less than half that amount. At the end of the century, therefore, the holdings of Russia's village communes (including lands rented from nobles and merchants) averaged about six acres for each peasant household resident. In Europe, a family might do well indeed if each member held that amount of land, but Russia's peasants were the least pro-ductive on the continent, with tragic results. For all but the most successful, it was almost impossible to grow enough grain to pay taxes and feed a family on the land available for their use.[29] In some regions, the poorest peasants began to supplement their grain with famine bread as early as October; nearly all had to do so by Easter.[30]

In an effort to be equitable in parceling out the limited lands within their boundaries, peasant communes divided their holdings into many small strips according to the land's fertility, water supply, and distance from the village, and then assigned to every household the use of a certain number of strips depending upon how many working hands lived within its walls. As in medieval Europe, the holdings of each family thus lay scattered over the commune's entire domain, and it was almost unheard of for a peasant in Russia's Black Soil provinces to have a farm in the sense that nineteenth-century American settlers had come to know the term. "Strips [of land] six feet wide are by no means rare," wrote one observer. "Of these narrow strips, a household may possess as many as thirty in a single field!"[31] Since every village held title to many fields, a peasant household might well have the use of a hundred or more of these tiny land fragments. That meant that peasants had to waste parts of each working day in moving their implements from one plot to another, and the number of valuable hours lost as a result must have been considerable in the course of a single season. That, however, was only one of the obstacles that made it impossible for any village to be as productive as it ought to have been.

Should one of the nineteenth-century American farmers to whom we referred earlier have been transported halfway around the globe to the *izba* of his Russian counterpart, he would have been appalled to learn not only that his host's lands were scattered over a wide area but that the actions of his fellows could deprive him of their use at any moment. Every commune held regular meetings to decide when to plow, plant, and harvest. At such assemblies, only the heads of households (a position that could be held by women as well as men) could vote, but every peasant had the right to speak his mind. Except in the Ukraine, the most important task of these communal assemblies was to reapportion the lands within their boundaries every few years in order to take account of each household's altered circumstances. As a result, a family whose numbers had been reduced by deaths or migrations of its sons to the cities might see its lands diminish drastically within a short span of time. That single fact took away any incentive most peasants might have had to fertilize their fields or improve them in other ways. Because they made no effort to replenish what their crops took from the soil, the fields of the Black Soil region yielded less and less per acre. It was a vicious circle that could be broken only when Russia's peasants became the real owners of the lands they tilled.[32]

Except for that handful of rural folk called *kulaki* who were beginning to prosper, the great majority of the men and women who produced Russia's single greatest source of wealth thus lived on the brink of poverty and starvation when Nicholas II became Emperor. Even though grain was their major crop, and even though Russia exported large amounts of grain to Western Europe, most peasants had to buy flour before the winter reached its end. In some parts of the Black Soil region, as many as nine out of every ten families had to buy flour in the spring at prices that were far higher than those at which they had been forced to sell their wheat and rye to pay their taxes the previous fall. Often such purchases were not mere supplements to the family larder, but a major portion of the year's food supply. Almost half of the peasant families in some parts of Russia's central grain-growing provinces had to purchase more than half of their flour in any given year.[33]

Flour, of course, was vital to the survival of every peasant family because from it the women baked the coarse rye bread that was the staple of its diet. Often there was little else to eat, although every peasant housewife endeavored to serve at least a watery cabbage soup called *shchi* at the evening meal to go with the bread. "The basic hot dish served almost daily was cabbage soup," wrote the Soviet sociologists who studied the village of Viratino. "Depending on the family's economic situation, it was made with or without meat and enriched with milk, sour cream, or lard."[34] But there were in fact many peasant families in Russia's grain belt for whom even *shchi* was a rare luxury. "There are many peasant households who do not have the means to buy cabbage, pickled cucumbers, or meat. There are some families who do not see milk in the course of an entire year!" Dr. Andrei Shingarev wrote in reporting conditions he found in parts of Voronezh province about a decade before the Revolution. "For someone like me, who was born and raised in a village, it was no surprise that very little meat was eaten by the peasants," he continued. "But to find families who had no cabbage for the winter was something I never expected. 'Then how do you manage to make *shchi?*' The question sprang from my lips even before I had time to think. . . . '*Shchi,*' an elderly and sick peasant said dully. 'It has been a year and a half since we've eaten any *shchi.*' "[35] Shingarev estimated that the combined daily consumption of meat, fish, and poultry among the peasants in some of the villages he visited averaged just over one ounce, produced chronic protein deficiency and left the peasants' diets acutely short of fats. With such basic foods in short supply, even the simplest luxuries stood far beyond the reach of all but the most fortunate peasant. In one village, annual sugar consumption totaled just less than three ounces per person, and, although vodka was thought to be Russia's traditional curse, Shingarev found the peasants there were so poor that they could buy about only one ounce each week. In the same village, the average annual consumption of tea was a half-ounce (the equivalent of about seven modern-day tea bags) for each person, even though tea drinking was a custom to which peasants were as dedicated as they were to the consumption of vodka.[36]

Monotonous diets overloaded with carbohydrates and consisting mainly of coarse rye bread and *shchi,* supplemented by limited quantities of dairy products and vegetables, took a toll upon the health of all peasants, but the impact was seen most dramatically in the terrible infant mortality rates that plagued Russia's villages. When their mothers were unable to nurse them, or could do so for only a few months before their milk ceased to flow, as many as two out of three infants died before their first birthday. Even under the best conditions, one out of every three peasant infants died before he was weaned. Wretched diets obliged mothers to supplement their milk even during the first months of their children's lives, and this caused more deaths. Such effective diet supplements as gruel were beyond the means of one out of every five peasant mothers, and they could do nothing but feed their nurselings the only food they had.

Morning and evening, hungry peasant mothers took a few bits of precious black bread from their own ration, chewed it briefly, wrapped the mush in a bit of rag, and gave it to their infants to suck. Half of the children fed in that manner died in their first year.[37]

Throughout the Black Soil region, rural communities were ravaged by diseases and maladies that sapped the strength of their undernourished residents. From lives of hard physical toil, many peasants developed kidney ailments, hernias, and rheumatism that often removed them from the village labor force in their forties. Infectious diseases struck villages on a regular schedule and often reached epidemic proportions. The new year usually found a typical peasant village in the grip of an influenza outbreak. In May, malaria usually struck, soon to be followed by cholera. In the late fall and early winter the annual wave of diphtheria arrived and, as the year closed, the village once again fell victim to influenza, which carried over into January to begin the cycle anew. Utter ignorance about the most elementary rules of sanitation allowed peasant water supplies to be contaminated by human and animal wastes, and debilitating parasitic infections of the gastrointestinal tract were commonplace. Tuberculosis struck often and at any season, as did dysentery, typhoid fever, scarlatina, measles, and smallpox, all of which often proved fatal in a peasant setting.[38]

Yet these were diseases from which the Russian land had suffered for centuries, and peasants had long since become reconciled to their ravages. During the second half of the nineteenth century, however, they faced a new infection that quickly reached near-epidemic proportions. In nineteenth-century Europe, syphilis often seemed common to those cities in which the surging Industrial Revolution had spawned an urban proletariat of sizable dimension. Demoralized by the impersonality of urban life, and freed from the moral and social constraints that had ruled their lives among family and friends in the village, tens of thousands of the country folk who had come to the city in search of work infected each other with venereal diseases at an alarming rate. The same was true of Russia's few industrial centers in the 1870s and 1880s. Unlike the West, however, syphilis also spread through Russia's peasant world during the second half of the nineteenth century. In an era before the discovery of antibiotics, and among a population never before exposed to the disease, doctors were powerless to halt its furious march.

Syphilis, of course, was not new among certain strata of Russia's population, for its ravages had been felt ever since her contacts with the European world had begun to broaden appreciably in the seventeenth century. Peter the Great had almost certainly contracted the disease in Moscow's Foreign Quarter, and, as the eighteenth century had progressed, a growing number of Russia's lords shared the affliction with their wives and mistresses. Because of their long-standing isolation from the outside world, however, many peasant villages had escaped infection during those years, especially because those among them who were drafted into the army, and most likely to become infected at one garrison or another, almost never returned to their native villages if they survived their quarter-century terms of military service. After the Emancipation Acts were promulgated in 1861, however, peasants began to move more freely. The best estimates are that traveling merchants and wholesalers who dealt in grain and cattle first spread syphilis into villages of the Black Soil region, especially those that boasted an inn or stood in the vicinity of a district fair. As acute land shortages forced more peasants to seek part-time work in Russia's cities and mines, or obliged them to join the annual migration of farm laborers to the far south, the disease spread more widely and young men carried its infectious spirochetes back to their villages when they returned in the spring or fall.

These new population movements left as many as one peasant family out of five infected with syphilis in some villages. But even that shocking statistic does not reveal the full extent of the disease's spread. Toward the end of the 1890s, appalled public health physicians began to find syphilis in as many as four out of every ten children in some parts of rural Russia. Because syphilitic mothers had infected them before birth, their disease often reached its tertiary stage even before they entered adolescence. An effective cure for the infection still was more than four decades away, and there was no way to halt its spread.[39] Russia's malnourished, syphilitic peasantry presented a dismal prospect indeed as the new century began.

Peasants' reluctance to consult those few doctors and clinics to which they might have turned for treatment magnified the impact of diseases caused by filth and malnutrition, as well as those occupational illnesses that stemmed from part-time labor in mines and factories. Superstitious and fearful about modern medicine, they clung to their centuries-old faith in folk medicine as practiced by a wide assortment of "wise" men and women. The chief weapon in the medicinal arsenal of such local healers was holy water, which did nothing to cure men, women, and children suffering from syphilis, cancer, or tuberculosis. Still, a number of folk cures proved surprisingly effective. Among the Russian peasantry, as among the American Indians and other primitive peoples, the knowledge of herbal infusions that passed from generation to generation had true curative value, and that was especially the case in the treatment of fevers and intestinal ailments that could respond well to medicinal herbs.

When their illnesses proved resistant to herbal remedies and holy water, most peasants suffered in silence, for it was only toward the very end of the nineteenth century that anything resembling the practice of scientific medicine came within their reach. Yet, even when provincial and district councils (zemstva) began to hire more doctors and public health personnel, most peasants could be persuaded to visit the small clinics and district hospitals that began to dot the Russian countryside only when they lay at death's door. That doctors proved unable to save the lives of those whose diseases had reached the terminal stage before they sought treatment reinforced the peasants' prejudice against modern medicine. Because so many who visited local clinics died, peasants feared that any visit to a clinic would prove fatal, so they stayed away.

Peasants' fears of modern medicine were especially tragic because so many of those who died from infectious diseases could have been saved by prompt treatment. During the last decade of the nineteenth century, about one Russian in two hundred died from smallpox, scarlatina, whooping cough, measles, or diphtheria. Among peasants, the mortality rate from those diseases was fully four or five times higher, and often accounted for as many as half of all the deaths in a peasant community in any particular year. As the twentieth century opened, those disastrous death rates of five or six out of every hundred that had so appalled educated Russians during the famine year still were common coin among the peasants.[40]

For most peasants, even those years that showed a "profit" were lean ones. After all farm expenses, costs for extra food, taxes, and other sums due the government were paid in an average year, according to one sampling of "typical" peasant budgets studied by Vladimir Lenin in the years just before he founded the Bolshevik party, two out of every three peasant households had less than 65 rubles (about $32) left over with which to buy clothing, lamp oil, and all other necessities. Nor was that the only measure of their poverty, for the value of their total assets in no way reflected lifetimes spent in heavy labor. At the end of the century, the average worth of such peasant households (including the value of the *izba,* farm buildings, implements, livestock, and all the family's clothing) was just less than 400 rubles—a mere $193![41] It was a damning statement about the failure of the Tsar and the Empire he ruled to provide even the most modest opportunities for most of his subjects. On the eve of the Revolution of 1905, Russian peasants could hope for little more than to find the means to survive for another year. With such minimal opportunities and limited resources, they made most of what they wore or used in the course of their daily lives with their own hands and bought only those few manufactured goods that they absolutely could not do without.

From spring to fall, peasants' lives were given over to incessant labor as they dedicated every hour of daylight to the single task of surviving for another year. "The one thing that the Russian peasant knows for certain is that a sunny summer working day must be cherished, that Nature allows him very little time in which to complete his agricultural labors, and that the brief Russian summer can be shortened still further by unseasonably bad weather," wrote the great nineteenth-century historian Vasilii Kliuchevskii. "Therefore, the Russian peasant must bend to his tasks," he continued. "He must work at top speed to get everything finished in time."[42] For the 79 million peasants who lived in the Empire that Nicholas II inherited from his father, the *ottepel*—the great annual spring thaw that turned Russia's primitive roads into seas of mud—heralded the onset of the season of frantic labor that Kliuchevskii described. Without a moment's delay, the peasants had to plow and harrow the land, sow their crops, and put the livestock out to pasture in the common meadow, all within a few short weeks. Every peasant household then had to tend its fields, harvest its crops, gather fuel for the winter, lay in a supply of pickled vegetables, dried fruits, mushrooms, and nuts, plant and harvest the flax, and shear the sheep. Entire families labored during this season from sunup to long beyond sunset, and eighteen-hour workdays were commonplace.[43]

Spinning, weaving, and sewing were women's work, and those tasks filled many of their hours before the *ottepel* came. Instead of using spinning wheels, most peasant women twisted thread on hand spindles that were fastened to the top of an L-shaped frame. Called *prialki,* such distaffs often were decorated with elaborately painted or carved designs that could be seen easily when the user tucked the tip of the frame's base under one thigh and sat on a bench near the window to let the winter light fall upon her work. Once the spinning was done in late winter, the weaving commenced and continued until Lent. When the weather grew warm, the women bleached their newly woven cloth (the equivalent of the American pioneers' "linsey-woolsey") with wood ash and boiling water in a process that had to be repeated some two dozen times before the product of their looms was ready to be dyed. Virtually all peasants produced black cloth in their own *izby,* but, for other colors, especially their favorite blues and reds, they took the bleached cloth to men more skilled in the dyer's trade than they. Only after that was done could the sewing begin.

From the cloth they had produced during the year, Russia's peasant women fashioned shirts, trousers, and coats for their men, as well as skirts, sarafans, aprons, blouses, and everyday kerchiefs for themselves. Men wore their shirts outside trousers that were amply cut and often made of blue and white striped material. Over these they wore the blackcloth coat that was a standard part of every peasant's wardrobe. Women's skirts usually were of dark blue, black, and white plaid, and their blouses were of coarse white linen.

Surrounded as they were by monotonous shades of gray, brown, blue, and black, peasants lived color-starved lives. Therefore they chose the most brilliant hues for their holiday clothing, and fiery shades of red, green, and pink were very much in vogue. All treasured their special holiday attire, which included elaborately embroidered blouses, skirts of finer wool decorated with braid and colored ribbons, and kerchiefs made of silk or satin for women, while men wore similarly embroidered shirts, brass belt buckles, and fancy caps. More affluent peasants added patent leather shoes. Almost all girls and women wore necklaces of glass beads with a small brass ikon pendant, as well as earrings made of brass or copper wire. *Kulak* women sometimes wore silver or even gold jewelry as evidence of their greater wealth.[44] Holiday dress was designed to be distinctive, yet, like so much else in the peasants' lives, and in spite of their best efforts, much of it remained poor and sparse.

During the spring and summer, everyone in the village wore slippers called *lapti* that the men and boys wove from thin strips cut from the inner bark of young linden trees. Such material could not long resist the soil's abrasions, and *lapti* wore out quickly. Several pairs therefore had to be woven for each member of the family during the winter months. Thin and porous bark shoes could not be worn in the cold and damp of autumn and winter, and, during those months, peasants donned felt boots that they called *valenki*. These usually were made by a village craftsman as were sheepskin coats and leather boots, the other major items in the peasant's wardrobe. Many peasant families had only one or two sheepskin coats, which the members shared among themselves; leather boots were treasured and given such special care that it was not unusual for them to last for several decades and be passed on to new generations by their proud possessors.[45] In such a world, where barter prevailed and cash was only infrequently available, prospects for the immediate development of all but the nation's heavy industries were indeed bleak. There simply was no domestic market that could encourage Russia's light industry to develop beyond the most rudimentary handicraft level.

Peasants observed a variety of festive occasions, and the lack of many simple necessities quite probably added to the intensity of their celebrations. Holidays were identified by a variety of customs that varied from province to province. Caroling at Christmas, fortune-telling among the village maidens at New Year's, and egg rolling at Easter were common to all peasants, as was the custom of holding weddings around the feast of St. Mikhail in November and during the week after Easter. Holidays were greeted with special foods, games, dancing, and fighting.[46] Most of all, however, they celebrated with vodka, that raw, fiery spirit that figured so prominently in all Russian festivities. "It's a sin to come home sober from a wedding," went an old folk saying. Not to have vodka to celebrate a holiday was a deprivation of body and spirit that few peasants were willing to accept, no matter how poor they were. "What would he do if he could not get drunk tomorrow?" wrote Vladimir Korolenko at the beginning of his famous tale about a peasant who faced Christmas without a drop of vodka in his *izba*. "How terrible life was! Here it was the greatest holiday of the winter and he had not a single bottle of vodka to drink!"[47]

Whatever the occasion, the consumption of vodka was more than a polite ritual among Russia's peasantry. No village enterprise such as planting or haying could begin, no business be transacted, no agreement made, no betrothal, wedding, birth, or funeral celebrated without it.[48] Virtually every peasant sought from time to time to attain that euphoric state of drunken stupor known as *zapoi* and, when he succeeded in that effort, he quickly threw all caution to the winds in an endeavor to preserve his intoxication as long as possible. Without hesitation, he would spend every kopek in his pocket and, when his money was gone, would sometimes exchange his clothes, livestock, even his right to use a portion of the village land, for more and more vodka. In the course of those periodic binges to which they were addicted, peasants sometimes ruined themselves and condemned their families to even greater poverty.[49] "I believe that no one will deny that we have started our civilization directly with debauch!" Dostoevskii lamented not long before he began to write *The Brothers Karamazov.*[50]

Although nature, the government, and even fate joined forces to raise many obstacles in their path, it is difficult to escape the conclusion that the peasants of Russia often were their own worst enemies. "They were crude, dishonest, filthy, and drunken," Russia's master of the short story, Anton Chekhov, once wrote. "Who tends the tavern and makes the peasants into drunkards?" he asked rhetorically. "A peasant! Who would steal from his neighbor, commit arson, and perjure himself in court, all for a bottle of vodka? Who is the first to speak out against the peasants in the district council and elsewhere? A peasant. Yes, to live among them was terrible," Chekhov concluded, "but they were human beings nonetheless. . . . They had no help and nowhere to turn for help."[51] Chekhov's was a view that many educated Russians shared. "Judge the Russian people [i.e., the peasants] not by those villainies which they frequently perpetrate, but by those great and holy things for which they long amidst the very villainy," Dostoevskii exhorted his readers. "A true friend of mankind," he added, "will understand and forgive all the impassable alluvial filth in which they are submerged, and will be able to discover diamonds in this filth."[52]

Peasants endeavored to escape their terrible world in *zapoi*, but they tried to explain it through a form of religion that embodied a curious and anachronistic mixture of paganism and Christianity. The relationship of the Russian peasant to the Orthodox Church was very different from the deep and fervent faith of the downtrodden Roman Catholic peasants of Ireland or Poland at the end of the nineteenth century. Russia's peasants lived closer to nature, nearer to those elemental forces that had kindled the pagan belief of primitive peoples in earlier times. "Mystical exaltation is not in their nature," wrote the great nineteenth-century literary critic Vissarion Belinskii in his famous letter to Nikolai Gogol. "They have too much common sense."[53] "Life on earth may be unbearable," went a peasant saying, "but death is not so pleasant either." Peasant belief thus combined fatalism with paganism upon which it imposed the rituals of Orthodoxy.

"Russia is probably the only European country where man has not lost the sense of the invisible, where he truly and really feels himself in touch with the denizens of the unseen world," wrote a French publicist in the 1880s.[54] Russia's peasants thus insisted that calamities stemmed directly from God's will. "God is angry and has sent them," the peasants of southern Russia reportedly concluded when their crops were attacked by locusts in 1880. "When the day of punishment is past, the locusts will go."[55] Likewise, drought, famine, and disease could be attributed to the same source. God and his saints therefore had to be appeased by prayer, invocation, and genuflection, and the peasants regarded these holy beings in very personal terms. God was always nearby in their imaginations, although he often assumed strange forms. "God has little green, red, and blue *lampady* just like tiny little eyes," one of Chekhov's peasants explained at one point.[56] The God of the Russian peasants, as well as the Holy Mother and all the saints, could bestow protection, wreak vengeance, and carry grudges that could have dire consequences. Therefore, no peasant dared enter his or anyone else's *izba* without making a proper obeisance to the ikons that hung in the "place of honor." None among them dared commit any sinful act within their sight, and peasant prostitutes and women about to commit adultery always hastened to cover the ikons before they abandoned themselves to intercourse with their clients or lovers. To please the ikons, peasants not only said prayers but also lit candles before the saints' images in the local church. Here, too, paganism combined with Christian devotion as in the oft-repeated account of the peasant who lit two candles at the festival of St. George. When asked why he had done so, he replied that one was for St. George and the other was for the dragon.

But God, the Holy Mother, and the many saints of the Russian Orthodox Church were not the only powers to whom superstitious peasants looked to account for the events in their lives. There were many other supernatural beings to whom they paid homage and endeavored to win to their cause. Chief among these were the *vodianye*, those water sprites who lived in the rivers and were most commonly found near millraces; the *leshnie*, or woods goblins, who lived in the forests, teased travelers, and made them lose their way; and the *domovoi*, the little demon who lived inside every *izba*'s oven and played all sorts of pranks upon unwary housewives. Rituals to appease the spirit world were as complex as any used to win God's favor. To protect themselves and their families against cholera, for example, peasant women were known to assemble in the dead of night and parade half-naked around the outskirts of their village. At the head of their procession they bore ikons, while they chanted folk incantations and spells in an effort to keep the demons who bore the disease from crossing a furrow that two maidens harnessed to a plow traced around the village's perimeter.[57] In addition to these lesser spirits that brought mischief and disease was the Devil himself, the most important in the peasants' pantheon of supernatural beings. Peasants invoked his name nearly as often as God's, and he often figured along with God in their folk sayings. "Light a candle to God, but light one to the Devil too. You never know," they were fond of saying. "Pray to God, but take care not to offend the Devil."

Peasants held such views about water sprites, house demons, and the Devil not only as a consequence of their distant pagan heritage, but because they knew so very little about the real teachings of the Church. Most could not recite the Lord's Prayer, even at the end of the nineteenth century, and were equally ignorant about all other aspects of Christian doctrine. When one peasant was asked to name the three Persons of the Trinity, he reportedly replied: "Of course, it is the Savior, the Mother of God, and St. Nicholas the Miracle-Worker!"[58] To Russia's rural masses, the rituals of the Church were a complex form of magic that, when properly applied, could bring success to any venture regardless of its nature. "Christ Himself appears to him [the peasant] as the mightiest and most benevolent of conjurors, and God is the supreme magician," wrote one observer at the time.[59] Therefore, one peasant thief in St. Petersburg was known to have visited a church to obtain the saints' blessing before he set out to rob and murder a young attaché at the Austrian Embassy, while another housebreaker was heard to promise his patron saint to light a whole ruble's worth of candles to his greater glory if only he would help him remove the tightly mounted precious stones from an ikon in a church.[60]

In no small measure, the amazingly primitive quality of the peasants' belief, and the equally primitive world in which they lived at the opening of the twentieth century, stemmed from their lack of education and their consequent inability to become integrated into that larger society of which they were a part. At the time of their emancipation, less than two out of every hundred peasants could read and write, and the battle for literacy moved at a veritable snail's pace for the next three decades. During the late 1860s and 1870s, literacy programs for peasant draftees were instituted in army garrisons. Some peasants who went to Russia's towns and cities also learned to read and brought their knowledge back to their villages. Nonetheless, the majority of Russia's peasants remained illiterate at the end of the nineteenth century, and only the concentrated efforts of Soviet planners eventually succeeded in reducing illiteracy in the decades after the Revolution of 1917.[61]

In any case, few among the peasants read to gain knowledge or for self-improvement. They had long since learned how to interpret weather signs, build an *izba*, thatch its roof, and drain a field. They knew when the rye should be planted and when it should be reaped. They knew which mushrooms could be dried for winter use and which would bring hallucinations, convulsions, or even death to the ignorant soul who consumed them. They knew which herbs had medicinal value and which bore deadly poison in their sap. They knew how to appease the *domovoi* that lurked in the *izba*'s oven so that he would not make the bread fall or cause the food to burn. What, then, could books tell them? In 1901, Dr. Shingarev reported that, at best, only one family in three actually had a book in its *izba*, and more recent studies by Soviet sociologists have borne out his findings in other parts of the Black Soil provinces. Literate peasants favored religious tales, volumes of fairy stories with colorful and fanciful illustrations, and, by 1900, had begun to develop a taste for the Russian equivalent of "penny dreadfuls."[62]

Because peasants saw no reason at all for a woman to know how to read, they especially resisted all urgings to send their daughters to school. As a result, villages where only one woman in fifty could read evidently were not uncommon, and government statisticians actually found villages in the Black Soil provinces where not even one female out of a population of several hundred could be classed as literate. One such village studied by Dr. Shingarev was located within a mile of a government school, yet not only were its women utterly unlettered but the literacy rates among its men and boys were only half the national figure. "Take the books back to the school," one peasant was heard to tell his son in another village. "We're going to plow."[63] Not even one school-aged peasant child in six was actually in a classroom when Nicholas II donned his father's crown in 1894.[64] To transform Russia into a nation of literate men and women would have required tens of thousands more schools and hundreds of thousands of new teachers. First, however, there would have had to be a far stronger commitment to mass education from Nicholas and his leading councillors. Most important of all, Alexander III's conservative program of education, which urged the Church to play a central role in elementary education and dictated that children should be educated "more in keeping with their social status," would have had to be abandoned.[65]

Superstitious, fatalistic, ignorant, and illiterate, Russia's peasants viewed the outside world in the same concrete and personal terms that ruled their everyday lives. Before the Revolution of 1905, political tracts and revolutionary propaganda did not make much headway in the peasant world. As one noted scholar wrote not long ago, peasants "could perceive only in terms of specific activity [or people]. 'State,' 'society,' 'nation,' 'economy,' 'agriculture,' all these concepts had to be filled with people they knew or activities they performed in order to be grasped."[66] "Spring" to peasants thus meant plowing and planting, just as "fall" meant harvest. "Government" meant the petty and corrupt officials they encountered, albeit infrequently, in their everyday lives. For them, the Tsar was the "state," and they thought of him in very personal terms. The Tsar was their "Little Father"—their *Batiushka*. They imagined him to be a benevolent and beneficent patriarch who would understand their wretched plight and would set it right if only they could reach him. Landlords and officials, the Russian peasants thought, were responsible for their misery, not the Tsar, for the Tsar was, in the words of Professor Richard Pipes, their "terrestrial father and protector."[67] Such a view was based upon an idealized image of the Tsar that peasants had held for centuries. At the same time, the Tsar and his ministers fervently believed that the peasants were unswervingly loyal to their "Little Father," and that belief played a central role in their efforts to formulate new state policies. As always, idealized images proved supremely unattuned to reality. Both Tsar and peasants were soon forced to readjust their views. Nicholas II and the millions of peasants who called him "Tsar-Batiushka" when he ascended the throne paid a great and dear price for their failure to comprehend each other's true nature.

The high rates of illiteracy in Russia became especially critical as the nation moved into the modern technological age, where the limits of time and space shrank dramatically. In a world where news could travel thousands of miles within minutes, where decisions about national policy and diplomacy had to be made quickly, and where armies could be brought to the battlefield in days, not weeks or months, the Russian government's inability to communicate with its subjects by means of the printed word posed far more complex and critical problems than it had a half-century earlier. As the government's international interests ranged ever wider, there simply was no effective means for it to generate support among a *narod* that could not read. The first consequences of that failure became evident very soon after the twentieth century dawned. Faced by an illiterate citizenry, Nicholas II and his advisers found it impossible to explain Russia's aims in the Far East to the men and women from whom they would demand the greatest sacrifices. As a result, they failed utterly to generate popular support for the Russo-Japanese War. Their failure helped to stir the popular discontent that was so important in bringing on the Revolution of 1905.

Although the great famine of 1891 had brought disease and starvation to Russia on a vast scale, the 1890s marked an era of economic recovery and growing prosperity for a number of Russians. Industry flourished, foreign investments increased, and exports grew in value. Sergei Witte, the brilliant and farsighted statesman who replaced Vyshnegradskii as Russia's Minister of Finance in the summer of 1892, moderated his predecessor's policy of squeezing a full

measure of the surplus capital needed for Russia's industrial development from the peasantry of the Black Soil provinces and repeatedly
urged that the peasants' level of prosperity be raised.[68] Peasant
prosperity, he insisted, was the key to Russia's success in the twentieth century for, if the peasantry could be taxed at the same rate
as their far more prosperous French and Austrian counterparts, the
state's income would be more than doubled. For Witte, private
enterprise offered the best chance for the peasants to prosper. "It
is in the nature of every man to seek to better himself," he wrote
to Nicholas in October 1898. "The well-being and prosperity of
society and the government are based upon this single quality in
man." Because he was convinced that "in a slave this instinct is
crushed," he urged his Emperor to free the peasantry of Russia from
that slavery of arbitrary authority that all levels of government imposed upon their lives. Everyone saw fit to meddle in the peasants'
affairs with the result that the peasantry had no control over its own
destiny. "The peasant question," Witte concluded, "is the most
critical issue in the national life of Russia at the present moment.
It is absolutely essential to deal with it effectively."[69] He proposed
that Nicholas establish a special commission of experts to consider
how the peasantry might be set firmly upon the path to modernization, progress, and prosperity. For the moment, his effort produced
no result.

Witte's bold plea urged a dramatic break with the government's long-standing dedication to the peasant commune as the
rural institution best suited to direct peasant life. What drove him
to take such a stand was the sad fact that Russia's peasantry reflected
so very little of the economic recovery enjoyed by other sectors of
the economy and society in the decade after the great famine. At
the close of the century that had seen their emancipation from
personal bondage to their lords, rural folk remained in ongoing
economic bondage to their government as they fell farther and
farther behind in their efforts to meet the annual payments for their
village lands that the Emancipation Acts of 1861 had imposed upon
them. By 1900, their arrears had reached the immense sum of 120
million rubles.[70] The time for action had long since come. Swift and

decisive measures were called for. Urgently, Witte prodded Nicholas and his conservative advisers to strike out onto new paths before it was too late. Only when the hour of doom appeared to have struck, when revolution surged across Russia in 1905, were they finally moved to act. As so often happened, their efforts produced too little too late.

CHAPTER III
Russia's New Lords

THE GREAT INDUSTRIAL SURGE THAT VYSHNEGRADSKII AND Witte fostered at such terrible cost to Russia's peasants during the 1880s and 1890s produced a new group of privileged men and women, the likes of whom had never before appeared on Russia's historical stage. These were the lords of the Empire's new industry. Conservative and nationalistic, their values emphasized above all that very "Russianness" against which St. Petersburg's European taste and tradition continued to stand as a monument, and their economic and social world centered in Moscow. They aimed to develop Russian industry to meet the demands of Russian markets, and the needs of foreign entrepreneurs played little part in their calculations. Unlike the industrialists of St. Petersburg, the iron and coal magnates of the Ukraine, and the oil barons of Baku, many of whom were themselves foreigners, the men and women of Moscow's business community resisted the glitter of foreign capital and developed their factories with their own, Russian, resources. Brilliantly successful, they grew immensely rich.

These new lords of native Russian industry sometimes had their beginnings among the Empire's old-fashioned and conservative merchants. Others traced their origins back to a particularly resourceful and energetic serf family whose members had begun to better themselves by buying and selling to their neighbors in the early days of the nineteenth century. As family members had prospered, they had bought their freedom from their noble masters and had moved to the Moscow quarter called Zamoskvoreche, that seventeenth-century world of Old Russian custom and religiosity that flourished in the midst of early-nineteenth-century Russia. There they formed a tightly knit community from which they excluded all but their own kind. When Nicholas II ascended the throne, educated Russians probably knew considerably less about these new lords of industry than they did about the workers who labored in their factories. Russia's great industrial magnates were, and to this day remain, one of the most enigmatic of all social groups in the Empire's history.

Among Russian writers and publicists, ignorance about the lives lived by such men and women bred contempt, and contempt bred yet greater ignorance, although most educated commentators masked that fact with statements bearing the stamp of far more authority than they had any right to claim. "They employ much trickery and fraud in trade," the Emperor Maximilian's ambassador, Sigismund von Herberstein, had written of Russian merchants even before the days of Ivan the Terrible. "In their dealings [Russian] merchants always resort to false oaths and fraudulent promises," confirmed Augustin von Mayerberg, ambassador of the Holy Roman

Emperor to Moscow, a century later, while a French visitor to Russia during the reign of Catherine the Great warned that "there is not the least vestige of good faith and honesty among Russian merchants."[1] Russians themselves echoed much the same refrain. "Just as an army cannot exist without merchants [to supply it], so the merchants cannot survive without the army [from which to enrich themselves]," one of Peter the Great's councillors warned him in the 1720s.[2] Others repeated variations on that theme for the next two centuries. "Like a field mouse in the crops . . . eats and destroys everything around it, so the . . . Russian bourgeoisie has created nothing," wrote one Russian publicist as the twentieth century opened. " 'Don't deceive and you won't sell'—here is their rule of life."[3]

Perhaps the most enduring portraits of Russia's old-school merchants sprang from the pen of the mid-nineteenth-century playwright Aleksandr Ostrovskii, whose father had forsaken his family's tradition of service to the nation's church in order to become a government official in Moscow. There his playwright son was born, raised, and educated in full view of those very merchants whom he immortalized in his many plays. Like his father, young Aleksandr Ostrovskii became a civil servant in Moscow's commercial court, where he saw much of the seamy side of life among the city's businessmen. For several years, he looked on in amazement while they filed bogus claims, pleaded fraudulent bankruptcies, and pursued their never-ending passion for petty cheating, before he abandoned his career at the age of twenty-eight to devote himself to writing about the world he had seen as a youth and civil servant in Zamoskvoreche. Making it his life's task to describe what the great literary critic Nikolai Dobroliubov called the "kingdom of darkness," the inner realm of Russian merchant life, Ostrovskii always portrayed his subject in its most unvarnished, true-to-life form, although he often did so with humor and sensitivity.[4]

Ostrovskii's comedies popularized the stereotype of "Kit Kitych," the quintessential Russian merchant. "Kit Kitych" was what Russians call an *arshinnik,* a tradesman who never looked beyond the *arshin** of cloth he was trying to sell at any particular moment. He was concerned only with the kopeks of the present; he gave little thought to how they might relate to the rubles of the future.[5] " 'You should also measure,' I say, 'a little more naturally,' " one of Ostrovskii's merchants confides. " 'Stretch and pull the material until it's ready—God help us—to split.' 'You know,' I say, 'we're not going to wear it later on.' 'Now if the customers stand around gaping, no one's to blame,' I say, 'if you'd count one yard as two.' "[6] The stereotypical "Kit Kytch" wanted only to "add a ruble or two to the price per yard"[7] and revel in dreams about declaring fraudulent bankruptcies that might cheat his creditors out of seventy-five kopeks on every ruble he owed.

Ostrovskii's "Kit Kityches" were tied to Old Russia by religion as well as habit and tradition. Many of the merchant men and women of Zamoskvoreche were Old Believers, passionate in their dedication to the precepts that had governed Russian religious practice before the Great Church Council of 1667. For something over a century after the council had outlawed the Old Belief, its adherents had borne intense persecution, but the religious toleration that Catherine the Great had instituted toward the end of the eighteenth century had allowed them to flourish anew. From Russia's more remote regions, where they had sought refuge during the long years of persecution, Old Believers returned to the shelter of Moscow's time-worn walls within which their forefathers had practiced the rituals sanctified by the first saints of the Russian land. There they began to prosper as traders, merchants, and industrialists. During the first half of the nineteenth century, their ranks increased almost tenfold until they numbered nearly half of Moscow's entire population.[8]

A close-knit society and a strong work ethic enabled these Old Believers to prosper in trade and industry throughout the Russian land. In the growing Ural mountain center of Ekaterinburg, they controlled most of the privately owned metallurgical enterprises and,

---

*An *arshin* was an Old Russian unit of measure equal to twenty-eight inches.

on the lower Volga, they dominated the shipbuilding industry, directed East-West overland trade, and controlled the great annual fairs for which the region had long been famous.[9] Most of all, however, they flourished in Moscow, the city whose spiritual traditions claimed their profound and unwavering allegiance. There, Old Believer communities founded industrial enterprises that rapidly accumulated the capital from which grew a number of great private fortunes.[10]

However deep their dedication to Old Russian religious precepts, Moscow's Old Believers never shunned the exploitation of their less fortunate countrymen. As they gave shelter, employment, and religious instruction to orphans, serving girls whose masters had sent them into the streets pregnant and penniless, and others among the urban poor, they readily congratulated themselves for performing good works for the glory of God. At the same time, they clearly appreciated the great economic profit that came from employing folk who were in no position to quarrel about the terms of their employment at particularly low wages. By the 1850s, this supply of ready cheap labor enabled such Old Believer entrepreneurs as the Guchkovs, the Morozovs, and the Ushkovs to build industrial establishments that each employed more than a thousand workers, while a number of their coreligionists such as the Alekseevs were not far behind.[11]

Yet there were limits upon the development of industrial and commercial enterprise within Moscow's Old Believer community in the 1840s and 1850s. Persecutions launched by Nicholas I broke down the isolationist character of their settlements. At the same time, they realized that their enterprises could develop further only if they could hire many more workers than they had been able to assemble through traditional means. New industrial development thus demanded methods that extended far beyond the closed world of Zamoskvoreche, and these generated new values, "a secularization of their faith in the form of a nativist culture," as one expert wrote not long ago.[12] Isolationist Old Believers, who had traditionally cursed both Tsar and government as instruments of the Antichrist, began to evolve into fervent Russian patriots. As the French publicist Anatole Leroy-Beaulieu observed toward the end of Alexander III's reign, "wealth, which has begun the [Old Believers'] social emancipation, will end by accomplishing [their] intellectual emancipation also."[13] By the latter years of the century, gypsy singers no longer could curse indiscriminately:

> The Moscow merchantry,
> Whose *arshins* fall short a few inches,
> You're not sons of your country,
> You're just sons of bitches.[14]

Russia's merchants had begun to assume a new role in the nation's life. "The merchant, who thinks in terms of a domestic national market, is no longer that *arshinnik* who used to give the mayor two large cones of sugar in return for letting him go on giving short weight and measure to his customers," wrote Prince Vladimir Mescherskii.[15]

Among the new lords of Russia's industry, perhaps none soared higher than Savva Vasilevich Morozov, a humble serf of Count Riumin who was born in 1770 in the village of Zueva, some eighty-five *versty** northeast of Moscow.[16] Life was especially hard for Russian serfs when young Savva was growing to manhood. Caught in the grip of soaring inflation, masters demanded ever-larger dues from their bondsfolk, and the pressure of these heavy payments served to crush any spirit of initiative that might have lingered among them. A year's extra effort could be wiped out by a single stroke of the master's pen if he chose to demand more dues from his serfs that fall. There was little that the average serf could do with extra money in any case. There were almost no ways in which he could save it or, more importantly, invest it so that it might one day enable him and his family to improve their lot. Beyond that, because serfs were at the mercy of their masters' whims in all things, the vast majority made no effort to better their position. If one had little to

---

*A *versta* was an Old Russian unit of distance that was equivalent to two-thirds of a mile.

begin with, then one stood to lose less if times grew worse or the master more greedy.

All of these obstacles were of little account to Savva Morozov, for he possessed a store of energy and wit rarely found in a serf. Well before he reached the age of twenty, he managed to hire himself as a weaver to Kononov, who ran a small silk factory in his village. The wage was small, and much of it had to be paid to Count Riumin, but such sacrifices were worth enduring in order to learn a valuable craft. Soon, he put his knowledge to good use. The road would be long and hard, but the prize that Savva Morozov sought would be worth the effort. For within three decades after he first went to work in Kononov's factory, he, his wife, and children no longer would be numbered among Count Riumin's serfs. All of them would be free.

From the start, Savva Morozov showed his amazing capacity for extracting advantage from adversity. Not long before his twentieth birthday, he faced his first great challenge, and it was one that required all of his determination and ingenuity to overcome. Ever since the days of Peter the Great, the first days of spring brought tragedy to Russia's peasants as each village had to yield up its quota of recruits for the Imperial army. In eighteenth-century Russia, serf lads were taken into the army for life. Once drafted, they were lost forever to their families and villages, and their loved ones marked their departure by holding a funeral service in their memory. So terrible was the prospect of a life in the army that peasant lads were known to cripple themselves in an effort to escape.

These were desperate measures, subject to severe punishment. But there also was one legitimate means of escape. According to Russian law, any peasant recruit was entitled to hire a substitute to take his place, but the cost was very high. Five hundred rubles—the amount of cash that the average eighteenth-century serf family generated in about a quarter of a century—was the amount often asked, and it was rare that anyone could pay it.[17] Since the burden of army service was so onerous, and because so few could pay to escape it, peasants often settled the fate of the young men in their village by casting lots. One spring, toward the end of the 1780s, the lot fell to Savva Morozov.

Morozov was not prepared to resign himself so readily to wielding musket and bayonet for Catherine the Great. With rare persistence, he convinced his employer to lend him the sum to hire a substitute. Kononov agreed that he should repay the loan by piecework to be done at a very low rate of pay and undoubtedly thought that he had assured himself of the services of a talented weaver for many years to come. He soon realized that he had underestimated Morozov's resolve.

Dedicated to bettering his lot, Savva married, and his wife proved his equal in every way. Uliana Morozova, reputed to be one of Count Riumin's bastards, was the first in a long line of remarkable women who defied the constraints of tradition and labored to build the Morozov family fortune. Although barely out of her teens, she already had shown great skill in dyeing fabrics, and Riumin had even sent her to England to study the latest innovations in her art. Resolutely, she dedicated her talents to her new husband's cause. Together, they labored long hours to repay the loan that had freed him from military service. Within two years, the debt was paid. Now free from his debt to Kononov as well as the army, and urged on by his energetic wife, Savva Morozov turned to pursue a new and daring course. In 1797, he petitioned Count Riumin for permission to found his own silk ribbon factory in Zueva. When Riumin granted his request, Savva Morozov embarked upon the entrepreneurial journey that would lead to wealth beyond his wildest dreams.[18]

Among the many oddities about life in Russia before the middle of the nineteenth century was the strange fact that extremely able serf artisans and traders could become millionaires yet remain enserfed to their masters. A number of such serf millionaires were concentrated in the growing textile center of Ivanovo, less than a hundred *versty* northeast of Zueva, and there were a few others to be found in St. Petersburg and Moscow. Although everything had to be purchased in the name of their masters, such serfs often held large tracts of land, shops with rich inventories, and manufactures producing hundreds of thousands of rubles worth of goods each year. As the price for being allowed to continue in their enterprises, they paid their masters tens of thousands of rubles annually. For all of them, the first and greatest goal was to buy their freedom, although many years often passed before a master would agree to part with what Prince Dmitrii Mirskii once so aptly called "a hen with golden eggs," especially when such eggs tended to grow larger as the years passed.[19] In 1795, the Grachev family became the first to accomplish their goal by paying Count Sheremetev cash, factories, and serfs valued at a quarter of a million rubles. In later years, others paid more than four times as much for freedom.[20]

With the help of Uliana and their four sons, Savva Morozov set out upon the path already taken by his contemporaries at Ivanovo. Success came remarkably quickly, not only because of the Morozovs' dedication but also because they had the immense good fortune to begin their enterprise at one of the most propitious moments in Russia's history. In 1807, exactly a decade after Savva and Uliana had established their silk ribbon factory, Russia's Emperor Alexander I entered into Napoleon's Continental System and cut Russia off from all trade with England. Because English merchants had been the major suppliers of the large quantities of luxury goods that Russia's nobles consumed, the ladies of Moscow soon found themselves in desperate need of silken ribbon to adorn the new "Empire style" gowns that were coming into fashion. Uliana's reputedly superb sense of color, combined with the family's willingness to work long hours, must have made it especially easy for the Morozovs to exploit the booming Moscow market for their wares. Although many Russian merchants and nobles suffered serious losses during this period, the Morozovs' fortunes flourished.[21]

When Napoleon invaded Russia in the summer of 1812, he brought ruin to many. None suffered more than the people of Moscow, who had greeted the Corsican conqueror's arrival with one of the greatest fires in their city's history. "One drew breath in a sea of fire," wrote one of Napoleon's adjutants. "The flames spread continuously and it was impossible to predict where or when they would stop."[22] The burning of Moscow and the flight of the Russian nobles who lived there temporarily destroyed the market that the Morozovs had found so lucrative. But eighty-five *versty* to the north and east, their factory had escaped devastation. The family had only to await that moment when Napoleon's army would leave. In the meantime, they increased their stock of goods.

Soon after Napoleon abandoned Moscow in October 1812, Savva Morozov returned to the devastated city with his wares. When Moscow's nobles came back to those residences that had survived the fire, they found Morozov waiting, his large peddler's pack filled with bolts of wool and linen, as well as lacy Orenburg shawls and brilliant silk ribbons that could bring a flash of longed-for color to the fire-blackened world to which they had returned. Muscovites clamored for his goods; on some of his trips, many of his customers went out to meet him before he even reached the city. Here was an opportunity that no good businessman could ignore, and the Morozovs resolved to expand their enterprises. They were intent upon accomplishing this by using as little of their own capital as possible; that was to be saved for the dream they cherished most of all: freedom.

Among the few better-off peasants in the nearby villages, they found some with small savings that they were willing to invest. With this capital, the Morozovs built a woolen mill on the high bluff across the river from their ribbon factory. This was to become the famous Nikolskaia Mill, the cornerstore of their great fortune.

In 1820, less than a decade after the Nikolskaia Mill had been built, Savva Morozov paid Count Riumin 17,000 rubles to free himself, Uliana, and their four sons from bondage. Riumin, however, included the strange stipulation that any other children born to the Morozovs still must be serfs. For three years, there were none. Then, in 1823, when they both were well into middle age, Uliana gave birth to a fifth son. Riumin insisted that his stipulation must apply and, although his parents and brothers were free, Timofei Morozov remained a serf until he entered his teens, for it took that long for his family to assemble the king's ransom that Riumin now required.[23]

With all of their children free from bondage, Savva and Uliana Morozov concentrated their energies on further expansion. Quick to see the vast potential that lay in the combination of cheap American cotton and the modern spinning and weaving machinery from which the British had just lifted export restrictions, they abandoned their silks and woolens in favor of cotton calico for which there was emerging a vast market among Russia's lower classes. In rapid succession, the Morozovs installed English power looms and spinning jennies at Nikolskaia to develop one of the largest textile enterprises in all of Russia. With industrial methods unlike anything yet seen in that part of the world, they centralized cloth production at Nikolskaia to such an extent that raw cotton was brought to the mills and finished cloth emerged. When Savva Morozov died at the age of ninety in 1860, the Nikolskaia mills employed over three thousand workers, spun over four million pounds of cotton thread valued at nearly two million rubles, and produced almost the same value of finished cloth.[24] The Morozovs had traveled a very great distance from the small enterprise that Savva and Uliana had begun in their small shed at Zueva a half-century before. During the next half-century, their family fortunes would rise incomparably higher still.

It was Timofei, rather than the elder sons, who became the guiding force in the Morozovs' growing empire after Savva's death. Like his father, he was unlettered, but endowed with the rare gifts of common sense and native cunning. Success never softened him, and he remained always a despot in the fullest sense of the term, allowing no one to question his judgment or discuss his decisions. He ruled his family and his workers with an iron hand.

Following his father's plan, Timofei allowed his elder brothers to direct branches of the family enterprises but held the ultimate control—and the management of the vast new Nikolskaia-Zueva mills—in his hands alone. He would build the Morozov holdings into Russia's largest family enterprise. By 1890, the Nikolskaia-Zueva mills alone encompassed some two and a half square miles, employed over seventeen thousand workers, and produced over thirteen million rubles worth of goods. There were other Morozov mills employing another twenty thousand workers and producing well over twenty million rubles worth of cloth in addition to those at Nikolskaia. The Nikolskaia-Zueva mills were ranked the second largest in all of Russia; the family's other cotton factories ranked sixth, tenth, and sixteenth in the Empire, and there were additional far-

flung interests that had grown considerably.[25] Under Timofei's nev-
er-wavering hand, the Morozovs had entered railroad development
and banking, just to name some of their better-known endeavors. An
estimate by one of the best Russian economic historians is that
Morozov family holdings were worth about 75 million rubles (about
$38 million) in 1913.[26]

It was a success story dazzling in its brilliance, but eventually
Timofei's heavy-handed despotic rule took its toll. Ever since Savva
and Uliana had produced their first brightly colored silken ribbons
at Zueva, Morozov fabrics had enjoyed an enviable reputation for
quality. As the great mills at Nikolskaia-Zueva had become mech-
anized and as they had employed greater numbers of semiskilled
workers, that standard of quality had become more difficult to maintain. Refusing to admit that mechanization and greater output must
inevitably bring some deterioration in quality, Timofei imposed
upon his workers one of the most vicious systems of penalties in all
of Russia. So stringent were the fines that even the most skilled of
his workers, men and women who had given decades of their lives
to the Morozovs' enterprises, suddenly found themselves obliged to
surrender a day's pay every week. Others were obliged to pay even
more. It was more than any workers could bear for long. Unaccustomed to hearing workers' protests, Timofei refused any concessions.
Very soon, he faced one of the largest strikes Russia had ever seen.[27]

In August 1883, Petr Moiseenko, a thirty-one-year-old former
serf from the western province of Smolensk, appeared at the Nikolskaia Mill in search of work. Because skilled weavers such as he were
always in demand, he was hired without question. Unknown to his
new employers, however, Moiseenko had just returned from Siberia,
where he had served several years of exile as punishment for the part
he had played in several earlier strikes in St. Petersburg. Already
hardened in the crucible of political struggle, Moiseenko would not
allow the despotic system of Timofei Morozov to go unchallenged.
"At Morozov's factory there reigned a capricious abuse of authority
such as I had never seen anywhere else," he recalled some decades
later. The looms were old and worn, requiring "a great deal of
knowledge and dexterity to keep them going," but Moiseenko knew

his trade and had little difficulty. All went well until the second day, when he was told that he would be fined.

"Let me have your paybook," one of the supervisors insisted.

"What for?" Moiseenko asked.

"To write down your fine. The selvages on the cloth you wove yesterday were poorly done."

"Show me the ones that were spoiled."

"We don't have them here anymore."

"If you can't show me the spoiled selvages, then you don't touch my paybook because they were properly done and were even approved by the foreman."[28]

Moiseenko walked away. He had struck the first note of protest. Over many months he prepared for a full-scale confrontation with Timofei Morozov.

Aided by two fellow labor activists named Vasilii Volkov and Luka Ivanov, Moiseenko schooled the Nikolskaia workers about the need for protest. Matters came to a head at the beginning of January 1885, when the factory manager told them all that they must work on January 7, the day after Epiphany, which was generally observed as a holiday by workers at other factories. "We decided to take advantage of this opportunity," Moiseenko remembered. He and his comrades resolved to lead the workers out on strike.[29] The violence of their response to his call for action took him by surprise.

Moiseenko later insisted that "we wanted to carry out an organized strike—to present our demands, but without any excesses of violence,"[30] but, once released from the constraints under which they had labored for so long, the Nikolskaia workers proved impossible to control. In a fury, they attacked the company store and then the factory. "To hell with them! They've robbed us long enough!" they shouted. "Now it's time for us to rob them!" In vain Moiseenko and Volkov urged them to stop plundering. "We're not thieves, but honest toilers," they shouted. But the mob of workers who swarmed through the factory were in no mood to heed their pleas. Windows were broken, machines smashed, and goods seized from the company store as the workers wrought their revenge.[31] Yet their victory was short-lived. As was to be expected during the firm regime of Alexander III, order was restored quickly. Moiseenko, Volkov, and Ivanov were arrested and more than six hundred workers were sent back to their villages. None of the workers' demands were met, and the system of excessive fines continued until Timofei Morozov's death four years later. In France, a socialist paper proclaimed that the Morozov strike was "the point of departure for a new phase of the workers' movement" in Russia. In a sense it was, for it was one of the first organized protests to be launched by the factory workers of the Empire.[32] Other strikes would come, but the Morozov Strike of 1885 would retain its symbolic significance. Timofei Morozov had raised his family's fortunes to new heights. He also had presided over the opening sortie in a conflict that ultimately would destroy them all.

Like his father before him, Timofei Morozov had relied for advice and counsel upon a wife who was his equal in many ways and whose manner and outlook were much like his own. Therefore, it was to Maria Fedorovna Morozova, not to either of their sons, that Timofei bequeathed a controlling interest in the Morozov enterprises, and it was in her hands that he left full command of the great Nikolskaia mills. Contemporaries expected Maria Fedorovna to reign in the stern manner of her husband, and she more than met their expectations. Dressed in the very latest style, she devoured modern novels during her moments of leisure, but, for all her contemporary appearance, she possessed the heart and soul of an old-fashioned merchantress from Zamoskvoreche. Superstitious and suspicious, she lived in semidarkness in a great mansion built in the Old Russian style because she feared to install the "diabolical force" of electricity to light its twenty cavernous rooms. She lived alone and let none but her treasured Old Believer priests visit her except on major holidays, when she opened the mansion's doors to her immediate family. With her traditionalist priests, she prayed and dreamed of Old Russia, a world in which, if the truth were to be admitted, her family could never have attained the position of wealth and power she so enjoyed. Yet despite her piety, her heart was cold. She never shed a tear at her husband's death, and her good works were done more from a sense of Christian duty than out of any love for her less fortunate fellows. "She devotes herself to charitable works, but not a single soul loves her," her elder son Savva Timofeievich once told a friend. Neither Savva nor his younger brother Sergei had any love for their mother; Morozova's loyalty to the Morozov enterprises stood far before them in her heart.

"She trusts absolutely no one, and surrounds me with her spies," Savva once lamented. Yet it was Savva whom she tried to school to manage the Morozov fortune. Still following her husband's stern, unyielding methods, Maria insisted that no concessions be made to workers' demands, while her son urged that they move with the times and accept some of their more urgent pleas. Never able to forget the raw and fearsome violence that his father's despotic methods had stirred among the Nikolskaia workers in 1885, Savva Morozov tried to better the wretched conditions under which they lived and worked. He built better housing, invested in expensive safety equipment, reduced accidents, and improved medical care. At every step, his mother opposed him bitterly, even though the annual net profits at Nikolskaia reached some three million rubles after she turned over management of the mills to him.[33]

Conflict between mother and son was heightened by Savva's support of undertakings that conflicted with her dedication to the Morozov enterprises. Vladimir Nemirovich-Danchenko, Konstantin Stanislavskii's copioneer in founding the avant-garde Moscow Art Theater, remembered Morozov's intense commitments to social, cultural, and political causes. "While the enchantment lasted," he later wrote, "he completely yielded his powerful will into the hands of the enchanter."[34] So long as such enchantments were cultural or social, Maria Fedorovna did not interfere, although she never approved of time taken away from business.

But it was not in art or culture that Savva found the ultimate enchantment. Some of his fondest memories were of a visit he had made to England as a young man. "I worked in a textile factory there," he liked to recall in later years. "I associated with the Fabians, a group something like Socialists."[35] From that, and in reaction to the Nikolskaia strike of 1885, Morozov developed a passion for radical social change. "His most tremendous, all-consuming attraction was [the Bolshevik writer] Maksim Gorkii, and later the revolutionary movement," Nemirovich-Danchenko remembered.[36] Boldly, Morozov would give shelter to political activists whose papers were not in order. "You'll spend the night in my study," he would say grandly. "It's dangerous to go to a hotel with papers such as yours." The next morning, he would add, "If you have any trouble with the governor about your papers, send me a telegram. We'll put a good scare into him!"[37] When his support for the revolutionary cause began to involve larger commitments, Maria Fedorovna's cold disapproval turned into seething rage. At the beginning of 1905, Savva Morozov put up ten thousand rubles to bail Gorkii out of jail and, at about the same time, proposed a profit-sharing plan for the Nikolskaia workers. Appalled, Maria Fedorovna struck in a manner worthy of her husband. Convinced that her son's first loyalty no longer was to the Morozov enterprises, she removed him from his position as director of the Nikolskaia mills. Soon afterward, he shot himself in Nice.[38]

During the two decades before his suicide in 1905, Savva Morozov showed that he had reconciled many of the contradictions between the old merchant realm of Zamoskvoreche and the new and vastly more complex world that had come into being at the end of the nineteenth century. A large man of powerful build, he resembled his peasant grandfather, but he moved more slowly and expressed himself with greater care. It was his eyes—"his mercurial eyes," in the words of one who knew him—that revealed the quickness of his thought and the acuity of his mind.[39] When he chose to marry, it was to a beautiful peasant girl who had once worked at a spinning machine in the Nikolskaia mills. Like his father and grandfather, his only concern was to find a wife whose talents matched his own. He gave little thought to her social origins.

Where Savva Morozov differed sharply from those Morozovs who had come before him was in his taste for life in the modern world. He supported Stanislavskii's Moscow Art Theater and took great pride in helping to construct its sets and design its lighting.

"Dressed in working apparel, he labored side by side with electricians and smiths, astounding specialists with his knowledge of electricity," a grateful Stanislavskii, himself from the wealthy Alekseev merchant family, later wrote. "He began to love the theater to such an extent that he gave all of his free time to it."[40] Yet, despite his many interests, there was nothing of the dilettante about Morozov, nor did he allow his passions for art, culture, and social justice to eclipse his passion for business, an arena in which he excelled above all others. "He understood the power of capitalism when applied on a broad national scale, and he worked with energy, often disappearing for weeks to spend the time at his factory which maintained 30,000 employees," Nemirovich-Danchenko wrote.[41] Savva Morozov may have proposed to share the profits of the Nikolskaia mills with the men and women who labored at its machines, but he knew how to make certain that there was a profit to share.

"He knew the good taste and value of that simplicity which is more costly than luxury," one of his friends commented.[42] Although Savva also knew the value of a well-placed bribe, he bowed to no man, not even to Grand Duke Sergei Aleksandrovich, Governor General of Moscow and Nicholas II's uncle. When the Grand Duke asked to see the new palace Morozov had built in Moscow, a building that had created a great stir, Savva urged him to come at his special convenience, but made it a point to have the Grand Duke shown through its rooms by a butler. He would not remain at home to greet his guest. Wrote Nemirovich-Danchenko, "This was a very subtle snub which was equivalent to saying: 'You have a desire to see my house, but you're not coming to see me. The house is at your service, then. Have a look 'round. But don't imagine that I'll be here to meet you with genuflections.' "[43]

The amazing, meteoric rise of the Morozov family from poor serfs to well-educated multimillionaires who patronized charity, education, the arts, and even radical politics, represented in microcosm the development of a powerful new class. Whether their origins were serf, free peasant, petty provincial trader, or, in rarer cases, more prosperous Moscow merchant, the fortunes of those who rose to become Russia's new industrial and mercantile lords underwent an impressive surge during the half-century between 1830 and 1880, when Russian industry began to develop. All had the foresight and daring to industrialize rapidly and on a very large scale during those years. It was in the 1850s that the Riabushinskii family decisively shifted the emphasis of their textile business from distributing yarn and collecting finished cloth from hundreds of peasant weavers who worked small looms on a piecework basis in their *izby* to ever-larger mills that wove cotton and woolen fabrics on a vast scale. At about the same time, the Khludovs founded their cotton-spinning mill, and, in 1866, the Tretiakovs opened their Great Kostroma Works, which boasted more spindles under a single roof than any other mill in Europe. The Guchkovs, Alekseevs, Prokhorovs, and Soldatenkovs all followed a similar course, while the Ushkovs established a large chemical plant, and the Mamontovs went on to invest some of the profits they had amassed from the state liquor trade in railroads and a large paint and varnish factory.[44]

In the cases of these families and a number of others, success in their first large-scale industrial ventures only provided the capital needed to expand into others on an ever-increasing scale. Drawn to the enterprise most of them knew best, they built more textile plants or bought control of others that had begun to falter in the hands of entrepreneurs less able than they. But these, too, marked only a beginning, as they went on to build broader and more diverse industrial empires. The Alekseevs bought land in Central Asia to grow their own raw cotton and then established several new plants to process the raw fibers before they were spun into thread. Even more imaginative and daring, Savva Mamontov bought up foundries in the Urals to produce rails and locomotives, in order to supply rolling stock for the railroads in which he held a controlling interest. Among Russia's new lords, Mamontov was unusual only in the intensity of his passion for railroads. Virtually all of them invested in railroads at some point, but expanded into other enterprises ranging from oil and chemicals to paper, lumber, and glass.[45] During World War I, the Riabushinskiis even began to build Russia's first automobile factory.[46]

To increase the amount of financial resources they could bring to bear at any particular time and to maximize their investment opportunities, many of these families established banks over which they maintained very close control. Most important among them were the Moscow Merchant Bank (the city's largest), the Moscow Trade Bank, and the Moscow Merchants' Mutual Credit Society, all founded between 1866 and 1870. Drawing almost exclusively upon the assets of these banks, they managed to finance their industrial expansion without the aid of that foreign capital with which Ministers of Finance Vyshnegradskii and Witte tried to spur the development of Russia's industry.[47] Partly with funds from these banks, the Morozov textile enterprises increased their work force by some 1,400 percent, and the total value of their annual output rose from under 2 million to almost 36 million rubles in the quarter-century before 1890. Although no other family's assets could match that stupendous achievement, the Prokhorovs' famous Trekhgornaia cotton mill increased the value of its annual output by well over 1,000 percent. By 1890, the Tretiakovs' linen factory employed almost two thousand workers, while the Khludovs' textile mills had grown to employ almost four times that number. The Khludovs' workers almost doubled in numbers during the next decade, while the number employed by the Prokhorovs in their Trekhgornaia mill more than quadrupled.[48]

In addition to a good measure of luck coupled with that ruthlessness shared by all founders of great entrepreneurial fortunes, Russia's new industrial lords possessed a work ethic uncommon to Russian tradition and experience. Indeed, the Russian Orthodox Church had never emphasized hard work and diligence as a virtue, nor did any of those other fundamental institutions that shaped the values that ruled Russians' lives. "Work is not a virtue, but a simple immutable responsibility," Ivan Morozov wrote to his son Savva around 1860. "A man must work from childhood until old age," he continued, "or otherwise turn into a parasite from the proletariat."[49] To the virtues of hard work, honesty, temperance, and thrift, these men added a passion for technological innovation.[50] In fact, so modern were some of their textile mills' machines at the opening of the twentieth century that the looms installed at the Prokhorovs'

Trekhgornaia mill were destined to survive not only the Revolution of 1917 but the Second World War and the decade following. Indeed, a good number of the looms installed in 1895 were still giving their Soviet users good service as late as 1955.[51]

One of the reasons the Prokhorovs and a number of their associates could indulge their fascination with technology was that Russia's rising captains of industry were spared the curse of taxation. In 1885, fewer than two hundred people in all of Moscow paid more than a thousand rubles ($500) in any form of direct taxes, and, despite the impressive growth of Ivan Prokhorov's Trekhgornaia cotton mill (it would become one of the twenty largest enterprises in all of Russia by 1890) Prokhorov barely qualified for membership in that group.[52] Such minimal tax liabilities and substantially growing profits soon left these emerging new lords with personal fortunes to devote to a variety of purposes, and it was in the manner of spending their surplus wealth that they differed so dramatically from their merchant and peasant-turned-entrepreneur forebears.

Although immensely proud of their families' rise to wealth and power, most of Russia's new lords also were extremely sensitive about the low esteem in which they were held by educated and high-born Russians. Russian aristocrats always had looked down upon men who made their living in trade, and their disdain intensified as they became more financially dependent upon the very men whom they had treated with such scorn. The last quarter of the nineteenth century found many Russian nobles painfully short of capital because they had failed to come to grips with the economic realities that the emancipation of 1861 had thrust upon them. "At that time, all of us were dreadfully in need of money," one of them remembered. "And the *kupets*—the merchant—had the money."[53] Newly admitted merchants and peasants-turned-entrepreneurs kept such formerly sacrosanct aristocratic establishments as Moscow's exclusive English Club from ruin in the 1870s and 1880s, and the same group supplied the city's near-indigent nobles with ready cash to pay their creditors. Russian aristocrats thus had no choice but accept such nouveaux riches into their clubs, restaurants, and, even, ballrooms and salons, even though they scorned them as men of little culture and consequence. To counter that general disdain, Russia's new lords began to support numerous cultural and philanthropic endeavors. For some, it was an effort to win esteem in the eyes of men and women who thought them inferior. For others, it became an all-consuming passion.

Pavel Mikhailovich Tretiakov, whose provincial merchant forebears had come to Moscow in the 1770s and had slowly risen to prominence during the next half-century, was among these new patrons of the arts.[54] Born in 1832, he began to soar far beyond the Old Russian world of his ancestral nest even as a young man of twenty. On a trip to St. Petersburg in 1852, he remarked about its sharp contrast with Moscow, but—unlike his contemporary Timofei Morozov, who cursed journeys to St. Petersburg as "trips to the Tatar Khan"—young Tretiakov saw value and attraction in Russia's new Europeanized culture. To his parents' irritation, he remained longer in St. Petersburg to look more closely at the new cultural world it represented. Tretiakov was fascinated by the theater, but it was the city's art galleries that truly seized his imagination. Again and again he returned to view the Hermitage art collection and the exhibitions of paintings at the Imperial Academy of Fine Arts.[55] Very soon after he returned to Moscow, he began an art collection that would one day become the most famous in all of Russia.

His first purchases were several grandiose paintings reputed to have come from the brushes of sixteenth- and seventeenth-century Flemish masters. Yet he quickly learned from sad experience that his poor education had not given him the training and knowledge to distinguish the genuine from the clever and artful counterfeit. He therefore resolved to begin by buying only works painted by living Russians so that he could more easily guarantee their authenticity.[56] In the mid-1850s, he bought two paintings by Vasilii Khudiakov and Nikolai Shilder, both students at St. Petersburg's Academy of Fine Arts. Almost immediately, he designated his paintings as gifts for the Moscow he loved above all other cities as a token of his gratitude for the success he and his family had found there. He was only twenty-eight, an age when few men think of death, when he drew up a will dedicating more than half of his personal fortune to founding "a national art gallery" in the city. Reflecting a Moscow merchant's characteristic distrust of St. Petersburg's army of officials, he insisted that any gallery founded with his bequest must remain private, "without any government paper-pushers," and that it be dedicated to the work of Russia's native masters.[57] "Even as a young man," he later confessed, "my idea was to become rich so that I could return that which had been taken from it back to society (to the narod) in the form of some sort of useful institution. This thought has never been far from my mind throughout my life."[58]

In 1865, Tretiakov wed Vera Mamontova, daughter of another Moscow merchant lord and a close relative of a man destined to become another great patron of *fin de siècle* Russian culture. With her encouragement, a month rarely passed without new additions to his collection: landscapes by Mikhail Klodt, seascapes by Ivan Aivazovskii, historical canvases by Valerii Jacobi, and many others. As his knowledge grew, Tretiakov sought earlier works to make his collection more representative of Russia's national achievement: ikons from the tumultuous time of Ivan the Terrible and brilliant portraits by the great eighteenth-century master Vladimir Borovikovskii and the even greater Dmitrii Levitskii, whose likeness of the Empress Catherine the Great was known throughout Europe.[59] By the early 1870s, Tretiakov's collection had outgrown his spacious Moscow townhouse. "I must tell you, it's crowded, terribly crowded here," Tretiakov would complain to his brother-in-law Aleksandr Kaminskii. "There's not an inch of space to spare. Not even any room to stack canvases, let alone hang them." "It's as I've been telling you for a long time," Kaminskii would reply wearily. "Either stop buying paintings or build a gallery for them."[60]

Late in the summer of 1872, Tretiakov decided to follow Kaminskii's advice. At a cost of almost thirty thousand rubles—a princely sum indeed for an era when Ministers of State earned only half that amount in a year—he built a gallery to house his treasures. By March 1874, it was done. Joyfully Pavel Tretiakov devoted the last days of Lent to supervising workmen as they rehung his treasured paintings, saving the best for the main gallery, which had a northern exposure. "What delight we experienced as we walked through the gallery," Vera Tretiakova later exclaimed. "It was truly a magnificent hall, all hung with paintings that seemed incomparably better to us now that they had the proper light."[61] Tretiakov had established the first gallery devoted exclusively to Russian art. Very soon, it became one of Russia's greatest national monuments.

A group of fourteen artists who had seceded from St. Petersburg's Academy of Fine Arts in 1863 in protest against the restraints that Russia's conservative artistic establishment had endeavored to impose upon their work found a patron in Tretiakov. Led by the great Ivan Kramskoi, they launched the beginnings of a brilliant national artistic movement. They called themselves the *Peredvizhniki* (the Itinerants) and insisted that, if Russia were to develop a truly national art, every artist must enjoy unrestrained freedom to paint all subjects in his own way. "I sincerely wanted freedom," Kramskoi later remembered, "and so sincerely that I was ready to use all means so that others would also be free."[62] At the urging of the amazingly energetic critic Vladimir Stasov, the work of the *Peredvizhniki* became passionately nationalistic as Stasov exhorted them to paint Russian landscapes, Russian historical themes, Russian people, and scenes from daily life.[63]

When the first *Peredvizhnik* exhibit of forty-six paintings opened in St. Petersburg late in 1871, Tretiakov bought the largest number; over the next quarter-century, he spent almost a million rubles on their works. Within a decade, his brilliant collection included landscapes by Ivan Shishkin, Mikhail Klodt, and Lev Kamenev, and magnificent portraits of Russia's greatest sons and daughters by Kramskoi, and Vasilii Perov. Quickly, these were joined by Vasilii Surikov's vast historical canvases, which commanded the attention of all Russians who loved their nation's history. Surikov's gripping portrayal of the ever-defiant *Boiarina Morozova*, patroness of the seventeenth-century Old Believers, being taken away in chains to prison and death dominated an entire room dedicated to his work. Perhaps most dramatic of all were the greatest works of Ilia Repin in one of the main galleries. There hung his *Ivan the Terrible and His Son Ivan Ivanovich*, unforgettable in its tragic portrayal of the terrible Tsar torn by anguish as he held the limp body of the son he had killed in a fit of rage. Nearby hung Repin's portrait of the great and tormented composer Modest Mussorgskii, along with the extraordinary canvas entitled *They Did Not Expect Him,* in which he had portrayed a political prisoner's sudden return after long years in Siberia. The depths of tragedy in this painting were so profound that Tretiakov begged him to soften the suffering he had etched so deeply in the returning exile's features.[64]

But it was to all Russian art, not merely to the work of the *Peredvizhniki,* that Tretiakov had dedicated his gallery, and he therefore sought first-rate works by artists of all schools and persuasions. During the 1870s and 1880s, at a cost of almost two hundred thousand rubles, he added nearly all the major works of Vasilii Vereshchagin, whose great canvases portrayed the life that Russian conquerors found when they descended upon Central Asia and, more pointedly, the horrors of the Russo-Turkish War of the same era. Vereshchagin, "a man of sensitivity and genius living through the horror of human carnage," as Tretiakov once said, was aghast at the brutality of war. The impact of what he had seen with the armies of General von Kaufmann in Central Asia and those of Grand Duke Nikolai Nikolaevich and General Skobelev in the Balkans remained with him always. "It was impossible to forget even for a moment, the heroic, tragic tendency expressed in his every word and action," Tretiakov's daughter Vera wrote in recollections of her adolescent years.[65]

When Tretiakov presented the entire collection to his beloved Moscow six years before his death in 1898, it numbered 1,757 paintings.[66] Perhaps more than any of Moscow's other new lords, he had left a monument to his nation's artistic achievement that was destined to survive the devastation of the wars, revolutions, and famines that would cast their dark shadows across the Russian land during the coming decades. Wrote the Soviet editor of Tretiakov's daughter's memoirs, "The man has passed on, but his work has remained to flourish magnificently . . . and immortalize his name."[67]

One who had urged Tretiakov to follow his passion at all costs had been the woman he had married when his fascination with Russian art was in its first bloom, Vera Nikolaevna Mamontova, whose family must figure prominently in any group portrait of Moscow's merchant lords. The Mamontovs had grown immensely wealthy as provincial agents of the state liquor trade and had ranked among the city's richest merchants from the moment the Mamontov brothers, Ivan and Nikolai, had moved to Moscow around the middle of the nineteenth century. Although the sources tell us little about their early lives, they seem to have been men who valued culture and respected learning. As friends of the historian and publicist Mikhail Pogodin, they soon entered Moscow's literary and scholarly world and helped to support Pogodin's Slavophile and nationalistic bimonthly journal *Moskvitianin*. Both Mamontovs fathered large families. Tretiakov's wife Vera was Nikolai's favorite daughter. One of her closest cousins was Ivan's son Savva, who became the most famous of their clan.[68]

Born in 1841, Savva Ivanovich Mamontov was almost a decade younger than Tretiakov. Therefore, he did not grow to adulthood in the reactionary decade after the revolutions of 1848, but in the far more liberal years that followed the Crimean War. Where Pavel Tretiakov formed his values in a world ruled by serfdom and aristocratic privilege, Mamontov's early adult experience reflected the new life that came into being with the serfs' emancipation. The contrast between their views was striking as a result. Like his contemporary Timofei Morozov, Tretiakov remained staunchly conservative and so deeply religious that he was known to pay high premiums for paintings that centered upon religious themes.[69] Mamontov was touched by the radical intelligentsia's growing fascination with the *narod* and even shared their sense of social mission to the extent that he saw art, literature, and music as instruments that could help raise the *narod* above its abysmal poverty and utter wretchedness. When he married, it was to a woman who held similar views; the former Elizaveta Saposhnikova was perhaps even more deeply committed than her husband to the populists' naïve idealization of the *narod*, and certainly more dedicated to aiding them.[70]

It was Savva's unshakable ambition to leave his name deeply engraved in the annals of Russia's cultural history. To train his rich baritone voice, he studied for several years in Italy, but never won fame in the opera. He also proved a moderately able stage manager and playwright, wrote opera libretti, and showed modest talent as a sculptor. His greatest talent (though not his greatest passion) was in business, especially in the business of railroad building, and he almost single-handedly opened up Russia's Far North. Yet Mamontov was well aware that he would win no lasting fame as an entrepreneur because of the low esteem in which Russian society held the nation's businessmen. "You live, you work, you overwork, and one fine morning they cart you off," he once lamented. "Your name becomes an empty sound and no one feels anything toward you." He therefore resolved to follow the path of Italy's great Medici family and patronize those arts in which he himself could claim modest achievements but never excel.[71]

In 1870, the Mamontovs' joint commitment to the *narod* and Savva's desire to become a notable patron of Russian culture led them to buy Abramtsevo, an estate of some 780 acres with a rambling summer house that had once been owned by the poet Sergei Aksakov, father of the great Slavophiles Konstantin and Ivan. Some fifty *versty* from Moscow, Abramtsevo stood in a glorious pastoral setting, surrounded by forests of birch and evergreen, through which the Voria River wound its way. These lands overflowed with historical and cultural meaning. Less than twelve *versty* beyond rose the crenellated walls and golden domes of the great Troitsa-Sergeevskaia Monastery, one of Russia's most revered ancient shrines. There, the Romanovs had come since 1613 to pray for divine guidance. More recently, Abramtsevo's drawing room and park had known the tread of such great Slavophile thinkers as Ivan Kireevskii, Aleksei Khomiakov, and Iurii Samarin.[72] For the grandson of a provincial merchant who had peddled vodka to the tavern keepers of central Russia, it must have been exhilarating to acquire such a domain. He paid the full asking price of 15,000 rubles in cash. "Life suddenly became filled with pleasant and happy concerns about how to arrange things, what to repair, what to build, and what to remodel," Mamontov wrote. "It seems there are no more pleasant and amusing concerns in life," he mused wryly, "than to arrange one's own nest."[73]

When the spring of 1871 brought cholera to villages nearby

Abramtsevo, the Mamontovs were shocked to find that the local peasants had neither clinics nor schools. With that same driving energy that had hewn a railroad empire out of Russia's Far North, Savva Mamontov built a hospital and school for the region's peasants, while Elizaveta spent her days and nights tending the sick and infirm. There, she gave substance to her dreams of aiding the *narod.* Her thin face and spare figure became known in every peasant household for miles around.[74] She was a plain woman, thin and dark, but a portrait that Repin painted of her in 1878 vividly captures her inner warmth.

If Elizaveta found her vocation at Abramtsevo, it was not long before the estate also became an instrument for fulfilling her husband's greater cultural aspirations. The stage was set not in Russia but in Rome, where the Mamontovs spent the winters of 1872–73 and 1873–74 in hopes of speeding their second son's recovery from a serious illness. In Rome, and in their brief travels to other European capitals, they assembled a brilliant circle of young Russian composers, artists, and sculptors who had come to the West to work and study. Vasilii Polenov, the young *Peredvizhnik* artist destined to win fame for such canvases as *The Lord of the Manor Claims His Prerogatives;* the sculptor Mark Antokolskii, whose marble statue of Ivan the Terrible had just won him academician's rank at the age of twenty-eight; and the young composer and music critic Mikhail Ivanov were the first to join their entourage.

When the Mamontovs went to Paris in the spring of 1874, Polenov introduced them to Ilia Repin. Mamontov invited Repin to spend summers at Abramtsevo, along with the young painter Viktor Vasnetsov, whose portrayals of folkloristic themes on canvas were about to raise him into the ranks of Russia's leading painters. Mamontov insisted that each work or vacation according to his inclinations, and this produced dramatic results. In the late 1870s and early 1880s, Repin painted his *Pilgrims* and *The Religious Procession* on Mamontov's estate, and began his *Ivan the Terrible* and *The Zaporozhtsy Cossacks,* while Vasnetsov produced some of his most important early canvases. At one point, Mamontov persuaded the artists to decorate a new church for the village. A humble peasant village near the center of Old Russia thus came to possess a church with an ikonostasis designed by Polenov, several facades and ikons painted by Vasnetsov, and an ikon of Christ painted by Repin himself. "How much this church has added to Abramtsevo," Elizaveta Mamontova exclaimed. And then she spoke of what made her happiest of all: "How joyously the ardent and devout *narod* came to offer up their prayers."[75]

Hospitality to painters marked only the beginning of Mamontov's patronage of the arts in Russia. Returning to what was probably his first cultural love, music, he founded a private opera company in 1885 and dedicated it to Russian national music and to the search for new native talent. Dargomyzhskii's *Rusalka* was first performed there, as were Rimskii-Korsakov's *Snow Maiden, Sadko,* and *Tsar's Bride.* Mamontov brought together an amazing array of recognized talent to provide a breathtaking backdrop for his new discoveries in the world of music, and artists from the Abramtsevo summer circle designed many of the sets. At his private theater, young Feodor Chaliapin first emerged from his obscure position at St. Petersburg's Imperial Opera to become the legendary soloist whose great voice captured all of Europe during the first decade of the new century.[76]

Meanwhile Elizaveta Mamontova continued to serve the *narod* at Abramtsevo. Helped by Vera Polenova, the painter Polenov's sister and a longtime student of peasant art and culture, she established a series of workshops that produced utensils and small pieces of furniture according to traditional peasant designs. There peasants pursued the crafts of their ancestors and decorated them with an array of folk motifs adapted to reflect art nouveau tastes by Vasnetsov and a number of other famous Abramtsevo artists. During the mid-1880s, a few of these Abramtsevo pieces were sold each year to friends and acquaintances at a sale held just before Christmas, and their fame soon spread. Princess Naryshkina, wife of the Grand Marshal of the Imperial Court, descended upon the Christmas sale of 1889, bought several pieces, and ordered thirty small carved mirror frames as gifts for the debutantes who were to be presented at her winter ball. Among St. Petersburg's lords and ladies who, as always, were caught up in a never-ending quest for the new, the innovative, and the unusual, the Abramtsevo frames caused a stir. So many orders poured into the Abramtsevo workshops that Elizaveta Mamontova's artisans opened a small shop in Moscow as a regular outlet for their work. Typical of the entire venture, the shop's interior was designed and decorated by none other than Mikhail Vrubel, the great artist of the 1890s, for whom Savva Mamontov had acted as a patron when the Russian artistic establishment had initially rejected his paintings.[77]

Savva Mamontov patronized Russian culture more broadly than Savva Morozov or Pavel Tretiakov, but his passion for railroads almost equaled his love of art, music, and theater. With a daring unmatched by his contemporaries, he drove the rails of his enterprise ever deeper into the vast expanses of Russia's Far North until his company's track reached the port of Arkhangelsk on the distant shores of the White Sea. But Mamontov was not content to lay new track into new lands. He envisioned a network of railroads in which Russian-made locomotives, freight, and passenger cars ran on Russian iron. He bought factories to build the equipment his railroads needed, but his entire enterprise crashed before his efforts at self-sufficiency had time to succeed. Accused of embezzling funds from his Moscow-Arkhangelsk Railroad, Mamontov was sent to prison late in 1899 to await trial. Before a Moscow court found him innocent of any wrongdoing, his creditors seized his townhouse and all the treasures he had assembled there, and the government took his railroads.[78]

Among those who witnessed Mamontov's enthusiastic attempts to produce innovative operas and plays during the 1880s and 1890s was Konstantin Alekseev, one of Elizaveta Mamontova's young relatives. The Alekseevs were one of Moscow's oldest merchant families, with extensive interests in the wool and cotton industry. "My father . . . [was] the owner of a mercantile firm a hundred years old . . . [and] a pure-blooded Russian," Konstantin once wrote proudly.[79] He was equally proud of his family's prominent role in the civic life of their native city. At the beginning of the nineteenth century, wealth had brought the Alekseevs into Moscow culture and politics even before the Morozovs and Mamontovs had settled there.

Between 1840 and 1890, the family produced two of Moscow's mayors and a dean of Moscow University's law faculty.[80]

In contrast to such men as Tretiakov, Mamontov, and Savva Morozov, Konstantin Alekseev, who soon took the theatrical name of Stanislavskii, represented an entirely new generation among the merchant lords of Russia, for he could recall no relatives who preserved remnants of their peasant or petty tradesfolk heritage in their daily lives and personal tastes. No one in his family even remotely resembled the crude and superstitious parents of Savva Morozov, or those Old Russian merchant parents and relatives who had filled the childhood world of Pavel Tretiakov. Stanislavskii's parents and relatives all lived urbane and cosmopolitan lives that had long since broken all connection with the world of Zamoskvoreche. Significantly, Stanislavskii entitled the introduction to his memoirs "Old Russia," but proceeded to describe a milieu that would have seemed very new—even avant-garde—to Savva Morozov, Pavel Tretiakov, or even Savva Mamontov.[81]

Stanislavskii was born in 1863, a moment in Russia's history that he very aptly called "a dividing point between two great epochs."[82] Serfdom, the institution that had played a central part in the Morozovs' family history, had just come to an end. With it had fallen the traditional life of aristocratic Russia. No longer would enserfed men and women provide most of the labor on the land. No longer would serf lads be called to give a quarter-century of their lives to the army. And no longer would Russia's population be sharply divided into free and unfree. It seemed to Russians of the 1860s that a new age had burst upon their nation, and Stanislavskii lived his adolescence in that heady atmosphere. Surrounded by parents and relatives who no longer thought only of business, his childhood horizons were infinitely broader than those that had spread out before most of Russia's new lords in their youth. He never knew the struggle that Pavel Tretiakov or Savva Morozov endured to break from traditionalist, even anachronistic, surroundings into the modern cultural world. Young Stanislavskii found all roads open; the only limits he knew were those set by his own imagination and talent. "We were taught many languages, we traveled very extensively, and, in a word, were plunged into the very heart of the maelstrom of culture," he wrote in recalling the excitement of his early life.[83]

From childhood, Stanislavskii was fascinated by the theater's eternal magic. As he grew to manhood, fascination became single-minded dedication to the portrayal of real life on the stage. Stanislavskii set about becoming an actor, yet more than a decade in the theater brought him only frustration in productions that seemed stilted and artificial.[84] Undaunted, this man who had mastered what he once called "the difficult art of being able to be rich,"[85] drove himself in quest of the elusive formula that would bring reality to the theater. He could not accomplish his difficult task alone. After much searching, he found his ally in the person of Vladimir Nemirovich-Danchenko, a teacher and director in the dramatic school of the Moscow Philharmonic Society. "It seems that Nemirovich-Danchenko had also dreamed of such a theater as I imagined and sought a man such as he imagined me to be," Stanislavskii later remembered.[86] A long and passionate meeting between these two men, both "poisoned by the same dream,"[87] Stanislavskii later confessed, marked the birth of the Moscow Art Theater, one of the landmarks in the history of modern theater, and a dream finally brought to life only by the great wealth and cultural patronage of Stanislavskii and others such as Savva Mamontov.

The historic meeting between Stanislavskii and Nemirovich-Danchenko took place on June 21, 1897, at a famous Moscow restaurant called the Slavianskii Bazar where, Nemirovich-Danchenko remembered, "we began our historic conversation at two o'clock in the afternoon and finished it at [Stanislavskii's] villa at eight o'clock the next morning." For almost eighteen hours the two men probed each other's mind, amazed at the unity of their views about art and theater. "The most remarkable thing about this conversation," Nemirovich-Danchenko wrote, "was that we did not once disagree."[88] His was a remembrance with which Stanislavskii fully concurred. "The peace conference of Versailles did not consider the world questions before it with such clarity and exactness as we considered the foundations of our future enterprise," Stanislavskii added in his account of their meeting.[89]

As their private table at the Slavianskii Bazar became cluttered from the remains of lunch, coffee, and dinner, Stanislavskii and Nemirovich-Danchenko discussed with total candor the merits of Russia's greatest living actors and actresses.

"And what will you say about actress B?"
"She is a good actress, but not for us."
"Why?"
"She does not love art, but herself in art."[90]

And so it went through the afternoon, evening, night, and early morning. Most important, Stanislavskii recalled, they spoke at length about "artistic ethics." Therein lay the principles upon which they founded their theater.

"There are no small parts, there are only small actors."
"One must love art, not one's self in art."
"Today Hamlet, tomorrow a supernumerary, but even as a supernumerary you must become an artist."
"The poet, the actor, the artist, the tailor, the stage hand serve one goal, which is placed by the poet in the very basis of his play."
"All disobedience to the creative life of the theater is a crime."
"Lateness, laziness, caprice, hysterics, bad character, ignorance of the role, the necessity of repeating anything twice are all equally harmful to our enterprise and must be rooted out."[91]

They agreed upon one final principle to which they swore always to remain faithful: "The literary veto belongs to Nemirovich-Danchenko, the artistic veto to Stanislavskii."[92] Neither abused the right, but both used it with decisive effect on rare occasions. "One of us would only have to pronounce the magic word *veto,*" Stanislavskii wrote, "and our debate would end in the middle of a sentence."[93]

"Seek your examples in life," Mikhail Shchepkin, the greatest of nineteenth-century Russia's actors, once had told Stanislavskii, and the union with Nemirovich-Danchenko brought a new type of theater into being based upon their perception of that "simple, yet profound dictum."[94] When it opened its doors in 1898, the Moscow Art Theater breathed life into the brilliant plays of Anton Chekhov, whose dramatic works had failed dismally when staged and directed by more traditional methods. Likewise, it brought new vitality to the works of Ivan Turgenev, that great novelist of the emancipation era, whose plays had never found a director able to bring out their inner meaning and depth. Perhaps most important of all, the theater of Stanislavskii and Nemirovich-Danchenko brought before audiences the work of Maksim Gorkii, a man from the slums of Nizhnii-Novgorod. His work, "a new tocsin to the joys of life . . . seized upon men's imagination," Nemirovich-Danchenko later wrote, and moved the founders of the Moscow Art Theater by its raw power and simplicity.[95] Thus it was the Moscow Art Theater that introduced the world to Gorkii's *Petit Bourgeois* and, above all, his greatest play, *Among the Dregs,* that dominated the 1902–3 theatrical season.[96]

It was perhaps one of the greatest ironies of Russia's early-twentieth-century cultural experience that one of the most profound statements ever made about the pain and bitterness of life in the world that the Empire's new lords had created was brought to life by an actor from their midst in a theater that owed its very being to their dedicated patronage. While creating the brilliant world of the Tretiakov Gallery and the Moscow Art Theater, they and their fellows had also created the tragic and deadly world encompassed by life in the lower depths of Russia's cities, where men and women could never think of truth and beauty, but only of the urgent need to feed themselves and their families that night in order to survive for one more day. To comprehend the world Russia's new lords created in their quest for wealth and fame, we must also examine the lives of the hundreds of thousands of men and women who labored in their factories and lived in those wretched workers' quarters that their great mills brought into being in the outskirts of the cities of the Russian Empire.

CHAPTER IV
Life in the Lower Depths

The dark, ominous world depicted by maksim gorkii took shape in the factory districts of Moscow and St. Petersburg, and in such newer industrial centers as Ivanovo-Voznesensk. It encompassed not only the burgeoning ranks of factory workers but, at its absolute nadir, those legions of unemployed, destitute, and disabled men and women who were the urban poor.

Factory workers, petty artisans, day laborers, whores, thieves, and beggars—these and all the others who crowded into the lower depths of Russia's industrial slums comprised the Empire's urban proletariat. Well known in the West, this class had figured prominently in the writings of Karl Marx and Friedrich Engels, but it was still unfamiliar to many educated late-nineteenth-century Russians. Statesmen, economists, philanthropists, and even revolutionaries were little acquainted with the proletariat's aspirations and unused to comprehending its needs. Indeed, those earnest young student radicals who had gone "to the people" in the 1870s to preach the gospel of socialism to the *narod* had been convinced that legions of peasants, marching by the tens of thousands, would one day form the rank and file of Russia's revolutionary armies, not the urban proletariat as in the West. They had hardly dreamed that the sufferings of that comparative handful of proletarian men and women in the cities might provide more fertile soil in which to sow the seeds of revolution than the impoverished peasants. They had been surprised, even apprehensive, to hear in 1877 from the lips of Petr Alekseev, one of those yet-unfamiliar urban workers, that "the strong arm of millions of working folk will be raised to smash the yoke of despotism, surrounded although it is by soldiers' bayonets, into smithereens."[1] As on a number of other occasions during the next several decades, a proletarian had been the first to state views that those revolutionary intellectuals, who had proclaimed themselves his mentors, would take up only at a later time. By the end of the decade, however, all but the most stubborn among them had to confess to the "utter lack of any sign of active struggle" in the peasant villages and admit "the obvious futility of having whole scores of people" continue their efforts to raise the revolutionary consciousness of Russia's peasant masses.[2]

As the 1880s dawned, Russia's revolutionaries faced the urban proletariat in confusion and without a program for action. Only during that decade did they come to grips with the obvious existence of this new class. Georgii Plekhanov, who at the age of twenty-seven had become the "father of Russian Marxism" and was perhaps its most brilliant theorist, became one of the first to perceive the proletariat's potential for providing the critical raw material needed to forge revolutionary weapons.[3] "The Russian revolution will triumph as a workers' revolution," Plekhanov proclaimed at the International

Socialist Congress in 1889.[4] Some seven years before, he had determined that he was ready "to make out of [Marx's] *Das Kapital* a Procrustean bed for all my comrades."[5] Yet the day when theory could be transformed into practice still lay in the future. Under the heavy hand of political repression that lay upon the land during the last years of Alexander III's regime, Russia's proletariat suffered in silence, and those revolutionaries who hearkened to Plekhanov's teachings remained unable to preach their new-found convictions. "During the six years I spent in the workshop [at Kronstadt, from 1888–94] I never once saw a single revolutionary leaflet or illegal pamphlet, and neither did any of the other men who toiled there," recalled Ivan Babushkin, a factory worker who later joined Lenin and his Bolsheviks in their struggle to overthrow the Romanovs.[6] Not many more years would pass, however, before Babushkin and his comrades would begin to exercise a dramatic influence upon their nation's political destinies. When revolution first struck Russia in 1905, the factory workers and the urban poor emerged as a potent political and social force. Who these proletarians were, where they came from, where they worked, and how they lived are complex and intriguing questions that we must explore in order to understand the part they played in Russia's national life before the Great War.

When Alexander II freed Russia's enserfed peasants in 1861, the men and women who could be called proletarians in his Empire numbered about 3.25 million, or less than 5 percent of all his subjects. During the next thirty years, their numbers more than doubled and, in the course of the next decade, doubled again.[7] Not all of these men and women labored in Russia's factories; a substantial portion worked in the building and service trades or in the iron foundries of the Ural Mountains where workers were surprisingly well off by Russian standards. While the malnourished peasants of Russia's Black Soil provinces lived in one-room *izby*, rarely saw meat, and existed from day to day on black bread, pickled cabbage, and a bit of onion, the iron workers of the Urals regarded meat, fish, butter, and vegetables as common daily fare.[8]

But these conditions were atypical. The vast majority of

Russia's proletarians in the 1860s lived on the edge of destitution in wretched barracks or tenements. As early as the 1840s, Russian statesmen had begun to sense a potential threat from St. Petersburg's lower classes when a commission appointed to investigate workers' living conditions reported that it was not unusual to find eighteen to twenty people crowded into one small tenement. In one extreme case, they found fifty men, women, and children, including several suffering from tuberculosis and syphilis, living in a single room that measured barely twenty feet on a side. Yet the government failed to act. As time passed, conditions grew even worse.[9]

By the 1870s, the housing shortage in St. Petersburg had become truly desperate, and there simply were no more places for the new waves of workers flowing into Russia's capital to find shelter. Even the city's damp and oozing cellars, never used for human habitation even in the cruelest days of serfdom, were pressed into service. For exorbitant prices, greedy landlords rented mere corners that filled with excrement-tainted liquid whenever it rained. Filth and excrement accumulated so rapidly in the courtyards of buildings in the city's poorer sections that, in 1869, one public health doctor estimated that more than thirty thousand tons of human feces were lying unattended throughout the city. Disease flourished. By the 1870s, St. Petersburg had earned the dubious distinction of suffering the highest mortality rate of any major city in Europe. Cholera, typhus, and, above all, the omnipresent scourge of tuberculosis, took a frightening toll.[10]

A variety of moral and social malaises ravaged the ranks of the urban poor as well. "Drunkenness is unprecedented, even for Russia," the famous censor and diarist Aleksandr Nikitenko lamented at the beginning of 1864. "Everywhere, drunken folk wander in crowds through the streets, loll about, and huff like cattle." Those among Russia's embryonic proletariat who sought such release from the burdens of their daily lives in *zapoi* drank the cheapest vodka, fiery and raw, which they usually tempered with gulps of sour, watery beer. The effect was instantly deadening, sometimes deadly. "A number of unfortunate accidents, some of them fatal, occur as a result of drunkenness," Nikitenko reported. "There have been cases of fatal alcohol poisoning, even among fourteen- and fifteen-year-olds."[11] According to some estimates, perhaps as many as one out of every four residents of St. Petersburg was arrested for crime, drunkenness, or disorderly conduct (usually drunken) toward the end of the 1860s.[12] Since government officials, army officers, and aristocrats almost always avoided such encounters with the police, the rate of arrests, especially for drunkenness, among St. Petersburg's proletarians was far higher. Nor was the situation in Russia's capital unique. There is every indication that the experience of St. Petersburg's workers was repeated by their fellows in other cities. Certainly those peasants who gravitated toward Moscow lived and worked in a similar environment.[13] Likewise, although the average worker in Odessa, Russia's great southern port city, received only 70 percent of what experts considered a survival wage, he nonetheless spent one out of every twelve rubles he earned on vodka.[14]

Most of this early wave of peasant factory workers were men who were unmarried or had left their wives far away in their native villages, and their arrival in Russia's cities caused prostitution to soar. Dostoevskii's gentle and long-suffering Sonia Marmeladova, who sold her favors in St. Petersburg's Haymarket to feed her consumptive mother and starving brothers and sisters, was but one among a veritable army of whores who plied their trade in St. Petersburg's worker districts. In just the three years between 1868 and 1871, for example, the number of registered prostitutes in Russia's capital more than doubled, and they represented only a portion of the women engaged in that trade. Public health authorities and the police found it impossible to control unregistered prostitutes, and these women especially spread syphilis among the city's workers at such a rate that the number of cases almost tripled in less than a decade. By 1870, the disease was so rampant in St. Petersburg that one physician found that three out of every ten randomly chosen workers were infected.[15]

In the last decade of the nineteenth century, every one of Russia's heavy industries—iron, steel, coal, oil, railroads, machine tools, and chemicals—doubled or tripled its output and then doubled it again by 1905. Avid European financiers poured capital into commercial and industrial ventures that seemed safe investments, realizing handsome dividends. For a time, Russian state bonds even enjoyed higher ratings than did those of such newly arrived industrial giants as Imperial Germany.[16] Such flourishing industries demanded veritable armies of new labor to stoke blast furnaces, lay railroad track, and man new machines. Not counting the men and women needed for labor in the expanding building and service trades, more than a million workers joined the industrial labor force in the 1890s alone. Russia's cities grew at twice the rate of her general population. By 1900, one out of every eight of Nicholas II's subjects lived in an urban setting.[17]

The serfs' emancipation in 1861 had made it difficult for them to leave the land because Russian statesmen wanted to keep a tight rein upon the men and women who produced the nation's leading export commodity and paid most of its taxes. Still, there was a reservoir of men and women less firmly tied to their native villages who could move more easily to industrial centers when there was work to be had. A number of these folk had been rented to factory owners during the days of serfdom and merely continued on as wage laborers after their emancipation. More numerous in Russia's potential industrial labor force, however, were men and women who had been "household serfs." These never had worked the land because they had been obliged to serve their lords and ladies as cooks, valets, coachmen, nursemaids, or in any number of other menial capacities. The emancipation made little effort to provide such folk with land and left them to their own devices. A few left their masters' service with marketable skills, as in the case of blacksmiths or cobblers, but most had little choice but to seek work in the cities or join the migrant labor army that flowed toward southern Russia in spring and summer only to return in winter to seek refuge in their native villages. In all, there were more than three million of these landless peasants in the 1860s. When the demand for factory workers began to grow in the next decade and then surged upward in the 1880s and 1890s, they were the first to leave for the cities. Russia's urban proletariat first developed from their ranks.[18]

Yet men and women left landless by the Emancipation Acts

of 1861 were not the only ones who joined the swelling tide. There were peasants from the north of Russia, where the land was too poor to farm, and there were young peasants from all over the Empire who went to the factories, at first sometimes only for a few months at a time, to earn those extra rubles that would enable their families to survive the poverty, crop failures, and misfortune that dogged their efforts in the Russian countryside. Clearly, these folk saw employment in Russia's new factories as an opportunity to better their desperate lives. Nonetheless, it was a fearsome first step that they took. "All day, we walked about the city, from morning till night. We were hungry. We had not even a single kopek left between us," recalled the young weaver Petr Moiseenko who had come to St. Petersburg with his brother in search of work. Some acquaintances from their native village who had already found work took the brothers in for the night, gave them food, and told them where to look for work. At first, there were only part-time jobs to be had. Finally, Moiseenko found a factory that would hire him on the night shift so that he could work steadily. "My rescue from the pangs of hunger had been accomplished!" he rejoiced.[19]

In the 1870s and 1880s, young men like Petr Moiseenko often were expected to sleep in barracks, cellars, or, in some cases, under the machines they tended. "The conjugal or nuclear family . . . was almost a rarity" in Moscow, one expert recently concluded,[20] and that was the case in other cities too. Men worked and ate, worked and slept, and were too exhausted to do much except visit the neighborhood tavern or whorehouse from time to time. "I did not live, but only worked, worked, and worked," recalled the metal-worker Ivan Babushkin, who came to Kronstadt in 1888. "I worked morning, noon, and night, and sometimes did not leave the factory for two days at a stretch." Even on holidays, there was little opportunity to enjoy life's little pleasures. One's only thought, Babushkin remembered, was that "it would be work again tomorrow—heavy, continuous, killing work—but there would be no real life and no real rest to look forward to."[21]

By the 1890s, increasing numbers of lower-class women began to appear on urban censuses. This would seem to indicate that the men who labored in Russia's factories were beginning to establish families in the cities. However, recent research in the Soviet archives by at least one young American scholar has shown that most workers still remained physically unattached in their new urban surroundings; the upswing in the numbers of proletarian women was the result of peasant widows and spinsters arriving to seek work as their male counterparts had a decade earlier.[22] Nevertheless, some of the men and women who congregated in worker barracks did marry, and a number kept their children with them. Some factory owners even began to make provision for housing couples with children in their crude barracks-dormitories. The Prokhorov merchant-princes were thought to be especially enlightened employers for that reason, even though it was not unusual at their great Moscow textile mill for two families to share a single room that measured no more than eight by fourteen feet. "The children slept in a trunk or on the floor," recalled Tamara Dontsova, who lived with her husband and two children in one such room around the turn of the century.[23]

The appearance of women and children in Russia's industrial centers was accompanied by all the abuses associated with female and child labor in the industrial revolutions of Western nations earlier in the century. Few factory owners provided any sort of child-care facilities and, despite laws that forbade it, managers and foremen encouraged parents to employ their children in the factory.[24] "Almost half the workers are children, many of whom are under the age of ten," reported Ivan Ianzhul, a government factory inspector charged with uncovering violations of Russia's primitive child labor laws in some fifteen hundred mills during the 1880s. He was particularly appalled at what he saw at the cotton-matting factories in Moscow. "One even finds tots no more than three years of age working alongside their mothers," he exclaimed.[25] At the same time, his colleague Pavel Peskov found that in the matchworks of Vladimir, where everyone suffered continual exposure to noxious phosphorus fumes, almost six out of every ten workers were under the age of fifteen, and an even higher percentage of the workers in the Vladimir spinning mills fell into the same age category.[26] All worked under terrible conditions. By the time the matting factories closed for the summer, Ianzhul told his superiors, the children all had grown so weak that "a gust of wind could blow them over."[27] The accident rate among children so weakened by hunger, disease, and overwork was frightfully high. At a factory in Bogorodskoe, almost 70 percent of the accidents involved children, many of whom had grown too tired or too weak to escape injury from the machines they tended.[28] "When I was twelve," one middle-aged woman told a Soviet historian during the 1930s, "they would wake me up at midnight, lead me by the hand so that I wouldn't fall, and take me to the factory. There I'd only be able to think of finding some place to crawl into so that I could go back to sleep but, if the night foreman found me, he'd dock my pay."[29] It was not unusual for these children to work more than twelve hours a day, including Sundays. Even after child labor was prohibited in 1882, factory owners shamelessly continued to exploit them. In St. Petersburg, one group of factory owners even dared to petition the Minister of Finance for permission to *lengthen* children's workdays more than a year after the use of child labor had been declared illegal![30] "In the vast majority of factories," Ianzhul wrote in May 1885, "the law on child labor still has not been put into effect."[31]

It was not uncommon for the children's mothers to work eighteen-hour days, from four in the morning until ten at night.[32] Although the government had limited work at night, on Sundays, and on holidays for women, it rescinded those restrictions in April 1890, when factory owners complained, and then actually left such decisions to the discretion of the owners themselves.[33] Russian women workers at the end of the nineteenth century still suffered all the abuses that Friedrich Engels had found in his study of the working conditions endured by their sisters in England some seventy years before, and they bore other indignities as well. Even in the "enlightened" Prokhorov cotton mill, pregnant women continued at their looms and spindles even after their labor pains began. "It would sometimes turn out that you'd begin to feel the pains and would tell the woman next to you that you were in labor," one working mother remembered. "She'd try to calm you down. 'Why not wait a bit?' she'd say. 'It's almost quitting time. Soon we'll be done and then you can leave.' "[34] Women who tried to forget labor pains and stay until the end of their shift sometimes gave birth on the factory floor, their cries drowned out by the roar and clang of the machines to which they had given their first allegiance. Fearful that they would lose their jobs for being absent, they usually returned to the factory within no more than two or three days, carrying their newborn infants because there was no other way to feed them. After the Revolution of 1905, when workers asked that women be given four weeks of maternity leave from their jobs, one factory director remarked: "Female workers will so enjoy having that much time off that they'll begin to give birth every six months."[35]

Whatever the factory, there was always considerable physical danger for workers of all ages, although few were as heedless of safety as the Briansk Ironworks where, according to one estimate, a labor force of five thousand sustained "not less than ten thousand accidents resulting in injury over the space of fifteen years."[36] It was Ivan Ianzhul, however, who in the course of his inspections produced a shocking catalogue of dangers that threatened workers in the factories and mills of Moscow province. In porcelain and pottery factories, workers were sickened by the poisonous compounds in the paints they used. At the matchworks in Kolomna, they had no protection from ever-present poisonous phosphorus and sulphur dust at work or in their barracks. "The workers' quarters were so strongly permeated by the smell of sulphur and phosphorus," Ianzhul reported, "that I was unable to stand it for more than half an hour."[37]

Poisonous chemicals and paints posed long-range threats to workers' health that few could comprehend in the 1880s and 1890s. The greatest immediate danger came from the plant machinery that had created the very jobs upon which Russia's growing industrial proletariat had come to depend for their daily bread. It was rare for employers to install any protective or safety devices, so that workers were constantly exposed to flying gears, wheels, and belts. "This is the greatest cause of accidents, ranging from minor cuts to death," Ianzhul wrote. Pavel Peskov, his colleague in Vladimir, secretly observed that the factories in his region were even worse than those in Moscow. Perhaps worst of all was the great Sokolovskaia Mill, which employed something over three thousand workers. There, an unbelieving Peskov discovered that more than six out of every ten lathe operators and almost eight out of every ten boilermakers had suffered work-related injuries during the previous two years.

Factory managers allowed machines to be stopped only after working hours and on holidays and expected workers to clean them at those times and without extra pay. The result was dirty, poorly maintained machinery with even greater risk of accident. Machine belts usually were replaced, minor repairs undertaken, and lubrication attempted while machines were running at full speed. Enterprising foremen and managers quickly discovered that children's small quick hands and nimble feet could be used to oil and clean clogged gears on moving machines. This became a murderous assignment for ten- and twelve-year-olds. "The result—maiming and death," Ianzhul warned. Employers posted signs that read:

IN THE EVENT OF AN ACCIDENT, THE OWNER AND DIRECTOR OF
THE FACTORY ASSUME NO RESPONSIBILITY

No accident records were kept, and employers freely admitted that the authorities learned about only those accidents that were too serious to be concealed. Workers in other areas of Russia suffered even more extreme danger than those in the textile mills and light industries of central Russia. The appalling number of fatal accidents in the Donbass coal mines earned that region the dubious honor of enjoying one of the highest accidental death rates anywhere in Europe.[38]

Workers who were tired and weak from overwork and hunger, of course, were especially accident-prone. At the beginning of the 1890s, a fourteen-hour workday was common in most Russian factories, although sixteen- and eighteen-hour days were far from rare. Workers in the cloth-printing factories of Ivanovo-Voznesensk and their counterparts in Łódż did not succeed in shortening their workday to eleven and a half hours until 1897. At Briansk, it continued to be twelve hours until the end of the century.[39] In parts of Vladimir province, the workday often extended to fifteen or sixteen hours, especially in the summer, as it did in Moscow. Only in St. Petersburg was the workday somewhat shorter. Because Russia's capital stood in the midst of a sparsely populated region, employers eventually had to offer shorter hours to induce prospective factory hands to make the long journey from the central provinces where they might have found work closer to their native villages. Workdays of ten and a half hours thus had become common in St. Petersburg by the late 1880s.[40]

If workers thought their jobs too dangerous or their hours too long, they had little recourse until an illegal strike movement gained strength in the mid-1890s. Until then it was as Ianzhul had reported: "The factory owner is the absolute sovereign and law-giver, who is constrained by no laws, and who often simply arranges things to suit himself. The workers owe him *unquestioning obedience* as the rules at Factory No. 18 [the matchworks of Hazen and Mitchinson in Moscow province] proclaim."[41] Those rules applied not only to those who spent their days and nights choking on the sulphur and phosphorus dust at Hazen's and Mitchinson's matchworks, but to the industrial proletariat of all Russia, wherever and for whomever they worked.

Proletarians in near-abject submission to employers who wielded absolute authority had little to say about the wages they received. According to one careful comparison, Russian mill hands usually earned less than half of what their counterparts received in England and America, and it was not unusual for an American or British factory worker to earn more in a week than a Russian did in an entire month. Yet Russian workers often did not receive wages every month, and it was rare indeed for them to be paid every week. "It depends entirely upon the owner's inclination and the amount of cash he happens to have on hand at any particular moment," Ianzhul observed. Very often the lords of Moscow's industries paid their factory hands on Christmas and Easter, deducted the amount they owed at the company store, and gave them what little was left. It was not unheard of for a man and a woman to labor long hours for an entire year in the mills of Moscow province and then, on the eve of the Christmas holidays, to receive from their employer no money at all and a statement that their year's wages were less than the cost of the food they had taken on credit from his store. Nor were conditions significantly better in the mills of nearby Vladimir. In another province, a government inspector found a mill in which several years had passed since the workers had been paid their full wages.[42]

Even when Russia's factory hands received wages regularly, they offered the worker "little more than the opportunity to continue a life in which he is more dead than alive," wrote Dr. Dementev, a public health official from central Russia.[43] In Moscow, Vladimir, and a number of other central Russian provinces, wages for men ranged between thirty and ninety kopeks (fifteen–forty-five cents) a day, and the wages of men in the factories and mills of Kiev were about the same. In other regions, workers sometimes earned a bit more, especially if they worked in skilled trades. Coal miners in the Donbass earned just over a ruble a day, and some of St. Petersburg's metal workers received even more, although the average workingman earned only about eighty kopeks in Russia's capital.

If he worked long hours, a man could support himself on such wages. If he had a family, he could not spare them from starvation unless everyone, including small children, took their place at his side in the mill. Women generally earned between one-third and one-half of what men did, and children received almost nothing. In the 1880s, some children in Moscow's spinning mills earned as little as fifteen kopeks a day, or the equivalent of about a half-cent for each frightening and dangerous hour they spent darting in and out among the machines to tie threads, replace spindles, and oil moving gears. In central Russia's peat bogs, they earned the equivalent of five cents a day while their mothers cut and carried peat for less than a penny an hour. Those children under the age of ten who coughed and struggled through the haze of sulphur and phosphorus dust in the matchworks of Vladimir received as little as a ruble and a half (seventy-five cents) *a month!* This grim picture of men, women, and children giving their labor for such pitifully meager wages did not change very substantially before 1905. In a quarter of a century, factory wages rose less than 20 percent on the average.[44]

Although Russia's factory workers toiled from dawn till dark for a mere handful of kopeks, they almost never received the full measure of their earnings. Fines levied by mill foremen and factory owners for all sorts of transgressions against a myriad of rules that governed their behavior in and out of the factory drained a substantial portion of their earnings. No worker escaped the foreman's watchful eye and, because fines provided a very comfortable supplement to the owner's profit, they were readily levied. Workers were fined for tardiness, for fighting, for being drunk at work, and for such apparently strange transgressions as "hunting in the forest" and "assembling several people together into a single group." Even more often, they were fined for breaking tools (even when the cause was normal wear, not abuse), spoiling the products they were manufacturing, and for producing inferior goods. Fines ranged from ten kopeks (well over an hour's pay for most workers) for minor offenses to as much as three rubles for serious ones. With the exception of food, fines often consumed one of the largest portions of a worker's wages. In Vladimir, inspector Peskov found factories where fines cost workers about a half-month's pay in the course of a year. "In the hands of factory owners, exorbitant fines have become a means for lowering wages when industrial activity is in a slump," Minister of Internal Affairs Tolstoi reported in 1886. At about the same time, Senator Plehve commented that "fines exacted from workers . . . have in some cases totaled as much as 40 percent of their total wages."[45]

Outside the factory, workers endured conditions nearly as wretched as those under which they labored. Many could not even dream about renting even the poorest tenement for themselves and their families, for the cost often was more than their wages. Sergei Gvozdev, a factory inspector in the late 1890s, estimated that nearly half of all the workers in central Russia lived in factory-owned barracks and that another 30 percent lived in crowded rented rooms. "The housing problem at our factories becomes more critical with each passing year," Gvozdev warned. He found mill hands living in places that were crowded and filthy beyond anything he had imagined. Most barracks featured plank platforms divided into sections where each worker was allotted a space about two feet wide and six feet long in which to sleep. Mattresses and blankets were rare, and most workers—men and women alike—simply wrapped their coats and whatever rags they could acquire around themselves for warmth in barracks that sometimes had neither light nor heat. Gvozdev even found one barracks where an enterprising factory owner had arranged for unmarried men and women to share the same sleeping spaces without violating any of the canons of Victorian morality: men were assigned to work the night shift while the women slept; at dawn they took over the sleeping places while the women worked during the day.[46] Some barracks were found to be "so poor and so filthy," wrote one commentator, "that they brought forth shudders of horror even from some factory owners themselves."[47]

That Gvozdev found such conditions in the late 1890s shows how little the workers' lot had improved. Ivan Ianzhul described some of the barracks he visited in the early 1880s as "worthless and filthy hovels." Yet Gvozdev found still other factories where there were no barracks at all and where young women slept on the floor next to their sewing machines.[48] To some of the barracks at the Prokhorovs' cotton mill, workers gave such nicknames as "Penal Servitude" and "Sakhalin" (an island off the coast of Siberia famous for its penal colony). "The plank platforms were infested with bedbugs and lice," remembered Feodor Dovedenkov. "Sometimes when I returned there from the factory at two or so in the morning, I almost choked from the foul stench."[49] "People were crammed in like herrings in a cask," added Ivan Kuklëv. "One could have filled up a whole convoy of wagons with filth and dirt taken from this barracks. That's why there were all sorts of vermin crawling everywhere."[50]

Public health officials and government inspectors agreed that there was an acute housing shortage in most industrial centers and that it grew worse in the early twentieth century. "I once was in one of the workers' barracks at the Thornton Factory [in St. Petersburg]," Lenin's wife Krupskaia remembered some years after the Bolshevik Revolution. "The noise was terrible . . . and the walls were green with mold. Two families lived in each tiny room. The air was so stale that the lamps kept flickering and almost going out."[51]

If the quarters that factory owners provided for their mill hands were filthy and crowded, other housing was no better, except that it freed workers from the regimented life in factory barracks. Yet greater freedom to come and go was about the only benefit gained from such independence, especially in St. Petersburg, where a two-room tenement, without firewood, water, kitchen, or toilet facilities, cost the equivalent of a month's pay even for a metalworker whose wages were among the highest in the country. By 1881, one out of every four Petersburgers therefore lived in cellars. Soon, attics were pressed into service in outlying parts of the city, while petty officials and tradesfolk often rented small inner rooms, closets, and even corners to workers. Sometimes as many as a hundred lived in one large room in the workers' districts of the city.[52] In describing typical St. Petersburg workers' quarters, one contemporary wrote: "The rooms are filthy and the walls and ceilings are thick with soot. Two rows of cots lined each room and two men are obliged to sleep in each one."[53] In fact, there were even worse accommodations, and a government study showed that there were between 2.4 and 2.8 workers for each available sleeping space in the city and its suburbs. Such appalling overcrowding and the filth that accompanied it caused the mortality rates in the workers' districts of Russia's capital to rise to fully twice what they were in the city's aristocratic quarters.[54]

The diet of the men, women, and children who labored in Russia's mills and factories during the first decades of her industrial revolution was scarcely better than that of the friends and relatives they had left behind in their native villages. Especially during the 1880s, workers were at the mercy of stores established by mill owners at which they were obliged to purchase food and other necessities at prices that sometimes were almost twice those on the open market. To ensure that workers would not buy elsewhere, their employers often paid them in scrip redeemable only at the factory store or, in other cases, actually insisted that they take a portion of their wages in food, which the management had purchased at wholesale and then calculated at retail prices when it was doled out to the workers.[55] Even after these practices were outlawed in 1886, factory owners frequently continued them. "To evade the law prohibiting them from paying workers in food and goods, they record such transactions in workers' paybooks as cash payments," fumed one irate inspector.[56] As late as 1901, almost one out of every four rubles that Moscow cotton mill workers earned was paid in that fashion. Even after the Revolution of 1905, Sergei Gvozdev found that about half of all the wages paid to mill hands in Moscow still were spent at factory stores.[57] Nor did reports and complaints by inspectors end such blatant violations of Russia's handful of factory labor laws. "Almost 10 percent of workers' wages in Moscow are paid in food and other products from the factory store," wrote Lenin on the eve of the Great War.[58]

Mill hands also had to contend with sharply rising prices while their wages remained low. Between 1890 and 1900, the price of bread, meat, fish, kerosene, and cloth all more than doubled in St. Petersburg while workers' wages rose by only about a fifth.[59] "A cup of milk cost five kopeks, so how could workers drink it every day?" asked the weaver Ivan Kuklëv. "You'd buy a cup for the children and then try to make it last for two days if you could."[60] Such prices forced many workers to spend well over half their earnings on food. Only by careful management could unmarried factory hands avoid borrowing against their wages, but workers with families faced the hopeless prospect of ending each year deeper in debt. On the eve of the Revolution of 1905, many workers found that they owed as much as a third of their annual wages to the men who owned the factories where they worked.[61]

Some workers formed cooperatives, sometimes with a hired manager and cook, to buy and prepare food more cheaply.[62] To keep the cost low, only the poorest grades of the cheapest foods were used. That way, workers could feed themselves for about five to nine kopeks (three to five cents) a day in the late 1890s. In bitter jest, some workers called such groups "cooperatives for the disposal of spoiled food," where hordes of maggots infested the rare servings of meat, bread was moldy, and cabbage often rotten. "The basic food was *shchi* made of pickled cabbage and water," one factory worker recalled. "Potatoes in *shchi* were a rarity, seen only on holidays." "Even if only once a month, one simply had to get out and eat something other than the eternal, never-ending *shchi* and buckwheat groats," another worker remarked. "You'd come from work and, long before you got to the dining room, the smell would clog up your nose," Tamara Dontsova told Soviet scholars who interviewed her after the Revolution. "You'd come in, they'd pour out that repulsive *shchi*, and you'd gulp it down as fast as you could and leave."[63]

According to one knowledgeable calculation, such fare provided sufficient carbohydrates, but only one-fifth of the fats and less than three-quarters of the proteins needed. Most of the minimal proteins that central Russian workers consumed came from vegetable sources, especially rye bread and buckwheat groats, a balance that most experts condemn as dangerously unhealthy. Even in St. Petersburg and in the oil fields of Baku, where workers enjoyed better diets than elsewhere in Russia, average daily consumption of animal protein was less than one and a half ounces, while in central Russia it was only about a quarter of that amount.[64] For such meals, some workers worked as much as seventeen days out of every thirty.

A worker rarely could afford to spend more than two or three days' earnings every month on clothing. That came to less than fifteen rubles every year for each family member, although unmarried workers sometimes spent more. But how much would fifteen rubles buy? How well could a hard-working weaver or spinner hope to clothe himself, his wife, and his children if he could spend no more than that sum on each of them? To answer that very question, one contemporary wrote that "a calico dress costing one and a half rubles ought to last, and does last, for five to seven years. The one jacket a woman has in her wardrobe costs twelve rubles and has a term of service only slightly less than an army conscript in the olden days, that is to say it has to serve for about twenty years."[65] Boots cost about half of one year's allowance, and an overcoat cost three or four times that sum. Unable to enjoy the luxury of new clothing, most workers patronized local rag merchants. Such clothing as they had was worn, patched, worn again, and then traded to the rag peddler for something else. A worn jacket might be exchanged for a slightly less worn dress or pair of trousers, which, in turn, might later be traded for a kerchief, belt, or scarf. Only a small elite among Russia's factory workers—mainly single men in some of the skilled trades—bought new clothing regularly.[66] It is not surprising that workers spent too many of their hard-earned kopeks on vodka at those taverns that infested their neighborhoods.[67] Only in the misty haze that came upon them in drunken stupor did many of them see reflections of a better, less unjust, world.

About one out of every seven Russian factory workers became seriously ill in the course of any given year. The law required owners of any mill with more than a hundred workers to have an infirmary, but they usually ignored it and left their hands to fend for themselves. In all of Moscow province, not even one large factory in ten had a place where sick workers could receive treatment by a physician. Those unfortunate enough to be sick could do little else but lie on their plank cots in the barracks and wait for fate to decide if they would live or die. Such neglect produced chilling statistics. One study showed that one out of every two adult workers died before the age of forty-five.[68] Even more appalling, most Russian proletarians never even reached adulthood. Children were especially vulnerable to accident and disease, and, in some cases, their mortality rates were even higher than in Russia's primitive country villages. "I had twelve children," Ivan Kuklëv recalled, "but only two of them survived." One of Kuklëv's coworkers, a woman weaver at the Prokhorov cotton mill, told Soviet scholars: "I had eleven, but only three grew up. You'd go to the factory, but your soul always was in torment. Your heart always grieved for your children."[69]

Even before they began to work in the mills, proletarian children faced hazards at every turn. As in country villages, they often died from diseases and infections for which there actually were effective medical treatments. But in the urban setting, dangers rarely found in the countryside took a further toll. "Children played in the barracks kitchens and latrines," one worker remembered. "In the kitchens there always was the danger of them getting burned, but in the latrines—well, you'd go in for just a minute and almost choke from the stench—but they'd play there anyway." There was considerable danger, as the following item, which appeared in a Moscow weekly just a few years before the Great War, makes clear:

> On October 15, 1909, just after noon, a four-year-old lad fell into one of the latrines on the fourth floor [of the Prokhorov mill barracks]. At the time of the accident, the adults were changing shifts at the mill. When the boy's father returned from work and ran to his son's aid, some thirty minutes had already passed and the boy was dead by the time they managed to pull him out.

In one factory, some parents tried to shield their infants from such dangers by placing them in a nursery that their employers had just opened with much fanfare. Later investigations found that "the nursery had not even one bed, and they simply laid the workers' babies in rows of five on planks. They also cut corners on food," one investigator reported. "As a result, three or four out of every ten infants in the nursery died."[70]

As wretched as the lives of Russia's industrial proletarians were, there were others in the Empire's cities who had descended to the lowest depths of mere existence. These were the urban poor—the unemployed, the beggars, the whores, and the petty thieves—who lived under conditions so appalling that no observer could fail to be astounded by the sight of human beings caught in such deprived circumstances. It was their world that the great turn-of-the-century novelist Aleksandr Kuprin described in his memorable novel, *Iama*. Iama was the deepest, most vicious of slums, a putrid wasteland peopled by men, women, and children whom stupidity, greed, or fate had transformed into the flotsam and jetsam of mankind. Life in Iama was brutal, without hope, and infected its victims with a hatred for humanity that was matched only by their disgust for themselves. Here lived those broken women who had resigned themselves to becoming what Kuprin sadly called "sewers to drain off the city's surplus lust," who sold their bodies to anyone willing to pay "fifty kopeks or less . . . to aimlessly perform the greatest and most beautiful of all human mysteries." "Look at me," exclaimed Kuprin's Zhenechka. "What am I anyway? Some sort of universal spittoon, a cesspit, a public shit-house! Think of it. . . . Think of the thousands and thousands of men who've taken me, pawed me, panted and grunted like pigs on top of me, and all those who were, and all those who might still have been, in my bed. Ach! How I detest them all!"[71] In Iama, hungry and desperate men also sought refuge from their cares in perpetual *zapoi*, killed their fellows for a glass of raw vodka, and stole for even less. In these lowest of the lower depths, children were exploited from the moment of their birth and entered upon lives of toil, beggary, or crime when most of their childhood years still lay before them.

Kuprin had situated his Iama "in the furthest outskirts of a large southern city," but it was part of all Russian cities, large or small, northern or southern. The Iama of which Gorkii had written in *Among the Dregs* was in Nizhnii-Novgorod, a great commercial entrepot that flourished where the Oka flowed into the great Volga, mother of Russian rivers. The great textile center of Ivanovo-Voznesensk also had its Iama, "like a bazaar, where everything ebbs and flows, where some depart and others enter . . . where you never see even one birch tree or a single bit of green anywhere," in the words of one early-twentieth-century observer.[72] St. Petersburg's Iama was the Haymarket, that grim and gloomy region that Dostoevskii had endowed with eternal notoriety in *Crime and Punishment*, not more than a quarter of an hour's walk from the Nevskii Prospekt, St. Isaac's Cathedral, and the Winter Palace. But the largest, most desperate Iama in all of Russia stood near the center of Moscow, less than twenty minutes' walk from the Kremlin, in a place called Khitrovka.

A perpetual haze hung over Khitrovka. Its fundamental element was the foul torpid fog that rose from the stagnant Iauza River. Added to it was the harsh smoke of burning *makhorka*, a cheap tobacco smoked by the habitués of Khitrovka's taverns and flophouses, mixed with the sourish-sweet odor of unwashed bodies garbed in filthy, sweat-sodden attire. The stench of rancid grease issued from open pots that boiled in the courtyards and on street corners to mingle with the noxious miasma of urine and feces that spilled each day from countless humans and animals into Khitrovka's hallways, alleys, and courtyards. Everything combined with a variety of alcoholic vapors generated by the ceaseless efforts of Khitrovka's residents to purge their consciousness of the misery and despair that engulfed them all.[73]

Khitrovka took its name from Major-General Nikolai Petrovich Khitrovo, a grandee who had owned an entire block of Moscow property and had erected a large townhouse upon it during the 1820s. After the General's death, his urban domain served to house a corps of lesser government officials until it was bought a few decades later by an engineer named Romeiko at the time when Moscow's city fathers purchased most of its grounds and outbuildings for a public market. Years of neglect had brought Khitrovo's townhouse to ruin, and Romeiko had no intention of spending the fortune needed to renovate it. Instead, he turned it into the worst sort of flophouse—what Russians call a *trushchoba*—where the city's beggars, thieves, twenty-kopek whores (called *marukhi* in the local slang), and unemployed workers of various sorts could buy a night's shelter for a few kopeks. Romeiko's was the first of four such buildings, each housing several *trushchoby* that enterprising slumlords established in the formerly elegant buildings that stood in the vicinity of the Khitrovo market. Each was known by the name of its owner. There was Bunin's, Rumiantsev's, and Stepanov's (later renamed Iaroshenko's). When Romeiko sold his property in the 1880s, it took the name of its new owner and became known as Kulakov's. By the 1890s, according to Vladimir Giliarovskii, a Moscow writer who made it his life's study, Khitrovka's *trushchoby* housed some ten thousand men, women, and children, each paying five kopeks a night for space on double- and triple-decked wooden platforms. Modern statistical analyses show that his estimate was remarkably accurate.[74] Twenty-eight inches separated each tier of rough planks from the one above it. Pairs of tenants had to share a space that was forty-two inches wide by six feet long, where all slept their fitful sleep with nothing for cover except their own rags.

Each of Khitrovka's buildings also housed one or more drinking dens, each dubbed by the locals with names that provided clues to the identity of its clientele. Iaroshenko's held the region's elite establishment, a den called the *Katorga* (Penal Servitude), which catered to the aristocrats of Khitrovka—thieves, escaped Siberian convicts, and other folk on the run from the law—who dedicated their evening hours to what Giliarovskii called "stormy and drunken debauchery." The *Katorga* closed its doors early, well before midnight usually, and its patrons had to continue their carousals elsewhere. Some moved on to the *Sibir* (Siberia), a den at Rumiantsev's that stood a step beneath the *Katorga* and typically catered to petty thieves, pickpockets, and fences who dealt in stolen merchandise on a grand scale. Patrons of the *Sibir* thought themselves well above those who frequented the *Peresylnyi* (Transit), a more disreputable den housed in the cellars of the same building. At the *Peresylnyi*, beggars, those who would do anything for a quick profit, and the homeless all gathered to guzzle raw vodka and cheap wine. For them, the *Peresylnyi* was especially well named, for many indeed stood at a crossroads. Either they would soon rise into the more select company that frequented the *Sibir*, or they would fall—finally and hopelessly—into the dens that lay at the very pit of life in Khitrovka. Collectively these lowest dens had been dubbed *Svinoi Dom*—the Swine's Quarters.

By the 1890s, Kulakov's had extended to include several buildings in addition to General Khitrovo's former townhouse, and their cellars housed *Svinoi Dom*, where every door opened upon someone or some place that sold vodka so raw that it seared the stomach. "In the walls, under the floors, even in fat table legs, liquor was stashed away" for ready sale, Giliarovskii reported. The two most notorious dens in *Svinoi Dom* were the *Ustiug* (Flatiron) and *Sukhoi Ovrag* (the Dry Gulch). The latter's patrons bore the ominous collective title: "Wolves of the Dry Gulch," and it was a name well merited. Even the most redoubtable policeman never ventured there. At the *Ustiug* and the *Sukhoi Ovrag* gathered men willing to sell their last ragged tatters of clothing for a glass of vodka, addicts desperate for a sniff of cocaine, and murderers ready to ply their craft for a small fee. There were tramps grown old in Khitrovka, and young girls who had every expectation of spending their lives there. All of these "Wolves of the Dry Gulch" made Khitrovka resound. Men roared in rage, while *marukhi* cried out in pain and fear. Desperate and compelling, their screams nonetheless went unanswered. Some whores would be beaten, others would be stabbed or have their necks broken, after which their bodies would be stripped and left naked where they fell. In the morning, the police gathered up the corpses, sent some to the coroner's office for further examination and carted the others over to the university's laboratories, where medical students cut them up and used them for their studies of anatomy.

Each of Khitrovka's dens held its corps of pimps, or "cats" as they were called, who sat surrounded by their stables of *marukhi*. From time to time a *marukha* would go off with a man who had bought her services for a few moments. If she were fortunate, he would buy her company for the entire evening, which meant that she might have a chance for a few hours' sleep. As one *marukha* left, another returned to bring in her earnings or to be assigned to another customer. It was rare for a *marukha* to earn more than fifty kopeks from the rent of her body, even for an entire evening. Such women often began their sad and lonely careers in childhood, easing the pain and indignity of life with alcohol so that, in Giliarovskii's words, "drunken ten-year-old whores were not a rarity" in Khitrovka's lowest dens. From time to time, a *marukha*'s trade yielded its inevitable fruit, and such offspring were put to immediate use. Many an enterprising whore rented her nurseling by the day to one among Khitrovka's legions of beggars who then carried the infant, hungry, often sick, and wrapped only in filthy rags, through Moscow's cold streets for hours on end as she called out to passersby to "have pity on a poor mother and her fatherless infant." Infants often died from such abuse. If one died during the day, it was not unusual for the beggar who had rented the infant to carry its tiny, snow-sodden corpse through the streets until night fell, in an effort to add further pathos to her cries for alms.

Children who survived the ordeal of infancy in Khitrovka soon took up the beggar's trade themselves. To stir up greater sympathy, they often hid away their boots and coats and stood in the snowy streets near the entrances to the city's better restaurants to beg from well-heeled patrons. Every possible ruse had to be employed to squeeze alms from Moscow's citizens because it was a general rule that any five-year-old beggar who failed to return to his elders at the end of the day with at least twenty kopeks—about twenty hours' wages for a child in one of Moscow's factories—would be beaten and starved. Child beggars also served as lookouts while their elders committed robberies and thus entered the world of crime to become what Giliarovskii called "future convicts." Children of unusual agility soon became *fortachi*, whose trade was to wriggle through the small hinged windows by which Russians let air into their dwellings in the winter. A clever *fortach* would spy an open window in an apartment in some prosperous part of the city, wait until its inhabitants left, and then slip inside to pass the valuables out to his accomplices. After a few years, *fortachi* often joined the ranks of young men who slipped out of the Dry Gulch at night with revolvers under their coats to try their hand at larger crimes.

Khitrovka's young thieves sold much of their booty to well-known fences, but they also turned to a group of clever tailors who lived at Bunin's and could quickly alter the form of the articles they had stolen. These men were called "crayfish" because they had long since sold their last stitches of clothing for vodka and could not venture out of doors. As quickly as they earned a few kopeks, they spent them on drink, and it was to them that Khitrovka's enterprising young thieves brought cloaks and pelisses of rich furs stolen from the homes of Moscow's wealthy citizens. A night then would pass in frenzied labor. By morning, fur coats had been transformed into jackets, hats, and muffs that appeared for sale in the nearby market stalls while the police searched in vain for the garments reported stolen the night before. How long one survived this dangerous life was a matter of skill, wit, and luck. But the end was the same. Death usually came well before forty in a gutter, a crumbling stairwell, or a charity ward. It often came violently. At other times, it came from the virulent infectious diseases that raged in the district's *trushchoby*. Rarely did it come from old age.

Because the life of those who lived in Khitrovka or in the slums of other Russian cities was the most desperate and hopeless of any in the Empire, it had predictable consequences over and beyond the many deaths from violence and disease. In 1911, more than eight hundred suicides were reported in Moscow alone, most of them among unemployed workers who had fallen into the gruesome world of Khitrovka and saw no escape.[75] The folk saying that "once you've eaten Khitrovka soup you'll never leave" proved grimly true all too often.[76]

Many who had tasted the soup of Khitrovka or of the deep slums in other Russian cities, of course, had done so through little fault of their own. Unemployment was the scourge of all those nineteenth-century proletarians for whom society and the government assumed no responsibility. It struck the diligent and the lazy alike, and loyalty to an employer provided no sure defense against it. Like their counterparts elsewhere, nineteenth-century Russian entrepreneurs hired and laid off workers with shameless abandon as the demand for their products rose and fell. They gave no thought for the terrible impact of their act upon their workers' hopes and lives. If demand suddenly rose, plant managers frantically hired as many new workers as they could employ at the factory's machines; if demand fell even briefly, or if raw materials were late in arriving, they laid them off with equal speed. Most factory jobs were not highly skilled, and managers found it a simple matter to rehire all the workers they needed a month, a week, or even a day hence. Laid-off workers received no support from any source. They had no savings. If they could find no work, they simply had to beg, steal, or starve.

By the end of the century, layoffs had become so common in Russia's factories that nearly one out of every two workers in St. Petersburg and Kiev knew the gripping fear that came with unemployment, and three-quarters of that number had to endure at least a month without wages before they found other work. In Moscow, the number of unemployed factory workers in the city passed eighteen thousand as the twentieth century opened, and their numbers swelled further as thousands of peasants abandoned their desperate struggle for survival on the land and left their villages to seek their fortunes in the city. Every fifth proletarian in Moscow was out of work in 1900, and at least twelve thousand more would join their ranks before the next decade passed. Even in Ivanovo-Voznesensk, a booming center of Russia's textile industry, one worker in seven was laid off for at least one month out of every twelve.[77]

Desperate for work, Russia's growing army of unemployed thronged primitive labor exchanges. In just one year (1909), more than twenty-five thousand workers registered at Moscow's central labor exchange, but less than one in four found work. Every day, hordes of men and women who asked for nothing more than a job at near-starvation wages gathered at the gates of factories and mills all over Russia "to beg for work," in the words of one historian, "as beggars begged for alms."[78] Hundreds often stood long hours each day in the snow and ice in anticipation of that moment when a foreman would appear at the gates, cast his eyes over the pleading crowd, and speak the magic words to a chosen handful:

"Do you know how to run the machines?"
"Yes, I know how."
"Good, then get to work!"[79]

The foreman might offer less than the going wage, and the work might not last more than a day or two. But it was work, the one thing that stood between a man or woman and the depths of the city's slums. Those who were not chosen would return on the morrow. Perhaps a new day would bring them better fortune.

Because the search for work often proved so arduous for all but the most skilled, workers laid off at Russia's mills and factories faced days and weeks without the means to buy a bowl of watery *shchi* or a crust of bread. Their desperation was all the greater because their places in the wretched factory barracks depended upon their continued employment. "It was especially hard on families," one commentator wrote. "People had no savings, and, when they were laid off, they faced hunger from the very first day. To make things worse, everyone who was laid off was hastily evicted from their rooms. They literally threw workers into the street."[80] Ivan Kuklëv remembered seeing women who had been laid off at the Prokhorov mill turn to prostitution just to find shelter and ward off starvation. Small wonder, then, that a woman who had worked in the mills later recalled that she had seen sister workers fall into a dead faint when they were told they had been laid off. Foremen simply ordered such unfortunates doused with water and shoved them out the factory's front gate.[81]

Workers desperate to feed themselves and their families were rarely willing to risk their slender sustenance in confrontation with their employers. Only at moments of deepest economic crisis might they pose even the most timid economic demands, but their situation had to be utterly desperate before they took that step. "It is impossible for our position to be any worse," declared Fedor Kozlov, a weaver who spoke out at a strike meeting at the Morozovs' mill in 1885. "It has become utterly impossible to live."[82] Had Kozlov's words touched only a minority of his fellows and those unfortunates who had already fallen into the depths of Khitrovka, they would have had little effect. Only because so many of his coworkers were crushed in the grip of soaring unemployment and plummeting wages did his pleas move them to strike.[83] Although dramatic reminders that even workers desperate for work could be pushed too far, such strikes had little impact upon factory conditions. Too many had to face the stark choice between survival at minimal wages or starvation to lodge effective protests during the early decades of Russia's industrial revolution. Only when hunger and ruin did not confront them squarely every day did a portion of the proletariat gain the minimal economic freedom needed to launch their struggle for higher pay, shorter hours, and better working conditions.

Even during the 1880s and 1890s, there were a handful in the ranks of Russia's proletariat who had grown more daring and had begun to envision a better life. The instrument of their liberation became the printed word. We have no accounts to tell us how clearly Russia's proletarians perceived the value of the written word in furthering their cause, but the speed with which they learned to read and write was little short of astonishing. By the end of the nineteenth century, six out of every ten male factory hands, and more than half that number of female factory workers, had achieved literacy. In Moscow, the figures were about 10 percent higher, while, in St. Petersburg, the portion of proletarian men and women who were literate rose to be fully three times greater than in Russia as a whole.[84] By 1900, the factory worker in Moscow and St. Petersburg who could not read had become the exception, while the reverse continued to be true in the villages whence they had come. "When I came in from work, I did not lie down to sleep immediately," recalled the newly literate Fedor Samoilov, an Ivanovo weaver who joined Lenin's Bolsheviks in 1903. "Instead, I picked up a book, lit a candle that I had bought with my own savings, and read until I no longer could keep my eyelids from closing."[85] "I read a great deal about various explorations and discoveries of new lands," added Semën Balashov, another Ivanovo worker who was among the first to join the Russian Social Democratic Labor party in 1898. "Here I caught sight of a new life, one very different from our life of servitude." Samoilov followed much the same path. "In the beginning," he wrote, "I read Jules Verne, Mayne Reid, and [James Fenimore] Cooper, and was captivated by their descriptions of journeys and discoveries." For some time, such readers wandered with no direction or purpose, caught up in the thrill of fighting Indians in America's wilderness, the excitement of life at twenty thousand leagues beneath the sea, and the mystery of travel to other planets.[86]

Especially during the reign of Alexander III, rigid censorship removed political writings from the hands of all but the most dedicated of revolutionaries among Russia's readers. Samoilov tells us that: "Over a period of five to six years, I read through the most diverse assortment of books imaginable . . . but I never encountered a single one that could have awakened my class consciousness." Yet there was perhaps an even greater reward to be drawn from their undirected, nonpolitical reading. "Books," wrote Samoilov, "taught me how to think."[87]

During the 1880s and early 1890s, growing numbers of Balashovs and Samoilovs became literate and rose to become part of a worker elite in material terms as well. No longer did the threat of hunger loom over tomorrow's horizon for such highly skilled men and women. Semën Kanatchikov, an unusually adept and adaptable peasant who became a master patternmaker at Moscow's great Bromley Factory at the age of eighteen, earned twice the wages of many factory workers.[88] The same was true of a number of others, especially metalworkers in St. Petersburg. Although wages rose slowly during the quarter-century after the assassination of Alexander II in 1881, the gap between the economic position of Russia's emerging worker elite and the mass of proletarians widened appreciably. Despite their enviable position in comparison with their less fortunate fellows, such highly skilled workers as Kanatchikov, Samoilov, and Balashov still did not live in even modest comfort, and it was probably that fact that stirred them to demand more from their employers once they were no longer obliged to live from meal to meal and from day to day. Trade unions and all forms of labor protest were outlawed; these men and women therefore turned to Russia's resurgent revolutionaries for guidance during the first years of Nicholas II's reign. They became Russia's worker intelligentsia, whose urgings became a powerful force in recruiting proletarians to the revolutionary cause as the twentieth century dawned in Russia.

These men and women ruled their lives with a new morality that made them very unlike most proletarians at the time. "We never drank spirits, never engaged in senseless destruction, and, in fact, did little else but read in our spare time," recalled one such worker who was employed at the Prokhorov mill.[89] But such puritanical virtue was not the claim of only a few individuals in one factory. By the 1890s, it had become something of a code of ethics among much of the worker intelligentsia in Russia's cities.[90] As Ivan Babushkin recalled: "We . . . were of the opinion that a good socialist ought not to drink vodka, and we even condemned smoking tobacco. . . . At this point in our lives, we preached morality in the strictest sense of the term. In a word, we insisted that a socialist must stand as the best example to people in all things, and we tried to set such examples ourselves."[91] It was men and women such as these that factory owners feared, not those who lived from day to day and spent their few extra kopeks on vodka. There was a good reason why the Prokhorovs asked each and every one of their workers: "Are you literate? What do you read? Do you go to church? What do you do after work?" and preferred those who were illiterate and wasted their free hours.[92]

The handful of skilled workers who began in the 1890s to envision a society and government more responsive to their needs, and who sought to govern their lives with a more rigid morality, needed guidance to give their strivings form and substance. This could not be found in James Fenimore Cooper's stirring tales of adventure in the American wilderness, nor was it part of Jules Verne's world of science fiction. Their awakening coincided with new stirrings of Russia's revolutionary movement, no longer composed of naïve young idealists but of hardened realists whose strength and dedication to the revolutionary cause had been forged in the reactionary crucible of Alexander III's Russia. By the mid-1890s, the leaders of these revolutionary men and women already had served the revolutionary cause for a decade, and their dedication to its goals had been tested by the trials of imprisonment, penal servitude, and exile. Their commitment to revolution was not the combination of youthful ardor and adolescent rebellion against the world of their elders that had been so characteristic of those revolutionaries who had gone to the *narod* in the 1870s. It was a consciously chosen dedication that consumed their lives from day to day and year to year.

These new revolutionaries would lead the Russian proletariat in a quarter-century of struggle against the autocracy and the capitalist order it had brought into being. Not only had these men and women envisioned the form of its replacement but they had calculated the means and the method to attain that end. For them, the 1880s had been a time in which they had developed the theory that would govern their actions, but repression and their own inexperience had prevented them from fully testing their conclusions in the arena of political struggle. By the mid-1890s, they were prepared to try again, and their effort carried them directly into Russia's factories to those elite and literate workers who stood ready to receive them. Together, these men and women began to forge the revolutionary alliance that brought them first into worker demonstrations and then into the revolutionary conflict that surged over Russia in the year of turmoil that came in 1905.

CHAPTER V
The Few Who Dared

BEFORE 1905, THERE SEEMED ALMOST NO HOPE OF REVOLUtion in Russia. Revolution meant the overthrow of the Tsar, a ruler who, most Russians believed, had received his autocratic power directly from the hands of God. To go against the Tsar's command thus seemed to flaunt God's will, and few were prepared to risk the fury of divine retribution. Against those few who dared, Russian Tsars had weapons other than divine sanction to defend their crowns. Throughout the nineteenth century, they were supported by the nobility, legions of state officials, and an army that numbered well over two million as the twentieth century dawned. Few revolutionaries in history ever faced such crushing odds. Even to contemplate such a course as theirs called for the sort of fortitude that lay in the breasts of only the most devoted disciples of a new order. Life as a revolutionary promised no immediate glory, no earthly rewards, only the most terrifying demands:

—"O, you who wish to cross this threshold, do you know what awaits you?"

—"I know."

—"Do you understand that yours will be a life of cold, hunger, hatred, ridicule, scorn, insult, imprisonment, sickness, even death?"

—"I do."

—"Can you face complete alienation, utter loneliness?"

—"I can. . . . I am ready to endure it all."

—"Even when this will come not just from enemies, but even from your family and friends?"

—"Yes, even then."

—"Good. But are you ready to make any sacrifice?"

—"Yes."

—"Even if your sacrifice shall be nameless? Are you prepared to die even if no one—not one soul—will remember or even know that you died?"

—"I need no thanks, no mourning. I need no monuments to my name."

—"Are you prepared even to resort to crime if necessary?"

—"Even for that I am ready."

—"Do you realize that at some point you might lose faith in your beliefs? That you might come to think that you were deceived and gave your young life in vain?"

—"I understand. Even so, I want to cross this threshold."

—"Enter, then!"

—"Fool!" someone in the background muttered through clenched teeth.

—"Saint!" the echo replied.[1]

In one form or another, educated young Russians of the 1870s and 1880s were familiar with this awesome litany of revolutionary life set forth by Ivan Turgenev in his *Poems in Prose*. But how could such a credo be put into practice? Revolution could not come in an instant. How, therefore, should would-be revolutionaries pave the way? To whom should they address their message? How many must give their lives as "nameless convicts" before their comrades could elevate them publicly to the pantheon of revolutionary heroes? *What Is To Be Done?* asked the title of Nikolai Chernyshevskii's radical utopian novel. "When Will That Day Come?" wrote Nikolai Dobroliubov in the title of one of his most important essays. From first to last, Russian revolutionaries asked and reasked these "cursed questions" to which the true answers seemed destined to remain ever elusive.

Russians always had known political radicals, but revolutionaries began to appear among them only in the 1860s. When the long-awaited Emancipation Acts of 1861 did not immediately free millions of serfs from the medieval constraints under which they had labored for so long, some of Russia's radical young men and women abandoned all hope that the Tsar ever would give "true freedom" to his people. "[The Emancipation Acts] have only given serfdom a new form," stormed Nikolai Ogarev, one of Aleksandr Herzen's closest collaborators on the radical émigré journal *Kolokol (The Bell). "The people have been deceived by the Tsar!"*[2] WHAT DO THE PEOPLE NEED? trumpeted the headline of a supplement to the July 1, 1861, issue. "Land and Liberty!" Ogarev proclaimed in reply.[3] But how could Land and Liberty be won? And who should lead the struggle? This time, it was Herzen who supplied the answer to those hundreds of student radicals who forced St. Petersburg University to close in the fall of 1861: "GO TO THE PEOPLE!"[4]

But clarion calls that rang from *Kolokol's* pages from 1861–62 failed to strike a responsive chord among Russia's radical youth. Impatient and romantic, they were not yet prepared to become "nameless sacrifices" for the people's cause. For them "The People" —the *narod*—was an abstraction. Few had ever seen a peasant village and fewer still had ever spoken at length with a peasant. Therefore, they at first found far more alluring those prophets who urged them to work for revolution or, at least, progress, equality, and social justice, within the arenas where they felt most at ease. They held various visions of their nation's future, and found a number of roles appealing, but nearly all included a passionate belief that the laws that determined human behavior could be discovered in the same fashion that scientists had discovered the laws that governed physical phenomena. Science therefore became their new god.

In 1862, Russia's radical youth found in the pages of Turgenev's *Fathers and Sons* the first model to seize their imaginations. The novel's central character, Evgenii Bazarov, personified their uncritical adoration of science. Bazarov was a nihilist, a term Turgenev used to describe a new breed of youth "who does not bow before any authority [and] who accepts nothing on faith." There was not a "single convention in our present-day family or civic life that does not demand complete and merciless rejection," Bazarov insisted. Yet such nihilism offered no positive vision. "At the present time, rejection is the most useful thing—therefore, we reject everything." When one of Turgenev's "fathers" asked if it were not necessary to build something to replace what he and his kind would destroy, Bazarov replied: "That isn't our business. First, it is necessary to clear the way."[5]

Many radicals bitterly rejected what they thought must be a caricature of their beliefs, but the literary critic and publicist Dmitrii Pisarev seized upon Turgenev's portrayal. For Pisarev and the "new men," whom he later christened "thinking realists," Bazarov personified the scientific mind at its best. "He recognizes no governing social force, no moral law, no sanctioning principle outside himself," Pisarev explained. "If Bazarovism is a sickness, then it is a sickness of the age in which we live."[6] Pisarev thought that Russia's Bazarovs need not serve society nor dedicate themselves to the *narod*. Simply by acting on their passion for science, they would serve the best interests of the people. To the ever-present cursed question "what is to be done?" Pisarev therefore replied: "Live while you're alive. Eat dry bread when there's no roast beef. Sleep with any woman when you can't have a particular woman and, in general, don't dream about orange groves and palm trees when you're standing in snow drifts on frozen tundras."[7] In 1862, Pisarev could offer nothing more. If Russia's restless youth hoped to find in his affirmation of Bazarov a plan for social or political action or even simple reassurances about the rightness of their course, they were to be disappointed.

For those to whom Pisarev's portrayal of the new men seemed too asocial, the novel *What Is To Be Done?* offered a vision of a new society as well as the first plan for its construction. Published in 1863, Chernyshevskii had written his book while a political prisoner in the Peter-Paul Fortress, that massive structure of brick and granite that lowers ominously from the Neva's bank opposite the Winter Palace. Like a number of Russia's most important revolutionary works, its publication resulted from a combination of good fortune and administrative error.* Nikolai Nekrasov, the poet and editor who was to publish the novel in serial form in *Sovremennik (The Contemporary)*, had lost the entire manuscript as he made his way home one night after a party. A well-meaning passerby found it, returned it intact, and a sympathetic censor allowed it to slip past the administrative hurdles that stood in the way of its publication.[8] In the realm of *belles lettres*, the novel failed miserably, and Chernyshevskii himself readily admitted that "I am an author without talent who doesn't even have a complete command of his own language."[9] Yet *What Is To Be Done?* had an immense impact upon Russia's youth, so much so that Georgii Plekhanov, the founding father of Russian Marxism, later claimed that "no printed work has had such

---

*The first instance occurred in 1790, when a negligent censor failed to make certain that Aleksandr Radishchev had removed a quantity of objectionable passages from his famous *Journey from St. Petersburg to Moscow*. Less than a decade after Chernyshevskii's novel appeared, a committee of censors passed the Russian translation of Marx's *Das Kapital* on the ground that its objectionable passages were not dangerous because "they are, as it were, buried in the immense mass of abstract, somewhat obscure, politico-economic argumentation that comprises the contents of this book." ["Sochineniia Karla Marksa v russkoi tsenzure (arkhivnaia spravka)," *Dela i dni. Istoricheskii zhurnal* 1 (1920): 323–24.]

success" in Russia.[10] For many of Russia's greatest revolutionaries, the novel became a bible.

Chernyshevskii was determined not only to raise the burning issues of the emancipation era but to provide answers. The pages of his novel drew a blueprint for a society ruled by equality and social justice, and its characters, although melodramatically, even laughably, drawn, provided models for youths who had to find their way along untrodden paths. The mere fact that the leading character was a woman was of great importance in encouraging many young women to follow the path of female liberation. Some were willing to pay as much as twenty-five rubles (more than a month's pay for a factory worker) for a copy, and a number tried to follow Vera Pavlovna's path to emancipation and sexual freedom through fictitious marriages and study for professional careers.[11] For men and women alike, Chernyshevskii portrayed a utopian socialist world where each labored for the welfare of all to create the best possible lives for themselves in which, as Vera Pavlovna proclaimed, "everyone lives as he wishes."[12] It was a society in which the full realization of one's individuality never impinged upon the well-being of others. Many of Russia's ardent youth took up Chernyshevskii's cause and vowed to follow his program as the government sent the author into Siberian exile.

It was never easy to be a "radical" in Russia, but it became especially difficult after January 1863, when a bloody revolt broke out in Russian Poland. Not only did the Tsar's government become more repressive but, once order was restored, numbers of lucrative new government sinecures opened up in the Russified regime that Alexander II and his advisers imposed upon the Empire's reconquered Polish lands. Well-educated young Russians, who had been alienated from the establishment because there were few career opportunities open to them in the 1850s and early 1860s were enticed away from radical idealism by the promise of material rewards. The minority who remained steadfast became more bitter, more alienated, and more radical. To them, the Tsar barred the way to freedom for the *narod* and darkened their dreams for a new society. For them, Chernyshevskii's gradualism seemed too slow, and they vowed to move history at a quicker pace. Led by Nikolai Ishutin, a number of them formed a secret group called "Hell," where they began to talk about killing the Tsar.[13] Among them was Dmitrii Karakozov.

Karakozov was the son of a minor official, one of those many desperately poor nobles who served in insignificant provincial posts to feed families that were noble in name only. They enjoyed none of that wealth and luxury so often associated with Russia's aristocracy by readers of *War and Peace*, and, after the emancipation of 1861, very little remained to distinguish them from the lesser folk among whom they lived and worked. Thus Dmitrii Karakozov grew up in straitened circumstances. In 1860, he entered the University of Kazan, the future alma mater of Lenin and scene of a number of revolutionary events during the second half of the nineteenth century. Worn, pale, careless about his appearance, he was expelled, made his way to Moscow, registered at the university there, and was expelled once again. He then joined Ishutin's circle where they spoke of regicide. To one who spoke of killing the Tsar, Karakozov once said: "Don't talk about it—do it!"[14] He suffered from psychological disturbances that made him think of suicide. He bought poison but did not take it because, according to one expert, "the thought of having to die before doing anything for the people plagued him so mercilessly that he could not take his own life."[15] Early in 1866, tormented in mind and body, he resolved to kill the Tsar. "The combination of regicide and suicide became deeply attractive," one scholar recently wrote of him. "He no longer wished to live and he wanted to make some kind of supreme sacrifice for the people."[16] When he made his decision, Karakozov was twenty-six years old.

Late in February, Karakozov went to St. Petersburg to fulfill his self-imposed mission. There is still some doubt about how much Ishutin (who also was Karakozov's first cousin) and "Hell" were involved in the plot. But it is quite certain that Karakozov bought an old double-barreled pistol, powder, and ball with money he had gotten from Ivan Khudiakov, an important member of the secret organization, and there is a very real possibility that Khudiakov helped Karakozov to draft several of the proclamations with which he hoped to announce his deed once the Tsar was dead. Ishutin and "Hell" may have been even more deeply involved, for we know that several of the group made hurried trips between St. Petersburg and Moscow as the weeks passed and Karakozov still had not begun to stalk his quarry. At one point, Ishutin even ordered Karakozov to return to Moscow. He obeyed, only to return to St. Petersburg in less than a week. Ishutin, Khudiakov, and their friends later insisted that their purpose in all these hasty comings and goings had been to dissuade Karakozov from the assassination attempt, but it is quite possible that during these critical weeks they were urging him to get on with his effort.[17]

Those Summer Gardens that Peter the Great had laid out with such care, and whose beautification had so occupied the eighteenth-century Empresses Anna and Elizabeth, were one of Petersburgers' favorite promenades, and it was Alexander II's custom to join them briefly on some afternoons. Like his father, the iron-willed Nicholas I, he enjoyed chance meetings with his subjects. On April 4, 1866, he strolled in the gardens for a short time, spoke briefly with the Duke of Leuchtenberg, and returned to his carriage. While the policemen on duty at the gardens' main gates were falling over themselves to be of service, Karakozov stepped from the crowd, raised his pistol, and fired at his unsuspecting sovereign. According to widely circulated official reports, a peasant—one of that very *narod* to whom the revolutionaries had dedicated their efforts—saved the Tsar by jostling Karakozov's arm, but it is more probable that his aim simply was poor. Angrily, violently, the police seized him and dragged him before Alexander.

—"Are you a Pole?" the Tsar asked, thinking that his would-be assassin came from the ranks of those rebels his soldiers had only recently suppressed.

—"Pure Russian," was Karakozov's reply.

—"Why did you try to shoot me?"

—"Because you promised to give the *narod* land but failed to do so."[18]

Karakozov remained stubbornly indifferent to his captors' efforts to learn his identity, although they eventually did so because he had carelessly left incriminating papers in the cheap boarding-house where he had rented a room. For months, he remained unrepentant, insisting that he had dedicated his life to the *narod* gladly. "If I had not one but a hundred lives, and if the *narod* demanded that I sacrifice all of them for their well-being," he wrote grandly to the Tsar, "then I swear, Sire, by all that's holy, I would not hesitate for a single moment to make such a sacrifice."[19] At his trial, however, Karakozov's nerve failed. He pleaded insanity and, when told that he was to be hanged, begged for mercy. Alexander replied that as a Christian he freely forgave him, but that as Autocrat of All the Russias he could not do so. On September 3, 1866, after spending long hours on his knees in prayer, Karakozov was executed. Before he was put to death, he implicated not only Ishutin and Khudiakov but most of his other friends and acquaintances in Moscow and St. Petersburg.[20]

The wave of public outrage that followed Karakozov's shot enabled the Russian authorities to tighten their grip on all forms of political dissent as much sterner men stepped forward to become the Empire's Minister of Public Instruction (controlling the schools and universities), Chief of the Third Section (controlling the political police), and Military Governor General of St. Petersburg. For several years, it was impossible for radical young men and women to exchange ideas or to spread their beliefs among the *narod*. What was to be done? Clearly very little *could* be done in the face of the conservative wave that had washed over Russia, and, for half a decade or so, young radicals could do little more than prepare themselves for professions that might someday enable them to better serve the people.

A number chose medicine. Among them were a substantial portion of young women acting upon the inspiration of *What Is To Be Done?* Yet all institutions of higher learning (and especially medical schools) remained closed to women in Russia, and this induced some to study in Western European cities, especially in Zurich, where the Swiss authorities made it a relatively simple matter for foreign students to enter the university. There, during the late 1860s and early 1870s, these young women and the men who followed them were caught up in the dizzying ideological crosscurrents that swirled from the writings and speeches of Marx, Lassalle, such émigré Russians as Lavrov and Bakunin, and those Communards who had sought refuge in Switzerland when the Paris Commune fell.[21]

No radical writings had a greater impact during these years than did those of Petr Lavrov, although, at first glance, he seems an improbable candidate for such an influential role. A wealthy nobleman and a colonel who served in the artillery for more than twenty years, he taught mathematics at several of the Imperial military academies, where the elite of the Russian officer corps were trained. He wrote poems critical of Tsar and government, but kept them to himself. Not until he was forty-five (a full quarter-century older than many of Russia's youthful radicals) did he publish the work that catapulted him to fame as the prophet of Russian populism.[22]

Lavrov set forth his message in a series of seventeen "Historical Letters" that were spread over fifteen installments in 1868 and 1869 in the St. Petersburg journal *Nedelia (Week)* and then published in book form the next year. More urgently than any of his predecessors, he insisted that Russia's revolutionary youth had both a debt and a mission. The debt was to the *narod;* the mission was an inescapable moral duty to repay the debt in the fullest measure. "Each of the material comforts I enjoy, each thought which I have had the leisure to acquire," Lavrov wrote, "has been bought with the blood, suffering, or toil of millions. . . . What progress there is depends exclusively upon critically thinking individuals [such as he considered himself to be] but . . . since it is precisely for *their* civilization that [this] terrible price . . . has been paid, it is upon them that the moral duty to repay the cost of this progress is incumbent."[23] As Lavrov's artful translator, Professor James Scanlan, so aptly put it, his message "was heard so clearly by the rebels because it both resolved their ambivalence and articulated their innermost ideals. . . . Lavrov supplied them with a unique amalgam—a *theory of action.*"[24] "This was the book of life, the revolutionary gospel, the philosophy of revolution," proclaimed Osip Aptekman, one of the hundreds of youths whom Lavrov's message moved to action.[25] For Aptekman, and many like him, Lavrov's "Historical Letters" gave direction to their deepest strivings in a far more realistic manner than had Chernyshevskii's blueprint for utopian communes.

Lavrov's call to action was soon to be put into practice. In May 1873, Alexander II's government issued a decree that, in the words of one writer, "fell upon the Russian students studying in Zurich like snow on one's head."[26] Clearly the Tsar and his advisers were disturbed by their visions of radical young Russians abroad, especially as their numbers increased around 1870:

> Coincidental with the increase of Russian students [in Zurich], the ringleaders of the Russian [radical] emigration chose this city as a center for revolutionary propaganda and directed all their energy toward recruiting these students into their ranks. Under their influence scientific pursuits were abandoned in favor of useless political agitation. Among these young Russian men and women various political parties with the most extreme goals developed. . . . Some of these youth travel from Zurich to Russia and back two or three times each year, carrying letters, messages, and proclamations, and they take an active part in criminal propaganda. Others are carried away by communist theories of free love, and under the protection of a fictitious marriage they consign to oblivion the most basic principles of morality and female chastity.

This decree was much more than an idle catalogue of grievances, and it could not be ignored by those accused of violating all the canons of moral and political virtue: "The government cannot accept the notion that two or three medical diplomas can compensate for the evil that is growing out of the moral corruption of the younger generation and therefore realizes that it is necessary to put an end to this abnormal situation." There would be no negotiation, no pleas, no exceptions to the government's decision. "All those who continue to attend lectures [in Zurich] after January 1, 1874," the decree concluded, would be barred from all Russian schools and prohibited from practicing their profession anywhere in the Empire.[27] Some chose to remain abroad; many others returned to Russia only to find that they could pursue neither educations nor careers because they were politically suspect. For them, the cry that Herzen and Ogarev had raised a decade before took on new meaning. They now resolved to go directly to the people.

Although important, the decree of May 1873 was not the only influence to turn radical youth toward the countryside. Within Russia itself there were small radical groups, the most notable being Nikolai Chaikovskii's circle who, in the early 1870s, determined that the most effective way to pay the debt about which Lavrov had written was to go directly to the *narod* and educate them in the principles and ideals of socialism.[28]

Still another strain of radical thought urged young Russians into the countryside in the early 1870s. Ever since the 1830s, Mikhail Bakunin had been a major figure in the ranks of Russia's radical intelligentsia, pleading, cajoling, arguing, even terrorizing his listeners with his powerful personality and bearlike physique. Bakunin's personal dedication to the cause of revolution was worldwide. He fought on the barricades of Paris in February 1848 and hastened to pursue revolution's red flags in Berlin, Frankfurt, and Prague before the year's end. After two years in Saxon and Austrian prisons, he was extradited to Russia in 1851 and exiled to the remote eastern regions of Siberia only to launch a daring escape that carried him down the Amur River, to Japan, San Francisco, across the isthmus of Panama, to New York and then on to London, where he joined his friend and fellow radical Herzen. Ever true to his conviction that revolution was "instinct rather than thought,"[29] he pursued his dream across the length and breadth of Europe during the 1860s: in Poland, in Italy, and, in 1871, in Paris. "What a man!" Paris's revolutionary Prefect of Police once exclaimed. "On the first day of a revolution, he is a perfect treasure; on the second he ought to be shot!"[30] As E. H. Carr, his greatest biographer, once wrote, "Bakunin preached destruction so long as there was anything left to destroy. He preached rebellion—even when there was nothing left to rebel against."[31] At one time or another, Bakunin engaged nearly every leading European revolutionary in rhetorical and ideological combat; his greatest struggle was with Karl Marx, whose passion for a new social order he shared, but whose methods he violently disputed. "Bakunin sought liberty in destruction and disintegration which, to Marx's orderly mind, seemed midsummer madness," Carr once explained.[32] "Political agitation is as necessary to him as the breath of life," an agent of the Tsar's secret police who knew him well concluded.[33]

All during Bakunin's participation in foreign revolutions, the situation in his native Russia never was far from his thoughts. He wrote often and with passion about his hopes for revolution in his homeland, and pointed to the Empire's countless peasant communes as its most fertile source. While some Russian writers found there a symbol of their nation's intolerable backwardness, others found in it a promise of Russia's greatness, either because it preserved Old Russian virtues (this was the claim of the Slavophiles in the 1840s and 1850s), or because it offered a crude model upon which to develop a society ruled by equality and social justice (Chernyshevskii). To Bakunin, the peasant commune was above all a reservoir of pent-up lower-class anger and hatred directed against established authority in Russia. This hatred resembled a bomb; it needed only to be lit by Russia's young revolutionaries to detonate the terrible, elemental force of a peasant war that would sweep everything before it. Like Lavrov, Bakunin urged Russia's youth to go to the people, but for a very different purpose. The radical intelligentsia could strike the spark that would ignite this dormant revolutionary force.[34]

Hundreds of radical youths, some committed to the teachings of Lavrov, others to the more impatient urgings of Bakunin, poured into the Russian countryside in the spring, summer, and fall of 1874 to "go to the people," whom they proclaimed to be "the natural allies of anyone who seriously and sincerely hates the present and longs for a better future."[35] They went with optimism and with a sense of deep urgency. "I cannot wait more than four years for a revolution," one insisted.[36] Therein lay the appeal of the passionate, violent Bakunin over the more cautious and sober Lavrov for the more restless among them. "We had an inner moral compulsion to immediately burn all our bridges and to break off all ties with a world we thought sunk up to its eyeballs in depravity," wrote young Pavel Akselrod, later to become one of Russia's leading Marxists. "There is no doubt," he added, "that Bakunin intoxicated us especially with his revolutionary phraseology and his flaming eloquence."[37]

But the peasants had no use for the ardent anarchism of Bakunin's disciples. Nor had they any interest in the more moderate propaganda of Lavrov's followers. As Sergei Kravchinskii later confessed, most peasants simply distrusted everyone and treated all revolutionaries with disdain, indifference, or hatred. Some years later, Kravchinskii recalled a winter day when he and a companion overtook a peasant driver as they trudged along a lonely country road. "I began to tell the peasant that he must not pay taxes," he recalled, "and I tried to convince him by quotations from the Bible that they must revolt." The peasant offered no reply. "He made his horse trot, and we began to trot behind him," Kravchinskii continued. "All the time I continued to talk to him about taxes and revolt. Finally, he made his horse gallop, but the animal was not worth much . . . so my companion and I did not fall behind but kept up our propaganda till we were quite out of breath."[38]

All over Russia, young Russian populists met similar rejections of their effort to spread socialist propaganda among the peasants, while those who had believed that the *narod* was ready to be led in a raging social war suffered beatings at the hands of irate listeners. For most of these young men and women, their first face-to-face encounters with the *narod* were shattering experiences; none returned unscathed. Some sixteen hundred of them were turned over by their beloved *narod* to the Tsar's police. Almost half that number (770 in all) were kept under arrest.[39] Those who were tried and convicted disappeared into prisons or into the wastes of Siberia, leaving behind only the echo of their ringing words of defiance. "I still am convinced that the day will come when even our somnolent and sluggish society will awaken and be ashamed," Sofia Bardina, aged twenty-three and a follower of Lavrov, told her judges. She knew that she probably would be condemned to exile in Siberia but, nonetheless, added a stern warning: "Torment us while you still have the power to do so. But we have moral power, the power of historical progress, and the power of ideas. And you cannot suppress ideas with bayonets!"[40] Despite such noble words, the efforts of these young radicals to repay their debt to the *narod* lay in ruins by the end of 1874. "Scientific socialism, the socialism of the West," Kravchinskii lamented, "bounces off the Russian masses like a pea off a wall."[41]

Nevertheless, Russia's revolutionary populists did not abandon their belief in the masses. Nor did they relinquish their deep hope that one day they would become the bearers of revolution in Russia. Their passion for the *narod* grew more intense. As Richard Wortman, author of one of the most sensitive and persuasive scholarly portrayals of the crisis that gripped these young radicals, wrote some years ago, "Like a rejected lover [the young populist] only longed the more powerfully after his beloved when rebuffed, and cast the blame for his failures upon himself. . . . Humbled, he began to look upon the peasants with even greater respect and admiration."[42] Those survivors of the arrests of 1874 took up the arduous task of rebuilding their movement. They called themselves *narodniki* to symbolize their greater admiration and deeper devotion and dedicated themselves to the people anew. "We are narrowing our demands to those that are realizable in the immediate future, that is, to the people's needs and desires at this moment," they proclaimed.[43] To best express those needs, they returned to Ogarev's reply to the question "What Do the People Need?" The *narodniki* now insisted, as had Ogarev in 1861, that the people needed "Land and Liberty." That became their slogan, and the name they gave to their new organization of activists.

The new leader of the *narodniki* was Mark Natanson, a young Jew in his mid-twenties, one of the handful of revolutionaries active in the 1870s who lived to see the Bolsheviks' triumph in 1917. His followers called him the "gatherer of the Russian lands," an expression of their hope that he, like the Tsars of Muscovy (who also bore that epithet), would summon all of Russia to their cause.[44] He

reassured his followers that the people's refusal to heed their preachings during the mad summer of 1874 was of little consequence
because "the Russian *narod* already holds those very ideas that the
intelligentsia considers the most advanced."[45] It was not necessary
to teach socialism to the masses, he insisted, because they were, by
the very nature of their life and experience, "so socialistic that, if
their desires and aspirations were realized at this moment, such
could become a firm underpinning for the further development of
socialism in Russia."[46]

Still, there was urgent work for the *narodniki* in the countryside, which they must not delay "because the development of capitalism . . . threatens the commune with destruction and a greater
or lesser distortion of the people's world view."[47] Thus Natanson
and his followers decreed that the *narodniki* must go to the people,
not for days or weeks, but for months, even years. They must become
like the *narod* and be accepted by them as faithful brothers and
sisters. The *narodniki* therefore went to the people in 1877 and 1878
to help them, to learn from them, but, at the same time, to turn their
thoughts toward revolution. They saw those diverse tasks as necessary and important preparations that would qualify them as leaders
of the *narod* when the inevitable national uprising broke out.[48]
Again cruel disenchantment awaited them. The Tsar's police
seemed to have eyes and ears everywhere, even in the most remote
corners of the Empire, and many were arrested and sent to prison
or exile. "How sorry I feel for these young people," Herzen's daughter Natalia wrote to a friend several years after her father's death.
"So much self-sacrifice, so much strength expended to no purpose!
One cannot but admire their courage, especially that of the women,
but at the same time I have to admit that they act like madmen."[49]

Narodniki who escaped arrests in 1877 and 1878 had to find
another path to revolution. At the same trial at which Sofia Bardina
had spoken so passionately, young Petr Alekseev, the lone factory
worker among the sons and daughters of nobles, army officers, state
officials, doctors, and merchants, spoke of "the millions of working
people who are only just beginning to stand on their own two
feet."[50] His words were not only a warning to his judges, but a plea

to Russia's many nonproletarian radicals to turn their attention to the men and women who lived such desperate lives in the Empire's factories. A handful of *narodniki* had gone to the factories when the *narod* expelled them from their villages and had found more eager listeners there. But their comrades could not yet admit that the proletariat in the capitalist cities should form the vanguard of the revolution in Russia. That moment soon was to come—even for such ardent disciples of Bakunin as Akselrod and such faithful followers of Lavrov as Plekhanov—but the Russian revolutionary movement was destined to live through yet another painful and tragic phase before its rededication to the industrial proletariat and devotion to the teachings of Marx.

Karakozov's execution had not erased his fateful shot from the minds of Russia's revolutionaries, and the debate about the efficacy of conspiracy and terror therefore continued to rage among them. Far more than any other form of revolutionary protest, terror required single-minded dedication. Above all, it demanded iron discipline, a quality of heart and mind that most Russian revolutionaries possessed in acutely short supply. The terrorism of Karakozov and his friends in Ishutin's circle had its disciples nonetheless. Their efforts to preserve Karakozov's heritage during the decade after his execution mark some of the most convoluted and sordid episodes in the history of Russian radicalism.

Peter Tkachëv had been only peripherally associated with Ishutin's circle, but Karakozov's testimony had led to his arrest along with its other members. At that time, he was twenty-two, widely read in the writings of Chernyshevskii, Herzen, and Dobroliubov, and already a veteran of political protest. At seventeen, he had taken part in the disorders at St. Petersburg University and had been sent to the Kronstadt fortress for two months. Within a year, he was arrested for having subversive literature in his room (among other things, he had a copy of Ogarev's pamphlet *What Do the People Need?*), sentenced to three years in prison, but released well before he had served the full term of his sentence. Beginning in March 1869, he spent nearly five years in prison and in Siberian exile. At the end of 1873, he fled to Western Europe. Not yet thirty, he had fifteen years of experience in revolutionary agitation in Russia to his credit. Once safe in Switzerland, he founded *Nabat (The Tocsin)*, a revolutionary newspaper that he used to offer others lessons drawn from his extensive revolutionary experience.[51]

Tkachëv condemned the teachings of Chernyshevskii, Lavrov, and Bakunin as equally ineffective. "Centralization, severe discipline, speed, decision, and unity in action," he wrote, were the essential elements for victory in the revolutionary struggle. "Any concession or doubt, any compromise, multiplicity of command, or decentralization of the forces in the fight, can only weaken their energy, paralyse their work and do away with any chance of victory."[52] These were ruthless revolutionary principles, and, as Russian history would prove, they were the only tactical and organizational principles that could work effectively in an actual revolutionary situation. To his quickness to understand that very fact, Lenin would owe much of his success; unlike his rivals, he would organize his Bolsheviks along lines very similar to Tkachëv's precepts.

Yet, despite his ruthless single-mindedness, Tkachëv never pursued conspiracy for its sake alone, nor terror merely for the sake of terror. Driven by the belief that the goal of conspiracy was successful revolution, he hoped to abolish private property, eliminate the state, grant equal status to women, and create a new order that would produce "the gradual abolition of physical, intellectual, and moral inequality among men, by means of a compulsory system of social education, equal for all, and inspired by the spirit of love, equality, and fraternity."[53] Tkachëv's dedication to the revolutionary struggle was sincere and complete. Tragically, there were others who saw conspiracy and terror as ends in themselves.

Sergei Nechaev, a young man for whom Tkächev served as a mentor and patron during the late 1860s, was the most unprincipled of them all. In contrast to Tkachëv, who was a nobleman of modest means, Nechaev was the son of former serfs and spent his childhood in the squalid mill town of Ivanovo. As a messenger boy at one of the local factories he learned to read and write while still a child.[54]

From this background—hardly comfortable, but certainly far from the wretched life lived by the peasants who labored in the mills— Nechaev constructed the legend that he was a former serf who learned to read and write only in his mid-teens.[55] Purposely confusing fact and fiction, he surrounded himself with an aura of dark mystery that heightened his appeal to the nonproletarian radicals of Moscow and St. Petersburg. For them, Nechaev became the man from the *narod* in whose existence they so ardently believed.[56] It proved an odd relationship from the start, for the mystique to which Nechaev dedicated so much effort simultaneously repelled and attracted those who met him. "The first impression Nechaev makes is unpleasant yet actually seductive," one of his St. Petersburg friends later confessed to the police. "The main traits of his character are despotism and self-esteem. . . . He stimulates interest in himself, and the more impressionable and naïve simply worship him, the latter a necessary condition to any friendship with him."[57] Vanity, despotism, deceit, utter dishonesty, and lack of principle: these were the characteristics that distinguished Nechaev as he set out to carve a place for himself in Russia's revolutionary annals.

Nechaev first appeared in St. Petersburg not long before Karakozov tried to kill the Tsar. What he did and whom he met during the next two years remain something of a mystery. Aside from a few personal details and the fact that he earned a license to teach religion at the primary school level in 1867, we know only that, by mid-1868, he had apparently dedicated himself to the revolutionary cause. Sometime in 1868, he met Tkachëv who, although only three years his senior, was closely connected with several important radical journals and already enjoyed a solid reputation as a revolutionary tactician and theorist. Still unknown in revolutionary circles and evidently seeking an entrée, Nechaev became his ready disciple. Together the two played a part in student disorders late that year. "Our protest is firm and united," they proclaimed. "We are sooner ready to choke in exile or in fortress cells than to become morally deformed and go on suffocating in our academies and universities."[58] Early in 1869, they drafted *A Program of Revolutionary Action*, which proclaimed that "social revolution is our final goal

[but] . . . political revolution is the only means for achieving it." In contrast to Bakunin's dreams, they insisted that revolution must be led from above, not engendered spontaneously from below. Therefore, they planned to finish training dedicated revolutionary cadres by May 1, 1869, and with them to launch a revolution that would sweep across all of Russia. According to their schedule, their revolution would break out in the spring of 1870, although they could not be more precise about its date.[59] Before they could act, Tkachëv was arrested late in March 1869, imprisoned, and sent into exile.

The year 1869, however, saw Nechaev give free rein to a variety of absurd, but extremely dangerous, terrorist fantasies. These began when he fled to the West soon before Tkachëv's arrest and concocted a series of dramatic incidents to explain his sudden departure to his comrades. It was all a ruse to enrich his mystique and to win greater stature among Russia's revolutionaries. Thus, at the beginning of February, Vera Zasulich, a young revolutionary who later won fame for shooting the Governor General of St. Petersburg, received an anonymous letter that read, in part: "While walking today along Vasilevskii Island, I encountered a carriage carrying a person under arrest. A hand thrust out and threw a note, and I heard a voice say: 'If you are a student, take this to the designated address.'" The letter enclosed a note written in Nechaev's hand: "They are taking me to a fortress," it read. "Let our cause continue."[60] Apparently victim of a secret police arrest, Nechaev became a hero overnight. In truth, no one had arrested him and he had simply slipped away to Moscow where he and a close friend continued to release rumors for the next month about his "escape," his "recapture," and yet another "escape." Each account was embellished with numerous tales of Nechaev's heroism and resourcefulness. That accomplished, he slipped across Russia's western frontier at the beginning of March.[61]

In Geneva, Nechaev had other tales to tell as he painted the size and strength of the revolutionary movement inside Russia in glowing and vastly exaggerated hues. He won Bakunin's favor and collaborated with him on a number of revolutionary pamphlets, the most amazing being their now-notorious *Revolutionary Catechism*, which prescribed for the dedicated revolutionary a life even more fearsomely ascetic than that portrayed in Turgenev's litany. "The revolutionary is a doomed man," they proclaimed. "He has no interests, affairs, feelings, attachments, property, not even a name that he can call his own. Everything in him is absorbed by one exclusive interest, one thought, one passion—the revolution. . . . He has severed all ties . . . with laws, decorum, all the generally accepted conditions and morality of this world. He stands as its relentless enemy and, if he continues to live in it, then it is only in order to be more certain of its destruction. . . . Day and night he must have but one thought, one single goal—merciless destruction. Striving only for this aim, coldly and tirelessly, he must be prepared to perish himself and to destroy with his own hands all that hinders its realization."[62]

Nechaev insisted that these uncompromising principles must apply to any who would bear the proud title of revolutionary—to all, that is, except himself. Proclaiming that "any secret society which does not have as its aim a series of actions capable of destroying something is a child's toy," he returned to Russia that fall to create a revolutionary organization that he grandly called The People's Revenge. Once in Moscow, he embarked upon the cruelest, most pointless, most deceitful course ever pursued by a Russian revolutionary. "Without sparing lives," he wrote, he and his followers would "fling ourselves into the life of the people . . . so as to shake it, unite it, and drive it toward the triumph of its own cause."[63] Only terror could achieve that goal. He justified his course on the ground of revolutionary security, but the truth was that he employed terror only to satiate his psychotic craving for self-aggrandizement and to satisfy his lust for killing. By the end of the year, one of his comrades was dead and some fourscore more in prison as a consequence of his efforts to embellish the elaborate cloak of myth and legend with which he endeavored to surround himself.

Living in Moscow under the pseudonym Ivan Pavlov, Nechaev set out to found a series of revolutionary cells, such as he and Bakunin had described in the *Revolutionary Catechism*. Although more than a hundred revolutionaries crossed his path during those months, most moved only briefly into his orbit and then drifted away. Nonetheless, Nechaev did establish at least one revolutionary cell, made up entirely of those "doomed" men and women in whom he and Bakunin had placed their faith.

First and foremost, there was the twenty-two-year-old Petr Uspenskii, married to the sister of Vera Zasulich and, in the fall of 1869, frantic with worry because his own fifteen-year-old sister had been arrested and confined in the Peter and Paul Fortress.* There also was the somewhat deranged forty-two-year-old Ivan Pryzhov who at the time of his arrest could only exclaim that "I have led a dog's life!"[65] There was, in fact, some justification for Pryzhov's complaint. Nearly twenty years older than any of his friends in the revolutionary movement, he had grown up surrounded by a torturous cloud of death and madness in Moscow's Mariinskaia Charity Hospital where his father was a clerk. Pryzhov became a petty clerk himself, but lost his position at about the time of Karakozov's arrest. He became a drunk, a well-known figure in the desperate world of Khitrovka and the author of a curious work entitled *A History of Russian Pot-Houses.* Nechaev saw him as an instrument for tightening the link between his terrorists and the urban masses.

Pryzhov and Uspenskii soon were joined by Aleksei Kuznetsov, son of a local merchant and a young man willing to squander his father's wealth on Nechaev's movement. There was also Elizaveta Beliaeva, timid, stupid, and barely able to read and write, who was so madly in love with Nechaev that, in the words of one witness, she was "ready to go with him through fire and water and endure any sacrifice for him."[66] The final recruit was Ivan Ivanov, a dedicated

---

*Although there seems to be no evidence that Uspenskii knew of it, Nechaev himself was indirectly responsible for his sister's arrest. Uspenskii's sister had been caught up in a police sweep of Feliks Volkhovskii's radical circle that had been set off by a letter Nechaev had sent to Volkhovskii from Switzerland. Like a number of other revolutionaries, Volkhovskii had snubbed Nechaev during the months prior to his flight to Switzerland in March 1869. While he was in Switzerland, Nechaev sent hundreds of letters (and packages of revolutionary propaganda) to scores of Russian students and radicals, leading to the arrests of a number of those who had spurned him during the early months of his revolutionary career.[64]

student activist of great physical strength, who has been called "irritable, limited, and stubborn."[67] Ivanov frequently disputed Nechaev's efforts to wield absolute authority.

Ivanov's refusal to subordinate himself to Nechaev's fanatical self-adoration set in motion a series of appalling and tragic events. By November 1869, Nechaev's hatred for the youth who would not accept his word as law had grown so intense that he announced to the others in his revolutionary cell that Ivanov must be executed. Together with Nikolai Nikolaev, the friend who had helped him escape to the West at the beginning of the year, Nechaev assembled Pryzhov and Kuznetsov to help him commit the murder and justified his unprecedented and pointless act by the outright lie that Ivanov had become a police spy. Together, they lured Ivanov into an isolated Moscow park, strangled him, and then shot him through the left eye as a symbol of his "execution" for "betraying" the revolutionary cause. They bungled the job badly and the police discovered Ivanov's body in a matter of days. Soon, they arrested most of the circle and a large number of the revolutionaries with whom its members had been in contact. Nechaev, however, escaped to the West. This time, Switzerland did not prove so hospitable a haven, and late in 1872 the Swiss authorities extradited their unwanted visitor to Russia. Tried by a Moscow court at the beginning of 1873, he was found guilty by a jury (an innovation established in Russian criminal law less than a decade before) and led away proclaiming, "Long Live the Assembly! Down With Tyranny!"[68] After a last-minute reprieve spared him from execution, Nechaev was confined in the Peter and Paul Fortress, where he spent the last decade of his life in its deepest and dankest dungeon.[69]

All of the publicity and controversy that surrounded Nechaev's unprincipled escapades discredited revolutionary terror in the eyes of many young men and women who joined in the Movement to the People in the 1870s. But terrorism nonetheless continued to have its advocates, especially in times of stress and frustration. As the Movement to the People foundered again in the mid-1870s, desperate young *narodniki* began to reconsider terror, this time as a weapon of last resort against the authorities who had paralyzed their efforts to lead the people. Russian revolutionaries felt an overwhelming sense of powerlessness as the authorities struck them down, and that feeling intensified as several leading tsarist officials distinguished themselves in brutality toward their new prisoners. For such bitter and desperate youths, terrorism was not an instrument to be abused in a quest for personal glory. They saw it instead as a potent weapon in their life-and-death struggle to break free from autocracy. Many revolutionaries now chose to fight to the death to resist capture, and, for the first time in Russia's history, both revolutionaries and police began to carry firearms. This ushered in a new era in Russia's revolutionary conflict that began with a single shot from a pistol hidden in a young woman's muff.

"Vera Zasulich was the mother of the terrorist struggle in Russia," recalled Lev Deich, a young man who went to the people and later rose to sit high in the councils of the Mensheviks.[70] Indeed, it was Zasulich, a young woman of excessively ordinary appearance but distinguished among her comrades for her courage and stern sense of justice, who fired the first shot in a campaign that would bring down the Tsar in little more than three years. Zasulich had been peripherally associated with Nechaev's circle through her sister's marriage to Petr Uspenskii. Arrested during the investigations that followed the discovery of Ivanov's corpse, she was sent to prison for two years even though she had no part in the killing and had not even been seriously involved with the group's discussions. Sent into exile after her release from prison, she slipped away to the Ukraine and joined the Movement to the People; like many of her comrades, she hoped to spark the peasant uprising that Bakunin had prophesied. When it did not come to pass, Zasulich rededicated her zeal to the grueling task of freeing comrades who had fallen into the hands of the authorities. Where liberation was impossible, she sought vengeance for their suffering.

On January 24, 1878, Zasulich set out to avenge the treatment of Ivan Emelianov (known to the police as Bogoliubov) who had been flogged on direct orders from St. Petersburg's Military Governor General Fedor Trepov. Zasulich went to Trepov's office posing as a petitioner. When her turn for an audience came, she drew from her muff a large-caliber snub-nosed revolver, popularly called a "Bull-dog," and shot him in the left side. Although five of its cartridges remained unfired, she calmly lay down her weapon and offered no resistance when Trepov's aides seized her.[71]

In a society racked by self-doubt, the Zasulich case immediately became a cause célèbre, all the more so because the government announced that she would be tried by a jury, not a military court-martial. Senior officials in the Ministry of Justice reasoned that if a civilian jury found her guilty (and no other verdict seemed possible because she readily confessed to the crime and there were a number of eyewitnesses), the revolutionary movement would stand publicly condemned.[72] Yet the government's hopes were dashed. Petr Aleksandrov, Russia's first great trial lawyer, rose to defend Zasulich, and his task was immeasurably easier because even conservatives had little use for Trepov. Amazingly, the trial judge allowed Aleksandrov to call blatantly sympathetic witnesses whose emotional testimony only raised the accused higher in the public eye. Tearfully, and needing to stop several times to regain her composure, Zasulich told a courtroom packed with partisan spectators how she had decided to punish Trepov for his cruelty. "I did not find—indeed I could not find—any other way to bring attention to this situation," she confessed once she had gained control of her emotions. "I could see no other way. . . . It is terrible to raise one's hand against a fellow human being, I know, but I concluded that this had to be done."[73]

In a passionate speech that relied far more upon emotion than fact, Aleksandrov spoke in Zasulich's defense. Appalled by Trepov's cruelty, "Zasulich waited for help to come from public opinion," he told the jury. "She waited, finally, for some word of justice. Justice!" —he paused to allow the word's dramatic effect to fill the courtroom —"Justice! But nothing was ever heard about justice." And so, Aleksandrov explained, Zasulich decided to bring Trepov to justice only after the government and society had failed to do so. "Yes," he concluded, "she may leave this court condemned, but she will not leave in disgrace. It remains only for us to hope that the events that caused this to happen will not be repeated and thereby allow us to prevent similar crimes from giving birth to similar criminals."[74] Anatolii Koni, the young judge who presided at the trial, instructed the jury to begin its deliberations. When they returned to announce that they found Zasulich "not guilty," the courtroom erupted with cheers, applause, and stomping feet.[75] "Many great lords and ladies from high society," Minister of War Dmitrii Miliutin wrote in his diary, "were in ecstasy at the court's verdict."[76] For the moment, Zasulich was the heroine and Trepov (and the government he represented) the villain.

Indirectly, public opinion in Russia had endorsed terrorism, although few realized the grave implications of that endorsement. The great novelist Count Lev Tolstoi was perhaps one of the very few who saw beyond the celebrations to the dark days that lay ahead for the old order when he warned that "the Zasulich trial is no joke. This is like a prophecy of revolution."[77] If the authorities had had their way, Zasulich would have been seized and sent to Siberia despite the jury's verdict, but her friends spirited her to the safety of Switzerland where she helped to found the first Russian Marxist party a few years later. She left behind a revolutionary movement turned onto a very different course. Within months, a number of high officials, including the chief of the security police, fell before the revolutionaries' attacks. "Political assassination *is the most terrible weapon for our foes*, against which neither a menacing army nor a legion of spies can help," one of them rejoiced.[78] Terrorism had become a major weapon in the arsenal of Russia's revolutionaries.

Although assassination made it possible to fight directly against their enemies, there were those in the ranks of Russia's revolutionaries who opposed terrorism because they feared it would divert their comrades' attention from the more important tasks of raising the peasants' revolutionary consciousness.[79] Nonetheless, advocates of terror and their opponents found it possible to coexist as *narodniki* until April 1879, when Aleksandr Solovev, whose experiences as a *narodnik* had convinced him that the Tsar was "an enemy of the people,"[80] fired five shots at Alexander II while he strolled in the Winter Palace gardens, missing his mark each time. Solovev was seized, tried, and hanged at a public execution to which a number of foreign correspondents were invited to make it clear to Russia and Europe that the Tsar intended to crush the revolutionary movement. Following the execution, Alexander raised three generals who had distinguished themselves in combat to positions of supreme command in the areas of his Empire where the terrorists were most active.[81] To Adjutant-General Iosif Gurko, he gave command of St. Petersburg; to Adjutant-General Count Eduard Totleben, Odessa; and to Adjutant-General Count Mikhail Loris-Melikov, Kharkov.

Faced with vicious repression, all *narodniki* were forced to confront the question of terrorism head on. If they chose terror, they must be prepared to pursue that course relentlessly to its ultimate conclusion—the assassination of the Tsar himself—for only that could justify the great losses their ranks would sustain in the assault. Otherwise, they must husband their resources and spread propaganda among the workers and peasants.[82] There were dedicated champions of both views. Perhaps the strongest advocate of moderation was Georgii Plekhanov, a young man with a sad, somber face whose statesmanlike mien, so very unlike the unkempt appearances of his comrades, was enhanced by a neatly trimmed chestnut Vandyke beard. Even at the age of twenty, a friend remembered, Plekhanov's eyes "looked out sternly from under extraordinarily thick eyebrows and long eyelashes with an ironical smile."[83] One of his greatest talents was his genius for arguing ideological and tactical questions in lucid, closely reasoned prose. He was fated "to live with a pen in his hand," one of his comrades wrote after the revolution, and, as a consequence, he became the Russian Marxists' first and greatest theoretician.[84]

Plekhanov's name had been unknown in revolutionary circles until December 6, 1876, when he unexpectedly gave a moving speech at a demonstration in front of St. Petersburg's Kazan Cathedral. He fled abroad, but soon returned to work in the provinces. When police surveillance became too intense, he moved to St. Petersburg and lost himself in the city's crowds. In those days, he slept with a revolver under his pillow and carried brass knuckles wherever he went. Nonetheless, he remained a passionate advocate of moderation and firmly opposed adding terror to the revolutionary arsenal.[85] Yet the terrible year of 1879, when every revolutionary in Russia seemed in danger, was not the time for Plekhanov's counsels of moderation. Violence was in the air. The terrorists' insistence that "terrorism is revolution in action" dramatically affirmed their struggle for survival.[86]

Plekhanov's confrontation with the terrorists took place at the Voronezh Congress, an assembly of twenty-one narodniki who slipped into the provincial city of Voronezh late in June 1879. Several days before the "congress" opened, the terrorists held a secret meeting at the nearby resort town of Lipetsk, organized themselves into an Executive Committee, and vowed to support terror as a major weapon against the forces of order.[87] They then went on to Voronezh for the general congress, where they presented Plekhanov and his followers with a fait accompli. Many years later, Nikolai Morozov, one of the leading terrorists, recalled that Plekhanov simply asked: "Is this really to be our program?" He "turned as white as a sheet" when told that it was. Ever polite, in sharp contrast to his comrades, Plekhanov then asked: "Can it really be, gentlemen, that you *all* think this way?" Some of the leading moderates had not learned of the congress in time, and there were only a handful there to support him. "In that case, gentlemen," Plekhanov concluded, "there's nothing more for me to do here. Farewell!" Morozov remembered that "it seemed that he stayed on his feet only with the greatest effort."[88] The old narodnik party that had called itself Land and Liberty since the middle of the decade was irreparably split.

Soon, Plekhanov and those who supported his view that educating the masses to play a role in the *future* revolution was their main task, formed a new group called *Chernyi Peredel,** while the

---

*The literal translation of Chernyi Peredel is "Black Repartition," and, although the phrase is utterly meaningless in English, it has often been used in accounts about the Russian revolutionary movement. The sense and meaning of Chernyi Peredel are probably best conveyed by the term "General Redistribution," a phrase that makes much more sense if we remember that it was chosen, as Plekhanov's leading biographer explains, to express the moderates' "solidarity with the old narodnik aspiration for an agrarian revolution which would divide [i.e., redistribute]

terrorists took the name *Narodnaia Volia* (the People's Will). For the next two years, the daring young men and women of *Narodnaia Volia* held undisputed command of the revolutionary stage in Russia while Plekhanov and his supporters (including Vera Zasulich) went into exile in Switzerland to redirect their efforts to transform Russia.

The tale of *Narodnaia Volia* has been told in a variety of languages because its drama and suspense make it well worth telling.[90] Its ranks never numbered more than a handful. When first organized at the apartment of Vera Figner, there were fifteen members. In the weeks immediately after the group was organized, a mere twenty-nine more were added to its rolls.[91] Its founders demanded utter dedication from each other. Following Tkachëv's precepts, they established a small corps of revolutionaries bound by iron discipline. Members could never resign; only death could free them from their vows.[92] All members swore allegiance to common goals and vowed to work for their realization. "We are convinced that only on the basis of socialist principles can mankind embody in its life freedom, equality, and brotherhood, and provide for the general material well-being and the complete all-around development of each individual's personality," their program began. Their goal was revolution; their instruments propaganda and terror "to destroy the most dangerous people in the government, to protect the party from spies, and to punish the most blatant excesses committed by the government."[93] Soon after they returned to St. Petersburg from Voronezh, the members of *Narodnaia Volia* made a decision that ruled their lives for the next eighteen months. On August 26, 1879, they agreed that "the will of the people" demanded the assassination of Alexander II. Thus began a deadly game of cat and mouse, in which the People's Will pursued the Tsar across the face of Russia, even into the corridors of the Winter Palace itself.[94]

Because every member of *Narodnaia Volia* was dedicated to

---

the land among the peasant communes and lay the foundation for a Russian agrarian socialism."[89]

its mission, it is perhaps unfair to name some as its central figures. Still, few historians would dispute that Aleksandr Mikhailov, Sofia Perovskaia, and Vera Figner were among its leading personalities and that its leader, unquestionably, was Andrei Zheliabov. Unlike his comrades, Zheliabov had been a serf, but his master—one of that handful of enlightened lords who cropped up from time to time in the annals of Russian serfdom—had provided him with a good education. After the emancipation, Zheliabov attended the university in Odessa on a government scholarship, and married the mayor's daughter. Fate seemed to be carrying him in exactly the opposite direction from the revolutionary course he would eventually follow.[95] But there was a deep restlessness in Zheliabov's spirit that drew him away from his comfortable and predictable life among Odessa's merchants. Although he remained on the periphery of the organized revolutionary movement for some years, he longed to aid those from whose midst he had sprung. Only on the eve of the Lipetsk meeting did he agree to set propaganda aside for terrorism, and only if Alexander II was the target.[96] Once committed, his dedication and single-mindedness surpassed that of any other in *Narodnaia Volia.*

During the eighteen months after the terrorists launched their campaign against Alexander II in the fall of 1879, they carried out seven attempts on his life. The fourth, which occurred in February 1880 after months of careful planning, was easily one of the most spectacular. Preparations began in September 1879, when a simple cabinetmaker in search of work appeared at the workmen's entrance to the Winter Palace. According to his passport, he was Batyshkov, a peasant from the northern province of Olenets. Pleasant and honest, not overly intelligent, but an able craftsman, he was taken on as a carpenter. Unknown to his new employers, however, he was none other than Stepan Khalturin, one of the leaders of St. Petersburg's nascent workers' movement and a key figure in *Narodnaia Volia's* battle organization. His task was simple, yet immensely hazardous. During the next few months, he smuggled bits of dynamite into the workers' cellar dormitory at the Palace and hid it beneath his mattress.

Toward the end of January, Zheliabov decided that Khalturin had enough explosives for his needs, although Khalturin angrily insisted that he needed more. At a meeting of the Executive Committee, Khalturin was overruled by his comrades and told to make his final preparations. Doubtful of success, but submissive to party discipline, he planted his charge in the cellar, two floors below the palace dining room. On February 5, 1880, he lit the fuse and calmly left by the workers' entrance. A few minutes later, a tremendous explosion shattered the guardroom on the floor above, killing eleven and injuring fifty-six. But Khalturin had been right all along. There had not been enough dynamite to destroy the Tsar's dining room above the guardroom, and Alexander escaped unharmed. Nonetheless, the psychological impact of the attack was immense, for it proclaimed to all Russia and to the world beyond that the Tsar of All the Russias was not safe from the revolutionaries' vengeance even within his own palace.[97]

Within days after the explosion, the People's Will laid new plans even though the police security around the Tsar had become nearly impenetrable. They hoped to attack Alexander in Odessa in the spring and, failing that, to strike again in St. Petersburg that fall. Both plots failed, and their ranks were further decimated by arrests, exiles, and executions. For one brief moment, even Zheliabov faltered and asked if they ought not to postpone further attacks. But Anna Iakimova, the child of a poor parish priest, and Sofia Perovskaia, daughter of a former Governor General of St. Petersburg and great-granddaughter of the Empress Elizabeth's lover Kyril Razumovskii, insisted they must press on. "Our girls are fiercer than our men," remarked Nikolai Kibalchich, their chief explosives expert. "The honor of the party demands that the Emperor must be killed," Zheliabov conceded, and his comrades prepared to launch one more attempt.[98]

Twenty young men and seven young women, all but six under the age of thirty and with somewhat less than two hundred rubles among them, prepared to bring down the Autocrat of All the Russias as 1880 drew to a close. Seven would be dead within six months. Another eleven would not survive the decade. Only six would live to see revolution come in 1917.[99] With Perovskaia to direct them, five terrorists watched Alexander's movements and noted his favorite routes. Their main weapon remained the dynamite charges that they had used in past attempts, but they now supplemented them with an untried, but daringly conceived new weapon. A brilliant scientist, Kibalchich had fashioned an ingenious fuseless hand grenade by carefully placing two thin glass vials of nitroglycerine against each other in the center of a receptacle filled with jagged metal fragments. The vials shattered upon impact and the grenade exploded with lethal effect. Kibalchich's grenades were designed to be almost suicidally volatile. A carrier need only have his arm jostled on a crowded street or lose his footing for a moment on an icy pavement and death would ensue, not only for the terrorist but for any bystanders within a radius of several meters. How many innocent victims could be tolerated? The People's Will had managed to sidestep that question in their attempt on the Winter Palace because the victims had been soldiers who, although peasants, were defenders of the regime. "So long as the army supports tyranny and does not realize that its sacred duty is to be with the people against the Tsar, such tragedies will remain inevitable," they warned.[100] But what about civilian onlookers whose ranks might include poor tradesmen, servants, peasants, or workers? With this question unresolved, the People's Will chose Kibalchich's invention as a second means of attack should their dynamite fail them again.[101]

To lay their dynamite mine, the terrorists rented a small basement shop at No. 56 Malaia Sadovaia Street, along which Alexander often drove. To allay suspicion, they opened a cheese shop in their new quarters and began to tunnel beneath the street from one of its unused rooms. They chose Anna Iakimova and Iurii Bogdanovich, both known for their ready wit, to play the part of cheese merchants under the assumed name of Kobozev. Very soon, servants, housewives, and other shopkeepers began to gossip aloud about this pleasant young couple who sold their merchandise so cheaply to neighborhood workers with no apparent thought for profit. In a city where many doormen and janitors were in the pay of the secret police and where each was on the alert to report anything out of the ordinary, not much time could pass before such idle chatter reached the ears of the authorities. Meanwhile, the danger of detection grew even greater as the excavation reached the sidewalk and street. At any moment, the sound of the picks and shovels might be heard by the police and watchmen who patrolled the street above.

Early in 1881, after eighteen months, the police began to penetrate the curtain of secrecy that had protected the People's Will. In January, three conspirators were arrested; a few weeks later, another fell into the authorities' clutches. At about the same time, Natalia Olovennikova suffered a nervous breakdown and had to be sent away to Moscow, and an inspection of the cheese shop by a general from the Imperial Corps of Engineers disguised as a municipal surveyor almost uncovered the nearly completed tunnel. Good luck and Iakimova's glib tongue and artful manner threw the inspectors off the scent for the moment. But on February 27, Mikhail Trigoni and Zheliabov walked into a police trap. For several days the police did not realize whom they had captured and their ignorance gave the terrorists a few more days' time.

Sofia Perovskaia stepped forward to fill the place of her lover Zheliabov after his arrest. Small and blond, almost childlike in appearance, she was nonetheless a revolutionary to the very depths of her soul. Under her fierce encouragement and watchful gaze, her comrades placed the dynamite in the tunnel and set its electric fuse. Kibalchich spent the evening of February 28 making four nitroglycerine grenades to be carried by Ignacy Hryniewicki, Nikolai Rysakov, Timofei Mikhailov, and Ivan Emelianov. Only by working for seventeen hours without rest did he complete the weapons in time.[102]

On the morning of March 1, 1881, the terrorists took up their attack positions. Of the three who were posted at the cheese shop, two were to leave just before the attack, while Mikhail Frolenko was to detonate the dynamite and probably die beneath the rubble. Vera Figner recalled with amazement the calm with which Frolenko faced almost certain death. "In astonishment I watched him take a bottle of red wine and a large sausage from a bundle he had brought with him, place them on the table, and prepare to eat," she wrote many years later. " 'What are you doing?' I asked, almost in horror, as I watched these very common and ordinary tasks being carried out by a man doomed to almost certain death beneath the rubble the explosion would produce. 'I must be in the full possession of all my faculties,' my comrade answered calmly, and imperturbably began to eat."[103]

As the terrorists in the cheese shop waited for the Tsar to pass above their mine, Perovskaia took command of the grenade throwers. If Alexander II did not follow his usual Sunday route, she planned to direct her comrades to other locations by using a series of prearranged hand signals. As it turned out, the Tsar did not drive along Malaia Sadovaia that day because his wife had been alarmed by the rumors flying through the city and had begged him to avoid that route. To allay her fears, he promised to go by way of the Catherine Canal Embankment instead. He reviewed a parade at one of the military riding schools, looked in briefly on his cousin, the Grand Duchess Ekaterina, and began his return to the Winter Palace. True to his promise, he drove by way of the Catherine Embankment.

When Sofia Perovskaia saw their quarry drive to the Grand Duchess's palace, she signaled her grenadiers to move quickly to the Catherine Canal Embankment because that was the most obvious alternate return route to the Winter Palace. All were in their new positions when the bombproof Imperial carriage, a gift from Napoleon III, came racing along the Inzhenernaia and turned onto the embankment. Rysakov's grenade damaged the carriage and wounded several bystanders, but Alexander was unharmed. Then, in the shock and confusion, the Tsar committed a fatal error. He left his carriage to inspect the damage and to comfort the injured. Nearby, leaning against a railing, stood Hryniewicki, a Pole sworn to avenge the conquest of his homeland by the Tsar and his armies in 1863. When his quarry was not two meters away, he hurled his grenade directly between Alexander's feet. A deafening explosion, blood-drenched snow, and the screams of some twenty wounded onlookers filled the air. When the heavy smoke cleared, Alexander lay mortally wounded, both legs ripped away by the blast. Not far away, Hryniewicki also lay torn and bleeding, a victim of his own grenade. "I'm cold, so cold," Alexander whispered as an aide bent over him. As his officers hastened to cover him with their cloaks, they heard him say: "Take me to the Palace . . . to die."[104] He died within an hour; his assassin followed him in death later that same evening. To the very end, he never told the police his name.[105]

Horrified by the terrorists' deed, Russians demanded their punishment. Vera Figner managed to elude the police for several years, but Zheliabov, Perovskaia, Kibalchich, Timofei Mikhailov, and Nikolai Rysakov died on the gallows. Hangings were particularly brutal in nineteenth-century Russia. Russian officials never bothered to construct drop platforms in the scaffold floor, and death therefore came by slow strangulation. This made the hangman's trade so unpopular that it had only one practitioner in all of Russia, a man named Frolov, who invariably deadened his scruples with large tumblers of raw vodka. On April 3, 1881, Frolov was even more besotted than usual, and it was only by chance that three of his victims died without incident. Zheliabov and Mikhailov met crueler deaths. Twice Mikhailov's noose slipped and he fell to the platform, only to be hauled up and hanged again by the cursing, drunken Frolov. To prevent the noose from slipping when he hanged Zheliabov, Frolov tied a double knot, which slowed his victim's strangulation even more.[106] It took several minutes for each man to die.

Even before their execution, Russia had embarked upon what is sometimes called the Era of Counterreforms. By one of those tragic ironies of history, Alexander II had signed a decree that granted a very limited form of representative government for Russians on the very morning of his death. Its nullification was one of his son's first acts from the throne.[107]

The repressive measures Vera Figner called "the White Terror" began the moment Alexander III stepped into his father's place. Arrests followed quickly, one after the other, until, as Figner wrote, the terrorists "had exhausted their entire stock of capital" of human resources.[108] For a short time, a few remnants of the People's Will kept the terrorist vision alive. In March 1882, Khalturin and a comrade assassinated General Fedor Strelnikov, the military prosecutor of Odessa who was responsible for sending several terrorists to their deaths on the scaffold or in fortress dungeons. Although the two men were executed within days, a handful remained at large. Soon even these no longer posed a danger. Colonel Grigorii Sudeikin of the secret police induced the terrorist Sergei Degaev to betray his comrades en masse, and by early 1883, Sudeikin had all that remained of the People's Will organization under close surveillance. Degaev's betrayal ultimately brought even Vera Figner, the last member of the original Executive Committee still at large in Russia, into police custody in March; she would spend a quarter-century in the Schlüsselburg Fortress.[109] With relief, Alexander III wrote on the report of her arrest: "Finally, she's been caught."[110] For the terrorists, the White Terror had finally borne its most bitter fruit.

"Boredom, grief, anguish, apathy, even despair—this was the mood of Russians in the middle of the 1880s," wrote one revolutionary in later years.[111] Yet echoes of the People's Will were to be heard once again, even though its organization was utterly destroyed and all of its founders executed, imprisoned, or exiled to Siberia. Its new rumblings were heard at a student demonstration organized in St. Petersburg to pay homage to the radical critic Dobroliubov on November 17, 1886, the twenty-fifth anniversary of his death. Surrounded by saber-wielding Cossacks, students had charged their vastly outnumbered tormentors and driven them in retreat. Savoring their brief victory, Petr Shevyrev, Pakhomii Andreiushkin, Vasilii Osipanov, Vasilii Generalov, and Aleksandr Ulianov chose to carry their defiance further. "Against the crude force upon which the government has chosen to rely, we also shall use force," they proclaimed, "but this force will be organized and joined by its spiritual unity."[112] During the next several days, they sent several hundred copies of their proclamation to cities all over Russia. After intercepting a large number of them, the government was left with the impression that it faced a serious revolutionary threat.[113] The students' challenge, however, was not destined to endure for more than a few months.

"When are we finally going to do something?" Andreiushkin asked. "Everything is words and more words, but no action!" "The time to act is now," Generalov insisted soon after they sent out their first proclamation. "I cannot wait," he added. "I stand on the side of bombs!"[114] To which young Ulianov added, "I do not believe [merely] in terror. I believe in *systematic* terror."[115] Passionately dedicated to the revolutionary struggle, none of these young men had yet developed a plan of action. That came from Shevyrev, son of a rich merchant from Kharkov and founder of a student cooperative where these young men and their friends ate their meals. Together with Ulianov, Shevyrev insisted that they must draft a program before taking any terrorist actions. During December 1886 and early 1887, they and a number of their friends often met at Ulianov's rooms to discuss their readings of Marx as a basis for action. Ulianov, in particular, one of them wrote, "followed the brilliant dialectic of Marx with rapture and passionately expressed his delight with it."[116] Under this new influence their program became "an effort to combine social-democratic and *narodnik* ideas,"[117] in effect a transition from the precepts of Lavrov and Bakunin to those teachings of Marx and Plekhanov that would guide the radicals of the 1890s.[118]

There was a crucial, and soon fatal, difference between the program of these young terrorists and the precepts of Marx and Plekhanov, nonetheless. Following in the steps of the People's Will, whose parenthood they readily acknowledged, Ulianov, Shevyrev, and their friends urged terrorism as an instrument of political struggle. For them, as Ulianov's more famous younger brother Vladimir (who would later be known as Lenin) wrote, "the term political struggle was synonymous with political *conspiracy.*"[119] Their chosen weapons were nitroglycerine grenades, each with almost two hundred metal balls packed within it, and dynamite bombs concealed in hollowed-out medical dictionaries.[120] With these, they planned to kill Alexander III on March 1, 1887, the sixth anniversary of his father's murder by the People's Will. They would stalk him along the Nevskii Prospekt, between the Winter Palace and the Kazan Cathedral.

At the end of January, Andreiushkin stupidly wrote about his terrorist beliefs to a friend in the provinces. The police read his letter as it passed through the Imperial post and placed him under surveillance. Once they learned that Generalov was one of Andreiushkin's frequent associates, they began to watch him as well.[121] As a result of this amazing ineptness, the police were waiting when Andreiushkin, Generalov, and Osipanov stepped onto the Nevskii Prospekt with their bombs on March 1.

As Minister of Internal Affairs Count Dmitrii Tolstoi reported to the Emperor later that day, "A student at St. Petersburg University . . . Pakhomii Andreiushkin aged twenty, arrested at the corner of Nevskii Prospekt and the Admiralty Square . . . found to be carrying a loaded revolver . . . and an oval-cylindrical metal bomb. . . . [Likewise] Vasilii Generalov, student at St. Petersburg University . . . aged twenty-two, arrested near the Kazan Cathedral . . . with the same sort of device on his person. . . . [And finally] Vasilii Osipanov, student at St. Petersburg University . . . aged twenty-six also arrested near the Kazan Cathedral . . . with a thick book, its pages glued together, the inside hollowed out and filled with dynamite."[122] Within a few hours, Ulianov and several others were also taken into custody. Shevyrev was arrested a week later at the Black Sea resort of Yalta.[123] In all, fifteen young men, most of them students at St. Petersburg University, were apprehended and charged.

Once arrested, none of the terrorists tried to conceal his guilt. "I recognize my guilt in that, belonging to the terrorist faction of the Party of the People's Will, I took part in a plot to deprive the Sovereign Emperor of his life," Aleksandr Ulianov confessed. "I prepared several parts of the fragmentation bombs meant to be used in carrying out this plot," he continued. "I knew who would carry out the attack, that is, who would throw the bombs."[124] Although the outcome was a foregone conclusion, a trial was held on April 15. When he addressed the court, Ulianov spoke of his reasons for turning to terrorism and what he had hoped to accomplish. "Terror is that form of struggle that has been created by conditions of the nineteenth century," he began. "It is the only form of defense to which a minority, strong only in terms of its spiritual strength and in its knowledge of the rightness of its beliefs, can resort against the physical strength of the majority." He had not chosen terrorism willingly; the oppressive policies of the government forced him to take that path. Nor, he insisted, was his reaction to the oppression that reigned in Russia unique: "Among the Russian people . . . there will always be those small groups of men and women who are so dedicated to their ideas and so passionately conscious of the unhappiness in their native land that it will not be a sacrifice for them to die for their beliefs."[125]

Ulianov's widowed mother had traveled more than a thousand miles from her modest home in the Volga River town of Simbirsk to attend the trial. "I was astonished at how well Sasha* spoke—how earnestly, how eloquently," she later remarked. "I did not know that he could speak like that."[126] But the strain of hearing her firstborn speak so ardently while on trial for his life was too great. Maria Ulianova therefore did not hear the court sentence ten of the defendants to long terms in prison. Nor did she hear them condemn her son, Osipanov, Andreiushkin, Shevyrev, and Generalov to death by hanging, the most dreaded form of execution. She had already made her peace with her son, his ideas, and his readiness to face death when the Tsar had allowed her to see Aleksandr some days before. Together they had wept, and Aleksandr had begged her forgiveness for bringing her such grief so soon after his father's death. He had tried to explain, and she had tried to comprehend:

—"It is the duty of every honorable person to fight for the liberation of his homeland," he had insisted.
—"But these methods are so terrible!"
—"What is to be done—if there are no other ways?"[127]

Once again, Aleksandr Ulianov had posed the terrible question. Like so many before him, he had not yet found the answer.

Nor would he. During the night of May 5, 1887, seven prisoners were taken from their cells in the Peter and Paul Fortress, placed aboard a small steamer, and taken forty miles upriver to the Schlüsselburg Fortress where Vera Figner and a number of her comrades

---

*Sasha is a Russian nickname for Aleksandr.

from the People's Will already were incarcerated. Among the prisoners taken from the Peter and Paul Fortress that night were Ulianov and four comrades. They reached their destination some six hours later. Wrote Iosif Lukashevich, one of the two not under sentence of death: "They hurried us through the courtyard, past the church, and through the guardhouse. We skirted the new prison, a two-storied brick structure with two tall smokestacks that I at first took to be some sort of factory, went on through the tall gates of the citadel, across its great courtyard overgrown with weeds and dotted with dandelion blossoms here and there, to a white, single story building—the old prison (called 'the barn')."[128] There, Lukashevich and his companion Novoselskii would spend the next twenty-five years, while Ulianov and the other four terrorists were executed three days later in the usual manner. "Thus ended our unsuccessful effort," Lukashevich recalled, "and the terrorist struggle died away for many years."[129]

Soviet hagiographers have paid much attention to the words that Aleksandr Ulianov's younger brother Vladimir supposedly spoke to his sister Maria when he learned that his adored elder brother had been hanged: "No, we shall not follow the same path. That is not the path to follow."[130] When she repeated her brother's words, Maria Ulianova was addressing the Plenum of the Moscow Soviet on February 7, 1924, just over a fortnight after he had died. *Pravda* printed them with suitable fanfare the next day, and they served as the subject for a painting by the Soviet artist Belousov showing a stern adolescent Vladimir Ulianov comforting his mother with the supposedly reassuring words: "We shall take a different path."[131] Since it took Maria Ulianova, but a child of nine at the time of Aleksandr's execution, more than thirty-seven years to recall these ringing words, the skeptical historian may reasonably doubt that Lenin ever made the remark, especially since it is unlikely that he had thought of any path to take at all at the age of seventeen. In fact, his elder sister Anna insisted that "he had no political beliefs at all" at the time.[132] Still, there can be no doubt that his elder brother's execution left a profound scar upon Lenin, and many who knew him agree that he became introspective, even morose, for the next several years.

The "different path" that Lenin would eventually take already had been blazed by Plekhanov, now in exile in Switzerland, who some four years before had founded the first Russian Marxist party, which he called the Emancipation of Labor Group. Of one thing Plekhanov was certain. The terrorists' efforts to force a democratic political transformation in Russia were doomed, even if the transformation actually occurred. Few in number, and weakened by their struggle against such immense odds, any revolutionaries who won a constitution for their homeland, he warned, would only exchange one group of oppressors for another because the bourgeoisie would rise to take the place of the autocracy and its minions. "A socialist 'party' without foundations and influence among the people is nonsense," Plekhanov wrote at the beginning of 1880. "Its enemies . . . could ignore its demands without any serious danger to themselves."[133] The sad experience of revolutionaries throughout the 1870s soon obliged Plekhanov and his comrades to raise the question that most Russian radicals had feared to ask ever since the first Movement to the People had shattered against the wall of peasant indifference: Who were The People? Revolutionaries had long been convinced that The People were the nation's peasant millions whose communes, they ardently believed, bore within them the seeds of primitive socialism. But were the peasants The People who would serve as the rank and file in a socialist revolution?

In 1879, the ethnographer and sociologist Maksim Kovalevskii had published *Communal Land Tenure: the Reasons, the Process, and the Consequences of its Disintegration*, a ponderous book in which he had demonstrated how peasant communes in more advanced countries had disintegrated because of the conflicts that occurred naturally and inevitably between the affluent and poor peasants who lived within them.[134] Would Russia repeat the experience of other nations? Ever since the 1840s, passionate believers in the commune's virtues had insisted that it differed from those found elsewhere. But they had argued on the basis of faith, not hard statistical data. Kovalevskii thought they were wrong.

A few months after Kovalevskii's conclusions had begun to circulate among the Russian intelligentsia, a thirty-one-year-old stat-

istician by the name of Vasilii Orlov published an immensely detailed book on *Forms of Peasant Land Tenure in Moscow Province,*
which, despite its tendentious title, offered the unlooked-for and
startling conclusion that the *Russian* peasant commune, in which
so many radicals had placed their deepest faith, was *already* rapidly
disintegrating.[135] Orlov had studied more than five thousand peasant settlements. His profoundly disturbing conclusions could not be
disputed. "It was impossible to disagree with the figures," Plekhanov's loyal wife Rosalia remembered. "It seemed that the question of whether the commune were to be or not—if it were to
disintegrate or not—was for [Plekhanov] a matter of life and
death."[136] As the very cornerstone upon which he had built *Chernyi
Peredel* shattered before the barrage of Orlov's indisputable data,
Plekhanov returned to the realm of economic and political theory.
"What do we know, basically?" he asked. "We must study."[137]

Plekhanov's closest comrade on his lonely intellectual odyssey
during these years was Pavel Akselrod, son of desperately poor Jews
from Shklov, who had helped lead Plekhanov into the *narodnik*
movement in the mid-1870s.[138] More than any of his revolutionary
contemporaries, Akselrod was drawn to the writings of Ferdinand
Lassalle and German Social Democracy; according to his leading
biographer, "no one played as decisive a role as he in familiarizing
other Russians with the doctrines and policies of that party."[139]
From Lassalle, Akselrod turned to Marx and found in his preface to
A Contribution to the Critique of Political Economy a profoundly
appealing message that he hastened to share with Plekhanov. "What
grandiose perspectives spread out before present-day mankind if all
its past, already so rich with great scientific discoveries and technical
inventions, as well as cultural and spiritual achievements, is only the
preliminary phase, the prehistorical stage, in the historical epoch of
its existence!"[140] But Plekhanov was more cautious than his friend.
Much impressed by Marx, he nonetheless required two more years
to make his conversion complete. Convinced that he had chosen the
wrong path once, he did not want to do so again. "We do not want
to go against history," he insisted, "but we do not want to stay
behind it one single step."[141] He therefore approached Marx with

extreme skepticism and caution, and this search added to the pain that he, Akselrod, and their families endured while they searched for spiritual nourishment in Switzerland. Plekhanov fell victim to tuberculosis, and at one point he and his wife had no food. "Send what you can but, for God's sake, send," he begged Akselrod at a time when his friend, his wife, and their three children tottered on the brink of starvation themselves.[142] For them all, it was a physically arduous, soul-shaking journey during which their common endurance bound them more closely together.

Two years of struggle and study finally produced results. "Anyone who did not live through that time with us will have difficulty imagining the passion with which we seized upon Social Democratic writings," Plekhanov later wrote. "Like Ariadne's thread, the theory of Marx led us out of the labyrinth of contradictions in which our ideas had struggled under the influence of Bakunin. In the light of this theory, it became completely clear why revolutionary propaganda had encountered a far more sympathetic reception from the workers than from the peasants." He came to see "the very *development of Russian capitalism*" as a vital "new guarantee of the revolutionary movement's success."[143] In setting forth a new theory to replace his shattered *narodnik* faith, Plekhanov argued that the peasant commune was bourgeois not socialist in nature and that Russia's revolutionaries must turn from the peasants to the nation's factory workers. The task of the Marxist revolutionary in Russia thus must be to instill the proletariat with class consciousness and to mold it into a revolutionary force.[144] As one scholar wrote some years ago, "The proletariat was to become a force capable of simultaneously supporting capitalism in its struggle against reaction [i.e., the forces of autocracy] and of opposing the very same capitalism in its struggle against the workers' revolution of the future."[145]

Plekhanov thought that Marx had discovered those very laws of social development that Russians had been seeking since the 1850s. Convinced that he had replaced his blind *narodnik* faith with what one student of Russian Social Democracy has called "the last word in the scientific study of society," he, like Akselrod, became a Marxist.[146] Together with Vera Zasulich, Lev Deich, and a young man by the name of V. I. Ignatov, Plekhanov and Akselrod formed the Emancipation of Labor Group in 1883.[147] Russia's first Marxist organization thus began with a mere five members.

Its early history was utterly inauspicious. Within two years, Ignatov had died from tuberculosis, Deich had been arrested in Germany, extradited to Russia, and sent to Siberia, and the membership of the Emancipation of Labor Group had fallen from five to three. Obliged to remain in exile, Plekhanov, Akselrod, and Zasulich were kept from any effective contact with the proletariat in whom they now placed their hopes. For the next decade, their chief concern was how to relate their newfound Marxist faith more precisely to Russian experience, while a younger generation of revolutionaries timidly and sporadically experimented with their theories on Russian soil. Efforts to explain the Russian situation in terms of Marxist theory thus utterly overshadowed revolutionary practice. "How unclear the forms of the future workers' movement still were for us," wrote one of those who carried the message of the Emancipation of Labor Group to Russia. "[We thought that] gradually the number of workers studying Marx would increase, and that they would bring into their circles still more new members. With time, all of Russia would be covered with such study circles and we would form a socialist workers' party. What it would do and how it would struggle [for the workers] still remained unclear."[148] Yet even within Russia there was an awareness that abstraction and theory could not continue as substitutes for action. With the rise of the weak-willed Nicholas II to the throne at the end of 1894, it became possible for Russia's revolutionaries to resume their struggle within Russia on a larger scale.

Two young men who had barely grown out of swaddling clothes at the time Plekhanov dedicated himself to the revolutionary struggle burst onto the Russian revolutionary scene to play a vital part in returning the Russian Marxist labor movement to the arena of revolutionary action. One was Vladimir Ulianov. The younger of the two was Iulii Tsederbaum, later to become internationally known by his revolutionary name Martov. Martov was a Jew born in Odessa in 1873. He enjoyed prosperity as a youth, but was driven

into the revolutionary struggle despite his well-educated family background. As a child of seven, Martov first felt the depths of Russian
hatred and the icy fear it engendered in the breasts of the Empire's
Jews when he lived through the terrible wave of pogroms that followed the assassination of Alexander II. He escaped injury, but could
not remain unmoved by the tales of horrors seen and suffered that
surged around him. "Would I have become what I am had not
Russian reality . . . hastened to impress its coarse fingers upon my
pliable young soul?" he asked many years later.[149] Certainly, Martov
had become bitterly hostile to the policies of Alexander III long
before 1891, when he entered St. Petersburg University and joined
with radicals there. Among Jews and Gentiles, joined in their common hatred for the tsarist regime, Martov found himself in the
company of friends who respected him as a person and did not scorn
him for his Jewishness.[150]

Immediately Martov felt those urgent stirrings that drove
young men and women to social activism in an effort to combat the
terrible suffering that the great famine of 1891 inflicted upon
Russia's masses. Although the government moved with commenda-
ble speed and effect, as we saw earlier, many still thought that
bureaucratic bungling had caused widespread starvation. Hundreds
of educated men and women dedicated their skills and knowledge
to the peasants' aid. Soon Martov found himself in the company of
a strange array of reborn populists and quasi-Marxists. Carried away
by enthusiasm, he naïvely urged his comrades to prepare for a coup
d'état while the state was weakened, as it must be, when "the famine
inevitably leads to spontaneous peasant uprisings" all over Russia.[151]
The risings never came. This was the Russia of Alexander III—not
that of his more tolerant father or weaker son—and Martov's revolutionary associations brought him not to the people but to a police
cell. On February 25, 1892, he was arrested, expelled from the
university, and sent into administrative exile for two years. Yet his
treatment was far from harsh; the authorities allowed him to live
anywhere in Russia except for Moscow, St. Petersburg, or any other
city that had a university.[152]

During the months after his first release from prison (and

before he began his administrative exile in Vilno), Martov studied Marx in earnest. In Paul Lafargue's translation of the first volume of *Das Kapital,* he found what he had been seeking: "a synthesis of subjective revolutionary ideals and scientific cognition of the laws of social development," to use his own words. "Very little of my naïve spirit of undisciplined revolt remained," he confessed. "It somehow suddenly became clear to me how superficial and sterile all my revolutionary sentiments had been up to that point."[153] With his friend Ivan Starskii, he proclaimed, "I am more of a Marxist than Marx himself,"[154] and threw himself into the writings that had flowed from the pens of Plekhanov, Zasulich, and Akselrod during the past decade. Symbolically, just before his departure for Vilno, he and his friends rechristened their circle the Petersburg Group for the Liberation of Labor.[155]

When Martov returned to St. Petersburg in 1895, he found himself at the forefront of the *molodye,* the "youngsters," of the Russian Social Democratic movement, as opposed to the *stariki*— the "old men"—most of whom were actually under thirty. The *stariki* were led by Vladimir Ulianov, who was just twenty-five at the time of Martov's return, although his short stature (five feet five inches) and receding hairline made him look older. Those who knew Lenin at the time called him "the Old Man." He had only recently come to the capital after spending the first twenty-one years of his life in the provinces.

Unable to face the scorn of Simbirsk society after her eldest son's execution, Maria Ulianova had moved her family in 1887 to Kokushkino, a small village between Simbirsk and Kazan. It was there that the seventeen-year-old Vladimir plunged into frenzied study in order to retrace his brother's road to radicalism. Especially Chernyshevskii's *What Is To Be Done?* burned deeply into his consciousness. "I spent not days but several weeks reading it," he told his one-time comrade Nikolai Volskii. "This novel provides inspiration for a lifetime!"[156] That fall (1887), Lenin entered the University of Kazan, was expelled for attending a protest meeting, and returned to the countryside where he spent the next four years in study, contemplation, and misdirected efforts to become a gentleman farmer.[157] During the long winters he returned to Chernyshevskii again and again. "I used to read greedily from early morning until late at night," his comrade Vatslav Vorovskii remembered him saying. "Only Chernyshevskii had a real, overpowering influence on me before I got to know the works of Marx, Engels, and Plekhanov, and it started with *What Is To Be Done?* Chernyshevskii not only showed that every right-thinking and really honest man must be a revolutionary, but he also showed—and this is his greatest merit—what a revolutionary must be like."[158]

For a brief moment in 1891, it seemed that Lenin's fascination with Chernyshevskii had passed and that his mother's pleas had deterred him from the revolutionary path his elder brother had followed to such an early death. In response to Maria Ulianova's petitions, the authorities decided to overlook her son's adolescent misadventures with radicalism and permitted him to take the bar exams. Lenin thus became a lawyer in Samara. But that proved to be only a brief stopping place along his way to a revolutionary future. As in the case of so many early-twentieth-century revolutionaries, the great famine of 1891 was a critical point in his experience, but he reacted very differently from his contemporaries. Samara's intelligentsia, an old-school populist remembered, all threw themselves into relief efforts "except for Vladimir Ulianov and his family and a little circle which followed him." This handful reportedly rejoiced at the peasants' suffering because they thought it would move Russia closer to the day when class conflict would break out.[159]

This seemingly callous view stemmed from Lenin's conversion to Marxism. Feeding the hungry and caring for the sick was a useless palliative, he contended. The only way to help Russia's peasants was for the revolutionaries to mount a new propaganda offensive against the government. A dogged adversary of Samara's born-again *narodniki*, Lenin even distinguished himself in debate against Nikolai Mikhailovskii, Russia's leading populist at that time. Yet populism remained the dominant current in the narrowly focused radical intellectual life of the provinces. Lenin longed for men and women who could see in the writings of Marx and Plekhanov a summons to action outside their study circles. In the fall of 1893, he left

Samara for St. Petersburg, the city that held the largest concentration of industrial proletarians in all of Russia.[160]

In the words of one scholar, "The foundation of the whole subsequent political career of Lenin" was laid during the two years he spent in St. Petersburg before his arrest at the end of 1895.[161] During this brief period, he formed some of the alliances and conceived some of the hatreds that remained with him to the end of his life. For Martov, he developed real respect and affection. Within a few months the two young men formed the city's isolated study circles into the Union of Struggle for the Liberation of Labor, which was no longer satisfied to debate theoretical issues. It now aimed to lead the workers of St. Petersburg against their employers, to demand shorter hours and better wages, and to push them farther along the road to heightened revolutionary consciousness.[162]

Martov's group in Vilno had been the first to exchange theoretical debates for direct agitation among factory workers, and their efforts had brought an amazing response. "The winter strike campaign," Martov wrote, "enjoyed great success," as he delightedly assembled reports of labor unrest in Moscow, Kiev, Kharkov, Minsk, Odessa, and a dozen other cities.[163] For the first time in more than a decade, Russia's radicals were on the move as they used the example of the first strikes to foment others.[164] Strikes in Moscow, in the southeast, in the Ukraine, in Lithuania, and in Russian Poland— these proved only the prelude to even greater worker protest in St. Petersburg itself.

Strike! Although well known in Europe and America, the shout was rarely heard in Russia's capital. It had first been heard in 1870, and the government of Alexander II had immediately declared all future strikes illegal. A few strikes had flared in the 1880s, but ruthless suppression had quickly restored peace. Then, in the spring of 1896, wave upon wave of unrest swept St. Petersburg's industrial suburbs to cast both factory managers and workers into the utterly unfamiliar realm of labor conflict. It was a time of testing and discovery for both, as old stereotypes broke apart and old axioms proved untrue. When workers demanded a workday of ten and a half hours, they were told that the Tsar himself had just such a decree on his desk. But workers of the mid-1890s were not as gullible as earlier generations had been. They now demanded more details:

—"When will this decree be signed?" they asked.
—"In a couple of years or so," came the vague reply from factory managers and government officials.
—"Well, then we'd better get on with our strike now!"
—"It's up to you," one plant manager replied with self-assured arrogance. "When you get hungry enough, you'll come back to work."
—"We'll die right here in the roadway," came the unexpectedly firm reply. "But we won't come back to work under the conditions we had before!"[165]

Clearly, the Union of Struggle had instilled in them an awareness that their numbers meant power if they stood firm. "What means do we have for improving our position?" one leaflet asked. "We have only ourselves to rely upon. But we have strength in unity. Our weapon—a unified, unanimous, and unyielding resistance to factory owners." The leaflet concluded: "The working men and women of the Russian land are beginning to rise up and soon shall strike fear into the hearts of the capitalists and all the enemies of the working class!"[166] This stirring message gave Russian workers a sense of identity they had never known before. They won concessions—a shorter working day and slightly better wages—and with these came a new sense of power.[167]

With the strikes of 1896, St. Petersburg's Marxists launched a political struggle against factory lords and the autocracy in Russia, but neither Lenin nor Martov could share their followers' fleeting glory. Nor could many of their lieutenants. Once they abandoned inconspicuous study circles to spread propaganda among the factory workers, their greater visibility dramatically increased the danger of arrest. No longer could their meetings be kept secret, and the security police, now called the Okhrana, took full advantage of that fact. In December 1895 and January 1896, the Okhrana struck.[168] They seized Lenin and some forty others in one well-planned swoop on

December 8. On January 4, they struck again to arrest most of the *molodye* including Martov. Only rank and file Marxists remained to bolster the workers' resolve when strikes broke out some weeks later.[169]

For Lenin and Martov, arrest meant imprisonment and Siberian exile. Lenin's term was three years spent in the Siberian town of Shushenskoe, part of it with Nadezhda Krupskaia, the woman who became his lifelong companion. Theirs was not the hard life of deprivation and suffering so often associated with Siberian exile, however. Surrounded by a formidable array of books, journals, and even foreign newspapers sent to him by family and friends, Lenin immersed himself in study and writing. He wrote a number of important works, among them his deservedly famous *Development of Capitalism in Russia.*[170] But Martov truly languished. While Lenin lived in the relatively moderate climate of Shushenskoe, Martov was sent some six thousand kilometers north and east from St. Petersburg to Turukhansk, a settlement at the very edge of the Arctic Circle. It was there that he contracted tuberculosis of the throat, the disease that eventually took his life. In Turukhansk, Martov received mail only nine times a year. He, too, tried to study and write, but he enjoyed much less success than his more fortunate comrade, whose tireless mother continued to pull all possible strings to ease her son's lot.[171]

On March 1, 1898, a "congress" of nine Marxists met at the west Russian city of Minsk to found the Russian Social Democratic Labor party.* Within two decades, one wing of the RSDRP would rule the Russian land, but none of its nine founders could have envisioned such success, even in their wildest dreams. Precisely because of the power of the old order, Plekhanov, Akselrod, Zasulich, Lenin, and Martov could not attend, and even those lesser lights who founded the party soon languished in tsarist jails. Led by the ruthlessly able Sergei Zubatov, himself a former revolutionary, the Okh-

---

*Its full Russian name was *Rossiiskaia Sotsialdemokraticheskaia Rabochaia Partiia* —hence the abbreviation RSDRP.

rana struck again in the late spring and early summer of 1898. By July, they had imprisoned the RSDRP's entire Central Committee and some five hundred of the most active Social Democrats from all over Russia.[172]

The arrests left the RSDRP dangerously adrift, buffeted by theoretical crosscurrents that threatened to drive it far from the Marxist orthodoxy of Lenin and Martov.* With cries of "dirt, triviality, and stupidity," Plekhanov and Akselrod railed against the "heresies" of Economism and Revisionism from Switzerland.[173] But they were too far removed from the mainstream of Russian experience to parry the threat these doctrinal controversies posed to the unity of Russian Marxism. During the last months of his Siberian exile, Lenin therefore laid plans for founding a Social Democratic newspaper, publishing it in Europe, and smuggling it into Russia, much as Aleksandr Herzen had done with *Kolokol* in the 1850s and 1860s.

"The fundamental task of Social Democracy is to instill socialist ideas and political self-consciousness in the mass of the proletariat and to organize a revolutionary party inseparably joined to the spontaneous workers' movement," Lenin wrote. "We must prepare men and women who will dedicate not merely free evenings to the revolution, but their entire lives." Such a newspaper could provide orthodox Russian Social Democrats with a weapon against the heresies of Economism and Revisionism, both reinterpretations of Marx that, Lenin insisted, "peddle old bourgeois ideas under a new label."[174] In the words of one scholar, the enterprise was "an imaginative and somewhat daunting prospect."[175] The moment they reached the West at the beginning of 1900, both Lenin and Martov threw themselves into it with characteristic dedication.

The newspaper *Iskra (The Spark)* took its name from the words

---

*Economism and Revisionism à la the German socialist Eduard Bernstein were the two most threatening of these new interpretations of Marx. Writings about them in Russian are extensive, but they need not occupy our attention here. Economism and Revisionism are briefly summarized by the noted scholars Leopold Haimson in *The Russian Marxists and the Origins of Bolshevism*, pp. 75–91, and J. L. H. Keep, in *The Rise of Social Democracy in Russia*, pp. 49–66, as well as by the former Menshevik Theodore Dan in *The Origins of Bolshevism*, pp. 209–20.

written by a Decembrist, one of the very first Russian revolutionaries, who had vowed that "from this spark" of the revolt he and his
comrades had incited against Nicholas I in 1825 "shall come the
flame" of a revolution destined to sweep the Russian land. Despite
the best hopes of Lenin and Martov, not to mention such leading
Marxist exiles as Plekhanov and Akselrod, the life of *Iskra* was
clouded with strife from the very beginning. Although Martov,
Zasulich, and Akselrod sought conciliation, there seemed no way to
blunt the violent clashes that inevitably arose between two men of
such powerful personality and monumental ego as Lenin and Plekhanov. At times it seemed that *Iskra* must succumb to the conflicts
that raged among its founders. Yet on each occasion it was somehow
salvaged. Once Plekhanov and Akselrod agreed to remain in Switzerland, while Lenin, Martov, and their comrade Aleksandr Potresov
printed the paper in Munich, *Iskra* began to run more smoothly. For
more than two years, copies of *Iskra* made their way clandestinely
across Russia's frontiers to give a sense of identity and unity to those
hardy men and women who struggled for Social Democracy in mill
towns and study circles all across the Empire of Nicholas II.[176] Very
soon, however, that budding sense of unity was shattered.

The "elemental battle about how the RSDRP should be con-
stituted," became, as one commentator pointed out recently, one of
the most critical struggles of Lenin's career.[177] The issues were clear
cut: what were the tasks of Russian Social Democracy, what role
should the party play, and how should it be organized? Lenin spoke
to these vital questions in a pamphlet, perhaps the most important
he ever wrote, that appeared in March 1902 under a title that
reiterated the cursed question—*What Is To Be Done?* If left to its
own devices, Lenin insisted, the working class could never develop
a socialist ideology and "could only fall victim to the ideology of the
bourgeoisie." Therefore, he urged, "our task, the task of Social
Democracy, must center upon diverting the workers' movement
from the spontaneous strivings of trade-unionism under the wing of
the bourgeoisie, and bring it under the protection of Social Democracy." The party, and the party alone, should guide the strivings of
the workers, *"bringing closer and merging into a single whole* the

spontaneous destructive force of the crowd and the conscious destructive power of the revolutionaries' organization." To accomplish
such diverse and difficult tasks, he insisted, "it is essential to have
a strong organization of professional revolutionaries [and] the more
secret this organization is, the stronger and more widespread the
faith in the strength of the party will be."[178] These were the keys
to Lenin's revolutionary organization and tactics, principles from
which he would never deviate. The revolutionary rank and file, he
insisted, must be organized and led by a general staff of men and
women who had dedicated their very souls to the revolutionary
cause. Such an elitist, "professional" approach to the people's revolution soon brought Lenin and Martov to a bitter parting of the
ways.[179] Their rift came at the Second Congress of the RSDRP, a
gathering that many Russian Social Democrats hoped would proclaim a united party and end the bitter conflicts that divided its
leaders.

With forty-three delegates in attendance, the Second Congress of the RSDRP opened in Brussels on July 30, 1903, in a rat- and
flea-infested abandoned flour warehouse, the interior of which was
festooned with red banners. Belgian police thronged the alleys of the
surrounding neighborhood, while Okhrana agents—part of that ev-
er-growing corps of spies the Russian government supported on
foreign soil—lurked in doorways and courtyards to see who came and
went, and with whom. From the first, there were bitter wrangles
over rules, interpretations, and meanings. Men and women clashed
in deadly earnest about issues that seemed utterly remote from the
life-and-death struggle against autocracy to which they all were
sworn. Neither Plekhanov nor Akselrod had set foot in Russia for
twenty-three years, and Zasulich had not been there in more than
a quarter-century. Isolated from life under the regime they had
vowed to overthrow, they focused upon revolutionary theory, not
practice. Less than fifty in number, with only the most fragile skele-
ton of an organization within Russia itself, the delegates therefore
spent days in wrangling about the finer points of the government
they would establish *after* the autocracy and bourgeoisie had been
overthrown. Should the death penalty be abolished? Plekhanov

agreed that it should, but sagely suggested that "a few reservations" must be made. "Should Nicholas II be permitted to live?" he asked in his best schoolroom manner. "I think that we should reserve for him a death penalty."

At another point, Lenin and Plekhanov insisted that "the essential condition for the social revolution is the dictatorship of the proletariat." But what of the democratically elected constituent assembly? their opponents asked. Again Plekhanov, in his self-appointed role as master and teacher of Russian Social Democracy, instructed the wayward delegates. Only if the assembly were one that supported the interests of Social Democracy, he insisted, could it be allowed to function. "If the elections should turn out badly for the working class, we might try to dissolve it, not at the end of two years, but in two weeks if possible." They must always remember to view all programs and tactics through one fundamental prism. "*The health of the revolution is the supreme law,*" he told them loftily. "If the safety of the revolution should demand the temporary limitation of one or another of the democratic principles, it would be a crime to hesitate."[180]

"The Russian [radical] intellectual is always dirty," Ivan Babushkin, one of the few nineteenth-century Russian Marxists to arise from the workers' ranks, once remarked. "He is incapable of tidying himself up."[181] Admittedly, Babushkin's comment had been directed at radical men and women whose concern with ideas and theoretical debates left them unconcerned, even unaware, of the more prosaic realities of daily life, but it also had a broader meaning, as the Second Congress of the RSDRP made clear. Perhaps nothing could have highlighted the delegates' utter isolation from the reality of Russian labor protest more than the fact that, while they intrigued in all-night cafés and exchanged well-aimed verbal thrusts from the podium, a general strike, the very first in the Empire's history, was sweeping through southern Russia, the Caucasus, and the Urals. While those who presumed to instruct them in the tactics of revolution debated the finer points of rules and programs, the workers of Rostov, Kiev, Odessa, Baku, Ekaterinoslav, and a score of other cities faced the thrusts of Cossack lances and sabers. Workers in the Urals, in Rostov, and in Kiev fell before volleys of infantry fire, and hundreds came to know the terror of being ridden down by Cossack cavalry.[182] As would happen in October 1905 and in February 1917, the workers themselves, urged on by men like Babushkin, led the way into the battle against the old order, while the Social Democrats followed, their leaders surprised and unprepared, frantically endeavoring to give their own direction to the workers' outrage.

After ten days of meetings, the wrangling revolutionaries in Brussels were reminded, in a more gentle fashion than were their brethren in Russia, of the reality of the world that lay beyond their dilapidated warehouse. In response to pressure from Nicholas II's government, the Belgian police ordered them to leave the country within twenty-four hours. In disarray, the Congress hastily loaded themselves, their belongings, and their squabbles onto a Channel steamer, and continued their disputes for another two weeks in London. There, in a church that had been made available for its meetings, Russian Social Democracy split before it was even fully formed.

The debate that split the RSDRP centered upon two closely related issues: the organization of the party and the qualifications for membership. Lenin had made it clear in *What Is To Be Done?* that he wanted to limit membership to an elite corps of dedicated professional revolutionaries and insisted that they be organized into a highly centralized, firmly disciplined party. "Our task," he explained in London, "is to protect the steadfastness, firmness, and purity of our Party. We must strive to raise the title and importance of a party member higher and higher."[183] By contrast, Martov urged that new members need only be sympathetic to the goals of Social Democracy, and proposed a looser, more democratic organization. On the vote about membership qualifications, Lenin lost to Martov by a narrow margin. Enraged, he forged a fragile majority to seize control of the party's Central Committee and the editorial board of *Iskra*. From these momentary victories, Lenin's supporters took the name *Bolsheviki* (those in the majority), while those who sided with Martov were called the *Mensheviki* (those in the minority). Although the names did not come into general use for another year or so, they made it clear that the RSDRP had split. Despite efforts at reconciliation, there always would be two wings of Russian Social Democracy.[184]

Volumes of scholarly analysis have been written and many more volumes of letters and memoirs published, about who was to blame for the split in the RSDRP. Yet the debates about who was to blame, and who might have repaired the breach, need not detain us unduly. In all these accounts, one incontrovertible fact emerges, and that is that at no time after mid-August 1903 were the ranks of Russian Social Democracy ever firmly united. "There is absolutely no hope for peace," Lenin told his *Bolsheviki* that October, and his words proved all too true.[185] Lenin's party, Martov warned his followers, "is divided into those who sit and those who are sat upon."[186] Many of the most gifted Russian Social Democrats, including a number who at first had supported Lenin, chose not to be sat upon and took Martov's side. The ranks of Martov's *Mensheviki* always were more numerous; even when the *Bolsheviki* seized power in October 1917, they still were outnumbered. Yet, in another sense, Lenin was clearly the victor. "[The name] Lenin rings all the time in your ears, Leninism sits in your heads and, whatever one may say to you, you can only comprehend it in terms of *pro* or *contra* Lenin," one revolutionary remarked a year or so after the split.[187] Certainly by that time, Lenin had become the central figure in Russian Social Democracy.

But was Leninism indeed the wave of the future for Russians? Or, for that matter, could any ideology based upon the principles of Social Democracy make that claim at the beginning of the twentieth century? During the decade in which Lenin and Martov had grown from radical novices to revolutionary leaders, there were other moral and political precepts that competed for Russians' loyalty. The vast majority during the last years of the nineteenth century remained steadfast in their loyalty to Tsar, Church, and Mother Russia. By the time of Nicholas II's accession, this primary allegiance had been worked into a defensive ideology in which most Russians believed, and with which many tried to counter the opponents of the old order.

CHAPTER VI
Defenders of the Old Order

"Is it not like a spirited troika that you, O Russia, dash onward, leaving all behind you? Whither are you rushing in such headlong flight?" Nikolai Gogol had asked as he concluded the first volume of *Dead Souls* in 1842.[1] Fifty years later, no one could yet give a confident answer to Gogol's question. As they struggled with those complex social and economic tensions that nourished the seeds of revolutionary Social Democracy, Russia's rulers and statesmen faced crises they could not even fully comprehend, let alone resolve.

Her direction ill-defined and yet unsure, Russia near the end of the nineteenth century still seemed like a troika hurtling without direction across the vastness of the Eurasian steppe, the driver unable to curb its unbridled steeds.

As the outdated political principles of autocracy and the traditional values that supported them came under attack during the quarter-century before the Revolution of 1905, Alexander III and Nicholas II rose to their defense by reviving blatantly chauvinistic forms of Orthodoxy, Autocracy, and Nationality, the precepts that Nicholas I had used to buttress Russia against revolution in the 1830s and 1840s. Best summed up by Alexander III's firmly stated conviction that "Russia should belong to the Russian people,"[2] this defense of the old order combined virulent anti-Semitism with militant Russification. While its disciples supported industrial development and encouraged economic progress, they were even more aggressive in prohibiting any political modernization in the Russian Empire. This defense drew its first support from the nobility of privilege and the lords of the Russian Orthodox Church, those conservative groups who were loyal by tradition to the Autocrat of All the Russias, but it also found ardent advocates among almost every social group in Russia.

One of the first organized expressions of this reactionary ideology was the Sacred Guard. Semiclandestine in nature (its full membership is still not known), its avowed purpose was to protect Alexander III and his family against terrorist attack, to undermine all attempts to spread revolutionary ideas, and, as Witte once said, "to fight the anarchists with their own weapons," including terrorism.[3] With each member sworn to be "ready at any time to offer up [his] life in defense of His [the Emperor's] safety and for the greatness and well-being of Russia," the Sacred Guard adopted Nechaev's principles of terrorist organization. Its ranks divided into hierarchically arranged cells of five, each member swore not only to "dedicate myself utterly to the defense of the Sovereign Emperor" but, with equal fervor, to seek "the exposure and eradication of all sedition that brings disgrace upon the good name of Russia."[4]

Witte once claimed that the idea for the Sacred Guard grew

out of the helpless frustration he felt when he first heard of Alexander II's murder. Accordingly, he had written to his uncle Rostislav Fadeev, a man close to the chief of His Majesty's security forces, Count Illarion Vorontsov-Dashkov, and proposed a secret organization that would guard the Emperor, pursue the terrorists in Russia, and even invade their previously sacrosanct havens in Western Europe. Witte was then the rising young manager of Russia's Southwestern Railway in Kiev, but was still without influence or even recognition in the inner circles of government. Certainly a letter from such a man did not spur Alexander III's courtiers to organize, for they already had begun to do so. But it did show them that they might profitably expand their privileged ranks by careful recruiting among Russia's new aristocracy of wealth. Witte's letter encouraged them to invite him, a man of common background, to join them. Vorontsov-Dashkov therefore summoned him to St. Petersburg and swore him into the ranks of the just-formed Sacred Guard. He was to be its chief in Kiev.[5]

Within a remarkably brief time, some of Russia's wealthiest and most powerful men joined the Sacred Guard. Many were generals in the Imperial Army and scions of Russia's hundred richest noble families.[6] As self-appointed guardians of Russia's conservative order, these men insisted that the Sacred Guard must "unite as closely as possible all conservative elements of Russian society, study those social revolutionary movements that are disrupting Russian life, and bring all means possible to bear in the fight against them." They looked for further support from other rich property owners and from the magnates of trade, industry, and finance. Whatever their economic means and social position, they insisted that every recruit must be "purely Russian." All Jews were rejected as unreliable, even those with conservative views.[7]

Fervent support of Tsar, country, and the old order did not mean that the ideologists of the Sacred Guard were mere obscurantists. They perceived that repression alone could not eradicate terrorism from Russia and urged their members also to become active in local affairs, to seek election to district and provincial boards, and to exert greater influence on national affairs.[8] In less than six months, the organization boasted more than seven hundred members and private donations of more than three million rubles, not to mention such resources as the palace guards and secret police that their commander Vorontsov-Dashkov controlled. It is little wonder indeed that one perceptive scholar recently called the Sacred Guard "a state within the state."[9] It became an awesome instrument. Pobedonostsev and Alexander's conservative Minister of Internal Affairs Count Dmitrii Tolstoi feared it as a potential threat to the absolute power of their sovereign.[10]

Pobedonostsev and Tolstoi may have been even more disturbed by the Sacred Guard's effort to subvert liberal and radical groups by publishing pseudorevolutionary and pseudoliberal newspapers than by the vast wealth and influence its members could assemble. Although these papers reflected the program of Alexander III's government to the extent that they fostered anti-Semitism and endeavored to undermine Russia's incipient liberal movement, they were published abroad in order to give them greater credibility among the groups they sought to undermine. Realizing that any independently funded newspaper published beyond the reach of government censorship could one day become a dangerous foe, these two statesmen therefore resolved to break up the Sacred Guard before it challenged them or the government in any way. Pobedonostsev took the lead by compiling a damning collection of carefully selected excerpts taken out of context from the organization's newspapers for the Emperor's attention; with this evidence they convinced Alexander to order the guard's dissolution.[11] Undoubtedly at the Emperor's request, one of the senior members of the guard's inner circle wrote to all members in December 1882: "By order of the Sovereign Emperor [Minister of Internal Affairs] Count Tolstoi is transmitting the monarch's thanks to all those who have joined the society for the purposes of protecting His Majesty's August Person and fighting against sedition. At the same time, and in view of the changes that have occurred in the situation, further activities of the society are discontinued by the Sovereign Emperor's order."[12] For the moment, the Sacred Guard had run its course. In 1905, however, it would reappear to enlist far greater numbers under the chauvinistic and virulently anti-Semitic banner of the Union of the Russian People. Until that time, many of its ideals were kept alive by those who stood closest to the Emperor and his Court.

Nowhere did the principles of loyalty to Tsar, Church, and Country find more ardent expression than in the person of Konstantin Petrovich Pobedonostsev, Director General of the Holy Synod, the supreme ruling body of the Russian Orthodox Church. A graduate of the Imperial School of Jurisprudence, Pobedonostsev had entered Russia's service in 1846 and was shocked by the injustice of Russia's legal system. "There is no just case that cannot be lost," he lamented while still in his twenties. "Nor is there any illegal case that cannot be won."[13] Soon he exchanged his chancery desk for a university lectern, wrote extensively about the law, and helped draft the great reform of 1864 that made trials public, introduced trial by jury, and bestowed lifetime tenure upon judges. At that point in his life, Pobedonostsev urged Russia to model her legal system upon that of Europe.[14]

Soon after the Judicial Reform of 1864 was decreed, however, Pobedonostsev's hopes soured. In the words of his leading biographer, he wrote to a close friend that "he was sick and tired of reform [and] had lost faith in reform programs."[15] By the mid-1870s, he had become the narrow, sober official that posterity still remembers. "Unmarked by any passions—even his hatreds were cold and harsh —he was a man of balance," Professor Robert Byrnes once wrote. "He had a positive dislike and distaste for any kind of enthusiasm or liveliness, and he lacked a sense of humor. He was a believer in painful, slow growth, and he was suspicious generally of grandeur, eloquence, and striking ability."[16] More and more Pobedonostsev seemed to prefer a life devoted to books and study, but circumstances always drew him in the opposite direction.

In the early 1860s, Pobedonostsev had been reluctant to abandon the scholarly solitude of Moscow to tutor Alexander II's eldest son in St. Petersburg, where he feared he might lose the integrity he so prized.[17] Nonetheless, he had heeded his Emperor's call and quickly earned the confidence and deep respect of Grand Duke Nikolai Aleksandrovich, Russia's dying heir.[18] When Nikolai Aleksandrovich died in 1865, his younger brother, the future Alexander III, asked Pobedonostsev to teach him as he had taught his brother. "Dear Konstantin Petrovich," he wrote not long after his marriage. "I want to begin my lessons with you again. Affectionately yours, Alexander."[19] By his own admission, Alexander at that time knew little beyond how to be "a conscientious regimental commander."[20] It became Pobedonostsev's task to instill in him the breadth of vision and the depth of judgment required of a ruler of the world's largest Empire. In the inner prejudices and not yet fully formed attitudes of the student, the teacher's view struck a particularly responsive chord. Although Pobedonostsev's teachings were not completely mirrored in Alexander III, they formed an integral part of his conservative, chauvinistic response to the conditions that Russia faced in the 1880s and 1890s.

Pobedonostsev viewed humanity through a misanthropic prism that portrayed men as evil, corrupt, subject to vile passions, and governed by base instincts. He called the public press "one of the falsest institutions of our time" and branded its readers "idlers for the most part, ruled less by a few healthy instincts than by a base and despicable hankering for idle amusement." The tastes of these people, he said, were governed by "intellectual pruriency of the basest kind." In his view, any parliament was "an institution serving for the satisfaction of the personal ambition, vanity, and self-interest of its members." "Parliament," he proclaimed, "is one of the greatest illustrations of human delusion." Men needed to be ruled by a stern, benevolent monarch, who took authority into his hands to spare them the temptations that might come from wielding it themselves. It was for the Russian Autocrat—paternal, all-powerful, stern, yet all-caring—to assume that "limitless, terrible strength of power, and its limitless and terrible burden" for the welfare and salvation of all Russians.[21]

The welfare and salvation of all Russians was a theme to which Pobedonostsev often returned, and it was his view as much as Alexander III's that Russia should belong to the Russian people. "I am a Russian living among Russians, and I know the Russian heart and what it wants," he insisted.[22] He condemned one statesman because he was "not a Russian patriot," praised another because he possessed "a Russian soul," and lauded yet another because "his heart is Russian." To reign for the true welfare of Russia, he said, a Tsar must be sensitive to "the general desires of all Orthodox Russian people." If he were so, and also remained humble before God, he would find that "an entire regiment of sturdy and true Russian men, ready to carry on the life and death struggle for Russia's future well-being" would assemble around him. For Pobedonostsev, these "sturdy and true Russian men" were the old landowning nobility who "as a result of their historical position are more accustomed than any other class, on the one hand, to serve and, on the other, to command," standing at the head of the *narod*. In the 1870s and 1880s, the *narod* was idealized not only by revolutionaries, but by conservatives as well. For Pobedonostsev, they were "people with a Russian soul, doing good works in faith and in hope."[23]

Such good people, Pobedonostsev thought, looked to Moscow, a Russian city, "a pure place," in contrast to St. Petersburg, "a city of extremely painful impressions," where people were "occupied with the petty concerns of their ego [and] submerged in intrigues fostered by personal vanity."[24] He loved Moscow's antiquity and the peace of the "little house on a narrow side-street" he had known as a child and as a young professor at Moscow University. As the traditional center of the Russian Church, Moscow also gave him a sense of closeness to his roots and to his God. "How I remember . . . my dear native street with all its churches," he wrote from St. Petersburg. "Every morning on my walks, I went first of all to pray in our parish church, where there were morning services and all stood in blessed quiet."[25] Moscow was Russian, St. Petersburg European. "This is a cursed place," Pobedonostsev had once said of Russia's capital. Moving there from Moscow, he lamented, was "like throwing myself into a grave."[26]

God and Russian Orthodoxy were the focus of Pobedonostsev's ascetic universe, just as they stood at the center of his image of Moscow. "In our churches all social distinctions are laid aside," he wrote. "The poorest beggar feels, with the greatest noble, that the church, at least, is his. . . . It is the only place where the rich may not say to the poor, 'Your place is not beside me, but behind.' " Man could not live by bread alone, Pobedonostsev insisted. Nor could the state be maintained only by temporal force. "However powerful the state may be, its power is based alone upon the identity of religious profession with the people [and] the faith of the people sustains it. . . . In spiritual sympathy with its rulers a people may bear many heavy burdens, may concede much, and surrender many of its privileges and rights . . . [but] the state must not demand concession, or the people concede, . . . the domain where believers . . . bind themselves with eternity. There are depths in this domain to which the secular power dare not descend."[27]

In 1880, when Pobedonostsev rose to the exalted office of Director General of the Russian Orthodox Church's Holy Synod,[28] he set out not only to propagate and defend the faith, but to increase the Church's role in secular affairs. The spirit of any institution, he insisted, was vital, and that was especially true of the Church. In Russia, that spirit lay within the ceremonial and ritual that expressed the essence of the masses' belief. "Destroy this ceremonial, and the people will think its institution destroyed," he warned. "The masses assimilate ideas only through direct sentiment." Yet he did not insist that the Church remain only a repository of feeling, belief, and ritual. "The Church is truly a lifeboat for inquiring minds, tortured by questions of what and how to believe," he once explained.[29] He found in the Orthodox Church the perfect balance of belief and intellectual stimulation to rule his life for eighty years.

As Director General, Pobedonostsev's deep belief and his unshakable faith in the greatness of Russia and the Russians led him to insist that the Empire "must become and remain a community of believers."[30] He wanted Russia to remain uninvolved with world affairs and to concentrate upon solving the problems posed by the many nationalities within her boundaries through a policy of strict and aggressive Russification. The Lutheran Church and native culture in the Baltic provinces and in Finland, the Roman Catholic Church and Polish culture in Poland, national churches and cultures in Armenia and Georgia, as well as Mohammedanism in Central Asia—all were to be overwhelmed by the power of the Russian

Church, Russian culture, and Russian administration. In the words of his biographer, Pobedonostsev "considered religion the homogenizing cement of society. He assumed that a society or state was an independent organism and could therefore have only one religion, because all other beliefs and churches could only be agents of disintegration."[31] To spread Orthodoxy among non-Russians, and to instill its beliefs still deeper into the hearts of the *narod*, Pobedonostsev launched an aggressive program to increase Russia's parish schools. By 1905, the number of children being taught to read and write by priests stood at two million, about twenty times what it had been when he had taken up his duties in 1880.[32]

Pobedonostsev was nowhere more unrelenting in his persecution of non-Russians than in his treatment of Jews, a small but almost universally despised minority in Alexander's domains. "What you write about the Yids is completely just," he told Dostoevskii in 1879. "They have undermined everything, but the spirit of the century supports them. They are at the root of the revolutionary socialist movement and of regicide, they own the periodical press, they have in their hands the financial markets, the people as a whole fall into financial slavery to them; they even control the principles of contemporary science and strive to place it outside of Christianity."[33] Pobedonostsev thought that Jews made untrustworthy converts to Orthodoxy and considered it far better to isolate them from contact with Russians wherever possible. Anti-Semitism was one of the areas of state policy in which he exercised his greatest influence.[34]

During the 1890s, Pobedonostsev's views diverged increasingly from the more dynamic conservatism that other Imperial counselors advocated. Witte, who had admired him and once called him "a wise old man," now began to fear him as the "last of the Mohicans," who stained everything he touched with a chilling stagnation.[35] Indeed, Pobedonostsev reportedly warned at one point that "the continuation of the regime depends upon our ability to keep Russia in a frozen state. The slightest warm breath of life would cause the whole thing to rot."[36] To have succeeded in this aim, however, would have gone directly counter to Russia's new path. Change and progress had become a central fact of life in the Empire by that time, and any ideology that refused to recognize their presence could not survive for long. A more positive vision was needed to defend the sacrosanct status of autocracy, and neither the privileged aristocratic founders of the Sacred Guard nor Pobedonostsev was well suited to supply one. In the 1890s, it therefore was Sergei Witte who attempted to reconcile the social and economic progress of the Industrial Revolution with the anachronistic political precepts of autocracy. Witte had conceived of the Sacred Guard as a means to carry the struggle against revolution into the enemy's camp, but, unlike most of Russia's leading aristocrats, he had never thought of it as a weapon to defend the privileged position of the old landowning nobility. "It is my belief that a Russian Tsar ought to lean upon the *narod*," he insisted, and saw that union as a means of opposing the nobility's unyielding traditionalism.[37]

Witte was certain that tradition must give way if Russia hoped to challenge the industrial hegemony of the West. Very quickly he earned the enmity of those Russian lords whose vision of progress encompassed only a society and economy in which great mill owners and patriarchal lords dealt paternalistically with humble and docile peasants. "In economic life," wrote one of Witte's opponents, "the chief and unconditional demand is for economic harmony, for planned relationships, for the proportionality and conformity of all parts." All modernization should take "the conditions of Russian life and the true psychology of the Russian people" into proper account.[38] Any other course threatened the very fabric of the economic and social order that supported the landowning nobility. A so-called "political fantasy" written by one of the archconservatives' leading spokesmen denounced Witte as a "state criminal" whose arrest and trial would bring about a "purification of Russia."[39] "I am a faithful follower of the ideas of the Emperor Alexander III," Witte replied,[40] and few would now dispute that his program more accurately reflected Alexander III's aspirations than did Pobedonostsev's.

First and foremost a defender of autocracy, Witte thought that Russia would prosper so long as her autocrat was strong. "Who made the Russian Empire what she was even a decade ago?" he asked at the beginning of the new century. "Of course, the unlimited autocracy. If there were no unlimited autocracy, there would be no great Russian Empire."[41] Witte believed that, together with the *narod*, autocracy was the source of Russia's strength, so long as the Tsar had the will to lead his people firmly along the path to progress. Without a strong Tsar, Russia would languish, for an autocrat "without firm will" could, in a very short time, "destroy all that had been accomplished by his predecessors."[42] Witte therefore feared Nicholas II's timidity and weak resolve. Those weaknesses in his sovereign eventually convinced him to recommend transforming Russia's ancient autocracy into a constitutional monarchy in October 1905. "No one knows his defects and weaknesses better than I," he lamented as he looked upon Nicholas II's flawed efforts to rule. With Russia caught between military defeat in the Far East and revolutionary attack at home, Witte knew that Nicholas II lacked the stern will to restore peace to his realm as his father had done after Alexander II's assassination. "The Tsar is ruining himself and his dynasty, and is inflicting wounds upon Russia," he warned. "I have come to the conclusion that there is no way out other than a wise limitation . . . of autocracy."[43]

That Russia's autocracy had survived so long in the face of the social and economic dislocations brought on by Witte's programs for the Empire's rapid industrialization was in large measure due to the Okhrana, Alexander III's large and effective political police force. The Okhrana's main task was to defend autocracy against all domestic dissent, and it employed a sophisticated system of counterintelligence to carry out its counterrevolutionary activities.[44] With amazing regularity, its agents infiltrated revolutionary organizations in Russia and Europe, read large amounts of foreign and domestic mail, and spied upon Russians from all walks of life. One expert has estimated that "Lenin made no move, wrote no letter, [and] sent no propaganda into Russia of which the Okhrana was not aware to some degree,"[45] and that claim applied to other prominent revolutionaries as well. So effective was the Okhrana in penetrating secret revolutionary organizations that Gregorii Zinoviev, one of Lenin's chief lieutenants, later confessed that "there was not a single local [revolutionary] organization into which some provocateur has not crept."[46]

One major element in the Okhrana's success was its ability to extract great amounts of information from the Imperial mails. Beginning in the 1880s, agents who sometimes read as many as eight languages opened, read, and copied out the contents of large numbers of foreign and domestic letters before resealing them and sending them on to their proper recipients.[47] Since the letters of leading statesmen were routinely examined to more accurately gauge the state of Russian public opinion, Pobedonostsev himself made it a rule to ask friends traveling to Moscow to carry with them the very candid letters that he wrote to his confidante Ekaterina Tiutcheva because he feared they would be read at the Post Office if he entrusted them to the Imperial mails.[48] After the Revolution of 1917, investigators even found extensive Okhrana surveillance files about Grand Duchess Elizaveta Feodorovna, the elder sister of the Empress Aleksandra, and a woman known throughout Russia for her saintliness, charity, and good works.[49]

The Okhrana supplemented the information its agents assembled from the Russian mails by personal observation whenever possible. For that purpose, there was a corps of about a thousand plainclothesmen, selected with the utmost care from the ranks of noncommissioned officers and trained in the difficult art of following their quarry under all conditions. According to General Pavel Zavarzin, who at various times served as commander of the Okhrana forces in Kishinev, Warsaw, and Moscow, their main targets were "terrorists, people with whom they had some connection, and those who played an active part in such underground activities as revolutionary parties, secret printing establishments, and the manufacture of explosives."[50] Outside the capital cities, their numbers ranged from between six and forty per province; in St. Petersburg and Moscow, anywhere from fifty to a hundred could be found on the street on any given day.[51] Their training was intensive and demanded superb powers of concentration and recollection. Even in large cities like Moscow, plainclothes Okhrana agents were expected to memorize such details as the location of all building entrances in their assigned territory so that suspects could not easily slip away from them. Once ordered to place an apartment or shop under surveillance, they noted all comings and goings during their watch. According to one of the best accounts we have, "the Okhrana loved truth. They valued it above all else and it went badly indeed for the agent who falsified his reports."[52]

To gain further information about known or suspected revolutionaries and their associates, the Okhrana frequently set what were known as "mousetraps." Some time after midnight, once it was certain that any visitors had departed, Okhrana agents would swoop down upon the apartment of a known revolutionary, place everyone under arrest, and take them away under the cover of darkness. Agents remained in the apartment for several days to arrest any person who knocked at the door for whatever reason. Once arrested, no one could be released without being interviewed at the Okhrana headquarters by a senior officer, and there are reports of ludicrous arrests that occurred as a result. Among them were several famous British correspondents, at least one high-ranking official who bore the civil rank equal to that of a major general, and even a personal courier whom the Grand Duchess Ekaterina Mikhailovna had sent on a special errand.[53]

According to the official instructions under which the Okhrana operated, "the single most important basis of political inquiry is covert surveillance that is completely secret and ongoing. Its task is to investigate criminal revolutionary associations for the purpose of bringing their members to justice."[54] To carry out such surveillance, the Okhrana employed a corps of double agents who actually became members of various revolutionary groups and reported what was done and said when the revolutionaries thought themselves the most secure. This information—what General Zavarzin called "the data of internal agents"—was the most prized of all, for it filled in those incomplete portraits of revolutionary suspects that surveillance of mail and personal movements could sketch in only the crudest fashion. "Not only was it difficult to recruit such an agent," Zavarzin recalled, "but it was even more difficult to direct him and make certain that he did not betray himself by attracting the suspicion of those among whom he worked."[55] To lessen the risk, the Okhrana usually placed agents near the bottom of revolutionary organizations so that they could work their way up through the ranks and could earn the confidence of their comrades. "Such [agents] are essential and exist in all nations without exception," Zavarzin once wrote. "No government has ever existed, nor could one exist, without a secret service."[56]

Most agents had good educations or some particular talents that enabled them to earn the confidence of those they betrayed.[57] A number were repentant revolutionaries seeking what the Okhrana's official instructions called "complete rehabilitation," and a few had some weakness that the Okhrana could exploit to induce them to serve as double agents.[58] The success of the police in such recruitment was amazing. Only after the Revolution of 1917 opened the Okhrana files was it learned that a number of leading revolutionary figures had been agents of the secret police.[59]

Among those who served the longest as double agents was the former serf Anna Serebriakova, who bore her Okhrana assignment faithfully for more than a quarter-century before her duplicity was discovered.[60] A typical "worker-intellectual," in the words of her Soviet biographer, she had liberated herself from many of the traditional constraints under which most Russian women lived. She supported herself and was an active worker in the semilegal Red Cross organization that aided political prisoners and Siberian exiles. As Marxism flourished among Russian workers and intellectuals near the turn of the century, her apartment became a meeting place at which aspiring Russian Marxists held stormy theoretical and tactical debates. Men and women who rose high in the years after the Bolsheviks seized power were her frequent guests, the most prominent being Anatolii Lunacharskii, who became the People's Commissar of Public Enlightenment, and Lenin's own sister, Anna Elizarova. "Serebriakova was the center of underground work," one revolutionary recalled. "She maintained and circulated a library of illegal books and pamphlets. Money and things for those sitting in prison were sent through her, and from all parts of Russia comrades maintained ties with her."[61] "She gave the impression of being a wise, well-educated woman who was deeply interested in the revolutionary movement and ready to offer any help that was in her power to give," the revolutionary Sergei Mitskevich wrote in his memoirs.[62] Mitskevich remembered her from a meeting in 1894. Another fifteen years passed before an Okhrana defector revealed how she had betrayed her revolutionary comrades.[63] During that crucial time, as one expert wrote, "Serebriakova knew a great deal. And everything that she knew, the Okhrana knew also."[64]

There was one double agent whose accomplishments surpassed even Serebriakova's. Few accounts of the Russian revolutionary movement fail to mention Evno Azef, son of a poor Jewish tailor, who rose to become Head of the Combat Detachment of the Russian Socialist Revolutionary party and a member of its Central Committee. Azef had volunteered to serve Russia's secret police while a student in Germany in the spring of 1893. The Okhrana investigated his character and background for two months and were not deceived. Azef was "intelligent and a clever intriguer," they concluded. "His covetousness and his present state of need will make him zealous in his duty."[65]

Azef's importance to the Okhrana grew when he joined with Grigorii Gershuni to help found the Russian Socialist Revolutionary party in 1901. Gershuni headed the party's terrorist Combat Detachment, whose chief task was to kill prominent officials, and Azef became his chief lieutenant. Secure in this high position of trust, Azef betrayed the entire Socialist Revolutionary membership in the southeastern city of Kharkov. None in the party seemed the wiser, especially after Azef went on to help Gershuni organize the assassination of Minister of Internal Affairs Dmitrii Sipiagin, a plot he did not betray to the Okhrana. Gershuni's arrest in 1903 (the double agent's role in his apprehension remains unclear) put Azef at the top of the Combat Detachment and, until 1908, he served and betrayed revolutionaries and Okhrana with equal efficiency.

Probably in revenge for their anti-Jewish policies, Azef allowed the assassinations of Minister of Internal Affairs Viacheslav Plehve (July 1904) and Grand Duke Sergei Aleksandrovich (February 1905) to take place unhindered by Okhrana interference. Both were killed by bombs thrown into their carriages. In both instances, their assassins used bombs so powerful that only scattered bits of victim and carriage could be found. Azef then boldly betrayed almost the entire Combat Detachment to the Okhrana in 1905 and repeated his audacious feat three years later, just a few months before he was unmasked.[66] He fled to the West and lived in fear of the revolutionaries' vengeance until his death a decade later. Even more than Serebriakova, whose exposure followed his by just a few months, he had shown how vulnerable the revolutionaries were to infiltration by talented police agents. A former revolutionary admitted some years later, "as a spy, Azef was truly without equal."[67]

At one time, Azef and Serebriakova had been in the employ of one of the most brilliant officers ever to serve in the Romanovs' political police.[68] This was Sergei Vasilevich Zubatov, Chief of the Moscow Okhrana from 1896 until 1902, who once praised Serebriakova for her long, "honorable, and brilliant" service to the Tsar.[69] Zubatov himself was something of a repentant revolutionary. He had led a radical circle in Moscow during the early 1880s and, as one of his contemporaries recalled, was "an extremely gifted propagandist, particularly [talented in] attracting youngsters."[70] For reasons that still are not clear, Zubatov became a double agent, probably some time in the summer of 1886,[71] but was unmasked very quickly by his revolutionary comrades. No longer able to continue in this role, he became an officer in the Moscow Okhrana in 1888.[72]

Zubatov joined the Moscow Okhrana just as it turned to face Russia's newly resurgent revolutionaries. Talented, energetic, and with what one expert has called an "unrivaled knowledge of the revolutionary movement,"[73] he had passionate and unshakable faith in monarchism. "Without the Tsar there cannot be a Russia," he often said. "The happiness and greatness of Russia lies in her Sovereigns and their work."[74] Proclaiming that "whoever goes against monarchy in Russia, goes against Russia herself, and we must fight such people . . . to the death,"[75] Zubatov developed brilliant counterrevolutionary techniques that made the Moscow Okhrana the most effective branch in all of Russia. Before long, his superiors took note of this young officer who quoted the socialist writings of Eduard Bernstein to his prisoners to support his exhortations that they "reconvert" from revolutionaries to monarchists. To dissuade the revolutionaries with their own ideological weapons was a daring undertaking, but it brought dazzling rewards in the way of "conversions." In 1896, Zubatov's success won him an appointment as Chief of the Moscow Okhrana at the age of thirty-two. His was one of the most meteoric rises ever to occur in the ranks of Russia's political police.[76]

In the long hours he spent with young men and women arrested for illegal political acts, Zubatov preached that a just society free from conflict and economic suffering could be achieved most quickly in Russia by a benevolent autocrat. "History calls upon the Russian autocracy to fulfill the task of eliminating the class struggle that is so dangerous for all society," he insisted. "The sovereign needs our help!"[77] After he himself had been interrogated by Zubatov, Grigorii Gershuni, Azef's first chief in the Combat Detachment, reported that his was "a theory of a democratic people's monarchy, which stands above classes and class struggle, which mitigates class antagonisms, which establishes social peace, national welfare, and the general happiness."[78] By concentrating especially upon those literate factory workers, whom Moscow's chief prosecutor once described as "the connecting link between [the intelligentsia] and the milieu of the workers,"[79] Zubatov set out to convert socialists into monarchist trade unionists who would abandon their revolutionary struggle in favor of more moderate and legitimate reform efforts. To those willing to admit the error of their ways, he offered pardon and freedom in return for their promise to inform the police about the revolutionaries' future plans. Soon, Zubatov's tactics were adopted throughout the Okhrana.[80]

Conversion of revolutionaries into monarchists did not fully satisfy Zubatov's passion to proselytize autocracy among Russia's factory workers. "So long as the revolutionary merely preaches pure socialism, one can deal with him by repressive measures alone," he wrote in 1898. "But when he attempts to exploit the minor defects of the existing order in an effort to advance his own cause, then repression itself is not enough. It then becomes necessary to cut the ground away from beneath his very feet. . . . The average worker," he insisted, "always prefers not so much the brilliant denouement as he does the peaceful, legal one."[81] Earlier than Lenin, Zubatov realized that rank-and-file workers instinctively preferred trade union negotiations to revolutionary struggle.[82]

In September 1900, Zubatov sent two memoranda to the Imperial Department of Police in St. Petersburg urging that factory workers be encouraged to organize under government control. It was for the proper authorities, he said, to maintain "the equilibrium among classes," and "for the supra-class autocracy to 'divide and rule.'"[83] As always, the autocracy held center stage in Zubatov's plan. "The properly understood monarchical idea," he had written elsewhere, "is in a position to provide everything that the nation needs while unleashing its civic forces, but without bloodshed and other unpleasantness."[84] To achieve that end, the urban proletariat could become a useful and effective instrument in the hands of the government. "A little more faith in the masses," he urged. "We will entice them and they will be ours."[85] Zubatov proposed that the Moscow Okhrana actually help the workers organize those very associations that had always been illegal in Russia and that the government use such "unions" to immunize the workers against the revolutionaries' propaganda. The program he implemented in the spring of 1901 was so clearly associated with his principles that it became known as the *Zubatovshchina*. For almost a year, Minister of Internal Affairs Dmitrii Sipiagin withheld his blessing; Zubatov went ahead without it, but with the warm approval of Grand Duke Sergei Aleksandrovich and General Dmitrii Trepov who, as Chief of the Moscow Police, was his immediate superior.[86]

The first of the Zubatov "unions" began as a mutual aid fund for Moscow's machine workers and was organized by several repentant Social Democrats led by the skilled patternmaker Mikhail Afanasev. At about the same time, Nikifor Krasivskii, another of Zubatov's converts, began to organize similar societies among the city's textile workers. Huge congregations of workers began to assemble to hear lectures about how their wretched living and working conditions might be bettered. By fall, the *Zubatovshchina* in Moscow was flourishing. Thousands of workers were involved, yet Zubatov and his chosen agents still seemed in complete control, to the absolute rage of their revolutionary opponents. "We have organized a seventeen-member Workers' Council composed entirely of our agents," Zubatov reported. "The whole business is moving brilliantly. . . . By controlling the Council we have at our disposal the key to the entire mass of workers."[87] Many St. Petersburg officials remained doubtful, for it seemed impossible that workers' assemblies would not lead to confrontations with factory owners and the authorities. Yet Zubatov adamantly defended his program. As if to prove his immense authority, he organized a march by some fifty thousand workers within the Kremlin's very walls on February 19, 1902, the anniversary of the emancipation of the serfs in 1861, and a date that had become a traditional day of radical protest in Russia. Yet none among those assembled in the Kremlin spoke a word of protest as they joined in prayers for the Imperial family's health and cheered as a band played "God Save the Tsar!" It was, perhaps, Zubatov's finest hour.[88]

Just when success seemed within Zubatov's grasp, radicals, bureaucratic reactionaries, and Moscow's industrial magnates attacked from all sides. Disgruntled radicals publicized the connections between the workers' associations and the Okhrana, and a number of prominent Moscow intellectuals hastened to withdraw their support from Zubatov's "unions." Fearful that even Okhrana-controlled associations might lead the workers to press for better wages and working conditions, the new lords of Russia's industry begged Minister of Finance Witte to end the Zubatov "unions." Witte feared that any threat of worker unrest could upset the stability of Russia's industrial development, but he could do little against Zubatov so long as Grand Duke Sergei Aleksandrovich and General Trepov, recently joined by Sipiagin, supported him.

In a futile effort to mollify government critics and conservative factory owners, Zubatov assigned a greater role in his "unions" to the Church. Religious readings by priests replaced the lectures that the intelligentsia had given so successfully the previous year. The workers' enthusiasm flagged quickly. Although the textile workers' faith in the new associations proved somewhat more durable, the machine workers' association shrank to fewer than forty dues-paying members by early 1904. In less than two years, the Zubatov experiment succumbed to the hatred of the Moscow industrialists, the jealousy of the revolutionaries, and the fears of ultraconservative senior officials in St. Petersburg.[89]

Zubatov himself fell into disgrace well before the *Zubatov-shchina* collapsed. Not long after he had agreed to support Zubatov's effort, Sipiagin had been killed by a terrorist. Viacheslav von Plehve, who replaced him in April 1902, at first seemed even more inclined to support Zubatov than his predecessor. He brought Zubatov to St. Petersburg, appointed him to head the Special Section of the Department of Police, and even spoke of extending the *Zubatovshchina* to other parts of the Empire. But in August 1903, an utter turnabout occurred. Plehve summoned Zubatov to his summer villa on Aptekarskii Island in St. Petersburg, accused him of betraying state secrets to revolutionary members of the Jewish labor movement, dismissed him from office, and gave him twenty-four hours to leave St. Petersburg.[90] It was an amazingly cruel end to a brilliant career and, from all accounts, utterly unexpected. Less than two months before, Plehve had expressed full confidence in Zubatov's abilities to none other than Witte.[91]

The intrigues that led to Zubatov's sudden disgrace have never been fully unraveled, but the best estimates are that Plehve dismissed him for outright insubordination.[92] Zubatov evidently had tried to bring about his superior's dismissal because he thought that Plehve was scheming against him in secret and hoped that another Minister of Internal Affairs might lend him even greater support. He even confessed as much to Serebriakova a few days after his disgrace.[93] To his particular misfortune, he was found out at the very moment when Plehve needed someone to blame for the strikes that had wracked the great Black Sea port of Odessa earlier that summer. When Plehve learned that Grand Duke Aleksandr Mikhailovich had told the Emperor that Zubatov himself had organized the Odessa workers, he hastened to turn the Tsar's remarkable gullibility to his personal political advantage.[94] "This is what your policy has led to," Plehve reportedly stormed at Zubatov at their meeting.[95] Zubatov calmly pointed out that he had merely proceeded according to the instructions he had received from Plehve's own office, but the Minister cut him short to announce that he had just become a retired State Councillor.[96] In one shrewd stroke, Plehve thus avoided all blame for bungling the government's efforts to crush the Odessa strikes and appeased the bitter and dangerous critics of *Zubatovshchina* among Russia's industrialists and high officials. Only the efforts of Grand Duke Sergei Aleksandrovich won Zubatov a modest pension. Zubatov refused several offers to return to the Okhrana after Plehve's assassination although he remained a dedicated defender of autocracy. Until 1917, he was a forgotten figure. That year, at the beginning of March, when he heard that Nicholas had abdicated, he calmly arose from the dinner table, went into his study, and shot himself.[97]

There were few activities the defenders of the old order pursued more frantically than persecution of Jews. Anti-Semitism had been a blot on Russian life and culture even before the Romanovs had ascended Russia's throne, but it had grown more intense in the mid-seventeenth century with the annexation of Polish and Ukrainian territories with large numbers of Jews. There were open massacres, and between 1648 and 1658, almost a quarter-million Jews perished. At the end of the First Northern War, a few Jews were allowed to settle in Moscow as part of the peace settlement, only to be expelled a decade later. By the time Peter the Great began to rule in his own right in 1689, only a handful remained in Russia. Peter's wife and successor, Catherine I, expelled those who had survived the massacres of the 1650s, although her expulsion was never totally effective. In 1772, Russia's part in the First Partition of Poland brought her lands containing some two hundred thousand new Jews. Further Russian seizures of Polish territory added more Jews, and they numbered almost a million at the end of the eighteenth century. It was then that Catherine the Great established the infamous Pale of Settlement, that kidney-shaped region that lay along her

Empire's western and southern frontiers, and most Jews were confined there for the rest of her reign.

During the first three-quarters of the nineteenth century, the fortunes of Russia's Jews continued to rise and fall. Alexander I followed a policy of moderate toleration, while Nicholas I instituted a more repressive regime. The spirit of liberation that freed the serfs in 1861 also produced an "emancipation" of sorts for the Jews. For the first time, they were admitted to the civil service and the legal profession, and some were allowed to leave the Pale. Numbers of Jews fought with distinction in the Russo-Turkish War of 1877–78 and won commendations for valor. They began to enter Russia's schools in large numbers; by 1881, one out of every twelve university students came from a Jewish family. Yet this apparent betterment of the Jews' situation did not reflect a change in Russian popular attitudes, and the masses continued to despise them as economic exploiters and Christ-killers.[98]

Alexander III's accession brought persecution to Russia's Jewish communities on a terrifying scale. The last eight months of 1881 saw seventy times more pogroms than had occurred in the entire first eight decades of the century, and these vicious anti-Jewish riots brought ruin to thousands.[99] *"Bei zhidov!"*—"Smash the kikes!" The cry struck terror into the hearts of Russia's Jews as pogroms swept the Empire's southern cities. *"Bei zhidov!"* The onset of a pogrom was usually signaled by a ragged shout from the ranks of an infamous "barefoot brigade," a gang of out-of-town ruffians with an insatiable thirst for vodka and violence, who made a sudden appearance at a local railway station.[100] Fanned by the shameful bigotry of the Russian masses, the shout quickly swelled into a fearsome roar that remained forever etched upon the minds of those who heard it. "Get the kikes! Get the kikes! Bash them!"[101] While the police stood idly by, hordes of Russian workers and peasants surged through the streets to pillage Jewish shops, rape Jewish women, and murder Jews who tried to bar their way. These cruel memories—he called them the "coarse fingers of Russian reality"—drove young Iulii Martov to become one of Nicholas II's most implacable revolutionary foes,[102] and they compelled countless thousands of other Jews to flee Russia for the unknown vicissitudes of life in New York City's Lower East Side tenements.[103]

In all fairness, it must be pointed out that there is no evidence that Alexander III personally ordered the pogroms against Russia's Jewry, and some historians have argued that the pogroms actually displeased him.[104] Still, it must be admitted that Alexander's "displeasure" was expressed in amazingly moderate language for a Tsar who characteristically spoke his mind in the bluntest of terms.[105] When one of his ministers urged him to end the legal disabilities that oppressed Russia's Jews, Alexander merely replied: "We must never forget that the Jews crucified our Lord and shed His precious blood."[106] Somewhat earlier, he had remarked to General Iosif Gurko that "it delights me to the very depths of my soul when they beat up the Jews, but, nonetheless, we cannot permit it."[107] Alexander III was uneasy about pogroms only as instances of public disorder and only to the extent that he shared the apprehensions of Count Mikhail Reitern who once warned him that "today they persecute and rob the Jews. . . . Tomorrow, the merchants and nobles may be next."[108]

The first pogrom of Alexander's reign broke out in the southern town of Elisavetgrad on April 15, 1881, just six weeks after he had ascended the throne. It began when a group of newly arrived agitators sent a drunken Russian into a saloon to insult the Jewish proprietor. When the tavern keeper tired of his ravings and threw his unwelcome customer into the street, his companions launched the first violence with a shout that "the Yids are beating up Russians!" At first, the police restored order but, when the mob's attack grew more vicious the next day, the authorities no longer attempted to intervene. "Clerks, saloon and hotel waiters, artisans, drivers, flunkeys, day laborers in the employ of the government, and soldiers on furlough—all of these joined the movement," one eyewitness reported. "The city presented an extraordinary sight," he continued. "Houses with broken doors and windows; a raging mob, running about yelling and whistling in all directions and continuing its work of destruction without let or hindrance, and, as a finishing touch to this picture, complete indifference displayed by the local non-Jewish inhabitants. . . . Toward evening the disorders increased in intensity, owing to the arrival of a large number of peasants from the adjacent villages, who were anxious to secure part of the Jewish loot."[109]

But worse was to come. As word spread about the ease with which the Jews at Elisavetgrad had been abused, and as the authorities made no effort to punish the mob, Kishinev, Berezovka, and Ananevo all suffered pogroms within the next ten days.[110] Then, on April 23, in Kiev, the most ancient of Russian cities, where Jews had lived for nearly a millennium, a crowd of out-of-town agitators again assembled. As in other cities, the mob responded to their urgings, but hesitated when a few policemen and three mounted Cossacks appeared outside the first Jewish store they approached. According to a Christian observer, who abhorred the violence but stood by powerless to stop it, the impasse ended when a well-dressed young man drove up and shouted from his cabriolet to the hesitating crowd: "Eh, what's wrong with you, brothers? Have you turned yellow, or what? What a bunch of old women you are!" He got out of his carriage, seized one of the Cossacks' lances, and began to smash the shop's windows. "The crowd surged after him," the witness continued. "Within a few moments, the shop was utterly stripped of its contents."[111]

Such apparent daring flamed the mob. The young man had seized a weapon from one of the Governor General's guards, a crime that promised serious punishment anywhere in Russia. However, General Aleksandr Drenteln, Governor General of Kiev, who was once described by a close associate as a man who "despised Jews to the very depths of his being,"[112] made no effort to interfere in any way. When they saw that no punishment fell upon the man who had turned the Cossack's lance against the Jews, the crowd began to pillage in deadly earnest. "Soon afterwards the mob threw itself upon the Jewish synagogue which, despite its strong bars, locks, and shutters, was wrecked in a moment," another witness reported. "The [Torah] scrolls were torn to shreds, trampled in the dirt, and destroyed with incredible passion."[113] When night fell, the violence increased. More than twenty women were raped and a number of others thrown into burning buildings or beaten to death. About a thousand Jewish homes and shops were destroyed; the property damage was estimated at several million rubles.[114] Reported the Austrian consul in Kiev, "The entire behavior of the police leads one rightfully to the conclusion that the disturbances are abetted by the authorities."[115]

Nowhere was such cooperation more evident than in the Ukrainian town of Balta, where a pogrom more vicious than any seen in 1881 broke out in March 1882. Local officials apparently knew of the event days in advance, and the local Marshal of the Nobility, a petty lord by the name of Bialogorodetskii, actually told the Jewish merchant to whom he rented a small shop that he was looking forward to the event. To a friend he confided, "I'll just smoke a cigarette and look on calmly, even when they loot the shop of my tenant."[116] The Jews in Balta outnumbered the Christians by a margin of two to one and, at first, defended themselves against the mob's attacks. But the tide turned against them when the police and an army detachment hastened to place their sabers and rifle butts at the mob's service. The next morning the mob's ranks were swelled by some five hundred club-wielding peasants who had hastened to Balta from nearby villages to seize a share of the spoils.[117] In the space of two days, over twelve hundred Jewish houses and shops were destroyed and forty Jews murdered or seriously wounded. A local rabbi claimed that the number of Jews left homeless exceeded fifteen thousand.[118]

Almost as appalling as this terrible destruction and injury was the reluctance of Russians to speak out in the Jews' defense. Even Count Lev Tolstoi made no protest at first; a decade later when the great Russian philosopher Vladimir Solovev drew up a petition against the government's anti-Semitism, Tolstoi minimized his signing by explaining that he would sign anything that Solovev saw fit to write.[119] Yet Tolstoi's reluctance to defend the Jews in the 1880s (he would do so more strongly in 1903) was part of a broad tradition of apathy and prejudice shared by many prominent Russians. For Aleksandr Pushkin, Russia's poet of freedom at the beginning of the nineteenth century, the Jew was "contemptible" and came stealthily as a spy and informer.[120] Two decades later, Turgenev saw in the

Jew an object of ridicule. "He really was absurd despite the desperate situation in which he now found himself," Turgenev wrote in one of his short stories about Herschel, a Danzig Jew about to be hanged by the Russian army. "The agonizing grief of bidding farewell to life, to his daughter, and to his family expressed itself in this unfortunate Jew by such strange, disjointed bodily movements, outcries, and gyrations that we all smiled in spite of ourselves."[121] Turgenev, Tolstoi, and Dostoevskii all spoke against anti-Semitism in a few private letters and a handful of journal articles, but they portrayed the Jew in the stereotypical Russian manner in *belles lettres* nonetheless.[122] Not until the turn of the twentieth century did such younger writers as Vladimir Korolenko feel compelled to speak out in protest against the anti-Semitism of the Russian government.[123]

As a number of Imperial advisers grew concerned that the pogroms' violent expressions of mass hatred might shift from the Jews to Russia's landowning aristocracy, the pogroms began to diminish.[124] By late summer 1882, they had burned themselves out completely. Over the next decade, to avoid the unfavorable attention of Europeans, especially the Rothschild bankers from whom Russia required large new loans, Alexander and his advisers persecuted Jews by means of confidential regulations, not public decrees. The first of these were the "Temporary Regulations" of May 3, 1882, destined to remain in effect until 1917.[125] These restricted the movement of Jews within the Pale, curtailed their rights to own property outside its boundaries, and, most oppressive of all, attempted to force Jews who had left the Pale to return. Determined to keep Jews out of the rest of the Empire, Minister of Internal Affairs Nikolai Ignatev proclaimed: "The Pale cannot be spread further East. The western border, however, is open for Jews."[126] Ignatev's meaning could not have been more clear. Jews were not free to move within the Russian Empire, but they were free to leave it. During Ignatev's tenure, it became a criminal offense for unbaptized Jews to bear Christian names. In 1887, Minister of Public Instruction Ivan Delianov ordered all school authorities to reduce the numbers of Jews admitted to their classrooms.[127]

At best, Ignatev's proscriptions were applied unevenly, nor

were they enforced more methodically by his successor Count Dmitrii Tolstoi. Only after Tolstoi's death and his replacement by his deputy Ivan Durnovo in 1889 did anti-Semitism find an unabashed champion in Russia's Ministry of Internal Affairs. Durnovo found staunch allies not only in the persons of the Tsar and Konstantin Pobedonostsev, but also in Grand Duke Sergei Aleksandrovich, Alexander III's younger brother and newly appointed Governor General of Moscow. "My brother Sergei does not want to go to Moscow before the Jews are cleaned out," Alexander reportedly told Durnovo in May 1891.[128] Durnovo already had taken steps to achieve precisely that end.

On March 28, 1891, he had published a decree that forbade Jews to live in Moscow. Most were to be expelled instantly, while that minority who had obtained special rights of residence were given three to twelve months to liquidate their business enterprises, move to the Pale some thousand miles away, or leave the Empire altogether.[129] Word of Durnovo's decree reached Moscow the next day, the first day of Passover. That very night, Cossack-reinforced police units surrounded the entire Zariade Quarter, where the poorest Jews lived in sprawling tenements just one step removed from the slums of Khitrovka. "The whole Quarter was ransacked, apartments forced open, doors smashed, every bedroom without exception searched, and every living soul, men, women and children, routed out," wrote Harold Frederic, the *Times* correspondent in Moscow. "Over seven hundred men, women and children were dragged at dead of night through the streets to the police stations. They were not even given time to dress themselves."[130] A few were sent to prisons, others exiled to Siberia, and most shipped directly to towns and cities in the Pale. None was given the opportunity even to pack clothing for the journey, let alone assemble what few valuables they might have possessed. Passover, 1891, had begun.

Within three months, some seventeen thousand Jewish artisans, petty shopkeepers, and workmen were driven from the city. Then it was the turn of the more prosperous Jewish merchants and traders, whose numbers totaled perhaps another four thousand. In return for large bribes, the police sometimes allowed them a few weeks of grace, but all except the richest merchants and those professionals with university educations had to face the inevitable expulsion within a year. Some were men of considerable property, but all had to dispose of their shops, businesses, and factories at a bare fraction of their recognized worth to Russians anxious to take advantage of their misfortune. Informers received liberal rewards for exposing Jews who attempted to escape expulsion.[131] In January 1892, when temperatures plummeted to thirty degrees below zero, "crowds of Jews dressed in beggarly fashion, among them women, children, and old men, with remnants of their household belongings lying around them, filled the [unheated] station of the Brest railroad," one observer remembered. "Jews who had lived in Moscow fifteen, twenty-five, and even forty years were forcibly removed to the Jewish Pale of Settlement."[132] In all, Moscow lost over twenty thousand Jews, some one hundred million rubles in trade and business production, and about twenty-five thousand jobs that Russians had held in Jewish enterprises. The production of silk, one of the city's most lucrative enterprises, was virtually wiped out.[133]

One commentator remarked that for that handful of Jews allowed to remain in Moscow, the restrictions were so extensive that "the only 'living' civic interest among the Jews of Moscow at that time was the cemetery." The lower orders of the Moscow police openly referred to the Jewish High Holy Days as the "kike-hunting season," because they were allowed to break up secret Jewish religious services in any way they chose during that time. Only in 1906, after a revolution had brought a constitution and a legislative assembly to Russia, was the Moscow Synagogue allowed to reopen. "This house, called 'the Moscow Synagogue,' saw many, many tears and much bitter sorrow," wrote the author of a brief history of the persecution that Moscow's Jews endured after 1891.[134]

Nicholas II did nothing to ease the persecution of Russian Jewry. As the tenth anniversary of his accession approached, the Jews of southern Russia suffered a pogrom more violent than any seen even in the 1880s. This time, government complicity was far more obvious. According to Count Sergei Witte, who played such a prominent role in Russian affairs between 1891 and 1906, "the immense pogrom in Kishinev [the capital of Bessarabia] was directly organized by [Viacheslav] Plehve," Russia's Minister of Internal Affairs at the time.[135] Even if Plehve did not actually take part in the pogrom's planning, it had, at the very least, the open and full support of Bessarabia's Deputy Governor Ustrugov, and a senior officer in the Okhrana by the name of Levendahl. Along with Plehve, these two men gave direct support to Pavolachi Krushevan, one of the most unsavory characters of the age. Krushevan was a Moldavian who had transformed himself into an ardent Russian chauvinist once he learned the generous rewards that lay in store for men who followed that path. With help from the Ministry of Internal Affairs's secret coffers, he founded the *Bessarabets (The Bessarabian)* in 1897 and, to the delight of his official benefactors, quickly made it into the Empire's most virulently anti-Semitic daily. The only daily newspaper in the entire province, with a circulation of almost thirty thousand, *Bessarabets* enjoyed a rare opportunity to mold public opinion. "The Jews are enemies!" it proclaimed. "The Jews must be destroyed!" One of its articles demanded a "crusade against the hated race" and even implied that such an enterprise would enjoy Imperial support.[136] The stage was set for an explosion. All that was needed was a spark to ignite a very short and volatile fuse.

As winter began to wane, fear gripped superstitious and ignorant Russians who lived in the Pale. For spring marked the approach not only of Easter but of the Jewish Passover, and they were convinced that Jews required blood drained from still living Christian children to properly prepare their holiday matzoth. Lower-class Christians were especially fearful in Kishinev, a city of about a hundred thousand, which held about equal numbers of Jews and Gentiles. On February 9, 1903, the body of fourteen-year-old Mikhail Rybachenko was found in the nearby village of Dubossary. According to his illiterate grandfather's testimony, his corpse contained twenty-four wounds, all placed in a clear pattern and made by the sort of grooved instrument that, according to popular belief, Jews used to drain blood from their victims. Rybachenko's grandfather also insisted that his grandson had been blinded before his blood was drawn "so that he could not offer any resistance to his torturers." Subsequent investigation by the Imperial Ministry of Justice proved that Rybachenko had in fact been murdered by a greedy uncle intent upon seizing his inheritance, but popular opinion was aroused. It was a perfect excuse for a pogrom, and *Bessarabets* played it to the hilt.[137] Smoldering popular suspicion grew more intense on Easter eve, when a Christian servant girl died in Kishinev's Jewish hospital under mysterious circumstances. It turned out that she had poisoned herself and had died despite desperate efforts by her Jewish employer to save her, but popular opinion preferred to believe that she too had become a victim of ritual sacrifice.[138]

The first act of this tragic final drama of Kishinev's Jews was played out on Easter Sunday, April 6, also the seventh day of Passover in 1903. That morning handbills announced that the Emperor had granted permission to local Christians to wreak "bloody punishment" upon the Jews.[139] In typical fashion, the authorities took no measures to protect the Jews, even though they knew that the proclamations were certainly false. At noon, some thirty bands of rioters, each with about fifty artisans, workers, and city employees, led by a student from the local seminary, struck at different points in the Jewish section of the city.[140] Forty-five Jews were murdered, some six hundred injured, and more than thirteen hundred homes and shops looted and destroyed before Plehve ordered in troops to halt the carnage.[141]

Some of the most gruesome tales of atrocities proved impossible to substantiate, and the dozens of letters, telegrams, and reports that flowed from government offices in Kishinev to St. Petersburg and back made little mention of them in any case. Michael Davitt, a native of Dalkey in Ireland and a correspondent for the Hearst newspapers in America, tried to separate fact from fiction when he visited Kishinev in May. By interviewing Russian officials, Jewish elders, survivors of the pogroms, and physicians at the hospitals that had treated the dying and the injured, he compiled an appalling tale of horror. "I have before me a record of thirteen girls and women of ages ranging from seventeen to forty-eight, who were assaulted by from two to twenty men and in many cases left for dead," Davitt wrote after he returned to Ireland. Several eyewitnesses told him how the mob drove nails into the eyes of one woman and then killed her by driving them deep into her brain. He interviewed a man in a Jewish hospital who had been blinded with a sharpened stake while the mob proclaimed, "you will never again look upon a Christian child." A devout Catholic who hesitated to think ill of the lords of the Church, Davitt was appalled to learn from Jewish and Christian sources that the Bishop of Kishinev actually had blessed a crowd of pogromists as he passed them in the street, while not far away the mob was raping sixteen women and girls they had found cowering in the loft of a small house at 13 Aziiatskii Alley. When the glazier Mottel Greenspoon tried to defend them, the mob castrated him and trampled him to death.[142]

The tale of Mottel Greenspoon and the atrocities committed at 13 Aziiatskii Alley also was told by Vladimir Korolenko, who wrote an emotional essay entitled "House No. 13" just a few weeks later. In a twenty-page account of the cruelty and anguish that had filled that small corner of Kishinev during those two terrible days, Korolenko painted for his readers what he called "a portrait of barbaric bitterness." "The moral is clear for each and every person in whom humanitarian feelings still live," he concluded. "But do they live in very many? This terrible question arises involuntarily when one looks upon what I saw in Kishinev."[143]

Korolenko's words were not mere rhetoric. He had every reason to question the humanity of the government and society of which he was a part. "From the Tsar and Plehve I heard that the Jews needed to be taught a lesson because they have been putting on airs and leading the revolutionary movement as well," General Aleksei Kuropatkin confided to his diary less than a week after the Kishinev tragedy.[144] Supporters of *Bessarabets* actually insisted that the Russians had only defended themselves against the Jews' vicious attacks. "All the Jews poured into the streets and squares of the city, having armed themselves beforehand with revolvers, clubs, crowbars, knives, and sulphuric acid," they insisted. "If the police and soldiers had not arrived, the Jews would have killed hundreds of Christians."[145] Plehve unabashedly included a milder version of the *Bes-*

sarabets claims in the official account of the pogrom he sent to the *Times* of London in mid-June.[146]

In any case, the government found other reasons to blame the Jews for the Kishinev atrocities and for those that followed a few weeks later in the town of Gomel. "You are yourselves to blame for all that has happened," the Governor of Mogilëv told them. "You propagate disobedience and opposition to the Government among an uncivilized population. But the Russian populace does not care for it and turns against you."[147] Father Ioann of Kronstadt, a priest renowned for his holiness and piety throughout Russia, announced that he had concluded that "the Jews themselves were the cause of those disorders, the wounds inflicted, and the murders committed," and that, despite the overwhelming contrary evidence, it was "the Christians who have suffered in the end."[148] "The Russian Government is the first to disapprove of such horrid acts of violence," Plehve assured the *Times*'s readers. Yet he insisted that it was impossible to better the Jews' situation in the Empire because "this is sure to drive the Russian populace to new excesses."[149] Even the sober Witte insisted upon extreme caution in discussing any lessening of the Jews' disabilities. "Any rapid, abrupt decisions will disturb the equilibrium," he warned. "The state is a living organism and therefore it is necessary to be extremely careful when operating upon it."[150] Russian Jews were better off to seek new lives elsewhere.

Superstition and deep-seated hatred lay behind the atrocities that mobs of lower-class Russians inflicted upon Jews, but these emotions do not easily explain why the Tsar and his chief ministers allowed pogroms to flourish. Nor does the Jews' role in Russia's emergent revolutionary movement explain the tolerance in high places for the great surge of pogroms; the number of revolutionaries was small, and the number of Jews in the revolutionary movement far smaller. Official tolerance of the pogroms was only one manifestation of a widespread malaise connected with the complex social and economic transformation that was taking place in Russia at the time.

Between 1861 and 1905, Russian society moved decisively and

irrevocably from the *ancien régime* world of privileged manor lords and enserfed peasants to one in which merchant princes, industrious peasants, and ambitious lawyers, scientists, and engineers—a new aristocracy of wealth and merit, in fact—began to rise to prominence. Their rise involved a fundamental economic challenge to the preeminence of Russia's old aristocracy for, in the new Russia that was emerging, these "new men" were coming to control the most fundamental sources of prosperity. No longer could wealth be measured in terms of land and serfs. Now, it was calculated in terms of goods and commodities produced, profits earned, and resources owned or controlled. The full measure of a man's worth no longer could be stated simply by the genealogy he claimed or the ranks he held. For many of Russia's old aristocracy, the measurement of value and accomplishment in terms of money and merit threatened tragedy, even ruin.

Nowhere was this confrontation between the old order and the new described with greater sensitivity than in some of the works of Anton Chekhov. The eldest son of a provincial grocer and grandson of a serf, Chekhov held an M. D. degree from Moscow University, but his passion to probe clinically and dispassionately the frailties of the human character and personality soon drew him into the world of literature. His stories and plays captured the tensions that pulled at the fabric of everyday Russian life at the close of the nineteenth century. With particular sensitivity, Chekhov probed the confrontation between the dying world of aristocratic privilege and the dawning order of money and merit in a clash that proved more pathetic and tragic than monumental.

In his play *The Cherry Orchard*, Madame Ranevskaia, a middle-aged aristocratic widow, faces ruin as the inevitable price she must pay for her profligate ways and her inability to comprehend the social and economic changes that swirl around her. Ermolai Lopakhin, a former family serf who has prospered in business, attempts to explain how she might save her ancestral home from the auction block. Ranevskaia need only say the word, he explains, and he will order the estate's large cherry orchard cut down and its lands divided into smaller parcels that then can be leased to those nouveaux riches from the nearby city who want to build summer cottages. The rent alone would stave off foreclosure and leave Ranevskaia with a comfortable income. Spread throughout the play's first three acts, their conversation about Lopakhin's scheme shows the unbridgeable chasm that stands between the dying world of Russia's elegant Ranevskaias and the vibrant, practical new one that is emerging to replace it. "You'd have an income of at least twenty-five thousand rubles a year," Lopakhin explains. "Summer cottages and summer visitors?" Ranevskaia exclaims in reply. "Oh, forgive me, but it's all too vulgar."[151] Inevitably, the new world triumphs. Despite Lopakhin's urgings, Ranevskaia does nothing. Unwilling to pass up the chance for a handsome profit, Lopakhin himself buys the estate and hastens to cut down the cherry orchard so that he can lease out the land. Their ancestral home and lands lost, Ranevskaia and her brother seem strangely relieved, for they have been spared the pain of making a decision that would have done violence to their most cherished values.

Ranevskaia's plight was a microcosmic expression of the dilemmas that faced many upper-class Russians as traditional ideologies, values, and institutions came under attack from many quarters. With the coming of a new century, the attack grew stronger as Russia's laboring men and women did violence not only to Jews, but to factories, factory owners, and landlords' estates. Nicholas II had seen only sixty-eight strikes involving a mere thirty-one hundred workers during his first year on the throne. By the end of 1903, the annual number of strikes had risen to well over five hundred, and the number of workers involved had soared to nearly ninety thousand.[152] No longer could sensible and sensitive statesmen believe Plehve's assurances that revolutionary discontent was confined to an insignificant handful of small groups that the police need only discover and destroy to eradicate any threat to the nation's domestic peace.[153] In fact, Plehve himself no longer believed it. More decisive action was needed.

On those rare occasions when he took a stand, Nicholas II often chose to follow the wrong advice given by the wrong minister, and his behavior toward the end of 1903 proved no exception to that sad rule. "In order to suppress revolution," Plehve declared, "we need a small victorious war."[154] War Minister General Kuropatkin confided to his diary that Plehve hoped a war "would get the masses' attention away from political questions,"[155] and that certainly seemed to be his purpose in urging this new course upon his Emperor. A worse reason for waging war could not have been found, and most of Nicholas's ministers realized that Russia's further development required peace at all costs. For almost a decade they had tried to impress upon their Tsar that Russia simply lacked the wealth and industrial capacity to join in the arms race that consumed the resources of the Great Powers in Europe and, for a brief moment in the late 1890s, it seemed that Nicholas had understood the awful consequences of their warnings.

Unfortunately, Nicholas had not, and Plehve's urgings carried the day. Throughout 1903, Plehve's "small victorious war" lay just below Russia's Far Eastern horizon. Very soon, it loomed darkly into full view. Less than a month after they had celebrated the advent of 1904, Russians were at war with Japan in a conflict destined to be neither small nor victorious.

CHAPTER VII

"A Small Victorious War"

For almost a hundred years before Nicholas II ascended the throne, Russia's Tsars had made it a rule to keep their army at least half again as large as any other in Europe. They had used it against the West to win great glory for their Empire. Like a relentless tide arising from deep within the Eurasian continent, hundreds of thousands of Russian infantry had surged westward in 1813 to crush Napoleon and free Europe from his tyrannical grasp. Grateful for their liberation but fearful of its cost, Europe's statesmen spoke in awed tones of the colossus that had arisen beyond their eastern frontiers. As in the days of Peter the Great, they began to doubt the security of their borders. Might not the armies of the Tsar march again? And might not their nations fall before the Russians' irresistible advance?[1]

At the time of the European revolutions of 1830 and 1848, even the combined might of Austria and Prussia, the two greatest land powers in Europe, was dwarfed by the million-man army of their eastern neighbor as Nicholas I took firm command of Eastern Europe's defenses against the onslaught of the new revolutionary forces that had arisen in France. Everywhere, kings and politicians called Russia the Gendarme of Europe. "Have thousands of men in the past sacrificed their lives and well-being to see Germany today governed by the grace of Russia?" the great philologist Max Müller asked bitterly.[2] "The Emperor Nicholas I is master of Europe," Queen Victoria's consort Prince Albert confessed,[3] while Russia's Foreign Minister Count Karl Nesselrode proudly told his master that he had "become for the world the representative of the monarchical ideal, the mainstay of the principles of order and the impartial defender of European equilibrium."[4]

Nesselrode's grandiose estimate soon proved to have far less substance than anyone had anticipated. As the nineteenth century's technological revolution worked an awesome transformation in the nature of warfare, command of the largest army no longer held a reasonable promise of victory in war. Now, the nation whose soldiers carried the most modern weapons and whose industry was best able to replace lost armaments and move weapons, ammunition, and supplies to the front with the greatest speed was the one that could anticipate victory on the field of battle. Russia's embarrassing defeat by a much smaller Allied army in the Crimean War had readily proved this new military truth. Muzzle-loading English and French rifles, whose effective range exceeded that of Russia's smooth-bore infantry muskets by a mere hundred meters, wrought utter havoc in the war's first battles. "Whole regiments melted . . . while they were [attempting to come] into musket range," wrote a chagrined and desperate Russian officer. "I am convinced," he added, "that [the

Allied infantry] will cut us down as soon as we fight in the open."[5] Almost overnight, the invincible Russian colossus seemed to have acquired feet of clay.

The Crimean War witnessed only the very beginnings of what proved to be the greatest revolution in the tactical arsenal of the world's armies before the advent of nuclear weapons. The next quarter-century saw repeating rifles become the standard infantry weapon; during these same years, automatic weapons, the most deadly and fearsome of which was the machine gun, also entered their arsenals. The discovery of more powerful explosives led armaments makers to produce new alloys strong enough to contain their force, and the result was longer-range artillery of immense caliber. With their rate of fire no longer calculated in minutes but seconds, and their effective range measured in tens of kilometers, the great guns of Europe's armies began to reach farther and farther behind the front lines of the enemy to those staging areas and supply depots once thought immune from all but surprise cavalry attack. Armies grew even larger as Europe's spreading network of railroads made it possible to mobilize reserves and transport them to the front in days. In 1850, Russia had been the only nation in the world with a million-man army. By 1900, every European power could mobilize forces of at least that size.

Alfred Nobel's discovery of smokeless powder in the 1890s also had a profound effect on the nature of modern warfare. No longer did infantry and artillery fight in that choking haze of black-powder smoke that had confined the soldier's view of combat to a few square meters in most of history's earlier battles. Men now faced much larger fields of combat. By 1900, the infantry of every army in Europe carried rifles powerful enough to shatter a human tibia at ranges up to 4,500 meters. Heavy naval and land artillery fired projectiles weighing hundreds of pounds at targets far beyond their gunners' vision and often well below the horizon. By the beginning of the twentieth century, infantrymen in the world's modern armies carried twenty times the ammunition, their rifles had twenty times the effective range, and they could be fired twenty times faster than the weapons of their counterparts a half-century before. Wrote one self-proclaimed Russian expert in the 1890s, "even with the weapons now adopted, the effectiveness of fire presents the possibility of total mutual annihilation."[6]

But weapons had also grown astronomically more expensive. According to the best calculations, the Crimean War had cost Russia something more than a million rubles a day. Thirty years later, experts estimated that it would cost her at least seven times that amount just to put her armies into the field in any European war. At that rate, three weeks of war would draw more from the Imperial Treasury than the entire 1812–15 campaign, from the moment Napoleon had invaded Russia until his final defeat at Waterloo. These estimates did not take into account the immense cost of the weapons themselves. Nor did they include any replacements for those that inevitably would be lost or destroyed in combat. Those costs soared with every year that passed as more complex weapons made even decade-old arsenals obsolete. In the mid-1890s, knowledgeable financiers estimated that to rearm *only the infantry* of Russia would cost over a billion rubles; artillery and naval costs were far, far greater. Even for heavily industrialized European nations, such expenditures were burdensome; for Russia they threatened fiscal ruin. Russia's inefficient and backward industry made weapons production more expensive, and the sheer size of her wartime forces (almost three million in 1896) promised to make hers the most costly army of any in Europe to keep in the field. Russia could not afford to go to war—as Witte and a number of other sensible Imperial ministers realized. She could scarcely pay the cost of rearming her infantry with modern rifles.

Perhaps the man most diligent in his efforts to deflect his country from what he thought was a ruinous course, was Ivan Stanislavovich Bliokh, a Warsaw-born converted Jew who had helped to develop Russia's railroads. A successful banker and a self-educated man with a passion to learn more, Bliokh devoted the last decade of his life to studying the state of the world's armaments. Toward the end of the 1890s, he published a monumental six-volume work, *The Future of War,* in which he drew disquieting, almost apocalyptic, conclusions about the future course of human history if the world's statesmen allowed the arms race to continue unchecked.

Unlike the pacifists of Europe and America, Bliokh did not direct his concern at the immorality of war and killing. He was certain that modern war would bring economic ruin to aggressor and victim alike and opposed the arms race for that reason. Quoting the oft-repeated words of the famous Habsburg General Count Montecuculli that "to wage war, you need first of all money; second, you need money, and, third, you also need money,"[8] Bliokh argued that the soaring cost of armaments already had made war a practical impossibility for smaller nations. Any war among major powers, he insisted, would prove suicidal because modern soldiers would kill each other by the millions at costs that would threaten the economic survival of all modern states. Rulers and statesmen thus must act soberly but quickly to avert catastrophe. In a truly prophetic preface to his work, he warned that a European war probably would lead to the destruction of the continent's reigning dynasties through revolution. "What the governments all will soon come to see more or less clearly," he once told the Manchester *Guardian*'s W. T. Steed, "is that, if they persist in squandering the resources of their people in order to prepare for a war which has already become impossible without suicide, they will only be preparing the triumph of the socialist revolution."[9]

Time has proved that Bliokh overestimated the destructive capability of the world's armaments and the economic dislocations that a European war would produce. Nonetheless, his warnings penetrated the inner reaches of the Russian government, where a number of statesmen, especially Minister of War Kuropatkin, realized that the arms race already had exceeded Russia's limited resources. In mid-1898, Kuropatkin learned to his chagrin that Austria had begun to reequip her artillery with rapid-firing weapons that rendered Russia's slower-firing field guns obsolete. At a cost that already strained her military budget to the limit, Russia had just begun to rearm her infantry with smaller-caliber repeating rifles that fired more rapidly and at much greater effective range than those clumsy breechloaders her foot soldiers had carried into the Russo-Turkish War of 1877–78. Unable to match the Austrians' resources, Kuropatkin sought a mutual agreement to slow the pace of an arms race in which Russia could not hope to catch up. Witte called

Kuropatkin's proposals "utterly childish" and vehemently opposed any discussions that might reveal the precarious state of the Imperial exchequer. Instead of Kuropatkin's proposed pact with Austria, he urged Foreign Minister Count Mikhail Muravev to support a general European conference on arms limitation. "I considered it to be in the very best interests of Europe in particular and of the world in general if some limits could be set upon armaments," he later wrote. In fact, Witte expected nothing to come from any such conference, but he thought that the effort could do Russia's interests no harm.[10] At his urging, Nicholas approved the plan, and in August 1898, Muravev appealed to all European powers to assemble at the Hague to discuss a moratorium on the development and production of new weapons.

Thus it was Russia and Nicholas II—a weak nation and a far weaker Emperor—who set in motion the forces that brought the first Hague Conference together in May 1899. Few took the effort very seriously. The Prince of Wales called the Russian proposals "the greatest rubbish and nonsense I ever heard of," while the Kaiser snorted that it was absurd to imagine a monarch "dissolving his regiments sacred with a hundred years of history . . . and handing over his towns to Anarchists and Democracy."[11] Ever realistic, Witte simply warned Nicholas not to expect much to come of the entire venture. "The sacred truths of Christianity were set forth by Christ and his Apostles some two thousand years ago and the vast majority of people are utterly indifferent to them still. . . . In the same manner," he went on, "it will require many centuries before the idea of the peaceful settlement of conflicts between nations will have any practical consequences."[12] True to all expectations, the Hague Conference produced no limits upon weapons production, and the quickening pace of Europe's first great arms race never faltered as the twentieth century opened. Nicholas, too, never seriously considered any limitations upon his Empire's armaments other than those imposed by fiscal and economic constraints; in fact, he seemed more attracted to war, as a number of ambitious and unscrupulous advisers turned his attention toward the Far East. There his Empire's superiority in armaments was thought to be fully as great as that of Europe's Great Powers in relation to Russia.

A decisive turn to the Far East had been a notable feature of Russian foreign policy from the moment Alexander III ordered construction to begin on the Trans-Siberian Railway, and it intensified throughout the first decade of Nicholas's reign. Like the other Great Powers, Russia became increasingly involved in the affairs of China, Korea, and Japan.[13] Unlike them, however, she was in a position to bring vast military and economic pressures to bear in the Far East once the completion of the Trans-Siberian Railway in October 1901 brought Moscow to within a mere thirteen days of Vladivostok, the Empire's bastion on the Pacific. No longer would it take eighteen months for troops to travel the arduous roads and water routes from European Russia to the Empire's Far Eastern territories.[14] Equally important, once the Trans-Siberian was completed, Russia's railroad system became the shortest, least expensive route from Western Europe to the Far East. The forty-five-day journey by sea through the Suez Canal had been shortened to less than three weeks' travel across the seven thousand miles of Nicholas's domains.[15] Russia had acquired a new and enviable position as intermediary in Europe's Far Eastern trade at the same time as she became uniquely able among European powers to defend her interests in the region.

Witte's precepts guided Russian policy in the Far East throughout the 1890s, and they were calculated to reap the most rewards at the least cost. Witte once warned that "militarism creates a class interested in war and thus promotes the likelihood of war."[16] No doubt he had the Kaiser and his Prussian lords in mind. He urged a policy of peace everywhere, including the Far East where he thought it especially suited to Russia's purposes. "In contrast with the Western powers, which aim at economic and frequently even political subjugation of the peoples of the East," he insisted, "Russia's mission in the East must be a protective and educational one. It is Russia's natural task to guard her neighboring Eastern lands which lie in her sphere of influence against the excessive political and colonial claims of the other powers."[17]

Such a policy demanded consistent firmness and unerring resolve from a Tsar who was singularly unable to provide either. Nor
were the Imperial Grand Dukes and the motley crew of hangers-on
with whom Nicholas and Aleksandra surrounded themselves of
much use. "No moral force whatsoever can be felt," lamented the
longtime State Council member Aleksandr Polovtsov. "The Emperor has not the necessary training, nor has he the experience in
affairs of state. In particular, he lacks strength of character. . . .
Among the members of the Imperial family, the majority work only
for personal gain."[18] Remarked Witte somewhat ruefully, "Ours is
a regime in which intrigue plays an unseemly role."[19] While strug-
gling to keep his complex policies in proper balance, Witte continu-
ally had to fight for his own political survival at Nicholas's Court.
Under the best conditions it was a difficult task; foreign crises whose
origins lay utterly beyond his control made it impossible for him to
succeed.[20]

Witte's Far Eastern policy suffered its first serious setback in
1897, when Russia seized Port Arthur on the Liaotung Peninsula
and forced China to grant her the concession to build a railroad
connecting it to Harbin, the key center in Witte's plan to strengthen
Russian economic influence in Manchuria. Instinctively, Witte
sensed that his nation had crossed the Rubicon and embarked upon
a more aggressive, more dangerous expansionist course from which
it would be immensely difficult to turn aside.[21] Then, when the
Chinese Boxer Rebellion of 1900 damaged parts of Russia's newly
built Manchurian railroads, even Witte found himself obliged to
urge further military occupation of the region. Greater numbers of
Russian troops in the Far East made it tempting to extend Russian
interests still further, a course ardently advocated by a group of
adventurers centered on Aleksandr Bezobrazov, a retired Imperial
Guards officer whose friendship with Minister of the Imperial Court
Count Vorontsov-Dashkov and a number of others who had led the
Sacred Guard in the early days of Alexander III's reign brought him
to Nicholas's attention. For many years, it was thought that the
shady dealings and shameless speculations that Bezobrazov and his
friends pursued in Korea actually dragged Russia into war with

Japan. Scholars have since acquitted them of that charge, but none would dispute that their plottings were important in causing Witte's fall from the Ministry of Finance in 1903 and in gaining for the incompetent Admiral Evgenii Alekseev an appointment as Russia's Viceroy in the Far East.[22] Both events left Russia less able to cope with the rapidly worsening diplomatic situation in Manchuria and Korea.

All of this added confusion to Russia's Far Eastern policy just when her aspirations in Manchuria and Korea came into serious conflict with those of Japan. Unlike China's tradition-bound Mandarins and corrupt warlords, Japan's rulers and statesmen had launched a remarkably effective modernization effort during the last third of the nineteenth century. As a result, Japan acquired a modern industrial establishment and a modern army and navy in the brief space of thirty years. Trained by German army officers and British sea captains, Japan's armed forces quickly overshadowed those of her Far Eastern neighbors and, even in the 1880s, she began to seek footholds on the Asian mainland. Their particular interest in Korea brought the Japanese directly into conflict with China and, soon afterward, with Russia. Throughout these early skirmishes, Japan's great weakness remained her need for foreign oil and foreign iron, both of which had to be brought in by sea, but that became a far less serious disability by 1902 when she signed an alliance with Great Britain that recognized her special interest in Korea.[23]

Although Russian statesmen consistently underestimated them, the Japanese had become a military force to be reckoned with by the opening of the twentieth century. According to the best estimates, Japan could mobilize an army of just over a million men, arm them with new Arisaka repeating rifles, and support them with artillery of the latest design. To be sure, the Japanese officer corps was young and still inexperienced, but many of its members boasted a glorious *samurai* heritage that guaranteed they would not flinch under fire.[24] On balance, it was an effective, well-armed force that Japan's leaders commanded to protect their new interests on the Asian mainland. To defend her vital interests in Korea, Japan had gone to war with China in 1894, quickly defeated China's army near

Pyongyang, destroyed much of her northern fleet near the mouth of the Yalu River, and won control of the Yellow Sea.[25]

Japan's victorious advance into Korea and the Liaotung Peninsula (from which she soon withdrew under pressure from the Great Powers) brought her into direct conflict with Russia's new policy of aggressive expansion in those same regions. Ostensibly in a last effort to preserve peace, negotiations continued throughout 1903 in St. Petersburg and Tokyo, although it seems quite possible that the Japanese pursued them only in order to provide some justification for their attack the following year.[26] Before he left the Ministry of Finance to take up his impressive-sounding but far less influential duties as President of the Council of Ministers, Witte had warned that "an armed clash with Japan would be a great disaster for us."[27] Nicholas, it seems, had belatedly realized the truth of Witte's words and seems to have honestly decided to work for peace. "I do not desire war between Russia and Japan, and I shall not permit it," he warned his Viceroy Alekseev in October.[28] "War is absolutely impossible [now]," he insisted to Kuropatkin some two months later. "Time—that is Russia's best ally. Every year strengthens us further."[29] Still, Russia remained so intractable in demanding that Japan cede her entire sphere of influence in northern Korea that there seemed little hope for any accommodation. In fact, there were those in the West who openly wondered why Japan even bothered to continue a diplomatic process that seemed utterly hopeless. "What is really wrong with us is that we have yellow skins," one Japanese remarked to a German visitor. "If our skins were as white as yours, the whole world would rejoice at our calling a halt to Russia's inexorable aggressions."[30]

Faced by Russia's unwillingness to compromise in Korea and her refusal to withdraw any of the troops she had agreed to remove from Manchuria some two years before, Japan's senior statesmen knew by 1904 that they had little choice but to go to war. Still certain that these "little short-tailed monkeys" would give way,[31] Nicholas once more warned them that there was a limit to what he thought of as Russia's overly generous forbearance, and he did so in a manner that made clear his disdain for those not of his race. He

was convinced, Witte later wrote, "that, although a few reinforce-
ments might be needed, Japan would be smashed to smithereens."[32]
When he heard these last warnings, Kurino Shinichiro, Japan's
Ambassador to St. Petersburg, already knew that his superiors' patience had been exhausted. As Kurino bowed respectfully before
Nicholas at the New Year reception at Tsarskoe Selo, the Japanese
General Staff had begun to mass transports and load troops at
Moji.[33] Only a Russian diplomatic capitulation could have changed
the orders at that point. "There is no peace party [in Japan] now,"
their ambassador confided to Britain's Foreign Secretary Lord Lans-
downe, who came away from their meeting certain that "nothing
short of a complete acceptance of the Japanese proposals [by Russia]
would avert war."[34] The myth of white supremacy was about to be
put to a true test for the first time in modern history as Europeans
and Asians armed with modern weapons faced each other in Manchuria.

At eight o'clock on the evening of January 26, 1904, Nicholas
and the Empress Aleksandra entered the Imperial box in St. Petersburg's Mariinskii Theater. The great painted ceiling, the blue walls
set off by ornate carvings covered with gold leaf, and the huge crystal
chandelier, now ablaze with the light of hundreds of recently added
electric bulbs, all projected a warm and comforting glow that contrasted sharply with the wet snow and icy wind that raged outside.
The performance that night was to be Aleksandr Dargomyzhskii's
Rusalka, an opera based on Pushkin's famous tale about a miller's
daughter seduced and betrayed by a young nobleman. It promised
to be a memorable performance, and one that Nicholas seemed quite
prepared to enjoy. The preceding days had been especially difficult,
and he must have been anxious to put thoughts of international
crises temporarily aside. Just two days before, Ambassador Kurino
had broken off negotiations and had left St. Petersburg with his
entire staff.[35]

Kurino's departure had left Nicholas in a fatalistic mood. "War
is war, and peace is peace. But this business of not knowing either
way is agonizing," he had told General Kuropatkin.[36] He seemed to
feel that it would be a relief just to have the decision made one way

or the other. "All day I was in an excited mood," he confessed when Minister of Foreign Affairs Count Lamsdorf, Kuropatkin, and several others assembled to discuss the situation with him. He found a certain consolation in their decision "not to start anything." At least for the moment, he could turn his attention to *Rusalka*, which he later pronounced "very good" indeed.[37]

Eight o'clock on the evening of that same day found Vice-Admiral Togo Heihachiro, commander of the Japanese fleet, far away from anything resembling the luxurious comfort of Nicholas's surroundings. In every direction, he could see only the cold, dark sea, as his fleet of eleven destroyers steamed west by northwest at full speed. At that moment, Togo's fleet was some fifty miles southeast of the southern tip of the Liaotung Peninsula. Unknown to anyone except himself and his superiors in Tokyo, Admiral Togo was going to begin the Russo-Japanese War in just a little less than four hours from that moment by an attack against Port Arthur, where most of the capital ships of the Imperial Russian Pacific Fleet lay at anchor. Among the vessels in the roadstead were seven battleships, led by the flagship *Petropavlovsk*, and including the *Tsesarevich*, one of the most modern ships in the fleet, purchased only a few months before from the shipyards of France. Togo's object was to destroy them all. To complete his mission, he needed speed, surprise, and a measure of very good luck.[38]

While Admiral Togo and his ships' crews steamed resolutely toward Port Arthur, the Russians against whom their guns and torpedoes soon would be directed were scandalously unprepared. Not one gun on the battleships was manned or loaded, and only one ship's searchlights were in use. Port Arthur's shore batteries stood immobile, still heavily coated with grease to help them withstand the fierce winter storms. The single battery of five permanently mounted long-range ten-inch guns on Electric Cliff could not be fired for several hours because they had no fluid in their recoil cylinders.[39] As Viceroy in command of Russia's defenses in the Far East, Admiral Alekseev was very well aware of his country's worsening relations with Japan. At least ten days before, he had received accurate reports that the Japanese had assembled enough naval transports and troop carriers to move up to six divisions, and he had even requested Nicholas to allow him to order a full-scale mobilization of all troops in the Far East.[40] But Alekseev had failed to order his commanders to prepare defensive measures in case the Japanese should attack. Rear Admiral Oskar Stark, commander of the fleet that lay in Port Arthur harbor, had given orders that no torpedo nets should be put in place. "Don't raise any alarm," he admonished those officers who protested. All ships, he added, were to leave all lights burning. As his superior, Alekseev raised no objections to these irresponsible orders.[41] Such shocking lapses in common sense came as no surprise to some in Russia's High Command. Not three weeks had passed since acting Naval Chief of Staff Admiral Zinovii Rozhestvenskii had warned Nicholas that Alekseev was a man who always placed his personal pride above duty to the Empire and that under his command Port Arthur would be defenseless if war broke out.[42]

Just as at Pearl Harbor, some thirty-eight years later, the Japanese struck without warning. Even more incredible than at Pearl Harbor, they attacked at much closer quarters, yet still took their enemy completely by surprise. At 11:35 P.M., Admiral Togo's destroyers steamed into the roadstead, pulled alongside the Russian battleships, fired torpedoes into their hulls, and turned away at top speed. Within minutes, the battleships *Retvizan* and *Tsesarevich* and several lesser ships including the cruiser *Pallada* had gaping holes blown in their hulls. Alekseev was reading a book in his palace study when he heard the first explosions. Not wanting to interrupt his reading, he sent an orderly to investigate and actually accepted his report that the firing was merely a part of a fleet exercise until he received word of the attack from other quarters.[43] Alekseev's was easily one of the most shocking command failures in Russia's military history. Not one of Togo's ships was damaged; in fact, he set up a blockade with them that put the surviving Russian ships out of action. Even before war was officially declared, the Japanese thus had seized command of the sea in the Far East. Now able to land troops and supplies on the mainland at will, they occupied all of Korea and drove northward toward the Yalu River and Manchuria without serious opposition from the Russians.[44]

Word of the Japanese attack on Port Arthur reached St. Petersburg some three hours after it began. It came not from Alekseev's headquarters but from a Far Eastern commercial agent, whose telegram his counterpart in St. Petersburg took to Witte. Although it was around midnight, Witte hastened to the home of an amazed and incredulous Kuropatkin who, in turn, hurried to confer with Admiral Avelan, Chief of Russia's Admiralty. By then more than five hours had passed since the *Tsesarevich* and *Retvizan* had been torpedoed, but Avelan still had no word from Alekseev.[45] At that point, some influential Russians had grown so disgusted with the Viceroy's incompetence that Prince Vladimir Meshcherskii, editor of the influential conservative newspaper *Grazhdanin*, reportedly got down on his knees and begged Nicholas to remove him from command.[46] The Tsar did nothing. From the moment Togo fired the first torpedo of the Russo-Japanese War, Russia's Far Eastern forces felt the dead weight of timid, slow-witted senior officers and the frustration of impossibly bad communications.

If inept field command, unreliable communications, and an Emperor who was hardly cut from the cloth that makes bold leaders were not sufficient handicaps, Russia's armed forces were burdened by training that had not prepared them to wage war against a well-trained, well-armed enemy in the Far East. At the same time, they faced awesome transportation and supply problems. A victim of its planners' shortsightedness, the Trans-Siberian Railway remained bisected by Lake Baikal, some thirteen thousand square miles of water that lay directly in its path in eastern Siberia. To save the expense of constructing the especially costly stretch of track around the lake's southern tip, the builders of the railway decided to ferry freight and passengers across it. That proved an adequate, though awkward, stopgap measure so long as no great amount of heavy freight had to pass across the lake. Like a number of senior officers, Kuropatkin foresaw the immense difficulties that this bottleneck would create for supplying troops should a war break out in the Far East. From the moment he became War Minister, he urged that the eastern and western banks of the lake be linked by rail with all speed. Of necessity, the work moved at a snail's pace, while upwards of forty tunnels were blasted through the mountains to complete a mere 250 *versty* of track. A month before war broke out, Kuropatkin estimated that another sixteen months would be needed to finish the link, even if work went ahead at top speed. Until then, enough ammunition, weapons, food, medicine, and clothing would have had to be laid in on Baikal's eastern shore before the end of the winter to last the army until after the spring thaw, when breaking ice stopped all movement on the lake.

Because neither Alekseev nor Nicholas expected Japan to attack Russia during the early months of 1904, no such stockpiles had been prepared, and Russia's soldiers would pay a heavy price for that neglect. The first reinforcements from European Russia did not reach the Far Eastern theater of the war until June, and more than seven months passed before they arrived in force. To take the place of the hundred thousand men killed, wounded, or sickened by disease during the first months of war in Manchuria, Russian commanders received a mere twenty-one thousand replacements. "With our troops reaching the front drop by drop, as it were, we lost all hope . . . of seizing the initiative," Kuropatkin later wrote.[47]

These problems notwithstanding, Nicholas approached the war with confidence. He did not like to think about the bloodshed and suffering that any war would bring to his people, but the thought that Japan might severely challenge Russia's armed might seems never to have crossed his mind. He also remained blissfully unconcerned about how the war would be financed. True, his treasury had begun to show a surplus after a decade of Witte's careful management, but its balance remained precarious. The cost of even a short war would undo all that Witte had accomplished, but Nicholas thought of the money needed to fight Japan as a short-term loan at best. It would be more than recovered, he assured Witte, by the reparations Russia would extract from the Japanese once the war was won.[48] In the meantime, Kaiser Wilhelm, Nicholas's cousin "Willy," preached about the Yellow Peril and Russia's great mission in the East. Nicholas seemed not to notice that the Kaiser reserved for himself the title of "Admiral of the Atlantic" when he began to call his cousin "Nicky" the "Admiral of the Pacific." Nor did Nicholas see fit to remember that every German Chancellor since the great Bismarck had turned Russia's attention from Europe to Asia whenever possible, a principle of diplomacy that the Kaiser considered almost sacrosanct. In strictest confidence, Wilhelm had told his ministers that "we must try to tie Russia down in East Asia so that she pays less attention to Europe and the Near East."[49]

However much the flattery of the Kaiser and the reassuring claims of such prowar advisers as Alekseev, Plehve, and Bezobrazov may have stirred Nicholas's confidence, nothing could have touched his emotions as deeply as the spontaneous popular demonstrations that greeted word of the attack on Port Arthur. On January 30, thousands of students gathered in St. Petersburg's Palace Square and went on to join an even larger rally that marched along the Nevskii Prospekt to the Anichkov Palace where they sang "God Save the Tsar!" and cheered Russia's army. "Everyone was mixed together," wrote the reporter of the weekly *Niva*. "Generals and tramps marched side-by-side, students with banners, and ladies, their arms filled with shopping. Everyone was united in one general feeling."[50] "The outpouring of feeling exceeded that of any recent war—the Crimean War, the Balkan encounters, the Turkish War," one commentator wrote recently.[51] That feeling was deeply tinged with a racism that war with the British, the French, or even the Turks had never awakened in the breasts of Russians. Russians were incensed that an Asiatic people, in their minds inferior by definition, should have dared to attack the great Russian Empire.

During those first euphoric days of war, when he felt that his people stood behind him against all enemies, Nicholas wanted to "share the danger and privations of the army," but allowed his uncle, Grand Duke Aleksei Aleksandrovich, to dissuade him from going to the Far East.[52] He settled for reviewing troops and passing out images of St. Seraphim to soldiers waiting to leave for the front,[53] while Aleksandra threw herself into the war effort in other ways. "We resigned ourselves to an almost complete cessation of balls and parties," her close friend Anna Vyrubova recalled. "The great salons of the Winter Palace were turned into workrooms, and every day society flocked to sew and knit for our soldiers and sailors fighting such incredible distances away. . . . Every day the Empress came to inspect the work, often sitting down at a table and sewing diligently with the others."[54] Images of St. Seraphim and mittens knitted by the Empress and her friends did little to offset the army's disabilities and privations in the Far East. Outgeneraled, outmaneuvered, and undersupplied, the Russians at first stood little chance against those *makaki*—"little short-tailed monkeys"—as the press, having seized upon Nicholas's phrase, now called the Japanese. The government might print tens of thousands of postcards with "gaudy representations in blue, and red, and yellow, of a giant Russian guardsman bayoneting a wizened Japanese," as the British correspondent Douglas Story reported,[55] but it could not change the fact that the Japanese continued to defeat the Russians in every major engagement.

In Port Arthur itself, Togo's attack against carelessly defended ships and unprepared land fortifications marked only the beginning of a debacle the Russians were obliged to endure for just one week short of eleven months. During the first two months of the war, catastrophe followed upon catastrophe as the Russians found that unwieldy ships and badly trained crews produced a wretched combat force. Although capable of much higher speeds, Russian ships could not hold their places in battle formation if they steamed faster than twelve knots. Even at that snail's pace, they could not take evasive action without risk of ramming each other, and that made them easy targets for Japanese gunners on those rare occasions when they steamed out to engage the enemy.[56] Although far from daring in the strategy he pursued after January 26, Togo thus took a heavy toll upon the ships that ventured out of Port Arthur to attack his formations. By the end of March, he could report three battleships—the *Tsesarevich, Pobeda,* and *Retvizan*—damaged, in addition to three cruisers and three destroyers, the *Baian, Pallada, Boiarin, Steregu-shchii, Vnushitelnyi,* and *Bezstrashnyi.* In March, Togo's gunners sank the destroyer *Strashnyi,* and a few days after the first Japanese attack, the minelayer *Enisei* had been blown to bits by one of her own mines. The *Enisei* proved to be a particularly costly loss, for it turned out that there was no record (aside from the one kept in the sunken ship's own log) of where she had laid her mines. For several weeks, the Russians had to search not only for Japanese mines but for those laid by one of their own ships. There was more disaster to come. After a brief engagement at the end of March, the flagship *Petropavlovsk* blew up, killing nearly all of her officers and crew, including Admiral Stepan Makarov, one of the most talented senior officers in Russia's navy. It is likely that one of the *Enisei's* still unlocated mines killed Makarov and sank his flagship.[57]

After Makarov's death, the Russian fleet remained under the shelter of the fortress guns while the Japanese prepared a land and sea operation that would place all of Port Arthur under siege. At the end of April, Alekseev moved to Harbin, far from any threat of combat. His last instructions to the senior naval officers who remained behind were that they should "talk over" how they might launch a sea attack against those Japanese transports that were landing troops to cut off Port Arthur's land communications to Manchuria.[58] As they assembled for that purpose, the first words of their new commander, Admiral Wilhelm Witheft, were far from reassuring: "Gentlemen, I expect you to assist me with words and deeds. I am no leader of a fleet."[59]

It was not until long after the Japanese transports had discharged their cargo and the troops had closed in upon Port Arthur that the Russian naval forces under Witheft's command attempted to engage the enemy once again. Acting upon orders from Alekseev that he take "every precaution" and attack the enemy at the "most favorable moment," Witheft announced on June 7 that "with the help of God and St. Nicholas the Miracle-Worker, the patron of all seafarers, we shall endeavor to do our duty, fulfill our oaths to the Sovereign, and defeat the enemy."[60]

Despite his apparent pessimism, Witheft commanded a powerful force of seven cruisers, six destroyers, and six great battleships: the *Poltava, Sevastopol,* and *Peresvet,* as well as the *Tsesarevich, Retvizan,* and *Pobeda,* all of which had been fully repaired and made ready for battle. With them all in formation, he sailed early on the morning of June 10 to do battle with Admiral Togo. At first sight of Togo's fleet, he turned and raced the twenty miles back to

Port Arthur. In hot pursuit, the Japanese fired almost forty torpedoes. Incredibly, not one found its mark, and Witheft's only casualty was the *Sevastopol*, which struck a mine as she sped into the harbor.[61] Russia's admirals had bungled again, and Togo could claim another victory.

After Witheft's resounding failure, the battle for Port Arthur shifted from sea to land. During the spring, General Baron Nogi Maresuke's entire Third Japanese Army had disembarked well to the north of Port Arthur and had begun to fight its way down the Liaotung Peninsula in an advance that was a carbon copy of the 1894 campaign in which they had seized Port Arthur from the Chinese. By the middle of July, Nogi had cut all land communication between Port Arthur and the Asian mainland and the siege was on. Blockaded by the Japanese navy, and with Nogi's four divisions standing between them and the main body of Russia's forces that General Kuropatkin now commanded in Manchuria, the fate of Port Arthur and its garrison of some forty-two thousand men lay in the hands of General Anatolii Stoessel. With large supplies of food, ammunition, and weapons ready at hand, Stoessel was far better prepared to face his foe than were many of history's siege commanders. Although there was less than a month's supply of fresh beef, the fortress storerooms bulged with enough flour, salt, dried vegetables, and fodder to feed the entire garrison and its forty-five hundred horses for at least half a year. At any point, the horses could be slaughtered and eaten.[62]

The general's main task was to strengthen and defend the twenty-nine kilometers of coastal and land defenses that surrounded Port Arthur. When they seized Port Arthur in 1898, the Russians had begun to modernize and extend its fortifications, but, in typical Russian fashion, very little seemed to have been accomplished. Stoessel therefore had no defenses that could withstand heavy artillery and mortar bombardment. Iron and steel plates to protect gun emplacements were scarce, and no one had thought to lay in stores of barbed wire, that hateful device that had recently become a part of modern defense perimeters. Nor was there much else to place as obstacles against an infantry advance, although at one point it occurred to an ingenious Russian engineer to run some four thousand volts of electricity through plain wires strung in front of Russian positions. It was an innovation whose potential its creator never appreciated, but it struck deathly fear into the hearts of the otherwise valorous Japanese infantry. After writing of the courage with which Japanese soldiers faced death, one correspondent reported that the electric wire, hidden among other wire entanglements, "spread terror in the ranks of the soldiers and caused even the bravest to hesitate."[63] Still, electrified wires could be cleared away with a few well-placed artillery rounds, and the Russians never bothered to use it on a large scale in any case.

The Russians' inability to erect physical barriers against infantry assault was a more serious impediment to Stoessel's defense plans than it would have been in other armies because his soldiers were such notoriously poor marksmen. "The Russian soldier is the worst shot in any great army in Europe," wrote the British military observer General Sir Ian Hamilton, as he described an earlier battle that had been fought near the Yalu River. "The river should have been filled with dead and wounded," he continued in his report. "The [Russian] defenders had the precise range, and it was only 300 to 800 yards from their trenches. Actually, no very serious damage was done."[64] Nonetheless, there were other factors in Stoessel's favor in addition to his large store of provisions. He had a total of 646 pieces of artillery, the largest being the great ten-inch guns on the Electric Cliff. A number of them were quick-firing weapons, and he had well over a quarter-million shells in his arsenal. Beyond that, his infantry's poor marksmanship could be somewhat compensated for by the sixty-two machine guns he placed in his defense perimeters.[65] Most of all, his men needed courage and fortitude, for they had lost battle after battle as they fell back before Nogi's attacks for dozens of kilometers along the Liaotung Peninsula. They could retreat no farther. "Dead or alive, you are to hold your assigned defensive positions," Stoessel ordered. "Remember that you are renowned Russian soldiers!"[66]

What General Stoessel required from the Port Arthur garrison was what Russia's soldiers always had done best. As their grandfathers had at Sevastopol a half-century before, they took up positions to defend one of the great fortresses on the fringes of their Tsar's domains. All the doubts and uncertainties that had plagued these Russian peasant infantrymen during Nogi's advance faded. They now knew the direction from which their enemy would attack, and they fought on terrain that was unchanging and familiar. The massed fire in volleys they had been trained to give could compensate for their poor marksmanship against assault troops at close range and, unlike most infantry, Russian foot soldiers relished hand-to-hand combat. Bayonets had been their favorite weapons since the days of Peter the Great; in the 1790s, the great Field Marshal Suvorov had built the tactics with which he defeated the armies of revolutionary France around them.

At exorbitant cost, General Baron Nogi learned these hard truths about Russian soldiers on August 6. In grand style, he assured a recently arrived group of European war correspondents that they had arrived "just in time to see the conclusion of a victorious campaign."[67] At 4:30 A.M. he opened his attack with a general bombardment from 360 guns ranging from the light mountain guns of his Ninth and Eleventh divisions to the heavy 6-inch howitzers and ultramodern 4.2-inch Krupp guns of his siege artillery battalions. He followed this up with massed assaults against the entire perimeter of Port Arthur's outer defenses. As the Russian defenders shredded the attackers' ranks with heavy machine-gun and point-blank artillery fire, the Japanese forces lost some of that cohesion and synchronization that they had used to such good advantage in earlier battles. Enormous casualties broke the Japanese assault into smaller, disconnected actions as Nogi's field commanders led their men forward again and again, only to be driven back by furious Russian counterattacks whenever they seized a brief advantage. When Nogi called off the assault six days later, his forces had seized a few Russian outposts at a cost of almost twenty thousand men. Clearly, the Third Japanese Army was in for a long and bloody siege. Weeks, even months, must pass before General Nogi could expect success from a general assault against the Russian defenses.[68] He proved to be more impatient than he should have been.

By September 6, Nogi was ready to try the Russians again. After a furious bombardment, he again unleashed his infantry battalions in assault after assault against the Russian positions. On both sides, dead and wounded mounted as the fighting grew more intense. Hospitals overflowed as wounded were brought in faster than doctors could treat them. For surgeons on both sides, the war had become especially horrendous because it saw the first large-scale use of the new weapons whose untested destructive power had led Bliokh to conclude that modern armies would annihilate each other in battle. Bliokh's predictions proved inaccurate, but the number of wounds, especially multiple wounds, sustained by Japanese and Russian soldiers was immense. Foreign medical observers found that the slightly larger and heavier Russian rifle bullet* was by far the more destructive, although its Japanese counterpart inflicted a slightly greater percentage of instant kills at ranges under 150 meters because of its higher initial velocity. "Wounds due to the Russian bullet were always of a much more severe character," reported Maj. Charles Lynch, an observer from the Medical Department of the U. S. Army's General Staff. "In fact, practically all bullet wounds involving bone caused by the Russian bullet suppurated, while many produced by the Japanese did not do so."[69]

For more than a decade, ordnance officers on the general staffs of the world's armies had advocated infantry weapons of ever-smaller caliber to enable their infantrymen to carry greater numbers of lighter cartridges into combat. Major Lynch's observations convinced him that the Japanese, who carried one of the world's smallest caliber infantry weapons, had reached the point of diminishing returns. One wondered, he wrote, "if the Japanese have not carried their desire for long range, flat trajectory, and lighter weight of cartridge too far, and have thus sacrificed the stopping power of the bullet to such an extent that their weapon does not yield the best

---

*Russia's standard infantry rifle fired a 7.6mm-caliber bullet weighing 13.7 grams at a muzzle velocity of 2,015 feet per second, while the Japanese Arisaka rifle was chambered for a 6.5mm 10.5 gram round that developed a muzzle velocity of 2,356 feet per second.

results in war."[70] Nonetheless, Japanese rifles inflicted their share of wounds upon the Russians and, if they tended to be less severe, that deficiency was more than offset by the clumsiness with which the Russians treated them. Russian surgeons usually employed far more radical procedures than their colleagues in Europe, the United States, or Japan. They performed amputations regularly in cases where careful surgery could have saved a limb and even returned a soldier to combat. "They've gotten so used to hacking and sawing at the human body every day that they discuss operations and human life like a bunch of cobblers talking about old boots!" one Port Arthur civilian said of the doctors he saw at work in the Russian military hospital.[71] Even when not doing amputations, Russian surgeons often cut extensively and carelessly, "without reference to the direction of the muscles, the fibres of which were ruthlessly cut traversely," according to Lynch's account. Himself a surgeon, Lynch was appalled and termed some Russian surgical techniques "so unjustifiable as to be almost criminal."[72] A far greater number of men were sent home as cripples than was necessary. Russians therefore had in their midst tens of thousands of living monuments to the dark shadow that modern war would cast across a nation as they entered the last decade before the outbreak of the Great War.

Crippled or not, none of the Russians wounded in Port Arthur were destined to move anywhere until their commanders or the Japanese admitted defeat. That time seemed very distant in mid-September as both forces continued to fight to a standoff. After four days of the most bitter fighting, the Japanese captured a few minor Russian positions, the most important of which was called the Waterworks Redoubt, a part of Port Arthur's water supply system. At best, it was but a small breach in the Russians' defenses for the redoubt occupied no significant strategic position and there were more than enough wells within Port Arthur to supply its defenders with water. Thus it was not the Japanese but the Russians who instantly cut off all water from the Waterworks Redoubt for fear that their enemy might try to poison their fortress water supply. In return for thousands of casualties, Nogi again had very little to show. He was especially disturbed that his attacks against the very important

203 Meter Hill, which overlooked part of Port Arthur's inner defenses from the northwest, had failed repeatedly. When he called off his attack on September 9, Nogi was not much closer to his objective than he had been when he closed the siege around Port Arthur in July.[73]

What made Port Arthur so difficult to take by siege was the depth and diversity of the fortifications that lay between its outer works and those heights that overlooked its inner fortifications. After his August and September assaults failed, General Nogi began to lay careful entrenchments to shield his troops' advance against the murderous massed fire that the Russians directed against them whenever they appeared above ground. At the same time, he brought up fresh reserves from Japan and strengthened his artillery. Eighteen great 11-inch howitzers taken from Japan's home defenses gave him added support for a new assault against Port Arthur's outer works. Each of the 11-inch guns could fire a 500-pound high explosive projectile up to a maximum range of 7 kilometers; before the siege ended, his gunners would fire 36,000 of them into Port Arthur. While the Japanese thus prepared for a new assault, the Russians strengthened their defenses and raised some of the outer works to a height of over 30 feet. One of their most effective new weapons proved to be the hand grenades that the resourceful ordnance officer Lt. Col. Ivan Krestinskii produced out of used 37mm and 47mm shell casings. Krestinskii had his men fill thousands of casings with explosives and fit each with a short length of Bickford fuse timed to explode before the Japanese could throw them back into the Russian redoubts.[74] When the Japanese attacked, Krestinskii's grenades rained down upon them to inflict what one American military observer described as "frightful injuries."[75]

With his new artillery, Nogi tried a third attack on October 17. Heavy bombardments, combined with infantry assaults that continued night and day for more than seventy-two hours, produced only very modest gains. Although by the end of the month, the Japanese had moved dangerously close to three outer defense works —Fort Sungshu, Fort Erhlung, and Fort Chikuan—they failed to seize any of them. Nor had they yet captured the 203 Meter Hill.

Murderously slow progress was being made, nonetheless. The Russians could replace none of their losses, while Nogi's reserves swelled with each week that passed. Inevitably, the balance would shift in his favor. By early November, his army numbered one hundred thousand men. When he threw more than fifty thousand of them against the Russian defenses on November 13, the disparity in resources began to tell when Stoessel's field commanders could marshal only 5,717 soldiers to man the outer defenses against the attacking Japanese divisions. Although outnumbered ten to one, the Russians held for ten days and drove the Japanese back from all three of the forts on the eastern side of Port Arthur. To the west, however, Nogi's First and Seventh divisions finally blasted their way into the defenses of the 203 Meter Hill using dynamite charges weighing up to a thousand pounds each to clear their way. The assaults of mid-November cost the Japanese another twelve thousand men, more than twice the entire force that opposed them at any one time in Port Arthur's outer works. But the 203 Meter Hill proved to be the gateway to the fortress. From its peak, Japanese observers could direct heavy artillery fire into parts of the fortress and onto the fleet itself. Between November 22 and November 26, the Japanese sank all that remained of the fleet Admiral Togo had first attacked ten months before.[76]

With the fleet and its heavy guns destroyed and the inner defenses of Port Arthur partly exposed to Japanese artillery fire, Nogi had finally weakened the Russians' position. Still, it was far from desperate. Japan's resources of men, money, and matériel had been stretched thin by almost a year of war, while the Russian buildup in the Far East was just beginning to show results. Kuropatkin's army in Manchuria finally began to show the effects of the shipments of men, weapons, and supplies that had flowed eastward along the Trans-Siberian Railway throughout the spring, summer, and fall of 1904. Even at sea, the explosion of a power magazine in one of Togo's few battleships, a bump against an unseen mine, or one or two well-placed twelve-inch shells from the capital ships that remained with Russia's Pacific Squadron at Vladivostok could have shifted the balance of power dramatically and, perhaps, have broken the blockade of Port Arthur. The defense of the fortress thus remained a viable military proposition, and everyone expected the siege to continue for some weeks or, even, months.

Having once proclaimed that "Port Arthur will be my grave,"[77] General Stoessel summoned his senior officers for a council of war on December 16. General Belyi reported that "there are still enough shells for a defense," and Colonel Irman added that "we still have ten thousand bayonets" ready to throw against the Japanese.[78] These men had made a realistic appraisal of their resources and all agreed that Port Arthur still could be defended. From the military point of view, theirs was the proper decision. What they did not know was that Stoessel and his two confidants, General Fock and Colonel Reuss, had secretly agreed to surrender and had already sent word of their decision to the Tsar. "The Fortress can hold out only a few days more," Stoessel reported to St. Petersburg. "The garrison has been laid low by scurvy. I have ten to eleven thousand still under arms, but they are all sick."[79] What he telegraphed to the Tsar simply was not true. Nonetheless, four days later Stoessel sent word to the Japanese that he was prepared to discuss the conditions of Port Arthur's surrender. "Taking into consideration the state of affairs in the seat of war in general," he wrote in English, "I find the future resistance of Port Arthur useless and in view of fruitless loss of men I would like to negotiate about the capitulation."[80] At the same time, he ordered General Fock to evacuate several of the remaining outer fortifications that the Russians still held. Once Fock had done so, defense of the inner fortress became far more difficult, something that Nogi obviously realized when, early the next morning, he agreed to Stoessel's request. At seven o'clock that evening, December 20, 1904, the Russians signed the articles of surrender and admitted Nogi's adjutants into Port Arthur as victors.

When they entered Port Arthur, the Japanese expected to find a handful of desperate defenders short of weapons, ammunition, and food. Not counting doctors, nurses, and noncombatants, they found 13,485 able-bodied men, another 5,809 suffering from scurvy or minor wounds, and 13,856 who were in the hospital or on light duty because of wounds or serious illness. There were over 600 pieces of artillery still in good firing order, over 200,000 shells still unfired, and about 2.5 million rounds of machine-gun and rifle ammunition. There were tons of food and fodder: flour for 27 days, groats for another 23 days, beans and lentils for 34 days, and dried vegetables for 88 days. There was nearly 200 days' supply of salt and tea. Most amazing of all, perhaps, there were 2,944 horses in the fortress, enough to supply the garrison with fresh meat for many days to come in view of the large quantities of fodder still remaining.[81] With their sense of honor that drove them to fight to the death for their Emperor, the Japanese were dumbfounded.

If the Japanese were amazed, Nicholas II and his advisers were beside themselves with anger when word of the vast stores Stoessel had surrendered eventually reached St. Petersburg. At a court-martial held after the war's end, Stoessel was convicted on no less than ten separate charges. Among other crimes, he was found guilty of sending false reports to the Emperor and of recommending General Fock and Colonel Reuss for the Order of St. George (given only for great bravery in battle) when they had done nothing to deserve it. Finally, the court's senior officers concluded that he "did not fulfill the obligations of his oath and military honor in that having delivered the fortress into the hands of the enemy, he did not share the lot of the garrison by becoming a prisoner of war with them."[82] It must have been only very small consolation for Stoessel that a few days after the surrender of Port Arthur, Kaiser Wilhelm had bestowed upon him Germany's highest military order. On the same day, Wilhelm also had awarded it to General Nogi.

Throughout history, great sieges have stirred the popular fancy, and the siege of Port Arthur was no exception. As never before, the world had become linked by transoceanic telegraph, faster ships, and railroads so that news of important events reached people half a world away with great speed and accuracy. Correspondents of the world's leading newspapers had joined General Nogi's headquarters even before the first assault against Port Arthur's outer defenses in August to file a steady stream of dispatches about the valor of the Japanese assaults and the tenacity of the Russian defense throughout the campaign. For the first time, what happened yesterday (not last year or last month) in the Far East became a matter of serious interest for men and women in Chicago, New York, London, Paris, and Berlin. Thanks to the speed of modern communications, they learned the outcome of assaults against strategic points just hours after they occurred. Port Arthur thus assumed perhaps a greater importance in the eyes of the world than its strategic position merited.

Port Arthur could not bar the movement of Japanese troops into Manchuria, nor did its fall impede any of Russia's supply routes into the same region. Yet the Japanese could not move safely into Manchuria with a large Russian force on their flank. That threat had to be eliminated before Nogi's superior, Marshal Iwao Oyama, could turn his full attention to Kuropatkin's army. Thus, what the Russian defense at Port Arthur accomplished in strategic terms was to tie up almost two hundred thousand Japanese troops. For the better part of six months the High Command in Tokyo was prevented from launching a full-scale invasion into Manchuria. By September 1904, the rail link around the southern tip of Lake Baikal was completed, and Kuropatkin's army became a far more formidable foe as supplies from European Russia began to flow more rapidly.

But during the previous months, things had gone badly for the Russians in Manchuria. In April, the Japanese had marched, unopposed, up the Korean peninsula; while holding General Zasulich's attention by a well-timed feint, General Kuroki Tametomo had brought most of his First Army regulars across the Yalu at Uiju to defeat the Russians at Kuliencheng. Although the number of troops involved was insignificant when compared with those that clashed later at Port Arthur and Mukden, the psychological impact of the Japanese victory at Kuliencheng had been immense. "For the first time regiments of the Island Empire have measured themselves in a serious battle with a European army and have decorated their colors with bloody laurels," proclaimed the *Allegemeine Zeitung.* [83] Sir Ian Hamilton, Britain's military observer with the Japanese, wrote that Kuropatkin had sent Zasulich to confront Kuroki "with a force too small to fight effectively [and] too big and too immobile to extricate itself easily once it had come into contact with the enemy's superior forces."[84] The fault lay in large part with the ongoing conflict between Admiral Alekseev as Russia's Viceroy in the Far East and Kuropatkin as Commander of the Manchurian Army. In no small measure, Nicholas's chronic inability to delegate command was at the root of their conflict.

Typical of weak men in positions of power, Nicholas preferred to leave partial authority in the hands of several men, to avoid recognizing any one of them as superior to the others. In the Far East, he allowed Kuropatkin and Alekseev each to claim some authority for military command but obliged each to seek his support to strengthen their position. In practice, the Kuropatkin-Alekseev conflict meant tangled lines of authority that weakened Russia's war effort for most of 1904. Kuropatkin especially was obliged to do battle on two fronts, the most crucial one sometimes centered in St. Petersburg. At the Yalu, Alekseev had insisted that Russia's armies must bar the Japanese from Manchuria at all costs, while Kuropatkin had argued that they must fight only a delaying action until Russia could assemble the men and armaments needed for a crushing counterattack. A useless and dangerous compromise—the force that was too large and not large enough with which Zasulich faced Kuroki in mid-April—was the result.

After Kuroki's First Army forced the Yalu, the Japanese turned their attention to the south where Nogi was preparing to close the ring around Port Arthur. Only in August did Oyama move decisively against Russia's Manchurian Army. Fearful that Kuropatkin's new shipments of men and weapons might tempt him to seize the initiative, Oyama ordered his First and Second armies under Kuroki and General Oku Yasutaka to attack at Liaoyang, a small city of some 60,000 astride the railroad that connected the now-besieged Port Arthur and Harbin. Kuroki struck first on August 11. To some, his impetuosity seemed foolhardy, for the Russians had spent an estimated five million rubles on Liaoyang's defense to construct what *The Standard*'s correspondent called a "terrible array of pits and wires and hills and trenches, bristling with rifles and guns."[85] Kuropatkin's Manchurian Army of 148,900 now outnumbered the combined First and Second Japanese armies by about 40,000 men, and he had more artillery.[86] "Confident that, with his fortified position and huge army, Kuropatkin would hurl back his foes and inflict a terrible defeat upon them, the entire Russian press awaited the coming struggle with impatience," wrote one commentator.[87]

The battle for Liaoyang raged for ten days. Although Kuropatkin did not suffer outright defeat, he could not claim a victory in any sense except that his army suffered ten thousand fewer casualties than the Japanese. Throughout the battle, his tactics were cautious, clumsy, and slow and he never managed to commit his vast reserves of forty-six thousand infantry and cavalry effectively. Repeated Japanese attacks eventually forced him to abandon Liaoyang and its considerable military stores, although he was able to withdraw with his entire army in good order. "If we are talking only about our military position, then there are no serious difficulties," he reported.[88] There were, of course, other positions to consider. In St. Petersburg, Kuropatkin's successor as War Minister put it more bluntly: "We did not attain the object aimed at [and] . . . were compelled by force of arms to relinquish it," he wrote. "Consequently, we suffered a defeat."[89] Kuropatkin's defeat, however, did not leave the Japanese in possession of a decisive victory. Carefully and deliberately, he pulled his army back to Mukden, the capital of Manchuria, some forty miles north. There he threw all his resources into preparations for a new and decisive offensive.

During the month after he withdrew to Mukden, Kuropatkin strengthened his forces until his army had grown to 213,325 men. As at Liaoyang, he outnumbered Oyama's combined armies by about 40,000 and commanded over 100 more field guns. On September 19, he exhorted his men to march "with the awareness of how important victory is for Russia"[90] and launched a new offensive against Oyama's combined forces. This time, both armies met at the Sha River, just north of Liaoyang. The battle began on September 22. By October 4, the outcome was clear. Although far from decisive, the victory lay with the Japanese, as Kuropatkin again withdrew to form a defensive line to the south of Mukden. Their victory had cost the Japanese over 20,000 killed and wounded. His defeat had cost Kuropatkin twice that number. As at Liaoyang, he blamed the men to whom he had assigned command of his major tactical units.[91] Never did he seem to understand that the greatest fault lay with his failure to prepare a clear plan of attack and, more generally, with the rigidly hierarchical command structure of his army that left field officers unable to respond directly to changing battle conditions. With his army spread out along a forty-mile front, Kuropatkin could not possibly direct all units himself, yet he gave none of his commanders authority to move against any of the unforeseen maneuvers that Oyama's more daring generals might make.[92]

The Sha River defeat finally forced Nicholas to unify the Manchurian Army's fragmented High Command. He relieved Alekseev and gave Kuropatkin full command of all Russian land forces in the Far East. "I do not rejoice," Kuropatkin confessed when he heard the news.[93] He now was free to direct Russia's war effort in the field. With that freedom came the heavy burden of full liability should he fail.

For the armies of Kuropatkin and Oyama, the battle on the Sha River marked the end of the fighting for 1904. Both went into winter quarters. Winter was pleasant for neither, but it proved particularly miserable for the Russians whose supply problems continued despite the new railroad link around Lake Baikal. Overcoats and winter boots sent out to Kuropatkin's soldiers early in the fall of 1904 took almost a year to make the journey and reached the Far East only after the war had ended. As winter wore on, morale plummeted. "Bureaucratic Russia has rotted through and through," lamented one correspondent. "We are living in terrible, disgraceful, shameful times."[94] No longer small, and far from victorious, Plehve's war spawned revolutionary discontent as crowds of workers in St. Petersburg greeted the new year with mass demonstrations. Although peaceful at first, these quickly turned violent as the Tsar's guards fired upon unarmed workers. By the beginning of February 1905, the victory that Plehve had so confidently predicted was needed desperately. At the same time, the Japanese also required a decisive victory, but for different reasons. By early 1905, Japan's resources of men, money, and matériel were stretched almost to

their limit, while those of the Russians, although plagued by bureaucratic bungling and command incompetence, swelled as the Trans-
Siberian Railway slowly did its work. Marshal Oyama therefore realized that if a decisive defeat was to be inflicted upon Russia it must
come soon. "It is essential that the enemy be dealt a heavy blow,"
he told his commanders at the beginning of February.[95] Among
those to whom he spoke stood not only Generals Kuroki, Oku, and
Nozu, who had served with him since the previous spring, but
General Kawamura, commander of the newly arrived Army of the
Yalu, and General Nogi, who had brought his battle-hardened Third
Army up the peninsula after its victory at Port Arthur.

Ponderously, and with appalling lack of imagination, Kuropatkin began to move his lumbering divisions into attack positions
toward the end of January 1905. In all, he had 300,000 men, 1,386
pieces of artillery, and 56 machine guns. Kuropatkin planned to
attack from his right flank, to the west of Mukden, against Nogi's
Third Army in what was to become history's first vast modern battle.
At Mukden, more than a half-million men clashed along 150 kilometers of front, parts of which the Russians had begun to fortify as early
as April 1904. In none of history's earlier wars would any general
have dared even to contemplate such a battle. Success demanded
boldness from corps and division commanders with the vision and
independence to move quickly and turn unforeseen shifts in the tide
of battle to their advantage. How utterly impoverished Kuropatkin's
command was in these vital elements was clear when, on February
6, Oyama caught him unprepared and utterly by surprise. While
some of Russia's senior generals squabbled among themselves,
scheming to seize Kuropatkin's command,[96] Oyama sent Kawamura
to strike against them in the east. The eastern attack, however, was
only a massive diversionary tactic. Oyama planned his main attack
in the west at precisely the point where Kuropatkin was preparing
to launch his own offensive. Thus General Nogi, not Kawamura or
Kuroki, was to strike the main blow. If Kuropatkin allowed himself
to be deceived by the feint in the east and moved to reinforce the
divisions on his left, Nogi could catch his massive troop concentra-
tions while they were in motion and unable to turn quickly to meet
a new assault from another direction.[97]

That any commander-in-chief could be so easily taken in was almost more than Oyama could have dared to hope. But Kuropatkin was wretchedly ill informed about his enemy's movements and fell completely into the trap. Lack of accurate information about his enemy's strength and position was Kuropatkin's Achilles' heel, yet he had the cavalry resources to develop reconnaissance far superior to that enjoyed by his Japanese foes. Because he did not know what forces faced him, Kuropatkin immediately weakened the army he had concentrated in the west to block Kawamura and Kuroki in the east because he assumed that theirs was Oyama's major assault. As Oyama closed his trap, Kuropatkin's situation was made worse because his senior generals—Linevich, Bilderling, and Kaulbars—did nothing to help each other. In any case, they had very little authority to make tactical decisions on their own. Each struggled in his own sector, awaiting decisive orders that never came. After only a day or two of fighting, Kuropatkin utterly lost touch with his armies' movements. His front was too long and Oyama's generals moved with far too much speed.

The battle of Mukden raged for twenty days, from February 6 until February 25, 1905. Again, Kuropatkin was pushed back along his entire front, as Oyama's energetic generals forced him to abandon well-fortified and long-held positions.[98] On February 25, he ordered a retreat, and the Japanese entered the city. By that time, both armies had been bled white by their immense losses. The total Russians killed and wounded numbered 60,093, with another 29,330 missing in action. The Japanese had lost 70,059 killed and wounded with only a handful more missing or taken prisoner. Taken together, three weeks of battle had reduced the ranks of both armies by over 160,000 men.

Although a major victory for the Japanese, Mukden did not prove a decisive defeat for the Russians. At the cost of his rear guard, which sacrificed itself to save Russia's main army, Kuropatkin withdrew the rest of his forces in good order to take up new positions at Tiehling, some forty kilometers to the north.[99] It was his last command decision in the Far East. On March 4, Nicholas replaced him with Gen. Nikolai Linevich. "Personally I used to consider the Japanese, like all Asiatics in general, to be inconsequential foes,"

Linevich wrote in his diary a week before he relieved Kuropatkin of command. "[Now] I have to confess that the enemy is clever, strong, and numerous. We always thought him weak. He has shown himself to be very strong and very brave."[100] Unable to press on, Oyama was obliged to settle for the victory at Mukden.

With Port Arthur lost and the Manchurian campaign at a standstill by the beginning of March, there remained one unknown factor that might still turn the tide in Russia's favor. In command of the Baltic Fleet, recently rechristened the Second Pacific Squadron, Rear Admiral Rozhestvenskii had steamed out of the Baltic harbor at Libau on October 2, 1904. He carried with him the Tsar's blessing and an exhortation to "uphold the honor of the Russian fleet . . . and take revenge . . . on the impudent enemy who has violated the tranquillity of our Mother Russia."[101] Each of Rozhestvenskii's ships carried a special ikon sent by the Empress Aleksandra, and each of the great guns in the fleet had been sprinkled with holy water. "All of Russia is looking to you with faith and with firm hope," Nicholas had telegraphed as the funnels of Rozhestvenskii's flagship, the *Kniaz Suvorov*, with its four great 305mm guns had slipped below the horizon.[102] As its new name implied, the destination of Rozhestvenskii's fleet was the Far East. With green crews led by officers with little or no combat experience, it was difficult to be optimistic about its chances against a fleet that had known only victory under Togo's command. Even more than an admiral who could bring it safely to its destination half a world away, the Second Pacific Squadron needed a battle-hardened commander with the genius and the will to use the arduous voyage that lay ahead to whip its crews into shape, hone its gunners' skills to a fighting edge, and instill in it that esprit de corps so desperately needed by demoralized men embarked on a dangerous mission.

Zinovii Petrovich Rozhestvenskii looked every inch the man for that task.

"Anyone meeting him for the first time was struck by the stern and powerful will expressed by his concentrated and never-smiling face, and by his steely penetrating glance," wrote one of his officers. "His way of talking with short precise phrases creates the impression of a man who knows where he is going and what he wants, and who will not be diverted from the road he has chosen."[103] Looks often are deceiving and they certainly were in Rozhestvenskii's case. Aged fifty-six at the time of his appointment, he was a naval gunnery and torpedo officer whose only combat experience had come as a junior officer on the *Vesta,* an armed steamer that had fought off an enemy cruiser in the Russo-Turkish War of 1877. There is some evidence that the *Vesta*'s victory was a hoax, but Rozhestvenskii's career had profited nonetheless. His promotion to Rear Admiral came soon after he had dazzled Tsar and Kaiser with a brilliant display of naval gunnery at the maneuvers near the Baltic port of Reval in the fall of 1902. Some of his less charitable colleagues were heard to say that he had rigged the demonstration by setting all targets at predetermined ranges. Still, Rozhestvenskii's effort won the Kaiser's enthusiastic admiration and his appointment as one of Nicholas's aides-de-camp. In that position, he never advised the Tsar, but merely did as he was told.[104] According to Witte, many of Nicholas's advisers doubted that the Baltic Fleet could accomplish anything beyond its own destruction if it sailed to the Far East, but Rozhestvenskii reportedly said only that "the voyage would be terribly difficult, but if the Sovereign Emperor ordered him to do so he would stand at the head of the fleet and lead it in battle against Japan."[105] Witte remembered that "the Emperor with his habitual optimism expected that Rozhestvenskii would reverse the entire course of the War."[106] Serafim, a famous monk whom Nicholas soon tried to appoint Metropolitan of St. Petersburg, predicted that peace would be concluded in Tokyo and that "only Kikes and intellectuals could think otherwise."[107]

"Everyone knows that the new ships have been finished in a hurry and that the others are veterans that should have been left to rest in peace," wrote the surgeon of the cruiser *Izumrud.* "In general, it's difficult to imagine how depressed we are."[108] A ship's surgeon, of course, should not be expected to make perceptive appraisals of the quality of a fleet, but Sergei Politovskii, the engineer-in-chief, was in a position to know much that others could not. "The torpedo-boat *Bystryi* rammed the [battleship] *Osliabia,* knocking a hole in her hull and damaging her torpedo tubes," he wrote to his wife the day the fleet sailed. Three days later, he added, "here we are at our first anchorage. Already there are masses of breakdowns. They have ruined the *Bystryi*, there are damages on the *Sisoi*, they have broken the davits on the *Zhemchug*, and sunk a cutter. The three Danish colliers that delivered coal to us were damaged in the process."[109]

Thus far, most of the damage had been caused by stupidity or carelessness that stemmed from poor training. Amazingly, some of the fleet's sailors were ignorant about even the most fundamental aspects of warfare. Just a few days before his ship sailed, the appalled (and somewhat terrified) surgeon of the *Izumrud* had written: "I attended today the funeral of our chief petty officer, who had died from the typhus. When the time came to fire a farewell volley, it was discovered that the squad did not know how to load their rifles. And we are going to war!"[110]

Paranoid fear of surprise Japanese attack overshadowed the crews' ineptitude and inexperience from the moment Rozhestvenskii's fleet steamed out of its Baltic harbor. They were no more than twenty-four hours out of port, with several days' voyage ahead before they would even leave the confines of the Baltic, when Politovskii wrote to his wife: "Tonight it will be dangerous. We'll all sleep in our clothes with all our guns loaded. We are passing through a narrow strait and are afraid of striking Japanese mines. . . . This strait is just perfect for torpedo-boat attacks and for laying mines."[111]

Such ludicrous delusions soon had tragic consequences. To the amazement of diplomats from St. Petersburg to Washington, D. C., at about 11:30 P.M. on October 8, a number of ships in the Second Pacific Squadron, including Rozhestvenskii's flagship, opened fire on the British fishing fleet that was trawling in the North Sea's Dogger Bank. Several ships were sunk by Russian shells, a number more damaged, and a serious diplomatic incident created. Yet the nervous and trigger-happy men of Rozhestvenskii's squadron were not yet finished with their night's work. "What a misfortune," Politovskii wrote three hours later. "Our division fired on the *Avrora*. . . . Evidently someone mistook her for Japanese and fired on her with the six-inch guns."[112] Not only had Rozhestvenskii's gunners sunk part of the Hull fishing fleet but they had managed to put six shells into one of their own cruisers and injure several of its crew, including the ship's chaplain whose hand was blown off—and all before the fleet had been at sea a full week.

The difficulties of Rozhestvenskii's first week at sea set the pattern for a voyage of almost thirty thousand kilometers that took most of his ships around the tip of Africa, across the Indian Ocean, and on toward the Sea of Japan where his mission was to destroy Admiral Togo's fleet and free the Russian warships still bottled up in the harbor at Port Arthur. On they went, great battleships displacing more than fifteen thousand tons, armed with huge twelve-inch guns that fired projectiles weighing over a thousand kilograms, accompanied by smaller cruisers, including the *Svetlana* with her magnificent mahogany staircase that had been installed in the days when she had served as the Grand Duke Aleksei Aleksandrovich's personal yacht. From Tangiers they steamed on through the tropics, to Dakar and on to Gabon, Libreville, Great Fish Bay, and Angra Peguina, where they learned that the Japanese had seized the 203 Meter Hill and that Port Arthur was in serious danger, and then on to Madagascar to learn that Port Arthur had fallen just a week before.

The arduous journey through burning heat was made far worse by Rozhestvenskii's obsession with the coal supplies his ships required. Ever fearful that coal might be denied them at some port and that his fleet might be caught without enough fuel to carry them to a friendly haven, he added coal whenever possible and, at times, took on far more than his ships were designed to carry. The added weight made his ships slower, more cumbersome, and did repeated damage to their engines. The continual labor of loading, stacking, and rearranging coal in every available nook and cranny left his crews worn and debilitated. Perhaps worst of all, with coal piled on ammunition trolleys, around gun turrets, and even on the decks, there was little opportunity for the gun drills that the Russians so desperately needed if they were to hold their own against the well-trained, well-equipped Japanese.[113]

On December 27, Rozhestvenskii's fleet reached Nossi Bé in

Madagascar. There they remained for some ten weeks to refit and repair before they began the long voyage across the Indian Ocean to the East Indies and Indo-China. Again Politovskii's letters to his wife told a tale that gave very few grounds for optimism:

January 13: "Twice during maneuvers today the *Borodino* and the *Aleksandr III* almost collided."

January 19: "During firing practice yesterday, a shell ricocheted into the *Donskoi.*"

January 26: "They say that during fleet maneuvers the *Suvorov* almost rammed the *Kuban.*"[114]

After more than three months at sea, such incidents were less than reassuring, and the morale of sailors and officers went from bad to worse. The heat was intense. The food was bad. Shore leaves were few, and news from home rare. Mail arrived at the most irregular intervals bringing many disappointments. "Again there is a mix-up in addresses," Politovskii lamented on January 27. "We received letters today that were addressed to the Emperor Aleksandr III Electrotechnical Institute [in St. Petersburg]."[115]

By the time he left Madagascar, Rozhestvenskii knew that Russia had lost the battle at Mukden and that he must face Togo's fleet alone. It seemed certain that the battle must be joined somewhere in the straits that separated Korea and Japan, and he must have had that thought increasingly in his mind as he passed Singapore and anchored briefly in Kamranh Bay to make his final preparations before sailing into Japanese waters. Politovskii used the days there to repair the damage caused by new collisions. "The *Blestiashchii* managed to tear a hole in the side of the *Bezuprechnyi,*" he wrote to his wife on April 1. "The sea has become too cramped for two Russian destroyers."[116] They were in the China Sea by the end of April when reinforcements sent out from the Baltic under Rear Admiral Nikolai Nebogatov joined them. Rozhestvenskii celebrated with a General Fleet Order that told his sailors of the dangers ahead and explained how to meet them. "The Japanese have an important advantage—long fighting experience and much gunnery practice in war conditions," he warned. "They are absolutely devoted to their throne and country: they cannot bear dishonor and die like heroes. But we bow before the throne of the All-Highest," he concluded. "The Lord will strengthen our right hand, will help us carry out the task of our Emperor and with our blood wash away the bitter shame of Russia."[117] Just over two weeks later, Rozhestvenskii and his crews faced their final challenge as they approached the Tsushima Strait. The time for the reckoning with Admiral Togo had come.

Rozhestvenskii never consulted with his division commanders and senior captains about strategy or tactics. So little did he communicate with these men, in fact, that on the morning of the great battle at Tsushima no one in the entire fleet aside from the captains of the *Kniaz Suvorov* (Rozhestvenskii's flagship) and the *Osliabia* (Rear Admiral Felkerzam's flagship) knew that Felkerzam, the fleet's second in command, had been dead for the past three days. Rozhestvenskii had not shared that vital information even with Nebogatov, the man designated to take Felkerzam's place in just such an emergency.[118] Nor had he issued precise orders about his plans for the coming battle. Once the fighting began, the Russians had to rely upon those ship-to-ship signals at which Rozhestvenskii's crews had time and again given dramatic demonstrations of their ineptitude. It was the inability of Rozhestvenskii's ships to signal accurately and maneuver precisely and his failure to take those deadly failings into account that spelled disaster when the two fleets met on May 14 in the first of the twentieth century's great naval battles.

Although both fleets had caught sight of each other in the early morning hours, what history remembers as the battle of the Tsushima Strait began in earnest at 1:35 P.M. when Admiral Togo reversed his ships' course so as to cross in front of the Russian line, a tactic known as "crossing the T," that brought all of his guns to bear on Rozhestvenskii's most powerful ships at a time when the Russians could bring only a few of their guns into play against him. Great Rising Sun battle flags flared from the Japanese ships' masts as crews took their battle stations. "The Empire's fate depends on the result of this battle," Togo signaled to his ships. "Let every man do his utmost duty."[119]

If successful, Togo's effort to reverse course and to "cross the T" of Rozhestvenskii's formation would bring vastly superior firepower to bear against the Russians, but it was a daring move nonetheless. For at the moment each of his ships reached the turning point and reversed course they made easy targets for the Russians' guns. They were spared the danger, however, because several Russian ships nearly collided as Rozhestvenskii's fleet frantically adjusted its formation. "At this time our formation, properly speaking, was nothing but a heap," Nebogatov later wrote in describing the moment when Rozhestvenskii's flagship opened fire.[120] Within the next few minutes, the Russians scored hits on Togo's flagship the *Mikasa* and the cruiser *Asama*, but they faced a return fire that was far more accurate and rapid. Wrote Commander Vladimir Semenov, who was aboard the *Kniaz Suvorov* that day: "I glanced around. Devastation! Flames on the bridge, burning debris on the deck, piles of bodies. Signaling, rangefinding, and shot-spotting stations swept away and destroyed. And astern, the *Aleksandr III* and *Borodino* also wreathed in smoke and flame."[121] The *Osliabia*, flagship of Rozhestvenskii's Second Division, took several waterline hits, and sank in less than half an hour. By that time, the bridge on the *Kniaz Suvorov* had been hit by a high explosive shell and Rozhestvenskii wounded several times by splinters. About to lose consciousness, he transferred command to Nebogatov.

The battle was far from over, and Togo's gunners had only begun to do their worst. Before night fell, the great battleships *Aleksandr III*, *Borodino*, and the *Kniaz Suvorov* all joined the *Osliabia* at the bottom of the sea, as did several Russian cruisers and destroyers. Nebogatov tried to lead the remaining ships north to Vladivostok, but suffered incessant Japanese torpedo-boat attacks all night. Unable to escape Togo's now overwhelming firepower, he surrendered the next morning. By that time, the Russians had lost 20 major warships and 5,045 men killed. The ranks of the Japanese fleet had been reduced by 3 torpedo boats and 116 men killed in action.[122] Weak from his wounds, Rozhestvenskii attempted to

escape to Vladivostok on the destroyer *Bedovyi* but was taken prisoner by two Japanese destroyers off the island of Matsu. It was left
to Nebogatov to carry out the act of surrender in a far more crushing
defeat than that which Kuropatkin had suffered at Mukden.

A good commander, though not a brilliant one, Nebogatov
possessed none of the courtier's arts, and it was he, more than any
other commander in the war, who suffered the wrath of Nicholas
and his advisers. Tried by a naval court, he was condemned to death.
His sentence was commuted to imprisonment, and he spent several
years in a fortress prison before he was pardoned. Since no other
Russian commander shared his fate, one therefore might want to
look more closely at the nature of his crime. He had not allowed
himself to be outmaneuvered as Kuropatkin had, nor had he grossly
misjudged the enemy and been caught unaware, like Alekseev and
Stark at the beginning of the war. Unlike Stoessel at Port Arthur,
Nebogatov had not surrendered while he still possessed hundreds of
guns, tens of thousands of shells, and millions of rounds of ammunition. Nor had he allowed himself to be tricked by simple tactical
maneuvers, entered a battle unprepared, and proved unable to exploit his enemy's moment of weakness as Rozhestvenskii had during
the first hour at Tsushima. Faced by overwhelming firepower, and
with most of the fleet's capital ships sunk or seriously disabled before
he assumed command, Nebogatov's first thought was for the lives
of the two thousand men who remained alive under his command.
He could not "commit these young lives to suicide," he later said.
"I had no right to take their lives [for no practical purpose]."[123]
Therefore, he surrendered.

Nebogatov's crime thus was that he had presided over yet
another inglorious defeat at a time when Russia and the Russians
could not tolerate another failure. None among his judges and accus-
ers thought he could have triumphed at Tsushima. According to the
official Russian view: "Continuation of the battle would not have
had the slightest effect on the result of the war, but the destruction
of a handful of brave men in an unequal fight with the enemy adorns
a nation's history. Descendants take pride in such feats of their
ancestors, and are inspired by an example of selfless service to the

Motherland."[124] Nebogatov had refused to spend two thousand lives to give Russia that glorious adornment to her military annals she desperately craved after so many humiliating losses to an Asian foe. To the shame of Nicholas, his admirals, and his generals, the Japanese had proved superior to Russia's forces on land and sea. To many, the only course now seemed to be a peace quickly concluded.

Even before Tsushima, both sides had begun to think seriously of peace. "While the enemy still has powerful forces in its home country, we have already exhausted ours," warned Field Marshal Marquis Yamagata Aritomo, Chief of the Army General Staff, a fortnight after the Mukden victory. "[If we decide to continue the war] the burden on the people will become much greater. . . . We must now be prudent."[125] Japan's victories thus had stretched her resources almost to the breaking point, while Russia's defeats had left her still with vast reserves of men and weapons that were only beginning to reach Manchuria. By the summer of 1905, the Trans-Siberian Railway was moving four times more men and equipment each week than it had at the war's outset, with the result that Russia's forces in the Far East increased dramatically after Mukden while the Japanese were hard pressed to replace their losses.[126] Perhaps more than the Russians, the Japanese therefore were anxious to accept President Theodore Roosevelt's offer to mediate the conflict while Nicholas procrastinated in the hope that the war might still turn in Russia's favor. "Did you ever know anything more pitiable than the condition of the Russian despotism," Roosevelt asked his ailing Secretary of State. "The Tsar is a preposterous little creature," he concluded. "He has been unable to make war, and he is now unable to make peace."[127]

Yet Nicholas could not delay peace for long. Although Russia still had great resources to devote to the struggle, she also had to face growing dissent at home. The demonstrations of Bloody Sunday—January 9, 1905—had unsettled Nicholas and his ministers, and the tension increased throughout the spring. On May 24, 1905, nine days after Nebogatov's surrender at Tsushima, Russia's military leaders met at Tsarskoe Selo and urged Nicholas to end the war. The next day, he informed George von Lengerke Meyer, U.S. Ambassador in St. Petersburg, that Russia was prepared to begin talks with the Japanese.[128]

Even with Roosevelt's energetic urging, an agreement to discuss the possibility of beginning discussions did not mean that a peace conference between Russia and Japan could begin immediately, and it was not until August 9 N.S. (July 27 according to the Russian calendar) that Count Witte as Russia's spokesman met his counterpart, Komura Jutaro, at Portsmouth, New Hampshire, where they stayed at the famous Wentworth Hotel as guests of the American Government. The Wentworth has been described as "one of the finest resort hotels in the United States" and was summer host to scores of wealthy and prominent Americans from the Eastern Seaboard at the turn of the century.[129] Witte immediately took a strong dislike to it, pronounced it immensely cramped, and described it as a "gross wooden hotel, built to accommodate people of modest means during their summer vacations." He thought the food "absolutely abominable" and insisted that it had made him sick. "Without doubt," he later remarked snidely, "this particular year was marvelously happy for the proprietors of the hotel!"[130]

For twenty days Witte, Komura, their advisers, and staffs labored in Portsmouth while telegraphic messages in cipher flowed constantly between them and their superiors in Tokyo and St. Petersburg. By August 28 N.S. both sides had reached a stalemate over Japan's insistence that Russia pay an indemnity and cede the island of Sakhalin. But time now stood on the side of the Russians. Realizing that Japan's General Staff could not begin to match Russia's buildup in the Far East, Witte was prepared to break off the negotiations and return his nation's disputes to the battlefield. According to some reports, he had even established a prearranged signal that would send a coded message on its way to St. Petersburg the moment the negotiations broke down. "Send for my Russian cigarettes," he would tell one of his secretaries, and that would release the signal that would let Nicholas and his General Staff know that they should order General Linevich to launch a new offensive.[131] But if the Russians knew the Japanese limitations, the Japanese knew them even better. Therefore, when Komura came to what many thought would be his last meeting with Witte at 9:30 A.M. on August 29, he already had instructions to give way on both the issues that had deadlocked the negotiations. Komura therefore withdrew Japan's insistence that Russia pay a war indemnity, and he and Witte agreed to divide Sakhalin between their two nations. That settled, Witte turned to his staff and exclaimed: "Gentlemen, peace!"[132]

Witte had achieved what few had thought possible. Opposed to the war from the very beginning, it was nonetheless he who negotiated the peace. Russia kept all of her Far Eastern possessions except for the Liaotung Peninsula (including Port Arthur), the South Manchurian Railway, and the southern half of Sakhalin Island.[133] Thus she remained a Great Power on the Pacific.

But even Witte could not shield Nicholas from the stigma of being the first ruler in Europe to admit defeat at the hands of Asians. For Nicholas that may have been the most bitter pill of all, but it had to be swallowed, for other crises now demanded his attention more urgently.

That spring, the cauldron of dissent and revolutionary protest had begun to seethe in the cities and great industrial centers of Russia and had overflowed during the summer and fall into the Empire's usually tranquil villages. Perhaps most frightening, there was even some reason to doubt the loyalty of the armed forces that had traditionally defended the Russian autocracy against all enemies. Some weeks before Witte had reached Portsmouth to begin his meetings with Komura, the sailors who served on the *Potëmkin*, one of the great battleships in the Black Sea fleet, had mutinied and raised the red banner of revolt. Although the mutiny ended rather ingloriously when the sailors surrendered to the Rumanian authorities at Constanza at the end of June, a new era in the Russian revolutionary movement had opened. A war in the Far East could have "dynastic consequences," Nicholas's brother-in-law Prince Petr Oldenburgskii had warned some six weeks before Togo's surprise attack. Now it was clear that he had come far closer to the truth than had Plehve's more optimistically expressed hopes.[134]

The "small victorious war" had failed to stem the revolutionary tide Plevhe so feared, and surging revolutionary dissent finally cost him his life when a terrorist threw a nitroglycerine bomb into his carriage on July 15, 1904. Other killings, including that of the Grand Duke Sergei Aleksandrovich in Moscow, followed Plehve's assassination. The year 1905 thus would be a year of unparalleled turmoil in which the future of Russia's autocracy and even the survival of its dynasty were called into question for the first time in almost three hundred years.

Nicholas and Aleksandra hunting in the Gatchina Woods, 1901
(THE MANSELL COLLECTION)

The Emperor Alexander III

(Opposite page above) *A provincial Russian noble family on a holiday* (T MANSELL COLLECTION)

(Opposite page below) *Russian fami victims, 1891* (BBC HULTON PICTU LIBRARY)

Konstantin Pobedonostsev

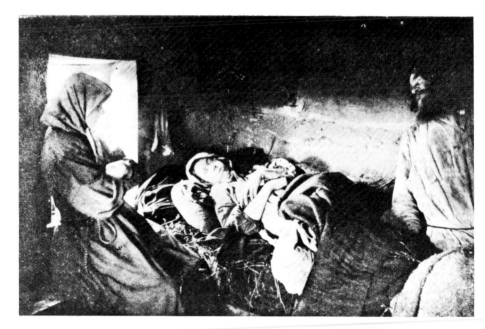

A victim of the 1891 famine (BBC HULTON PICTURE LIBRARY)

Inside the Putilov Factory

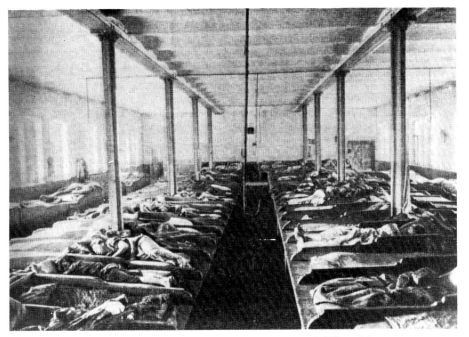

The Men's Dormitory at the Prokhorovs' Trekhgornaia Mill in Moscow

A Resident of a Truschchoba in Moscow's Khitrovka

Father Georgii Gapon (BBC HULTON PICTURE LIBRARY)

Jewish victims of pogroms in Russia (BBC Hulton Picture Library)

The Police arrive to arrest the revolutionaries at the first printing press of Narodnaia Volia

Sofia Perovskaia

Nikolai Kibalchich

Vera Zasulich as a young woman

Dmitrii Karakozov

Vera Figner, 1883

Vladimir Ulianov (Lenin), 1892
(The Bettmann Archive)

(Opposite page below) *Lenin with members of the St. Petersburg League for the Emancipation of the Working Class, the nucleus of the Communist party* (The Bettmann Archive)

Russian peasant settlers en route to Siberia

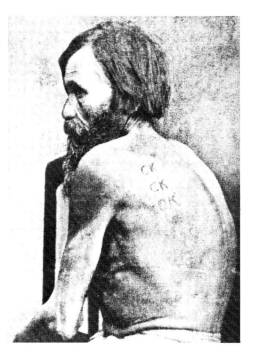

A convict branded with the initials "C.K."—Siberskii Katorzhnik—(Siberian Convict)—for attempting to escape (THE MANSELL COLLECTION)

An executioner at a Siberian prison holding the knut (whip) used to punish prisoners (THE MANSELL COLLECTION)

Maksim Gorkii

Aleksandr Blok

Aleksandr Benois

Vladimir Solovev

Zinaida Gippiu

right-wing caricature titled "The Dictatorship of the Proletariat" (THE UNIVERSITY OF ILLINOIS SLAVIC COLLECTION)

Workers being fired upon on Bloody Sunday, January 9, 1905 (THE MANSELL COLLECTION)

Soldiers being mobilized for the Russo-Japanese War, 1904 (BBC HULTON PICTURE LIBRARY)

(Below) Russian infantry preparing to meet a Japanese attack during the Russo-Japanese War (BBC HULTON PICTURE LIBRARY)

Russian artillerymen getting a six-inch Howitzer into firing position, October 190 (BBC HULTON PICTURE LIBRARY)

Buildings in Moscow's Presna district destroyed by artillery shelling during the December 1905 uprising

(Below) Soldiers from one of the government punitive expeditions burning the izba of a peasant suspected of sympathizing with the revolutionary cause in 1905 (BBC HULTON PICTURE LIBRARY)

The Empress Aleksandra receiving France's Foreign Minister and Premier Raymond Poincaré at Tsarskoe-Selo, August 1912 (THE MANSELL COLLECTION)

A caricature directed against the October Manifesto, 1905. The enema apparatus is marked "The Promised Reforms" and the chamber pot is labeled "Their Results" (THE UNIVERSITY OF ILLINOIS SLAVIC COLLECTION)

"The Machine-Gun." Caricature of General Dmitrii Trepov, Governor-General of St. Petersburg in 1905 (THE UNIVERSITY OF ILLINOIS SLAVIC COLLECTION)

Caricature of the so-called "Bulygin Duma," 1905 (THE UNIVERSITY OF ILLINOIS SLAVIC COLLECTION)

Russian soldiers attending a field mass after the outbreak of the First World War (BBC HULTON PICTURE LIBRARY)

CHAPTER VIII

1905: The Year of Turmoil

BEFORE 1905, RUSSIA'S MASSES SAW THE TSAR AS THEIR "*Batiushka*"—the "Little Father" of them all—who cared for them and answered to God for their welfare. If he did not act as a "*Tsar-Batiushka*" should, then it stood to reason, in the popular mind, that he was an impostor to be driven from the throne. Time and again in the seventeenth and eighteenth centuries, the oppressed *narod* of Russia had marched against the ruler beneath the banners of rebel Cossack leaders—first behind Ivan Bolotnikov during the Time of Troubles; then in the hordes of Stenka Razin; still again when Kondratii Bulavin protested against Peter the Great's revolution from above and its dedication to destroying the Old Russian ways; and finally, in the rebellious serf legions of Emelian Pugachev. With their scythes and broad-bladed peasant axes— sometimes with lances, muskets, and even cannon—they marched to challenge those Tsars and Tsarinas whose policies of extreme oppression, they insisted, branded them as "false" rulers. Violent and destructive in their anger, the *narod* nonetheless never challenged autocracy as the ruling principle of Russian life. Always, a pretender marched with the rebel legions to be proclaimed the "true" Tsar.

Only in 1905 did the masses in town and country turn from their traditional path of protest. That summer and fall, tens of thousands of peasants stormed from their villages to inflict almost thirty million rubles worth of damage upon the lands, barns, and manor houses of well-to-do lords,[1] while their city brethren took to the streets of Moscow, Odessa, Łódź, and St. Petersburg to wrest political concessions from Nicholas and his startled advisers. For the first time in her history, Russia came to know revolution as Western Europeans had known it in the century since the Parisian crowd had stormed the Bastille in 1789. For the first time, some among the Russian *narod* uttered the fateful words: "There is no Tsar!" As the poet Boris Pasternak later wrote, it was "The tearing apart/ Of the joints/ Of oaths/ To the dynasty sworn."[2]

The strains that threatened to rend the fabric of Russian society were no secret to those who spoke in the name of the masses. "Groaning is the hunger-swollen Russian peasantry," wrote young Iosif Djugashvili. "Groaning are the small town dwellers, petty employees.... Groaning, too, is the lower and even middle bourgeoisie . . . and the oppressed nationalities and religions in Russia. . . . Groaning are the unceasingly persecuted and humiliated Jews . . . the Georgians, and the Armenians . . . [who] are compelled to submit to the shameful and oppressive policies of Russification."[3] This was the first published statement by a young man who spoke directly to the people in a way that such revolutionary theorists as

Lenin, Martov, and Plekhanov could not. A quarter of a century later, he would use frightful terror to drive the people to amazing feats of endurance and achievement. Then, he would be known by a different name—Iosif Stalin.

Stalin, of course, was not alone in his condemnation of Nicholas's policies. From Siberia, young Trotskii spoke of villages "devastated economically by the *kulaki* [and] physically by syphilis and all sorts of epidemics. . . . In thoughtful silence," he lamented, "our village is dying from disease."[4] Soon he would proclaim that "the real monarch has destroyed the idea of the monarch" in Russia.[5] At the newly founded University of Chicago half a world away, Pavel Miliukov, renowned professor of history from the University of Moscow and soon to become a prominent political figure, warned that "material want [is] growing more and more acute." Nicholas's government, he insisted, had "shown itself to be incompatible with the gratification of the most elementary social needs."[6]

"Criticism of the existing order bursts forth roaring and whistling through every crack and gap," proclaimed a young lawyer in the provincial town of Saratov,[7] and police statistics seemed to bear out that claim. In Russia's capital alone, some sixteen thousand Petersburgers out of a population of almost 1.5 million were sent into exile in 1901. Although only slightly more than 1 percent of the city's residents, their numbers equaled about a third of its population growth that year.[8]

But Nicholas himself could not perceive the magnitude of the crisis that faced his Empire—even though the misery of the people was proclaimed by the intelligentsia and the police drove nearly fifty men and women every day from the capital for fear their anger would provoke violence. Not long after he became Emperor, Nicholas had sworn "to preserve the principles of autocracy as firmly and as steadfastly as did my late and unforgettable father," who for him had been a true *Bogatyr,* one of those folk heroes who loomed larger than life in the legends of olden times. Even after a decade on the throne, however, he still rarely took firm positions, and those he took too often proved tragically wrongheaded.

Perhaps it was coincidence, or perhaps it was indeed an omen, that Nicholas II had been born on the feast day of Job the Sufferer, May 6, 1868.[9]

In the 1880s, while his father ruled Russia, Nicholas worked a few hours each day under the misanthropic guidance of Pobedonostsev, who set out to school the timid son as he had tutored the stern father. Otherwise, the Tsarevich lived a carefree life, unconcerned—indeed, unacquainted—with affairs of state. He went skating with his sister and built snowhouses in the winter, gardened and planted saplings in the spring and summer and chopped wood in the fall. He adored the theater, the opera, and the ballet, and had the immense good fortune to live in the brilliant age of Tschaikovsky, Rimskii-Korsakov, Balakirev, and Borodin, whose newest compositions could be heard at the Imperial Mariinskii Theater, the Italian Opera, and the Imperial Conservatory. Nicholas saw Tschaikovsky's *Sleeping Beauty* three times in the month after its premiere. He dined, drank, sang, and danced night after night, sometimes until dawn, as he took in all the pleasures that the vibrant culture of Russia's great capital had to offer. Like so many Romanovs, he loved the order and precision of Russia's army. "I now am happier than I can say to have joined the army," he wrote to his "dear, darling Mama" in June 1887, soon after he turned nineteen.[10] "It appealed to his passive nature," remarked his brother-in-law, Grand Duke Aleksandr Mikhailovich. "One executed orders and did not have to worry over the vast problems handled by one's superiors."[11] Significantly, Nicholas II never wore a general's rank until he assumed command of Russia's armies in 1915.[12]

Nicholas's first assignment of consequence as Russia's Tsarevich began in the fall of 1890, when his father sent him on a world tour that carried him from St. Petersburg to Egypt's pyramids, to the jungles of India and Ceylon, and to the exotic cities of Singapore, Bangkok, and Hong Kong. Everywhere, he was met with pomp and ceremony that obscured the true nature of the world he was seeing for the first time. "My trip is senseless," he told Grand Duke Aleksandr Mikhailovich when they met in Ceylon. "Palaces and generals are the same the world over, and that's all I am permitted to see. I could just as well have stayed at home."[13] Others in his place had endeavored to penetrate the shroud of ceremony that surrounded them; Nicholas did not. From Hong Kong, he went on to Tokyo and visited some of Japan's most scenic regions. His Asian journey, however, ended in Otsu on a sour note—a narrow escape from the sword of a would-be assassin. Shaken by this sudden brush with death, Nicholas hastened to the safety of Vladivostok, where he turned the first shovelful of earth to begin the eastern terminus of the Trans-Siberian Railway. He then made his way back to St. Petersburg across Siberia's vastness. Nicholas, the last Romanov, thus became the first to travel from one end of his Empire to the other. Yet he returned to St. Petersburg in the late summer of 1891 with no clear political impressions of the world he had seen. He seems to have formed no estimates of the people he met and the nations he visited, except to come away from the Far East with a bitter hatred for the Japanese as a result of the assassination attempt he had suffered at their hands.[14]

One of the greatest influences upon Nicholas during his life as Tsarevich was his mother, the vivacious, strong-minded, fiercely maternal Empress Maria Feodorovna. That influence began to wane somewhat in 1894, only to be replaced by one that was even stronger and more enduring. Princess Alix of Hesse Darmstadt, the young woman Nicholas called "Sunny," was to rule him in a manner his mother could not hope to match. Alix—lovely, regal Alix with the flaming red hair and the soulful blue eyes—was the granddaughter of Queen Victoria and younger sister of the Grand Duchess Elizaveta Feodorovna, who had married Nicholas's uncle, the Grand Duke Sergei Aleksandrovich. Alix had all the will, the fire, and the dedication to follow difficult courses that her "Nicky" so obviously lacked, and from the moment she agreed to become his wife in April 1894, she engulfed him with a jealous passion. She was "a religious *exaltée* with a strong sexual drive," one historian wrote not long ago —and Nicholas loved her deeply, though far less aggressively, in return.[15] From the first moments of their life together, Alix offered the man she called her "darling boysy" her everlasting love (and eternal care) as lover, mother, and truest friend. When in mid-July 1894, she wrote in his diary that "your Guardian Angel is keeping watch over you,"[16] it was no longer clear whether she referred to the celestial or terrestrial variety of that peculiar species.

The best documentary record we have of this relationship on a day-to-day basis comes only during the dreadful days of the Great War, but it shows that the pattern Alix established in 1894 had endured and strengthened over the intervening two decades. "I kiss you all over," she wrote, while Nicholas replied, "I love you and long for your caresses!"[17] "Don't laugh at silly old wify, but she has 'trousers' on unseen," Alix reassured him when he found the pressures of war and political crisis difficult to bear.[18] "I suffer over you as over a tender, softhearted child—wh[o] needs guiding," she confessed. "Be Peter the Great, John [Ivan] the Terrible, Emperor Paul —crush them all under you," she urged him the next day.[19] "Tender thanks for the severe written scolding," was Nicholas's grateful reply. "God bless you, my darling, my Sunny! Your 'poor weak-willed' little hubby Nicky."[20] The long-enduring love between Nicholas and Aleksandra thus was based upon a very unequal partnership in which she demanded that he submit to her will in all things—their family life, their moments of passion, and their politics. Nicholas always couched his submission in words of love and tenderness, but it was near-total submission nonetheless. Alix's demands were expressed in a flurry of love words as well, but it was submission, not equality, that she demanded.

If their months of courtship in the spring and summer of 1894 were a time of bliss, their marriage bore the blemish of deep sadness when Nicholas and Aleksandra exchanged their vows just a week after Alexander III had been laid to rest in the great Cathedral of the Peter and Paul Fortress. It was a strange, bittersweet sort of day, so typical of their life together for the next twenty-four years. Now Emperor and Autocrat, Nicholas donned the uniform of the Hussar Life Guards in which he had found such happiness as a junior officer, while Aleksandra, wearing a gown of silver brocade and the diamond wedding crown of Imperial Grand Duchesses, joined him before family and a few friends in the Winter Palace chapel. "Our marriage seemed to me a mere continuation of the masses for the dead, with this difference that I now wore a white dress instead of a black one," she later wrote.[21] When she had first entered St. Petersburg a week before, old peasant women in the crowd, those ever-present harbingers of good and evil, joy and sadness, had seen her, crossed themselves, and muttered darkly, "She has entered our land behind a coffin. She brings misfortune with her."[22] Such gloomy predictions seemed out of place and even wrong when Nicholas and Aleksandra emerged from the Winter Palace chapel after their wedding and a rare note of warmth illuminated their first day as Tsar and Tsarina of Russia. When they made their way to the Anichkov Palace a mile or so away, Nicholas ordered that the guardsmen who stood shoulder to shoulder along their route be removed in what the correspondent of France's *Journal des Débats* called "a daring and beautiful gesture" as hordes of Petersburgers crowded around the Imperial sleigh.[23] George, Duke of York, and a future King of England, reported to his mother that Nicholas was "very popular already."[24]

It was perhaps a measure of Russians' longing to be rid of the heavy-handed regime of Alexander III that they appeared so anxious to bestow their hearts upon their new sovereign. But Nicholas proved utterly inept at cultivating that loyalty so generously and readily offered by his people. "We look forward, Sire, to its being possible and rightful for public institutions to express their views on matters concerning them, so that an expression of the . . . thought of representatives of the Russian people . . . may reach the heights of the throne," wrote the representatives of the *zemstvo*, the provincial assembly, of Tver.[25] In response, Nicholas lashed out with an inept and crushing reply that any such hopes were "senseless dreams." According to future Minister of Foreign Affairs Count Aleksandr Izvolskii, the phrase—indeed, the entire speech—was Pobedonostsev's, and Nicholas was so unacquainted with its contents and the issues involved that he scarcely knew what he was saying.[26] But the damage was done. Russian public opinion, and especially Feodor Rodichev, the influential chairman of the Tver *zemstvo* whose summary removal Nicholas had ordered, would never forget the seemingly arrogant words with which their new Tsar had greeted their expressions of responsible concern for Russia's welfare.[27] The gleam that Russians had seen in Nicholas's apparent modesty and quiet personal charm had been quickly tarnished. Very soon, it would be extinguished altogether.

Nowhere was Nicholas's ineptitude more blatantly evident than during his coronation festivities in the spring of 1896. More than any previous Romanov, he wanted the *narod* to feel that they were a part of his coronation, and he planned a mass banquet for them on a gargantuan scale. There would be dancing, circus performers, tables piled high with food, and twenty booths to dispense thousands upon thousands of gallons of beer. Nicholas sent proclamations throughout his Empire to invite his subjects to this great outdoor celebration to be held on May 18, the fourth day after his coronation. The *narod* were to assemble at Khodynka Field just outside Moscow, where the Imperial Army Corps of Engineers held summer maneuvers and practiced constructing entrenchments.[28]

Even before the spring thaws began, peasants and workers from all parts of Russia began moving in the direction of Moscow, intent upon seeing their Tsar and Tsarina and celebrating their coronation. More could do so than ever before because of the vast railroad-building program that Witte and Alexander III had championed. Russia now had over forty thousand *versty* of track over which passengers could travel distances that had seemed all but impassable just a few decades earlier. Such western Siberian towns as Tomsk and Tobolsk had been many weeks' journey from Moscow in earlier times. In 1896, even a peasant with a third-class ticket could make the journey in less than a week. It took only about three days to travel to Moscow from Kiev in the heart of the Ukraine. It cost less than nine rubles (about $4.40) to travel a thousand *versty* on the cheapest slow train, and the greater the distance one traveled the lower the rate became.[29] The railroad was beginning to bring Russia together as never before. Two decades later, these same improved means of travel would bring workers and peasants to St. Petersburg to proclaim Nicholas's overthrow.

As third-class passengers in slab-seated railroad cars, as deck passengers of riverboats, in rough, two-wheeled carts, and on foot, the Russian *narod* flowed toward Moscow in the spring of 1896. As one historian wrote not long ago, "all of Russia [was in Moscow]—

that is the Russia of bast shoes, of linen foot-wrappings, of shapeless blouses, blue pantaloons, *tulepy* (greasy sheepskin jackets), heavy capes, kaftans, and worn blackcloth coats."[30] Before dawn on the morning of May 18, almost a half-million had assembled at Khodynka. For days, they had eaten poorly—a crust of bread, a bowl of watery *shchi*, a raw onion, or a half-cooked potato—as they made their way to Moscow. Now, they were ready to fill their stomachs with their newly crowned Tsar's bread, sausage, and pastries and to slake their never-ending thirst for alcohol with the free beer to be drunk as toasts to Nicholas and Aleksandra from special commemorative mugs.

While tens of thousands of the *narod* were beginning to assemble at Khodynka Field during the waning hours of May 17, Pierre d'Alheim, Russian correspondent for *Le Temps* of Paris, was just leaving the Bolshoi Theater after a special performance of Glinka's *A Life for the Tsar*. D'Alheim found the streets outside the theater jammed with people, all moving purposefully away from the city's center. It struck him as strange: the Tsar in Moscow and the *narod* leaving? Then he remembered. "Ah, yes! Tomorrow is the people's celebration at Khodynka Field." He joined the crowd and found himself among old women and children, the halt and the blind, the infirm and the robust. He let himself be carried along by the surging throng, impressed by its calmness and deep religious fervor. "From time to time," he reported, "hands would be raised [in prayer] as they came to a chapel or a church, and, for an instant, one caught a glimpse of that white spot on every breast on which they wore emblems of the cross. Women even stopped, crowded together, and offered up brief prayers, bowing low before these sacred places. I was ecstatic," he continued. "How wonderful it was not to be considered a foreigner in this crowd and to be able to walk in the midst of these people!"

D'Alheim moved with the masses through "broad streets, sparsely lit by electric streetlamps, through dark alleys, and then along the *chaussée* outside the city." Suddenly, they were in the open countryside in the vicinity of Khodynka. The surging stream of people, until that point held in by buildings and trees along their route, "spread out into a wide river, and then became lost in a veritable sea of people into which its noise was absorbed." Here was everything that a foreign correspondent in search of the "real" Russia and the "real" Russians could have hoped for, and d'Alheim waxed poetic in his description of the way in which the throng passed the predawn hours. There were "old men lying on their stomachs and chatting peacefully. Maidens doing folk dances in a ring. Peasant lads lustily singing humorous ditties and everyone roaring with laughter."

Much to d'Alheim's amazement, the crowd's mood changed abruptly just before dawn broke. "Without any warning, something seemed to seize the crowd," he wrote. Suddenly fearful, d'Alheim pushed sideways, finally broke free, and took refuge in an all-night restaurant from which he could look out upon the mass of common folk from whose ranks he had just escaped. He watched the crowd grow larger, surging toward the stalls they knew would dispense beer and food at the far side of the field. "Suddenly, there was a terrible, long, drawn-out wail," he recalled. "I caught sight of a small girl, saw her rise above the heads of the crowd, and saw her disappear suddenly. Women and men, somehow being disgorged from the mass, broke away in utter terror." D'Alheim heard them shouting, "There are ditches and trenches in there! People are falling into them! They say that people are simply vanishing!"[31]

That day, d'Alheim got no closer than the edge of Khodynka Field. Vladimir Nemirovich-Danchenko, Stanislavskii's partner in founding the Moscow Art Theater and, in 1896, special correspondent for the St. Petersburg weekly *Niva*, went to Khodynka later that morning to investigate his cook's hysterical account of "thousands" being crushed to death in the ditches and trenches that crisscrossed the field. By the time he reached Khodynka, the crowd was gone, and he found row upon row of trampled, broken, battered corpses that just a few hours before had been men, women, and children, happily preparing to greet their Tsar.[32] According to official estimates, 1,389 people lost their lives in the stampede, and another 1,300 suffered injuries.[33] As with all official statistics published about disasters in Imperial Russia, these numbers were very low, and it is generally agreed that the numbers of killed and wounded were several times greater.

Ever the tough-minded and practical statesman, Witte urged Nicholas to cancel the rest of the coronation festivities.[34] Again, Nicholas made the worst decision possible. He and Aleksandra went on to attend the French ambassador's ball that evening, an event held at Moscow's exclusive Hunt Club upon which the French Government reportedly spent nearly a quarter-million rubles. Russians and foreigners alike were aghast at what many termed the young Tsar's callous disregard for the tragedy that had come so unexpectedly upon his people. The next day, Nicholas and Aleksandra hastened to attend a funeral service for the victims of Khodynka and visited several hospitals to offer their sympathies to those who had been injured. Nicholas donated a thousand rubles (several years' earnings for a peasant and most workers) to the families of each victim and founded a special orphanage for the children whose parents had perished in the disaster.[35] These were noble gestures, but their impact was diminished greatly by Nicholas's order to continue with plans for a great military review. Just eight days after Khodynka Field had been stained by the blood of innocent workers and peasants, Nicholas stood again on its reviewing stand to receive the salute of 40,592 men, including 67 generals, in a grand finale to his coronation celebrations.[36] By the end of May, articulate and progressive men and women who were dedicated to Russia and to Russia's well-being, many foreign observers, and a large segment of public opinion in Moscow—all had begun to condemn their young sovereign as insensitive, even arrogant.

During the first decade of his reign, Nicholas's advisers urged further industrialization, more railroad construction, and continued fiscal conservatism. As during the time of Alexander III, these policies produced impressive results, but left very pressing problems unattended. We have already seen that most Russians were still illiterate and therefore beyond the reach of the men who ruled them in an age in which the printed word was the only means of mass communication. They remained out of contact with the modern world in other crucial ways as well. Only a small percentage of

Nicholas's subjects ever saw a doctor in their entire lives. Almost none of the *narod* ever experienced any of those pleasures that educated men and women ranked in the category of "the finer things of life." Most Russians, in fact, were so impoverished that economists had begun to express reservations about the future of Russia's industrial development. The great surge of industrial activity in the 1880s and 1890s had been confined almost exclusively to the heavy industrial sector. "Upon what basis could light, consumer-oriented industries develop?" knowledgeable experts asked. As Nicholas's tenth anniversary approached, there was still no widespread demand for consumer goods in Russia because most Russians were too poor to buy them. As the pressures of the war with Japan weighed upon them, the plight of Russia's masses grew even more desperate.

Concerned about autocracy's apparent failure to recognize so many ominous signs of discontent and desperation, Count Lev Tolstoi urged Nicholas to "give the masses an opportunity to express their desires and demands," because, as he wrote in a famous open letter of 1902, "autocracy . . . no longer answers the needs of the Russian people." Above all, Tolstoi warned the Tsar not to be lulled into false confidence by the fabled love of the *narod,* for that was an anachronistic dream at best.[37] Nicholas ignored the warning and chose instead to heed Pobedonostsev's counsel that "the continuation of the regime . . . depends upon our ability to keep Russia in a frozen state."[38] Very soon, he faced the anger of a *narod* too long suppressed. This time, the people's anger did not burst into flame in some distant part of the Russian countryside as it had in the seventeenth and eighteenth centuries. In 1905, the men and women who demanded better conditions in which to live and work marched in the streets of St. Petersburg itself. Their appearance posed a new and very frightening threat to Russia's established order.

Like their predecessors, Nicholas and his advisers had buried their heads deeply in the sand whenever anyone spoke of controlling the abuses factory owners inflicted upon their workers. Even so perceptive a statesman as Witte self-assuredly remarked in 1895 that "in Russia, fortunately, there is no working class in the western sense; therefore, there is no labor problem."[39] At the time, Witte thought (or so he said) that relations between workers and their employers ought to be governed by "moral laws and Christian feelings" and went on to insist that "in our industry, a patriarchal order prevails in the relations between factory owner and his workers." Such paternal concern, he explained, was "expressed in many cases by the mill owner's care for the needs of the workers and other employees in his factory."[40] Less than half a decade later, he had to revise his views dramatically as factory workers began to organize into unions, and strikes became more frequent and widespread.

In the first year of Nicholas's reign, there had been sixty-eight strikes in all of Russia. By 1903, the number had risen above five hundred, and almost ninety thousand workers were involved. Perhaps even more dangerous for the established order, during those years, nearly half a million workers had taken part in at least one strike.[41] No longer were Russian proletarians novices in the arena of labor protest. Nor were they helplessly disorganized. During the so-called political "spring" that followed the assassination of Plehve in July 1904, the workers in St. Petersburg took great strides toward making a citywide union of laboring men and women a reality. "In two or three years, all two hundred thousand Petersburg workers will be members of our union," exclaimed their leader, Father Gapon.[42] But already Gapon had begun to look far beyond that objective. That March, he had told a small gathering of radical workers: "We shall unite the workers in all of Russia!"[43] A dream such as his was both daring and dangerous, and one that all Russian statesmen feared.

A slightly built man, with dark hair and piercing black eyes, Georgii Gapon came from a well-to-do Ukrainian peasant family. As a youth, he set out to become a priest, was momentarily deflected from his path by a brief flirtation with some of Tolstoi's forbidden spiritual musings, but managed to graduate from St. Petersburg's Seminary in 1898 at the age of twenty-eight. He discovered then that he could charm the masses with his words and set out to work his art upon the city's laboring folk. He spent many hours in the harbor district, a part of St. Petersburg "where the poorest people

lived in the greatest poverty," he later wrote. To this flock, he began
to preach a new message and was enthralled by their response.
"Often more than two thousand people gathered to hear me," he
recalled a few years later. "I told them that they might achieve better
results for themselves by some sort of workingmen's organization
than by clashes with the authorities."[44]

The organization Gapon urged his followers to form owed its
beginnings to none other than Zubatov, whose protégé he was. As
such, the young priest won official permission in August 1903 to
found the St. Petersburg Assembly of Russian Factory and Mill
Workers—known more simply as the Assembly—and then gained
a surprising amount of independence from the Okhrana, which in
turn gave him greater authority with the masses to whom he
spoke.[45] Under Prince Petr Sviatopolk-Mirskii's more progressive
policies as Plehve's successor in the Ministry of Internal Affairs,
Gapon further broadened his Assembly's influence among Petersburg's millhands. But with success came new dangers as factory
owners began to fear that Gapon might one day unite their entire
labor force into a citywide organization. In response to their heated
complaints, the briefly mild political climate began to chill.[46]

At the very beginning of 1905, workers went on strike at the
Putilov Works, where twelve thousand men and women labored in
arms productions and shipbuilding. "The workers of the Putilov
Plant demand that the factory management deal with their demands
openly, and not resort to tricks, promises that are meant to be
broken, and the assistance of the police," they announced.[47] They
called for an eight-hour day, the abolition of compulsory overtime
work, higher wages for unskilled workers, better medical facilities,
and free medical care.[48] What at first had seemed nothing more
than a minor dispute over a few firings burgeoned into a massive
labor protest as thousands of workers from other factories joined the
Putilov men. By the middle of the first week of January, twenty-five
thousand men and women were on strike in St. Petersburg.

A strike on this scale would have disturbed the government at
any time, but it made the authorities particularly nervous because
of the impending festival of Epiphany, when the Emperor tradition-

ally took part in a ceremonial blessing of the Neva's waters. Persistent rumors about possible assassination plots kept police and army on edge during these days, especially because the recent killings of Ministers of Internal Affairs Sipiagin and Plehve gave them considerable substance. Clearly the Combat Detachment of the Socialist Revolutionary party that Azef had taken over from Grigorii Gershuni in 1903 was a far deadlier instrument than earlier terrorist organizations had been.

As Epiphany, January 6, 1905, dawned, it seemed that St. Petersburg's police had perhaps overemphasized the threat of attacks by revolutionary terrorists. With the capital's high-ranking officials and diplomatic corps looking on from the windows of the great Nicholas Hall in the Winter Palace, the Metropolitan Antonii blessed the waters, while Nicholas performed his traditional ceremonial role. From across the river, the guns at the Peter-Paul Fortress fired in salute. Suddenly, terror seized the onlookers. "At the third or fourth shot, pieces of broken glass shattered from the window above our heads," wrote Dmitrii Liubimov, who witnessed the scene. "Someone shouted in Russian: 'They are firing live ammunition!' And the shout was repeated in other languages. Small holes could be seen in the upper portions of the windows that left no doubt about what was happening."[49] "It seemed that this was an attempt on the lives of the Tsar and the high officials who were at the ceremony in great numbers," wrote Grand Duke Konstantin Konstantinovich, who was standing with Nicholas on the embankment when the salutes were fired.[50] Many must have had the same fear. Frantic inquiries revealed that a few live rounds had gotten mixed in with the blanks by accident and that no one's life had been in danger because the salutes had been aimed high above the heads of the crowd. Yet the mood had been set. Police officials and the officers who commanded the Petersburg garrison grew more on edge, especially when the city's printers joined the Putilov men and newspapers did not appear the next day.[51] The stage was set for more dramatic events, and they followed very quickly.

To give better direction to the workers'. discontent, Father Gapon planned to lead them directly to the Winter Palace on

Sunday, January 9, where they would present their petition to the Tsar. "We, the workers of St. Petersburg, our wives, children, and helpless old folk, have come to you to seek justice and protection," were its first words.[52] The workers wanted to express their hope that Nicholas, their Tsar and *Batiushka*, would defend them against the factory owners and plant managers.

During the days that separated Epiphany from January 9, Father Gapon seemed to be everywhere in St. Petersburg's workers' districts exhorting followers to join his march to the Palace Square. In the workers' clubs of the Narva Quarter where the stale air and stench from hundreds of unwashed bodies made breathing difficult, in the smoke-filled cafés, teahouses, and taverns where workers drowned their sorrows in watery beer and fiery cheap vodka, and even in the streets where men and women huddled against the biting wind and fierce cold, Gapon asked the same question. "Supposing the Tsar will not receive us and will not read our petition?" Everywhere, the same answer was shouted back with unmistakable resolve: "Then we have no Tsar!"[53] Wrote one eyewitness, "Like an echo the phrase repeated itself from all sides: 'No Tsar! No Tsar!.' "[54] Had he heard the vehemence of their replies, Nicholas might have responded in a different manner when the working men and women of St. Petersburg marched to the Palace Square that Sunday.

The workers who marched with Father Gapon knew that they might be fired upon, but they had sworn to lay down their lives in the cause of freedom. "It is better for us to die for our demands than to live as we have lived until now," proclaimed one worker. "Do you swear to die [if necessary]?" he asked those who stood before him. "We swear!" some seven hundred working men and women called back. "But what about those who swear to die [for our cause] today, but get cold feet and don't march with us tomorrow?" he asked again. "Let them be damned!" the crowd roared back.[55] "Suppose that the workers do not show up tomorrow?" some of the leading revolutionaries in St. Petersburg asked each other in worried tones.[56] The workers had no such doubts about themselves. Not knowing what lay ahead, they made ready for their march. "If I am killed, then do not weep," wrote one of them in a farewell note to his wife and infant son that night. "Raise Vaniura," he begged, "and tell him that I died a martyr for the freedom and happiness of the people."[57] Only a few hours remained before the march began. "Many turned their attention that evening to the huge blood-red moon that rose above the horizon," one eyewitness remembered. "On this night, Petersburg was the very heart of Russia."[58]

While workers in their crowded slums slept fitfully, paced nervously, wrote notes to loved ones, or prayed to a God in whom some of them no longer truly believed, the forces of St. Petersburg's Governor, General Ivan Fullon, were busy with their own last-minute preparations. Just that afternoon, battalions had arrived from Pskov and Reval, so that the capital now held some twelve thousand cavalry and infantry. "Petersburg resembled a city that had been seized by enemy soldiers," one commentator wrote. "Bivouacs were laid out in its streets and squares, and campfires burned brightly.[59] Ambulances stood ready to take on the wounded, and great kettles of soup steamed in company mess kitchens that had been set up in the open. At about midnight, orders came down from Guards Commander Prince Vasilchikov to issue live ammunition and extra rations of vodka. The soldiers were told that the workers were preparing to destroy the Winter Palace, and murder the Tsar, his family, and many leading officials.[60] Before daybreak, General Fullon's "twelve thousand bayonets and sabers" stood waiting for the workers' advance. "The workers made ready to go to the Tsar," one historian remarked, "while the Tsar prepared his forces for a mass slaughter."[61]

The morning of January 9 dawned bright and clear, the temperature about five degrees below freezing. It was one of those rare Petersburg winter days when there was no wind. Gapon assembled his marchers at several points in the workers' suburbs and, from there, planned to march them along the great avenues that converged on the Winter Palace Square. The workers and their wives and children came dressed in their best, looking sober, serious, and purposeful. "Put on your best dress," they had been told. "Take your children and your wives. No arms, not even penknives."[62] All revolutionary symbols were to be excluded from the demonstration. Workers were to sing religious hymns, not revolutionary songs. They were to carry ikons, not revolutionary placards. Portraits of Nicholas and Aleksandra, not red banners and revolutionary slogans, were to rise above their heads. They were even urged to be careful about taking red handkerchiefs from their pockets.[63] Nothing was to be done that could give the authorities the least cause for alarm. "Save us, O Lord, your people!" they sang as they marched. "How glorious is our Lord in Zion!"[64] Some thirty thousand strong, they marched to carry their petition to Nicholas, the "Little Father" who, peasants had believed for centuries, was their protector against the strong and cruel masters who ruled their lives. On they came, "Like a powerful rising tide/ The *narod* kept coming," wrote the anonymous author of *Red Snow.*[65] "The crowd reminded one of the ocean's dark billows," the Bolshevik writer Maksim Gorkii added. "The gray faces of the people were like the turbid, foamy crests of the waves."[66]

To stop the workers' march upon the Palace Square, General Fullon had thrown barricades across the great avenues that connected the workers' districts with the center of the city. At each of these points, soldiers tried to turn back workers; at several of them, officers ordered their men to fire into the defenseless crowds. The worst slaughter took place on the Winter Palace Square itself, where a company of Preobrazhenskii Guards, their captain acting on direct orders from Guards Commander Prince Vasilchikov, shot several hundred workers. Among the first to fall was an old man who had marched confidently forward, proudly bearing the Tsar's portrait aloft. Beside him fell a small child who had been carrying a lantern.[67] When the day's bloody work was done, between 150 and 200 men, women, and children lay dead, and another 450 to 800 had been wounded.[68] Among the dead lay Ivan Vasilev, the worker who had left his wife a note that morning begging her to raise their son in the knowledge that his father had died for freedom.

While sabers cut through padded jackets to the flesh beneath and rifle shots rang out in St. Petersburg's streets, Nicholas remained at Tsarskoe Selo with Aleksandra and their children. When he received the first reports from Fullon and Vasilchikov, he wrote in his diary: "Many were killed and wounded. God, how painful and heartbreaking!"[69] He hastened to receive a carefully chosen delegation of thirty-four workers whom he lectured in the manner of a stern father about the need for order and the evils of revolutionary propaganda. "I believe in the honest feelings of the working people and in their unshakable loyalty to me," he told the workers who stood unwillingly before him. "Therefore, I forgive them."[70] "The Russian people are deeply and truly devoted to their Sovereign," Aleksandra assured her sister, Princess Victoria of Battenberg, later that month.[71] Nicholas and Aleksandra would have been far less smug in their confidence about the workers' loyalty had they seen the letter from Father Gapon, by then in hiding, that Gorkii read out at a meeting a few days later. "There is no Tsar!" Gapon proclaimed. "Between him and the people lies the blood of our comrades. Long live then the beginning of the popular struggle for freedom!"[72] Great cheers greeted Gorkii's reading. Workers had died on that terrible day of January 9, 1905. The most momentous casualty of all, however, was the death of the people's belief that Nicholas was their "Little Father." That myth, for so long a vital bulwark in defenses of the Romanovs' autocracy against all enemies, could never be resurrected.

Bloody Sunday marked the beginning of what the Dowager Empress Maria Feodorovna called the "year of nightmares."[73] Tragedy followed tragedy, crisis piled upon crisis, as Russian workers and revolutionaries struck their first blows in the cause of freedom. The first Romanov casualty, literally blown to bits by a nitroglycerine bomb thrown by a member of the Socialist Revolutionary Combat Detachment, was Grand Duke Sergei Aleksandrovich, commander of the Moscow military region and former Military Governor General of Moscow, who had publicly sworn his hatred for revolutionaries. Members of his own family thought him "obstinate, arrogant, disagreeable," a man who "flaunted his many peculiarities in the face of the entire nation, providing the enemies of the regime with inexhaustible material for calumnies and libels."[74] He was both Nicholas's uncle and brother-in-law, the husband of Aleksandra's elder sister, and one of those several senior uncles about whom

Nicholas felt apprehensive, even fearful. As Moscow's Governor General he had proved utterly incompetent. Nonetheless, Nicholas had allowed him to remain in office until he himself resigned over a policy dispute late in January.

Neither Nicholas nor Aleksandra attended Sergei Aleksandrovich's funeral on February 6 because their advisers thought it dangerous for them to leave the safety of Tsarskoe Selo. After one brief decade on the throne, the Tsar who had insisted that the troops be removed from his route so that the people of St. Petersburg could greet him and his bride on the day of their marriage no longer dared go among his subjects even in the company of armed guards. "These terrible events seem like a dream of some kind," the Grand Duke Konstantin Konstantinovich wrote in his diary on the day of Sergei Aleksandrovich's funeral. "Here in Russia, things get worse all the time. If you look back to the fall—to September and October—you simply can't believe how quickly we have advanced toward an encounter with disaster, with unknown misfortunes."[75]

Yet the assassination of Sergei Aleksandrovich signaled only the beginning of a broader wave of popular unrest that had been sparked by the events of Bloody Sunday. As the war in the Far East went from bad to worse and as Nicholas stubbornly refused to heed pleas that he grant a constitution and summon a national Duma (parliament), agitation and revolutionary activity increased. Yet demonstrations, strikes, and even terrorism posed no serious threat to the autocratic regime of Nicholas II so long as his armed forces remained loyal. Soldiers had fired upon workers and peasants on January 9. So long as they continued to do so, Nicholas's crown remained secure. Suddenly, the balance seemed to shift. On June 14, the crew of the battleship *Potëmkin* mutinied in the Black Sea harbor of Odessa.

That Russia's first serious military dissent should occur in the navy rather than the army may seem surprising. The navy usually required more training, more education, and longer terms of service from those who served in its ranks, and even draftees were obliged to stay on active duty for seven years before they were released to the reserves. During such long terms of service, sailors grew accustomed to the navy's severe discipline. It was almost unthinkable for a sailor to refuse an order, and doing so meant almost certain death by firing squad. In an army weakened by bloody fighting in the Far East and plagued by shortages of weapons, supplies, and medicine that cost thousands of lives, mutiny seemed a far more real possibility than it did in the well-disciplined Black Sea Fleet, whose sailors had been spared the peril of battle because international conventions denied their ships entrance into the Mediterranean Sea and the oceans that lay beyond. Yet safety from battle had another consequence for men more literate than their counterparts in other branches of Russia's military service. The lower decks of the Black Sea Fleet included a well-developed network of radical discussion groups and revolutionary cells. Sailors of this fleet were no strangers to revolutionary propaganda, and a number were deeply attracted by it.[76]

With a crew of 768, the *Potëmkin* was one of the newest and most modern ships in the Black Sea Fleet. So many of her senior sailors and petty officers had been taken off to serve on Admiral Rozhdestvenskii's shorthanded Baltic cruisers when they were sent to the Far East that, by early 1905, only one crewman out of five was an experienced hand, while the rest had only recently been taken from their native villages. These men were neither well disciplined nor well trained, and they were unaccustomed to the hardships of navy life. Their commander, Captain E. N. Golikov, was a notoriously stern disciplinarian who made no allowances for the difficulties faced by awkward peasant lads in learning to become sailors. As word of disorders elsewhere in Russia began to reach the Black Sea ports, Golikov endeavored to isolate the *Potëmkin*'s sailors from revolutionary contamination by confining them aboard ship whenever they docked, and his restrictions became especially severe when a general strike broke out in Odessa that spring. On June 12, a number of workers were killed by rifle fire in confrontations between strikers and troops while the *Potëmkin* was anchored in Odessa harbor, and the next day, a party of seamen who had been sent ashore to buy provisions returned and brought word of the killings. They also brought meat that was crawling with maggots from which Golikov ordered the ship's kitchen to prepare the sailors' midday meal. That night, the men resolved not to accept worm-filled rations the next day. When they carried out their resolution, Golikov ordered his guards to open fire, and the sailors' peaceful protest became a violent mutiny.[77]

Led by a handful of revolutionary sailors, the *Potëmkin*'s crew arrested Golikov and seized his ship. For the first time in Russia's history, the red banner of revolt waved from the mast of an Imperial ship of war, while, for two days, Odessa suffered what may have been the bloodiest fighting of the entire year. Yet the *Potëmkin* sailors were involved in the Odessa street battles only incidentally, and most of the nearly two thousand who fell in the conflict were strikers and their sworn enemies on the far right, the Black Hundreds. The *Potëmkin* sailors tried to bring their heavy guns to bear in support of the strikers but failed. Nor were their efforts to win over the rest of the Black Sea Fleet any more successful. Unable to turn their mutiny into the beginning of the armed rebellion of which Russia's revolutionaries had dreamed so long, the *Potëmkin*'s crew sailed out of Odessa harbor. Ten days later, they docked at the Rumanian port of Constanta to take on water and provisions. Unable to obtain supplies, they surrendered to the local authorities. The Rumanians refused irate Russian demands for extradition of the *Potëmkin* mutineers, and most of them emigrated to the United States, Canada, and Brazil. Although the *Potëmkin* mutiny did not mark the beginning of a larger rebellion, the ship, its crew, and the strikers of Odessa became much-needed symbols for revolutionaries at home and abroad in their struggle against Nicholas's government. As summer approached, that struggle shifted to the Russian countryside and to a number of provincial cities, where it became more fragmented, more destructive, and more brutal.[78]

Between May Day and the beginning of September, the Russian countryside was swept by violence while strikes held many towns and provincial manufacturing centers in their grasp. Almost three-quarters of a million workers were on strike during those months. In Ivanovo-Voznesensk a strike of about fifty thousand workers lasted for seventy-two days. Tbilisi was hit by a general strike at the end of June and had to be placed under martial law. There were strikes in Nizhnii-Novgorod, Minsk, Kharkov, Rostov-on-the-Don, Riga, Revel, Kovno, Belostok, and Pinsk, and outbreaks of violence among the peasants in more than half of Russia's provinces. By the beginning of September, the year had seen 3,129 strikes and 1,194 peasant disturbances.[79] Everywhere, troops fired upon striking workers. Sixty-five were killed and wounded in Stavropol, another forty in Nizhnii-Novgorod, and thirty-five more in Novorossiisk. In Belostok, the figure rose to over a hundred, and so it went throughout the summer as Nicholas and his ministers proved that, while Bloody Sunday had been the first bloodletting of the year, it was by no means the last.[80] Between Bloody Sunday and the late fall, Nicholas and his military advisers assigned 15,297 companies of infantry and 3,665 squadrons of cavalry, with 224 cannon and 124 machine guns, to suppress strikes and peasant riots.[81]

The summer of 1905 saw yet another phenomenon enter the arena of Russian labor protest. Those newly built railroads Witte had called the key to Russia's economic development also spread the strike movement across the Empire. No longer was it only the railroad workers of St. Petersburg and Moscow who protested. There were strikes in distant Krasnoiarsk, in the Siberian centers of Omsk and Irkutsk, and at stations along the Trans-Siberian line to the east of Lake Baikal.[82] By September, there had been over two hundred strikes among railroad workers, more than in all of Russia's history.[83] Numbers were cut down by Cossack sabers and infantry bullets, as desperate officials tried to get tens of thousands of tons of stalled freight moving in order to prevent shortages of flour and bread in Russia's cities. Very quickly, it became clear that railroad workers could play a very important part in developing regional or even national strike movements.

By summer's end, Russian workers no longer were isolated from each other as the railroads tied revolutionary organizations together across the Empire. Even more disturbing from the government's point of view, these groups were no longer defenseless. "There began to be formed small squads of workers armed with pistols," wrote the Bolshevik Sergei Mitskevich in his memoirs about

Moscow in September 1905.[84] For the first time, an armed uprising of workers in some of Russia's industrial centers became a real possibility, and the nature of the revolutionary movement shifted accordingly. No longer could revolutionary groups dedicate themselves mainly to theoretical debates, propaganda, and agitation designed to convince the workers to strike. At least part of their resources had to be directed to obtaining weapons and training their members to use them.

Yet arms were costly and very difficult to obtain in Russia. A number of revolutionaries therefore turned to foreign sources, especially to Brussels, headquarters of the International Socialist Bureau, and Lièges, which boasted a colony of over a thousand Russian émigrés. Browning and Mauser pistols were the favored weapons, and they were purchased by students with revolutionary sympathies who then smuggled them across Russia's long borders. Through Finland, across the Baltic, through the Balkans, and across the Austrian border these weapons made their way into Russia. The cartridges they required were made in secret during the evenings from materials stolen from Russian weapons factories. They were then distributed in packets of fifty, wrapped in such a way to resemble a newly purchased book wrapped in brown paper.[85] By the end of September, they found their way into the jacket pockets of revolutionary agitators who went among the workers to stir them to further deeds of labor protest.

In early October 1905, Lenin was in Switzerland and Martov was in Vienna. Neither saw the approach of revolution and neither was prepared for it. Then, before either of them realized it, revolution had all of Russia in its grip. Its outbreak had not been planned; like most mass upheavals, it had burst forth spontaneously. For a fortnight, a printers' strike in Moscow had ebbed, surged forward, and ebbed again as other workers joined it briefly and then returned to work.[86] By October 5, the strike seemed to lose force and the momentum of the workers' movement appeared to be lost. This proved to be only the deceptive calm before a storm unlike any Russia had ever seen.

Between October 7 and October 17, the entire Russian Empire was paralyzed by a spontaneous strike movement that involved millions of workers. The railroad men struck the Moscow-Kazan Railroad on the morning of October 7, and, in support of their effort, some eleven thousand printers and silversmiths left their presses and benches.[87] "Into the fray! Join the struggle for freedom, comrades!" they proclaimed. "Moscow is the heart of Russia. It . . . will become the heart of a mass rebellion!"[88] Almost as if someone had set up vast strings of dominoes along all the rail lines that spread out from Moscow like the spokes of a wheel and then had knocked over the one standing in the very center, the strike spread outward in scarcely more time than it took for the trains to travel. It reached Kursk, Nizhnii-Novgorod, Kiev, Riazan, and Voronezh on the 9th; St. Petersburg and Kharkov on the 10th. By October 14, it had breached the Urals and the Caucasus Mountains and flowed into Georgia, Central Asia, and Siberia. Traffic came to a standstill along some twenty-six thousand miles of track as three-quarters of a million railroad employees laid down their tools and walked away from their work.[89] In a number of provincial towns and cities, workers took up pistols and sabers and went into the streets to meet force with force. The red banners of revolution rose above their ranks as they sang the "Marseillaise" and proclaimed "Freedom, Life or Death!" "Down with Autocracy!" and "Long Live the Revolution!"[90] No longer were Russia's laboring men and women willing to settle for better pay and working conditions. In October, they called for the right to determine their fate and that of their fellows. While political demands had been notably absent from workers' protests earlier in the year, well over half of the strikers in October demanded that Nicholas grant political concessions.[91] As the protests continued, Nicholas continued to do nothing to meet the workers' demands.

By the time the railway workers' strike had reached Siberia and Central Asia, much of European Russia was in the grip of one of the greatest and most effective general strikes in the history of labor protest anywhere in the world. All of Russia's industry ground to a halt. All of her public services ceased to function. In St. Petersburg, virtually everyone left work. Factory workers, servants, postal workers, telegraph operators, janitors, and hackney drivers all walked off their jobs, as did bank clerks, shop clerks, and clerks in government offices. Doctors, lawyers, schoolteachers, university professors, even the entire corps de ballet of the great Imperial Mariinskii Theater —all joined the strike. There were no newspapers, no streetlights, no tramcars. Food and fuel soon grew scarce.[92]

Throughout these momentous days in St. Petersburg, Sergei Mintslov, novelist, rare book dealer, and bibliographer, dutifully recorded his impressions in a diary to leave us a record of the reactions of a man who generally stood apart from politics.

> October 12th. Piter* is now cut off from the rest of Russia. . . . Panic is beginning to spread throughout the city. People are certain that by evening all shops will shut their doors and go on strike. . . . Sausage shops, bakeries, and grocers' shops are all besieged by customers as everyone tries to lay in a stock of provisions. The price of meat has soared [during the course of one day] from 16 to 22 kopeks a pound. . . .

> October 14th. Shop windows are all boarded up for protection. There is no electricity today. Shop interiors are dully lit by a few candles or by some sort of cheap oil lamps. Everything looks as if it has been fixed so that, with the very first tremors, the proprietors need only shut their doors and douse the lights in order to turn their shops into little strongholds.

> October 15th. Reinforcements have arrived in Piter. They say that infantry have been brought from Pskov and the Guards' Cavalry from Tsarskoe Selo. . . . There are no newspapers today. . . . The Tsar is at Peterhof where the Imperial yacht, "Polar Star," remains under

---

*"Piter" was a slang term for St. Petersburg, comparable to the popular American usage of "Frisco" for San Francisco.

full steam and ready to take him aboard and flee to Denmark.

October 16th. Evening. The electricity has been playing tricks. One minute the streets are pitch dark. Suddenly, there is a crackling sound and all the streetlamps flame with light only to go out again in a few minutes. A huge searchlight illuminates the Nevskii Prospekt. . . . Rumors are flying that the "revolution" will break out on the 20th, and now all workers and revolutionaries are laying in weapons.

October 17th. The mood of alarm continues. . . . All institutions of higher education are occupied by soldiers and machine guns. . . . Everyone is convinced that the Tsar does not want to hear of any concessions, and that, in the highest circles of government, they are firmly resolved to "spill the blood of the revolution."[93]

The rumors about decisiveness among Nicholas's ministers were far from accurate. In fact, they were almost paralyzed. "Instead of acting with quick decision, the ministers only assemble in council like a lot of frightened hens and cackle about providing united ministerial action," the Tsar complained to his mother a few days later.[94] At the same time, the revolutionaries organized a new body to coordinate the striking workers and express their economic and political demands. This was the St. Petersburg Soviet of Workers' Deputies, a unique organization of laboring men and women that would become an important feature of the revolution of 1905 and would reemerge to play an absolutely central role in the February Revolution of 1917. In both instances, soviets were found not only in the capital, but all over Russia, although the St. Petersburg Soviet held the most authority because of its proximity to the centers of Russian administrative and political power.

Forged in the crucible of revolutionary struggle, the Soviet of Workers' Deputies captured the imaginations of workers and revolutionaries alike. "Soviets of workers' deputies," Lenin later wrote in the Bolshevik newspaper *Novaia zhizn (New Life)*, "are not workers' parliaments. . . . They are fighting organizations created to achieve certain specific ends."[95] Somewhat surprisingly, they were born not of theorists' fertile imaginations but of workers' practice in the midst of labor protest. The first Soviet of Workers' Deputies in Russia thus was formed by the striking workers of the great textile center of Ivanovo-Voznesensk on May 15, 1905, in an effort to impose their demands more effectively upon the factory owners of the entire region. The Soviet had evolved spontaneously from a mass meeting on the banks of a nearby river, but it proved effective. The workers of Ivanovo revered it as their own revolutionary instrument, and it commanded intense loyalty among them.[96] As such, it was not surprising that it should emerge to play a central part in the experience of the St. Petersburg workers when the great October strikes began.

Convened on October 13, with a membership of about thirty workers' deputies, the St. Petersburg Soviet's leading organizers were *Mensheviki,* and its numbers soon grew to 562. Its leading figure was Lev Davidovich Bronshtein, the fiery young son of a Jewish farmer from the southern Ukraine. Although just turned twenty-six, Bronshtein was well known in radical circles by his revolutionary nom de guerre—Trotskii. A relative newcomer to the revolutionary movement, Trotskii was not firmly allied with either the *Bolsheviki* or *Mensheviki.* Unlike their leaders Lenin and Martov, however, he had had the good fortune (or, perhaps the great foresight) to have spent much of 1905 in Russia. By early summer, he had been forced to flee, but he went no further than Finland. October 1905 thus found Trotskii only a few hours away from the center of Russia's revolutionary events, and he moved quickly to take advantage of his fortunate situation.[97] Proclaiming, "Citizens! Our strength is in ourselves," he took command of the Petersburg Soviet, and it became a testing ground for the platforms and tactics of all revolutionary groups in Russia.[98] "By placing many disconnected organizations under its control," Trotskii later wrote, "the Soviet united the revolution around itself."[99]

Even if it had been as united as Trotskii claimed, the workers' revolution had no chance for success in 1905, for Nicholas still had the support of the Imperial army. Fearful that the workers might try to overthrow the government, Nicholas gave General Dmitrii Trepov full authority to deal with all outbreaks of violence and disorder in the capital. Unlike Tsar and ministers, Trepov suffered no lack of resolve, nor had he any doubts about his course of action. Hastily he reinforced the Petersburg garrison and issued his first and most famous order: "Use no blanks and don't skimp on bullets!"[100] As Nicholas wrote to his mother soon afterward, "Trepov made it quite plain to the populace by his proclamations that any disorder would be ruthlessly put down; and, of course, everybody believed that." But Trepov's firm decree did not end the October crisis. What Nicholas called "the ominous quiet days" began. "Everybody knew that something was going to happen," he wrote. "The troops were waiting for the signal, but the other side would not begin."[101] To break the impasse without great bloodshed, Nicholas had to give way to some of his people's demands for a voice in their own, and Russia's, destiny.

Once again, it was Witte who became the man of the hour. "I am sure that the only man who can help you now and be useful is Witte," the Dowager Empress had written to her son a few days before. "He certainly is a man of genius, *energetic*, and clear-sighted."[102] Nicholas did not readily share his mother's wise opinion of the man who had served him and his father so well, but he turned to Witte because he could think of no other alternative. While he discussed with Witte the course they must follow, he lamented to his mother that "I have nobody to rely upon except honest Trepov!"[103]

Faced by a general strike, the newly formed Soviet of Workers' Deputies, and crowds of demonstrators in the streets, Witte was not inclined to soften the stern message he delivered to his Emperor. As Nicholas understood his blunt explanation, "There were only two ways open: to find an energetic soldier [to lead the army] and crush the rebellion by sheer force. There would be time to breathe then but, as likely as not, one would have to use force again in a few months; and that would mean rivers of blood, and in the end we should be where we had started. . . . The other way out," he continued, "would be to give to the people their civil rights, freedom of speech and press, also to have all laws confirmed by a State Duma —that, of course, would be a constitution."[104]

Nicholas much preferred bullets to ballots, but Witte refused any part in a military dictatorship. Nicholas therefore called in his uncle, Grand Duke Nikolai Nikolaevich, six feet five inches tall and every inch a soldier's soldier. He proposed to make Nikolai Nikolaevich military dictator of Russia.[105] According to the oft-repeated tale, the Grand Duke swore to shoot himself on the spot if Nicholas insisted and urged him to follow Witte's advice and grant a constitution.[106] Nicholas gave in. On October 17, 1905, Witte published the famous October Manifesto by which Nicholas granted to all Russians civil rights, agreed to summon a Duma (national assembly) elected by a wide (but not universal) suffrage, and agreed that all laws must be approved by the Duma.[107] "God Almighty will be our help," wrote Nicholas. "I feel Him supporting me and putting strength into me, which gives me courage and does not allow me to lose heart."[108] Wrote the Grand Duke Konstantin Konstantinovich from Tashkent when he received word of Nicholas's manifesto: "It's the end of Autocracy! This new freedom does not come as a benevolent expression of a powerful sovereign's free will, but only as a concession, torn from him by force." To grant such concessions in a moment of weakness and at a time of crisis, the Grand Duke lamented, "produced a very painful impression."[109] Nonetheless, a new era in Russia's history had begun. Nicholas had just proclaimed himself his country's first constitutional monarch, but he found the role an awkward one. His new regime brought violence, terror, and bloodshed to Russia.

Russians greeted the October Manifesto in different ways and with a variety of emotions. "Hurrah! We are now free people!" the usually staid Mintslov exclaimed from his study.[110] But most reactions were more subtle and complex. To his left-wing liberal followers, Miliukov proclaimed the Tsar's manifesto a victory, but one that easily could be lost. "Will this be our last and final victory?" Miliukov asked when he heard of Nicholas's agreement to Witte's proposals. "We must not abandon our battle stations," he warned. "We must continue the struggle for freedom in order to prove ourselves worthy."[111] Together, Miliukov and his associates formed the *Kadety*, a party that stood to the left of center but still favored change through legal and peaceful means. They shared that aspiration with the men who stood on their immediate right, moderates who accepted Nicholas's decree at face value and eventually built a political platform for the Octobrist party upon it. Although often in conflict, both groups nonetheless dedicated themselves to nurturing the fragile seed of constitutionalism in order to make it bear in Russia the harvest it had yielded in the West. As we shall see in the next chapter, their dream proved more difficult to preserve, and the seed more costly to nourish, than any of them had expected.

In contrast to the liberals and moderates, reactionaries in Russia were aghast at what Nicholas and Witte had done. "Fear has driven them out of their minds in St. Petersburg!" ranted Dmitrii Pikhno, editor of the *Kievlianin*, a provincial newspaper so reactionary that it had been the only one in all of Russia to continue its publication during the October general strike. "God alone knows what they are doing! They're actually making the revolution themselves!" Pikhno thought that the October Manifesto had destroyed the very foundations upon which Russia had been built. "People have laid down their lives 'For the Faith, the Tsar, and Country'— and this is how Russia was created," he exclaimed. "But who is going to lay down his life 'For the State Duma'?" A loyal Russian reactionary could not blame the Tsar for long, however. There were other scapegoats upon whose heads anger could fall more easily. To Pikhno's mind, there was a very simple explanation for the Tsar's behavior during the October crisis. "It's the Jews!" he told the young conservative lawyer Vasilii Shulgin.[112]

Such reactionaries as Pikhno immediately organized groups of bigoted and brutal men into Black Hundreds. Their program, as Pikhno indicated in his first outburst against the October Manifesto, was a narrow vision of Orthodoxy, Autocracy, and Nationality, which the Black Hundreds used to justify their hatred for all non-

Russians in the Empire, especially Jews. Beatings, even murder, were how they dealt with any who opposed them. In less than a week after the October Manifesto was published, the people of Moscow felt their wrath as these vengeful reactionaries killed or wounded some two dozen workers and students on the city's streets. In other Russian cities, more casualties followed. The urban masses blamed the Tsar. Wrote Mitskevich, "They began to call him Bloody Nicholas and Nicholas the Swindler."[113]

In St. Petersburg, Trotskii voiced sentiments shared by all revolutionaries in the uncertain days of late October. "A constitution is given, but the autocracy remains," he warned. "Everything is given and nothing is given." As if clearly remembering the detachments of Cossack cavalry whose whips and truncheons broke the ranks of striking workers, he threw down a ringing condemnation: "The proletariat . . . does not want a *nagaika,* a Cossack whip, wrapped up in a constitution!"[114] Trotskii and other revolutionaries urged workers into the streets to "stand guard over our freedom." After all, he cried, "isn't Trepov's order to spare no bullets hanging by the side of the manifesto about our freedoms?"[115] Together, they urged the workers to collect money to purchase more weapons, to defend their rights against the agents of autocracy. More Brownings quickly made their way into proletarian pockets.[116]

With weapons in the hands of revolutionary workers as well as those of the reactionary small shopkeepers, tradesmen, and petty government officials who filled the ranks of the Black Hundred mobs, further bloodshed in the streets of Russia's cities was inevitable. Left and Right often came to blows, and murder became common. Of necessity, the energies of the workers were turned away from the government to parry the very real physical danger they faced. That brief unity the opposition had enjoyed early in October had been eroded by Witte's manifesto, and they could no longer present a united front against the government or reactionary assaults from its civilian agents. If only briefly, Nicholas began to see the wisdom of Witte's program. "More voices are heard protesting that the time has come for the government to take matters firmly in hand," he wrote at the beginning of December. "It is just what

Witte has been waiting for—he will now begin to deal with the revolutionary movement energetically."[117] Witte did precisely that. On December 3, troops surrounded the building in which the St. Petersburg Soviet of Workers' Deputies had held their meetings for more than a month and arrested some three hundred of its members, including most of its Executive Committee. The Revolution of 1905 in St. Petersburg passed into history. "The Revolution is dead," Trotskii proclaimed. "Long live the Revolution!"[118]

The death of revolution in St. Petersburg did not mean its immediate interment elsewhere in the Empire. During the exciting days of October and November, some fifty Soviets of Workers' Deputies had been formed in towns and cities across Russia, and a number of them had gathered arms for self-defense. As Nicholas's government stepped up its attacks against the revolutionaries at the beginning of December, some of these groups prepared to defend themselves and their revolution by force of arms. Especially in Moscow, the Soviet of Workers' Deputies proclaimed a general strike for December 7 in an effort to recapture the initiative that the workers' movement had lost when Nicholas's guards closed the St. Petersburg Soviet four days earlier. This time, Nicholas faced the ultimate revolutionary weapon, an armed workers' uprising in the streets of Moscow.

On the eve of the Revolution of 1905, Moscow was one of Russia's largest industrial centers, with almost 850 factories and mills within its city limits. Nearly a quarter of its population—some three hundred thousand men and women—were numbered among its factory workers. Taking their families into account, the number of proletarians in Moscow exceeded six hundred thousand, spread throughout the city, but concentrated in the sections of Zamoskvoreche, Rogozhskoe, Khramovki and, especially, Presnia, where the Prokhorov merchant princes had built their great Trekhgornaia cotton mill, the largest in all of Moscow. As the size of the Trekhgornaia mill suggested, cotton spinning and weaving were one of Moscow's major enterprises; metallurgical industries were another. Metalworkers—the *metallisty*—were the elite of the Russian proletariat.

Their living conditions still were scarcely even comfortable, but they earned the highest pay and enjoyed the highest living standard of any Russian workers, while spinners and weavers earned far less and lived much more poorly. Even though their standards of living were so different, workers from both industries had played a very visible part in the history of Russian labor protest.[119] If they joined forces in the city's streets, cotton workers and *metallisty* would present an awesome spectacle of opposition, and one about which General Fedor Dubasov, Moscow's Governor General, was especially apprehensive. Even before the strike began, he telegraphed the Tsar for more troops because he feared that as many as two-thirds of his own command might go over to the workers should fighting break out. Almost immediately, he received Grand Duke Nikolai Nikolaevich's curt reply: "There are no extra troops in St. Petersburg available for assignment to Moscow."[120] Like Dubasov, the authorities in Russia's capital awaited a new general strike and feared the outbreak of an armed uprising in St. Petersburg. Their fears proved unfounded; in Moscow, Dubasov's apprehensions turned out to be all too accurate.[121]

The Moscow uprising—what the Bolshevik memoirist Sergei Mitskevich called "the unforgettable twelve days . . . the supreme culmination of the Revolution of 1905"—began as a general strike at noon on December 7.[122] A few hours after the factory whistles sent out their screeching signals, more than four hundred plants and mills had closed, their hundred and fifty thousand workers spilling into the streets of the city. From the first, there was more hatred and more violence in the Moscow general strike than that which had swept Russia in mid-October; and there were clashes between troops and workers, with casualties on both sides. People rushed to buy stocks of food; fearful of the conflict's outcome, shopkeepers demanded payment in gold. In panic, Muscovites withdrew some two million rubles in gold from the city's banks. By the evening of December 8, there remained enough reserves of gold coin to last only a couple of days more.[123] If neither side launched an offensive, there was some hope that the general strike might not turn into a full-scale confrontation between workers and the city authorities.

Dubasov, however, destroyed any chance for peace and transformed the protest into an armed uprising by an ill-advised attempt to seize the leaders of the strike. On the night of December 8, he marshaled the few troops of whose loyalty he was absolutely certain and surrounded the Aquarium Theater where several thousand workers had assembled. He hoped to arrest all of the workers' leaders. Some were seized, but many escaped. A few shots were exchanged, and the armed uprising began.[124]

On December 9, angry working men and women threw up barricades across Moscow's main streets. In the Arbat, on Tverskaia, on Bolshaia and Malaia Bronnaia, on Sadovaia, Lesnaia, and several other arterial streets, these universal harbingers of revolution arose without warning and without any apparent plan. Behind their protective cover, pistol shots rang out, and government troops began to return the fire. "What did you hit with your Browning?" "What did you get with the five bullets you fired?" workers began to ask each other on street corners and in cafés.[125] There were cries of "Victory or Death!" "Boldly into the fray, comrades!" and "Down with the criminal tsarist regime!"[126] Utterly ignorant of military strategy and tactics, a number of revolutionaries tried to draw hasty lessons from Bliokh's ponderous volumes on *The Future of War*, which, despite its author's efforts to proclaim war's futility, contained elementary lessons in tactics.[127] "Act in small groups. . . . Put one or two marksmen against a hundred Cossacks," urged handbills posted by Bolshevik and Menshevik combat detachments. "Let our fortresses be courtyards with entrances front and back, and all other places from which it is easy to fire and withdraw."[128] Such tactics were most effective when the city's masses supported the insurgents. General Dubasov's first counterattack was calculated to weaken that support by instilling terror in all but the most dedicated soldiers of the revolution.

At noon on December 10, Dubasov established a command post in the belfry of the Strastnoi Convent, moved artillery into the square below, and mounted a machine gun in the belfry itself. One by one, he began to blast away the barricades with artillery, while the machine gun mounted high above the square drove back any who tried to rebuild them. Within a few hours, fifty workers were killed and another hundred wounded.[129] Soon, revolutionary combat detachments began to return Dubasov's fire as a few proletarian marksmen armed with Mauser and Winchester rifles began to fire and run from rooftops, apartment windows, and courtyard entrances. Clearly, artillery, Cossacks, and massed infantry could have little effect against such urban partisans, but that was not Dubasov's purpose.[130] He continued to use artillery in a futile effort to convince the masses to abandon their support for the insurgents. For the next several days, his artillerymen continued to clear away barricades with high explosive shells. Gradually he confined the conflict within an increasingly constricted area. By December 15, revolutionary combat detachments were contained within Presnia. Narrow streets lined with slum housing, with barricades hastily thrown up to block each and every one, became fortresses that Nicholas's commanders knew must be taken by storm.[131] As they prepared to make their final stand against the Tsar's troops, the revolutionary defenders of Presnia made a final count of their weapons: 200 rifles, about 600 revolvers and pistols, 150 sabers, and about 50 hand grenades.[132] With these they faced the entire Moscow garrison, its loyalty now stiffened by elite regiments that the Grand Duke Nikolai Nikolaevich had sent from St. Petersburg.

Preparations for the storming of Presnia began on December 15, when the Semenovskii Guards were dispatched from the capital. Unknown to these troops, the very train on which they rode carried dramatic testimony to the revolutionary dedication they were about to face. With them rode "Natasha," an attractive and lively young woman, who was taking her three-year-old daughter "Lizka" to Moscow. None of the Semenovskiis suspected that, using "Lizka's" childish charm to divert attention from her luggage, "Natasha" was carrying a traveling bag filled with desperately needed grenades for the rebels in Presnia.[133] In Moscow, "Natasha" and the Semenovskiis went their separate ways—they to take up assault positions, she to deliver the grenades that would deter them a few moments longer.

The Semenovskii Guards were led to Moscow by Colonel

Georgii Min, a man whose mind worked very much like General Trepov's, and an officer in whom Nicholas had complete confidence. With troops whose loyalty was absolute, Min and Dubasov no longer worried that civilian casualties might stir up excessive sympathy for the rebels among their soldiers. During the evening and night of December 16, they surrounded the entire Presnia Quarter with artillery and at seven o'clock the next morning ordered a general bombardment. For the better part of the day, with the guns sometimes firing as many as five shells per minute, Nicholas's commanders subjected Presnia to intense barrages of high explosive and incendiary shells. By nightfall, the entire quarter was ablaze. Most of the revolutionary guards had fled, but hundreds of civilians had fallen. The following morning, Min issued his final general orders: "Act without mercy. There will be no arrests. Every building from which soldiers are fired upon will be destroyed by burning or by artillery fire."[134] The battle of Presnia—henceforth to be remembered in revolutionary annals as Red Presnia—had ended. Of its defenders, 922 men and 137 women—workers, peasants, students, and servants —were dead; among them lay 86 small children. On its side, the government lost over a hundred soldiers to revolutionary snipers.[135] "Thank you, Petersburgers, for your support," one working woman in Moscow was heard to say. "You sent us the Semenovskii Regiment."[136]

Although Nicholas had thought the killing of workers on Bloody Sunday "painful and heartbreaking," he was not overly disturbed by the bloodshed in Moscow that December. In fact, he was determined to spill as much blood as necessary to restore order throughout his Empire, and he was ready to spill it quickly. "Terror must be met by terror," he wrote.[137] What especially concerned him was the continuing violence in Russia's countryside, where bands of peasants burned manor houses and murdered nobles, landlords, and officials. The solution, Nicholas was now convinced, lay in Punitive Expeditions, well-trained detachments of professional soldiers led by tough, dedicated officers, who were to be sent into the countryside to restore order. Punitive Expeditions simply operated as if they were invading the land of a foreign foe, where every living soul was an enemy. They executed many villagers at random, burned entire hamlets without mercy, and left thousands of people wounded, starving, and homeless. Again came the implacable order: "Don't skimp on bullets, and make no arrests!"[138]

With orders to give no quarter, Generals Sollogub, Orlov, and Meinhard fanned their regiments across Russia's turbulent Baltic provinces where they unleashed a weeks-long reign of terror and shot hundreds of suspected rebels without trial. At the same time, Generals Pavel Rennenkampf and Baron Aleksandr Meller-Zakomelskii moved to crush all insurgent activity along the Trans-Siberian Railway. Carrying Witte's order to succeed, "whatever the cost," Meller-Zakomelskii struck with particular fury.[139] Within weeks, the Trans-Siberian was cleared of all rebels, and calm was restored. Pleased with the results of their work, Nicholas wrote to his mother that "many seditious bands have been dispersed, their homes and property burnt."[140] As he received more reports of burnings and executions, he remarked to one of his aides that "this really tickles me!"[141] Some of the Punitive Expeditions executed at least eight out of every ten peasant men and women they arrested.[142] No Romanov before Nicholas II had ever crushed his subjects on such a massive national scale. For the time being, he could do so because the army remained loyal. "In December 1905," Trotskii lamented, "the Russian proletariat foundered . . . on the bayonets of the peasant army."[143]

Even before the Punitive Expeditions had finished their work, Nicholas's best advisers turned their attention to the immense problems the Revolution of 1905 had left in its wake. Most pressing of all, Witte's October Manifesto had embodied very clear promises of a parliamentary regime for Russia, and those promises could not be broken or ignored. Therefore, these men had to create the apparatus for a constitutional monarchy, bring political parties into being, set down the rules for the election of deputies, and arrange for eligible voters to be registered, all in the space of less than four months between late December 1905 and April 1906, when the Duma—the new national assembly—was to meet for the first time. These were overwhelmingly complex tasks, but at least some of Nicholas's advisers turned to confront them with a sense of optimism nonetheless, for they saw limited constitutional government as a means to tap vast reservoirs of talent that men outside the government possessed. Their hopes were perhaps best summed up by the dynamic Petr Stolypin, soon to become known for his dogged efforts to move Russia more quickly into the twentieth century. "What *we* want," Stolypin proclaimed to friend and foe alike, "is a GREAT RUSSIA!"[144]

CHAPTER IX

"What We Want Is a Great Russia!"

I F STOLYPIN AND WITTE SAW SOME GROUNDS FOR CAUTIOUS optimism in the promises of the October Manifesto, there were others in Russia who saw in Nicholas's proclamation the dawn of a new era. These were the men and women who served in the *zemstva*, those modest instruments of local self-government that Alexander II had established in 1864 as part of the Great Reforms.[1] For a quarter of a century, the resources of the *zemstva* had remained as small as their responsibilities were immense, for they had shouldered the burden of developing programs for public health, education, and poor relief in Russia's villages at the same time as they had struggled to encourage local agriculture, industry, and trade. Repeatedly, they had called for the most able and best-educated of Russia's men and women to join them; as the 1890s began, their efforts brought greater success. As their ranks grew, dedicated *zemstva* doctors, teachers, and agronomists began to envision programs that were nationwide in scope. They appealed for more men and women to join them and looked for ways to make their influence felt in St. Petersburg itself.[2]

Of all the *zemstva* urgings that reached St. Petersburg during the last third of the nineteenth century, the one to which Emperors and statesmen remained the most stubbornly opposed had been any suggestion that elected representatives of the people might play a part in national affairs. Obviously, a national *zemstvo*—"the crowning of the edifice," as it was sometimes called—remained the liberals' fondest dream.[3] But the *zemstva* could never hope to mount a national assault against the conservative bastions of the autocrat's power in St. Petersburg so long as they remained scattered over the face of Russia, separated and isolated from each other. Finally, a number of daring *zemstva* leaders organized the first all-Russian congress in Moscow in May 1902. This was followed the next month by the appearance of *Osvobozhdenie (Liberation),* the constitutionalists' own biweekly newspaper that was published in Stuttgart by Petr Struve, a thirty-two-year-old Marxist-turned-liberal. "Our task is not to divide but to unite," Struve announced. "The cultural and political liberation of Russia . . . must become a national cause."[4] To further the development of their national movement, *zemstva* politicians summoned a second congress in April 1903. Because their first effort had been met by a stern rebuke from the authorities, they now gathered in semisecrecy in several St. Petersburg apartments to repeat their urgings that the government grant them a larger role in state affairs.[5]

Semiclandestine national meetings that produced sporadic semipublic pronouncements supported by an émigré newspaper forbidden by the censors to enter its homeland offered small comfort to the constitutionalist cause in Russia. At Schaffhausen in Switzerland, twenty *zemstva* politicians, university professors, and journalists met during the summer of 1903 to form a coalition of all liberal elements in Russia, including even a number of revolutionary socialists. They proposed to use demonstrations, petitions, and public criticism of the government's failings to launch a broad assault against Nicholas's autocratic regime.[6] At the beginning of January 1904, they formed themselves into the Union of Liberation at a secret meeting in St. Petersburg and proclaimed that "the liquidation of autocracy and the establishment in Russia of a constitutionalist regime" was their chief goal.[7]

Born during the reactionary regime of Plehve, the Union of Liberation chose an extremely difficult moment to enter the political arena. Yet its members had not long to wait for a dramatic shift in the atmosphere of Russian politics that might have bettered their prospects. After Plehve's assassination in July 1904, Nicholas named Prince Petr Sviatopolk-Mirskii as Russia's new Minister of Internal Affairs. At the time Governor General of the turbulent western provinces of Vilna, Kovno, and Grodno, Mirskii was known for his personal charm and policies of conciliation and moderation. "Everywhere Mirskii served, they loved and respected him," Witte remembered.[8] Sviatopolk-Mirskii entered office at the end of August in a flurry of decrees that brought tax relief to the peasants and amnesty to political dissidents. He spoke of "sincere benevolence and sincere confidence . . . toward the population in general,"[9] and announced that his policies would "conform to the spirit of true and broad progress," so long as it "did not conflict with the existing order."[10] With only two exceptions, the Russian press greeted his appointment with a warm sense of anticipation. Progressive men and women called it a time of "governmental springtime."[11] Proclaimed one poet: "The cherry orchard/ Stands fairylike, bedecked with blossoms./ The air is full of warmth and light,/ And everything is gowned in the garments of spring."[12]

Sviatopolk-Mirskii's policies seemed to herald a new era of toleration, but they also were fraught with danger because they raised Russians' expectations faster than the new minister could respond. "The most dangerous moment for a bad government is when it suddenly starts to yield to public opinion," a historian once wrote,[13] and so it proved with Mirskii's well-intentioned efforts. Even before he was established in office, progressive Russians had begun to expect more than he could possibly give, and, in their disillusionment, they reacted bitterly. Therefore, when Mirskii turned to seek an accommodation with the Union of Liberation at the end of 1904, its leaders refused their support. "There are no intermediary positions between autocracy and constitutionalism," Miliukov stubbornly insisted. The Union of Liberation, he announced, could be satisfied with nothing less than "a formal abolition of autocracy."[14] Within five months, Mirskii left office, his efforts at conciliation buried in the gore-stained debris of Bloody Sunday. "Everything has failed," he lamented as he went into retirement. "Let us build jails."[15] "Petr has already left the government," his wife confided to her diary on January 19, 1905. "Thank God."[16]

Sviatopolk-Mirskii's resignation did not lessen Russians' clamor for a voice in their government. The "banquet campaign" of late 1904 and early 1905 saw the Union of Liberation organize thirty-eight public banquets in more than two dozen Russian cities to marshal support for its program. From these banquets, a series of politically active professional unions were born, and by the middle of the year they had merged into a powerful Union of Unions. When the general strike broke out in October, they could claim more than a hundred thousand members.[17] Including as it did the Engineers' Union, the Union of Railway Employees and Workers, and the Union of Journalists and Writers, to mention only a few of the most powerful, the Union of Unions continued to play an influential role in directing political protest against Nicholas's tottering government for the rest of the year.[18]

During the first nine months of 1905, the resolve of *zemstva* liberals and all those who joined with them in the Union of Liberation and the Union of Unions was strengthened by the indecisive responses with which Nicholas and his advisers met their demands for a voice in national affairs. On February 18, Nicholas issued several contradictory decrees that condemned all political opposition but urged private citizens to submit plans to the Council of Ministers about ways to make life better in Russia. At the same time, he announced his intention, "with the help of God, to draw into the preliminary examination and discussion of legislative proposals the most worthy individuals holding the public confidence, and elected by the people."[19] Aleksandr Bulygin, Sviatopolk-Mirskii's lackluster successor, eventually proposed that a very limited number of Russians—excluding all Jews and most city folk, factory workers, and professionals—be allowed to elect a consultative assembly. This so-called "Bulygin Duma"* would be permitted to offer advice to the Tsar and his ministers on only those matters about which they chose to seek the Duma's counsel.[20] At best, Bulygin conceded far too little much too late.

Should progressive men and women take part in Bulygin's consultative Duma in the hope of transforming it into a national legislative assembly once it began its deliberations, or should they simply shun it altogether? The debate that raged over this question during the spring and summer of 1905 split the Union of Liberation. Miliukov and his allies proclaimed "a new era of free political life in Russia"[21] and resolved to take part in the coming elections, but the great majority of the Union's membership refused to follow their example. Events negated the debate's outcome in any case. Weeks before the elections could take place, the October Manifesto promised to recast Bulygin's impotent consultative assembly into a more broadly elected Duma with real legislative authority.[22] No longer was it a question of *if* Russia would have a constitutional monarchy. Men and women now turned to debate the form that new monarchy would take. In a number of important ways, Witte held the key, for it became his task to prepare drafts of the decrees that would give shape to the October Manifesto's promises. A firm believer in autocracy, Witte now had to preside over its legislative abolition.

---

*Among other things, the term *duma* in Russian means a council or an assembly. Historically, it implied a body with consultative, not legislative, functions as, for example, in the case of the *Boiarskaia duma* (The Council of Great Lords) that advised the Tsar in the sixteenth and seventeenth centuries.

Witte had urged the October Manifesto upon Nicholas for one simple reason: he had lost all faith in his Emperor's ability to rule Russia as an autocrat. He had held his faith longer than many, far longer than those who had doubted Nicholas from the very first. "Remember what I say, Sergei Iulievich," Ivan Durnovo had warned him soon after Nicholas took Alexander's place on the throne. "This [new Tsar] will be something like a modern-day version of the Emperor Paul I," a monarch notorious in Russia for his ineptitude and tyranny.[23] As the fall of 1905 came and went, Durnovo's words must have seemed prophetic to the men who had to deal with their frightened and uncertain Emperor from day to day. "I was under no illusions about the character of my sovereign," Witte sadly confessed some years later. "I knew that, lacking any strength of will, and unable to pursue any sort of consistent policy, he would become the plaything of each and every foolish influence that came along and that, therefore, his personal qualities could only make worse an already difficult situation. . . . The history of my brief premiership, from October 20, 1905, until April 20, 1906, fully confirmed all my forebodings."[24]

As Witte took up his duties, Russia was in the grip of strikes, mutinies, nationalist revolts in her outlying lands, pogroms in the towns and cities of the south and west, and peasant riots in the central and Baltic provinces. At the same time, there were problems of a more endemic nature that threatened to be even more difficult to resolve over the long term. How was the newly enfranchised, largely illiterate, intensely parochial Russian electorate to be induced to think in terms of national issues rather than village ones, especially when there were no political parties to develop constituencies or foster discussions about questions of national significance? And how could debates on national policy even take place, given the constraints that censorship had traditionally imposed upon such discussions?

Beginning in late October, Witte tried to enlist respected public figures to help him resolve these problems, but many refused their support. Conservatives still cursed him as a traitor, the author of the manifesto that had destroyed autocracy, while many liberals condemned him as a vicious and willing instrument of reaction. With public opinion still polarized on the extreme left and far right, Witte thus faced the impossible task of forming a cabinet that would hold both the Tsar's and the people's confidence. As Sviatopolk-Mirskii had done a year earlier, he turned to the leaders of the zemstva, hopeful that this time they would be more willing to seek a common path. Most of all, he placed his hopes in Dmitrii Shipov, a man deeply respected in progressive circles, who soon helped to found the Union of October 17th, a moderate political party that stood in the center of Russia's political spectrum. Shipov and his allies were the only ones with whom Witte might have joined, yet he clumsily destroyed any chance for such an alliance by his unexplained insistence that the archconservative Petr Durnovo be appointed Minister of Internal Affairs.

It has been suggested that Witte may have planned to add Durnovo to his cabinet in addition to such moderates as Shipov in the hope that Durnovo might then be blamed for any repressive measures needed to restore order.[25] If that was his plan, it failed miserably, for Shipov and his associates flatly refused to join any cabinet in which Durnovo was included. The appointment cost Witte even more than the loss of Shipov's moderates, however, because Durnovo soon began to report directly to the Tsar in an effort to weaken his superior's position and better his own.[26] By mid-November, Witte had lost any hope of drawing prominent and respected public figures into his government. He then had no choice but turn to the very bureaucrats and generals that so many Russians despised.

By the end of 1905, Witte had managed to prepare a law about general elections, even though the Tsar had now grown even more hostile to reform and had demanded narrower limits upon suffrage than his chief minister probably would have preferred. Landowners, industrialists, merchants, and senior officials were given the greatest say in choosing delegates to the new Duma, while factory workers were to have almost no say at all.[27] As one account put it, "The vote of one landowner was equivalent to that of three and one-half city dwellers [i.e., merchants, industrialists, and officials], of fifteen peasants, and of forty-five workers." These, of course, were average figures. In the province of Voronezh, only six out of every thousand voters were factory workers.[28]

Witte's task still was far from done as the new year opened. As progressive Russians were only too ready to point out, the October Manifesto was only a series of unsecured promises, not a constitution. It pledged reforms, but offered no guarantees about when, in what form, or even *if,* they would take place. Witte therefore had to define the framework within which the elected Duma would function as a legislative body. He was forced to argue his case for limited constitutional monarchy just when Nicholas began to think that it might be possible to avoid renouncing his unlimited power as autocrat. Confident that he now had the upper hand in town and country, the Tsar began to think about breaking the promises he had made to his people in October. "This is the most important issue of all," Nicholas warned his ministers. "The question still torments me: do I have the right to change the form of that authority which my ancestors bequeathed to me? I was fully aware of what I was doing when I issued the Manifesto of October 17," he continued, "and I am firmly resolved to see it through to the end. But I am not convinced that this requires me to renounce the right of supreme power and change the definition of it that has existed for 109 years in the first article of the Fundamental Laws. . . . I am convinced that eighty percent of the people would stand with me in this."[29]

What Nicholas had in mind was a clear violation of the spirit, if not the actual letter, of both the October Manifesto and the decree of February 20, 1906, with which Witte had just convinced him to establish the structural framework within which Russia's new government was to function. "This question will decide the entire future of Russia," Witte warned him. "It was you, Sire, who desired to limit your power [by the October Manifesto]," Count Konstantin Pahlen, a member of the State Council for almost thirty years, remarked. Minister of Justice Mikhail Akimov warned that to insist that autocratic power remained unlimited "means to throw down the gauntlet" to those very individuals and political groups whom the October Manifesto had lured away from the revolutionary cause.

Even the supremely reactionary Durnovo, whom Nicholas thought was "doing splendid work" in sharp contrast to Witte,[30] admitted that "after the Manifestos of October 17th and February 20th, unlimited monarchy has ceased to exist." Four days later, Nicholas finally heeded his ministers' warnings and agreed that his autocratic power was no longer "unlimited," although he insisted that it remained "autocratic."[31] He never really understood what that very fundamental alteration meant, and his personal view of autocracy continued as before, even though the new Fundamental Laws that Witte prepared as his last service to Russia before Nicholas sent him into retirement made the Emperor's altered position clear. Nicholas retained the "supreme autocratic power" in Russia, but that power no longer was described as "absolute" or "unlimited."[32]

By the time the new Fundamental Laws were published on April 24, 1906, Witte was gone, "cast off from one shore and not yet having reached the other," in Miliukov's graphic phrase. "Count Witte's greatest service," Miliukov remarked in a truthful but uncharitable moment, "was that he proved that it is impossible to create the necessary basic conditions for a free political life so long as autocracy is preserved."[33] Miliukov thought the Fundamental Laws "a conspiracy against the people,"[34] while his colleague Fedor Rodichev proclaimed that "in Russia there is no justice! In Russia law is made into a joke!" "During this year," he continued, "Russia has lived through sufferings such as she has not seen since the time of Batu Khan."[35] "All Russia is an absolute madhouse," Witte confided to a friend, and then hastened abroad for a long rest.[36] He left behind a host of political enemies and a profoundly ungrateful sovereign. Witte's ministry was "like a nightmare," Nicholas wrote to his mother. *"As long as I live,"* he concluded bitterly, "I will never trust that man again with the smallest thing."[37] The events of the next eighteen months confirmed him in his hatred of Witte, constitutional government, and electoral politics, as Russia took her first awkward steps along the painfully rough road toward establishing a constitutional regime.

The first national election in Russia's long history took place between February and April 1906. Somewhere between 20 million and 25 million Russians voted to elect deputies to the lower legislative house, the State Duma.[38] A fraction of these then were allowed to elect a limited number of upper-class and deeply conservative representatives to the Council of State, the upper house to which Nicholas appointed the remaining half of its members. Many were not certain why they voted; many more did not understand for what or whom they were to cast their ballots. "Some thought they were voting for the Tsar," explained one recent account. "Many thought they were voting for more land, and others were convinced they were voting for freedom and for a new order for Russia."[39] Anxious politicians, many of them uncertain of their role, hastened to form political parties that reflected an amazing myriad of views and aspirations. More than two dozen parties managed to elect deputies to the Duma, as did some sixteen national minority groups. Out of almost five hundred elected deputies, there were only eighteen Social Democrats to represent the extreme left; there were none at all who clearly spoke for the far right.[40]

What shocked Nicholas and his ministers when the First Duma assembled was the peasant delegates' decisive rejection of their government. Witte and his assistants had made certain that large numbers of peasants would be elected in the hope that such deputies could be used to establish a bloc of progovernment sentiment in the Duma and thus make the task of working with it much easier. Few realized that the carnage of Bloody Sunday had destroyed the peasants' belief in the Tsar as their "Little Father." When more than two hundred peasants were elected to the Duma, most joined the coalition that opposed the government. When Ivan Goremykin, Witte's successor, and Petr Stolypin, the then little-known provincial governor who had been called in to replace Durnovo, turned to deal with Russia's first elected assembly, they faced a large bloc of peasants who demanded that the huge estates of Russia's great lords be broken up so that their brethren in the village could purchase more land at affordable prices.

Disgruntled but politically naïve, peasants hesitated to form a party of their own, but allied with others who seemed best able to defend their interests. These often were the Constitutional Democrats, the *Kadety*, who were the Duma's largest and best-organized political party.[41] A somewhat amorphous coalition of liberal and left-wing elements, the *Kadety* had evolved from the Union of Liberation in October 1905. Their leader Pavel Miliukov, easily one of the most impressive and compelling political figures to emerge from Russia's year of revolutionary turmoil, was a nobleman who had become a famous historian and professor at the University of Moscow. For his part in several political protests, he had been exiled to the provinces during the first years of Nicholas's reign and then had spent much of the next decade lecturing in Great Britain and the United States. Bloody Sunday had found him delivering lectures at the University of Chicago, then less than a decade old, but already renowned for the world-famous scholars who assembled there. When he returned to Russia in April 1905, Miliukov found it very different from the country he had left many months before. Freedom was in the air and change in the making. Without a moment's hesitation, he turned from history to politics and continued to follow his long-held ties to the Union of Liberation. Although his wife and children still lived near St. Petersburg, he spent the first months of his return in Moscow, the city he had left as an exiled professor a decade before. "I felt more comfortable with myself there," he later explained, "and freer from influences and decisions dictated by outside forces."[42]

Along with Struve, Rodichev, and Vasilii Maklakov, Miliukov had presided over the birth of the Constitutional Democratic party. Together they called for a constitutional monarchy, political amnesty, and a ministry to be responsible to the yet-to-be-elected Duma. Later they demanded social and economic reforms, including the breakup of Russia's great latifundia, with proper compensation paid to the great lords who held title to them. These were in fact revolutionary demands, although the *Kadety* insisted upon the "liberal" character of their platform. It was the Moscow uprising, and their painful refusal to support its destructive violence, that finally obliged Miliukov and his followers to commit themselves to realizing their program "only *within* the institutional bounds set by the regime."[43]

Firmly committed to achieving the *Kadet* platform by the ballot box and the legislative process, Miliukov led his party to a resounding victory in the general elections of 1906. "We are certain," he wrote wryly, "that the government is our most faithful ally, and we shall leave it to continue its work in the interests of the Russian opposition."[44] He could well afford to be smug; the government's efforts to sway public opinion had produced a backlash that had worked to his party's advantage. The *Kadety* had captured more than a third of the seats in the Duma, half again as many as their nearest competitor, the Labor Group, who also were their most frequent allies. Together they controlled more than half of the Duma seats and could readily count on its support for their program.[45] Such a victory exceeded their wildest dreams and brought them to the Duma demanding a government of *Kadet* ministers. "The strict constitutional principle would require that a ministry now be formed by those who have emerged victorious from the general elections," Miliukov wrote on the day of Witte's resignation.[46] "Perhaps only the *Kadet* party, and the *Kadet* party alone, can lead Russia out of its fateful impasse," he added arrogantly.[47] "We go to the Duma conscious of our strength, conscious that behind it stands the might of Russia," Rodichev proclaimed as he and his colleagues prepared to take their seats. Others commented more uncharitably that the *Kadety* had begun to suffer from being "drunken with success."[48] Certainly their victory had partially blinded them to Nicholas's intense hatred for their principles and political demands. Then, in Witte's place, the Tsar appointed not one of the victorious *Kadety*, but Ivan Goremykin, a reactionary who openly supported those militant Black Hundred mobs who roamed the streets in search of radicals, liberals, and Jews.[49] "The most important thing is that Goremykin never will go behind my back," the Tsar told his Minister of Finance Count Kokovtsev. "I can trust him completely and there will be no unlooked-for surprises."[50] The *Kadety* thus had to face a dismaying array of conservative and reactionary ministers. The greatest irony of all, perhaps, was that Miliukov, architect of the *Kadet* victory and politician par excellence, had been unable to stand for election because he was under indictment for censorship violations.[51]

Russia's first parliament opened on April 27, 1906, just one week after Witte's departure, and with the victorious *Kadety* in full control. Among this group sat some of Russia's most able politicians and most brilliant minds. These were men who had studied their nation's history with care and knew well the innermost workings of her government. They were thoroughly schooled in the political experience of Europe and had carefully studied the political theory upon which that experience was based. They had journeyed through Russia and had traveled in the West. Some spoke foreign languages fluently and were as much at home in London, New York, Paris, or Berlin as they were in St. Petersburg or Moscow. Yet, when it came to leading their countrymen in their first halting steps toward parliamentary government, they proved rigid doctrinaires and wretched failures. Miliukov and the more conservative Shipov had refused to work with Witte in the early days of his ministry; their allies now refused to work with his successors. "Compromise and gradual achievements were regarded as 'lowering the flag,' " explained Vasilii Maklakov, a *Kadet* who lived to regret his party's tactics at that critical historical moment. "Concessions were regarded as betrayal."[52] The Duma, and especially the *Kadety* who dominated it so completely, should have worked for "the reconciliation of the old and the new," he insisted in retrospect.[53] Their best course would have been "to make use of the prestige of the monarchy, not reject it," but that was not the purpose of the *Kadety* in 1906. Victims of what would become a major failing of their revolutionary successors two decades later, they became prisoners of their own ideology. Spurred on by what Maklakov called "the demands of theory," they used the tactics of deliberate confrontation to provoke the authorities at every turn and made little effort to seek any common ground. "The irresponsible year 1906," Maklakov lamented later in his life, was a lost opportunity and a terrible tragedy in the annals of parliamentary government in Russia.[54]

Nicholas, it seems, actually may have been more willing to seek a modest accommodation with the Duma, although admittedly within very narrow limits, than they were to seek common cause with his government. To be sure, in December 1905 he had told Witte, "I know perfectly well that I am creating an enemy, not an

ally," when they discussed the new electoral law.[55] Yet he still may
have hoped to find common ground upon which to stand with the
men whom he had called "the best people" in Russia at the Duma's
opening ceremonies.[56] Less than a week before the Duma opened,
Minister of Finance Count Kokovtsev recalled, "His Majesty told
me of His hopes that, once it became involved with responsible
duties, the Duma would become less revolutionary as a result."[57]
Whatever the Tsar's hopes may have been, they were dashed
quickly. Even the opening ceremonies at the Winter Palace provoked antagonism. In the words of Vladimir Gurko, at the time a
high official in the Ministry of Internal Affairs, "there was a certain
lack of tact on both sides." The Duma members appeared "dressed
in a deliberately careless fashion," while the Court overemphasized
its brilliance and splendor. "The Court and the government, flourishing gold-laced uniforms and numerous decorations," Gurko
wrote, "was set opposite the gray, almost rustic group representing
the people of Russia." The scene produced an unfortunate contrast,
he concluded, and "set in juxtaposition the boundless Imperial luxury and the poverty of the people."[58]

The poverty of the people was only one of several themes upon
which the Duma deputies chose to focus their attack against Nicholas and his government. As soon as the deputies left the opening
ceremonies at the Winter Palace, they formulated an address to the
throne that destroyed almost all hope for cooperation between
crown and parliament. Led by Sergei Muromtsev, the deputies'
choice as their president, and assisted by Ivan Petrunkevich, who
had been in the thick of zemstva conflicts with the government since
the 1870s, the Kadety and their allies chose to meet the government
head on.[59] "The greatest ulcer of our public life," they wrote, "is
the despotism of the government's officials, which separates the Tsar
from the people." If constitutional government was to flourish and
Russia's still uneasy civil peace remain secure, they insisted that "the
destruction of all barriers between the Sovereign and his people"
must be accomplished quickly. They went on to demand freedom
of speech, the press, and assembly; the legalization of unions; the
right to strike; the elimination of all forms of class privilege; and the

abolition of the death penalty. Treasury, Crown, and Church lands must be offered for sale to the land-hungry and poverty-stricken peasants of the Empire, and amnesty granted to all who had taken part in the revolutionary upheavals of the previous year.[60] Theirs was a maximalist program of such scope that the government could not hope to accept it, and even Europeans sympathetic to the liberals' cause were taken aback by its audacity. "What of the crimes?" asked the amazed Russian correspondent of the *Revue des deux Mondes*. "What of the robberies? What of the killings?"[61] Nicholas refused to receive the deputies or their address, leaving it to his ministers to reply.

According to an eyewitness who sat in on the meetings of the Council of Ministers over which Goremykin presided each afternoon in the hulking Ministry of Internal Affairs building that stood near St. Petersburg's famous Chain Bridge, the Prime Minister "was inclined to entirely disregard the Duma's address." Nonetheless, some response had to be made. Neither Tsar nor government could accede to the Duma's demands, and Goremykin's colleagues all agreed that Nicholas should be shielded from direct conflict with the people's representatives. Some preferred to respond with platitudes and noncommittal reassurances, but Vladimir Gurko urged a response that answered the Duma's outright demands with forthright rejections.[62] Goremykin chose to follow Gurko's advice when he went to the Duma on May 13 to present his colleagues' reply. "His hands shaking with emotion," he read the message Gurko had written "in a voice that was scarcely audible, devoid of all expression, and in a flat, passionless tone," one of his colleagues remembered.[63] Miliukov later wrote that "May 13th became the date which marked the beginning of an open struggle" between Duma and government."[64] Instantly, the *Kadety* rose to condemn the government and, as the ministers left the Duma chamber in the Taurida Palace en masse, the *Kadety* led the deputies in passing a meaningless vote of censure.

The lines of struggle thus were clearly drawn, and tragically so. In their inexperience with parliamentary politics, neither side had left itself room to maneuver in Russia's treacherous new political currents. Left with the options only of capitulation or of firm opposition, Goremykin and his colleagues unhesitatingly took the latter course. That left the Duma in the same difficult position as their ministerial opponents. They, too, must capitulate before the ministers' rejection of their address or give no ground and oppose the government totally. Like Goremykin and his associates, they also chose the unyielding course. Still the prisoners of their own ideological preconceptions, the *Kadety* continued to utterly misjudge their political power. In his new daily newspaper, *The Duma*, Struve proclaimed that "the final political triumph" was near and that "the fate of the monarchy itself depends on how soon the ministry of bureaucrats will be replaced by a ministry of the Duma." He dismissed as "mindless" all talk that the government might simply dissolve the Duma and insisted that any attempt to do so would lead to "the most brutal and pitiless struggle." Should the Tsar and his ministers persist in their "stubborn refusal to concede power," he warned, "the raging waves of the people's irresistible anger . . . will inundate the ancient edifice of the Russian monarchy."[65]

Struve's optimistic arrogance was undoubtedly fed by his knowledge that Stolypin and Nicholas's special assistant General Dmitrii Trepov already had discussed with Miliukov, Shipov, and Muromtsev the conditions under which the Tsar might permit their participation in the government. The sincerity of both sides in these discussions remains entirely open to question, and the *Kadety* continued to press for a radical solution to the agrarian question while the government searched for a middle ground. Ignoring a number of obvious warning signals, Struve pressed on and urged the Tsar's ministers to give way to the Duma without delay lest "anarchy erode, burn, and perish that force which is still capable of . . . saving the Crown."[66] But Struve's confidence proved grossly misplaced, and his estimate of *Kadet* power even more so. How far his estimate was off the mark became dramatically clear on July 9. While Miliukov and Muromtsev confidently awaited an Imperial invitation to form a ministry, Nicholas dissolved the Duma and replaced the aged Goremykin as President of the Council of Ministers with Stolypin.[67]

When soldiers closed the Taurida Palace gates to draw history's final curtain over the First Duma, the *Kadety* resolved to fight back. Some 200 deputies, including 120 *Kadety,* hastily retired to Vyborg, a town that lay just across the Finnish border, where they were out of reach of the Russian police. Most of these men thought the dissolution illegal, but were at a loss to answer the government's stern actions. With the demonstrations and riots of late 1905 well behind them, they had no force with which to respond. Yet they could not allow the dissolution to pass unchallenged precisely because, in their own words, "symbolic gestures" were "essential in dealing with the unsophisticated and uneducated masses."[68] Unsure of their course, but certain that a response was needed, 147 of them heeded Miliukov's plea and signed the Vyborg Manifesto urging all Russians to refuse taxes and army recruitment until the Tsar summoned the Duma back into session. Their protest proved more costly than any had expected. To their chagrin, the masses did not respond, and the government disenfranchised them all. That winter, the cream of the *Kadet* party had to stand aside while their enemies campaigned for the seats they had lost. Miliukov and most of his colleagues vowed to continue the struggle nonetheless, but a disillusioned Struve rejected their pleas. Calling the Vyborg Manifesto and the events surrounding it "the darkest page in Russian history," he sought a more moderate course;[69] that fall, he urged that his colleagues' costly protest be "interred with all honors" and forgotten.[70]

Unlike Goremykin, Stolypin understood that the Duma must remain a part of Russia's new political system. To stifle any cries that the Tsar had destroyed the Duma, he wisely urged Nicholas to proclaim the convocation of the Second Duma when he announced the demise of the First. The Second Duma was to assemble on February 20, 1907, and Stolypin used the intervening six months to wage a merciless campaign against the *Kadety* and their Labor Group allies. While the authorities sent some thirty-five thousand men and women into administrative exile, the government suppressed over three hundred opposition journals and newspapers, including seventy-seven during the month of January 1907 alone.[71] But Stolypin's brutal tactics had unlooked-for and unpleasant consequences for the government as well as the *Kadety.* His energetic campaign brought far more radical *Bolsheviki, Mensheviki,* and Socialist Revolutionaries into the fray, for their leaders had repented their unwise boycott of the First Duma elections. At the same time, when Stolypin began to subsidize the militant right to the tune of some three million rubles a year, their candidates surged into the political arena in unprecedented force.[72] The campaign of 1906–7 thus pitted the extreme left against the far right for those many seats emptied by the government's attack against the *Kadety.* The politics of that winter were more vicious and the conflict more violent than any witnessed in the previous year's elections.[73]

The ultraconservatives and extreme reactionaries whose strident political rhetoric echoed across Russia toward the end of 1906 owed their first quasi-independent political organization to the Sacred Guard that had flourished during the early days of Alexander III's reign. During the first years of the new century, they had reappeared on the occasions of various pogroms, but had never formed a political organization because the government was scarcely more receptive to pressure from the right than it was to demands from the left. Unwilling to oppose official injunctions against political activity, Russian conservatives spoke only of their common loyalty to Tsar, Church, and Homeland, and the turmoil of 1905 thus found the militant right far less prepared than their opponents. Not until early November did a group of ultraconservatives led by Vladimir Purishkevich (later to become famous as one of Rasputin's assassins) and Dr. Aleksandr Dubrovin (a St. Petersburg physician whose shadowy past remains unexplored) form the Union of the Russian People, possibly with some help from Grand Duke Nikolai Nikolaevich and the Deputy Director of the Ministry of Internal Affairs's Police Department, Petr Rachkovskii.[74]

From the first, the Union of the Russian People had arrayed itself firmly against Witte and his efforts to set Russia on the path to constitutional government. Even after he left office, they pursued him, their hatred still so intense that they evidently supported an attempt on his life early in 1907.[75] They had always insisted that Witte was guided by Jews, an opinion that Nicholas himself soon came to share,[76] and they set out in search of vengeance. According to some estimates, more than ten thousand Jews thus were killed and wounded in pogroms that swept more than a hundred towns and cities in the south during the month after Nicholas issued the October Manifesto.[77] In Odessa, marchers bearing ikons and portraits of Nicholas and Aleksandra turned on Jews with particular fury. During violence that lasted almost four days, somewhere between five hundred and a thousand Jews were killed or wounded, and almost four million rubles' worth of their property destroyed. One Russian physician looked on in horrified disbelief as the pogromists threw Jewish children from upper-story windows; one of them actually seized a child by its feet and broke its head against a wall.[78] From the Ministry of Internal Affairs, an appalled Prince Sergei Urusov insisted that "patriotic" Russians had been responsible for these terrors and urged that they be punished. Nicholas refused, welcomed the leaders of the Union of the Russian People to Tsarskoe Selo, and even accepted badges of membership for himself and the Tsarevich Aleksei.[79] "Because nine-tenths of the troublemakers are Jews," he explained to his mother, "the people's whole anger turned against them. That's how the pogroms happened."[80]

Basking in the Tsar's unofficial favor, Union candidates had spoken vaguely about social justice and economic reform in the political campaign of early 1906, but had emphasized much more the need to crush revolution, defend private property, and terrorize Jews. Tsar and people must be cemented into one. Together, they would form an invincible bulwark against the petty tyranny of government officials, the greed of Jews, and the immoral strivings of all revolutionaries. Russians might cheer such rantings on street corners, but evidently did not carry their enthusiasm to the polls. The Union of the Russian People won only one vote out of every twenty cast in the conservative city of Moscow, and even fewer in the capital itself. (However, the First Duma had assembled without a single Union candidate in its midst.)[81]

Anxious to build a strong body of progovernment sentiment in Russia's new legislature, Stolypin reversed Witte's policy and lavished secret government funds upon the Union of the Russian People's candidates in the elections for the Second Duma. The Union's appeals to the masses grew more demagogic, their urgings more violent, as they called their revolutionary opponents to account. Those who had led the Revolution in 1905, they insisted, now must be made to pay "an eye for an eye and a tooth for a tooth" for the injuries they had inflicted upon Russia.[82] With such paramilitary organizations as the infamous "Yellow Shirts" in Odessa included in its ranks, the Union closely resembled Italy's Fascists after the Great War, and their leader Purishkevich has been called one of the world's first Fascists.[83] Yet even government support and demagogic appeals to the baser instincts of the masses could win only ten seats in the Second Duma for the Union of the Russian People.[84] Clearly, they entered the Duma not to build Russia's new constitutional future but to destroy it, and they did their utmost to disrupt the Duma's work.[85]

Far stronger than the militant right when the Second Duma assembled were the forces of the radical left. Sixty-five Social Democrats (with the *Mensheviki* outnumbering the *Bolsheviki* by about two to one) and thirty-seven Socialist Revolutionaries won seats in the Duma as did 120 candidates of the Labor Group and Popular Socialist parties. Many of these left-wing deputies were under the age of thirty, and most had not yet passed forty. The leading Menshevik orator, a young Georgian by the name of Iraklii Tsereteli, was only twenty-five, while Grigorii Aleksinskii, his counterpart among the *Bolsheviki*, was just two years older.[86] Their youthful dedication unhindered by any political realism or common sense, they saw the Duma only as a new obstacle to revolution. Ardently committed to their cause, they shared a deep hatred for Nicholas's government in both its autocratic and constitutional forms.[87] For them, the end of revolution in 1905 had signaled a new stage in the revolutionary struggle.

Bitterly contested elections in early 1907 thus produced a Duma that was weaker in the center but far stronger at the extremes of the political spectrum than its predecessor. The *Kadety* saw their ranks halved, and the Labor Group allied no longer with them but with the Social Democrats and Socialist Revolutionaries with whose aims they felt more in sympathy. The Second Duma thus had about two hundred deputies who voted on the radical left to outnumber the *Kadety* and their handful of regular allies by almost two to one.[88] Stolypin's pious hope that the Second Duma would be more moderate had been dashed even before it assembled. The prospects for cooperation between Duma and government now seemed utterly remote. "On the day after the elections, it was clear that the days of the Second Duma were numbered," Miliukov wrote. "A chamber, two-fifths of whom are known to reject the constitutional means of struggle, would be in continual danger of dissolution even in countries with more stable constitutional structures."[89] The left had no purpose but "to criticize and discredit those who supported Russia's constitutional development," he insisted, while the militant right did not "see themselves as true popular representatives and demanded the restoration of the autocracy." The left wanted to destroy what they called Russia's "bourgeois democracy" in order to construct a socialist order upon its ruins, while the right threatened "to spill blood if their desire for the destruction of popular representation was not satisfied." It was the "Sisyphean task" of the *Kadety*, Miliukov explained, to defend Russia's new constitutional structure against attacks from both extremes.[90]

Whatever chance the *Kadety* may have had to succeed in the difficult task that Miliukov outlined depended especially upon their ability to strike an alliance with the Octobrists, some of their former conservative associates in the *zemstvo* movement, who now made up the Duma's only moderate right-wing party. Formally called the Union of October 17th, the Octobrists had emerged on the eve of the December Moscow uprising as a party of merchants, industrialists, and provincial landowners to take their stand squarely upon the October Manifesto, which they called "a precious achievement for the Russian people."[91] Like the Morozovs, Tretiakovs, and Mamontovs, a number of the Octobrists' founding fathers—including the Riabushinskii brothers and Grigorii Krestovnikov—were among those new lords of industry who had begun to dominate Moscow's cultural and political life in the 1880s. Their leader was Aleksandr Guchkov, wealthy and talented scion of one of Moscow's greatest merchant families, whose parents and grandparents had built an industrial empire from capital supplied by Moscow's Old Believer community.[92] In his mid-forties when his party was founded, Guchkov remained a powerful and energetic figure who guided the Octobrists for more than a decade. His early political experience accustomed him to adversity and defeat, and he carried those hard lessons with him into the far more desperate years of war and revolution.

Only a handful of Guchkov's Octobrists won seats in the First Duma, and they seemed painfully out of step with the times as they opposed *Kadet* efforts to move the government further to the left in its social and economic programs. Still, they persisted in their moderate course. Proclaimed Guchkov stubbornly, "The doctrinaire attitudes of the extreme parties, and their isolation from the entire historical life of Russia, alienate us from them."[93] The Octobrists opposed any expropriation of land, even with proper compensation to former owners, and urged the government to make every effort to turn the peasants away from any hope that such a program could be realized. "The Russian peasantry no longer needs mindless destruction, which will draw down upon them the justifiable retribution of the law for riot, robbery, and arson," one of their pamphlets stated. "They now need to reach an understanding about whom to elect to the State Duma."[94]

In sharp contrast to its treatment of all other parties except the Union of the Russian People, Nicholas's government recognized the Octobrists as a legitimate political party. That rare recognition, in addition to the generous donations the party's merchant lords lavished upon it, allowed them to use the press to great advantage. Although formed only in late 1905, the Octobrist party could claim the support of almost forty provincial newspapers by the beginning of 1906. Its brochure *About the State Duma,* which explained its views about the Duma's limited role in assisting Russia's government, appeared in an edition of several million copies,[95] and, by the end of the year, its leaders had collected nearly a half-million rubles to found the Moscow Company for the Publication of Books and Newspapers. Among other things, the Octobrists published *The Voice of Moscow,* a newspaper they called "a counterweight to the agitational intrigues of the extreme left's press among the working masses."[96]

Like their counterparts in Europe and America, Guchkov and his followers defended public order and held private property sacred. After a terrorist attempt upon Stolypin's life, Guchkov threw his full support to the government's new effort to meet terror with terror,[97] as many Russians wearied of violence and moved slowly to the right. That worked somewhat to the Octobrists' advantage in the elections for the Second Duma, and they won fifty-four seats.[98] Still, in return for the resources expended, they had done less well than they had expected. Disputes in their ranks kept them from becoming clearly situated in Russia's fluctuating political spectrum as the spring of 1907 approached.[99]

The history of the Second Duma was one of bitter conflict and constant confrontation. On the very first day, Social Democrats and right-wing deputies clashed over such symbolic gestures as cheering for the Tsar and wearing red lapel ribbons. The Social Democrats soon fell to squabbling among themselves, and that left the first days of the session surprisingly free from inflammatory speeches and accusations. "They were not prepared for serious [legislative] commission work [and] they found it boring in the Duma," Miliukov later wrote. "The Duma did not 'besiege Stolypin' [as some of the Social Democrats had threatened during their campaign speeches]; instead, Stolypin 'laid siege' to the Duma and encircled it with a 'tight blockade.' "[100] The government, the Premier insisted, wanted to establish a dialogue with the Duma and work toward common goals, but, first of all, order must be preserved and revolutionary attacks upon the members of the government ended. "These attacks," Stolypin told the assembled deputies, "all come down to two words directed against authority: 'Hands up!' To these two words," he warned them, "the government . . . can reply: 'You will not frighten us!' "[101]

Stolypin conciliated some Duma deputies but alienated others during the first days of its session. Unlike Goremykin, he took the Duma seriously, presented an impressive collection of draft legislation for its consideration, and urged it to get on with discussing the budget because the reforms he proposed depended upon the healthy state of the treasury. He attended Duma sessions often, and debated vigorously. Yet he was unwilling to give way on policy issues. "He displayed disturbing characteristics of the old bureaucratic type," a leading expert on the Duma's history once wrote. "He would cooperate with the Duma, but basically on his own terms."[102] Stolypin was angered by the deputies' clumsiness in dealing with Russia's legislative processes almost as much as by their growing antagonism on policy questions. "It will soon be evident how far the Duma intends to get down to serious work or to squander its time and small prestige in useless chatter and abuse," Nicholas wrote to his mother.[103] After several weeks, the results seemed even less promising. There were almost 150 workers and peasants in the Duma, few of them educated much beyond the level of elementary literacy, and for them legislative work proved especially awkward and unfamiliar. But unfamiliarity with parliamentary debate and the means of connecting it with Russia's bureaucratic legislative heritage made legislative work almost as difficult for men with more education and experience. The Duma was "rotting on its stem," Stolypin told Nicholas at one point, and that was because of a "lack of preparation and the inability to work in general."[104] Coupled with the left's festering hatred for the government, the intractable opposition to parliamentary government by the right made legislative progress impossible. After three months, the Duma still had not begun to discuss the state budget.

Nowhere was the conflict between Duma and government more intense than in its debates about the agrarian question, easily the most pressing issue it faced during the late spring of 1907. As in many underdeveloped nations, the critical problem centered upon the peasants' obvious and desperate need for more land in a nation where vast tracts lay idle. In some parts of Russia, more than one out of every two peasants now faced the terrible specter of hunger.[105] During 1905 and 1906 Nicholas's agents had found rural revolts far more difficult to quell than urban violence. Even into 1907, Punitive Expeditions still roamed the countryside to snuff out the flames of peasant rebellion that continued to flare up in more than five hundred districts of Russia. Like the embers of a dying fire, the sparks scattered each time the Tsar's agents tried to crush them out, and some of them inevitably burst again into flame.[106] "The people are awakening and beginning to rage like the waves of a tempest," said one Cossack Duma deputy.[107] The tempest had begun to calm as the Second Duma assembled, but the chance that it could begin to ravage the countryside again still seemed very real indeed.

Government officials and Duma deputies came to St. Petersburg in February 1907 convinced that the crisis in Russia's countryside needed serious attention. Their sense of urgency was all the greater because Russia was in the grip of the worst famine since 1891. According to the best contemporary estimates, and not taking into account the grain needed for livestock, rent payments, and taxes, the average peasant needed about 650 pounds of grain to survive for a year. Peasants could live on less, but anything below 550 pounds threatened famine. Government statistics, which habitually tended to portray difficult situations in optimistic terms, showed that almost 45 million peasants had less than 430 pounds of grain to live on in 1906, and more than 16 million of them did not have even half that amount.[108] Experts could point to the primitive agriculture of the peasantry, insufficient fertilizer, crude implements, and bad weather as reasons for recurring famine. All had an impact and all posed serious problems. But the fact remained that European Russia was filled with desperately poor peasants who could not hope to afford modern implements, fertilizers, or hybrid seed, and who could not get enough to eat even though they planted grain and potatoes on more than eight out of every ten acres they farmed.[109] From whatever point one viewed the dilemma, peasants accounted for 84 out of every 100 people who lived in European Russia, but they held only a bit over a third of the land[110]—they needed more.

The agrarian debate became so thorny in the Second Duma that every Monday and Friday was set aside for it from late March until mid-May. Although they differed bitterly about particulars, left-wing deputies all demanded nationalization of the land, including that held by the government and the Imperial family, as a way of putting more land at the peasants' disposal. *Kadety* now rejected any nationalization program and offered instead a more complex plan to expropriate great private latifundia but pay the former owners proper compensation. Stolypin himself proposed a unique program designed to turn peasants into small farmers, each with a solid stake in the existing order of things. Unfortunately, he would accept no compromise and would make no concession, thus forcing the Duma into the impossibly awkward political position of having had its entire agrarian program rejected by the government out of hand.[111]

Clearly, Stolypin and the Duma could not work together to resolve Russia's agrarian crisis if the majority of the deputies insisted upon solutions that required a social revolution. Long before they reached that impasse, however, Stolypin resolved to dissolve the Duma and change the electoral law in order to return deputies with whom the government could work more harmoniously. What remained to be decided was when the dissolution should occur and for what reason. "One must let them do something manifestly stupid or mean, and then—slap! And they will be gone!" Nicholas explained gleefully to his mother.[112] For Stolypin, that time came in May.

The key to the government's "discovery" of an alleged plot by Social Democratic Duma members to foment a mutiny in the Russian army was Ekaterina Shornikova, a young woman who had forsaken the revolutionary cause to work for the Petersburg Okhrana. On instructions from her superiors, Shornikova joined the St. Petersburg Military Organization of the Social Democratic party and worked her way into an important position because of the reputation she had earned as a loyal comrade during her days in the provincial city of Kazan. Very soon she was invited to a meeting attended by a few soldiers, several radical students, and some Social Democrats, including at least one Duma deputy. After the meeting, young Vladimir Voitinskii, one of the students who had helped to arrange the meeting, drew up a petition to the Social Democrats in the Duma in which the soldiers pledged to rally parts of the army behind them if need be. When Shornikova obtained a copy of Voitinskii's petition for her superiors and told them of another meeting planned between the deputies and the soldiers, the Okhrana immediately saw the chance to embarrass their radical opponents. All that remained was to raid the deputies' apartment when the soldiers were there. That, combined with the incriminating petition, might serve as evidence that some of the Social Democrats in the Duma were taking part in illegal revolutionary activities and abusing the immunity privileges that had been granted them as deputies.[113]

On the evening of Saturday, May 5, Okhrana agents raided the apartment of Ivan Ozol, a Social Democratic deputy who used his lodgings on the Nevskii Prospekt as the party's St. Petersburg office. There, in the company of thirty-five other Social Democratic Duma members, they found forty soldiers whom they immediately searched and arrested. Likewise, they searched several deputies before the remainder protested that such acts violated their privileges as members of the Duma. The raid and the searches posed a variety of complex questions about the immunity of the deputies, their personal effects, and, even, the inviolability of Ozol's apartment itself. Meanwhile, it was not clear that an illegal meeting had taken place or that a conspiracy was actually afoot. For several weeks, these issues were debated in the Duma while the government stated its case and the deputies counterattacked. Stolypin saw in the incident the pretext for dissolving the Duma that he had sought for several weeks. With Nicholas's approval, he went to the Duma on June 1, accused the Social Democrats of plotting the violent overthrow of the government, and insisted that the Duma cancel the parliamentary immunity of fifty-five Social Democrats who sat amongst them. He warned that the government must have an immediate answer to its request and that it would tolerate no delay. For the better part of two days, the deputies debated the issue, but with a growing sense of futility. Clearly, they could not abandon fifty-five of their members to the government on the basis of the limited evidence Stolypin and his ministers presented. Yet Stolypin was adamant: without the deputies' surrender, the life of the Duma was limited to a few hours at most. The die was cast. On June 3, the Second Duma passed into history, like its predecessor, the victim of a dissolution order.[114]

Like the First Duma, the Second Duma had accomplished very little. Nor had the government learned much more about working in harmony with the people's elected representatives. Further efforts, however, would be made on a new basis. "At the moment, the elections are under the control of the peasantry," Stolypin had said that spring. "The rights of control must be given to someone else."[115] Therefore, on the same day that he announced the Duma's dissolution, Stolypin published a new electoral law that enabled the government to draw much closer to the conservative nobility, its traditional bulwark in times of crisis.[116] The implications of this new direction were far-reaching and, from the point of view of many, ominous. For, whenever the government had been pressed to make common cause with the nobility, it always had done so by making important concessions to them. This time would be no exception. The result, one of the greatest experts on turn-of-the-century Russian politics wrote not long ago, was that a small group of nobles "found itself in a better position to resist the government's administrative and legislative initiatives in the last decade of the tsarist regime than it had been since the late eighteenth century."[117] As another scholar concluded, "The revolutionary period of 1905 to 1907 had come to an end. The state and its supporters were in firm control."[118]

Stolypin, one of the most able statesmen ever to serve any Russian sovereign, now proceeded to forge the Tsar, his ministers, and the Duma into a workable system of government. Unlike most Imperial statesmen, he had not built his early reputation at Court or in St. Petersburg's chanceries, but as an energetic, efficient, and hardheaded provincial governor who had never been shielded from the reality of Russia's myriad problems by mountains of bureaucratic red tape and reports. He knew the provinces, and he knew their problems. By the time he replaced Durnovo as Minister of Internal Affairs in April 1906, Stolypin had amassed an impressive record of successes in dealing with famine, epidemic, and revolt in some of the most impoverished and unruly provinces in the Russian Empire.[119]

Stolypin traced his noble lineage back to the time of Ivan the Terrible. When he rose to national prominence in the days of the First Duma, he was just forty-four, a barrel-chested bear of a man who commanded respect from friend and foe alike. "Stolypin had a talent for arousing in everyone with whom he dealt a feeling that he was sincere in everything he said," wrote Vladimir Gurko, an associate who was far from being a friend. "He inspired confidence and even affection."[120] Sir George Buchanan, Britain's ambassador to Russia, recalled that "he combined with rare strength of character a simple, gentle nature" and thought him the "ideal Minister to transact business with." Buchanan called Stolypin "a true patriot" and a "great Minister,"[121] a judgment with which his predecessor, Sir Arthur Nicolson, heartily concurred. Nicolson admired Stolypin's "ardent love for his country" and called him "the most notable figure in Europe."[122] "From the very outset, he has made a most excellent impression," Nicholas confided to his diary two days after Stolypin replaced Goremykin as chairman of the Council of Ministers.[123] "I cannot tell you how much I have come to like and respect this man," he added in a letter to his mother some three months later.[124] Perhaps most surprising of all, Nicholas's belief in his Prime Minister endured for half a decade. Not until 1911, when Stolypin attacked Rasputin, did Nicholas begin to doubt him.[125] By that time Rasputin was firmly ensconced in Aleksandra's confidence as a holy man whose prayers might cure the Tsarevich's hemophilia, but the Prime Minister very rightly feared that his sordid escapades were undermining Russians' confidence in the monarchy. Aleksandra was so enraged at Stolypin's attempt to exile the bogus holy man, whom she regularly referred to as "our Friend," that she saw Stolypin's tragic assassination that September as an act of divine retribution. "Those who have offended God in the person of our Friend may no longer count on Divine protection," she explained to the young Grand Duke Dmitrii Pavlovich.[126]

As an Imperial statesman and politician, Stolypin's principles were straightforward and unambiguous. "I believe in Russia's brilliant future with all my heart," he once said.[127] Yet he knew that that future must be very different from the past because of the changes wrought by the momentous events of 1905. He therefore understood that the government must work with the Duma and tried to form an alliance with the forces of the right and center, while attacking and weakening the militant left. "What you want are great upheavals," he told the left scornfully. "But what *we* want is a GREAT RUSSIA!"[128] Insisting that "all the concern of the government must be directed toward putting a program of progressive reforms into effect,"[129] Stolypin proposed some of the most dramatic social and economic reform legislation in Russia's history. His program proved so promising that Lenin lamented in 1908 that "if this should continue for very long periods of time . . . it might force us [*Bolsheviki*] to renounce any agrarian program at all. . . . It would be empty and stupid democratic phrasemongering to say that the success of such a policy in Russia is impossible," he warned. "It *is* possible!"[130]

In contrast to Lenin and other radicals, Stolypin devoutly believed that "a strong peasant proprietor can serve as an obstacle to the march of revolution" in Russia; he felt the government had a mission to "rescue the masses from poverty, ignorance, and lawlessness." Because he was convinced that "the land is the guarantee of our strength in the future, that the land *is* Russia," he staked his government's survival upon "the wise and the strong, not the drunken and the weak" among the peasantry.[131] "The small farmer who holds title to his own land will be the defender of order and a buttress for the existing social order," he insisted. "This is our great task—to create a strong individual property owner as the most reliable bulwark of the state and our culture. . . . Our next main task will be to strengthen all the lower classes, for the entire strength of the nation lies in them! More than a hundred million strong, they will become the healthy and strong foundation of our nation!"[132] Yet the masses to whom Stolypin was about to turn were so poor that the average yearly income in Russia stood at a mere ninety-eight rubles, or $49.[133] If they were to become his hoped-for shield against revolutionary propaganda in tens of thousands of Russia's villages, they must have land to achieve the minimal prosperity needed to transform them into "defenders of order." Agrarian reform thus had to be Stolypin's most pressing and immediate task, but it could not be the revolutionary reform program of his adversaries in the Duma.

Stolypin's program took the form of several Imperial edicts issued between 1906 and 1911 that gave millions of Russian peasants title to the scattered strips of land they previously had held in common as members of a commune and then made it possible for them to consolidate those strips into separate, self-contained farms. At the same time, Stolypin convinced Nicholas to open large tracts of Crown lands for purchase by peasants and to encourage especially poor peasants to emigrate from crowded parts of European Russia to new homesteads in Siberia. Above all, he set out to destroy the peasant commune, which for so long had dampened Russia's agricultural development by discouraging individual initiative and penalizing private enterprise, and to establish in its place a class of small farmers, each with a solid stake in the existing order.[134] The result was a rapid and very dramatic increase in Russia's agricultural production during the next decade, as the *kulaki*, the "rich" peasants, achieved a level of production on the eve of the Great War that the Soviet state, which soon exterminated them as the insidious bearers of rural capitalism, would not be able to match until the 1960s.[135] Largely because of their efforts, Russia's average national income rose to 130 rubles by 1912.[136]

Despite the apparent success of his programs, Stolypin was not destined to see them through. He had been Prime Minister for scarcely a month when terrorists blew up his summer house on St. Petersburg's Aptekarskii Island in an assassination attempt that rivaled their efforts to dynamite the Winter Palace a quarter-century earlier. Gurko was one of the first to arrive at the scene, and he later penned a vivid recollection of the damage. "The house was in ruins," he wrote. "The facade was entirely demolished. The front wall had fallen, exposing to view the large vestibule and the little reception room. The ceilings of both these rooms had crashed, and had carried with them the furniture of the two rooms above occupied by Stolypin's children."[137] Fifty-four were killed or wounded, among them Stolypin's daughter Natalia, who suffered two broken legs. Stolypin himself emerged unscathed and remarkably in control of the situation.[138] It was not the first attempt against his life; nor was it to be the last.

What Stolypin had developed during his years as the most effective Prime Minister in Imperial Russia's history was a scheme of political accommodation between Tsar and Duma that came to be known as the System of June Third, the date in 1907 on which he dissolved the Second Duma and published the new electoral law by which Russians would elect their representatives until the Revolution. Central to the System of June Third, the number of peasant Duma deputies was halved, while those who represented the great landowners were increased by 50 percent to ensure that the moderately conservative Octobrists and the parties that stood to their right would be the ones with whom Stolypin's government struck their political alliances. It was an effort "to pick and choose, bit by bit, from the Russian chaos those elements in which the feeling of loyalty to the regime still lived," wrote Sergei Kryzhanovskii, who drew up the new electoral law for Stolypin. It was an attempt "to tear the State Duma from the hands of the revolutionaries, to fuse it with Russia's historical institutions, and to squeeze it into the system of state administration."[139]

Nobles, priests, rich merchants, and wealthy industrialists thus became the social groups with whom Stolypin cast his lot to overwhelm those workers, peasants, and urban intelligentsia who had so energetically barred the way to moderately conservative reforms in the First and Second Dumas. Yet the System of June Third did not allow the extreme right to dominate. In fact, as the ultrareactionary *Kievlianin* newspaper confessed somewhat later, Stolypin's "coup d'état" of June 3 had marked the beginning of a precipitous decline for the Union of the Russian People precisely because it freed the nobility from any further need to curry favor with the lower classes.[140] Moderate conservatism was the key in Stolypin's system, and for more than two years the Octobrists held the balance in the Duma. "Bonapartism," Lenin called it. "The objectively inevitable . . . evolution of monarchy in every bourgeois country."[141] Put another way, Stolypin's System of June Third marked an effort by the Tsarist government and the social order that supported it to accommodate the many and complex pressures that grew out of the vast industrialization program that Alexander III and his advisers had launched a quarter-century before, but preserve as much of the old social and political order as possible.

Yet Stolypin's new system also produced new and bitter conflicts. Conflicts between the government and those men and women who had sustained the revolutionary movement between 1905 and 1907 were of course neither surprising nor unexpected. More unforeseen, and perhaps more politically damaging to the Imperial government in the long run, were the conflicts that the System of June Third provoked between the government and those noble landlords to whom Stolypin turned for support. In retrospect, such conflict seems unavoidable, even inevitable, because the aspirations of the landed nobility stood against the goals Stolypin set for his reform program. To implement the moderate reforms that had been spurned by Russia's liberals and radicals, he conceded greater political power to the very group whose social and economic future the reforms most directly threatened.[142]

Because the System of June Third embodied the makings of such stark conflicts, it is perhaps surprising that the entente between Stolypin and the Octobrists survived as long as it did. But, as public sentiment shifted to the right in 1909, the Octobrists began to lose ground. In local *zemstva* elections, the Empire's noble lords tightened their grip on Russian politics, while the peasantry grew apathetic and disillusioned by their first experiences with Russia's new political processes.[143] These ultraconservative aristocrats numbered a mere thirty thousand families out of over 130 million Russian subjects, but they exercised a formidable influence,[144] especially when they gained added authority in the Council of State, the legislature's upper house. In Stolypin's words, these men opposed the system itself because they thought it was "no longer necessary to legislate, but only to administer."[145] In doing so, they undermined the System of June Third as Stolypin had envisioned it.

Beginning late in 1909 and continuing into 1911, a series of crises left Stolypin's System of June Third impotent to pursue further reforms. A number of issues were involved, but the most dramatic confrontation between Stolypin and his enemies occurred over his efforts to extend the *zemstva* into Russia's western provinces. Stolypin therefore strongly supported the Western *Zemstvo* Bill, and it contained provisions that the extreme right had supported on several earlier occasions. But Russia's great lords saw an opportunity to weaken Stolypin, his system, and the Duma if they opposed in the Council of State a bill that the Duma had passed at the Prime Minister's urging.[146] Led by Senator Vladimir Trepov and Petr Durnovo, the right carried the day in the upper house. Convinced that his authority had been undermined by the growing strength of the ultraconservatives, Stolypin offered to resign at the beginning of March 1911. Nicholas insisted that he stay. Stolypin said that he would do so only if the Emperor recessed the Duma and Council of State for a few days so that he could use the extraordinary powers granted under Article 87 of the new Fundamental Laws to enact the Western *Zemstvo* Bill by decree. He also insisted that Nicholas furlough Durnovo and Trepov, both of them Imperial favorites, for the remainder of the year.[147]

Stolypin's clearly were dictatorial acts, and he had not bothered to cloak them in even a shred of constitutionality. He had become convinced that, when opposition became too strong, the Prime Minister's will must prevail and that those who opposed it too vigorously must be sent away. This revealed the central weakness of the system he had created, for Stolypin had not replaced the capricious power of autocratic politics with constitutional instruments. Instead, he had perpetuated it under a thinly veiled constitutional guise that slipped away the moment it confronted resolute political pressure. There followed a dramatic four-day pause while Nicholas considered the near ultimatum he had received from his Prime Minister. And then he succumbed. "Dear Petr Arkadevich," he wrote from Tsarskoe Selo, the refuge to which he and his family had retired during the upheavals of 1905, "I do not wish you to resign. Your devotion to me and to Russia, your five years' experience in the post you hold, and, most of all, your courageous upholding of Russian political principles on the borders of the Empire, move me to retain you at all costs."[148]

For the moment, Stolypin had seemingly triumphed, but he knew that a price must be paid. "The Emperor will never forgive me if he has to fulfill my conditions, but that is a matter of indifference to me," he had told his friend Kokovtsev while Nicholas considered his offer to resign.[149] What he had not counted on was the deep animosity that his high-handed tactics stirred in the Duma among such moderate former allies as the Octobrists. Almost to a man, Guchkov and his Octobrists, as well as Maklakov and some *Kadety,* turned against him for his open violation of the constitutional principles by which Russia was supposed to be governed. Warned Maklakov, "There is no such thing in politics as revenge, but there are consequences."[150] Those consequences took the form of the Duma's formal censure of the Prime Minister they had often supported before. For Stolypin, now only a few months away from assassination, it marked the end of his ability to govern Russia by constitutional and parliamentary means. "Something had snapped inside him," Kokovtsev later wrote. "His former belief in himself was gone."[151]

For just over five years, Stolypin eluded the terrorists' efforts as he continued to work with the Third Duma to establish an effective working relationship between parliament and the Tsar. In late August 1911, he accompanied Nicholas and his daughters Olga and Tatiana to Kiev to dedicate a memorial to Alexander II, the Tsar who had freed the serfs and had been assassinated by terrorists in 1881. On the evening of September 1, they and a number of other ministers attended a festival performance of Rimskii-Korsakov's *Tale of Tsar Saltan* at the Kiev Opera House. As was always the case when Nicholas or any of his family appeared in public, extraordinary security precautions were in force, and no one thought seriously that anyone's life could be in danger. Suddenly, during the second intermission, a double agent by the name of Dmitrii Bogrov walked up to Stolypin and shot him at point-blank range.[152] Nicholas was so near that he almost saw it happen. "We had just left the box," he wrote a few days later, "when we heard two sounds as if something had been dropped. I thought an opera glass might have fallen on somebody's head, and ran back into the box to look." From the box, he saw Stolypin standing in the first row of the orchestra. "He slowly turned his face toward us and, with his left hand, made the sign of the cross in the air. Only then did I notice that he was very pale and that his right hand and uniform were bloodstained. He slowly sank into his chair."[153] Four days later, Stolypin died in agony from the chest wounds he had received. Bogrov was mysteriously and hastily killed before a full inquiry could be made into his murderous act, thus giving rise to speculation that he was part of a plot involving high-ranking reactionaries who hated Stolypin almost as much as the revolutionaries did.[154] After Stolypin's assassination, Nicholas turned with relief to that narrow circle of reactionary great lords whom Durnovo and Trepov led in the Council of State. So strong was their influence that Kokovtsev, who succeeded Stolypin as Prime Minister, soon thought himself isolated and helpless.[155] "By the eve of the Great War, the Tsarist regime appeared more dependent on the landed nobility," Leopold Haimson wrote recently, "than at any time since the Pugachev Rebellion of the late eighteenth century."[156]

By 1910, Stolypin had brought calm and stability back to Russia, but neither he nor any others among Nicholas's advisers perceived the astronomical cost of those two cherished political commodities. Indeed, the future seemed very promising as Russia entered a new era of growth and prosperity. At the same time, the once-powerful revolutionary movement seemed to have faltered. Even most of its leaders appeared tired and despondent. Government repression had left them little room in which to maneuver, the workers now seemed uninterested in their preachings, and the peasants appeared to be slipping quickly and certainly into the ranks of the much-despised petty bourgeoisie as Stolypin's reforms offered them a stake in the Tsarist regime.[157] In terms of Russia's political modernization, the clock had stopped; it even seemed to have turned back.

CHAPTER X

"The Children of Russia's Dreadful Years"

D URING THE YEARS OF THE THIRD DUMA, THE TURMOIL THAT had been so much a part of Russia's political life shifted to the arts as many of the intelligentsia abandoned social and political activism. Turning to philosophy, religion, art, and literature, they launched Russia upon one of the most explosive cultural eras in her entire history. The new art they created, especially after 1905, no longer was judged by the rigid criterion of social utility that had been axiomatic ever since the literary critic Vissarion Belinskii had proclaimed in 1841 that the artist must be the conscience of his time and his society.[1] "Aestheticism, idealism, mysticism, and apocalypticism became the dominant themes of art and thought," one scholar wrote. "All sought a purely sensuous effect."[2]

Russia's avant-garde found themselves cast into a world where the dimensions of space and time had shrunk to a fraction of what they had been in their parents' day. Even as they struggled to comprehend the everyday world, they saw the present become transformed into the past, while they hurtled into the future with frightening speed. This Silver Age, when all seemed possible and nothing improbable in the world of Russia's avant-garde, was marked by extreme debauchery, frenzied searching, and deep, passionate belief. Life held equal measures of exaltation and despair, as men and women groped for moorings in a brave new world where science and technology seemed destined to become the gods of an increasingly cynical and present-minded society.

If life's pace and setting had shifted as the old century closed, many of the questions that consumed thinking men and women remained the same. What was art, and what was its relation to life? What was sin, and could a sinner still find salvation? Who (or what) was God? Was there any God at all? What was the destiny of man in this new and complex world? With their ungovernable passion for debate, Russia's intellectuals struggled with these age-old questions. As always, they searched for definitive answers. When answers eluded them, and their eagerly grasped credos failed, their vision grew more ominous until, in a flood of apocalyptic imagery, they proclaimed the Antichrist's coming and warned that a final struggle between Good and Evil soon must engulf mankind. "The children of Russia's dreadful years" the poet Aleksandr Blok called these searching and tormented men and women.[3] Like the White Nights that washed the palaces and canals of St. Petersburg with pale sunlight during summer's midnight hours, there was an ethereal quality about Russia's Silver Age. It ripened all too quickly during the last days of peace. It was "a feast of delicacies tinged with foreboding," one historian wrote. "Sunlight at midnight in one season led to darkness at noon in the next."[4]

Russia's passionate writers and artists were consumed by an urgent frenzy to explore all realms, to experience and attempt everything, as war's dark shadow hovered over them. Fatalists thought its descent unavoidable, even inevitable. Others, like Dmitrii Merezhkovskii, insisted that "if 'divine ecstasy' (sex) is not satisfied, the soul seeks the 'satanic ecstasy' of war."[5] Such beliefs drove artists and intellectuals to embark upon voyages of unrestrained sexual exploration. Suicide, murder, sexual perversion, opium, alcohol—all were part of Russia's Silver Age, from the soundless, timeless St. Petersburg "Tower" of the poet Viacheslav Ivanov to the lowest cellars of prostitution and depravity that Gorkii depicted in *Life Among the Dregs*.

The nineteenth-century writer whose thought had set the tone for the Silver Age had tasted none of these excesses. A gentle thinker, whom Dostoevskii may have used as his model for Alësha Karamazov, Vladimir Solovev was the first—and only—philosopher that nineteenth-century Russia produced.[6] Like Alësha Karamazov, he was a monk without a monastery, a man of many complexities, who "spoke like a prophet, lived the life of a monk, yet, like a child, could not resist the temptation of a bonbon or a jelly tart."[7] He preached the ideal of a "free theocracy" in which total freedom would be reconciled with the supreme authority of God in a temporal realm where the Russian Tsar, "in whom resides the supreme spiritual strength of the entire Russian people,"[8] ruled as the ideal Christian prince.

Sophia, the beautiful lady who first came to him in an aura of shining light when he was a child of nine, occupied the center of Solovev's thought and writing.[9] He saw her as the divine feminine principle, the principle of "all-in-oneness,"[10] of which beauty and sexual pleasure were important parts. Sexual pleasure, he once wrote, "is the highest flowering of the individual life" and must be connected with the "true nature of universal existence."[11] Beyond that, Solovev endowed sexual pleasure with a mystical significance because, as one critic explained, it previewed "the eventual union of flesh and spirit in the God-Man."[12] This ideal, which man could attain through a mystical and erotic union with Sophia, must be sought through all forms of art and artistic creation.[13] "Every sensuous expression of any object or event from the point of view of its final state or in the light of the *world to come* is a work of art," Solovev insisted. Prince Trubetskoi called this Solovev's "erotic utopia," in which the "direct *task* of love" was to create a "higher unity" of man and woman that became an "individualization of the total-oneness."[14]

Solovev's vision of a "free theocracy" in which men and women would seek a state of "total-oneness" through sexual love and artistic expression darkened as the nineteenth century approached its end. Like such great Silver Age symbolists as Aleksandr Blok and Andrei Belyi, he envisioned a vast and violent tide arising in Asia. Foreshadowing Blok's *Scythians* by a quarter of a century, he wrote in *Pan-Mongolism* of a new Mongol horde forming in the East to sweep over Russia. At the opening of the new century (he died in 1900), he spoke in even more explicit and remarkable terms of Japan arising to unite the peoples of the East before going on to conquer the world and usher in the reign of the Antichrist.[15] Soon, Solovev's apocalyptic symbolism took on a fearsome note of reality as Japan's army and navy defeated Russia's forces throughout the Far East.

Solovev's philosophical and aesthetic preachings breathed new life and creativity into writers and artists long grown weary of Russia's fifty-year dedication to realism. "His idea that the world is but a symbolic reflection of a more vital ideal world all around us," James Billington wrote some years ago, "gave poets a new impulse to discover and proclaim these higher beauties and harmonies."[16] Solovev's emphasis upon symbols—above all his image of the beautiful lady Sophia—was important in stimulating the ideas and literary images of Belyi and Blok and may also have had considerable significance for Dmitrii Merezhkovskii, the writer who served as their mentor at the turn of the century.[17] At the time of Solovev's death, Merezhkovskii and his talented and beautiful wife Zinaida Gippius had become part of an enterprise that would serve as the first vehicle for the ideas and images of the Silver Age, one that readily acknowledged its intellectual and aesthetic debt to the philosopher.

Mir Iskusstva (The World of Art), a journal founded in 1898 by the impresario Sergei Diaghilev and the painter, theatrical designer, and producer Aleksandr Benois, was the first voice of the new art and writing, the mouthpiece for what Diaghilev called "a generation thirsting for beauty."[18] Its pages filled with some of the most brilliant art and poetry ever to appear in Russia, it was the very antithesis of those ponderous "thick journals" that had published the great works of Tolstoi and Dostoevskii thirty years before. Turning aside from questions of civic reform and social justice, *Mir Iskusstva* proclaimed that "Art is Free; Life is Paralyzed"[19] and condemned the "enemies of art" who, Diaghilev warned, wanted to turn "everything lofty which humanity possesses . . . into a dull mirror of their own mediocre activities."[20]

Mir Iskusstva had its beginnings among a group of Benois's Petersburg friends who called themselves the "Nevskii Pickwickians" and met several times a week to discuss art, literature, and music. At first dominated by Benois and the young literary critic Dmitrii Filosofov, the group soon was joined by the painters Lev Bakst and Nikolai Rerikh and by Filosofov's provincial cousin Sergei Diaghilev, who soon became the journal's editor.[21] Insisting that "the artist is neither a servant, nor a guide, does not belong to the people or to the world, does not serve any idea or any society,"[22] they rejected both the "official" art of the Academy of Fine Arts and that of the nineteenth century's first artistic rebels, the *Peredvizhniki*, whose work continued to be dominated by the great canvases of Ilia Repin. Determined to chart a new course and opposed to "everything which reflected a literary, political, or social tendency," these young men embraced art for the sake of art alone.[23] "The *World of Art* is above all earthly things," Bakst proudly announced just before the first issue was published. "It stands among the stars, where it reigns arrogantly, enigmatically, and alone, like an eagle on a snowy crag."[24]

The Nevskii Pickwickians and their new allies gathered in the afternoons at Diaghilev's apartment on the corner of Liteinyi Prospekt and the Simeonovskii, where they drank tea served by the old nanny Bakst later captured in the background of his famous portrait of Diaghilev, and they planned future issues of *Mir Iskusstva* amidst their host's eclectic collection of antique Italian furniture, casts of Renaissance bronzes, Max Liebermann's neo-Impressionist land-scapes, and the many signed photographs of European artists that Diaghilev had so avidly sought during his early foreign travels.[25] With unabashed daring, they announced that it was the task of the coming century to "establish the first principles for Russian art, Russian architecture, Russian philosophy, Russian music, and Rus-sian poetry."[26] Although their diverse convictions and complex per-sonal relationships kept them in constant turmoil, they all agreed that art was "a form of mystical experience, a means through which eternal beauty could be expressed."[27] Both Bakst and Rerikh em-braced that creed in their early work, although its full expression came only a decade later when they joined with Diaghilev and Benois to create the amazing *Ballets russes* productions of *Prince Igor, Cléopatre,* and *Schéhérezade* with which they took Paris by storm in 1909 and 1910.

Efforts to capture the fleeting essence of eternal beauty and mystical experience stretched far beyond the confines of any artist's canvas and cried out for other forms of expression. Zinaida Gippius, her husband Dmitrii Merezhkovskii, and Vasilii Rozanov, their tor-mented friend who stood as the high priest of the Silver Age's new cult of sex, all penned vividly conceived works for the pages of *Mir Iskusstva.* Proclaiming that "the tie of sex with God is far stronger than the tie of intellect, or even conscience," Rozanov frequently likened himself to a fetus and preached a new "sexual transcenden-talism."[28] During what one commentator aptly called Russia's "spiritual Time of Troubles,"[29] Rozanov came to see Christ as a "God of Death," as he embraced what one scholar has called "a religion without faith, hope, or charity."[30] Only in sex did he see the key to man's existence. "A person comes into being only where there is sex," Rozanov once wrote.[31] He boldly went on to preach that "there is no spiritual friendship without carnal attraction," that "the body is the beginning of the spirit," that "the spirit is the smell of the body," and that "Christianity ought, at least in part, to become phallic."[32] A critic once wrote that "some of his pages have a distinct aroma of bedchamber and bathroom,"[33] and Rozanov himself proudly declared that "my works are blended with neither water nor blood, but with semen."[34] Finally, when revolution and civil war seethed around him and his own death approached, Rozanov concluded that there was more theology "in a bull mounting a cow" than in all of Russia's seminaries.[35] In one final contradictory act, he retired to spend his last days in a monastery, where he died before he finished his monumental *Apocalypse of Our Time.*[36]

Rozanov once recalled that, as he preached about "sexual transcendentalism" in Diaghilev's apartment, Benois usually sat like "a black beetle, deeply burrowed into an armchair."[37] During the early days of *Mir Iskusstva,* Merezhkovskii and Gippius were often there as well to join in the debate. While Rozanov argued that sex "is man's soul" and that man was a "transformation of sex,"[38] Merezhkovskii, whose ugliness and eccentricity appalled some and intrigued others, insisted as Solovev had that sex was the manifestation of God's worldly presence. There could be no salvation without sex, and he believed that sexual pleasure was "the anticipation of the Resurrection of the flesh." He lauded the ancient Babylonians whose "temple prostitution was the institutionalization of sex as a means of reaching God."[39] Sex need not be monogamous, Merezhkovskii insisted, because all love was a reflection of the love men and women had for Christ. Marriage must be a spiritual union, not a confining legal bond.

Gippius shared many of her husband's convictions, but added subtle and contradictory dimensions to them. Andrei Belyi was certain that "Gippius stood a full twenty-five heads higher than Merezhkovskii in the subtlety of her thoughts and feelings."[40] Convinced, in the words of her leading biographer, that "sexual love may lead to salvation by restoring the lost unity of two individuals," she also claimed that "only in physical love is it possible to realize the truth and significance of one's own being."[41] Yet she found humiliation in the traditional female sexual position and once wrote to Filosofov that the sex act was "merely a seizure."[42] Recently, literary historians have concluded that she disliked the sex act in any form and therefore dreamed of a brave new world in which love would find other means of expression, so that she could attain her ultimate goal, which one expert has defined as "the final merging with God in the meantime, she urged a ménage à trois upon Merezhkovskii, convinced that only in a relationship that reflected the Trinity in some fashion could the "mystery of the flesh" be resolved.[44] With Merezhkovskii and Filosofov, she set out to resolve the ultimate mystery Rozanov once had compared to an "enchanted forest" destined ever to remain beyond their comprehension.[45] Soon afterward, in the fall of 1901, she persuaded them to join her in founding the Religious Philosophical Society. "Our symbols have not yet been translated into actions," she lamented to her husband. "Don't you think that we should start a new cause, a real action?"[46]

Together with Rozanov and a few others, they obtained Pobedonostsev's permission to establish a society in which they urged a reconciliation between the official church and Russia's tormented intelligentsia.[47] Theirs was a scheme without hope for success. Gippius bitterly disapproved of the representatives of the Russian church, except for a handful who she thought "believed blindly, in the old way, with true childlike holiness." The rest she dismissed as "half-believing prelates and real bureaucrats" and rejected them as allies in her quest because they were "totally uncultured, and this defect was impossible to repair."[48] Perhaps in revenge, she set out to shock them by appearing at meetings of the society in an especially revealing black dress whose many pink-lined pleats separated whenever she moved to give the impression that she was naked beneath it.[49] Within eighteen months, Pobedonostsev closed the Religious Philosophical Society when it condemned his excommunication of Tolstoi as an attack against all who loved freedom and when Merezhkovskii urged that the relationship of the Holy Synod to the Orthodox Church and Russia's faithful ought to be questioned. As a consequence, the Silver Age intelligentsia turned still further from Russia's "establishment." "Autocracy is from Antichrist," Merezhkovskii announced.[50]

The *Dom Muruzi*—the salon of Gippius and Merezhkovskii—served their purposes far better than the Religious Philosophical Society. There Gippius was in her element; Petersburg's artists, writers, and poets flocked to these Sunday assemblies, attracted partly by Merezhkovskii's reputation, partly by her exotic and well-known beauty, and partly by rumors of wild sexual orgies that stemmed from the Merezhkovskiis' talk about "holy flesh" and its mysteries. Shrouded in a haze of cigar smoke, his face somewhat greenish, Merezhkovskii greeted his guests with exclamations: "We are yours, you are ours!" Her long blond hair dyed a flaming red, her sensuous mouth and green eyes set off by dramatic and bizarre fashions that some thought rivaled the dress and dazzling beauty of the Bolshevik feminist Aleksandra Kollontai,[51] Gippius smoked cigarettes through a long holder and peered at the world through an ornamental lorgnette. She had her dresses (almost always white ones) cut so that they fitted her body like a second skin, and she sometimes dressed in male attire. Andrei Belyi wrote that she seemed to dissolve in mistiness. She held many of the Petersburg intelligentsia under her spell, although the best evidence indicates that she never gave herself to any of them.[52]

An irregular, though prominent, visitor to the *Dom Muruzi* during its early days was Valerii Briusov, the recently emerged leader of Moscow's Decadents, who was approaching the peak of his fame. "Neither handsome nor the reverse," Gippius pronounced with decisive finality after she met him. "He had an interesting face and lively eyes. But if you look at him long enough, he begins to remind you of a chimpanzee."[53] Nonetheless, Briusov was a powerful figure with a magnetic personality that exuded an aura of mystery. "In this man," Belyi wrote, "one sees Prince Hamlet."[54] Briusov commanded attention, and his public appearances were dramatic events. Some thought he was a "black magician," a poet with powers beyond those held by mortal men.[55] He had been introduced to the work of the French Symbolists by Aleksandr Dobroliubov, a tortured young poet who was addicted to opium and lived in a windowless, gray-ceilinged room surrounded by walls draped with black velvet, where he held forth about French poetry, magic, and demonism.[56]

Despite his poetic references to carnal delights and great passions, Briusov's poems have been characterized as being tempered by "the icy sheen of rational invention." He often drew upon historical themes, which led one critic to remark that "the titles of his poems resound with the mouth-filling names of Chaldean shepherds, Pompeiian girls, Cretan builders, and Macedonian warlords." His most famous poem was "The Pale Horse," written in 1903, which was an early expression of the doom-filled vision that would descend upon many Russian poets and writers as the Great War approached. In 1905, he warned of the tramping iron boots of Huns and Scythians; in less than a decade, some of his poetic images became reality.[57]

The literary historian Konstantin Mochulskii once wrote that "for Briusov it was not enough to be an artist—he needed to be a conqueror."[58] When Briusov began to appear at the Merezhkovskii's "Sundays," he had already begun to assume that role as the founder and chief editor of Skorpion, a new publishing house that helped him to organize Moscow's turbulent Decadent writers into a more coherent and cohesive artistic group, who began to see art as an end in itself. He extended that remarkable organizational achievement to include a number of the Petersburg Symbolists, despite their insistence that art was a "metaphysical means of apprehending a higher reality,"[59] and found support at the *Dom Muruzi*. "They could not have received us more kindly," Briusov confided to his diary after he first visited Merezhkovskii and Gippius. "Merezhkovskii preached about the time for unity having come, that all who were seeking a new path ought to join together."[60] This marked the beginning of a rare and all-too-brief unity between the poets and writers of Moscow and St. Petersburg. "At a time when everyone thought that he was forcing his way through the darkness, without hope, and with a feeling that ruin lay on all sides—it turned out that others were following the same path," Belyi wrote in one of his first letters to Aleksandr Blok.[61] Soon, Merezhkovskii and Gippius enlisted Briusov's support for their new journal *Novyi put* (*The New Way*), and, a year later (in 1904), Briusov started *Vesy* (*The Balance*), a journal dedicated entirely to the Symbolist and Decadent movements. "He ruled Skorpion and *Vesy* with absolute power," one of his contemporaries wrote. "He conducted polemics, concluded alliances, declared wars, united and divided, made peace, and quarreled."[62] Yet he directed, threatened, insulted, and cajoled to good purpose, as he labored to increase the numbers of men and women who believed in his precepts.[63]

In December 1901, Merezhkovskii and Gippius visited Moscow, where Briusov introduced them to Boris Bugaev, a young writer who published under the name of Andrei Belyi so as not to embarrass his father, the famed mathematician Nikolai Bugaev, who shared academics' well-known scorn for the Decadents' work. Belyi was still a student at Moscow University in those days. "Thin, slight, with a high forehead and a chin that jutted forward, with his head always slightly tilted back, he seemed not to walk, but to 'fly,' " was the way a friend remembered him. "People especially remembered his eyes —not simply blue, but azure-enamel, the color of the very 'heavens,' with extremely thick, marvelous eyelashes that shaded them like fans."[64] He was a passionate disciple of Solovev, whom he had met just a few months before the philosopher's death. "This marked the beginning of the biography of 'Andrei Belyi,' " he later wrote. He had spent all of 1901, "the year of the dawn,"[65] spellbound, "under the sign of Solovev's poetry," and he dedicated all his soul's passion to the philosopher's Beautiful Lady.[66]

Just turned twenty-one at the time of their meeting, he was both captivated and repelled by Gippius. "A wasp in human attire," he called her. She reminded him of Aubrey Beardsley's then-famous "Enchantress," and it seemed to him that she and Merezhkovskii "bore an alien spirit derived from the green mists of the Neva." He had expected Merezhkovskii to be a "Russian Luther," but he seemed more like "a cross between a sexton and a petty official," a small, thin, brown man who "bleated" like a sheep.[67] The Merezhkovskiis saw Belyi as a valuable ally in their effort to win supporters in Moscow; they smothered him with their charm and, briefly, Belyi succumbed.

The Merezhkovskiis' campaign to enchant Belyi was reflected in the young poet's critique of Merezhkovskii's *Lev Tolstoi and Dostoevskii*, which he published under the intentionally transparent pseudonym, "A Student of Natural Science." In a series of articles that appeared in the very first issue of *Novyi put*, Belyi stated his apocalyptic credo. He felt the approach of a final struggle between "the Lady Clothed in the Sun" and the "great whore." "The storm is near," he warned. "The waves rage in tempest; something disturbing is arising from the waters." Merezhkovskii hastened to flatter him with the admonition: "Go then, teach us." Gippius called his work "remarkable and new" and begged him to come to St. Petersburg to help them with *Novyi put.* "You're a close friend," Merezhkovskii whispered to him the next time he and his wife visited Moscow. "Believe in us."[68] Belyi was attracted to Merezhkovskii, one critic wrote not long ago, "as a living example of the 'new man,' but soon realized that Merezhkovskii was just as confused as he."[69] His collaboration with *Novyi put* was destined to be brief, as was that of another of Solovev's passionate disciples, young Aleksandr Blok.

Blok had grown up on his mother's family estate enveloped in an aristocratic cocoon of comfort and culture.[70] His eighteenth summer (1898) awoke two great passions: the writings of Solovev and the person of Liubov Mendeleeva, the daughter of the world-famous scientist. Blok's quest for Solovev's Beautiful Lady quickly became confused with his burning love for the talented and strong-willed Liubov, whose beauty lured his thoughts from the upper realms of philosophical speculation to the region of fleshly, earthly pleasures. "Her Titian and ancient Russian beauty was further set off by an elegant taste in clothes," a friend remembered. "White suited her best, but she looked very well in black, too, and in bright red."[71] As with so many of the Symbolists, Blok's earthly passion was tormented by a conflict with spirituality. Under the influence of these diverse passions, Blok began his *Verses about the Most Beautiful Lady,* which occupied him throughout a long and stormy courtship until he and Liubov were wed in 1903.

In March 1902, at the height of the Merezhkovskiis' effort to win Belyi into their circle, Blok called on Gippius (he respectfully referred to her in his diary as Madame Merezhkovskaia) at the *Dom Muruzi* to ask for a ticket to one of Merezhkovskii's public lectures. He was then still a student at St. Petersburg University and his poetry had only begun to circulate in manuscript. A few poems had passed through Gippius's hands, and Belyi (who would not meet him for another two years) had recommended Blok's work to her enthusiastically. "Boria [Belyi] is in such raptures that he literally rolled on the floor," she wrote at the time. Gippius was instantly drawn to the well-mannered, soberly dressed youth who stood at her door that late winter's afternoon. "He did not seem handsome," she remembered. "His face was straight and motionless, as calm as if it were made of wood or stone. . . . Blok pronounced every word slowly, and with effort, precisely as if he were tearing himself away from some meditation." Yet she found "something endearing in the entire appearance of this student," quickly drew him into their circle, and encouraged him to confide in her about his poems, his hopes, and his love.[72] When she showed him Belyi's first long letter about Merezhkovskii's *Lev Tolstoi and Dostoevskii,* Blok reacted with the same intense passion with which Belyi had greeted his first unpublished poems. For the rest of the year, Gippius served as an intermediary. The two young men began to correspond at the beginning of 1903; yet another year passed before they finally met.

During 1902 and 1903, Blok remained under the spell of Gippius and Merezhkovskii. For almost two years, he had labored to find the meaning of art and religion, while he struggled to fit his love for Liubov Mendeleeva into his quest for Solovev's Beautiful Lady. At the *Dom Muruzi,* Merezhkovskii spoke with authority about those subjects, and his apparent erudition gave his pronouncements even greater weight. Blok was dazzled by Merezhkovskii's *Lev Tolstoi and Dostoevskii,* and hastened to reread the works of both masters from his new perspective. He scattered excerpts from the essays of Merezhkovskii and the poems of Gippius throughout his notebooks during the long summer of 1902. Yet, even in his enthusiasm for their works, a certain reserve held him apart. For Blok gave himself to no one and to no ideology with that total passion so common among those whom Oleg Maslenikov once called Russia's "frenzied poets."[73] "Even when he was right there with you, he always was somewhere else too," Gippius confessed at one point.[74]

Blok later wrote that the Merezhkovskiis had freed him from "philistine attitudes" during these years. As yet, he had published none of his poems, but was beginning to gain a broader awareness about the problems that troubled him. In the words of Avril Pyman's brilliant recent account, "Blok was becoming convinced that, though his way *to* God might lie through art, his art was not *of* God, but altogether of the fallen world."[75] Like Belyi, he tried to believe that art was "the realization of another, a higher will." Yet, even as he sought a path to God through art, he was beginning to realize that he, unlike his new friend, never could hope to escape the dictates imposed by poetic intuition. Unwilling to abandon his early belief, Blok married Liubov late in the summer of 1903 and lived with her in what she later described as "a fine-strung tenderness" that grew "more painful, more tender, and more impossible" as the months went by. Blok insisted that their love must remain above the profane touch of sex, and Liubov at first agreed.[76] For a year, they succeeded—he more insistently celibate than she. Then, in the autumn of 1904, "with malice aforethought on my part, unpremeditatedly on his," Liubov later confessed, Blok and his terrestrial Beautiful Lady became man and wife in the more prosaic sense. For both, the next two years of sporadic sexual searching brought only torment until Blok abandoned any further attempt to reconcile physical love for Liubov with his exalted Solovevian dreams.[77]

Thus, Blok's search for Solovev's Beautiful Lady came to an end. "I have fallen, betrayed, and now I really am an 'artist' and live not from that which makes life full but from that which makes it black and terrible," he confessed.[78] Unable to sublimate his longing to taste the profane to his quest for the divine, both in life and in poetry, Blok concluded that the poet's inner will must always prevail. At that point (1907), Belyi lamented that his friend's "Lady Beautiful had disintegrated into a prostitute, into an imaginary quantity something like the square root of minus one."[79]

After they had exchanged passionate, rambling letters between St. Petersburg and Moscow for a year, Blok and Belyi finally met in the latter's native Moscow in January 1904. "From their very first contact, the two friends sensed how close they were—and yet, how very far apart," Mochulskii wrote.[80] Belyi had imagined Blok as "a dark joyless monk," ethereal, medieval, otherworldly.[81] Instead, he found him very worldly indeed, "very stately, tall, and broad shouldered. . . . Everything about him was in good taste."[82] For two weeks, Blok and his young wife—"a marvelous pair," in Belyi's words —remained in Moscow, while their proud host introduced them to the city's world of Decadent culture, where poets vied with each other to make them welcome. "They shout that I am the first poet in Russia," Blok wrote to his mother.[83] Belyi's circle proclaimed him "superior even to Briusov" and dedicated poems to a delighted Liubov.[84] They pressed her to speak, but she refused: "No, I cannot speak. I—shall listen."[85] Delightedly, the Bloks basked in the enthusiasm of Moscow's Decadents. They dined at the famous Slavianskii Bazar, wandered around the Kremlin and the famous Virgins' Convent where Peter the Great had incarcerated his half-sister Sofia, visited Tretiakov's new gallery, and saw Stanislavskii's production of Chekhov's new and already famous *Cherry Orchard*.[86]

The Bloks returned to St. Petersburg at the end of January to find Russia at war with Japan, the Asiatic giant of Solovev's dark warnings. Some saw the war as the Beginning of the End, the first of many struggles foretold in the Book of Revelation,[87] from which Briusov had taken the title of his famous poem the year before. The St. Petersburg group began to live only for the moment.

Both Belyi and Briusov became enmeshed with Nina Petrovskaia, a minor poet passionately dedicated to living out the Decadents' creed in the bed of one poet after another. She was one of those whom Belyi once called those "modernistic girls—thin, wan, fragile, enigmatic, and languid—like the heroines of Maeterlinck," who flocked to Symbolist poetry readings at the turn of the century in Russia.[88] Konstantin Balmont, one of the first Decadents, who proclaimed that "I experienced my first passionate thought about women at five,"[89] had been her lover, but she soon tired of him and turned to Belyi for solace. Certain that he was blessed with "the wisdom to heal broken hearts,"[90] Belyi became her confidant in a stormy relationship that lasted for several years. One of his friends later insisted that Belyi "fled from Nina, lest her too earthly love should soil his immaculate robe,"[91] and Briusov became her new champion. Together they sank into a turgid morass of spiritualism, black magic, and narcotics. Eventually, she tried to shoot him at one of Belyi's public lectures—some accounts insist that she had set out to kill Belyi but turned upon her lover at the last moment—but Briusov managed to wrest her "dangerous toy" from her grasp.[92]

Briusov's affair with Nina Petrovskaia was but one expression of the despair that seized Russia's Silver Age poets, writers, and painters.[93] As Russia's political tension increased, Blok began to describe the "outward form" of his work as "cries, madness, and—often—painful dissonances." His devoted friend Evgenii Ivanov had a vision of the clouds lifting "like a curtain to open up a strip of the dawn above the earth, a field with puddles of bog water and blood. We stood at a crossroads," he concluded.[94] No one knew which road led to salvation, and which to damnation. Blok's Lady Clothed in the Sun began to change into a "Woman Arrayed in Purple and Scarlet."[95] He wrote of "The Nocturnal Violet," and "The Unknown Woman" of the streets who lived in a dark, sordid realm thick with the smells of stale smoke, soot, raw liquor, and steaming, unwashed bodies. "You're right, you drunken monster!" he exclaimed. "I know the truth lies in the wine."[96] "The violet-hued universe of the first revolution [of 1905] seized us and bore us into the maelstrom," he wrote much later.[97] "There, on the filthy street, where people gather,/ A whore—just arisen from her cot of lust—/ Knelt, clad only in a shirt, her hands raised aloft in supplication."[98] Blok's new realm of pain and lust and pleas that went unheard was filled with female figures—no longer even shades of the Beautiful Lady of his early years, but women, "their breasts adorned with a crumpled rose . . . with their heads tilted back, their lips half-parted."[99] "Christ was never there, and is not there now," he explained to Belyi as he described his newfound world. "He is walking somewhere very far away."[100]

Like Blok, Belyi reacted sharply to the political events of those years. "The year 1904 seems very gloomy to me," he wrote in his literary memoirs. "From 1904 until the very end of 1908, I felt as if the ground was slipping away beneath my feet."[101] His forebodings of impending disaster intensified when he finally visited St. Petersburg. He recalled it vividly in later years: "The *Dom Muruzi,* the stairwell, the door at the fourth-floor landing, the doorplate with the Gothic letters that spelled out 'Merezhkovskii.' " He was let in as soon as he rang. "Well, you've certainly chosen quite a day to come," Gippius remarked when she first saw him.[102] Belyi was at first puzzled, but soon learned the reason. By an amazing stroke of fate, he had made his first visit to Petersburg on Bloody Sunday. As he had taken a hackney cab to the *Dom Muruzi* from the train station that morning, the blood, whose shedding he, Solovev, Briusov, and Blok all had foretold, was staining the cobblestones that paved the Winter Palace Square. All day, friends came and went at the *Dom Muruzi*, bringing news of events to Gippius who, as the decadent lioness of St. Petersburg's avant-garde world, often never emerged from her elegant lair for days on end. "Everyone was outraged—and with good reason," she wrote. "Imagine firing upon an unarmed crowd simply out of a blind fear of any assembly of peaceful people!"[103] Gippius, Merezhkovskii, and their friends planned a "protest" that night at the Aleksandra Theater. To the delight of these people, for whom the masses had had no place in their lives or art, Father Gapon addressed them. "It *really was* Gapon," Gippius later assured her readers.[104]

Not long before Belyi came to St. Petersburg, the Merezhkovskiis and Blok had come to an intellectual and artistic parting of the ways. Blok saw "nothing at all in Dmitrii Sergeevich [Merezhkovskii]" and pronounced Gippius to be "a complete blank."[105] Belyi visited both camps—again and again—sad that the people he loved had grown so far apart. In a flurry of artistic and literary activity, the Merezhkovskiis introduced Belyi to the leading lights of the capital's avant-garde, and he soon came to know them well. Especially with Gippius, he developed a warm and deep friendship. They spoke every night—long into the small hours—about religion, the Trinity, and the flesh. "Zina, for God's sake, let Boria alone!" Merezhkovskii would call out from the other room. "It's four o'clock in the morning. You're not letting me sleep!"[106] In hushed voices, they would continue. Gippius never went to bed before dawn, and Belyi, searching for new guidance and direction, desperately tried to draw hope from their common musings.

Yet, perhaps even to his own surprise, Belyi found the Merezhkovskiis' preoccupation with theory devoid of the new substance he was seeking. For he wanted not only to see the raw reality of life, but to touch it, to experience its force. As the days of his Petersburg visit passed, he was drawn to Blok with ever-greater urgency. "Without ideology, even without his 'Beautiful Lady,' he came to life for me as a 'brother' during those days," Belyi remembered. Together, they explored the city that Blok already had made a part of his apocalyptic vision. During their evenings together, Blok suddenly would urge: "Let's go. I'll show you the back streets." Then they would walk, sometimes for hours, hands thrust deeply into their pockets, to see worn, tired people "shuffling from the factories. Sometimes, we'd catch sight of an exhausted prostitute, as the lights of cheap eating places shone forth," Belyi wrote. Blok never seemed to tire of this world. It fascinated him, seized his imagination. "It's a rotten life, very sad indeed," he would lament. *"They*—the Merezhkovskiis—don't even notice!"[107]

Although Blok's Beautiful Lady became a cardboard doll and then a whore as political tempests wracked his nation and personal crises buffeted his soul, Belyi let go of his earlier dreams in a very different fashion. In sharp contrast to Blok, his Lady Clothed in the Sun remained beautiful, ethereal, and chaste during those turbulent days, but she underwent an apocalyptical transformation nonetheless. "The earth began to tremble underfoot," he wrote when he recalled the events of January 1905 and described the fate of his Solovevian feminine ideal. "In agony, she tore her soul, and gave up her pure body to crucifixion before the fixed gaze of thousands. . . . And the streets of Petersburg still held the remains of the recent rebellion."[108] While Blok's Beautiful Lady became a harlot and very much of this earth, Belyi's image remained a virgin and rose above the stress and strife of everyday life.[109]

Just as he and Blok seemed closest in January 1905—"Sasha and Boria, not Blok and Belyi," he recalled—a new force drove them apart.[110] As Belyi's Lady Clothed in the Sun rose to the heavens, he replaced his quest for the metaphysical ideal with a search for the real. Tragically for "Boria and Sasha," the real woman Belyi turned to pursue was Blok's wife. Blok and Liubov were at that time at the height of their struggle to reconcile physical sex with the poet's shifting, increasingly pessimistic, vision of life. Exhausted by their effort, they sought refuge late in the spring of 1905 in the pastoral calm of Shakhmatovo, the family estate where they often spent their summers. There, Belyi and his friend Sergei Solovev (the philosopher's nephew and devoted disciple) joined them. It was a miserable, disastrous visit. Urged on from afar by Gippius, who resented Blok's defection from the *Dom Muruzi* circle, Belyi decided to rescue Liubov from the husband he now thought had betrayed her in his poetic ideals, and the two friends embarked upon several stormy years of quarrels punctuated by joyous reconciliations and bitter new outbursts. "How wicked and nasty we all were then!" Belyi later lamented.[111] Blok called it a time when "everything, whirling, disappears into darkness."[112] The two friends never would be quite the same again. "I have slammed shut the oven doors of my own soul," Blok exclaimed at one point.[113] Both men felt themselves lost and adrift, yet each hoped that the other might somehow lead the way to rescue. "If I am a traitor—then curse me, and forget me," Blok wrote in one of the many letters they exchanged. "But, if you see any hope," he pleaded, "then teach me."[114] Neither was able to give clear direction to the other, and their bitter feuds burst forth again and again. Each challenged the other to at least one duel. On three separate occasions, Liubov swore that she was ready to accept Belyi's "rescue" and flee with him to Italy, only to recant at the last moment. Several times, Belyi contemplated suicide and showered his friends with letters announcing his intention. Not until the end of 1909 did he and Blok finally make a lasting peace, when Belyi's new passion for Asia Turgeneva made it possible to end their quarrel.[115] By then, both had begun to come to grips with the world that the turmoil of 1904–5 had left in its wake.

Belyi and Blok were not the only ones among Russia's Silver Age poets, writers, and artists to be touched profoundly by the revolutionary events of 1905. In the *Dom Muruzi*, Merezhkovskii hastened to draw stark contrasts between Russia and Europe: "You are sober, we are drunk; you are rational, we are frenzied; you are just, we are lawless. . . . For you, politics is knowledge; for us it is religion."[116] The tension Merezhkovskii described was felt acutely by many others. "The air bore the destructive currents of revolution, and they percolated through all the new literature," Blok's aunt wrote. "Balmont, Briusov, the Merezhkovskiis, Viacheslav Ivanov . . . all said the same thing, summoning [society] to a protest against the calm and balanced life, . . . urging people to renounce happiness."[117] In the words of one expert, many of the Symbolists, profoundly apolitical until 1905, "sought a new faith in which artist and people would be one."[118]

For some of them, the famous "Tower" of Viacheslav Ivanov became the temple of their new faith. A man who drew his guiding principles from Friedrich Nietzsche's view that the philosopher was a "physician of culture,"[119] Ivanov defined Decadence as "an escape from life," while he thought that "Symbolism was the anticipation of and the striving toward the 'new' life."[120] "Idealistic symbolism is a musical monologue," he wrote. "On the other hand, realistic symbolism, in the final analysis, is both the chorus and the dance." Ivanov's language evoked obvious sexual images (a verb derived from *khorovod*, his term for "dance" is *khorovodit'sia*, meaning to have an affair), and he paid homage to Dionysus, patron of the drama and the chorus and god of fertility and wine. *Pilot Stars*, his first book of verse, published in 1903 when he was forty, featured a cycle of poems on the Dionysian myth. Ivanov was living in Europe at the time, and visited Russia only long enough to take Moscow's salons by storm. For a few weeks it was: "Ivanov said!" "Ivanov was here!" "Don't tell me you haven't met Ivanov yet!" "Where are Briusov, Balmont? Belyi? Blok?" Belyi asked. "There's only Ivanov, Ivanov, Ivanov!"[121] And then, Ivanov left abruptly and returned to his life in Italy and Switzerland where he remained for almost two years. In the words of one scholar, he had concluded by then that "every individual would become an artist in his own right. Art then would become a broadly communal enterprise."[122]

Late in 1905, Ivanov and his wife, the writer Lidia Zinoveva-Annibal, moved to St. Petersburg and rented a seventh-floor penthouse at No. 25 Tavricheskaia Street. Their new home overlooked the Taurida Palace, soon to become the home of the Duma, and its famous gardens. There, Ivanov, called "Viacheslav the Magnificent" by some, held his "Wednesdays" in a snug haven high above the city's streets, from which all boundaries of space and time were erased. Three apartments were combined into one to create the Ivanovs' "Tower." "Capriciously interlaced corridors, rooms, and doorless anterooms: square rooms, rhomboids, and sectors, where thick rugs swallowed up the sounds of footsteps," was the way Belyi described it. "Once there, you'd forget what country you were in and what time it was. Day became night, and night became day." People came and went. According to inclination and impulse, some stayed several days; Belyi once stayed for five weeks. The talk went on day and night. As one samovar was emptied, another appeared. "This brilliant but insane life destroyed the very foundations of time," Belyi recalled. "You'd blink and a month would have passed."[123] Mikhail Kuzmin, a minor poet known for his rhapsody to 333 different sexual positions (a theme upon which Ivanov later embroidered), came for a visit and remained for several years.[124]

One of those who knew him claimed that Ivanov "loved not so much poetry as power over poets."[125] Certainly, poets formed the core of those who came and went in his timeless, soundless "Tower." There, Georgii Chulkov, a poet of lesser talent but great popularity, developed his vision of mystical anarchism with which he hoped to transcend the "antinomy of freedom and necessity" by means of Eros.[126] For Chulkov, love was the universe's prime mover. Ivanov himself proselytized this notion more aggressively. "Anyone who does not love is dead," he wrote. "Life—is love,"[127] a view in which he received frequent support from the often-present Rozanov. This soil fostered Kuzmin's verses in praise of pederasty, and Zinoveva-Annibal's lesbian novel, whose first reviews Ivanov greeted with the ecstatic pronouncement: "My dear, I *congratulate* you. . . . Your novel has been banned as PORNOGRAPHY."[128]

The most impressive of Ivanov's guests was Blok himself. Belyi brought him to the first of the "Wednesdays," and he continued to be a frequent visitor in the years after the revolutionary events of 1905. At that point, Blok was drawn to the mystical and religious themes that figured so prominently in the discussions among the "Tower's" habitués. "Religion and mysticism," he wrote in his notebook at the beginning of 1906. "They have nothing in common. Although mysticism may become one of the ways to religion. Mysticism is the bohemian part of the soul. . . . Mysticism requires ecstasy. Ecstasy is solitude."[129] It was on the "Tower's" gently sloping roof during one of St. Petersburg's magical white summer nights that Blok first read his poem "The Stranger" in which he revealed his fallen Beautiful Lady's new identity. "Blok's poetry affected us as the moon affects lunatics," the young critic Kornei Chukovskii wrote in his memoirs.[130] Yet even amidst the adulation of Ivanov's guests, Blok did not find complete satisfaction. Almost as soon as it had begun, he wrote to Belyi that "this gathering of such cultivated people as Viacheslav Ivanov . . . is beginning to torment me."[131]

However, Blok found his growing estrangement from his "brother" Andrei Belyi a far greater torment than the sometimes oppressive adulation heaped upon him by the residents of Ivanov's "Tower." Belyi in particular endeavored to "legitimize" their personal differences by garbing them in the rhetoric of literary dispute. In the pages of Briusov's *Vesy*, he launched a series of vitriolic attacks against Blok, Chulkov, and Ivanov for their part in a new literary venture called *Zolotoe Runo (The Golden Fleece)*. Because success in the literary and artistic milieux of Russia's Silver Age meant winning disciples, every major group (and a number of minor ones) sought a journal to publicize its views. A search for a following had been important in the efforts of Benois and Diaghilev to found *Mir Iskusstva,* and it had been equally central to the beginnings of the Merezhkovskiis' *Novyi put* and Briusov's *Vesy*. As the chief propagators of mystical anarchism, Ivanov and Chulkov set out in 1906 to establish a new forum, and they quickly recruited Blok into their ranks. Soon afterward, as one critic later wrote, "Belyi went into action with the fanatic frenzy of a Savonarola."[132]

A lavishly designed magazine, with French and Russian texts on facing pages and original illustrations by leading avant-garde artists, *Zolotoe Runo* rivaled the brilliance of *Mir Iskusstva* from the moment its first issue appeared in January 1906. Its patron and proprietor was Nikolai Riabushinskii, one of those great Moscow industrial lords who, like Mamontov, Morozov, Tretiakov, and Alekseev-Stanislavskii, dedicated himself and his wealth to financing the art and literature of Russia's Silver Age. Riabushinskii dreamed of using *Zolotoe Runo* to consolidate the Symbolists' fragmenting ranks, and he encouraged the followers of both Briusov and Ivanov to join him in his new enterprise. The first issue of *Zolotoe Runo* boasted the contributions and editorial support of (to name just a few of the most diverse and important) the artists Benois, Vrubel, Bakst, Rerikh, Somov, and Serov, while its literary section listed the names of Blok, Belyi, Balmont, Briusov, Gippius and Merezhkovskii, Leonid Andreev, Ivanov, and even the notorious Nina Petrovskaia.[133]

The remarkable, but obviously artificial, unity that Riabushinskii imposed upon the turbulent artists and writers of Moscow and St. Petersburg did not survive his journal's first year. Fearful that Riabushinskii's achievement might diminish the stature of his own *Vesy*, Briusov was the first to leave, proclaiming that "we have multiplied too fast and it remains only for us to devour one another."[134] At his insistent urging, Gippius, Merezhkovskii, Sergei Solovev, and Belyi all joined him to launch a campaign against Chulkov and Ivanov, whose gospels of mystical anarchism, they insisted, threatened to vulgarize the remarkable achievements of Russian Symbolism. When Blok remained behind, Belyi bitterly branded him a "strikebreaker";[135] in reaction to Blok's defense of Andreev and Gorkii in an essay on Russian realism, Belyi's scorn turned to raging fury. "I hasten to inform you about a piece of news that will be pleasant for us both," he wrote at the beginning of August 1907. "As of this moment, our relations are severed for all time."[136] Belyi then saturated Moscow with vicious rumors about Blok, and the poet challenged him to a duel in response. Only with difficulty did their friends' cooler heads prevail.

The ease with which Russia's Symbolists made and broke friendships and alliances resulted not only from their mercurial tempers and tormented personalities but also from the lack of clear boundaries between various segments of the avant-garde. The decade after the Revolution of 1905 thus saw the arts explode in kaleidoscopic splendor, as the most brilliant talents in Russian art, literature, poetry, music, and the ballet combined and recombined their genius to produce a dazzling and ever-changing array of new creations that overwhelmed the senses. There seemed to be no end to the brilliance and variety that Russia's Silver Age could achieve, and no limits to the heights to which its creations could ascend. James Billington once pointed out that, of all the arts to flourish in Russia at this time, music was in some ways preeminent. Blok, the great painters Vasilii Kandinskii and Mikolojus Čiurlionis, and the revolutionary Futurist poet Viktor Khlebnikov all used musical terms and imagery to describe their work, and one art historian has recently reminded us that "the biographies of Benois, Somov, and Diaghilev each reveal a frustrated musician."[137]

Frequent use of the language of music to describe poetry and painting also reflected the remarkable way in which various artistic media flowed into each other during those years. Futurism, for example, began with the paintings of Mikhail Larionov and then moved into the poetry of Vladimir Maiakovskii and Khlebnikov, where profanity, eroticism, and street slang conveyed an artistic message that was calculated to shock Russia's highly cultured intelligentsia and art patrons in what proved to be a naïve attempt to reconcile art and society.[138] Much of this was misunderstood—or not understood at all—as ludicrous and frenzied antics of young men and women unable to communicate with society and utterly alienated from it. But, if the attempts of Maiakovskii, Larionov, and Khlebnikov at first often missed their mark, there were other, somewhat more conventional, efforts that enjoyed dramatic success.

Under the guiding genius of Diaghilev, who had bid farewell to the revolutionary events of 1905 with a daring toast to "a new and unknown culture, which will be created by us, and which will also sweep us away," the Russian ballet soared to unimagined heights.[139] After testing the ground by exhibitions of Russian painting, music, and opera in 1907 and 1908, Diaghilev launched his assault on Paris in 1909 and 1910. "I had already presented Russian painting, Russian music, and Russian opera in Paris," he later said. "Ballet contained in itself all those other activities."[140] Denied the stage at the Opéra, he could obtain only the city's old Châtelet Theater, once described as a place accustomed to "orange-eating, villain-hissing audiences."[141] To create the proper setting for the artistic gems he intended to display, Diaghilev refurbished the entire theater before he dazzled the city's audiences with totally new and unexpected productions of *Les Sylphides* (a ballet to the music of Chopin, but inspired by Isadora Duncan), *Cléopatre,* and *Schéhérazade,* and a small selection of operas that featured Mussorgskii's *Boris Godunov,* with Chaliapin singing the role of Boris.

The artistry of Nizhinskii, Karzavina, Ida Rubinstein, and Pavlova astounded Parisian theatergoers night after night. In an instant, emotion was restored to the ballet, only to be combined with exotically staged spectacles highly suggestive of erotic themes. The sets for *Schéhérazade,* Bakst insisted, must suggest "dreadful deeds of lust and cruelty."[142] Parisian critics vied to match passion with passion in their reviews. Nizhinskii was "an angel, a genius, a divine *danseur.*" Everything about Karzavina "was poetry," the most exquisite union possible between "classical tradition and an artistic revolution," while Rubinstein was "too beautiful, like a perfume that is too powerful." Pavlova, already proclaimed immortal, was "to the dance what Racine is to poetry, Poussin is to painting, and Gluck is to music."[143] But the real virtuosity of Diaghilev's achievement stemmed not simply from the brilliance of the stars that flashed across the Châtelet's newly rebuilt stage but from the manner in which music and the dance were combined with the artistry of sets by Rerikh, Benois, and, above all, Bakst, and the choreography of the young Russian rebel Mikhail Fokin. "The *Ballets russes* was a triumph in unity," proclaimed a leading French critic. It was "born of the music, melting into the colors of the *décor.*"[144]

Diaghilev's remarkable creations stemmed from unique Russian roots. The principles that Stanislavskii and Nemirovich-Danchenko had developed at their Moscow Art Theater were important in Fokin's new choreography, and those, in turn, had been drawn in part from Stanislavskii's experience with Savva Mamontov's enthusiastic efforts to produce innovative operas in which

Chaliapin had first learned to merge singing with acting in the 1890s.[145]

In the two decades before the Great War, the role of Russia's new merchant lords in fostering the explosion and blending of the arts was far greater than even our earlier remarks about Mamontov, Stanislavskii, Morozov, and Tretiakov would indicate. Their more publicized efforts encouraged men of lesser wealth to follow their example, as in the case of Andrei Shemshurin, a merchant who kept open house for Moscow's young artists at the turn of the century and fostered the discovery of some of the most brilliant of Russia's Primitivist painters. Shemshurin invited the unrecognized young artist David Burliuk to Moscow in 1907 and made it possible for Natalia Goncharova and Kazimir Malevich to show some of their early paintings. These and any number of others lived on Shemshurin's generosity, for any artist who could reach his anteroom before its doors swung shut at precisely 5:30 in the afternoon was assured of a place at his dinner table.[146]

Ivan Morozov and Sergei Shchukin made the works of Postimpressionist French painters better known in Moscow than in Paris. Of the two, Morozov approached French art with more caution, with the result that his collection was dominated by the works of Monet, Cézanne, Gauguin, and Renoir; he collected some of Matisse's early work, but only one Picasso. Shchukin, however, never attempted to curb his unquenchable thirst for modern French painting. A small man, with piercing jet black eyes and somewhat Oriental features, his interest in Impressionist art first was stirred in 1897, when his friend Mikhail Botkin convinced him to buy Claude Monet's *Argenteuil Lace*. Shchukin fell in love with the painting and all it represented, and that kindled a passion that grew more intense with each year. During the next eighteen years, he added on the average of one major painting every month to assemble the largest and most important collection of the Postimpressionists anywhere in the Empire. Shchukin introduced Russians not only to Manet and Renoir, but to Pissarro, Degas, and Monet. He probably did not buy his first Cézanne until 1904. Quickly he added more and complemented them with important works by Van Gogh, Gauguin, and Derain. Like Tretiakov, he filled his Moscow mansion with art and opened it to the public on Saturday afternoons. Muscovites flocked to stare at his amazing canvases whose numbers increased so rapidly that young Russian painters could scarcely absorb the flood of new impressions and influences.[147]

In 1904, the same year he began to collect the work of Cézanne, Shchukin probably bought his first Matisse, but he did not meet the painter until 1906. Their meeting marked the beginning of one of the most fertile unions between artist and patron in the history of modern art. Shchukin quickly began to purchase most of Matisse's most important works and gave him outright commissions for *Music* and *Dance,* two monumental canvases that the artist installed himself in the winter of 1911. Shchukin's efforts to make Matisse's work known to Russians resulted in a special issue of *Zolotoe Runo* devoted to the artist and his work. There, Matisse himself stated his credo that, "in my work, the expression of emotion is not confined to the feelings expressed in the face or in the body's fleeting movement. Rather, it is set forth in the entire composition of the painting, in the spaces that bodies occupy, in the background surrounding them, and in the proportions in general."[148] Shchukin's enthusiasm for Matisse's work stirred his passion for the artist's contemporaries. In the six years after 1908, he bought over fifty of Picasso's early canvases. These served as direct models for the Cubist works that the young Kazimir Malevich produced from 1913–14.[149]

The Shchukin and Morozov collections stirred a revolution on the canvases of Russia's young painters, and the hope of patronage from these rich industrialists encouraged them to strike out in new directions. In vivid contrast to Russia's golden literary age of the previous century, which was heavily influenced by European Romanticism, these new directions were neither clear nor even defined. The former Nevskii Pickwickian Dmitrii Filosofov proclaimed that each and every tendency must be sternly rejected if Russians hoped to create an art that could be comprehended by any but an elite.[150] Art thus became supreme in and of itself, while the values and prejudices of its creators were proclaimed to be utterly without consequence.

"A poet can be honorable or a villain, moral or debauched, a blasphemous atheist or devoutly Orthodox," Blok wrote in 1907. "A poet must be totally free in his creative work, and no one has the right to demand that he like green fields better than whorehouses." A year later, Filosofov insisted that Blok's dictum must apply to all art forms.[151]

Among Russia's young painters, it was Mikhail Larionov and Natalia Goncharova in particular who assimilated the diverse influences of the Postimpressionists. Both had been involved with exhibitions that *Mir Iskusstva* and *Zolotoe Runo* had sponsored, but their work had moved rapidly beyond the styles favored by such arbiters of taste as Benois and Riabushinskii. In conjunction with the brothers Dmitrii and Vladimir Burliuk, they therefore launched a new "Primitivist" Russian style of painting. The Burliuks, who came from the brawling, turbulent Black Sea port of Odessa, where Russian and European influences clashed at every imaginable level of life and culture, began their work well beyond such turn-of-the-century limits as those within which Larionov and Goncharova had first worked. Together, and in the amazingly brief span that separated their first meeting in 1907 from the outbreak of the Great War, these artists turned Russian painting onto a dramatic new course. "So much happened, so fast, in so many places, that it is difficult to piece it together so as to make a pattern of the whole," a leading expert on the period once confessed.[152]

The confusion and searching torment that drove Larionov and Goncharova during these years was in itself a vital part of the movement they created. Larionov became notorious in more conventional circles for his distorted drawings of soldiers and prostitutes across which he scrawled obscene remarks, and he, Goncharova, and the Burliuks could be found from time to time on Moscow's main streets, bedecked with flowers and with algebraic signs painted on their cheeks and foreheads. Brilliant blues, reds, and yellows blazoned their canvases in sharp contrast to the more subdued tones used by even Rerikh and Bakst. Yet, their union (in a group of artists that called themselves the "Knave of Diamonds") broke up very quickly when Larionov and Goncharova formed themselves into a new association, called the "Donkey's Tail," with Kazimir Malevich and Vladimir Tatlin. Closely allied with the famous *"Blaue Reiter"* group in Munich that at the time included the older and more famous Vasilii Kandinskii, these young artists joined Larionov on the eve of World War I to proclaim their allegiance to Rayonnism (Maiakovskii defined it as a Cubist interpretation of Impressionism), which endeavored to base painting upon rays of color that crossed as they were reflected from various objects. "We deny that individuality has any value in a work of art," they insisted boldly. "We go hand and hand with house painters. . . . From here begins the true freeing of art," Larionov concluded, and looked forward to "a life which proceeds only according to the laws of painting as an independent entity, painting with its own forms, color, and timber."[153] Although Rayonnism was very short lived (Larionov produced Rayonnist works only between 1911 and 1914), the "Donkey's Tail" group included within its four founders not only the main creators of Russian Primivitism (Larionov and Goncharova), but also the founders of Cubo-Futurism (Malevich, who drew his inspiration from Picasso's Synthetic-Cubist work), and Constructivism (Tatlin).[154]

Especially after the Revolution of 1905 did away with censorship, Russian culture reflected a new fascination with sex. Sexual degradation—especially the exploitation of women in any number of shameless and shocking ways—had become an obvious fact of urban life and a common theme in art and literature. Statistics rarely tell an unvarnished tale, but they can place this new preoccupation of Russia's writers and artists into a crude perspective. Out of a population of about 1.5 million in St. Petersburg, there was 1 policeman for every 150 inhabitants, and 1 tradesman (including everyone from cobblers and tailors to butchers and greengrocers) for every 75. By contrast, somewhere between 1 out of every 30 and 1 out of every 50 Petersburgers was a whore, and that figure does not take into account any of those bored well-bred ladies who pursued the trade as a form of amusement from time to time. The best estimates are that about 7 out of every 10 Petersburg men, some women, and even a few husbands and wives together, availed themselves of services offered by the city's prostitutes. Almost any whore could expect to earn 40 rubles a month. That was almost twice the average wage for all Petersburg factory workers in 1905, and almost three times what women earned for long hours spent in the city's mills. A few prostitutes reportedly earned as much as 700 rubles a month, a sum that was more than fifteen times greater than the wages earned by those highly skilled metalworkers who stood among that elite handful who received more than 1 1/2 rubles a day.[155] When two whores, both under the age of twelve, accosted the author of *Children of the Streets* and offered what he delicately reported as "perverted fulfillment of sexual requirements" at a nearby public bath for the sum of 5 rubles, they were hoping to earn in one evening more than they could have earned in a mill in about two weeks.[156]

White slavery flourished from Odessa to St. Petersburg, drawing girls from all parts of the Empire into shattered lives in urban brothels. As one expert wrote, the typical Russian establishment was nothing more than "a prison house for sexual slaves."[157] Far from being government-regulated instruments employed to relieve pent-up sexual tension in order to shield society from its awkward or violent consequences, prostitutes were, as Aleksandr Kuprin made clear in *Iama*, debased victims of a cruel and unjust system.[158]

Kuprin drew his grimly told tale of the women he called "deceived and corrupted children"[159] from a careful examination of public health records and police reports, and his account destroyed the officially propagated myth that prostitution was a carefully regulated trade, where frequent medical inspection assured the health of clients and whores alike. Yet *Iama* also pandered to the tastes of a reading public that was beginning to revel in sordid accounts of rape, incest, and sadism.[160]

Transferred into the more ethereal realm of high culture, Russia's new sensualism found particular expression in Ivanov's "Tower," where not only the proprietor but his wife and their guests spoke in sexual metaphors and pursued sexual themes in their poetry and prose. Mikhail Kuzmin's depictions of homosexual sex in *Wings* (1907), a brief tale about an older man and a youth, took up a theme long banned in Russian letters.[161] Far more shocking, however, was Lidia Zinoveva-Annibal's volume, which appeared in the same year and was filled with descriptions of lesbian sex. Never had Russians read such accounts as those that filled the pages of her notorious *Thirty-Three Abominations,* which began with a woman's tender description about how the heroine had "kissed my eyes and lips and breasts and caressed my body."[162]

Although shocking (and immensely titillating) to Russians who lived on the eve of the Great War's outbreak, Zinoveva-Annibal presented her account of lesbian love with obvious intelligence and considerable delicacy. Yet it was but a very short step to what Belyi called *tryn-travizm,* an attitude of utter, mindless debauchery that pervaded segments of Russia's educated youth, who shrugged off all concerns for society, morality, or justice with the phrase *"tryn-trava"* — "It makes no difference. Who cares? Why bother?" Belyi described this supremely fatalistic view as *ogarochnyi,* an adjective meaning to burn a candle stub at both ends with no thought for the consequences.[163] Russia's *ogarochnyi* youth claimed to hold the future in utter disdain. They lived as if there would be no future at all.

The handbook of Russia's *ogarochnyi* youth was Mikhail Artsybashev's *Sanin,* a tale of unvarnished lust in which the hero attempts to seduce his beautiful sister while other willing virgins are being deflowered by men who claim to be drawn to them by "the sexual instinct and nothing else." Artsybashev insisted that men and women should seek sexual pleasure with no thought for its consequences because "conceptions of debauchery and purity are merely as withered leaves that cover fresh grass." There could be no middle ground. "We must either remain perpetually chaste," the recently expelled university student Iurii insists at one point, "or else enjoy absolute sexual liberty, allowing women, of course, to do the same." Despite such grandiose pronouncements, men and women remained far from equal in *Sanin's* world, where men enjoyed their liberation to the fullest while women suffered tragic pregnancies and bitter abandonments as they endeavored to exercise their "right to plunge into the stream of sexual enjoyment." For some, self-gratification led to self-destruction, with three suicides marking the novel's climax. Nonetheless, Artsybashev's women spoke daring words despite the exploitation they suffered in their quest for sexual liberation. "It has always pained and grieved me that we women should care so much for our reputation and our chastity, being afraid to take a step lest we—well, lest we should fall, while men almost look upon it as an heroic deed to seduce a girl," one of them insisted. "If I like, I'll give myself to the Devil!"—this cried defiantly by Sanin's sister a moment or two before she saw her brother gazing greedily at her naked body through a ground-floor window.[164]

Tryn-travizm glorified vulgar Saninist notions of self-gratification, carnal excess, and self-destruction, as young Russians formed sex clubs to which they gave such obviously ogarochnyi names as "The Burned Down Candles" and "The League of Free Love." There were reports of a Temple of Eros, where men and women joined with children in sexual orgies.[165] Following the publication of Sanin, other novels took up similar themes as heroines began to insist that there was "nothing more memorable about where, under what circumstances, and with whom they satisfied a natural [sexual] function than about a chance dinner companion and the menu in the restaurant where they happened to dine."[166] Such sensuality survived the Great War and Revolution to appear in an early Soviet novel where an aristocratic girl, after becoming head of the local secret police, is able to use her new authority to satisfy her sexual appetites and exclaims: "The revolution is all permeated with sex for me!"[167] Combined with a true concern for winning total liberation for women in the new society, early Soviet sensualism found its most famous expression in the writings and activities of Aleksandra Kollontai, director of the Zhenotdel, the Women's Section of the Bolsheviks' Central Committee.[168]

Any literary and artistic merit that remained in the surge of sensualist writing that flourished in Russia after 1905 generally had disappeared by 1911, however. "The literary circles in Petersburg have reached the last stages of putrefaction," Blok lamented. "They are beginning to stink."[169] Life seemed to be slipping out of focus. "There was a sort of sickness in the soul. Drunkenness without wine, food that does not satisfy," his friend Elizaveta Kuzmina-Karavaeva later wrote.[170] "It was as if something was in the air hovering over each and every one of us," Gippius added. "People hurried and rushed about, never understanding why they did so, nor knowing what to do with themselves."[171] There was a sense of foreboding, of a rootlessness stronger than any that had led Russia's reckless youth to seize upon *tryn-travizm* as a debauched glorification of the present. Groping to give some new direction to his life, Ivanov took his stepdaughter Vera into his bed soon after her mother's untimely death, and then married her a few years later. All over Russia, people seemed poised on the brink. They had explored the lower depths of human emotion and experience, but still did not know what lay in the dark forest that stood beyond the fringes of that strange new world.

Perhaps the most dramatic hint of what lay in those unexplored regions came from the pages of *The Silver Dove*, a strange, awkward novel (his first) that Belyi wrote in 1909, during five weeks of self-imposed isolation in the tiny village of Bobrovka. *The Silver Dove* was an extraordinary work, in which Belyi combined eroticism, asceticism, and sadism with the mysteries of peasant life to produce an allegory of tragedy whose broader dimensions he himself could not even begin to comprehend at the time. The tale itself centered upon the fictional Symbolist poet, Darialskii, who became "lost in the black pit of Russia's ignorance, superstition, hatred, and evil," where the spirit of Russia's artists and poets was "extinguished by the black force of the earth and the forest."[172] Engaged to the beautiful, gentle, and noble Katia, Darialskii abandoned her serene, exalted love for the raw, primeval passion of the pockmarked peasant Matrëna. Matrëna was an earthly, sensual version of Solovev's divine Sophia, an incarnation of Blok's fallen Beautiful Lady. For Belyi, she was the "great whore" who had emerged triumphant from the struggle with the Lady Clothed in the Sun. Matrëna's features "expressed anything but beauty or a maiden's well-preserved chastity. The movement of her breasts, her thick legs with their white calves and the dirty soles of her feet, her big belly, and her sloping rapacious forehead—all frankly bore the imprint of lust."[173] She enslaved Darialskii with an elemental lust such as he, as a civilized man of culture, had not even imagined. "Now she herself was upon him," Belyi wrote in describing their meeting. Instantly, she was "pawing him and pressing her plump breasts against him—a grinning beast."[174]

For Matrëna, Darialskii forsook his fiancée, his art, and, even, civilization, to live in the dark forest. But not even her body could be his to command because she did the bidding of the carpenter Mitia Kudeiarov, "a wizard of the evil eye," who intended for her to conceive a "spiritual offspring" from her couplings with Darial-skii.[175] In the world of *The Silver Dove*, Kudeiarov reigned as leader of a mystical sect of men and women (Doves) who committed strange and violent acts in the seclusion of the forest's depths. Kudeiarov, a man with a face that "always looks like half a face; one side of it craftily winking at you, while the other is always spying on something, always afraid of something,"[176] occupied what Belyi once called "a still empty place" in Russian life.[177]

Four years earlier, that "still empty place"—evil, destructive, yet, like Matrëna's lust, holding out a false promise of salvation— had in fact been filled in the lives of Russia's Emperor and Empress by a man from Siberia, whose strength of will and power to do evil were unique among Russians of his day. He had appeared in the wake of the cataclysms of 1904 and 1905, and he would be wiped from the face of the earth on the eve of the even greater cataclysm of 1917. "We've made the acquaintance of a man of God, Grigorii, from the Tobolsk Gubernia," Nicholas wrote in his diary. The date was November 1, 1905.[178]

A scholar once wrote that "the dark form of Rasputin remains the most characteristic symbol and symptom of the sinister spiritual Time of Troubles" that Russia endured during the first two decades of the twentieth century.[179] Variously called a saint, a sinner, and a devil by those who knew him, Grigorii, later to be known as Rasputin, had lived the life of a Siberian peasant until one day in 1891 when he left his village, wife, and children, and set out for Mount Athos in Greece. "Grigorii has turned pilgrim out of laziness," his father is supposed to have remarked at the time.[180] Grigorii insisted that he had seen a vision of the Virgin and that he must follow the path she set. Thus, he began his career as a holy wanderer, whose pronouncements excited ecstasy or contempt wherever he went. Rasputin claimed to be what Russians call a *starets*, a holy man. A true *starets* was a man of God, who had renounced the world to pray for the salvation of all who still lived in it. "And so, what is a *starets?*" Dostoevskii had written in the fifth chapter of *The Brothers Karamazov*. "A *starets* takes your soul, your will, into his soul and his will. In choosing a *starets*, you renounce any will of your own, and you surrender it to him in complete obedience and with total self-abnegation." Dostoevskii explained further that one surrendered one's soul to a *starets* in the hope that "after a life of complete obedience, one could attain complete freedom, that is, freedom from one's self."[181]

Far from approaching Dostoevskii's image, Rasputin was a fraudulent *starets*, who set out to capture the minds and souls of simpleminded believers, high and low, rich and poor, in order to bend them to his will. He preached a doctrine of salvation through sin and reminded his flock, especially the women who flocked to him, that sins of the flesh were especially efficacious for achieving God's forgiveness and, thereby, salvation. "The first word of the Savior was 'Repent,' " he told them. "How can we repent if we have not first sinned?" "Man must sin in order that he have something to repent of," he continued. "If God sends us a temptation, we must yield to it voluntarily and without resistance, so that we may afterwards do penance in utter contrition."[182] Not long after he appeared in St. Petersburg in 1903, Rasputin began to assemble a flock of empty-headed noblewomen who sought his company and, through his rude caresses, his blessings. These women found it titillating to be ravished by a smelly peasant, who ate with his hands, tore at his food with blackened teeth, used the foulest language in their presence, described in coarse detail the sexual acts of the horses on his father's farm in Siberia,[183] and violated them quickly and brutally, with the vaguely muttered assurance that "now, Mother, everything is in order."[184] This was in real life the same sort of bizarre compulsion, the same attraction of repulsive opposites, that Belyi described in *The Silver Dove*.

As speculation about Rasputin's relationships with the Imperial family spread into the country beyond Petersburg between 1910 and 1914, thoughtful men and women were consumed by a sense of foreboding. "In the house of the Romanovs, a mysterious curse descends from generation to generation," Merezhkovskii warned. "Murders and adultery, blood and mud . . . the block, the rope, and poison—these are the true emblems of Russian autocracy. God's unction on the brows of the Tsars has become the brand of Cain."[185] Taking hope from the fact that the twentieth century had begun with "hatred and murder, famine and blood . . . salvoes of fire and the rumbling of guns,"[186] the young revolutionary Trotskii kept his faith during these years of spiritual upheaval, but other Russians who had been dedicated revolutionaries lost heart. Nowhere was this disillusionment more evident than in the collection of essays that appeared in the spring of 1909 and bore the title *Vekhi (Signposts* or *Landmarks)*. *Vekhi* was an amazing exercise in self-criticism (and, even, self-condemnation) undertaken by men who had formerly committed themselves to the cause of far-reaching social and political change. Three of its leading contributors—Nikolai Berdiaev, Sergei Bulgakov, and Petr Struve—who had accepted the Marxist gospels in their youth now turned to Solovev and Tolstoi and urged others to follow their example before it grew too late.

"We are not men, but cripples," exclaimed Mikhail Gershenzon, a prominent literary historian and critic who edited the collection. "Nowhere in the world does radical opinion reign so despotically as it does among us."[187] The intelligentsia "were a throng of sick folk, isolated in their native land," Gershenzon warned. The *narod*, whom Russian radicals had so long idealized, courted, and championed, had again rejected them in 1905 and would continue to do so because the gap between revolutionary precepts and the people's aspirations was so vast. "They do not sense a human soul in us, and therefore they detest us with a passion," he lamented. "Not only can we not dream of merging with the *narod*, but we must fear them more than all the government's executions. We must give thanks to that very regime which, with its bayonets and prisons, still protects us from the rage of the *narod.*"[188] Politically, socially, and, above all, morally, the revolutionary fervor that had ruled the intelligentsia for three-quarters of a century had led Russians into a hopeless cul-de-sac, the *Vekhi* contributors insisted. Predictably, their essays evoked impassioned denials; enraged cries of betrayal were heard from Miliukov and Lenin. Even Merezhkovskii denounced the *Vekhi* group as men who, in the words of one historian, were "flogging an exhausted horse to death."[189] Nonetheless, *Vekhi* was widely read, its pleas heard by many; it expressed a widespread response to that rapidly emerging apocalyptic vision that gripped the minds of many Russians.

Images of the Apocalypse have long been a part of the literature of Europe and Russia, but, in Russia, these assumed a new urgency as the twentieth century opened. "Nowhere else in Europe," a leading scholar once wrote, "was the volume and intensity of apocalyptic literature comparable to that found in Russia during the reign of Nicholas II."[190] In 1900, Vladimir Solovev had raised the first alarm, warning of a new Mongol horde forming in Asia and of the approaching end of civilization. When the turmoil of 1905 brought both defeat by the Japanese and revolution to Russia in the brief space of a few months, Belyi and Merezhkovskii concluded that the Apocalypse really had begun. "The great mystic [Solovev] was right," Belyi announced, now convinced, like so many of his friends, that the world as they knew it was approaching its end.[191] "Where are you, you marching Huns?" Briusov called out. "I hear your iron tread!" The Huns' approach, he warned, would drive "thinkers and poets, keepers of mysteries and the faith" into hiding "in catacombs, in deserts, and in caves," while everything else might "perish without a trace."[192]

In the rapidly changing new world of science and technology, the prime manifestation of the coming Apocalypse became the industrialized modern city. Briusov sounded a first dramatic note in his famous "Pale Horse," in which he moved Solovev's apocalyptic images from the faraway reaches of Asia into the very center of Russia's urban life. "The street was like a storm. Crowds passed by,/

As if pursued by Fate's inevitability./ Omnibuses, cabs, and automobiles rushed past,/ And the surging torrents of humanity flowed on endlessly," he began. In this turmoil, Death appeared astride a pale horse as foretold in Revelation 6:8. The fearsome vision lasted only a moment and then, as quickly as it had come, it vanished. "Omnibuses, cabs, and automobiles rushed past," Briusov concluded. "And the surging torrents of humanity flowed on endlessly."[193] For Briusov, the Apocalypse was not yet to be, but the warning had come. It remained for others to take up his tortured themes and apply them to the near, not distant, future.

Thoughtful Russians believed that the years 1910 and 1911 heralded the approaching end of an age. The spring of 1910 witnessed the reappearance of Halley's Comet, a potential cataclysm that Blok imagined might cause all mankind to "quietly pass into sleep and death after an exquisite moment of universal reconciliation."[194] But the drama of a passing comet marked only the beginning of events that seemed tragic and awe-inspiring to Russians. In that same year, the great Lev Tolstoi died, as did the artist Mikhail Vrubel and the famous actress Vera Kommissarzhevskaia, whom one critic called the "poetic image" of the Symbolist theater and "the emblem of the times."[195] To Blok and his friends, such deaths were signs of greater catastrophe to follow. "One could already begin to sense the smell of burning, blood, and iron in the air," Blok recalled a decade later. "In the spring of 1911, Miliukov gave an interesting speech about 'An Armed Peace and the Reduction of Armaments.' In one of the Moscow newspapers, a prophetic article entitled 'The Nearness of a Great War' appeared. . . . The summer heat was so intense that even the grass withered and died, while in London huge strikes of railroad workers broke out. . . . Then, in the fall, Stolypin was murdered in Kiev."[196]

If these events boded ill, there were others. The year 1911 brought the trial of Mendel Beilis and a new wave of anti-Semitic hatred in Russia. In Morocco, the German gunboat *Panther* probed the resolution of the Triple Entente at Agadir. "[Kaiser] Wilhelm is looking for a fight, and by all the signs he *will get his war*," Blok wrote grimly at one point.[197] In anger, but with a sense of growing excitement as he prepared to witness the coming conflagration, he told his mother that "the governments of all nations finally have gone too far. Perhaps we are yet fated to see three great wars, our own Napoleons, and a new map of Europe."[198] Art, life, and politics, Blok concluded sadly, could never be reconciled.[199] To Belyi, who had just embarked upon a long journey with Asia Turgeneva, he urged: "Come back to Russia. It may turn out that there is not much time left in which to know her as she is now!"[200]

While Blok warned of the grim fate that awaited a world poised on the brink of cataclysmic conflict, Belyi combined his personal sense of foreboding with Briusov's tormented themes to produce *Petersburg,* a novel of startling apocalyptic imagery, which he began in the fall of 1911 after he and Turgeneva returned from their European and North African travels. "There will be a leap across history," he wrote near the end of his second chapter. "Great will be the strife, strife the likes of which there has never been seen in this world. The yellow hordes of Asians . . . will encrimson the fields of Europe in oceans of blood." "As for Petersburg," he added on the same page, "it will sink."[201]

Belyi's Petersburg was a phantom city peopled by specters. Its buildings, bridges, and streets, "ashy and indistinct," could only be glimpsed, but rarely clearly seen, through "yellow-green fog" or "greenish murk." "Petersburg streets possess one indubitable quality," he explained. "They transform passersby into shadows."[202] In the words of one prominent critic, this strange realm of Belyi's creation was "incredible, fantastic, and monstrous, a world of nightmare and terror, a world of perverted perspectives, of disembodied people and moving corpses."[203] This was the terrible modern industrial city of which Briusov and Blok had already warned, the city of "gray human streams," of the "many-thousand human swarm" of wage slaves who labored for pitiful sums in "many-chimneyed factories." Belyi's Petersburg had become a realm of "bodies, bodies, and more bodies: bent, half-bent, bent hardly at all, and not bent," with "utterly smoke-sodden" faces, faces sometimes marked by "bluish veins," faces that often bore greenish or yellowish tinges. The city, an "un-Russian-but nonetheless-capital city," was wet and cold and filled with germs that settled upon men and women as they made their way against a biting wind that always seemed to whip along its gray, icy streets. Only after the Armageddon between Asia and Europe would the sun appear. "On that day," Belyi promised, "the final Sun will rise in radiance over my native land."[204]

Belyi's tale centered upon the actions of a terrorist son who had been ordered to kill his reactionary father by planting in his study a time bomb concealed in a sardine can. It was the bomb's urgent ticking that dominated *Petersburg* much as the time bomb of war and revolution had fixed itself deeply into the minds of the author and his Symbolist friends.

When *Petersburg* first appeared in serialized form in 1913, only a few months remained before the outbreak of war. At that point, the great struggle between city and countryside, between factories and farms, between pastoral calm and urban turmoil, seemed to be leading to what James Billington once called "the final struggle between 'iron and the land.' "[205] But the greater, more immediate threat to Russia was to come from outside. For Europe had become an armed camp of distrusting and hostile nations, whose burgeoning arsenals rendered peace more insecure with each month that passed. Even before the last installment of Belyi's *Petersburg* appeared, the drums of war had begun to sound. The conflagration that Belyi and his friends feared, but awaited with a thrill of anticipation, was about to burst upon them.

CHAPTER XI
The Last Days of Peace

FEBRUARY 21, 1913, BEGAN WITH AN ARTILLERY SALUTE FROM the fortress of Saints Peter and Paul to mark the passing of the 300th year since Russia's Assembly of the Land had chosen the first Romanov to be Tsar of All the Russias. That morning the front pages of St. Petersburg's newspapers all bore Nicholas's tercentenary manifesto praising Russians for their accomplishments and sacrifices: "By the combined labors of Our crowned predecessors on the Russian throne and the labors of all true sons of Russia . . . the Russian State was founded and grew strong. More than once, Our Homeland faced grave ordeals, but the Russian people, firm in their Orthodox faith, strong in the undying love they bore for their Motherland, and selfless in their loyalty to their Sovereigns, overcame adversity and emerged renewed and strengthened." Nicholas spoke of the heroism of Russia's soldiers, the achievements of her scientists and writers, and the labors of "tens of millions of ploughmen, whose endurance and labor continues to better our nation's agriculture and increases the basic sources of national wealth," but it was nonetheless a cold proclamation, somehow unlike those of his predecessors.[1] The great manifestos of Alexander I had stirred Russians to their very souls, and they had pledged their fortunes and lives to drive Napoleon from their land. Nicholas's words left the people of his capital unmoved.

This impression was shared by many in St. Petersburg as the day's events unfolded. That afternoon, Nicholas, Aleksandra, and their children rode to the great Kazan Cathedral for a memorial Mass. Standing beneath more than a hundred of Napoleon's eagles captured by Russian valor a century before, and in the presence of the ashes of Field Marshal Prince Kutuzov, the popular hero who had driven Napoleon from Russia at the end of 1812, the Romanovs celebrated their dynasty's past glories. Meriel Buchanan, the British Ambassador's daughter, was astounded to see that Nicholas's face displayed an "almost stern gravity [that] gave to the celebration no sense of national rejoicing" and that the crowds of onlookers remained "strangely silent."[2] Anna Vyrubova, Aleksandra's ever-loyal companion, called them "undemonstrative masses of people, a typical Petersburg crowd,"[3] a description that contrasted starkly with the accounts of those Petersburgers who had greeted Nicholas and Aleksandra on their wedding day, or of the crowds that had cheered the war with Japan at the beginning of 1904. The tercentenary, Meriel Buchanan recalled, "had been eagerly looked forward to and discussed for months beforehand. It had been hoped that these festivities would force the Imperial Family to come out of their seclusion [at Tsarskoe Selo, where they had moved during the upheavals of 1905] and that the Emperor, when he attended the

Duma, would make some public announcement that would relieve the internal situation."[4] But Nicholas and Aleksandra took no advantage of the opportunity for reconciliation with their subjects that the celebration offered. Nicholas did nothing unusual to celebrate his family's centuries upon the Russian throne; there were not even any special balls given at the Winter Palace to brighten the social season. Perhaps indicative of the confusion that surrounded the event, postage stamps bearing the portraits of all Romanov autocrats were issued to commemorate the occasion, but postal clerks at first refused to cancel them for fear of "defacing the Tsar's portrait."[5]

If Nicholas seemed aloof during the Petersburg celebrations, Aleksandra preserved an almost total detachment from the events that went on around her. At the performance of Glinka's *A Life for the Tsar* at the Mariinskii Theater, she appeared in the Imperial box for the first time in several years. "Her lovely, tragic face was expressionless, almost austere, as she stood by her husband's side during the playing of the National Anthem, her eyes, enigmatical in their dark gravity, seemed fixed on some secret inward thought that was certainly far removed from the crowded theater and the people who acclaimed her. Not once did a smile break the immobile somberness of her expression when, the Anthem over, she bent her head in acknowledgment of the cheers that greeted its conclusion," wrote Meriel Buchanan. It evidently proved beyond the Empress's emotional strength to remain in her subjects' view even for that one evening performance. "Sitting so close," Miss Buchanan continued in her account, "we could see that the fan of white eagles' feathers the Empress was holding was trembling convulsively, we could see how a dull, unbecoming flush was stealing over her pallor, and could almost hear the laboured breathing which made the diamonds which covered the bodice of her gown rise and fall, flashing and trembling with a thousand uneasy sparks of light. Presently, it seemed that this emotion or distress mastered her completely, and with a few whispered words to the Emperor she rose and withdrew to the back of the box, to be no more seen that evening."[6] Nor was she seen in public for the next several weeks as she was seized by deep feelings of persecution, bitterly certain that her subjects found perverse pleasure in misunderstanding her actions. When she was "exhausted," she was convinced that they thought her cold. When she was concerned about her son's fragile health, they thought her insensitive to their needs. She tried to do philanthropic work, but knowledge of her goodness never seemed to reach the outside world.[7] By 1913, Aleksandra had retreated so deeply into her cocoon of paranoia and wounded self-pity that she simply could not return to the real world of St. Petersburg and the Winter Palace. The Imperial yacht *Standart,* the gleaming new white limestone summer palace at Livadia in the Crimea, and the cozily arranged family quarters of the Alexander Palace at Tsarskoe Selo had become her refuges. On the rare occasions when she ventured outside them with her husband, she rarely found pleasure.

The spring of 1913 was one of those pleasureless times. After the great *ottepel* passed, the royal couple traveled to the lands of Old Russia—to the ancient towns of Vladimir, Suzdal, and Bogoliubovo that had stood at the center of the tiny duchy from which their vast Empire had sprung—to continue their dynasty's celebrations. Vladimir Kokovtsev, Stolypin's successor as President of the Imperial Council of Ministers, was amazed by "the absence of any real enthusiasm and the comparatively small crowds of people" that greeted them. The first part of the Imperial progress, he confessed, was "all very attractively arranged but somehow empty."[8] At Nizhnii-Novgorod, home of Russia's greatest summer fair, Nicholas and Aleksandra boarded the specially refurbished river steamer *Midsummer,* only to remain much of the time in their staterooms as they made their way down the great Volga River. Often they did not even appear on deck to greet those whom the authorities had assembled to cheer them on their way. The strange emptiness that had so amazed Kokovtsev continued.

Only when they reached Kostroma, site of the Ipatiev Monastery where young Mikhail Romanov and his mother had found shelter during the Time of Troubles, did Nicholas and Aleksandra stir real enthusiasm among their subjects. On May 19, they were joined by thirty Imperial Grand Dukes and Grand Duchesses, and all of Kostroma turned out to greet perhaps the most impressive assembly of Russian royalty ever to visit a provincial city. Nicholas and his entourage passed through gates adorned with the words: "Let Your Sovereign Family Live Forever!" that had been written in the Old Russian characters of the seventeenth century. Throngs of commonfolk lined their route and cheered whenever they appeared. With tears of joy streaming from her eyes, an old woman approached the Imperial carriage on her knees, gnarled hands outstretched. Deeply moved, Aleksandra gave her the shawl she carried, while the crowd roared *"Bozhe Tsaria khrani!"*—"God Save the Tsar!" The crowd followed the Imperial family back to the dock. As their steamer drew away, hundreds waded after them until the water became too deep.[9]

But the enthusiasm of the people of Kostroma did not follow Nicholas and Aleksandra for the rest of their journey. Disquieting impressions intruded upon their private world as a gnawing sense of their subjects' terrible poverty began to penetrate the curtain of official receptions and festivities.[10] They reached Moscow in time for Alexandra's birthday on May 25. "The weather was perfect," Vyrubova remembered. "Under the clear sunshine the floating flags and banners, the flower-trimmed buildings, and the numberless decorations made up a spectacle of unforgettable beauty."[11] Many special ceremonies were planned, but the police feared the Moscow crowd. Terrorists had killed several high officials and one Grand Duke in the city in recent years, and the memories of Stolypin's assassination in Kiev were still painfully fresh. Thus, the only time that Nicholas came near the *narod* was during a ceremonial procession through Red Square in which the Tsarevich Aleksei, suffering from an acute bout with hemophilia, had to be carried in the arms of a burly Cossack. "The crowd seemed to feel some sort of deep impending tragedy in the helpless condition of the Sovereign's only son," Kokovtsev remembered. The emptiness he had felt in Vladimir and Suzdal returned with a rush. "I cannot note anything remarkable about the Sovereign's visit to Moscow," he later wrote.[12] The next day, Nicholas and Aleksandra returned to their refuge at Tsarskoe Selo.

The pall that hung over Russians' muted response to the

Romanovs' 300th anniversary was but part of the ominous cloud that loomed above the Empire in 1913. Many educated young men and women continued to abandon themselves to the devil-may-care decadence of *tryn-travizm.* The few still willing to believe in mankind's better future rededicated themselves to revolutionary ideals; this path, however, was fraught with more perils than ever before. Just in Russia's capital alone, one out of every thirty Petersburgers on the eve of the Great War was a soldier, a policeman, or an official assigned to the city's courts.[13] Inevitably, more and more revolutionary leaders were condemned to long terms in Siberia or forced to flee into lonely foreign exile. In Switzerland, Lenin was overcome by pessimism. "I do not expect to live to see the revolution," he confided to several of his lieutenants.[14] Driven from France, Switzerland, England, and Spain, and thus unable to cross Europe to reach Scandinavia, Trotskii would finally cross the Atlantic at the beginning of 1917 to join Kollontai and Nikolai Bukharin in the United States.[15] "We are poor with the accumulated poverty of over a thousand years," he wrote in comparing his native land with Europe. "A thousand years we have lived in a humble log cabin and filled its crevices with moss—did it become us to dream of vaulting arcs and Gothic spires?"[16]

Within Russia, conditions in the factories may well have filled many peasant proletarians with nostalgia for Trotskii's metaphoric log huts. By 1913, a small number of factory workers actually were beginning to rise out of that terrible poverty into which they had been cast when they had abandoned their rural *izby* ten or fifteen years before, but at their backs stood tens upon tens of thousands of unskilled newcomers. Poverty, disease, wretched working conditions, and chronic unemployment still plagued most factory workers in Russia. Wages rose by about a fourth in the decade after 1905, but the prices of most necessities rose far higher. In St. Petersburg, eight out of every ten workers earned less than the amount a government commission had just set as the minimum sum needed to survive in the city.[17]

Many workers actually saw their wretched standard of living fall during these years, and they became desperate when they found that strong backs and willing hands were not enough to feed their families. The last days of peace thus found the Russian Empire in the grips of the greatest wave of strikes it had ever seen. There had been 466 strikes involving a bit more than 100,000 workers in all of Russia during 1911. Strikes quadrupled the next year, and the number of workers involved rose sevenfold. By the first half of 1914, strikes had begun to break out at the rate of more than 16 new ones each day. When war came in August, every other worker in Russia had taken part in some type of labor protest within the past twelve months.[18] Russia's proletarians thus turned to face war's harsh demands as hardened veterans of labor strife.

Bitter revolutionaries and desperate workers would provide little solid support for a sustained Russian war effort. Neither would the several million Jews who lived in the Empire's western lands that were about to be invaded by the armies of Germany and Austria-Hungary. Stolypin's social and political peace had brought more persecution for this long-suffering segment of Russia's population, and scarcely a month went by when the government did not issue new anti-Jewish decrees. Beginning in 1911, a number of reactionary politicians and government officials began to talk about the need to "clear Russia of Jews, to clear it consistently, without hesitation." One Duma deputy publicly denounced Jews as "a criminal race" and insisted that their suppression "*is never in contradiction* with the ideals of sound statesmanship."[19] Delighted at the opportunity to proclaim its anti-Semitic hatred, the reactionary press equated Jews with parasites and vermin. "Kikes," the Union of the Russian People insisted, "are dangerous to the life of mankind in the same measure as wolves, scorpions, reptiles, poisonous spiders, and similar creatures which are destroyed because they are deadly for human beings. . . . Kikes must be placed under such conditions that they will gradually die out."[20]

With the help of high-ranking reactionary officials, the Union of the Russian People set out to indict each and every Russian Jew of a crime so vile that all Russians would turn against them. They chose ritual murder, in which Jews were thought to drain the blood from still living Christian children, as the crime that best suited their purpose. Suspicions of ritual murders had sparked pogroms in the past, the most notable being the terrible Kishinev pogrom in 1903. Jews had even been indicted on such charges by hysterical local authorities from time to time, but, in 1911, the indictment came from none other than Ivan Shcheglovitov, the Imperial Minister of Justice. His victim was Mendel Beilis, a humble Jewish clerk in a brickworks that stood on the outskirts of Kiev.[21]

The troubles of Mendel Beilis began on the night of March 12, 1911, far from the poor room over the brickyard office in which he usually slept. Some days before, a woman named Vera Cheberiak, leader of a notorious gang of thieves in Kiev, had learned that some of their crimes were known to Andrei Iushchinskii, a thirteen-year-old schoolboy who sometimes played with her son. Fearful that young Andrei would betray them to the police, her men killed him, dumped his body in a cave near the brickworks where Beilis worked, and thought no more about the matter until the corpse, with forty-seven stab wounds, was discovered eight days later.[22] The reactionary press in Kiev and St. Petersburg hastily proclaimed Iushchinskii the victim of ritual murder by Jews and demanded retribution. "Our slobbering liberals seem not to understand what kind of species the Jews are with whom they are dealing," one editorial lamented, and the Empire's entire right-wing press leaped to condemn Jews for "their rapacity and parasitic instincts."[23]

Neither incompetents nor fools, the police of Kiev soon learned who had actually killed Iushchinskii, but they held their tongues while their superiors searched for a Jew who could be made to bear the blame. When a local journalist also traced the murderers, the Chief Justice of the Supreme Appellate Court of Kiev gave the Cheberiak gang official protection. By that time, Beilis already was in prison. Months before, on the night of July 21, a detachment of police, supported by fifteen gendarme officers and Okhrana officials, had arrested him. Of the nine Supreme Appellate Court judges who voted on the indictment presented against him, only two had bothered to study the evidence; they were both so appalled by its flaws that they wrote dissenting opinions. No one in authority actually thought Beilis was guilty, but, on Shcheglovitov's orders, they set out to convict him nonetheless. Foreign opinion first looked on aghast, then became irate, and, finally, turned against Russia in disgust. All across Europe, eminent politicians, scholars, and writers denounced Russia's medieval (some said barbaric) prejudice. With just one dissenting vote, the entire United States Congress urged President Taft to break America's commercial treaty with Russia.[24]

For almost two years, Shcheglovitov's underlings struggled to prepare their case. When the trial began in the fall of 1913, the Minister appointed a noted anti-Semite to preside, and promised him a promotion if Beilis were convicted. The jury was exclusively made up of traditionally anti-Semitic peasants, and the judge was so quick to remind prosecution witnesses of their testimony and to explain it to the jurors that Nicholas gave him a gold watch as a special reward. To the government's surprise, the twelve peasant jurors proved less biddable than expected, and none voted for Beilis's conviction. For justice in Russia, it was a brilliant victory; for the government, a bitter defeat. Desperate to recoup their prestige, the authorities tried to indict other Jews on other ritual murder charges.[25] In their most notorious effort, the Kiev city prosecutor publicly laid the blame for the murder of a child at the door of Jewish ritual murderers only to learn that the victim was a Jew himself. Incredible as it may seem, when the Great War broke out a few weeks later, a Jewish newspaper proclaimed that "Russian Jews will manfully step forward to the battlefield and do their sacred duty," and some Jews actually marched to defend the land whose people and government had persecuted them for so long.[26] Their support did not survive the first weeks of the war. Bigoted Russian authorities responded to Jewish patriotism by bringing massive accusations of espionage against their families and friends. Throughout Russia's western provinces, thousands of Jews were driven from their homes, falsely accused as spies and saboteurs, as the Empire's war effort got under way.[27]

By repressing political dissidents, persecuting Jews, and exploiting factory workers, Stolypin's political and economic programs had made bitter enemies for Nicholas's government. Among the peasantry, however, his policies had begun to transform land-poor tillers of Russia's soil from revolutionary sympathizers into conservative supporters of the government. Some among them actually began to prosper, although they were relatively few and their prosperity still meager. A mere half-decade after Stolypin launched his program in 1906, almost three million families had applied to exchange their shares in the commune for lands of their own, and a number of them had begun to buy even more land from other peasants.[28] Peasants who worked their own land became better farmers very quickly. It began to seem that Russia had at long last discovered how to bring her tens of millions of peasants into the modern age.

Before the Stolypin reforms were enacted, peasant communes had purchased about forty-nine out of every fifty acres of land sold on the peasant land market in Russia. Seven short years later, in 1913, that figure had shrunk to a mere one out of every three. More land went up for sale as thousands of poor peasants pulled up stakes and moved to the cities.[29] The ranks of the urban proletariat grew by more than six hundred thousand in just the four years before the war, and those of St. Petersburg's workers—men and women especially given to labor protest—almost doubled.[30] These new factory workers had not been chastened by defeat in 1905. Nor had they known the repression that striking workers had suffered in those days. Often young, frequently "hotheaded and impulsive," they began to radicalize anew those working men and women grown apathetic from political repression and long hours of toil.[31] Less than a month before Russia went to war in 1914, more than a hundred thousand Petersburg toilers went on strike. While France's President Poincaré discussed questions of war and peace with Nicholas and his ministers early in July, strikers from the great Putilov Works, one of Russia's most important weapons factories, tried to break out of the city's workers' districts to demonstrate at the Winter Palace. "The government is fighting with bayonets, the capitalists—with money, and the clergy—with sermons," they proclaimed. "Down with capital! Comrades, get ready! Hail socialism!" Only rigid lines of Cossacks and mounted police halted their march.[32] As a precaution, the Russians entertained the French President at Peterhof for most of his three-day visit.[33] More than twenty miles away from St. Petersburg's turbulent workers' districts, amidst the seaside splendor for which the palace and its gardens were famous, there was no danger that he would see the workers' red banners or hear their revolutionary songs. From Peterhof, Poincaré was taken to Krasnoe Selo, scene of the army's summer maneuvers, where the Russian army, always brilliant on parade, gave an impressive day's performance. "Fine troops," Poincaré remarked. "All in all, their appearance was good."[34] After the review, President and Tsar continued their discussions. Their voices spoke of peace, but their thoughts were of war.

As August 1914 approached, Russia thus stood midway in a transition that could have carried her toward either revolutionary upheaval or peaceful evolution along a path already marked out by the more advanced industrial nations of Europe. Between some Russians and their government, there was bitter antagonism, while others dared to be cautiously optimistic about their future. The outcome could not be known, but it was certain that Russians needed peace if they were to resolve the urgent problems they faced on every side.

At the beginning of 1914, peace hung by the slenderest of threads. Offensive military alliances, long-standing national enmities, and bitter competition for new markets and new empires—all had brought the nations of the European continent to the brink of war at a time when the world had never seen larger armies and navies or more destructive weapons. Exactly seventy years earlier, during a period of international crises, Nicholas's great-grandfather had regretted the almost unbearable tensions that sometimes develop in the affairs of men and nations. "So many powder barrels close to the fire," he had said to Britain's Lord Aberdeen. "How shall one prevent the sparks from catching?"[35] In 1914, no one knew the answer and few statesmen dared to ask the question. "Europe lived in a repressed fear of itself," a great historian once wrote. "Few people wanted war . . . but all took it for granted that war would come some day."[36]

Volatile new alliance systems had divided Europe's nations into hostile armed camps. In diplomatic terms, these new alliances had been cast in the 1890s, when the Franco-Russian Entente and the Triple Alliance of Germany, Austria, and Italy had replaced the system that had divided the continent between the "liberal" and "constitutional" governments of France and England and the conservative, absolute monarchies of Austria, Prussia, and Russia since the days of Napoleon. For more than a decade, England had remained aloof from both systems, but, in 1904, she entered an entente with France when Germany had rebuffed Colonial Secretary Joseph Chamberlain's feelers for an alliance.[37] Three years later, the combined efforts of Aleksandr Izvolskii, Sir Edward Grey, and Sir Arthur Nicolson settled some of the disputes between Russia and England over their spheres of influence in Persia; by the end of August 1907, the separate ententes between France and England and France and Russia were loosely joined into one.[38]

As a wise statesman, Grey saw the need for the entente once Germany and England had become locked in a naval arms race. "An entente with Russia is now possible," he had written to King Edward's secretary Lord Knollys, "and it is the thing most to be desired in our foreign policy. It will complete and strengthen the entente with France and add very much to the comfort and strength of our position." Nonetheless, he found the thought of tying England's fortunes to those of Russia unsettling. "The real rock ahead is the prospect in Russia itself," he had confessed to Ambassador Nicolson at one point. "If the Duma is dissolved, and there is a regime of pogroms and courts-martial, feeling here will be very adverse."[39] Yet Grey's thoughts did not follow a single track, and there were other factors in his calculations. Beyond the need to protect Britain's colonial empire against Germany, he feared other threats to his nation's far-flung interests. The vast subcontinent of India was never far from his thoughts, and, like all British statesmen since the eighteenth century, he worried that Russian expansion into Central Asia posed a threat to India's northern frontier. It was his hope "to secure ourselves . . . forever from further Russian advances in the direction of the Indian frontier."[40] To do so, and to secure England against Germany on the high seas, Grey thus had taken his nation out of her "splendid isolation" and plunged her into the political maelstrom that swirled across the European continent.

Even before Foreign Minister Izvolskii and Ambassador Nicolson had put their pens to the Anglo-Russian agreement of August 1907, the nations of Europe had allowed themselves to be drawn into one final and demonstrably futile effort to break away from the arms race that threatened to plunge them, and perhaps all the world, into war. For that futile exercise, 256 delegates from 44 nations assembled in mid-June 1907 for the Second Hague Conference to discuss peace and disarmament. None of the Great Powers of Europe took the effort seriously, but none was willing to bear the onus of rejecting the attempt. Izvolskii thought disarmament "a craze of Jews, Socialists, and hysterical women" and named as acting chief of Russia's delegation Professor Fedor Martens, a diplomatic historian who, in the words of an American diplomat, "does not believe . . . there is the slightest likelihood of any steps toward practical reduction of armaments being taken." Kaiser Wilhelm let it be known that he "devoutly hoped the Conference would not take place." He wrote to President Theodore Roosevelt that he thought the idea of disarmament a "humbug,"[41] to which the King of Italy added that he was certain that the Kaiser would never discuss "clipping the wings of Krupp," the master of Germany's armaments industry.[42] Germany's Chancellor Prince von Bülow rejected "any thought of sacrificing the safety of our country to the sanctimonious assurances of our enemies and . . . to the hollow phrasemongering of unsophisticated, and occasionally dishonest, fanatics."[43] "First England isolates us and now wants to disarm us," complained a Reichstag deputy for many of his fellow Germans.[44] Britain's new Liberal Prime Minister, Sir Henry Campbell-Bannerman, supported disarmament in principle, but saw it chiefly as a means to hinder Germany's challenge to his nation's naval supremacy, while his master, King Edward VII, "entirely disapproved" of the conference and found his Prime Minister's espousal of any sort of arms limitation irritating.[45]

Resigned to failure even before they met, the delegates at the

Hague spent four months going through empty motions. Hardly calculated to endear himself to Russians, Germany's chief delegate, Baron Marschall von Bieberstein, cynically remarked that his counterpart from St. Petersburg was a "charlatan . . . with an explosive lack of tact," while Roosevelt's new Secretary of State Elihu Root sadly concluded that "the tendency is toward war." As von Bieberstein left the Conference in October, he asked: "Was it a Peace Conference or a War Conference that took place?" Britain's poet laureate Alfred Austin urged his government to adopt military conscription without delay and quoted Lord Tennyson's famous line: "Form! Form! Riflemen, form!"[46] Most Europeans left the Hague convinced of Germany's bellicose intentions, even though at least a part of her fault had been her candor, not her policy. Nonetheless, it was the Kaiser's bluster, not his frankness, that stuck in the minds of Europeans. "We appeared as the obstacle to a better organization of the world," lamented Theodor Wolff of the Berliner Tageblatt. "All that they had heard from afar of a militarist Germany, steeped in the spirit of caste and of barrack discipline, bowed under the absolute will of a monarch, rigid in his mighty armour, found confirmation under their very eyes."[47]

In a broader sense, it was almost as if the Russo-Japanese War had freed Europeans from the specters that Ivan Bliokh had raised on the eve of the First Hague Conference. Clearly, Bliokh's prediction that armies simply would annihilate each other in battle had proved inaccurate, and, as Europe's generals always had insisted, even automatic weapons would leave enough men living on the field of battle to fight another day. Europeans therefore went to the Hague in 1907 convinced that the best guarantee of peace was not fewer armaments but more, and more powerful ones. "We are ready, and the sooner the better for us," the Chief of the German General Staff von Moltke remarked, while Nicholas later proclaimed that "it is at the very heart of Germany that we should strike."[48] In fact, the commissioning of H.M.S. Dreadnought just before the conference began marked the beginning of a new era in the arms race.

A high-speed naval fortress propelled by steam turbines and armed with ten 12-inch guns, the Dreadnought's speed and firepower rendered other battleships obsolete overnight. When Britain's First Lord Admiral Fisher announced plans to build three more of the awesome fighting ships, Germany hastened to challenge England's newly won advantage by planning similar ships for her own sea forces. The chances for conflict grew in proportion, while the area left for nations to maneuver narrowed. "Each year that passed bound all more closely to the Wheel of Fate," Bernadotte Schmitt once wrote.[49]

In 1908, just a few months after the Second Hague Conference, the nations of Europe faced a grave crisis in the Balkans. This crisis had been in the making ever since the Byzantine Empire had fallen in 1453, and Turkish oppression of their new subjects had caused Europeans and Russians to bemoan the fate of their fellow Christians forced to bend beneath the infidel yoke. In the eighteenth century, Russians' concern for their coreligionists was further complicated by their efforts to seize the Black Sea's northern shore and gain access to the Straits that governed passage into the Mediterranean. The century that brought Peter and Catherine the Great to the Russian throne thus saw several conflicts between Russia and the Ottoman Empire, and, after each war, Russia gained more authority. Clearly, the balance between the two enemies had shifted in Russia's favor by the end of the century, but the disputes were by no means settled.

The issues of the Straits and the Balkans had taken on more pressing importance in the nineteenth century as the Ottoman Empire grew weaker. Statesmen began to speak about "The Sick Man of Europe" and asked what would happen to the Ottoman lands if the Sick Man's illness took a fatal turn.[50] Most European rulers and statesmen were convinced that the Russians harbored dark plans to seize Constantinople and claim the Straits for themselves, and the Treaty of San Stefano, which ended the last Russo-Turkish War in 1878, made them even more certain of Russia's intent. Only Bismarck's efforts to assemble a congress at Berlin averted the very real prospect of a larger war.

For the next thirty years, the Balkans continued to harbor all those sources of conflict that had made them so explosive in 1878. Russia, Austria, England, France, Italy, and, after Bismarck, Germany—all tried to play larger roles in the seething cauldron of Balkan politics, while the Serbs, Croats, Slovenes, Bosnians, Bulgarians, and Greeks vied to realize inflated nationalist cravings at some-one else's expense. To make matters worse, after two Russian fleets had been sunk in the Far East, Nicholas's advisers thought it urgent that their nation's third fleet, long confined within the Black Sea by the Treaty of Berlin, be allowed free access to the Mediterranean. Likewise, Austria grew anxious to annex Bosnia, a Balkan state that still belonged to the Ottoman Empire and was a center of virulent South Slav nationalism whose advocates dreamed of an independent South Slav nation made up of Serbia, Bosnia, and lands that lay within Austria's frontiers. At its most grandiose, their plan would have cut Austria-Hungary off from the Adriatic. On the other hand, Austria could lengthen her short Adriatic coastline and deny Serbia, to whom South Slav nationalists looked as the leader of their movement, all access to the sea if she could annex Bosnia.

The situation in the Balkans turned even more volatile when Aleksandr Izvolskii and Baron Aloys Aehrenthal took over the foreign offices of Russia and Austria in 1906. Known for their shrewd and unscrupulous characters, these men urged more aggressive policies upon their governments. Acutely self-conscious about their backgrounds, both therefore were unusually sensitive about their stature in the capitals of Europe. "A snob first and foremost," and "not very prudent," Prince von Bülow said of Izvolskii, who tried to conceal his modest provincial origins and was anxious to marry well. A number of St. Petersburg's wellborn heiresses evaded his efforts. "I have regretted it every day [that I did not marry Izvolskii]," one of them remarked after he had risen to become Foreign Minister. "But I congratulate myself on not having done so every night." At one point, London society pronounced Izvolskii "a great bore," and the Parisians, no less lacking in generosity than the British, branded him "a nuisance."[51] By contrast, Aehrenthal boasted a well-titled background. His grandmother was the Countess Wilczek, and his mother, Countess Thun, came from the higher aristocracy of

Austria. Aehrenthal himself married Countess Szechenyi, a proud daughter of one of Hungary's greatest families. A baron and later a count, Aehrenthal nonetheless was plagued by the awkward remembrance that one of his grandfathers had been a Jewish grain merchant from Prague.[52] Arrogantly, he once claimed that "I have the Russians in my pocket."[53] If Aehrenthal was certain of anything in the uncertain world in which he lived, it was that he could best Izvolskii in any diplomatic exchange, and he was prepared to test that conviction at any point. "Here were two political adventurers, equally ready to fish in troubled waters to satisfy their ambitions," one astute commentator remarked.[54] It was only a matter of time before their aggressive scheming placed the peace of Europe in jeopardy.

Of the two nations that Izvolskii and Aehrenthal served, the Russians were more fearful of an aggressive policy. Still shaken by their loss to Japan and attempting to recover from the Revolution of 1905, most Russian statesmen rejected any thought of adventures abroad before the situation at home had been stabilized. At a secret council meeting toward the end of January 1908, Izvolskii pleaded for an aggressive policy in the Balkans and warned that Russia risked "losing the fruits of her centuries-long efforts all at once" if she did not act decisively. He urged his fellow ministers to allow him to pursue "the realization of Russia's historic mission in the Near East," but met with an unsympathetic response. Neither the army nor the Black Sea Fleet was ready for war, Deputy War Minister General Polivanov insisted. The final and conclusive warning was Stolypin's: "At the present time, the Minister of Foreign Affairs cannot count on any sort of support for a decisive foreign policy. After a few years, once we have completely restored peace and order at home, Russia can begin again to speak as she once did [but] it is essential for Russia to have a breathing space for the time being."[55] Izvolskii was thus put on notice that any effort to recoup Russia's fallen prestige by new exploits in the Balkans must wait. If he heeded his colleagues' warnings, his dreams of winning glory for himself would have to be set aside.

In Austria, Aehrenthal's resources were not so restricted, but the imperatives pressing upon him were no less insistent. Austria had lost no wars since 1866 and had not suffered the turmoil of revolution since 1849, but her lands were a hornet's nest of searing nationalist hatreds that threatened to tear her asunder at any moment. Wherever Austrian statesmen turned, there were nationalities who clamored for autonomy or independence and looked across Austria's borders to men and women of similar language and custom for support. The wise prudence of Aehrenthal's predecessor, the Polish Count Goluchowski, had spared Austria the stress of unwanted crises but had made her position as Germany's inferior partner in the Triple Alliance all too plain. Despite Austria's political instability, Aehrenthal therefore was determined to reestablish her as Germany's equal in the alliance. His aspiration was all the more dangerous because it was so far out of step with his country's military strength and economic resources. Toward that end, he employed "a mixture of pretensions and subtlety, of force and ruse, of realism and cynicism," one biographer wrote. "His readiness to cheat, to circumvent, to outwit, hid a harsh and ruthless will." The Kaiser once remarked that "Aehrenthal has fancies,"[56] but he was considerably better equipped to give them substance than was his more blunt Russian counterpart. Prince von Bülow, who knew and claimed the friendship of both during his years as Germany's Chancellor, once confessed that "Aehrenthal stood in utter contrast to the shorter, more restless and excitable, and occasionally pushing Calmuck, Izvolskii."[57]

In the Ottoman Empire, itself a turbulent conglomeration of nationalist and religious strivings, an unexpected revolution led by the Young Turks opened new vistas at the beginning of 1908 that neither Izvolskii nor Aehrenthal could resist exploring, and the two met at Buchlau Castle, home of Austria's Ambassador to St. Petersburg Count Berchtold, in September. Precisely what passed between them probably never will be known, but at least Aehrenthal seems to have left with the understanding that, if Austria went ahead and annexed Bosnia-Hercegovina, "Russia would assume a friendly and benevolent attitude."[58] In return, Izvolskii expected Austria to react in a similar fashion if Russia sent ships through the Dardanelles, brought her fleet into the Mediterranean, and violated the Treaty of Berlin that had denied all warships the use of the Straits. Apparently the two men agreed upon their mutual acquiescence in each other's aggressive acts. What was not agreed upon was the timing and, most particularly, the moment at which Austria would annex Bosnia-Hercegovina.

Izvolskii therefore left Buchlau thinking that he and Aehrenthal had reached only an agreement in principle and that it would not be implemented before proper diplomatic preparations were made. Aehrenthal, however, annexed Bosnia-Hercegovina within three weeks, long before Russia was ready to act, and even before Izvolskii had told his fellow ministers and allies the details of his discussions. Izvolskii therefore first learned of Aehrenthal's action from a newspaper he bought just before his train reached Paris at the beginning of October. Enraged, he exclaimed to Prince von Bülow: "That dirty Jew has betrayed me! That hideous Jew has really taken me in!"[59] But no amount of cursing could repair the damage that Russia's reputation had sustained to no purpose. Suspicious and irate, the statesmen of England and France thought Izvolskii had discussed an issue of major consequence behind their backs, and there was not even a remote chance that Russia could breach the Dardanelles while European opinion was so inflamed. "It is not, we think, the moment to discuss the Dardanelles question," sniffed Sir Edward Grey.[60]

For a moment, it seemed that Aehrenthal had done well indeed at Izvolskii's expense. Austria had gained a better foothold in the Balkans at no cost, while Izvolskii and the Russians had lost a good deal of face. But South Slav nationalism had been dangerously inflamed, for the Serbs, who had dreamt of a "greater Serbia" that included Bosnia-Hercegovina, were furious at Austria's bold move. Bosnia-Hercegovina was "the sensitive spot of all political minded Serbs, the center round which revolves their aspirations and their hopes," one of them wrote, and the Serbs rallied to its defense.[61] The government mobilized 120,000 men, and the *Skupština*—the Serbian national assembly—voted a war credit of 16 million dinars.[62] It was time "for us to risk all in defense of the future even if the result is defeat," Nikola Pašić, Serbia's special envoy to St. Petersburg proclaimed. "Blood shed on behalf of our brethren and of our own existence will bear good fruit."[63] For a time, it seemed that armed conflict might break out, and Nicholas felt obliged to warn Austria's Emperor Franz Joseph that any outbreak in the Balkans would cause "a great effervescence . . . that would put an end to all possibility of good relations between Russia and Austria-Hungary and might lead Europe into a general war."[64] Before matters went too far, cooler heads prevailed. Temporarily, the best efforts of Europe's statesmen kept the conflict localized, but it would not be for long. As one historian concluded, Aehrenthal's policy toward Bosnia-Hercegovina and Serbia had launched Austria-Hungary "on a course leading straight to the catastrophe of 1914."[65]

Izvolskii's failure in the Balkans did not dampen Russian interest, nor daunt her resolve, and his successor Sergei Sazonov remained deeply committed to an active policy in those regions. Sazonov was hardly the sort of hardheaded diplomat needed to steer a firm course in the treacherous shoals of Balkan politics, however. He "often lacked a sense of reality and objectivity," Maurice Paléologue, France's ambassador to Russia during the Great War recalled.[66] Thought by diplomats who knew him to be a man given to about-faces—usually for no apparent reason, and often in the midst of diplomatic crises—Sazonov found it difficult to make up his mind.[67] About one thing, however, he was certain. "Russia cannot and ought not to withdraw her attention from Europe," he insisted, "no matter how important and widespread the tasks of her civilizing mission on the Asiatic continent." Unhappily, Sazonov also had drawn some firm and very dangerous conclusions from the Bosnian crisis of 1909. Convinced that Austria was "hostile to Balkan Slavdom and to Russia," he thought that her annexation of Bosnia-Hercegovina "displayed with indisputable clarity the aims of Austro-German policy in the Balkans and laid the bases for an inevitable conflict between Germanism and Slavism." The interests of the two, he insisted, "were irreconcilable."[68]

Fearful of Austro-German influence in the Balkans, Sazonov and his ambassadors were nonetheless expected to observe the same caution that Nicholas and his ministers had urged upon Izvolskii with such resounding lack of success. "Listen to me," Nicholas told Anatolii Nekliudov, when he named him Russia's new ambassador to Sofia at the beginning of 1911. "Do not for one instant lose sight of the fact that we cannot go to war. . . . It would be out of the question for us to face a war for five or six years."[69] Sazonov therefore asserted that Russia's chief aim in the Balkans must be "to guarantee the free development of those Balkan peoples whose independent political existence Russia had called forth."[70] When Serbia and the newly independent Bulgaria began to discuss an alliance in 1911, Sazonov thought it the ideal instrument to achieve these aims. "Perfect!" he exclaimed to Nekliudov when he first learned that Bulgaria and Serbia had discussed such an alliance in September. "Five hundred thousand bayonets to guard the Balkans would bar the road forever to German penetration and Austrian invasion."[71] Within a year, Sazonov had his wish. Bulgaria, Serbia, Greece, and Montenegro had concluded an alliance by the spring of 1912.[72]

Sazonov's support of an alliance, in which the independent Balkan states secretly agreed that they would discuss joint military action if disorders broke out in Turkey that threatened the status quo in their region, set in motion a chain of events that the Russians could not hope to control. When his efforts to direct Balkan affairs foundered in the spring and summer of 1912, Sazonov tried to reverse their course, but that only transformed a volatile situation into an utterly explosive one. "He tries to put on the brake, but it is he who started the motor," Poincaré remarked acidly.[73] When Poincaré visited St. Petersburg in August 1912, Sazonov showed him the treaty's secret clause, and the French minister grew more appalled with each line he read. "I could not prevent myself from exclaiming: 'Why, it is a *convention de guerre!*' " he later wrote.[74]

Poincaré's fears proved all too well founded. Not long before he visited St. Petersburg, an uprising in Albania against the Turks had provoked a series of vicious reprisals and massacres.[75] Seeing these as the very threat to the status quo toward which the new Balkan alliance was directed, Montenegro therefore declared war against the Ottoman Empire on October 8, 1912. Nine days later, the armies of Greece, Bulgaria, and Serbia followed Montenegro into battle.[76] Izvolskii called it "the struggle of Slavdom not only against Islam but against Germanism."[77] As Poincaré had feared, the Balkans had been ignited by acts over which none of the Great Powers had control. "This is the first time in the history of the Eastern Question," wrote the French chargé d'affaires in St. Petersburg, "that the small states have taken a stand so independent of the Great Powers and have felt so capable of getting along without them and even taking them in tow."[78]

War between the Balkan allies and the Turks came as no surprise to Europe's diplomats, but none anticipated the speed with which the allied armies advanced toward the heart of the Ottoman domains. Within a month, the Bulgarians breached the last defenses that barred the road to Constantinople while the Greeks entered Salonika. At the same time, the Serbs reached the Adriatic, and the Montenegrins surrounded Scutari.[79] Except for a few scattered fortresses, virtually all of European Turkey had fallen into the allies' hands by the beginning of November. Victory seemed certain. Far less certain—and far more critical—was the Great Powers' ability to confine the conflict to the Balkans. Austria and Russia must be kept from any head-on confrontation in a region where both had very pressing political interests. All called for mediation, but statesmen again had to face Sazonov's vacillation. At first, he had urged that the territorial status quo be preserved. Then, as the allies won major victories and as public pressure to support their grandiose war aims mounted in Russia, he began to speak of dividing the fruits of victory. Sazonov's actions, Sir George Buchanan wrote sarcastically from St. Petersburg at the end of October, could "hardly enhance his reputation for diplomatic foresight," all the more so because, as he reported a few weeks later, the Russian Foreign Minister was far too "prone to see things in the light in which he would like to see them."[80]

Nonetheless, Sazonov recognized "the necessity of preventing this [Balkan] conflict from assuming the dimensions of a European war." Despite strong support for the Balkan Slavs in Russia's press and the inevitable "street demonstrations and meetings at which patriotic speeches demanded war in defense of Slavdom's interests," he was unwilling to be drawn into any military confrontation with other European nations. Sentiment was especially strong on behalf of the Montenegrins (Alexander III once had called her king "the only friend of Russia") who demanded Scutari, but Sazonov insisted that "it would be criminal to risk the life of a single Russian soldier" to support such a claim.[81] "In all our conversations of this year," France's ambassador reported, "Sazonov has never ceased to repeat . . . that the age of Russian armed intervention on behalf of the Slav Powers of the Balkans was closed. He [Sazonov] added: 'We have given them their independence, our task is finished.' "[82] In any case, Sazonov had little choice. From the very beginning, Sir Edward Grey had insisted that "the Powers in general, and France, England, and Germany in particular," must remain in close consultation about the Balkan crisis,[83] and, in November, Izvolskii reported from Paris that Poincaré had told him "that local—that is, purely Balkan —events can bring only diplomatic support from this government, but in no case will they result in military support."[84] Austria found herself in a very similar situation. "Our treaties and agreements do not pledge us to support Austria in her eastern plans," Germany's new Foreign Minister von Kiderlen-Wächter announced even before the allied advance against the Turks began. "We will not be her satellite in the Near East."[85]

Still fearful that the conflict might burst out of its Balkan containment, the ambassadors of Austria, Russia, Italy, Germany, and France met with Sir Edward Grey in London on December 17, 1912. Austria insisted that Scutari be made a part of Albania because its population was Albanian, while Russia opposed the plan because of Montenegro's aspirations to control the city herself. At the same time, the discussions were complicated still further by Austria's rigid opposition to Serbia's equally unyielding demand for a coastline on the Adriatic.[86] "Serbia will someday set Europe by the ears and bring about a universal war on the continent," Sir Fairfax Cartwright lamented from Vienna. "It will be lucky if Europe succeeds in avoiding a war as a result of the present crisis."[87] In an even more ominous remark, Germany's Chief of Staff von Moltke wrote to his

Austrian counterpart Baron Conrad von Hötzendorff that "a European war must come sooner or later." When it came, he insisted, it would be a conflict between the irreconcilable forces of Slavdom and Germanism.[88]

Already apprehensive about the Balkan War's consequences, Europe's statesmen grew more fearful when fighting resumed on February 3, 1913. Again the allies pressed forward and the key cities of Adrianople and Scutari fell to them. Before the end of the month, the Turks agreed to mediation. By May 30, a "perpetual peace" was signed, and Turkey ceded her remaining European territories to the Balkan allies.[89]

Twenty-nine days after the "perpetual peace" had been signed, Bulgaria's armies struck at Serbia and Greece. Within a week, Rumania joined the Serbs and Greeks in a crunching counterattack, and the Turks returned to the fray to recapture Adrianople. In vain, Sazonov tried to restrain fellow Slavs, whose antagonisms had been born of centuries-long rivalries. In utter exasperation, he finally confessed to the British ambassador that "Russia is powerless to exercise effective pressure at either Sofia or Belgrade."[90] The new battle in the Balkans would be bitter; but it would not be long, for Bulgaria's was a mad and hopeless attempt.[91] Within a month, a peace conference convened at Bucharest to strip Bulgaria of what she had gained in the war against the Turks. "Bulgaria, whose army had been so effective and essential to the defeat of the Turks, was allowed no access to the sea," Sir Edward Grey wrote. "Rumania got some territory that had belonged to Bulgaria, and Greece and Serbia got territory and ports that had been hitherto looked upon as legitimate objects of Bulgarian aspiration if Turkey were driven out of Macedonia."[92] Concluded the diplomatic historian G. P. Gooch, "The Treaty of Bucharest, signed on August 10, 1913, ended one of the shortest and fiercest conflicts in modern history."[93]

Both victory and defeat bore ominous overtones. Bulgaria was bound to try to regain the territories so quickly snatched from her grasp, and Serbia was determined to make further efforts toward establishing the "greater Serbia" that her statesmen had so long envisioned. "The first round is won," Serbia's Prime Minister Pašić remarked after he and his allies finished dividing the spoils of the Second Balkan War. "Now we must prepare for the second against Austria."[94] Sober statesmen nonetheless congratulated themselves for having averted a great European conflagration, at least for the moment. But this time, it was Nicholas who saw closer to the truth. "There is no such thing as European unity—merely Great Powers distrusting each other," he wrote to his mother in a moment of rare insight.[95] During the next eleven months, that distrust would fester and grow. "The aftermath of the Balkan wars," one historian wrote not long ago, "witnessed the darkening rather than the brightening of the prospects for peace."[96]

The incident that provoked the deepest suspicion and stirred the most bitterness during the eleven months that separated the silencing of the guns in the Balkans and their renewed firing on Europe's eastern and western fronts in August 1914 was a military mission headed by General Otto Liman von Sanders that Germany sent to Turkey at the end of the Second Balkan War.[97] Certainly the Turks desperately needed sound military advice to retrain and reequip their shattered land forces. Yet, it was equally certain that any large-scale German incursion into Turkish affairs would provoke a strong Russian response just when better relations between Russia and Germany were needed to strengthen Europe's unstable peace. When Liman von Sanders arrived in Constantinople with forty-two German military aides to assume extensive command authority in the Turkish army in December 1913, the Russians were incensed. Their anger turned to outrage when they learned that Major Kübel, one of Liman's staff, was under direct orders from the German General Staff to adapt Turkey's railways to the needs of war within six months.[98] The entire crisis affected Sazonov in much the same fashion as Austria's annexation of Bosnia had Izvolskii. Baron Taube, one of his subordinates in the Foreign Office, remarked some years later that Sazonov's increasing lack of "sangfroid," which appeared to stem directly from the Liman von Sanders affair, was a major factor in the worsening relations between the Entente and the Triple Alliance during the first half of that year.[99]

There were some good reasons for Sazonov's short-tempered

suspicion. No Russian statesman could tolerate such an obvious German move into a region so long thought vital to Russia's national interests. "Everything that transpires in Constantinople and the Straits is of the highest importance to Russia," Sazonov's deputy announced when he first learned of the secret negotiations that had paved the way for the mission.[100] Constantinople, Sazonov later wrote, "stood at the junction of Europe and Asia and was predestined by Nature to become the main distribution point of that vast movement of commerce" that flowed by sea and land from Europe and Russia to the Persian Gulf and Mesopotamia. He was convinced that Germany was about to seize control of that vital commercial and diplomatic hub and to throttle Russian commerce. It was "an old truth," he remarked, that "economic factors determine the course of international politics." The purpose of Liman von Sanders' mission, he concluded, was "to establish a firm basis for German power in the Ottoman Empire."[101]

In stating Russia's concern to her friends and foes in Europe, Sazonov insisted that the "single fundamental proposition" of his nation's policy toward Constantinople and the Straits had long been "the preservation of the political status quo" and that "any compromise on this absolutely fundamental point in Russian foreign policy was thought by us to be utterly intolerable."[102] Turning to Russia's partners in Europe, he insisted that "this question must be the test of the value of the Triple Entente."[103] He was dismayed when both the British and the French counseled caution. The Turks had named a French general to reform the Ottoman gendarmerie, and a British admiral commanded the Turkish Fleet. Neither government dared insist that Germany withdraw Liman von Sanders while their own officers remained. They had other reasons for caution as well, not the least of which was their fear that Sazonov, as Nicolson wrote, had "completely lost his head."[104] "The difficulty in dealing with Sazonov," Nicolson warned Britain's chargé d'affaires in St. Petersburg, "is that one never knows precisely how far he is prepared to go. . . . We should look very foolish if we took the question up warmly and then found that Sazonov had more or less deserted us. In fact there is a certain disinclination on our part to pull the chestnuts out of the fire for Russia."[105] Eventually, the dispute was settled peace-

ably though a variety of meaningless concessions. "One more settlement of this sort," exclaimed a German diplomat in Constantinople,
"and we lose face."[106] Sazonov was left feeling that Russia had been
ill served by her allies and was more convinced than ever of Germany's bellicose intent. "If there was anyone left in Russia who still
had doubts about the real purpose of German policy in the Near
East," he concluded, "the conditions under which the Liman von
Sanders mission were conceived and implemented put an end to all
uncertainties and misunderstandings on that score."[107]

Nowhere was the deep-seated bitterness between Russians and
Germans more evident than in the vitriolic diatribes that poured
from their national presses during the spring of 1914. "Ought we to
wait until our enemies are ready?" the Berlin *Post* asked on February
24. "The task of German policy is not to preserve peace as long as
possible, but on the contrary to prepare for the inevitable war with
energy and foresight and to begin it under the most favorable conditions."[108] An even more resounding salvo was fired on March 2 by
the *Kölnische Zeitung* when it published "Russia and Germany," an
inflammatory dispatch in which its St. Petersburg correspondent
reported that, although Russia was not then ready for war, "in three
or four years, the political weight of Russian military power will be
estimated quite differently." If Russia were allowed to complete
those preparations, the article's author hinted darkly, she would
launch a war against Germany at the first suitable pretext.[109] Germany should strike while she still held the advantage. In reply, St.
Petersburg's highly conservative *Novoe vremia* urged that the day of
full Russian preparedness must be moved closer. "The hour draws
near," it warned its readers. "It is essential to work day and night
to prepare the army."[110]

The Foreign Ministry's Baron Taube and his highly placed
friends discussed these articles among themselves in what he remembered as "an elegant, small St. Petersburg salon" and found themselves divided about whether sober statesmen could pursue such a
catastrophic course.

"We are at the mercy of a handful of adventurers or Slavophile
fanatics," one of them insisted.

"A purely formal child's game," a retired general huffed. "No one is mad enough to face a war with Turkey, Austria and, probably, Germany with an army that is still in the process of reorganization and with a fleet that is not even capable, as all of you know only too well, of transporting a single army corps to the other side of the Black Sea."

"War is simply impossible," another agreed. "For at least another three or four years it would be an act of political suicide."

"Unhappily, it is all too possible," cautioned a member of the Duma. "[Minister of War] General Sukhomlinov is personally preparing a vehement article . . . for the purpose of declaring, *urbi et orbi*, that we are ready for anything and that we fear no one."[111]

Was Russia ready for war in March 1914, or must she be resigned to several years of giving in to the threats of her enemies if she hoped to avoid a crushing defeat? The article by General Sukhomlinov to which Taube's friend from the Duma referred gave a ringing reply to these questions in St. Petersburg's *Birzhevye vedomosti* a few days later. "The time for threats is past," Sukhomlinov began. "Russia no longer fears foreign threats, and Russian public opinion has no further reason for uneasiness. . . . Russia as well as her ruler desires peace," he insisted, "but she is also armed for an emergency."[112] According to the War Minister, the army was well prepared and ready to face any crisis that might come upon the Empire from any direction.

Sazonov and the German ambassador discussed the inflammatory articles that had appeared in the Berlin and St. Petersburg papers in February and March in a sober fashion. Each accepted the other's assurances that neither he nor his government had been involved and that neither shared the views that the articles expressed.[113] Yet the battle of words had only just begun. More, and more bitter, statements were to follow.

When Baron Taube's friends, including at least one cabinet minister, assembled for their next discussion, he found them gripped by a deepening sense of doom. "During the past few days, I have given a great deal of thought to this avalanche that is carrying us toward war," their host said at one point. "At all costs we must try to open our Emperor's eyes to the danger. . . . Someone—someone among us—must have the courage, as in [Hans Christian] Andersen's fairy tale, to tell the Emperor that he has no clothes!"[114] All agreed that the subject of Russia's foreign policy ordinarily could not be raised unless the Emperor asked their opinion and that he was unlikely to do so. They therefore decided that Taube, who had been invited to speak about the history of Austro-Russian relations at the annual meeting of the Imperial Russian Historical Society, which the Emperor always attended, should add a few remarks that related to the dangers of Russia's present situation.

Baron Taube thought his friends were "grasping at straws," but agreed to make the attempt. He found Nicholas "particularly cheerful, animated, and friendly" as the evening began. Then, as he began to discuss the events of the months leading up to the Crimean War's outbreak—events that offered "a very close analogy to our present-day diplomatic history"—the Emperor grew "anxious, uneasy, almost displeased. I saw him in front of me," Taube remembered, "his head bent over a scrap of paper on which he doodled nervously." Apprehensive, and somewhat unsure of his course, Taube told himself that "the wine has been poured; it must be drunk," and continued. After the meeting, Nicholas thanked him politely for his remarks and noted that they "merited particular attention."[115] Yet neither Nicholas nor his chief ministers profited from the lessons that could be learned from the earlier failings of Russian foreign policy. The battle of words continued, and tension between Russia and Germany mounted.

On April 12, 1914, Professor Pavel Mitrofanov, a St. Petersburg University historian who may well have been present at Taube's lecture a fortnight earlier, sent an open letter to Hans Delbrück, his former professor at the University of Berlin. The German Empire, he insisted "was the principle enemy of Russia. . . . The Russia of today demands respect for its honor and consideration of its interests," Mitrofanov continued. "War with Germany would be a misfortune, but we shall not shrink from the bitter necessity, if it becomes really necessary." Professor Delbrück hastened to publish his former student's letter in the *Preussische Jahrbücher* at the beginning of June. His reply concluded with the warning that "if

Russia sees it as her mission to dominate Europe and Asia—well, we
see it as the mission of Germany to guard Europe and Asia from this
domination of the Muscovites."[116]

Delbrück's use of the term "Muscovite," which recalled a time
when Russia had been a backward nation bemired in medieval superstition beyond the eastern fringe of Europe, had been readily chosen
to give the greater offense, and the outraged statements by two
respected professors created a sensation throughout Europe. Yet
Europeans and Russians had hardly begun to discuss these polemics
before even more offensive and bellicose statements appeared. In
mid-June, *Birzhevye vedomosti* published another article assumed to
have been inspired, if not actually written, by Sukhomlinov, which
bore the ominous title "Russia is ready; France must be ready too!"
After comparing the size of the peacetime armies of Europe's major
powers, and noting that Russia's recruit levies had increased by
almost 30 percent that year, the article explained that "these army
increases in peace time are exclusively intended to effect a rapid
mobilization. . . . Russia and France want no war, but Russia is ready,
and France must be so, too."[117] This was a gauntlet crudely thrown
before a German sovereign inordinately proud of his army and
neurotically sensitive about his honor. "At last the Russians have
shown their hand!" the Kaiser exploded when he read a translation
in the German press. "Anyone in Germany who still does not believe
that Franco-Russia is not working at high pressure for an early war
against us . . . deserves to be sent straight to the Dalldorff lunatic
asylum."[118]

Only a fortnight separated Europe from the tragedy at Sarajevo
that brought the tensions of European affairs to a new fever pitch.
"Any insignificant conflict of interests between Russia and Austria-
Hungary may set the torch of war alight," Germany's Chancellor
warned the Kaiser.[119] But few were prepared to heed his words, and
all of Europe seemed caught up in a moment of breathless waiting.
"War is terrible," said an article in *Utro Rossii*, the Moscow daily
published by the great merchant lord Pavel Riabushinskii. "But
more terrible is the nightmare of constantly expecting war."[120] The
phrase was sadly reminiscent of those fatalistic words Nicholas him-

self had uttered a few hours before the Japanese had attacked Port Arthur a decade before. "War is war, and peace is peace," he had told General Kuropatkin then. "But this business of not knowing either way is agonizing."[121] By midsummer 1914, the lines of conflict in Europe were drawn with irrevocable firmness. "All right!" exclaimed Kaiser Wilhelm on July 25. "On with it!"[122] He had less than a week to wait.

CHAPTER XII
The Drums of War

"Some damned foolish thing in the Balkans," Bismarck once had said, would set off the next great war in Europe.[1] In the twenty-five years following his retirement from European affairs, Balkan politics had grown more complex, their tensions more explosive, as a new alignment of forces filled the vacuum left by Turkey's recent retreat from the European continent. These new Balkan nations had trod long and arduous paths to freedom. Now they were impatient to realize those cherished dreams of self-aggrandizement that infidel legions had dashed a half-millennium before. Not content to await the slow turning of history's pages, the newly independent Balkan states unsettled the grand scheme of alliances and alignments that had charted the course of European affairs and preserved the peace for many decades.

Of all the new Balkan nations, Serbia was perhaps the most volatile. Certainly her national policy was the most directly attuned to irredentist aims, and she harbored some of the most ardent nationalist sentiment on the continent. Serb nationalism was particularly intense because it combined contradictory revolutionary and evolutionary hopes. Col. Dragutin Dimitriević, a man known for his daring and magnetic personality, who still bore in his body the three bullets that had struck him when he helped to murder Serbia's King Alexander Obrenović and Queen Draga in 1903, insisted that assassination and political violence must be the chief instruments for effective political action. Nikola Pašić, the founder of the Radical party who later became Serbia's Minister of Foreign Affairs and Prime Minister, urged his nation to become the "Piedmont of the Balkans," the leader of a rising tide of moral and political forces that would eventually flow together into a large Yugoslav state. Sometimes able to join in common action, but more often torn by conflict, these currents of Serb nationalism were embodied in two famous political organizations founded at the time of the Bosnian annexation crisis and the Balkan wars.[2]

The more moderate of the two was *Narodna Odbrana* (the People's Defense), which took its name from its avowed intention to drive Austrians from the Balkans. It was formed the day after Austria annexed Bosnia-Hercegovina. On October 7, 1908, Serbia's Foreign Minister Milovan Milanović and Nikola Pašić held a meeting at Belgrade's town hall to announce its formation "to protect and promote our interests in the annexed provinces."[3] Certain that Serbia and Austria-Hungary soon must go to war, the founders set out to prepare all Serbs for the coming conflict. "Union with our brothers near and far across the frontier, and our other friends in the world is one of the chief tasks of *Narodna Odbrana*," they announced.[4] Not content to give public lectures about the "duties of

Serbia and its people," *Narodna Odbrana* planned special insurgent groups "for fighting as independent units" against Austrians everywhere. These were to operate, the founders explained, "in advance of our regiments and strike terror into the enemy rear."[5]

When international opinion urged *Narodna Odbrana* to renounce insurgent activities after the Bosnian crisis had passed, Colonel Dimitriević refused.[6] With several of the comrades who had proved their loyalty in the 1903 assassinations, he formed *Ujedinjenje ili Smrt* (Unification or Death) in 1911. More commonly known as the Black Hand, *Ujedinjenje ili Smrt* acclaimed "terrorist action over intellectual propaganda" and swore to fight all enemies outside Serbia with every weapon at its disposal. Secrecy and loyalty governed every act. Sponsors of new members had to pledge their own lives to guarantee the loyalty of the men they recruited. In a dark room lit by a single candle, the new men swore an oath upon dagger, pistol, and crucifix "to be faithful unto death" and to "be ready to make any sacrifice" for the cause of Serbian liberation and unity. Once they had sworn the oath, members received a number by which they were identified. Only the handful who sat on the Black Hand's Central Council knew their real names.[7]

The *Narodna Odbrana* and the Black Hand soon established ties with *Mlada Bosna* (Young Bosnia), a revolutionary group in Austrian-held Bosnia-Hercegovina dedicated to assassination, terrorism, and South Slav unity. More a loosely connected assortment of secret revolutionary cells than an actual political organization, *Mlada Bosna* was led by Vladimir Gaćinović, the son of a local priest, who had won overnight fame for his *Death of a Hero*, a pamphlet that glorified the first Yugoslav revolutionary martyr Bogdan Žerajić. "The Serb revolutionary," Gaćinović wrote, "must be an artist and a conspirator, must have a talent for strength and suffering, must be a martyr and a plotter . . . who will wage war for the unfortunate and downtrodden. Revolution never comes from despair," he insisted, "but out of revolutionary thought."[8] The Black Hand supported Gaćinović's efforts to establish a network of revolutionary cells *(kružoci)* in Bosnia-Hercegovina with advice and money. With Black Hand support, *Mlada Bosna* terrorists slipped into Serbia, where some of the Black Hand's leading members held high army posts and could give them special training. Once they had become trained killers, these young men slipped back into Austrian-held Bosnia to found new revolutionary cells. Led by Gaćinović's friend, the schoolmaster Danilo Ilić, an especially strong cell grew up in Sarajevo, for five hundred years Bosnia's capital and still its principal city.[9]

Toward the end of 1913, Ilić and his best friend Gavrilo Princip decided that the Sarajevo cell must carry out some dramatic assassination to show their hatred for the Austrians and to proclaim their devotion to the cause of South Slav unity. They first chose the governor of Bosnia-Hercegovina, General Oskar Potiorek, as their target, and there is some considerable evidence that the Black Hand's Colonel Dimitrievic was deeply involved in their plot from its beginning. Several months later, they learned to their delight that Archduke Franz Ferdinand, heir to the Austrian throne, would visit their city, and they shifted their attention to him.[10] At that point, Princip was studying for his final examinations at Belgrade's gymnasium. Quickly, he recruited Nedeljko Čabrinović and Trifko Grabež, like himself ardent Bosnian patriots, who had pledged their lives to the struggle against the Austrians. As sons of desperately poor peasants, all had good reason to hate the Austrians who ruled their land. "I have seen our people being ruined more and more," Princip later confessed. "That is why I decided to take revenge. I have no regrets at all."[11] Black Hand agents supplied them with four 9mm Browning semiautomatic pistols and six hand grenades, taught them how to use them, and arranged for them to return to Bosnia with their weapons undetected by the Austrian border police. Once in Sarajevo, they planned their attempt for June 28, when Franz Ferdinand and his wife, formerly the Countess Sophie Chotek, now Duchess of Hohenberg, would be in the city to celebrate their fourteenth wedding anniversary after having observed the nearby maneuvers of the Austrian army the day before.[12]

On Sunday, June 28, 1914, South Slavs celebrated *Vidov Dan* —the Festival of St. Vitus—as a day of national sadness and patriotic rejoicing. It was the sad 525th anniversary of Kossovo, the battle at which their army had been overwhelmed by the Turks in 1389, but it also was the joyous anniversary of the moment when, just hours after their defeat, a Serb hero had gone to the tent of the victorious sultan and killed him. Quite probably it was the day's significance as the anniversary of the assassination of a foreign oppressor that was foremost in the minds of Princip and his group.

The weather was radiant, a glorious early summer day. At 10:00 A.M., a procession of four automobiles entered Sarajevo from the south and drove along the Appel Quay toward the town hall, where a formal reception was planned. Tall and stern, the monotony of his features broken by a moustache every bit as luxuriant as the Kaiser's, Franz Ferdinand was in full dress uniform, bedecked in all his orders, while his wife, a tall, striking woman with flashing dark eyes that hinted at her proud Czech heritage, wore a white gown that almost sparkled in the brilliant sunlight. It seemed the beginning of a happy celebration as the royal couple chatted with General Potiorek and waved to the cheering crowds that lined the street. As the Archduke's auto passed the Čumurja Bridge that spanned the Miljačka River across the quay from the Austro-Hungarian bank, Čabrinović struck the detonator of his grenade against a lamppost and tossed it at his target. It struck the auto a glancing blow, rolled under the one that followed, and exploded. One of Potiorek's aides was wounded, but the royal party continued safely on its way, the Archduke now grim and angry. When the police told him that Čabrinović had been arrested, he muttered: "Hang him as soon as you can, or Vienna will send him a decoration," probably thinking of those Hungarian lords at the Austrian court who despised him and of the ardent Austrian nationalists who opposed his plans to give the South Slavs more rights within the empire.[13]

Although convinced that there was no further danger, General Potiorek decided to cancel the rest of the day's celebration and gave orders to proceed directly from the town hall to the railway station. On the way, there was a mix-up and the Archduke's auto had to stop for a moment near the Lateiner Bridge. As fate would have it, Princip, armed and waiting, stood just a few meters away. Calmly he stepped forward and fired at point-blank range. His first shot severed Franz Ferdinand's jugular vein, and a thin jet of blood spurted from his mouth. Quickly, Princip fired again. Later he insisted that his second shot was meant for Potiorek, but it was the Duchess Sophie who collapsed in a crumpled heap on top of her husband as the echo died away. Both were fatally wounded. Princip then tried to shoot himself, but the police seized him. "They began to beat me," he complained at his trial. "They dragged me away, covered with blood, to the police headquarters, where I was beaten again."[14] Long before the police got their captive to their headquarters, both of Princip's victims were dead.[15] It was "one of the most amateurish regicides of modern times," one expert recently wrote. "The success of the conspiracy was due mainly to sheer luck."[16] Reported the British consul general from Budapest, "It is surely the irony of fate that the future ruler who was commonly regarded as a champion of South Slav rights [within the Habsburg monarchy] should have fallen a victim to the criminal propaganda of Pan-Serbian agitation."[17]

"War against Austro-Hungary was our principal objective," the Black Hand's Colonel Božin Šimić later confessed. "We aimed at the creation of a single Slav state."[18] Soon they were to have their war. As word of the Sarajevo murders flashed along the telegraph wires that crisscrossed the Eurasian continent, men and women around the world waited with bated breath to know the outcome. Everywhere, stern and sober statesmen urged moderation and restraint upon the justifiably outraged Habsburgs. Heinrich von Tschirschky, German ambassador to Vienna, "calmly but very emphatically and seriously . . . [warned Austria] against hasty measures."[19] Similarly in Berlin, Under-Secretary of Foreign Affairs Alfred Zimmermann, who unexpectedly found himself in charge of the German Foreign Office, urged "great prudence" upon the Austrian ambassador and strongly advised "against making humiliating demands on Serbia."[20] "The sympathy of the world was with Austria," Sir Edward Grey recalled some years later. "There seemed to be good reason for the hope that [Austria] . . . would handle it in such a way as not to involve Europe in the consequences."[21]

Yet Grey reckoned without the virulent nationalism that had

long permeated the Austrian high command and that now began to spread to those very moderate groups that once had helped to hold such extremism in check. England's consul general in Budapest was struck by "the wave of blind hatred for Serbia and everything Serbian that is sweeping over the country" and warned that, despite their long-standing dislike for the dead Archduke, the Hungarians seemed "willing to go to any lengths . . . to revenge themselves on the despised and hated enemy."[22] From Vienna, the British ambassador added that "there is ground to regard almost all sections of the population as being just now blindly incensed against the Serbians" and warned that "many persons holding quite moderate and sensible views on foreign affairs" had begun to insist that Austria must strike "such a blow [against Serbia] as will reduce that country to impotence for the future."[23] More ominous, General Conrad von Hötzendorff, the Austrian Chief of Staff, had long advocated a war against Serbia and thought of the Bosnian annexation crisis and the Balkan wars as tragically missed opportunities. Conrad now insisted that "Austria-Hungary cannot let the challenge pass with cool equanimity. . . . The Monarchy has been seized by the throat and forced to choose between letting itself be strangled and making a last effort to defend itself." Conrad insisted that "the Habsburg Monarchy is left no other device than to cut the Gordian knot" if she hoped to prevent "her enemies within and without" from bringing about "the disintegration of the ancient empire."[24] To his delight, he received the Kaiser's full support. "It is solely the affair of Austria, what she plans to do in this case," Wilhelm remarked. "Serbia must be disposed of, *and* that right *soon!*"[25]

At lunch with Austria's Ambassador Count Szögyényi on July 5, the Kaiser issued his famous "blank check" that gave Austria almost unrestrained freedom to settle her differences with the Serbs. "His Majesty authorized me to convey to our august Sovereign," Szögyényi telegraphed to Vienna that evening, that "we may reckon on full support from Germany." He went on to add that the support was especially certain "in respect to any measure we might take against Serbia" and that "he would deplore our not taking advantage of the present moment which is so favorable to us." Nothing could have been more to General Conrad's liking. The Kaiser had even said that "if matters went to the length of a war between Austria-Hungary and Russia," Austria could be certain that "Germany in her customary loyalty as an ally would stand at our side."[26] With an appalling lack of good sense and foresight, Wilhelm took his ambassador to task for urging moderation upon the Austrians. "Who authorized him to do so?" he wrote angrily in the margin of a report that described Tschirschky's sober efforts to calm the inflamed passions that raged in Vienna. "It is high time a clean sweep was made of the Serbs."[27]

Thus the stage was set for a drama, the likes of which the world had yet to see. Convinced that Serbia had supported the assassins at Sarajevo and certain of Germany's full support, Austria's response would be neither moderate nor restrained as her statesmen set out to draft an ultimatum that was tantamount to a declaration of war. "Better a fearful end than endless fears," one of them exclaimed as they set down a list of demands that the Serbs could not possibly accept without complete humiliation.[28] So that France and Russia would not be able to consult immediately once their ultimatum was delivered, the Austrian government instructed its ambassador in Belgrade to present it precisely at 6:00 P.M. on July 23. At that hour, France's President Poincaré would have just ended his state visit to St. Petersburg and would be en route to Paris. The Serbs were to be allowed no more than forty-eight hours to reply. There was little that could be done in that time other than capitulate or go to war. "Now we'll settle scores with Serbia," Austria's Foreign Minister Count Berchtold is supposed to have rejoiced at that point.[29]

"It means a European war!" Russia's Foreign Minister Sazonov exclaimed when he learned of the Austrian ultimatum the next morning.[30] Immediately, he summoned Austria's Ambassador Count Szápáry. "You are setting fire to Europe," Sazonov warned. "The fact is you mean war and you have burnt your bridges."[31] So convinced was he that Austria intended "to crush Serbia, with no concern for Russia's interests whatsoever,"[32] that Sazonov had told England's Ambassador Buchanan a week before that "an Austrian ultimatum at Belgrade could not leave Russia indifferent, and she might be forced to take some precautionary military measures."[33] Indeed, orders for those measures were about to be given. By the time the Austrian ambassador delivered his government's ultimatum to the Serbian authorities in Belgrade, Sazonov, a number of senior General Staff officers, and even Nicholas himself had begun to talk of war. That very day, Sazonov told Buchanan privately that "he personally thought that Russia would at any rate have to mobilize," and the worried ambassador warned Sir Edward Grey that "an Austrian attack on Serbia would in all probability force Russia to intervene."[34] Within thirty-six hours, Nicholas himself declared that "it was necessary to support Serbia, even if it were necessary to proclaim mobilization and begin military operations."[35] In a very dangerous sense, the Russians had given their Serb allies a check that was every bit as blank as the one the Kaiser had so thoughtlessly bestowed upon his equally unstable Austrian partner at the beginning of July. Even before the Serbs drafted their reply, war was very near to breaking out in the Balkans.

For Serbia's statesmen, the Austrian ultimatum left no room for honest diplomatic negotiation. As one expert remarked many years ago, it had been "deliberately framed with the expectation that it would be rejected,"[36] and, indeed, there was no other course that Serbia could follow and still preserve a decent measure of self-respect as an independent nation. "Well, there is nothing to do but die fighting," Minister of Public Instruction Ljuba Jovanović said as he arose from the table around which he and his colleagues were sitting to discuss the ultimatum. Quickly, they informed Serbia's ambassadors that "the demands are such that no Serbian Government could accept them in their entirety."[37] Then, Prime Minister Pašić and several other ministers settled down to prepare a reply that would preserve Serbia's national honor, yet concede enough ground to win sympathy from European public opinion for their apparent moderation.

Once certain of Russian support, their resolve stiffened. Until the afternoon of July 25 they worked, crossing out and adding words and phrases in a feverish effort to prepare by that evening a reply that would give ground on all reasonable points, but not violate their

nation's laws or impinge upon her sovereignty. They were still edit-
ing the final text at 5:00 P.M. Forty-five minutes later—just fifteen
minutes before Austria's deadline—they sealed the fateful envelope.
"Well, who will take it?" Pašić asked. None of his colleagues spoke
a word. "Very well, then I shall take it myself," he said and marched
off for what would be his last meeting with Austria's Ambassador
Baron Giesl.[38] Giesl gave the Serbian reply only the most cursory
glance and pronounced it unacceptable. In less than an hour, he, his
wife, and his entire legation staff were en route to Vienna. Before
seven o'clock that evening, their train had crossed the frontier. "So
it has come after all," muttered the aged Habsburg Emperor Franz
Joseph sadly when he received the news some two hours later.[39]
Serbia had already mobilized her armed forces; Austria hastened to
do the same. If their allies could not pull them back from the
crumbling precipice on which they stood, all of Europe would be
plunged into a holocaust.

On July 28, Austria declared war on Serbia, and the attention
of the world shifted to Russia. Would Nicholas order a mobilization
of his armies against the Austrians? And, if so, what would be
Germany's response? At that point, Russia's statesmen and military
planners concentrated their attention upon what the *General Staff
Gazette* called the "premobilization period," or, in the precise language of the regulation that Nicholas himself had approved early in
1913, "the period preparatory to war."[40] When Russia entered that
phase of preparation on July 25,[41] France's Ambassador Paléologue
remarked, almost with a sense of fatalistic resignation, "This time,
it is war."[42]

Yet the Russians claimed that "premobilization" was not war
or, even, partial mobilization, and they insisted that nothing in their
actions was directed against Germany. For several days, Russian
planners debated whether to take the next step and order a partial
mobilization against Austria or—knowing that if Austria mobilized
against her, Germany must do likewise—to go ahead with plans for
a full-scale mobilization. The sad truth was that effective plans for
a partial mobilization against Austria had never been prepared. "Any

partial mobilization," General Danilov later explained, "would have been an improvisation at best," and would have thrown any subsequent general mobilization into utter chaos.[43] Knowing all too well the havoc that any such order would create, most General Staff officers simply assumed that, when it came, the mobilization would be a general one. The necessary orders had already been signed, and only the Tsar's signature was needed to put them into effect. By July 25, almost no one in the inner circles of Russia's government seriously thought that war could be avoided, but Chief of Staff General Nikolai Ianushkevich pursued the charade for several days more nonetheless. As late as 3:00 P.M. on July 29, he swore to Germany's military attaché that no order for any sort of mobilization had been given and even offered him written assurances. "I considered that I had a perfect right to put such a statement into writing," he later explained. "No mobilization had taken place up to that moment [for] I still had the decree for mobilization in my pocket."[44]

By July 29, patience in Berlin had worn dangerously thin. "Further continuation of Russian mobilization measures [that is, the activities actually connected with the "premobilization period"] would force us to mobilize and in that case a European war could scarcely be prevented," Germany's Chancellor Bethmann Hollweg telegraphed to Count Friedrich Pourtalès, the German ambassador in St. Petersburg, early that afternoon.[45] Yet to heed Germany's stern and urgent warning would have left Russia unprepared to face an attack from the partly mobilized forces of Austria and would have made it impossible for her to defend her Serb allies whose capital already was under heavy Austrian artillery bombardment. "We cannot accede to Germany's wishes," Sazonov telegraphed later that day to Izvolskii in Paris. "We have no alternative but to hasten our own military preparations and assume that war is probably inevitable."[46]

Reluctantly, Nicholas consented to a general mobilization of Russia's armies on July 29. About nine o'clock that evening, less than six hours after Ianushkevich had assured Germany's military attaché that no mobilization order had been given, General Dobrorolskii, Chief of the General Staff's Mobilization Section, ordered the Director of St. Petersburg's Central Telegraph Office to make ready to send the general mobilization order. At just that moment, a desperate and frustrated Ianushkevich called to tell him that the Tsar had changed his mind.[47] "I think a direct understanding between your government and Vienna possible and desirable," the Kaiser had telegraphed him that evening. "My government is continuing its exertions to promote it."[48] Timid in war and vacillating in peace, Nicholas had drawn back at the last moment and had left Russia's final military preparations in danger of plunging into hopeless disarray.

Convinced that the Kaiser still might mediate the crisis, Nicholas now would agree to no more than the partial mobilization that, as his generals knew all too well, could be nothing more than "an improvisation at best."[49] "Everything possible must be done to save the peace," he told Count Frederiks, Minister of the Imperial Court. "I will not become responsible for a monstrous slaughter."[50] Stern and tight-lipped, Ianushkevich and Minister of War Sukhomlinov set out to change his mind once again. "Mobilization is not a mechanical process that one can arrest at will, as one can a wagon, and then set it in motion again," Sukhomlinov warned.[51] At the same time, Ianushkevich tried to explain that "such a counterorder would throw our whole plan into confusion from top to bottom, and that a new mobilization would not only be slow, but impossible."[52] For the moment, Nicholas could not be persuaded. The clock moved past midnight to July 30. Two more days of peace remained.

Ianushkevich, Sukhomlinov, and the archconservative President of the Duma Mikhail Rodzianko were fearful that if Germany, with her well-known ability to mobilize rapidly, should declare war, Russia would be caught in a terrible twilight zone between the "period preparatory to war" and mobilization. They now urged Sazonov to try his hand at persuading the vacillating Tsar to order full mobilization. "War has already become inevitable and we are in danger of losing it even before we have time to draw our sword from its sheath,"[53] Ianushkevich warned. Nicholas must be made to understand, Rodzianko added, that "the Russian people will never forgive any delay that might throw the nation into fatal complications."[54] Rodzianko had just returned to St. Petersburg from Germany and had seen "German cavalry in battle dress and ready for action" all along the frontier.[55] The Kaiser had not yet given the order for general mobilization, but Rodzianko's description of troop columns made Sazonov think of Field Marshal von Moltke's remark that "the German army is always in a state of continual mobilization."[56] Certain that Russia faced mortal danger, Sazonov begged his Emperor for an audience and Nicholas agreed to receive him at three o'clock that afternoon. If he succeeded in persuading the Tsar to withdraw his last-minute postponement of general mobilization, Sazonov was to telephone Ianushkevich immediately, after which, the determined Chief of Staff swore that he would issue the necessary orders and then "retire from sight [and] smash my telephone . . . so that I cannot be found to give any orders for a new postponement of general mobilization."[57]

Just a few moments before the appointed time, Sazonov stepped into Nicholas's anteroom at the Peterhof summer palace. "You think that it is too late to save the peace?" the Tsar asked. Sazonov replied that it definitely was.[58] He then spoke for the better part of an hour about the danger Russia faced and the even greater danger that would befall her if a German mobilization order caught her forces entangled in the terrible confusion that any partial mobilization order was bound to create. "We had been driven into a dead end from which there was no escape," Sazonov recalled. "We either had to unsheath the sword to defend our vital interests and await the enemy's attack with weapons in hand . . . or cover ourselves with everlasting shame, refuse to fight, and throw ourselves upon his mercy." The time for war had come. "You are right," Nicholas finally said. "There is nothing left for us to do but await the attack. Give my order for mobilization to the Chief of the General Staff."[59]

Fearful about "the outcome of that terrible struggle that had been thrust upon Russia and for which she was not yet prepared," but convinced that Russia's best defense now lay in full and rapid mobilization, Sazonov went down to the ground floor of the Peterhof Palace and telephoned General Ianushkevich. "Now you can smash your telephone," he said. "Give your orders, my good general, and then—disappear for the rest of the day."[60] Once again Ianush-kevich sent General Dobrorolskii to have the Ministers of War, Admiralty, and Internal Affairs countersign the mobilization order. About 5:30 P.M. Dobrorolskii returned to the Central Telegraph Office, the machines stilled and ready to send his orders. This time, there were no telephone calls, no sudden instructions to turn back. At six o'clock the order went out, flashing simultaneously along a dozen lines, to all parts of the Russian Empire:

> HIS MAJESTY ORDERS: THE ARMY AND NAVY TO BE PLACED ON WAR FOOTING. TO THIS END RESERVISTS AND HORSES TO BE CALLED UP ACCORDING TO THE MOBILIZATION PLAN OF THE YEAR 1910.[61]

In less than two hours, the confirmations began to come in. At 7:55 P.M., the first military commander in the Warsaw Military District, whose units faced those of Germany, sent his reply. At 8:02, another confirmation came from the western front, and at 8:15, another. Throughout the night, local officials in tens of thousands of Russian hamlets put up the red cards that signaled mobilization to millions of illiterate peasant reservists. For Russia, there was now no turning back. Only if Austria and Germany made concessions and dared to face Russia's general mobilization with the forces not yet assembled on their eastern fronts could war be avoided. That was a risk almost too grave to be contemplated. As the calendar turned to August 31, peace in Europe no longer hung by a slender thread but by a filament so fine that it could scarcely be discerned. "The lamps are going out all over Europe," Sir Edward Grey told a friend. "We shall not see them lit again in our lifetime."[62]

While Grey continued to view the drama from his particular perspective, the *Kadet* leader Miliukov noted that in the depths of rural Russia, "an eternal quiet," a calm born of undisturbed insularity and supreme indifference, reigned supreme. "We are *ka-lutskie*"—we are natives of Kaluga province—Miliukov recalled some of the peasants saying, and that simple statement offered dramatic proof of the obstacles that stood in the way of any effort to stir up a sustained sense of outraged nationalism among the hundred million peasants who filled the Russian land.[63] They could just as easily have said, "we are from Tobolsk," or from Kazan, or Kostroma, or Tambov. "We are *kalutskie*" was a poignant, yet disturbing, reminder that Russian peasants were concerned only about what happened in their native regions. They had little understanding about what distinguished Germans from Frenchmen, or Frenchmen from Austrians, or Austrians from Serbs; nor did they care. For them, all foreigners were *nemtsy*—a term derived from the Russian verb meaning to become dumb—and they had little interest in them. Serbia was unknown. That its capital city continued to shudder under Austrian bombardment was of no more concern to them than what might be happening on the surface of the moon.

"God is high above, and the Tsar is far away," Russian peasants had said for centuries as they tried to explain their isolation from divine and temporal authority. Certainly, the Kaiser, the French President, the Habsburg Emperor, and the English King were even farther away and much less important. Russia's *narod* had emotional attachments to Mother Russia and the Blessed Virgin. But no one dared predict how long they could sustain their patriotism under the withering fire of the German and Austrian machine guns and heavy artillery they would have to face in Russia's Polish provinces in 1914 and 1915. "A Tambov peasant is willing to fight to defend the province of Tambov, but a war for Poland, in his opinion, is foreign and useless," Ianushkevich would write in 1915. "The soldiers therefore surrender en masse."[64]

If peasants viewed their world in insular terms, the comparatively more sophisticated, more literate workers who filled the cities and factories of the Empire focused their attention on other issues. While peasants so often seemed supremely indifferent, peasants-turned-workers were filled with indignation, even hatred, for the managers and mill owners who pressed them to labor in terrible conditions. For them, the first half of 1914 had been a time of great turmoil, as they had launched strike after strike against their employers. Convinced that factory owners and plant managers, not Germans and Austrians, were their greatest enemies, and their faith in the Tsar long since shattered by Bloody Sunday, they could not be expected to bear the burdens of war with sustained enthusiasm.

The Russians also faced technological and logistical problems that could not be dealt with by stirring speeches and ardent prayers. Urged on by General Iakov Zhilinskii, Commander of the Warsaw Military District, whose men would be among the first to face Germany's advancing divisions, Russian military planners had promised to have twenty-seven infantry and twenty cavalry divisions (about eight hundred thousand men) at the Empire's western front ready to meet any German attack by the fifteenth day of mobilization.[65] These were dreams born of an almost criminal disregard for the simple fact that Russia's railway network could not hope to move such numbers of men and supplies in the space of a fortnight. Germany had seven times more railroads for every hundred square kilometers of territory than did European Russia, and her quartermasters were estimated to be sixteen times more efficient in moving troops and supplies along them. Such statistics were disturbing in themselves. Coupled with Russia's need to move every soldier a distance of 900 to 1,000 *versty* during mobilization, while Germany and Austria needed to move theirs only 200 to 300, they promised disaster.[66]

Knowing many of these failings, Sazonov wrote of a time not long before the war when he "had the conviction that, although we could foresee the course of events, we were powerless to change them. . . . A vast gulf stood between our declared aims and their achievement. This always was Russia's greatest misfortune."[67] That misfortune now was transformed into catastrophe. At 12:23 P.M. on July 31, just eighteen hours after General Dobrorolskii had sent out the mobilization orders from St. Petersburg's Central Telegraph Office, the Habsburg Emperor announced the general mobilization of all Austrian forces. Then, at 11:35 P.M., Count Pourtalès presented an ultimatum in St. Petersburg. The Kaiser, he informed Sazonov, demanded that Russia halt her general mobilization by noon on August 1. "We are only a finger's breadth from war," Pourtalès wrote to his friend Count Frederiks early the next morning. "I seek everywhere means to avert a misfortune."[68] However, he had already received secret coded instructions to declare war on Russia regardless of her reply to the ultimatum.[69] At seven o'clock that evening, Pourtalès returned to the Foreign Ministry to present Sazonov with a declaration of war.

There could be no turning back as war's dark shadow settled irrevocably across the continent of Europe. Still, there were a few who took heart from the carnage. The Empress Aleksandra assured the man who soon would call himself her "poor weak-willed little hubby" that the war had "lifted up spirits, cleansed the many stagnant minds, brought unity in feelings, and is a 'healthy' war in the moral sense."[70] Her absurd exaltation, expressed after almost two months of bloody fighting, only showed how isolated she was from the land and people the Romanovs ruled. For the Empire of Nicholas and Aleksandra, the end had not yet come, but it was very near from the moment the first shot was fired across the frontier that separated Russian Poland from East Prussia.

Afterword

O<small>N THE WINTER PALACE SQUARE WHERE SOLDIERS HAD SHOT</small> down unarmed workers and peasants on Bloody Sunday, the masses gathered with ikons and portraits of their Tsar and Tsarina on the afternoon after Germany declared war on Russia. This time, Nicholas appeared on the Palace balcony and asked for their help in the struggles that lay ahead. In reply, the people knelt as one to sing *"Bozhe Tsaria khrani!"*—"God Save the Tsar!"[1] Then, they stormed the German Embassy, a gross edifice newly built of red

Finnish granite that stood on St. Isaac's Square as a monument to all that was rude and tasteless in the Germany of Wilhelm II. As the enraged crowd turned it into a shambles, the police looked on in the benevolent manner they usually reserved for those times when they faced pogroms against the Jews.[2]

The Great War thus began, as all wars began in Russia, with indiscriminate outbursts of outraged national feeling. Even reactionaries and extreme liberals in the Duma proclaimed their unity in the common cause of victory. Vladimir Purishkevich, leader of the right wing, hastened to embrace Miliukov, his longtime enemy on the left. In return, Miliukov's newspaper, *Rech,* urged his followers to set aside their "domestic disputes" with Purishkevich and his allies for the higher purpose of national unity. "Our first duty is to preserve our nation's unity and integrity, and to defend her position as a world power," *Rech* proclaimed. "Our first and only task at this moment is to support our soldiers."[3] In contrast to the Russo-Japanese War, when they had proclaimed "the worse the better" to support their struggle for political concessions, Petersburg's intelligentsia now rallied to their nation's side.[4]

But the war's outcome did not hinge upon Miliukov, Purishkevich, or their allies in the Duma. As in all of Russia's wars, it was the peasants who did the fighting and the dying, and any hope for victory depended very heavily upon their resolve to fight for Tsar and Country. That fall, hundreds of thousands of peasants mobilized all over Russia in answer to their nation's call. In the villages of the Far North where early frosts were about to turn the birch forests a rich gold, in Siberia, in the Black Soil lands, in the Ukraine where the rich harvest still stood ripening in the fields, and in the lands of New Russia along the Black Sea, the same sad scene was repeated as sturdy peasant lads solemnly shouldered their rucksacks and bade clumsy farewells to their loved ones. Most would never see their mothers, wives, or sweethearts again. Those who marched away in the late summer and early fall of 1914, with their knee-high boots, their rough smocks gathered at the waist by sturdy cord belts, were soon to die in the marshes and forests of Poland, East Prussia, and Galicia.

Very soon, these peasant soldiers faced battle against the armies of the Central Powers without even the weapons to defend themselves. Russia entered the war only to find that there were one million fewer rifles in her arsenals than the number of men who were mobilized, and the same arsenals proved to hold almost 600 million rounds of rifle ammunition less than expected. Soon, the shortage of rifles soared beyond the limits of all belief. According to the best estimates, between August 1914 and the end of 1917, Russia's soldiers needed 17.7 million rifles, while domestic production, foreign imports, and diligent efforts to salvage abandoned weapons on the battlefield produced only 11,365,000, for an overall shortage of more than 6 million.[5] According to Nicholas's own admission little more than three months after the war began, reinforcements regularly arrived at the front unarmed. "Half of them have no rifles," he lamented to Aleksandra. "The troops are losing masses and there is nobody to collect them on the battlefields."[6]

Not only rifles were in short supply at the end of July 1914, however. The entire Russian army had only sixty batteries of heavy artillery with which to face the Austrians and the Germans, while the Germans alone had 381 to direct against the Russians. None of Russia's heavy artillery equaled the German weapons in range and caliber. Every German infantry division was supported by exactly twice as many batteries of light artillery as its Russian counterpart, and the Germans had ample shells, while the Russians sometimes had none. Even under the unrelenting pressure of desperate quartermasters and army commanders, Russia's factories could raise their output of three-inch shells to only *one-seventieth* of the battlefield commanders' *lowest* estimate of the numbers required.[7]

A few farsighted Russian officers had seen these deficiencies well before the last days of July 1914, but a limited budget and the failings of the High Command made it impossible to set them right. In absolute terms, Russia's military budget was the smallest of any of the four major continental powers that fought the Great War, and only slightly more than half of Germany's.[8] Nor were her senior generals much more distinguished than her budget. In 1914, General Vladimir Aleksandrovich Sukhomlinov, who celebrated his sixty-sixth birthday on the fourth day of the war, still reigned over Russia's War Ministry. Sukhomlinov had seen combat for the first and last time in the Russo-Turkish War of 1877–78, in which he had served as a cavalry commander, and had won the much-coveted Cross of St. George for bravery. Thirty-six years later, that campaign remained his fondest memory and the basis of all the limited military knowledge he possessed. "As war was then, so it still remains," he would say to officers who urged the army to increase its firepower. "All these things are merely dangerous innovations." Sukhomlinov took pride in not having read a military manual of any sort in a quarter of a century. Like the great eighteenth-century Russian commander Suvorov, he still thought that cold steel—the saber, the lance, and the bayonet—was the key to victory. Machine guns, he insisted, could never stand against the bayonet assault and the cavalry charge. Russia's infantry therefore had less than one machine gun for every six hundred foot soldiers.[9]

"It was very difficult to make him work," Sazonov once said of Sukhomlinov. "But to get him to tell the truth was almost impossible."[10] In response to an offer of aid from France when Russia's armies were nearly paralyzed by shortages of weapons and ammunition, Sukhomlinov insisted that "Russia needed nothing and that she was provided with an abundant supply of guns and ammunition that would last a long time."[11] In fact, between 1908 and 1914, procurement officers had been obliged to place orders for weapons and ammunition abroad because Russia's own factories could not produce enough even to supply the needs of her peacetime forces. So shortsighted and inept were Sukhomlinov and his chief aides that they had not even the sense to prohibit such orders from going to the industries of unfriendly nations. "We had not even laid down the sound principle that orders like these should be placed only with countries allied to us," General Vasilii Gurko later confessed. Just before war broke out, Sukhomlinov's ministry actually was torn by a violent dispute about whether to order the new field artillery that would be needed to halt the Kaiser's armies from the French firm of Creusot or the gigantic Krupp works of Germany![12]

Week after week, month after month, men died by the tens of thousands on Europe's Eastern Front. In the first year of the Great War, nearly three million Russians were killed, wounded, or taken prisoner. Yet the slaughter continued with no end in sight. A small incident included in a report sent back to London by General Sir Alfred Knox, Britain's military observer with Russia's land forces, best described the terrible situation Russia's soldiers faced toward the end of the first year of fighting. Knox reported that he had seen eighteen hundred raw infantry replacements arrive at the front during a lull in a German artillery barrage. None had rifles, and therefore they were sent to wait in reserve trenches, according to Knox's flat, official prose, "until casualties in the firing line should make rifles available" for them. While they waited, the German guns began to fire again, and Knox watched in horror as "sixteen hundred of these unarmed drafts [were] churned into gruel by the enemy's guns."[13] After a year of fighting, this shameful waste of men, weapons, and supplies reached inhuman, if not outright criminal, proportions. General Knox now estimated that such slaughter had reduced the Russian army facing the Germans and Austrians to "only 650,-000 rifles, 2,590 machine guns, and 4,000 three-inch field guns" to defend a front that stretched from the Baltic port of Reval to the Carpathians.[14] If his figures were reasonably correct, it meant that Russia began the second year of the Great War with only one armed man, not always with bullets, for about every two and a half meters of front, and only three machine guns for every two kilometers along which her armies faced a well-armed enemy. Worst of all, the army of Russia, Europe's greatest producer of grain, was beginning to fight with empty bellies.

By the fall of 1915, it was clear that Russia's war effort faced collapse. "Considering the present situation at the front and in the rear of the armies," the new War Minister General Aleksei Polivanov reported to the Council of Ministers, "one can expect an irreparable catastrophe momentarily." But, he went on, "a far more horrible event threatens Russia." While his fellow ministers sat in grim anticipation of word about a crushing defeat or some new failure on the part of the General Staff, Polivanov concluded: "This morning,

His Majesty told me of his decision to personally assume the supreme command of the army."[15] Nicholas II, the Tsar who once had commanded a squadron of Hussars on summer maneuvers more than twenty years before, now was to command all of Russia's armies. The plan's absurdity was outweighed only by its tragedy. "Into what an abyss Russia is being pushed!" lamented Foreign Minister Sazonov.[16] He was not mistaken.

With the Tsar in command there was no hope—only endless dying on the part of brave soldiers who went to their deaths without boots, without food, sometimes without weapons. On the home front, France's ambassador noticed that people's faces had begun to take on a "sinister expression."[17] In February 1917, revolution came again to Russia, and this time the proletariat did not founder upon the bayonets of peasant soldiers as it had in 1905. Glimpsing their first rays of hope in almost three years, peasant soldiers this time turned their weapons against the defenders of the old order; in less than a week, neither the Romanovs nor their throne remained.

"The Revolution is dead! Long live the Revolution!" Trotskii had exclaimed when Nicholas's soldiers crushed the revolution in 1905.[18] History now proved the truth of his bold revolutionary faith. Yet, when the Revolution of 1917 freed Russians from the inept reign of the Romanovs, war's dark shadow settled heavier upon them still. The Great War ground on for another year only to be supplanted by more years of bitter civil war that raged from the Polish frontier to Russia's Pacific shores. Not until 1921 did Russians again know peace. Only then did war lift its dark shadow from the Russian land. In its wake, the people of Russia found new dreams and brighter visions—and new shadows.

Notes

CHAPTER I
1891: The Fateful Year

1. F. M. Dostoevskii, "Belye nochi," in *Polnoe sobranie sochinenii F. M. Dostoevskogo* (Leningrad, 1972), 2: 105.

2. Quoted from *Sanktpeterburgskie vedomosti*, in Paul de Laboulaye, "Souvenirs: L'Amiral Gervais à Cronstadt," *Revue de Paris* 45, no. 2 (April 15, 1938): 749.

3. Quoted in ibid., p. 752.

4. Quoted in William Langer, *The Franco-Russian Alliance, 1890–1894* (Cambridge, Mass., 1967), p. 186.

5. Paul de Laboulaye, "Souvenirs," p. 751.

6. Philippe Deschamps, *Livre d'or de l'alliance Franco-Russe* (Paris, 1898), pp. 8–9.

7. Paul de Laboulaye, "Souvenirs," p. 751.

8. Baron Boris Nol'de, *L'Alliance Franco-Russe. Les origines du système diplomatique d'avant-guerre* (Paris, 1936), p. 625.

9. Paul de Laboulaye, "Souvenirs," pp. 756–57.

10. Ibid., pp. 757–70.

11. V. N. Lamsdorf, *Dnevnik, 1891–1892* (Moscow-Leningrad, 1934), p. 159.

12. Langer, *Franco-Russian Alliance*, p. 185.

13. Anatole Leroy-Beaulieu, *Études russe et européenes* (Paris, 1897), p. 47.

14. Quoted in Robert F. Byrnes, *Pobedonostsev: His Life and Thought* (Bloomington, 1968), p. 341.

15. André de Laboulaye, "L'ambassade de Paul de Laboulaye à Saint-Pétersbourg," *Revue de Paris* 45, no. 2 (April 15, 1938): 738.

16. Nol'de, *L'Alliance Franco-Russe*, pp. 321–32.

17. Quoted in Langer, *Franco-Russian Alliance*, p. 49. See also pp. 48–49.

18. Quoted in ibid., pp. 48–49.

19. G. Giacometti, "Cinq mois de politique italienne, février–juin, 1891," *Revue des deux mondes* 107 (September 15, 1891): 403–4; George F. Kennan, *The Decline of Bismarck's European Order: Franco-Russian Relations, 1875–1890* (Princeton, 1979), pp. 398–410.

20. Quoted in Langer, *Franco-Russian Alliance*, p. 195, note 67.

21. Ibid., pp. 255–56; Ernest Daudet, *Histoire diplomatique de l'alliance Franco-Russe, 1873–1893* (Paris, 1894), pp. 281–331.

22. Lamzdorf, *Dnevnik, 1891–1892*, pp. 346–52; Nol'de, *L'Alliance Franco-Russe*, pp. 660–92.

23. George Kennan, *Siberia and the Exile System* (New York, 1891), 1: 56.

24. Harmon Tupper, *To the Great Ocean: Siberia and the Trans-Siberian Railway* (Boston and Toronto, 1965), pp. 6–7.

25. R. H. Fisher, *The Russian Fur Trade, 1550–1700* (Berkeley and Los Angeles, 1943), pp. 112–14.

26. Kennan, *Siberia and the Exile System*, 2:304.

27. A. I. Dmitriev-Mamonov and A. F. Zdiarski, *Guide to the Great Siberian Railway* (St. Petersburg, 1900), p. 71.

28. Kennan, *Siberia and the Exile System, passim;* and M. M. Gromyko et al., "Sibir'," in *Sovetskaia istoricheskaia entsiklopediia* (Moscow, 1969), 12: 830–50.

29. Quoted in Tupper, *To the Great Ocean*, p. 85.

30. V. F. Borzunov, *Proletariat Sibiri i dal'nego vostoka nakanune pervoi russkoi revoliutsii* (Moscow, 1965), pp. 21–22.

31. Quotes from ibid., pp. 125–26.

32. Quoted in ibid., p. 92.

33. Ibid., pp. 132–47.

34. Quoted in Tupper, *To the Great Ocean*, p. 4.

35. Quoted in S. V. Sabler and I. V. Sosnovskii, *Sibirskaia zheleznaia doroga v eia proshlom i nastoiashchem. Istoricheskii ocherk* (St. Petersburg, 1903), p. 448.

36. Quoted in ibid., p. 443.

37. Ibid., appendix, diagram no. 5.

38. Quoted in ibid., p. 445.

39. V. P. Semennikov, ed., *Za kulisami tsarizma. Arkhiv tibetskogo vracha Badmaeva* (Leningrad, 1925), pp. 77–80; Theodore von Laue, *Sergei Witte and the Industrialization of Russia* (New York and London, 1963), pp. 80–88.

40. Quoted in Sabler and Sosnovskii, *Sibirskaia zheleznaia doroga*, p. 443.

41. John P. McKay, *Pioneers for Profit: Foreign Entrepreneurship and Russian Industrialization, 1885–1913* (Chicago, 1970), pp. 4–5.

42. P. A. Khromov, *Ekonomicheskoe razvitie Rossii v XIX–XX ve-kakh* (Moscow, 1950), pp. 456–62.

43. Quoted in von Laue, *Sergei Witte*, p. 149, n. 46.

44. Michael Florinsky, *Russia: A History and An Interpretation* (New York, 1968), 2: 1106.

45. Quoted in von Laue, *Sergei Witte*, p. 24.

46. Ibid., p. 106; P. I. Liashchenko, *Istoriia narodnago khoziaistva SSSR* (Moscow, 1956), 2: 180–81; Khromov, *Ekonomicheskoe razvitie*, pp. 384–86.

47. Quoted in Richard G. Robbins, Jr., *Famine in Russia, 1891–1892* (New York and London, 1975), p. 6.

48. P. Kh. Shvanebakh, *Nashe podatnoe delo* (St. Petersburg, 1903), pp. 11–15; Khromov, *Ekonomicheskoe razvitie*, pp. 468–69; A. P. Pogrebinskii, *Ocherki istorii finansov dorevoliutsionnoi Rossii* (Moscow, 1954), pp. 85–88.

49. Robbins, *Famine in Russia*, pp. 5–8; von Laue, *Sergei Witte*, pp. 26–27.

50. L. Maress, "Pishcha narodnykh mass v. Rossii," *Russkaia mysl'* (October 1893), p. 66.

51. Robbins, *Famine in Russia*, pp. 1–12.

52. Quoted in ibid., pp. 34–35.

53. Ibid., p. 37.

54. L. N. Tolstoi, "Strashnyi vopros," *Russkie vedomosti*, no. 306 (November 6, 1891).

55. Karl Baedeker, *Russia, with Teheran, Port Arthur, and Peking: A Handbook for Travellers* (Leipzig, 1914), p. 102.

56. Quoted in Robbins, *Famine in Russia*, p. 43.

57. A. A. Polovtsov, *Dnevnik gosudarstvennogo sekretaria A. A. Polovtsova*, ed. P. A. Zaionchkovskii (Moscow, 1966), 2: 382.

58. John Maynard, *The Russian Peasant and Other Studies* (London, 1942), 1: 48–52.

59. I. Sukhopluev, "Posledstviia neurozhaev v Rossii," *Russkaia mysl'* (June 1906), p. 151.

60. Ibid., p. 152.

61. Edward Ames, "A Century of Russian Railroad Construction, 1837–1936," *American Slavic and East European Review* 6 (December 1947): 64–65.

62. Robbins, *Famine in Russia*, p. 58.

63. Ibid., pp. 58–60; V. A. Zolotov, *Khlebnyi eksport Rossii cherez porty chernogo i azovskogo morei v 60–90e gody XIX veka* (Rostov-na-Donu, 1966), p. 165.

64. Robbins, *Famine in Russia*, pp. 71–72.

65. J. H. Clapham, *The Economic Development of France and Germany, 1815–1914* (Cambridge, 1951), pp. 339–40; Khromov, *Ekonomicheskoe razvitie*, p. 462; Robbins, *Famine in Russia*, pp. 80–81, and appropriate gazetteers.

66. Quoted in Robbins, *Famine in Russia*, p. 93. See also pp. 79–94.

67. S. Iu. Witte, *Vospominaniia* (Moscow, 1960), 1: 254–55.

68. Robbins, *Famine in Russia*, pp. 171–87.

69. Queen Victoria to Leopold, King of the Belgians, June 11, 1844 (n.s.), in A. C. Benson and Viscount Esher, eds., *The Letters of Queen Victoria: A Selection of Her Majesty's Correspondence between the Years 1837–1861* (London, 1907), 2: 16.

70. Emile Joseph Dillon, "Aleksandr III," *Golos minuvshago*, nos. 5–6 (May–June 1917): 85.

71. Quoted in W. Bruce Lincoln, "Alexander III of Russia," *History Today* 26, no. 10 (October 1976): 645.

72. Grand Duke Aleksandr Mikhailovich, *Once a Grand Duke* (New York, 1932), p. 174.

73. Quoted in Dillon, "Aleksandr III," pp. 87, 92.

74. Quoted in Aleksandr Mikhailovich, *Once a Grand Duke*, pp. 66–67.

75. Quoted in ibid., p. 67.

76. Vera Figner, *Zapechatlennyi trud* (Moscow, 1964), 1: 268.

77. Quoted in David Footman, *Red Prelude, The Life of the Russian Terrorist Zhelyabov* (New Haven, 1945), p. 218.

78. Aleksandr Mikhailovich, *Once a Grand Duke*, p. 61.

79. Quoted in Dillon, "Aleksandr III," p. 92.

80. Quoted in Florinsky, *Russia*, 2: 1087.

81. Witte, *Vospominaniia*, 1:408.

82. Witte, *Vospominaniia*, 1: 408.

83. Ibid.

84. Konstantin Pobedonostsev, *Reflections of a Russian Statesman* (Ann Arbor, 1965), p. 265.

85. Ibid., pp. 32, 26, 35.

86. Quoted in Florinsky, *Russia*, 2: 1089.

87. Quoted in Aleksandr Mikhailovich, *Once a Grand Duke*, pp. 168–69.

88. Robbins, *Famine in Russia*, p. 100.

89. Quoted in Witte, *Vospominaniia*, 1: 435.

90. Florinsky, *Russia*, 2: 1142.

CHAPTER II
In the Wake of Famine

1. Anatole Leroy-Beaulieu, *The Empire of the Tsars and the Russians* (New York, 1969), 1: 148–49.

2. A. N. Radishchev, "Puteshestvie iz Peterburga v Moskvu," in *Izbrannye filosofskie i obshchestvenno-politicheskie proizvedeniia* (Moscow, 1952), pp. 125–26.

3. See, for example, the portrayals in N. M. Karamzin, "Bednaia Liza," *Izbrannye sochineniia* (Moscow, 1964), 1:605–21; and A. S. Pushkin, "Baryshnia-krest'ianka," *Polnoe sobranie sochinenii v desiati tomakh* (Moscow, 1964), 6: 145–70.

4. P. A. Zaionchkovskii, *Otmena krepostnogo prava v Rossii,* 3rd ed. (Moscow, 1968), pp. 7–62.

5. W. Bruce Lincoln, *Nicholas I: Emperor and Autocrat of All the Russias* (London, 1978), pp. 180–95.

6. Many English translations of this volume have appeared over the years and under a variety of titles. Among the most common, in addition to *Notes of a Huntsman,* are *Hunting Sketches* and *A Sportsman's Notebook.*

7. Terence Emmons, *The Russian Landed Gentry and the Peasant Emancipation of 1861* (Cambridge, 1968), p. 30.

8. Marc Slonim, *The Epic of Russian Literature: From Its Origins Through Tolstoi* (New York, 1964), p. 253.

9. Martin Malia, *Alexander Herzen and the Birth of Russian Socialism, 1812–1855* (Cambridge, Mass., 1961), pp. 285–88, 310–11.

10. Ibid., pp. 311–14.

11. M. I. Mikhailov, "K molodomu pokoleniiu," published in Mikhail Lemke, *Politicheskie protsessy M. I. Mikhailova, D. I. Pisareva, i N. G. Chernyshevskago* (St. Petersburg, 1907), pp. 36–54. Here, pp. 43–44.

12. Peter Lavrov, *Historical Letters,* translated with an introduction and notes by James P. Scanlan (Berkeley and Los Angeles, 1967), pp. 141–42.

13. Leopold H. Haimson, *The Russian Marxists and the Origins of Bolshevism* (Cambridge, Mass., 1955), p. 12.

14. Vera Figner, *Zapechatlennyi trud* (Moscow, 1964), 1: 153–55.

15. I. S. Turgenev, *Dym,* in *Sobranie sochinenii* (Moscow, 1961), 4: 26–27.

16. A. N. Engel'gardt, *Iz derevni: 12 pisem,* quoted in Richard S. Wortman, *The Crisis of Russian Populism* (Cambridge, 1967), p. 58.

17. Maksim Gorkii, *O russkom krest'ianstve*, quoted in Richard Pipes, *Russia Under the Old Regime* (New York, 1974), p. 160.

18. A. I. Livanov, "Kakoe polozhenie naibolee udobno dlia sblizheniia s narodom?" in *Revoliutsionnoe narodnichestvo 70-kh godov XIX veka*, ed. B. S. Itenberg (Moscow, 1964), 1: 145–51. Here, p. 151.

19. Jerome Blum, *Lord and Peasant in Russia from the Ninth to the Nineteenth Century* (Princeton, 1961), pp. 504–6.

20. The description of daily peasant life that follows is taken from a variety of sources. Most important among them are the following: A. I. Shingarev, *Vymiraiushchaia derevnia* (St. Petersburg, 1907), republished as an appendix to K. M. Shuvaev, *Staraia i novaia derevnia* (Moscow, 1937), which describes village life in the province of Voronezh on the eve of the Revolution of 1905; P. I. Kushner, ed., *The Village of Viratino*, ed. and trans. Sula Benet (New York, 1970), a translation of a Soviet work that describes life in a village in Tambov province before and after the Revolution of 1917; A. M. Anfimov, *Rossiiskaia derevnia v gody pervoi mirovoi voiny* (Moscow, 1962); A. A. Kaufman, *Agrarnyi vopros v Rossii* (Moscow, 1919); Petr Lokhtin, *Bezzemel'nyi proletariat v Rossii* (Moscow, 1905); Pipes, *Russia under the Old Regime;* S. N. Prokopovich, *Krest'ianskoe khoziaistvo* (Berlin, 1924); Geroid T. Robinson, *Rural Russia under the Old Regime* (New York, 1957); and P. M. Ekzempliarskii, *Istoriia goroda Ivanovo*, vol. 1 (Ivanovo, 1958). In addition, brilliant literary portraits of village life at the turn of the century can be found in A. P. Chekhov, "Muzhiki," in *Sobranie sochinenii v vos'mi tomakh* (Moscow, 1970), 6: 196–227, and I. A. Bunin, "Derevnia," in *Sobranie sochinenii v deviati tomakh* (Moscow, 1965), 3: 12–132.

21. Kushner, ed., *Village of Viratino*, p. 72.

22. Shingarev, *Vymiraiushchaia derevnia*, p. 198. See also Mary Matossian, "The Peasant Way of Life," in *The Peasant in Nineteenth-Century Russia*, ed. Wayne S. Vucinich (Stanford, 1968), pp. 5–7.

23. Shingarev, *Vymiraiushchaia derevnia*, p. 195.

24. Quoted in Kushner, ed., *Village of Viratino*, p. 60.

25. Shingarev, *Vymiraiushchaia derevnia*, p. 200.

26. *Vysochaishe uchrezhdennaia 16 noiabria 1901g. kommissiia po izsledovaniiu voprosa o dvizhenii s 1861g. po 1900g. blagosostoianiia sel'skago naseleniia sredne-zemledel'cheskikh gubernii sravnitel'no s drugimi mestnostiami Evropeiskoi Rossii. Materialy* (St. Petersburg, 1903), 1: 210–11.

27. P. Maslov, *Agrarnyi vopros v Rossii* (St. Petersburg, 1905), 1: 368–72; Robert E. Johnson, *Peasant and Proletarian: The Working Class of Moscow in the Late Nineteenth Century* (New Brunswick, 1979), pp. 39–50.

28. Robinson, *Rural Russia*, pp. 105–7.

29. Ibid., pp. 97–99, 268–77; *Obshchii svod po Imperii rezul'tatov razrabotki dannykh pervoi vseobshchei perepisi naseleniia, proizvedennoi 28 ianvaria 1897 goda* (St. Petersburg, 1905), 1: 161–63; Francis M. Watters, "The Peasant and the Village Commune," in *The Peasant*, ed. Vucinich, pp. 153–55.

30. Kushner, ed., *Village of Viratino*, pp. 18–19.

31. Sir Donald Mackenzie Wallace, *Russia* (London, Paris, New York, and Melbourne, 1905), 1: 173–74.

32. Blum, *Lord and Peasant*, pp. 523–27.

33. Shingarev, *Vymiraiushchaia derevnia*, pp. 339–41.

34. Kushner, ed., *Village of Viratino*, p. 98.

35. Shingarev, *Vymiraiushchaia derevnia*, p. 239.

36. Ibid., pp. 239–45.

37. Ibid., pp. 341–42.

38. Ibid., pp. 256–63; Kushner, ed., *Village of Viratino*, pp. 95, 145.

39. Shingarev, *Vymiraiushchaia derevnia*, pp. 263–69; Kushner, ed., *Village of Viratino*, pp. 145–46.

40. Robbins, *Famine in Russia*, p. 188; Shingarev, *Vymiraiushchaia derevnia*, pp. 293–97.

41. V. I. Lenin, *Razvitie kapitalizma v Rossii*, in *Sochineniia*, 4th ed. (Moscow, 1946), 3: 120–34.

42. V. I. Kliuchevskii, *Sochineniia* (Moscow, 1956), 1: 313.

43. K. M. Shuvaev, *Staraia i novaia derevnia* (Moscow, 1937), pp. 12–14.

44. Ibid., pp. 81–90.

45. Kushner, ed., *Village of Viratino*, pp. 75–82.

46. Ibid., pp. 130–45; Kliuchevskii, *Sochineniia*, 1: 311–13.

47. V. G. Korolenko, "Son Makara," in *Sobranie sochinenii v desiati tomakh* (Moscow, 1953), 1: 104–5.

48. *Vysochaishe uchrezhdennaia 16 noiabria 1901g. kommissiia. Materialy*, 1: 40–45.

49. Pipes, *Russia under the Old Regime*, p. 157; Kushner, ed., *Village of Viratino*, pp. 144–45.

50. F. M. Dostoevskii, *The Diary of a Writer*, translated and annotated by Boris Brasol (New York, 1954), p. 205.

51. A. P. Chekhov, "Muzhiki," in *Sobranie sochinenii v vos'mi tomakh* (Moscow, 1970), 6: 225–26.

52. Dostoevskii, *Diary of a Writer*, p. 202.

53. V. G. Belinskii, *Sobranie sochinenii*, ed. Ivanov-Razumnik (Petersburg, 1919), 3: col. 825.

54. Leroy-Beaulieu, *Empire of the Tsars and the Russians,* 3: 10, 20–21.

55. Ibid., p. 20.

56. Chekhov, "Muzhiki," p. 206.

57. Wallace, *Russia,* 1:103.

58. Ibid., p. 82.

59. Leroy-Beaulieu, *Empire of the Tsars and the Russians,* 3: 36.

60. Wallace, *Russia,* 1: 80.

61. I. M. Bogdanov, *Gramotnost' i obrazovanie v dorevoliutsionnoi Rossii i v SSSR* (Moscow, 1964), pp. 20–22, 94–105.

62. Shingarev, *Vymiraiushchaia derevnia,* p. 173; Kushner, ed., *Village of Viratino,* pp. 153–55.

63. Shingarev, *Vymiraiushchaia derevnia,* p. 171; Kushner, ed., *Village of Viratino,* pp. 150–51.

64. Florinsky, *Russia,* 2: 1237.

65. Quoted in ibid., p. 1114.

66. Pipes, *Russia under the Old Regime,* p. 157.

67. Ibid., p. 162.

68. S. Iu. Witte, "Obïasneniia Ministra Finansov komitetu ministrov po povodu zaiavleniia gosudarstvennago kontrolera o naprazhenii platezhnykh sil naseleniia," in S. Iu. Witte, *Samoderzhaviia i zemstvo: konfidential'naia zapiska Ministra Finansov stats-sekretaria S. Iu. Vitte,* 2nd ed. (Stuttgart, 1903), pp. 216–18.

69. S. Iu. Witte, *Vospominaniia,* 2: 523–24, 527.

70. *Vysochaishe uchrezhdennaia 16 noiabria 1901g. kommissiia, Materialy,* 1:290–93.

CHAPTER III
Russia's New Lords

1. Quoted in P. A. Buryshkin, *Moskva kupecheskaia* (New York, 1954), pp. 11–15.

2. I. T. Pososhkov, *Kniga o skudosti i bogatstve i drugie sochineniia,* ed. B. B. Kafengauz (Moscow, 1951), p. 113.

3. Quoted in JoAnn Ruckman, "The Business Elite of Moscow: A Social Inquiry" (Ph.D. diss., Northern Illinois University, 1975), p. 36, n. 19.

4. K. N. Derzhavin, "Ostrovskii," in *Istoriia russkoi literatury: literatura shestidesiatykh godov,* ed. M. P. Alekseev et al. (Moscow-Leningrad, 1956), 8 (2): 407–15; K. I. Arabazhin, "Aleksandr Nikolaevich Ostrovskii," in *Istoriia russkoi literatury XIX veka,* ed. D. N. Ovsianiko-Kulikovskii (Moscow, 1909), 3: 425–28; A. A. Fomin, "Cherty romantizma

u A. N. Ostrovskogo," in S. K. Shambinyi, *Tvorchestvo A. N. Ostrovskogo: iubileinyi sbornik* (Moscow-Leningrad, 1923), pp. 92–138.

5. Ruckman, "The Business Elite of Moscow," pp. 14–15.

6. A. N. Ostrovskii, "It's a Family Affair—We'll Settle It Ourselves," in *Five Plays of Alexander Ostrovsky*, ed. and trans. Eugene K. Bristow (New York, 1969), p. 56.

7. Ibid., p. 55.

8. William L. Blackwell, *The Beginnings of Russian Industrialization, 1800–1860* (Princeton, 1968), pp. 212–29; Alfred J. Rieber, "The Moscow Entrepreneurial Group: The Emergence of a New Form in Autocratic Politics," *Jahrbücher für Geschichte Osteuropas* 25, no. 1 (1977): 8–10.

9. Blackwell, *Beginnings of Russian Industrialization*, p. 213.

10. Ibid., pp. 212–23; Leroy-Beaulieu, *Empire of the Tsars and Russians*, 3: 339–57; Louis Menashe, "Alexander Guchkov and the Origins of the Octobrist Party: The Russian Bourgeoisie in Politics, 1905" (Ph.D. diss., New York University, 1966), pp. 11–15.

11. P. G. Ryndziunskii, "Moskovskaia burzhuaziia," in N. M. Istoriia Moskvy: period razlozheniia krepostnogo stroia, ed. N.M. Druzhinin and M. K. Rozhkova (Moscow, 1954), 3: 302; Blackwell, *Beginnings of Russian Industrialization*, p. 222; G. S. Isaev, *Rol' tekstil'noi promyshlennosti v genezise i razvitii kapitalizma v Rossii, 1760–1860* (Leningrad, 1970), pp. 162–63.

12. Rieber, "The Moscow Entrepreneurial Group," p. 13. See also Menashe, "Alexander Guchkov," pp. 19–21.

13. Leroy-Beaulieu, *Empire of the Tsars and the Russians*, 3: 343.

14. Quoted in Buryshkin, *Moskva kupecheskaia*, p. 47.

15. Quoted in ibid., p. 81.

16. Valentine Tscherbotarief Bill, "The Morozovs," *The Russian Review*, 14, no. 2 (April 1955): 109; P. P. Semenov, *Geografichesko-statisticheskii slovar' rossiiskoi imperii* (St. Petersburg, 1865), 2: 290.

17. A. A. Zaleskii, "Rekrutskaia povinnost'," in *Sovetskaia istoricheskaia entsiklopediia* (Moscow, 1968), 11: col. 1004.

18. Ruckman, "The Business Elite of Moscow," p. 107; Valentine T. Bill, *The Forgotten Class: The Russian Bourgeoisie from the Earliest Beginnings to 1900* (New York, 1959), pp. 18–19.

19. Prince D. A. Mirsky, *Russia: A Social History* (London, 1952), p. 215.

20. Ekzempliarskii, *Istoriia goroda Ivanova*, 1: 48–55, 70–72, 97–98; A. I. Kopanev, *Naselenie Peterburga v pervoi polovine XIX veka* (Moscow-Leningrad, 1957), p. 94; P. A. Berlin, *Russkaia burzhuaziia v staroe i novoe vremia* (Moscow, 1922), pp. 87–89.

21. Bill, *The Forgotten Class*, pp. 19–20.

22. Armand de Caulaincourt, *With Napoleon in Russia: The Memoirs of General de Caulaincourt, Duke of Vicenza* (New York, 1935), p. 120.

23. Berlin, *Russkaia burzhuaziia*, p. 88; Bill, *The Forgotten Class*, pp. 17–18.

24. Buryshkin, *Moskva kupecheskaia*, pp. 113–14; P. P. Semenov, *Geografichesko-statisticheskii slovar' Rossiiskoi imperii*, 3: 469.

25. S. G. Budagov and P. A. Orlov, eds., *Ukazatel' fabriki i zavadov evropeiskoi Rossii. Materialy dlia fabrichno-zavodskoi statistiki* (St. Petersburg, 1894), pp. ix, 41–43; Bill, *The Forgotten Class*, pp. 21–24; Buryshkin, *Moskva kupecheskaia*, pp. 112–14; Ch. Ioksimovich, *Manufakturnaia promyshlennost' v proshlom i nastoiashchem* (Moscow, 1915), 1: 11–42.

26. Liashchenko, *Istoriia narodnago khoziaistva SSSR*, 2: 442.

27. V. I. Nevskii, "Povorotnyi punkt rabochego dvizheniia v Rossii," in *Morozovskaia stachka 1885g.*, ed. A. Lozovskii (Moscow, 1925), pp. 4–6; Bill, *The Forgotten Class*, pp. 23–24.

28. P. A. Moiseenko, *Vospominaniia starogo revoliutsionera* (Moscow, 1966), p. 69.

29. Ibid., p. 74.

30. Quoted in M. Balabanov, *Ocherki po istorii rabochego klassa v Rossii* (Moscow, 1925), 2: 290.

31. Ibid., pp. 290–91; Moiseenko, *Vospominaniia*, p. 80.

32. Balabanov, *Ocherki po istorii rabochego klassa v Rossii*, 2: 310–12; Nevskii, "Povorotnyi punkt rabochego dvizheniia," pp. 11–12.

33. Aleksandr Serebrov, *Vremia i liudi. Vospominaniia, 1898–1905* (Moscow, 1955), p. 180; Buryshkin, *Moskva kupecheskaia*, pp. 114, 118; Bill, *The Forgotten Class*, pp. 26–28.

34. Vladimir Nemirovich-Danchenko, *My Life in the Russian Theatre*, trans. John Cournos (Boston, 1936), p. 132.

35. Quoted in Serebrov, *Vremia i liudi*, p. 178.

36. Nemirovich-Danchenko, *My Life*, p. 132.

37. Serebrov, *Vremia i liudi*, pp. 172, 175.

38. Bill, *The Forgotten Class*, pp. 30–32.

39. Nemirovich-Danchenko, *My Life*, p. 129.

40. Constantin Stanislavsky, *My Life in Art*, trans. J. J. Robbins (Boston, 1935), p. 386.

41. Nemirovich-Danchenko, *My Life*, p. 131.

42. Ibid.

43. Ibid., pp. 130–31.

44. Ruckman, "The Business Elite of Moscow," pp. 105–12; Rieber, "The Moscow Entrepreneurial Group," pp. 6–10.

45. Ruckman, "The Business Elite of Moscow," pp. 111–17.
46. Liashchenko, *Istoriia narodnogo khoziaistva SSSR*, 2: 459.
47. Ibid., pp. 454–55; I. F. Gindin, "Moskovskie banki v period imperializma, 1900–1917gg.," *Istoricheskie zapiski*, 58 (1956): 39, 51–52; I. F. Gindin, "Moskovskie banki," in *Istoriia Moskvy: period promyshlennogo kapitalizma*, ed. Koz'min and Iatsunskii (Moscow, 1954), pp. 208–10; Ruckman, "The Business Elite of Moscow," pp. 12–122; Roger Pourtal, "Industriels moscovites: le secteur cotonnier (1861–1914)," *Cahiers du monde russe et soviétique*, 4, nos. 1–2 (January–June 1963): 33–34.
48. Ruckman, "The Business Elite of Moscow," pp. 127–32; Pourtal, "Industriels moscovites," pp. 31–46; Ioksimovich, *Manufakturnaia promyshlennost', passim*.
49. Quoted in Ruckman, "The Business Elite of Moscow," p. 140.
50. Ibid., pp. 141–42.
51. Von Laue, *Sergei Witte*, p. 269.
52. A. S. Nifontov, "Naselenie kapitalisticheskoi Moskvy," in *Istoriia Moskvy*, ed. Koz'min and Iatsunskii, 4: 254–55.
53. Quoted in Ruckman, "The Business Elite of Moscow," p. 91.
54. Buryshkin, *Moskva kupecheskaia*, p. 134.
55. Pis'mo P. M. Tret'iakova k A. V. Tret'iakovoi, 17 oktiabria 1852g., in A. P. Botkina, *Pavel Mikhailovich Tret'iakov v zhizni i iskusstve* (Moscow, 1960), p. 21.
56. Ruckman, "The Business Elite of Moscow," p. 176.
57. Botkina, *Pavel Mikhailovich Tret'iakov*, pp. 55–57.
58. Quoted in ibid., p. 270. See also p. 6.
59. Ibid., pp. 38–80.
60. V. P. Ziloti, *V dome Tret'iakova* (New York, 1954), p. 116.
61. Quoted in Botkina, *Pavel Mikhailovich Tret'iakov*, p. 249.
62. Quoted in Elizabeth Valkenier, *Russian Realist Art. The State and Society: The Peredvizhniki and Their Tradition* (Ann Arbor, 1977), p. 33. See also pp. 34–37.
63. Ibid., p. 57.
64. Ibid., pp. 65–67; Botkina, *Pavel Mikhailovich Tret'iakov*, pp. 249–52.
65. Ziloti, *V dome Tret'iakova*, p. 238; Botkina, *Pavel Mikhailovich Tret'iakov*, pp. 174–85, 273–74.
66. Valkenier, *Russian Realist Art*, p. 64.
67. Botkina, *Pavel Mikhailovich Tret'iakov*, p. 298.
68. Ibid., pp. 58–59; Buryshkin, *Moskva kupecheskaia*, pp. 166–69.
69. Valkenier, *Russian Realist Art*, p. 68.
70. Stuart R. Grover, "Savva Mamontov and the Mamontov Circle,

1870–1905. Art Patronage and the Rise of Nationalism in Russian Art" (Ph.D. diss., University of Wisconsin, 1971), pp. 365–66; N. V. Polenova, *Abramtsevo. Vospominaniia* (Moscow, 1922), p. 46.

71. Quoted in Grover, "Savva Mamontov and the Mamontov Circle," p. 42. See also pp. 43, 365; Bill, *The Forgotten Class*, pp. 126–31; Ruckman, "The Business Elite of Moscow," pp. 208–9.

72. N. V. Polenova, *Abramtsevo*, pp. 5–16; Buryshkin, *Moskva kupecheskaia*, pp. 170–71.

73. Quoted in Polenova, *Abramtsevo*, p. 18.

74. D. Z. Kogan, *Mamontovskii kruzhok* (Moscow, 1970), pp. 9, 60, 66.

75. Quoted in Polenova, *Abramtsevo*, pp. 42–43. See also pp. 22–41; Kogan, *Mamontovskii kruzhok*, pp. 5–111; Tamara Tabot Rice, *Concise History of Russian Art* (New York, 1967), pp. 242–43; V. S. Mamontov, *Vospominaniia o russkikh khudozhnikakh* (Moscow, 1950), pp. 22–25.

76. Kogan, *Mamontovskii kruzhok*, pp. 112–22; Bill, *The Forgotten Class*, pp. 128–29; Mamontov, *Vospominaniia*, pp. 20–21, 46–47.

77. Polenova, *Abramtsevo*, pp. 72–96; Kogan, *Mamontovskii kruzhok*, pp. 164–73; Bill, *The Forgotten Class*, pp. 128–29.

78. Grover, "Savva Mamontov and the Mamontov Circle," pp. 343–51; Bill, *The Forgotten Class*, pp. 130–33.

79. Stanislavsky, *My Life in Art*, p. 21.

80. Buryshkin, *Moskva kupecheskaia*, pp. 147–48; Kogan, *Mamontovskii kruzhok*, p. 82.

81. Stanislavsky, *My Life in Art*, pp. 3–11.

82. Ibid., p. 3.

83. Ibid., p. 20.

84. E. I. Polenova, *Stanislavskii—akter* (Moscow, 1972), pp. 9–103.

85. Stanislavsky, *My Life in Art*, p. 20.

86. Ibid., p. 293.

87. Stanislavsky, *My Life in Art*, p. 292.

88. Nemirovich-Danchenko, *My Life*, pp. 76, 83.

89. Stanislavsky, *My Life in Art*, p. 294.

90. Ibid., p. 295.

91. Ibid., pp. 298–99.

92. Ibid., p. 295.

93. Ibid., p. 296.

94. Nemirovich-Danchenko, *My Life*, p. 230.

95. Stanislavsky, *My Life in Art*, p. 292.

96. S. N. Durylin, "Moskovskie teatry," in *Istoriia Moskvy: period imperializma*, ed. Pankratova, pp. 566–69.

CHAPTER IV
Life in the Lower Depths

1. "Rech' P. A. Alekseeva na zasedanii suda Osobogo prisutstviia pravitel'stvuiushchego Senata (protsess '50-ti')," in *Revoliutsionnoe narodnichestvo 70-kh godov XIX veka*, ed. S. N. Valk et al. (Moscow, 1964), 1: 366–67.

2. Vera Figner, *Zapechatlennyi trud* (Moscow, 1964), 1: 177.

3. Samuel H. Baron, *Plekhanov: The Father of Russian Marxism* (Stanford, 1963), pp. 59–116.

4. Quoted in Theodore Dan, *The Origins of Bolshevism*, ed. and trans. Joel Carmichael (New York, 1964), p. 153.

5. Pis'mo G. V. Plekhanova k P. L. Lavrovu, early 1882, in *Dela i dni* 2 (1921): 91.

6. I. V. Babushkin, *Vospominaniia Ivana Vasil'evicha Babushkina, 1893–1900* (Moscow, 1951), p. 21.

7. L. M. Ivanov, "Vozniknovenie rabochego klassa," in *Istoriia rabochego klassa Rossii, 1861–1900gg.*, ed. L. M. Ivanov (Moscow, 1972), pp. 16–18; A. G. Rashin, *Formirovanie rabochego klassa Rossii: Istorikoekonomicheskie ocherki* (Moscow, 1958), pp. 24–25, 30, 117–19, 172.

8. V. Iu. Krupianskaia and N. S. Polishchuk, *Kul'tura i byt rabochikh gornozavodskogo Urala (konets XIX–nachalo XX v.)* (Moscow, 1971), pp. 103–42; W. Bruce Lincoln, *Petr Petrovich Semenov-Tian-Shanskii: The Life of a Russian Geographer* (Newtonville, 1980), pp. 24–25.

9. Reginald E. Zelnik, *Labor and Society in Tsarist Russia: The Factory Workers of St. Petersburg, 1855–1870* (Stanford, 1971), pp. 52–56; "O polozhenii chernorabochikh v S.-Peterburge," Tsentral'nyi Gosudarstvennyi Istoricheskii Arkhiv v Leningrade, fond 869, opis' 1, delo no. 350/1–16.

10. Zelnik, *Labor and Society*, pp. 241–44.

11. A. V. Nikitenko, *Dnevnik* (Moscow, 1955), II, pp. 393, 454.

12. Zelnik, *Labor and Society*, p. 250.

13. S. Lapitskaia, *Byt rabochikh trekhgornoi manufaktury* (Moscow, 1935), pp. 29–30; A. S. Nifontov, "Ostrota sotsial'nykh kontrastov v burzhuaznoi Moskve," in *Istoriia Moskvy: Period promyshlennogo kapitalizma*, ed. B. P. Koz'min and V. K. Iatsunskii (Moscow, 1954), 4: 257–59.

14. S. Ia. Borovoi, "Polozhenie rabochego klassa Odessy v XIX i nachale XX v.," in *Iz istorii rabochego klassa i revolutsionnogo dvizheniia. Pamiati akademika Anny Mikhailovny Pankratovoi*, ed. M. V. Nechkina et al. (Moscow, 1958), p. 310.

15. Zelnik, *Labor and Society*, p. 251; p. 414, n. 45.

16. P. P. Mikulin, *Nasha bankovaia politika, 1729–1903* (Kharkov, 1904), pp. 236–37; P. V. Ol', *Inostrannye kapitaly v khoziaistve dovoennoi Rossii* (Leningrad, 1925), pp. 24–26.

17. Lenin, *Razvitie kapitalisma v Rossii*, p. 495; P. I. Liashchenko, *Istoriia narodnogo khoziaistva SSSR* (Moscow, 1956), 2: 141–43.

18. P. I. Liashchenko, *Ocherki agrarnoi evoliutsii Rossii* (Moscow-Petrograd, 1923), pp. 143–59; Petr Lokhtin, *Bezzemel'nyi proletariat v Rossii* (Moscow, 1905), pp. 28–36.

19. P. A. Moiseenko, *Vospominaniia starogo revoliutsionera* (Moscow, 1966), p. 17.

20. Robert E. Johnson, *Peasant and Proletarian: The Working Class of Moscow in the Late Nineteenth Century.* New Brunswick, 1979. p. 53.

21. Babushkin, *Vospominaniia*, pp. 27–28.

22. Johnson, *Peasant and Proletarian*, pp. 55–57.

23. Quoted in Lapitskaia, *Byt rabochikh trekhgornoi manufaktury*, p. 35.

24. I. I. Ianzhul, "Zhenshchiny-matery na fabrikakh," in I. I. Ianzhul, *Ocherki i izsledovaniia* (Moscow, 1884), 1: 390–91.

25. I. I. Ianzhul, *Fabrichnyi byt moskovskoi gubernii. Otchet za 1882–1883g.* (St. Petersburg, 1884), p. 44.

26. P. A. Peskov, *Fabrichnyi byt vladimirskoi gubernii. Otchet za 1882–1883g.* (St. Petersburg, 1884), p. 20.

27. Ianzhul, *Fabrichnyi byt*, p. 44.

28. Lapitskaia, *Byt rabochikh trekhgornoi manufaktury*, p. 52.

29. Quoted in ibid.

30. M. Tugan-Baranovskii, *Russkaia fabrika v proshlom i nastoiashchem* (Moscow, 1938), p. 327; V. Iu. Gessen, *Istoriia zakonodatel'stva o trude rabochei molodezhi v Rossii* (Leningrad, 1927), pp. 92–93.

31. I. I. Ianzhul, *Iz vospominanii i perepiski fabrichnago inspektora pervago prizyva. Materialy dlia istorii russkago rabochego voprosa i fabrichnago zakonodatel'stva* (St. Petersburg, 1907), p. 73.

32. F. Pavlov, *Za desiat' let praktiki. Otryvki vospominanii, vpechatlenii, i nabliudenii iz fabrichnoi zhizni* (Moscow, 1907), pp. 5–6; S. Gvozdev, *Zapiski fabrichnago inspektora. Iz nabliudenii i praktiki v period 1894–1908gg.* (Moscow, 1911), pp. 58–59.

33. *Polnoe sobranie zakonov rossiiskoi imperii.* Sobranie 3-oe. Law of April 24, 1890, no. 6743.

34. Quoted in Lapitskaia, *Byt rabochikh trekhgornoi manufaktury*, p. 50.

35. Quoted in ibid., p. 51.

36. D. Kol'tsov [V. A. Ginzburg], "Rabochee v 1890–1904gg.," in

Obshchestvennoe dvizhenie v Rossii v nachale XX-go veka, ed. L. Martov, P. Maslov, and A. Potresov (St. Petersburg, 1909), 1: 202.

37. Ianzhul, *Fabrichnyi byt,* pp. 125–26.

38. Ibid., pp. 126–33; Peskov, *Fabrichnyi byt,* pp. 125–30; O. A. Parasun'ko, *Polozhenie i bor'ba rabochego klassa Ukrainy (60–90e gody XIX v.)* (Kiev, 1963), pp. 184–85.

39. Kol'tsov [Ginzburg], "Rabochie v 1890–1904gg.," pp. 195, 199, 202; Ekzempliarskii, *Istoriia goroda Ivanova,* 1: 177–78.

40. Tugan-Baranovskii, *Russkaia fabrika,* pp. 325–26; I. A. Baklanova, "Formirovanie i polozhenie promyshlennogo proletariata. Rabochee dvizhenie 60-e gody–nachalo 90-kh godov," in *Istoriia rabochikh Leningrada,* ed. V. S. Diakin et al. (Leningrad, 1972), 1: 133–34.

41. Ianzhul, *Fabrichnyi byt,* p. 83.

42. Ibid., pp. 114–15, 90–91; Peskov, *Fabrichnyi byt,* pp. 77–78; Gvozdev, *Zapiski fabrichnago inspektora,* pp. 96–101.

43. E. M. Dement'ev, *Fabrika: Chto ona daet naseleniiu i chto ona y nego beret* (Moscow, 1897), p. 182.

44. Gvozdev, *Zapiski fabrichnago inspektora,* pp. 81–94; Peskov, *Fabrichnyi byt,* pp. 78–79; Ianzhul, *Fabrichnyi byt,* pp. 108–13; N. K. Druzhinin, ed., *Usloviia byta rabochikh v dorevoliutsionnoi Rossii* (Moscow, 1958), pp. 28–34, 102–4; M. Balabanov, *Ocherki po istorii rabochego klassa v Rossii* (Moscow, 1925), 2: 127–29, 190–92; Borovoi, "Polozhenie rabochego klassa Odessy," pp. 315–17; M. I. Gil'bert, "Dvizhenie zarabotkov rabochikh v kontse XIX v.," in *Iz istorii rabochego klassa,* ed. Nechkina et al., pp. 319–32; M. K. Rozhkova, "Zarabotnaia plata rabochikh trekhgornoi manufaktury v 1892–1913gg.," in ibid., pp. 333–41.

45. Peskov, *Fabrichnyi byt,* pp. 67–76; Ianzhul, *Fabrichnyi byt,* pp. 84–85; quoted in Tugan-Baranovskii, *Russkaia fabrika,* pp. 322–33, 338.

46. Gvozdev, *Zapiski fabrichnago inspektora,* pp. 155–56.

47. K. A. Pazhitnov, *Polozhenie rabochego klassa v Rossii* (Leningrad, 1924), 2: 93.

48. Gvozdev, *Zapiski fabrichnago inspektora,* pp. 119–20.

49. Quoted in Lapitskaia, *Byt rabochikh trekhgornoi manufaktury,* p. 54.

50. Quoted in ibid.

51. N. Krupskaia, *Iz dalekykh vremen* (Moscow-Leningrad, 1930), pp. 9–10.

52. D. G. Kutsentov, "Naselenie Peterburga. Polozhenie peterburgskikh rabochikh," in *Ocherki istorii Leningrada,* ed. B. M. Kochakov et al. (Moscow-Leningrad, 1957), 2: 202–3; Ianzhul, *Fabrichnyi byt,* pp. 116–17.

53. Quoted in Baklanova, "Formirovanie i polozhenie promyshlennogo proletariata," p. 143.

54. Kutsentov, "Naselenie Peterburga," pp. 204–6.

55. Peskov, *Fabrichnyi byt*, pp. 101–7; Ianzhul, *Fabrichnyi byt*, pp. 101–6.

56. A. A. Mikulin, *Ocherki iz istorii primeneniia zakona 3-go iiulia 1886 goda* (Vladimir, 1893), p. 70.

57. Balabanov, *Ocherki po istorii rabochego klassa v Rossii*, 3: 156; Gvozdev, *Zapiski fabrichnago inspektora*, p. 144.

58. V. I. Lenin, "Iazyk tsifr," in *Sochineniia*, 4th ed. (Moscow, 1954), p. 325.

59. P. N. Stolpianskii, *Zhizn' i byt peterburgskoi fabriki za 210 let ee sushchestvovaniia, 1704–1914* (Leningrad, 1925), pp. 120–21; Gil'bert, "Dvizhenie zarabotkov rabochikh," pp. 319–32.

60. Quoted in Lapitskaia, *Byt rabochikh trekhgornoi manufaktury*, p. 62.

61. Druzhinin, ed., *Usloviia byta rabochikh*, pp. 55–58.

62. Ianzhul, *Fabrichnyi byt*, pp. 94–101; Peskov, *Fabrichnyi byt*, pp. 98–101, 108–10.

63. Quotes from Lapitskaia, *Byt rabochikh trekhgornoi manufaktury*, p. 63. See also Gvozdev, *Zapiski fabrichnago inspektora*, pp. 147–48.

64. Gvozdev, *Zapiski fabrichnago inspektora*, pp. 147–48; Druzhinin, ed., *Usloviia byta rabochikh*, pp. 13–14.

65. M. Davidovich, "Peterburgskii rabochii v ego biudzhetakh," *Zapiski russkago tekhnicheskago obshchestva*, no. 1 (1912), p. 38.

66. Druzhinin, ed., *Usloviia byta rabochikh*, pp. 49–51.

67. Ibid., pp. 14–16, 52–53.

68. Balabanov, *Ocherki po istorii rabochego klassa v Rossii*, 2: 176–78; 3: 109.

69. Quotes from Lapitskaia, *Byt rabochikh trekhgornoi manufaktury*, pp. 67–68.

70. Ibid.

71. A. I. Kuprin, "Iama," in *Sobranie sochinenii v deviati tomakh* (Moscow, 1964), 6: 84, 7–8.

72. Quoted in Ekzempliarskii, *Istoriia goroda Ivanova*, 1: 179.

73. The description of Khitrovka that follows is especially indebted to V. A. Giliarovskii, *Moskva i Moskvichi* (Moscow, 1979), pp. 18–38, 43–60, 275–304, a brilliant account of Moscow life based upon many years of firsthand observation. See also V. A. Giliarovskii, *Trushchobnye liudi*, in *Sochineniia* (Moscow, 1967), 2: 74–80, 167–75; L. N. Tolstoi, "O perepisi v Moskve," in *Sobranie sochinenii* (Moscow, 1964), 16: 84–93; Joseph C.

Bradley, Jr., "*Muzhik* and Muscovite: Peasants in Late Nineteenth-Century Urban Russia" (Ph.D. diss., Harvard University, 1977), pp. 122–29; Joseph C. Bradley, Jr., " 'Once You've Eaten Khitrovka Soup You'll Never Leave!': The Slum in Pre-Revolutionary Moscow" (unpublished paper, 1981); M. N. Petrov, "Gorodskoe khoziaistvo," in *Istoriia Moskvy: period imperializma*, ed. Pankratova, pp. 690–717; and A. N. Sysin, "Sanitarno-lechebnoe delo," in ibid., pp. 718–29.

74. Bradley, "*Muzhik* and Muscovite," pp. 125, 128, 341.

75. G. G. Morekhina, "Razvitie promyshlennosti i polozhenie proletariata v gody reaktsii i novogo revoliutsionnogo pod'ema," in *Istoriia Moskvy: period imperializma*, ed. Pankratova, p. 223.

76. Quoted in Bradley, " 'Once You've Eaten Khitrovka Soup,' " p. 18.

77. Druzhinin, ed., *Usloviia byta rabochikh*, pp. 22–23; Iu. Z. Polevoi, "Sostav i polozhenie moskovskogo proletariata," in *Istoriia Moskvy: period imperializma*, ed. Pankratova, pp. 61–64; Morekhina, "Razvitie promyshlennosti i polozhenie proletariata," p. 223; Ekzempliarskii, *Istoriia goroda Ivanova*, 1: 177.

78. Lapitskaia, ed., *Byt rabochikh trekhgornoi manufaktury*, p. 38.

79. Ibid.

80. Ibid., p. 40.

81. Ibid., p. 41.

82. Quoted in Iu. Z. Polevoi, "Na puti soedineniia s sotsializmom," in *Istoriia rabochego klassa*, ed. Ivanov, p. 134.

83. Balabanov, *Ocherki po istorii rabochego klassa v Rossii*, 2: 261–93.

84. *Obshchii svod po Imperii rezul'tatov razrabotki dannykh pervoi vseobshchei perepisi naseleniia*, 1: 40–41; S. N. Semanov, "Chislennosti, sostav, i polozhenie peterburgskikh rabochikh," in *Istoriia rabochikh Leningrada*, ed. Diakin, 1: 184–85; Rashin, *Formirovanie rabochego klassa Rossii*, pp. 593–95.

85. Quoted in Ekzempliarskii, *Istoriia goroda Ivanova*, 1: 184. See also Bogdanov, *Gramostnost' i obrazovanie*, pp. 26–29.

86. Quoted in Ekzempliarskii, *Istoriia goroda Ivanova*, 1: 184. See also Moiseenko, *Vospominaniia*, p. 15.

87. Quoted in Ekzempliarskii, *Istoriia goroda Ivanova*, 1: 184.

88. Reginald E. Zelnik, "Russian Rebels: An Introduction to the Memoirs of Semen Kanatchikov and Matvei Fisher," *The Russian Review*, 35, no. 3 (July 1976): 271.

89. Quoted in Lapitskaia, *Byt rabochikh trekhgornoi manufaktury*, p. 78.

90. Zelnik, "Russian Rebels," p. 276.

91. Babushkin, *Vospominaniia*, p. 50.

92. Quoted in Lapitskaia, *Byt rabochikh trekhgornoi manufaktury*, p. 41.

CHAPTER V
The Few Who Dared

1. I. S. Turgenev, "Porog: son," in *Sobranie sochinenii*, 10: 24–25.

2. *Kolokol*, June 15, 1861, republished in *Kolokol. Gazeta A. I. Gertsena i N. P. Ogareva. Vol'naia russkaia tipografiia, 1857–1867gg.* (Moscow, 1962), 4: 848.

3. "Chto nuzhno narodu?" Supplement to *Kolokol*, July 1, 1861, republished in *Kolokol*, 4, insert following p. 860; Ia. I. Linkov, *Revoliutsionnaia bor'ba A. I. Gertsena i N. P. Ogareva i tainoe obshchestvo "Zemlia i Volia" 1860-kh godov* (Moscow, 1964), pp. 151–98.

4. *Kolokol*, November 1, 1861, republished in *Kolokol*, 4: 918. See also Abbott Gleason, *Young Russia: The Genesis of Russian Radicalism in the 1860s* (New York, 1980), pp. 114–59, and Daniel Brower, *Training the Nihilists: Education and Radicalism in Tsarist Russia* (Ithaca, 1975), pp. 127–31.

5. I. S. Turgenev, *Ottsy i deti*, in *Sobranie sochinenii*, 3: 139, 162, 159.

6. D. I. Pisarev, "Bazarov," in *Sochineniia* (Moscow, 1955), 2: 11.

7. Ibid., p. 50.

8. Adam B. Ulam, *In the Name of the People: Prophets and Conspirators in Prerevolutionary Russia* (New York, 1977), p. 136.

9. N. G. Chernyshevskii, *What Is To Be Done? Tales About New People* (New York, 1961), p. 12.

10. Quoted in Ulam, *In the Name of the People*, p. 135.

11. Richard Stites, *The Women's Liberation Movement in Russia. Feminism, Nihilism, and Bolshevism, 1860–1930* (Princeton, 1978), pp. 89–99.

12. Quoted in Ulam, *In the Name of the People*, p. 137.

13. Gleason, *Young Russia*, pp. 308–9; E. S. Vilenskaia, *Revoliutsionnoe podpol'e v Rossii (60-e gody XIX v.)* (Moscow, 1965), pp. 394–414; Franco Venturi, *Roots of Revolution: A History of the Populist and Socialist Movements in Nineteenth Century Russia* (New York, 1960), pp. 334–36.

14. Quoted in Gleason, *Young Russia*, p. 325.

15. Venturi, *Roots of Revolution*, p. 345.

16. Gleason, *Young Russia*, p. 326. See also pp. 324–25.

17. E. S. Vilenskaia, *Khudiakov* (Moscow, 1969), pp. 102–9; Ulam, *In the Name of the People*, pp. 156–62; Gleason, *Young Russia*, pp. 126–27.

18. Quoted in I. Khudiakov, *Zapiski Karakozovtsa*, with an introduction by M. Klevenskii (Moscow-Leningrad, 1930), p. 114.

19. Quoted in Vilenskaia, *Khudiakov*, p. 102.

20. Venturi, *Roots of Revolution*, pp. 348–49; Gleason, *Young Russia*, pp. 330–31.

21. Vera Figner, *Zapechatlennyi trud: vospominaniia* (Moscow, 1964), 1: 114–28; Stites, *Women's Liberation Movement in Russia*, pp. 131–38.

22. Philip Pomper, *Peter Lavrov and the Russian Revolutionary Movement* (Chicago, 1972), pp. 1–93.

23. Peter Lavrov, *Historical Letters*, translated with an introduction and notes by James P. Scanlan (Berkeley and Los Angeles, 1967), pp. 139–41.

24. Ibid., p. 54.

25. O. V. Aptekman, *Obshchestvo "Zemlia i Volia" 70-kh gg.* (Petrograd, 1924), p. 122.

26. V. Bogucharskii, *Aktivnoe narodnichestvo semidesiatykh godov* (Moscow, 1912), p. 213.

27. B. Bazilevskii [Iakovlev], *Gosudarstvennye prestupleniia v Rossii v XIX veke* (St. Petersburg, 1906), 1: 252–53.

28. B. S. Itenberg, *Dvizhenie revoliutsionnogo narodnichestva. Narodnicheskie kruzhki i "khozhdenie v narod" v 70-kh godakh XIX v.* (Moscow, 1965), pp. 138–72.

29. Quoted in E. H. Carr, *Michael Bakunin* (New York, 1961), p. 175.

30. Quoted in ibid., p. 157.

31. Ibid., p. 156.

32. Ibid., p. 453.

33. Quoted in ibid., p. 339.

34. B. S. Itenberg, ed., *Revoliutsionnoe narodnichestvo 70-kh godov XIX veka. Sbornik dokumentov* (Moscow, 1964), 1: 45–53.

35. Quoted in Richard S. Wortman, *The Crisis of Russian Populism*, p. 16.

36. Quoted in Ulam, *In the Name of the People*, p. 235.

37. P. B. Akselrod, *Perezhitoe i peredumannoe* (Berlin, 1923), p. 111.

38. Quoted in Prince Peter Kropotkin, *Memoirs of a Revolutionist* (Cambridge, Mass., 1899), p. 321.

39. Stites, *Women's Liberation Movement in Russia*, p. 139.

40. Bardina's speech at her trial in 1877 is published in Bazilevskii [Iakovlev], *Gosudarstvennye prestupleniia v Rossii*, 2: 327–31, here p. 331.

41. Quoted in Dan, *Origins of Bolshevism*, p. 101.

42. Wortman, *Crisis of Russian Populism*, p. 18.

43. S. S. Volk, ed., *Revoliutsionnoe narodnichestvo 70-kh godov XIX veka* (Moscow-Leningrad, 1965), 2: 33.

44. Quoted in Ulam, *In the Name of the People*, p. 246.

45. Lev Tikhomirov, *Vospominaniia L'va Tikhomirova* (Moscow-Leningrad, 1927), p. 86.

46. Volk, ed., *Revoliutsionnoe narodnichestvo*, 2: 30.

47. Quoted in Wortman, *Crisis of Russian Populism*, p. 22.

48. Tikhomirov, *Vospominaniia*, p. 86.

49. Natalie Herzen to Nikolay Ogarev, May 14, 1877, in *Daughter of a Revolutionary: Natalie Herzen and the Bakunin-Nechayev Circle*, ed. Michael Confino (Lasalle, Ill., 1973), p. 347.

50. Bazilevskii [Iakovlev], *Gosudarstvennye prestupleniia v Rossii*, 2: 331.

51. B. P. Koz'min, *Iz istorii revoliutsionnoi mysli v Rossii* (Moscow, 1961), pp. 349–72; Deborah Hardy, *Peter Tkachev: The Critic as Jacobin* (Seattle and London, 1977), *passim*.

52. Quoted in Venturi, *Roots of Revolution*, p. 419.

53. Quoted in ibid., p. 420.

54. N. Bel'chikov, "S. G. Nechaev v s. Ivanove v 60-e gody," *Katorga i ssylka*, no. 14 (1925), pp. 152–56.

55. Philip Pomper, *Sergei Nechaev* (New Brunswick, 1979), pp. 15–16; Ulam, *In the Name of the People*, p. 178.

56. B. I. Gorev and B. P. Koz'min, eds., *Revoliutsionnoe dvizhenie 1860-kh godov* (Moscow, 1931), pp. 220–25.

57. Quoted in Pomper, *Sergei Nechaev*, p. 24.

58. Quoted in B. P. Koz'min, ed., *Nechaev i Nechaevtsy: Sbornik materialov* (Moscow-Leningrad, 1931), p. 9.

59. Koz'min, *Iz istorii revoliutsionnoi mysli*, pp. 356–59. Quoted from p. 357.

60. Quoted in Pomper, *Sergei Nechaev*, p. 65.

61. Ibid., pp. 65–66.

62. Bazilevskii [Iakovlev], *Gosudarstvennye prestuplenie v Rossii*, 1: 183–84.

63. Quoted in Venturi, *Roots of Revolution*, p. 371.

64. B. P. Koz'min, "Novoe o S. G. Nechaeve," *Krasnyi Arkhiv* 14 (1926): 148–58; Pomper, *Sergei Nechaev*, pp. 69–74; Gleason, *Young Russia*, p. 361.

65. Quoted in Ulam, *In the Name of the People*, p. 187.

66. Quoted in Pomper, *Sergei Nechaev*, p. 109.

67. Ibid., p. 104.

68. Bazilevskii [Iakovlev], *Gosudarstvennye prestuplenie v Rossii*, 1: 252.

69. Ibid., pp. 160–78; Koz'min, ed., *Nechaev i Nechaevtsy*, pp. 101–16; Pomper, *Sergei Nechaev*, pp. 99–186; Gleason, *Young Russia*, pp. 361–85; Ulam, *In the Name of the People*, pp. 185–200; Venturi, *Roots of Revolution*, pp. 374–88.

70. L. Deich, "Valer'ian Osinskii," *Katorga i ssylka* 14 (1929): 27.

71. A. F. Koni, "Vospominaniia o dele Very Zasulich," in *Sobranie sochinenii* (Moscow, 1966), 2: 105–7.

72. N. K. Bukh, *Vospominaniia* (Moscow, 1928), pp. 160–63.

73. Koni, "Vospominaniia," p. 120.

74. Ibid., pp. 152, 157.

75. Ibid., pp. 173–74.

76. D. A. Miliutin, *Dnevnik D. A. Miliutina* (Moscow, 1950), 3: 41.

77. Quoted in the introduction to Koni, "Vospominaniia," p. 19.

78. Quoted in Baron, *Plekhanov*, p. 36.

79. S. S. Volk, *Narodnaia Volia, 1879–1882* (Moscow-Leningrad, 1966), pp. 76–77.

80. Quoted in Venturi, *Roots of Revolution*, p. 632.

81. S. S. Tatishchev, *Imperator Aleksandr II: Ego zhizn' i tsarstvovanie* (St. Petersburg, 1911), 2: 558–59.

82. Volk, *Narodnaia Volia*, pp. 82–84.

83. Quoted in Baron, *Plekhanov*, p. 17.

84. Dmitrii Kuz'min, "Kazanskaia demonstratsiia 1876g. i G. V. Plekhanov," *Katorga i ssylka* 44 (1928): 10.

85. Baron, *Plekhanov*, pp. 16–29.

86. Quoted in G. V. Plekhanov, "O bylom i nebylitsakh," *Sochineniia*, 24: 307.

87. M. F. Frolenko, "Lipetskii i Voronezhskii s"ezdy," *Byloe*, no. 13 (January 1907), pp. 67–77.

88. Quoted in Plekhanov, "O bylom i nebylitsakh," pp. 306–7.

89. Baron, *Plekhanov*, p. 44.

90. Two of the best accounts are Volk, *Narodnaia Volia*, and David Footman, *Red Prelude, The Life of the Russian Terrorist Zhelyabov* (New Haven, 1945).

91. V. Bogucharskii [Iakovlev], *Iz istorii politicheskoi bor'by v 70-kh i 80-kh gg. XIX veke. Partiia "Narodnoi Voli," eia proiskhozhdenie, sud'by, i gibel'* (Moscow, 1912), pp. 38–46; Frolenko, "Lipetskii i Voronezhskii s"ezdy," pp. 85–86; O. S. Liubatovich, "Dalekoe i nedavnee," *Byloe*, no. 6 (June 1906), pp. 108–9.

92. Footman, *Red Prelude*, p. 102.

93. "Programma ispolnitel'nogo komiteta," published in Figner, *Zapechatlennyi trud*, 1: 397, 399.

94. Ibid., pp. 191–208; Volk, *Narodnaia Volia*, pp. 94–99.

95. Ulam, *In the Name of the People*, pp. 333–34; Venturi, *Roots of Revolution*, pp. 644–45.

96. Frolenko, "Lipetskii i Voronezhskii" s"ezdy," pp. 70–73.

97. Figner, *Zapechatlennyi trud*, 1: 219–27; Volk, *Narodnaia Volia*, pp. 102–4; Bogucharskii [Iakovlev], *Iz istorii*, pp. 58–60; Footman, *Red Prelude*, pp. 130–37.

98. Quoted in Footman, *Red Prelude*, p. 167.

99. Those who lived to see the Revolution were Vera Figner, Mikhail Frolenko, Natalia Olovennikova, Arkadii Turkov, Mikhail Trigoni, and Anna Iakomova.

100. Quoted in Ulam, *In the Name of the People*, p. 341.

101. M. F. Frolenko, *Sobranie sochinenii* (Moscow, 1932), 2: 63.

102. Figner, *Zapechatlennyi trud*, 1: 247–48, 258–66; Footman, *Red Prelude*, pp. 171–87.

103. Figner, *Zapechatlennyi trud*, 1: 267.

104. Quoted in Bogucharskii [Iakovlev], *Iz istorii*, p. 75.

105. "Protsess 17-ti narodovol'tsev v 1883 godu," *Byloe*, no. 10 (October 1906), pp. 206–13; Venturi, *Roots of Revolution*, pp. 712–13; Footman, *Red Prelude*, pp. 194–200; Ulam, *In the Name of the People*, pp. 354–56.

106. Footman, *Red Prelude*, pp. 242–43.

107. P. A. Zaionchkovskii, *Krizis samoderzhaviia na rubezhe 1870–1880 godov* (Moscow, 1964), pp. 300–13, 322–40; V. G. Chernukha, *Vnutrenniaia politika tsarizma s serediny 50-kh do nachala 80-kh gg. XIX v.* (Leningrad, 1978), pp. 127–32; Daniel T. Orlovskii, *The Limits of Reform: The Ministry of Internal Affairs in Imperial Russia, 1802–1881* (Cambridge, Mass., 1981), pp. 191–96.

108. Figner, *Zapechatlennyi trud*, 1: 269, 304.

109. Ibid., pp. 368–70; "Protsess 17-ti narodovol'tsev," pp. 216–25; A. N. Bakh, *Zapiski narodovol'tsa* (Leningrad, 1931), pp. 30–31.

110. Quoted in Volk, *Narodnaia Volia*, p. 148.

111. O. M. Govorukhin, "Vospominaniia O. M. Govorukhina," *Golos minuvshago na chuzhoi storone* 16 (1926): 215.

112. Quoted in B. S. Itenberg and A. Ia. Cherniak, *Zhizn' Aleksandra Ul'ianova* (Moscow, 1966), p. 108.

113. Ibid., pp. 105–12.

114. Quoted in Govorukhin, "Vospominaniia," pp. 236–39.

115. Quoted in ibid., p. 230.

116. Quoted in Itenberg and Cherniak, *Zhizn' Aleksandra Ul'ianova,* p. 120.

117. Iu. Z. Polevoi, *Zarozhdenie marksizma v Rossii, 1883–1894gg.* (Moscow, 1959), p. 316.

118. A. I. Ivanskii, ed., *Zhizn' kak fakel. Istoriia geroicheskoi bor'by i tragicheskoi gibeli Aleksandra Ul'ianova rasskazannaia ego sovremennikami* (Moscow, 1966), pp. 294–303.

119. Quoted in Itenberg and Cherniak, *Zhizn' Aleksandra Ul'ianova,* p. 125.

120. I. Lukashevich, "Vospominaniia o dele l-go marta 1887 goda," *Byloe,* no. 1 (July 1917), pp. 32–39.

121. Ivanskii, ed., *Zhizn' kak fakel,* pp. 378–80.

122. Ibid., p. 391.

123. Itenberg and Cherniak, *Zhizn' Aleksandra Ul'ianova,* pp. 136–40.

124. Ivanskii, ed., *Zhizn' kak fakel,* p. 400.

125. A. I. Ivanskii, ed., *Molodye gody V. I. Lenina po vospominaniiam sovremennikov i dokumentam,* 3rd ed. (Moscow, 1960), pp. 230–31.

126. *Aleksandr Il'ich Ul'ianov i delo 1 marta 1887 goda. Sbornik vospominanii i materialov* (Moscow-Leningrad, 1927), p. 122.

127. Ibid., p. 123.

128. Lukashevich, "Vospominaniia," *Byloe,* no. 2 (August 1917), pp. 128–29. See also Mikhail Novorusskii, *Zapiski Shlissel'burzhtsa, 1887–1905* (Moscow, 1933), pp. 361–63.

129. Lukashevich, "Vospominaniia," p. 129.

130. Ivanskii, ed., *Molodye gody,* p. 237.

131. See, for example, the reproduction in Ivanshin, ed., *Zhizn' kak fakel,* facing p. 433.

132. Quoted in Harrison Salisbury, *Black Night, White Snow: Russia's Revolutions, 1905–1917* (New York, 1978), p. 31.

133. Quoted in Haimson, *The Russian Marxists and the Origins of Bolshevism,* p. 38.

134. M. M. Kovalevskii, *Obshchinnoe zemlevladenie: prichiny, khod, i posledstviia ego razlozheniia* (Moscow, 1879).

135. V. I. Orlov, *Sbornik statisticheskikh svedenii po moskovskoi gubernii: formy krest'ianskago zemlevladeniia v moskovskoi gubernii* (Moscow, 1879).

136. Quoted in Baron, *Plekhanov,* p. 55.

137. Quoted in Haimson, *Russian Marxists and the Origins of Bolshevism,* p. 42.

138. Akselrod, *Perezhitoe i peredumannoe*, pp. 156–57.

139. Abraham Ascher, *Pavel Axelrod and the Development of Menshevism* (Cambridge, Mass., 1972), p. 25.

140. Akselrod, *Perezhitoe i peredumannoe*, p. 421.

141. Quoted in Haimson, *Russian Marxists and the Origins of Bolshevism*, p. 44.

142. Quoted in Baron, *Plekhanov*, p. 131. See also pp. 130–33, and Ascher, *Pavel Axelrod*, pp. 82–84.

143. G. V. Plekhanov, "Pervye shagi sotsial-demokraticheskogo dvizheniia v Rossii," in *Sochineniia*, 24: 178–79.

144. G. V. Plekhanov, "Our Differences," in *Selected Philosophical Works* (Moscow, n.d.), 1: 373–83.

145. Haimson, *Russian Marxists and the Origins of Bolshevism*, p. 45.

146. J. L. H. Keep, *The Rise of Social Democracy in Russia* (Oxford, 1963), p. 16.

147. Plekhanov, "Pervye shagi," p. 178.

148. S. I. Mitskevich, *Revoliutsionnaia Moskva, 1888–1905* (Moscow, 1940), p. 143.

149. Iu. Martov, *Zapiski sotsialdemokrata* (Berlin, Petersburg, Moscow, 1922), p. 19.

150. Israel Getzler, *Martov: A Political Biography of a Russian Social Democrat* (Cambridge and Melbourne, 1967), pp. 1–11.

151. Martov, *Zapiski*, p. 94.

152. Getzler, *Martov*, pp. 13–19.

153. Martov, *Zapiski*, pp. 138, 137.

154. Ibid., p. 138.

155. Getzler, *Martov*, pp. 21–26.

156. Nikolay Valentinov [N. V. Volsky], *Encounters with Lenin* (London, 1968), p. 64.

157. Bertram Wolfe, *Three Who Made a Revolution: A Biographical History* (New York, 1948), pp. 65–85.

158. Valentinov, *Encounters*, p. 67.

159. Quoted in Wolfe, *Three Who Made a Revolution*, p. 90.

160. Polevoi, *Zarozhdenie marksizma*, pp. 407–22; Adam B. Ulam, *The Bolsheviks. The Intellectual and Political History of the Triumph of Communism in Russia* (New York, 1965), pp. 96–110; Neil Harding, *Lenin's Political Thought* (London, 1977), 1: 18–28.

161. Ulam, *The Bolsheviks*, p. 112.

162. Ibid., pp. 110–27; Haimson, *Russian Marxists and the Origins of Bolshevism*, pp. 103–9; Polevoi, *Zarozhdenie marksizma*, pp. 422–34;

Harding, *Lenin's Political Thought*, pp. 59–78; Richard Pipes, *Social Democracy and the St. Petersburg Labor Movement, 1885–1897* (Cambridge, Mass., 1963), pp. 40–75.

163. Martov, *Zapiski*, pp. 253–54.

164. See, for example, the illegal brochure entitled "Stachki i ikh znachenii dlia rabochikh," in *Rabochee dvizhenie v Rossii v XIX veke. Sbornik dokumentov i materialov*, ed. L. M. Ivanov (Moscow-Leningrad, 1961), 4: pt. 1, pp. 72–101.

165. Quoted in K. M. Takhtarev, *Rabochee dvizhenie v Peterburge (1893–1901gg.)* (Leningrad, 1924), p. 66.

166. Ibid., pp. 56–58.

167. Balabanov, *Ocherki po istorii rabochego klassa v Rossii*, 3: 207–21; Pipes, *Social Democracy*, pp. 99–116.

168. Martov, *Zapiski*, pp. 275–98.

169. Allan K. Wildman, *The Making of a Workers' Revolution: Russian Social Democracy, 1891–1903* (Chicago, 1967), pp. 64–80; Pipes, *Social Democracy*, pp. 94–98; Takhtarev, *Rabochee dvizhenie v Peterburge*, pp. 79–83.

170. Ulam, *The Bolsheviks*, pp. 127–38.

171. Martov, *Zapiski*, pp. 349–64; Getzler, *Martov*, pp. 37–41.

172. Wildman, *Making of a Workers' Revolution*, pp. 174–88; V. Levitskii [V. O. Tsederbaum], *Za chetvert' veka. Revoliutsionnye vospominaniia* (Moscow, 1926), 1: pt. 1, pp. 84–86.

173. Quoted in Haimson, *Russian Marxists and the Origins of Bolshevism*, p. 89.

174. V. I. Lenin, "Nasushchnye zadachi nashego dvizheniia," in *Sochineniia*, 4: 344–45, 342.

175. Keep, *The Rise of Social Democracy in Russia*, p. 68.

176. Ibid., pp. 67–95; Ulam, *The Bolsheviks*, pp. 160–76; R. H. W. Theen, *Lenin: Genesis and Development of a Revolutionary* (Philadelphia and New York, 1973), pp. 97–103; Haimson, *Russian Marxists and the Origins of Bolshevism*, pp. 117–36; Jonathan Frankel, ed. and trans., *Vladimir Akimov on the Dilemmas of Russian Marxism, 1895–1903* (Cambridge, 1969), pp. 43–60.

177. Harding, *Lenin's Political Thought*, p. 159.

178. V. I. Lenin, "Chto delat'?" in *Sochineniia*, 5: 348, 356, 478, 438.

179. Getzler, *Martov*, pp. 68–75.

180. Wolfe, *Three Who Made a Revolution*, pp. 232–40. Quotes from pp. 237, 235, 236.

181. Quoted in Nadezhda Krupskaia, *Memories of Lenin* (London, 1930), p. 83.

182. Balabanov, *Ocherki po istorii rabochego klassa v Rossii*, 3: 293–346.

183. Quoted in Ascher, *Pavel Axelrod*, p. 188.

184. Ulam, *The Bolsheviks*, pp. 176–93; Wolfe, *Three Who Made a Revolution*, pp. 232–62; Haimson, *Russian Marxists and the Origins of Bolshevism*, pp. 165–81; Keep, *Rise of Social Democracy in Russia*, pp. 107–48; Baron, *Plekhanov*, pp. 231–53.

185. Quoted in Haimson, *Russian Marxists and the Origins of Bolshevism*, p. 185.

186. Quoted in Getzler, *Martov*, p. 87.

187. Quoted in ibid., p. 89.

CHAPTER VI
Defenders of the Old Order

1. N. V. Gogol, "Mertvye dushi," in *Sobranie sochinenii* (Moscow, 1959), 5: 259–60.

2. Quoted in Louis Greenberg, *The Jews in Russia: The Struggle for Emancipation, 1881–1917* (New Haven, 1951), 2: 5.

3. Witte, *Vospominaniia*, 1: 129, 132–33.

4. M. Fedorova, "Moskovskii Otdel Sviashchennoi Druzhiny po dannym Arkhiva Sekretnago Otdeleniia Kantseliarii Moskovskago General-Gubernatora," *Golos minuvshago* 6, no. 1–3 (January–March 1918): 144–45.

5. Witte, *Vospominaniia*, 1: 128–30, 521–22; A. S. Suvorin, *Dnevnik A. S. Suvorina* (Moscow-Petrograd, 1923), pp. 25–26.

6. Gary M. Hamburg, "Russian Noble Families and the Terrorist Movement, 1878–1882" (unpublished scholarly paper, 1981), pp. 13–14; Stephen Lukashevich, "The Holy Brotherhood, 1881–1883," *American Slavic and East European Review* 18, no. 4 (December 1959): 493.

7. P. A. Sadikov, "Obshchestvo 'Sviashchennoi Druzhiny,'" *Krasnyi arkhiv* 21 (1927): 210–11.

8. Ibid., p. 211.

9. Hamburg, "Russian Noble Families," pp. 13–14; Zaionchkovskii, *Krizis samoderzhaviia*, pp. 310–11; V. N. Smel'skii, "Sviashchennaia Druzhina (iz dnevnika eia chlena)," *Golos minuvshago* 4, no. 1 (January 1916): 226.

10. K. P. Pobedonostsev, *Pis'ma Pobedonostseva k Aleksandru III* (Moscow, 1925), 1: 392–96.

11. Shmuel Galai, "Early Russian Constitutionalism, 'Vol'noe Slovo' and the 'Zemstvo Union.' A Study in Deception," *Jahrbücher für*

Geschichte Osteuropas 22, no. 1 (1974): 53–55; Lukashevich, "Holy Brotherhood," pp. 506–9.

12. Bogucharskii, *Iz istorii politicheskoi bor'by*, p. 383.

13. K. P. Pobedonostsev, "Graf V. N. Panin," *Golosa iz Rossii*, no. 7 (1859), pp. 137–38. Reprinted Moscow, 1974–75.

14. A. E. Nol'de, *K. P. Pobedonostsev i sudebnaia reforma* (Petrograd, 1915), pp. 10–12; K. P. Pobedonostsev, "O reformakh v grazhdanskom sudoproizvodstve," *Russkii vestnik* 22 (1859): 27–32.

15. Robert F. Byrnes, *Pobedonostsev: His Life and Thought* (Bloomington and London, 1968), p. 69.

16. Ibid., p. 106.

17. Richard S. Wortman, *The Development of a Russian Legal Consciousness* (Chicago and London, 1976), p. 216.

18. Konstantin Korol'kov, *Zhizn' i tsarstvovanie Imperatora Aleksandra III, 1881–1894gg.* (Kiev, 1901), pp. 16–17.

19. Pis'mo Tsesarevicha Aleksandra Aleksandrovicha k Konstantinu Petrovichu Pobedonostsevu, 22 noiabria 1866g., in *K. P. Pobedonostsev i ego korrespondenty* (Moscow-Petrograd, 1923), 1 (2): 1003.

20. Quoted in W. Bruce Lincoln, *The Romanovs: Autocrats of All the Russias* (New York, 1981), p. 448.

21. Konstantin P. Pobedonostsev, *Reflections of a Russian Statesman* (Ann Arbor, 1965), pp. 62, 65–66, 35, 254.

22. Quoted in Byrnes, *Pobedonostsev*, p. 154.

23. K. P. Pobedonostsev, *Pis'ma Pobedonostseva k Aleksandru III* (Moscow, 1925), 1: 316–18, 321; 1: 46.

24. Ibid., 1: 317, 275.

25. Quoted in Byrnes, *Pobedonostsev*, p. 19.

26. Quoted in ibid., pp. 78, 35; Pobedonostsev, *Pis'ma Aleksandru III*, 1: 317.

27. Pobedonostsev, *Reflections*, pp. 206, 137, 1–2.

28. B. B. Glinskii, "Konstantin Petrovich Pobedonostsev. Materialy dlia biografii," *Istoricheskii vestnik* 108, no. 4 (April 1907): 254.

29. Pobedonostsev, *Reflections*, pp. 186, 184, 150.

30. Byrnes, *Pobedonostsev*, p. 130.

31. Ibid., p. 210.

32. Ibid., pp. 188–203, 271–79.

33. Quoted in ibid., p. 205.

34. Ibid., pp. 204–9.

35. Witte, *Vospominaniia*, 2: 548; quoted in Byrnes, *Pobedonostsev*, p. 365.

36. Quoted in Aleksandr Mikhailovich, *Once a Grand Duke*, p. 177.

37. Quoted in V. V. Vodovozov, *Graf S. Iu. Vitte i Imperator Nikolai II* (Petersburg, 1922), p. 107.

38. Quoted in von Laue, *Sergei Witte*, pp. 286, 284.

39. Quoted in Vodovozov, *Graf S. Iu. Vitte*, p. 110.

40. Quoted in ibid., p. 103.

41. Quoted in ibid., p. 105.

42. Quoted in ibid., p. 106.

43. Quoted in ibid., pp. 106–7.

44. N. I. Faleev, "Rossiia pod Okhranoi: Istoricheskii ocherk," *Byloe* (October 1907), pp. 28–29.

45. Edward Ellis Smith, *"The Okhrana." The Russian Department of Police* (Palo Alto, 1967), p. 18.

46. Quoted in Wolfe, *Three Who Made a Revolution*, p. 535. See also Smith, *"The Okhrana,"* pp. 18–19.

47. P. P. Zavarzin, *Rabota tainoi politsii* (Paris, 1924), pp. 42–46.

48. Byrnes, *Pobedonostsev*, p. 86.

49. V. Zhilinskii, "Organizatsiia i zhizn' okhrannago otdeleniia vo vremena tsarskoi vlasti," *Golos minuvshago*, nos. 9–10 (September–October, 1917), p. 258.

50. General P. Zavarzin, *Souvenirs d'un chef de l'Okhrana, 1900–1917* (Paris, 1930), p. 41.

51. Ibid., pp. 36–42.

52. Zhilinskii, "Organizatsiia i zhizn'," p. 255.

53. George Kennan, "Russian 'Mouse-Traps,'" *The Century Illustrated Monthly Magazine* 88 (November 1911–April 1912): 745–52.

54. Quoted in Zhilinskii, "Organizatsiia i zhizn' okhrannago otdeleniia," p. 252.

55. Zavarzin, *Rabota tainoi politsii*, pp. 16–17.

56. Ibid., p. 21.

57. Ibid., pp. 20–21.

58. Quoted in Zhilinskii, "Organizatsiia i zhizn' okhrannago otdeleniia," pp. 281–82.

59. Wolfe, *Three Who Made a Revolution*, pp. 535–57; Boris Nikolaevskii, *Aseff the Spy: Russian Terrorist and Police Stool* (New York, 1934), *passim*.

60. I. V. Alekseev, *Provokator Anna Serebriakova* (Moscow, 1932), pp. 18–22; S. I. Mitskevich, *Revoliutsionnaia Moskva, 1888–1905* (Moscow, 1940), p. 284.

61. Quoted in Alekseev, *Provokator Anna Serebriakova*, p. 28.

62. Mitskevich, *Revoliutsionnaia Moskva*, p. 284.

63. Ibid., p. 286.

64. Alekseev, *Provokator Anna Serebriakova*, p. 31.

65. Quoted in Nikolaevskii, *Aseff the Spy*, p. 26.

66. Ibid., *passim*. See also Oliver H. Radkey, *The Agrarian Foes of Bolshevism. Promise and Default of the Russian Socialist Revolutionaries, February to October 1917* (New York, 1958), pp. 71–74, 77–80; Maurice LaPorte, *Histoire de l'Okhrana. La Police secrète des Tsars, 1880–1917* (Paris, 1935), pp. 61–82.

67. L. P. Men'shchikov, *Okhrana i revoliutsiia. K istorii tainykh politicheskikh organizatsii v Rossii* (Moscow, 1929), 2: pt. 2, p. 118.

68. Ibid.

69. Quoted in Mitskevich, *Revoliutsionnaia Moskva*, p. 285.

70. Quoted in Dmitrii Pospielovskii, *Russian Police Trade Unionism: Experiment or Provocation?* (London, 1971), p. 67; M. R. Gots, "S. V. Zubatov: Stranichka iz perezhitago," *Byloe*, no. 9 (September 1906), pp. 63–66.

71. B. P. Koz'min, *S. V. Zubatov i ego korrespondenty* (Moscow-Leningrad, 1928), pp. 52–54.

72. Jeremiah Schneiderman, *Sergei Zubatov and Revolutionary Marxism. The Struggle for the Working Class in Tsarist Russia* (Ithaca, 1976), pp. 51–53.

73. Ibid., p. 53.

74. A. I. Spiridonovich, "Pri tsarskom rezhime," in *Arkhiv russkoi revoliutsii*, ed. I. V. Gessen, 15 (1924): 123.

75. Ibid.

76. Schneiderman, *Sergei Zubatov*, p. 55.

77. Quoted in Alekseev, *Provokator Anna Serebriakova*, p. 126.

78. Quoted in Schneiderman, *Sergei Zubatov*, p. 80, n. 38.

79. "Raport prokurora Moskovskoi sudebnoi palaty N. P. Postnikova Ministru Iustitsii N. V. Murav'evu ob agitatsii Moskovskogo 'Rabochego Soiuza' sredi moskovskikh rabochikh za vseobshchuiu stachku dlia podderzhki rabochikh g. Peterburga" (classified as "Completely Secret"), 20 June 1896, published in *Rabochee dvizhenie v Rossii v XIX veke. Sbornik dokumentov i materialov*, ed. L. M. Ivanov (Moscow, 1961), 4: pt. 1, p. 348.

80. Schneiderman, *Sergei Zubatov*, pp. 78–82.

81. Quoted in Alekseev, *Provokator Anna Serebriakova*, p. 125.

82. Pospielovsky, *Russian Police Trade Unionism*, pp. 72–73.

83. Quoted in Schneiderman, *Sergei Zubatov*, p. 97.

84. Quoted in N. A. Bukhbinder, "Zubatovshchina v Moskve," *Katorga i ssylka* 14 (1925): 97.

85. Quoted in Schneiderman, *Sergei Zubatov*, p. 96.

86. Schneiderman, *Sergei Zubatov*, pp. 97–98.

87. Bukhbinder, "Zubatovshchina v Moskve," p. 111.

88. Schneiderman, *Sergei Zubatov*, pp. 99–133.

89. Ibid., pp. 136–208; Pospielovsky, *Russian Police Trade Unionism*, pp. 98–143.

90. S. V. Zubatov, "K istorii zubatovshchiny," *Byloe* 23, no. 1 (July 1917): 95–97.

91. Kuropatkin, "Dnevnik," *Krasnyi arkhiv*, 2: 82.

92. Ibid., pp. 81–82.

93. Alekseev, *Provokator Anna Serebriakova*, p. 136.

94. Spiridonovich, "Pri tsarskom rezhime," p. 153; Witte, *Vospominaniia*, 2: 220.

95. Quoted in Alekseev, *Provokator Anna Serebriakova*, p. 136.

96. "K istorii Zubatovshchiny," p. 95.

97. Schneiderman, *Sergei Zubatov*, pp. 358–61.

98. Greenberg, *The Jews in Russia*, 1: 70–118; S. M. Dubnow, *History of the Jews in Russia and Poland from the Earliest Times until the Present Day* (Philadelphia, 1918), 1: 153–87, 242–365.

99. Mark Vishniak, "Antisemitism in Tsarist Russia," in *Essays on Antisemitism*, ed. Pinson, p. 131; "Pogromy v Rossii," *Evreiskaia entsiklopediia*, 12: cols. 611–12.

100. S. M. Dubnow, "Anti-Evreiskie dvizhenie v Rossii v 1881–1882gg.," *Evreiskaia starina* 1 (1909): 92.

101. P. Sonin-M., "Vospominaniia o iuzhnorusskikh pogromakh 1881 goda," *Evreiskaia starina* 2 (1909): 213.

102. Martov, *Zapiska sotsialdemokrata*, p. 19.

103. Samuel Joseph, *Jewish Immigration to the United States from 1881–1910* (New York, 1914), pp. 90–95.

104. Vishniak, "Antisemitism in Tsarist Russia," pp. 132–33; Greenberg, *The Jews in Russia*, 2: 23.

105. R. Kantor, "Aleksandr III o evreiskikh pogromakh, 1881–1882gg. Novye materialy," *Evreiskaia letopis'* 1 (1923): 150–52.

106. Quoted in Vishniak, "Antisemitism in Tsarist Russia," p. 135.

107. Quoted in P. A. Zaionchkovskii, *Krizis samoderzhaviia*, p. 419.

108. Quoted in ibid., p. 417.

109. Published in Dubnow, *History of the Jews in Russia and Poland*, 2: 250.

110. "Pogromy v Rossii," col. 612.

111. P. Sonin-M., "Vospominaniia," p. 213.

112. Quoted in Zaionchkovskii, *Krizis samoderzhaviia*, p. 379.

113. Published in Dubnow, *History of the Jews in Russia and Poland*, 2: 253.

114. Ibid., p. 255.

115. Quoted in Greenberg, *The Jews in Russia*, 2: 21.

116. Quoted in Dubnow, "Anti-Evreiskie dvizhenie v Rossii," p. 95.

117. Ibid., pp. 93–97.

118. Dubnow, *History of the Jews in Russia and Poland*, 2: 302.

119. Salo W. Baron, *The Russian Jew under Tsars and Soviets* (New York, 1964), p. 61.

120. A. S. Pushkin, "Chernaia shal'," in *Polnoe sobranie sochinenii* (Moscow, 1956), 2: 16.

121. I. S. Turgenev, "Zhid," in *Sobranie sochinenii* (Moscow, 1961), 5: 102–3.

122. D. Zaslavskii, "Evrei v russkoi literature," *Evreiskaia starina* 1 (1923): 78–81.

123. V. G. Korolenko, "Dom No. 13," in *Sobranie sochinenii v desiati tomakh* (Moscow, 1955), 9: 406–22.

124. Zaionchkovskii, *Krizis samoderzhaviia*, p. 379, n. 2; E. A. Perets, *Dnevnik* (Moscow, 1927), pp. 131–34.

125. P. A. Zaionchkovskii, *Rossiiskoe samoderzhavie v kontse XIX stoletiia. Politicheskaia reaktsiia 80-kh–nachala 90-kh godov* (Moscow, 1970), p. 131.

126. Quoted in Vishniak, "Antisemitism in Tsarist Russia," p. 154.

127. Zaionchkovskii, *Rossiiskoe samoderzhavie*, pp. 131–36.

128. Quoted in A. A. Polovtsov, *Dnevnik gosudarstvennogo sekretaria A. A. Polovtsova* (Moscow 1966), 2: 370.

129. *Polnoe sobranie zakonov Rossiiskoi Imperii*, sobranie 3-oe, no. 7581.

130. Harold Frederic, *The New Exodus: A Study of Israel in Russia* (New York and London, 1892), p. 200.

131. "Evrei v Moskve po neopublikovannym dokumentam," *Byloe*, no. 9 (September 1907), pp. 153–57.

132. Quoted in Dubnow, *History of the Jews in Russia and Poland*, 2: 406.

133. "Evrei v Moskve," pp. 154–56.

134. A. Katsnel'son, "Iz martirologa Moskovskoi obshchiny. Moskovskaia sinagoga v 1891–1906gg.," *Evreiskaia starina* 1 (1909): 183, 186, 188.

135. Witte, *Vospominaniia*, 3: 327.

136. Quoted in Michael Davitt, *Within the Pale* (London, 1903), pp. 98, 211; Greenberg, *The Jews in Russia*, 2: 51; Dubnow, *History of the Jews in Russia and Poland*, 3: 69–71.

137. Testimony of Konon Vasil'evich Rybachenko in *Materialy dlia istorii antievreiskikh pogromov v Rossii*, ed. G. Ia. Krasnyi-Admoni and S. M. Dubnow (Petrograd, 1919), 1: 1–3. See also pp. 4–124.

138. Dubnow, *History of the Jews in Russia and Poland*, 3: 70–71; *Materialy dlia istorii antievreiskikh pogromov*, ed. Krasnyi-Admoni and Dubnow, 1: 135–36.

139. Dubnow, *History of the Jews in Russia and Poland*, 3: 71–72; Davitt, *Within the Pale*, p. 213.

140. *Materialy dlia istorii antievreiskikh pogromov*, ed. Krasnyi-Admoni and Dubnow, 1:130–31; Davitt, *Within the Pale*, pp. 125–26.

141. Vishniak, "Antisemitism in Tsarist Russia," p. 136.

142. Davitt, *Within the Pale*, pp. 169, 167, 135, 129.

143. Korolenko, "Dom No. 13," pp. 409, 420.

144. A. N. Kuropatkin, "Dnevnik A. N. Kuropatkina," *Krasnyi arkhiv* 2 (1922): 43.

145. "Kto vinovat?" in *Materialy dlia istorii antievreiskikh pogromov*, ed. Krasnyi-Admoni and Dubnow, 1: 266.

146. Published in Davitt, *Within the Pale*, pp. 182–85.

147. Quoted in Dubnow, *History of the Jews in Russia and Poland*, 3: 89.

148. Published in Davitt, *Within the Pale*, pp. 276–77.

149. Ibid., p. 185.

150. Witte, *Vospominaniia*, 2: 214.

151. A. P. Chekhov, "Vishnevyi sad," in *Sobranie sochinenii v vos'mi tomakh* (Moscow, 1970), 7: 325, 338.

152. S. Piontkovskii, ed., "Novoe o Zubatovshchine," *Krasnyi arkhiv* 1 (1922): 289.

153. Pospielovsky, *Russian Police Trade Unionism*, p. 145.

154. Quoted in Witte, *Vospominaniia*, 2: 292.

155. Kuropatkin, "Dnevnik," *Krasnyi arkhiv*, 2: 94.

CHAPTER VII
"A Small Victorious War"

1. W. Bruce Lincoln, *The Romanovs*, pp. 552–53.

2. Quoted in Constantin de Grunwald, *Tsar Nicholas I*, trans. Brigit Patmore (London, 1954), p. 255.

3. Quoted in Lincoln, *Nicholas I*, p. 329.

4. "Rapport presenté par le comte Charles de Nesselrode à S. M. l'Empereur Nicolas Ier, au jubilé de sa 25-e année de règne," 20 novembre 1850, in Count K. V. Nesselrode, *Lettres et papiers du Chancelier Comte de Nesselrode, 1760–1850*, 10: 2–3.

5. Quoted in John S. Curtiss, *The Russian Army under Nicholas I, 1825–1855* (Durham, 1965), p. 127.

6. I. S. Bloch [Bliokh], *The Future of War in its Technical, Eco-*

nomic, and Political Relations (Boston, 1902), p. 6. See also pp. 150–53, 329.

7. Ibid., pp. 5, 128–42; I. S. Bliokh, "Budushchaia voina, eia ekonomicheskie prichiny i posledstvie," *Russkii vestnik* 224, no. 2 (1893): 208–11.

8. Bliokh, "Budushchaia voina," p. 201.

9. Bloch, *Future of War*, pp. lxviii, lxxi, lxii.

10. Witte, *Vospominaniia*, 2: 159–61.

11. Quotes from Barbara Tuchman, *The Proud Tower: A Portrait of the World before the War, 1890–1914* (New York, 1966), pp. 239, 241.

12. Witte, *Vospominaniia*, 2: 162.

13. I. I. Rostunov, "Proiskhozhdenie voiny," in *Istoriia Russko-Iaponskoi voiny, 1904–1905gg.*, ed. I. I. Rostunov (Moscow, 1977), pp. 26–31.

14. A. A. Svechin, *Evoliutsiia voennago iskusstva* (Moscow, 1928), 2: 457–59.

15. Rostunov, "Proiskhozhdenie voiny," p. 36.

16. Quoted in von Laue, *Sergei Witte*, p. 191.

17. Quoted in ibid., p. 189.

18. A. A. Polovtsov, "Iz dnevnika A. A. Polovtsova, 1895–1900gg.," *Krasnyi arkhiv* 46 (1931): 121.

19. Quoted in John Albert White, *The Diplomacy of the Russo-Japanese War* (Princeton, 1964), p. 49.

20. Von Laue, *Sergei Witte*, pp. 240–42.

21. *Russko-Iaponskaia voina: iz dnevnikov A. N. Kuropatkina i N. P. Linevicha* (Leningrad, 1925), pp. 5–6; White, *Diplomacy*, pp. 18–21.

22. Andrew Malozemoff, *Russian Far Eastern Policy, 1881–1904. With Special Emphasis on the Causes of the Russo-Japanese War* (Berkeley and Los Angeles, 1958), pp. 177–207; B. A. Romanov, *Russia in Manchuria 1892–1906*, trans. Susan Wilbur Jones (Ann Arbor, 1952), pp. 248–308; Von Laue, *Sergei Witte*, pp. 243–48; Hugh Seton-Watson, *The Russian Empire, 1801–1917* (Oxford, 1967), pp. 587–89.

23. Rostunov, "Proiskhozhdenie voiny," pp. 48–54; William L. Langer, *The Diplomacy of Imperialism* (New York, 1965), pp. 747–86.

24. A. Svechin, *Russko-Iaponskaia voina, 1904–1905gg. po doku-mental'nym dannym truda voenno-istoricheskoi komissii i drugim istoch-nikam* (Oranienbaum, 1910), pp. 20–24.

25. Ibid., pp. 2–4; Malozemoff, *Russian Far Eastern Policy*, pp. 52–58.

26. Malozemoff, *Russian Far Eastern Policy*, p. 237; Romanov, *Russia in Manchuria*, pp. 294–322.

27. Quoted in David Walder, *The Short Victorious War: The Russo-Japanese Conflict, 1904–1905* (London, 1973), p. 43.

28. Kuropatkin, "Dnevnik," *Krasnyi arkhiv,* 2: 78.

29. Ibid., p. 95.

30. Quoted in White, *Diplomacy,* p. 121.

31. Witte, *Vospominaniia,* 2: 292.

32. Ibid.

33. Malozemoff, *Russian Far Eastern Policy,* pp. 237–49; White, *Diplomacy,* pp. 112–31; Walder, *Short Victorious War,* pp. 40–42.

34. Quoted in Malozemoff, *Russian Far Eastern Policy,* p. 248.

35. Nicholas's diary for 26 January 1904. Quoted in Salisbury, *Black Night, White Snow,* p. 89; Malozemoff, *Russian Far Eastern Policy,* pp. 248–49.

36. Kuropatkin, "Dnevnik," *Krasnyi arkhiv,* 2: 106.

37. Nicholas's diary for 26 January 1904. Quoted in Salisbury, *Black Night, White Snow,* p. 89.

38. Svechin, *Russko-Iaponskaia voina,* pp. 49–50; *The Official History of the Russo-Japanese War* (London, 1909), 1: 43–44.

39. Newton A. McCully, *The McCully Report: The Russo-Japanese War, 1904–1905,* ed. Richard A. von Doenhoff (Annapolis, 1977), p. 268; Walder, *Short Victorious War,* p. 58.

40. I. I. Rostunov and Iu. I. Chernov, "Nachalo voiny i strategicheskoe razvertyvanie," in *Istoriia Russko-Iaponskoi voiny,* ed. Rostunov, pp. 110–11.

41. Ibid., p. 118.

42. Kuropatkin, "Dnevnik," *Krasnyi arkhiv,* 2: 100.

43. McCully, *McCully Report,* p. 50; A. fon Shvarts and Iu. Romanovskii, *Oborona Port-Artura* (St. Petersburg, 1908), 1: 146–48.

44. Svechin, *Russko-Iaponskaia voina,* pp. 49–58.

45. Kuropatkin, "Dnevnik," *Krasnyi arkhiv,* 2: 109–10.

46. Ibid.

47. Ibid., p. 105; A. N. Kuropatkin, *Zapiski generala Kuropatkina o Russko-Iaponskoi voine. Itogi voiny* (Berlin, 1911), pp. 237–39, 242; Baedeker, *Russia,* p. 533.

48. Witte, *Vospominaniia,* 2: 292.

49. Quoted in Robert K. Massie, *Nicholas and Alexandra* (New York, 1978), p. 84.

50. Quoted in Salisbury, *Black Night, White Snow,* p. 91.

51. Ibid.

52. Nicholas to the Dowager Empress Maria Feodorovna, 23 September 1904, *The Letters of Tsar Nicholas and Empress Marie,* ed. Edward J. Bing (London, 1937), p. 177.

53. Massie, *Nicholas and Alexandra*, p. 88.

54. Anna Viroubova, *Memories of the Russian Court* (New York, 1923), p. 9.

55. Douglas Story, *The Campaign with Kuropatkin* (London, 1904), p. 299.

56. Rostunov and Chernov, "Nachalo voiny," p. 132.

57. Ibid., pp. 133–44; P. Larenko, *Stradnye dni Port-Artura. Khronika voennykh sobytii i zhizni v osazhdennoi kreposti s 26-go ianvaria 1904g. po 9 ianvaria 1905g.* (St. Petersburg, 1906), pp. 69–73; Walder, *Short Victorious War*, pp. 69–70.

58. A. Belomor, *Port-Arturskaia eskadra nakanune gibeli* (St. Petersburg, 1908), pp. 62–74; Walder, *Short Victorious War*, p. 88.

59. Quoted in Vladimir Semenov, *Rasplata* (London, 1909), p. 151.

60. Fon Shvarts and Romanovskii, *Oborona Port-Artura*, 1: 279–80.

61. V. P. Glukhov, "Oborona Port-Artura," in *Istoriia Russko-Iaponskoi voiny*, ed. Rostunov, pp. 174–77.

62. Voenno-istoricheskaia komissiia po opisaniiu Russko-Iaponskoi voiny, *Russko-Iaponskaia voina 1904–1905: Oborona Kvantuna i Port-Artura* (St. Petersburg, 1910), 8: pt. 2, prilozhenie no. 1, pp. 2–3; Svechin, *Russko-Iaponskaia voina*, pp. 266–70; fon Shvarts and Romanovskii, *Oborona Port-Artura*, 2: 1–5.

63. Ellis Ashmead-Bartlett, *Port Arthur: The Siege and Capitulation* (London and Edinburgh, 1906), p. 185.

64. General Sir Ian Hamilton, *A Staff Officer's Scrap-Book during the Russo-Japanese War* (London, 1912), p. 75.

65. Voenno-istoricheskaia komissiia, *Russko-Iaponskaia voina*, 8: pt. 2, prilozhenie no. 1, pp. 2–4; Walder, *Short Victorious War*, p. 125.

66. Quoted in fon Shvarts and Romanovskii, *Oborona Port-Artura*, 2: 6–7.

67. Quoted in Glukhov, "Oborona Port-Artura," p. 209.

68. Ibid., pp. 204–18; Voenno-istoricheskaia komissiia, *Russko-Iaponskaia voina*, 8: p. 2, pp. 130–238; fon Shvarts and Romanovskii, *Oborona Port-Artura*, 2: 133–200.

69. *Reports of Military Observers attached to the Armies in Manchuria during the Russo-Japanese War* (Washington, 1907), 4: 192–93; 2: 196–98. See also V. B. Giubbenet, *V osazhdennom Port-Arture. Ocherki voenno-sanitarnago dela* (St. Petersburg, 1910), pp. 221–40; and Raymond Spear, *Report on the Russian Medical and Sanitary Features of the Russo-Japanese War to the Surgeon-General, U. S. Navy* (Washington, 1906), pp. 64–67.

70. *Reports of Military Observers*, 4:192.

71. Quoted in fon Shvarts and Romanovskii, *Oborona Port-Artura*, 2: 311.

72. *Reports of Military Observers*, 4: 196.

73. Glukhov, "Oborona Port-Artura," pp. 224–29; *Official History*, 3: 54–64; Voenno-istoricheskaia komissiia, *Russko-Iaponskaia voina*, 8: pt. 2, pp. 318–404.

74. Glukhov, "Oborona Port-Artura," pp. 218–24; Voenno-istoricheskaia komissiia, *Russko-Iaponskaia voina*, 8: pt. 2, pp. 282–318; Ashmead-Bartlett, *Port Arthur*, pp. 158–62.

75. *Reports of Military Observers*, 4: 192.

76. Voenno-istoricheskaia komissiia, *Russko-Iaponskaia voina*, 8: pt. 2, pp. 550–645; *Official History*, 3: 81–99; Glukhov, "Oborona Port-Artura," pp. 236–43.

77. Quoted in Walder, *Short Victorious War*, p. 239.

78. "Zhurnal voennago soveta 16 dekabria 1904 goda," in Voenno-istoricheskaia komissiia, *Russko-Iaponskaia voina*, 8: pt. 2, prilozhenie, pp. 176, 174.

79. Glukhov, "Oborona Port-Artura," p. 248.

80. Voenno-istoricheskaia komissiia, *Russko-Iaponskaia voina*, 8: pt. 2, prilozhenie, p. 180.

81. Ibid., pp. 181–86; *Official History*, 3: 139–40.

82. *Official History*, 3: 141–43.

83. Quoted in White, *Diplomacy*, p. 151.

84. Hamilton, *Staff Officer's Scrap-Book*, p. 54.

85. William Maxwell, *From the Yalu to Port Arthur. A Personal Record* (London, 1906), p. 244.

86. V. I. Vinogradov and Iu. F. Sokolov, "Operatsii v Man'chzhurii," in *Istoriia Russko-iaponskoi voiny*, ed. Rostunov, p. 270; M. Pavlovich, "Vneshniaia politika i russko-iaponskaia voina," in *Obshchestvennoe dvizhenie*, ed. Martov et al., 2: 24–25.

87. Pavlovich, "Vneshniaia politika," p. 24.

88. Quoted in N. A. Levitskii, *Russko-Iaponskaia voina, 1904–1905* (Moscow, 1938), p. 164.

89. Quoted in Walder, *Short Victorious War*, p. 158.

90. Quoted in V. Marushevskii and P. Orlov, *Boevaia rabota Russkoi armii v voinu 1904–1905gg.* (St. Petersburg, 1913), 2: 7.

91. Kuropatkin, "Dnevnik," *Krasnyi arkhiv* 69–70 (1935): 114–17.

92. Marushevskii and Orlov, *Boevaia rabota*, 2: 1–103; Vinogradov and Sokolov, "Operatsii v Man'chzhurii," pp. 283–93.

93. Kuropatkin, "Dnevnik," p. 117.

94. Quoted in Vinogradov and Sokolov, "Operatsii v Man'chzhurii," p. 294.

95. Quoted in Walder, *Small Victorious War*, p. 268.

96. *Iz dnevnikov A. N. Kuropatkina i N. P. Linevicha*, pp. 64–73.

97. A. N. Kuropatkin, *Opisanie boevykh deistvii Man'chzhurskikh armii pod Mukdenom s 4-go fevralia po 4-e marta 1905 goda* (Moscow, 1907), 1: 3–12; Vinogradov and Sokolov, "Operatsii v Man'chzhurii," pp. 295–306; Voenno-istoricheskaia komissiia, *Russko-Iaponskaia voina*, 5: pt. 1, pp. 1–5, 20–39; prilozheniia nos. 1 and 3, pp. 4–63, 78–90.

98. Voenno-istoricheskaia komissiia, *Russko-Iaponskaia voina*, 5: pt. 1, pp. 40–197. For a detailed, almost hour-by-hour, account of the Russian forces during the battle, see Kuropatkin, *Opisanie boevykh deistvii*, vols. 1–3, *passim*.

99. Voenno-istoricheskaia komissiia, *Russko-Iaponskaia voina*, 5: pt. 2, pp. 315–16; Vinogradov and Sokolov, "Operatsii v Man'chzhurii," pp. 305–19.

100. *Iz dnevnikov A. N. Kuropatkina i N. P. Linevicha*, p. 87.

101. Quoted in J. N. Westwood, *Witnesses of Tsushima* (Tokyo and Tallahassee, 1970), pp. 82–83.

102. Voenno-istoricheskaia komissiia, *Russko-Iaponskaia voina*, 7: 3.

103. Quoted in Westwood, *Witnesses*, p. 54.

104. Witte, *Vospominaniia*, 1: 266–68; Walder, *Short Victorious War*, pp. 175–77.

105. Quoted in Witte, *Vospominaniia*, 2: 386.

106. Ibid., p. 384.

107. Ibid.

108. Quoted in Westwood, *Witnesses*, pp. 70–71.

109. E. S. Politovskii, *Ot Libavy do Tsusimy* (St. Petersburg, 1908), pp. 2, 5.

110. Quoted in Westwood, *Witnesses*, p. 73.

111. Politovskii, *Ot Libavy do Tsusimy*, p. 3.

112. Ibid., p. 11.

113. Iu. I. Chernov, "Tsusima," in *Istoriia Russko-Iaponskoi voiny*, ed. Rostunov, pp. 326–29; Westwood, *Witnesses*, pp. 14–32, 115–34; Walder, *Short Victorious War*, pp. 226–30.

114. Politovskii, *Ot Libavy do Tsusimy*, pp. 111, 119, 128.

115. Ibid., p. 128.

116. Ibid., p. 212.

117. Quoted in Westwood, *Witnesses*, p. 153.

118. Walder, *Short Victorious War*, p. 278.

119. Quoted in Westwood, *Witnesses*, p. 176.

120. Quoted in ibid., p. 170.

121. Quoted in ibid., p. 183.

122. Voenno-istoricheskaia komissiia, *Russko-Iaponskaia voina*, 7: 205–29; Chernov, "Tsusima," pp. 332–47; V. A. Anushkin, *Russko-Iaponskaia voina, 1904–1905* (Moscow, 1911), pp. 197–98.

123. Quoted in Westwood, *Witnesses*, p. 262.

124. Quoted in ibid., pp. 270–71.

125. Quoted in Shumpei Okamoto, *The Japanese Oligarchy and the Russo-Japanese War* (New York and London, 1970), p. 111.

126. A. N. Kuropatkin, *The Russian Army, and the Japanese War*, trans. A. B. Lindsay (London, 1909), 1: 256–63, 233–34.

127. Quoted in Eugene P. Trani, *The Treaty of Portsmouth: An Adventure in American Diplomacy* (Lexington, 1969), p. 53.

128. N. I. Rostunov, "Zakliuchenie," in *Istoriia Russko-Iaponskoi voiny*, ed. Rostunov, p. 364.

129. Trani, *Treaty of Portsmouth*, pp. 69–70.

130. Witte, *Vospominaniia*, 2: 424–25.

131. White, *Diplomacy*, p. 308.

132. Ibid., 309.

133. Ibid., pp. 206–309; Okamoto, *Japanese Oligarchy*, pp. 150–63; Trani, *Treaty of Portsmouth*, pp. 118–55.

134. Quoted in Kuropatkin, "Dnevnik," *Krasnyi arkhiv*, 2: 94.

CHAPTER VIII
1905: The Year of Turmoil

1. P. Maslov, "Krest'ianskoe dvizhenie," in *Obshchestvennoe dvizhenie*, ed. Martov et al., 2: pt. 2, pp. 260–61.

2. Boris Pasternak, "Deviat'sot piatyi god," quoted in Walter Sablinsky, *The Road to Bloody Sunday* (Princeton, 1976), p. 272.

3. Quoted in Isaac Deutscher, *Stalin: A Political Biography* (New York, 1967), pp. 40–41.

4. Quoted in Isaac Deutscher, *The Prophet Armed. Trotsky: 1879–1921* (Oxford, 1954), p. 47.

5. Quoted in ibid., p. 115.

6. Paul Miliukov, *Russia and Its Crisis* (Chicago and London, 1906), p. 434.

7. Quoted in ibid., p. 179.

8. Ibid., p. 196; E. E. Kruze and D. G. Kutsentov, "Naselenie Peterburga," in *Ocherki istorii Leningrada*, ed. Kochakov et al., 3: 104–5.

9. A. Mosolov, *Pri dvore Imperatora* (Riga, n.d.), pp. 6–7; *Nikolai II: Materialy dlia kharakteristiki lichnosti i tsarstvovaniia* (Moscow, 1917), pp. 40–42.

10. Nicholas to the Empress Maria Feodorovna, 25 June 1887, in *The Letters of Tsar Nicholas and the Empress Marie*, ed. Edward J. Bing (London, 1937), p. 33.

11. Alexander, Grand Duke of Russia [Aleksandr Mikhailovich], *Once a Grand Duke* (New York, 1932), p. 166.

12. Ibid. See also Lincoln, *The Romanovs*, pp. 603–7.

13. Alexander, *Once a Grand Duke*, p. 167.

14. Lincoln, *The Romanovs*, pp. 608–10.

15. Edward Crankshaw, *The Shadow of the Winter Palace: Russia's Drift to Revolution, 1825–1917* (New York, 1976), p. 308.

16. Quoted in Sir Bernard Pares, *The Fall of the Russian Monarchy: A Study of the Evidence* (New York, 1961), p. 36.

17. Aleksandra Feodorovna to Nicholas, 4 April 1915, *Letters of the Tsaritsa to the Tsar, 1914–1916*, ed. Sir Bernard Pares (Hattiesburg, 1970), p. 115; Nicholas to Aleksandra Feodorovna, 17 June 1916, *Letters of the Tsar to the Tsaritsa, 1914–1917*, trans. A. L. Hynes (Hattiesburg, 1970), p. 212.

18. Aleksandra Feodorovna to Nicholas, 22 August 1915, *Letters of the Tsaritsa to the Tsar*, p. 114.

19. Aleksandra Feodorovna to Nicholas, 13 and 14 December 1916, ibid., pp. 454–55.

20. Nicholas to Aleksandra Feodorovna, 14 December 1916, *Letters of the Tsar to the Tsaritsa*, pp. 307–8.

21. Quoted in René Fülöp-Miller, *Rasputin: The Holy Devil* (New York, 1928), p. 80.

22. Quoted in Pierre Gilliard, *Le Tragique destin de Nicolas II et de sa famille* (Paris, 1938), p. 35.

23. Quoted in S. S. Ol'denburg, *Tsarstvovanie Imperatora Nikolaia II* (Belgrad, 1939), 1: 47.

24. Quoted in Harold Nicolson, *King George the Fifth: His Life and Reign* (New York, 1953), p. 57.

25. P. B. Struve, "My Contacts with Rodichev," *Slavonic and East European Review* 12, no. 35 (January 1934): 350.

26. Crankshaw, *The Shadow of the Winter Palace*, p. 311.

27. George Fischer, *Russian Liberalism: From Gentry to Intelligentsia* (Cambridge, Mass., 1958), pp. 74–76.

28. Salisbury, *Black Night, White Snow*, pp. 51–53; Alexander, *Once a Grand Duke*, p. 171.

29. Baedeker, *Russia*, p. xxii.

30. Salisbury, *Black Night, White Snow*, p. 53.

31. *Nikolai II: Materialy*, pp. 106–8.

32. Ibid., pp. 111–13; Vitte, *Vospominaniia*, 2: 67–68. For a summary of Nemirovich-Danchenko's account, see Salisbury, *Black Night, White Snow*, pp. 54–56.

33. N. P. Eroshkin, "Administrativno-politseiskii apparat," *Istoriia Moskvy*, ed. A. M. Pankratova (Moscow, 1955), 5: 665–66.

34. Witte, *Vospominaniia*, 2: 68–70; Alexander Izwolsky, *Memoirs* (London, 1920), pp. 258–60.

35. Ol'denburg, *Tsarstvovanie Nikolaia II*, 1: 61.

36. Salisbury, *Black Night, White Snow*, pp. 57–58.

37. L. N. Tolstoi, "Pis'mo Nikolaiu II," *Sobranie sochinenii* (Moscow, 1965), 18: 289–97.

38. Quoted in Alexander, *Once a Grand Duke*, p. 177.

39. Quoted in ibid., p. 3.

40. S. Iu. Witte, "Tsirkuliar Ministra Finansov 'chinam fabrichnoi inspektsii' o merakh bor'by so stachkami rabochikh," in *Rabochee dvizhenie*, ed. Ivanov, 4: pt. 2, p. 824.

41. Ivanov, ed., *Rabochee dvizhenie*, 4: pt. 2, pp. xx–xxi; Sablinsky, *Road to Bloody Sunday*, p. 29.

42. Quoted in Gerald D. Surh, "Petersburg's First Mass Labor Organization: The Assembly of Russian Workers and Father Gapon," *Russian Review* 40, no. 3 (July 1981): 259.

43. A. E. Karelin, "Deviatoe ianvaria i Gapon," *Krasnaia letopis'*, no. 1 (1922), p. 107.

44. G. A. Gapon, *Zapiski Georgiia Gapona. Ocherk rabochego dvizheniia v Rossii 1900-kh godov* (Moscow, 1918), pp. 27–28. See also pp. 11–27.

45. Surh, "Petersburg's First Mass Labor Organization," pp. 243–44, 249–54; Sablinsky, *Road to Bloody Sunday*, pp. 85–118.

46. Gapon, *Zapiski*, pp. 52–54; Sablinsky, *Road to Bloody Sunday*, pp. 143–50.

47. Quoted in A. El'nitskii, *Tysiacha deviat'sot piatyi god* (Kursk, 1925), p. 23.

48. V. I. Nevskii, *Ianvarskie dni v Peterburge v 1905 g.* (Kharkov, 1905), p. 19.

49. D. N. Liubimov, "Gapon i 9 ianvaria," *Voprosy istorii* 40, no. 8 (August 1965): 123.

50. Grand Duke Konstantin Konstantinovich, "Iz dnevnika Konstantina Romanova," *Krasnyi arkhiv* 43 (1930): 105.

51. Sablinsky, *Road to Bloody Sunday*, pp. 198–99; A. V. Bogdanovich, *Tri poslednykh samoderzhtsa: Dnevnik A. V. Bogdanovicha* (Moscow-Leningrad, 1924), pp. 328–30; V. I. Gurko, *Features and Figures*

of the Past: Government and Opinion in the Reign of Nicholas II (Stanford, 1939), pp. 344–45.

52. Quoted in Liubimov, "Gapon i 9 ianvaria," p. 126.

53. L. Gurevich, "Narodnoe dvizhenie v Peterburge 9-go ianvaria 1906 goda," *Byloe* 1, no. 1 (January 1906): 210; El'nitskii, *Tysiacha deviat'- sot piatyi god*, pp. 33–34.

54. Quoted in El'nitskii, *Tysiacha deviat'sot piatyi god*, p. 34.

55. Quoted in S. Ainzaft, *Zubatovshchina i Gaponovshchina* (Moscow, 1925), p. 143.

56. Quoted in Sablinsky, *Road to Bloody Sunday*, p. 228.

57. Quoted in ibid., p. 222.

58. Gurevich, "Narodnoe dvizhenie," p. 213.

59. S. N. Semanov, *Krovavoe voskresen'e* (Leningrad, 1965), p. 72.

60. Ibid., pp. 72–73.

61. L. K. Erman, *Intelligentsiia v pervoi russkoi revoliutsii* (Moscow, 1966), p. 46.

62. Quoted in Sablinsky, *Road to Bloody Sunday*, p. 214.

63. Ibid., p. 215.

64. P. M. Rutenberg, "Delo Gapona," *Byloe*, nos. 11–12 (July– August 1909), p. 33; Semanov, *Krovavoe voskresen'e*, p. 86; Liubimov, "Gapon i 9 ianvaria," *Voprosy istorii* 40, no. 9 (September 1965): 114.

65. El'nitskii, *Tysiacha deviat'sot piatyi god*, p. 43.

66. M. Gor'kii, "9-e ianvaria," in I. P. Donkov, I. M. Mishakova, and N. V. Senichkina, *Pervaia russkaia. . . . Sbornik vospominanii aktivnykh uchastnikov revoliutsii, 1905–1907gg.* (Moscow, 1975), p. 10.

67. Nevskii, *Ianvarskie dni*, p. 55.

68. V. I. Nevskii, *Rabochee dvizhenie v ianvarskie dni 1905 goda* (Moscow, 1930), pp. 124–27; Liubimov, "Gapon i 9 ianvaria," no. 9 (September 1965), pp. 114–21.

69. Quoted in Sablinsky, *Road to Bloody Sunday*, p. 278.

70. Quoted in ibid., p. 281.

71. Aleksandra Feodorovna to Princess Victoria of Battenberg, 27 January 1905, in Baroness Sophie Buxhoeveden, *The Life and Tragedy of Alexandra Feodorovna, Empress of Russia* (London, 1928), p. 109.

72. Quoted in Sablinsky, *Road to Bloody Sunday*, p. 269.

73. Bing, *Letters of Nicholas and Marie*, p. 139.

74. Alexander, *Once a Grand Duke*, p. 139.

75. Grand Duke Konstantin Konstantinovich, "Iz dnevnika," *Krasnyi arkhiv*, 43: 114.

76. I. Ponomarev, *Geroi "Potemkina"* (Moscow, 1955), pp. 45–63; A. M. Pankratova, *Pervaia russkaia revoliutsiia, 1905–1907gg.* (Moscow,

1951), pp. 104–6; L. K. Erman, "Potëmkin," *Sovetskaia istoricheskaia entsiklopediia*, 11: cols. 475–76.

77. E. Maevskii, "Massovoe dvizhenie s 1904 po 1907gg.: Obshchaia kartina dvizheniia," in *Obshchestvennoe dvizhenie*, ed. Martov, 2: 65–69; Pankratova, *Pervaia russkaia revoliutsiia*, pp. 108–11; I. Lychev, *Vospominaniia Potemkintsa* (Moscow, 1925), pp. 22–25.

78. Sidney Harcave, *First Blood: The Russian Revolution of 1905* (London, 1965), pp. 150–51; Pankratova, *Pervaia russkaia revoliutsiia*, pp. 110–11; Lychev, *Vospominaniia*, pp. 26–39.

79. P. I. Klimov, *Revoliutsionnaia deiatel'nost' rabochikh v derevne v 1905–1907gg.* (Moscow, 1960), pp. 89–90.

80. Maevskii, "Massovoe dvizhenie," pp. 69–71; Ekzempliarskii, *Istoriia goroda Ivanova*, 1: 232–45; N. N. Iakovlev, *Narod i partiia v pervoi russkoi revoliutsii* (Moscow, 1965), pp. 128–29.

81. Klimov, *Revoliutsionnaia deiatel'nost'*, pp. 107–8; N. Karpukhin, ed., *1905 god v riazanskoi gubernii* (Riazan, 1925), p. 18.

82. D. Kol'tsov, "Rabochie v 1905–1907gg.," in *Obshchestvennoe dvizhenie*, ed. Martov, 2: 216–26; N. S. Trusova, ed., *Revoliutsionnoe dvizhenie v Rossii vesnoi i letom 1905 goda: aprel'–sentiabr'* (Moscow, 1959), 1: vi–xvii, 77–253.

83. I. M. Pushkareva, *Zheleznodorozhniki Rossii v burzhuazno-demokraticheskikh revoliutsiiakh* (Moscow, 1975), pp. 90–108.

84. Mitskevich, *Revoliutsionnaia Moskva*, p. 371.

85. M. N. Pokrovskii, ed., *1905: Materialy i dokumenty* (Moscow, 1927), pp. 57–60, 72–74, 100.

86. V. I. Nevskii, *Sovety i voorushennye vosstaniia v 1905 godu* (Moscow, 1931), pp. 193–220.

87. L. M. Ivanov, ed., *Vserossiiskaia politicheskaia stachka v Oktiabre 1905 goda* (Moscow-Leningrad, 1955), 1: 417–19.

88. Quoted in Mitskevich, *Revoliutsionnaia Moskva*, p. 392.

89. Pushkareva, *Zheleznodorozhniki Rossii*, pp. 152–56; Wolfe, *Three Who Made a Revolution*, pp. 320–21.

90. Ivanov, ed., *Vserossiiskaia politicheskaia stachka*, 1: 610–14.

91. Ibid., pp. vi–vii.

92. Wolfe, *Three Who Made a Revolution*, pp. 320–21; Leon Trotsky, *1905*, trans. Anya Bostock (New York, 1971), pp. 92–94.

93. S. P. Mintslov, *Peterburg v 1903–1910 godov* (Riga, 1931), pp. 161–64.

94. Nicholas to the Dowager Empress Maria Feodorovna, 19 October 1905, *Letters of Nicholas and Marie*, p. 187.

95. Quoted in Nevskii, *Sovety i vooruzhennye vosstaniia*, p. 15.

96. Ekzempliarskii, *Istoriia goroda Ivanova*, 1: 235–38.

97. Deutscher, *The Prophet Armed*, pp. 117–25.

98. Trotsky, *1905*, p. 117.

99. Ibid., p. 111.

100. Ivanov, ed., *Vserossiiskaia politicheskaia stachka*, 1: 354.

101. Nicholas to the Dowager Empress Maria Feodorovna, 19 October 1905, *Letters of Nicholas and Marie*, p. 187.

102. The Dowager Empress Maria Feodorovna to Nicholas, 16 October 1905, in ibid., p. 184.

103. Nicholas to the Dowager Empress Maria Feodorovna, 19 October 1905, in ibid., p. 188.

104. Ibid., pp. 187–88.

105. Iu. N. Danilov, *Velikii kniaz' Nikolai Nikolaevich* (Paris, 1930), pp. 55–56.

106. Witte, *Vospominaniia*, 3: 14–38; Sir Bernard Pares, *The Fall of the Russian Monarchy*, pp. 85–86.

107. V. I. Gurko, *Features and Figures of the Past: Government and Opinion in the Reign of Nicholas II* (Stanford, 1939), p. 399.

108. Nicholas to the Dowager Empress Maria Feodorovna, 19 October 1905, *Letters of Nicholas and Marie*, p. 189.

109. Grand Duke Konstantin Konstantinovich, "Dnevnik," *Krasnyi arkhiv* 40 (1931): 139.

110. Mintslov, *Peterburg*, p. 166.

111. P. N. Miliukov, *Vospominaniia, 1859–1917* (New York, 1955), p. 311.

112. V. V. Shul'gin, *Dni* (Belgrad, 1925), pp. 6–7.

113. Mitskevich, *Revoliutsionnaia Moskva*, pp. 409–10.

114. Quoted in Wolfe, *Three Who Made a Revolution*, p. 323.

115. Trotsky, *1905*, p. 117.

116. Salisbury, *Black Night, White Snow*, p. 164.

117. Nicholas to the Dowager Empress Maria Feodorovna, 1 December 1905, *Letters of Nicholas and Marie*, p. 197.

118. Quoted in Florinsky, *Russia*, 2: 1183.

119. N. N. Iakovlev, *Vooruzhennye vosstaniia v dekabrie 1905 goda* (Moscow, 1957), pp. 82–84.

120. Quoted in V. Storozhev, "Dekabr'skoe vooruzhennoe vosstanie po arkhivnym materialam," in *Dekabr'skoe vosstanie v Moskve*, ed. Ovsiannikov, p. 79.

121. A. Chebarin, *Moskve v revoliutsii 1905–1907 godov* (Moscow, 1955), pp. 179–81; V. Iakovlev and Ia. Shorr, *1905 god v Moskve*, pp. 152–56.

122. Mitskevich, *Revoliutsionnaia Moskva*, p. 449.

123. Chebarin, *Moskva v revoliutsii*, pp. 182–83.

124. E. Iaroslavskii, *Vooruzhennoe vosstanie v dekabre 1905 goda* (Moscow-Leningrad, 1926), pp. 40–41; Iakovlev, *Vooruzhennye vosstaniia*, pp. 164–66.

125. V. Kostitsyn, "Dekabr'skoe vosstanie 1905g.," in *Dekabr' 1905 goda na Krasnoi Presne*, ed. V. I. Nevskii (Moscow, 1925), p. 44.

126. Iakovlev, *Vooruzhennye vosstaniia*, p. 167; Mitskevich, *Revoliutsionnaia Moskva*, p. 447.

127. Kostitsyn, "Dekabr'skoe vosstanie," p. 25.

128. Quoted in Trotsky, *1905*, p. 240.

129. Iakovlev, *Vooruzhennye vosstaniia*, pp. 170–71.

130. Z. Dosser, "Na Presne i v Moskovskom komitete bol'shevikov v dekabr'skie dni 1905 g.," in *Dekabr' 1905 goda na Krasnoi Presne*, ed. Nevskii, pp. 13–15.

131. Iakovlev, *Vooruzhennye vosstaniia*, pp. 195–97; Mitskevich, *Revoliutsionnaia Moskva*, pp. 467–73.

132. Iakovlev and Shorr, *1905 god v Moskve*, p. 208.

133. Elizaveta Drabkina, *Chernye sukhari* (Moscow, 1963), pp. 31–32.

134. Quoted in Mitskevich, *Revoliutsionnaia Moskva*, p. 480.

135. L. T. Senchakova, *Boevaia rat' revoliutsii. Ocherk o boevykh organizatsiiakh RSDRP i rabochikh druzhinakh 1905–1907gg.* (Moscow 1975), pp. 134–35; Iakovlev and Shorr, *1905 god v Moskve*, pp. 213–14; Iaroslavskii, *Vooruzhennoe vosstanie*, pp. 65–67; Chebarin, *Moskva v revoliutsii*, pp. 204–7.

136. Quoted in Salisbury, *Black Night, White Snow*, p. 173.

137. Nicholas to the Dowager Empress Maria Feodorovna, 29 December 1905, *Letters of Nicholas and Marie*, p. 207.

138. Quoted in *Nikolai II: Materialy*, p. 23.

139. Witte, *Vospominaniia*, 3: 153; Mehlinger and Thompson, *Count Witte*, pp. 110–11.

140. Nicholas to the Dowager Empress Maria Feodorovna, 29 December 1905, *Letters of Nicholas and Marie*, p. 207.

141. Quoted in *Nikolai II: Materialy*, p. 23.

142. N. I. Faleev, "Shest' mesiatsev voenno-polevoi iustitsii," *Byloe* (2 February 1907), pp. 71–81; N. N. Polianskii, *Tsarskie voennye sudy v bor'be s revoliutsiei 1905–1907gg.* (Moscow, 1958), pp. 191–215.

143. Trotsky, *1905*, p. 296.

144. "Rech' P. A. Stolypina, 10 maia 1907 goda," in M. P. Bok, *Vospominaniia o moem ottse P. A. Stolypina* (New York, 1953), p. 248.

CHAPTER IX
"What *We* Want Is a *Great Russia!*"

1. S. F. Starr, *Decentralization and Self-Government in Russia, 1830–1870* (Princeton, 1972), *passim.* See also, N. A. Miliutin, "Zapiska po voprosu o preobrazovanii zemskikh uchrezhdeniiakh" (22 maia 1862g.), TsGIAL, fond 869, opis' 1, delo no. 397/28.

2. Boris Veselovskii, *Istoriia zemstva za sorok let* (St. Petersburg, 1903), 3: 47–368.

3. S. Iu. Witte, *Samoderzhavie i zemstvo. Konfidentsial'naia zapiska,* 2nd ed. (Stuttgart, 1903), pp. 195–97, 210–11. Quote from p. 211.

4. Quoted in Richard Pipes, *Struve: Liberal on the Left, 1870–1905* (Cambridge, Mass., 1970), p. 319. See also pp. 310–20, and N. M. Pirumova, *Zemskoe liberal'noe dvizhenie. Sotsial'nye korni i evoliutsiia do nachala XX veka* (Moscow, 1977), pp. 118–22.

5. D. N. Shipov, *Vospominaniia i dumy o perezhitom* (Moscow, 1918), pp. 215–20.

6. I. I. Petrunkevich, *Iz zapisok obshchestvennago deiatelia: vospominaniia,* ed. A. A. Kizevetter, vol. 21 in *Arkhiv russkoi revoliutsii,* I. V. Gessen, general editor (Berlin, 1934), pp. 338–40; Pipes, *Struve: Liberal on the Left,* pp. 333–34; E. D. Chermenskii, "Zemsko-liberal'noe dvizhenie nakanune revoliutsii 1905–1907gg.," *Istoriia SSSR,* no. 5 (1965), pp. 50–52; Shmuel Galai, *The Liberation Movement in Russia, 1900–1905* (Cambridge, 1973), pp. 177–87.

7. Quoted in Pipes, *Struve: Liberal on the Left,* p. 335.

8. Witte, *Vospominaniia,* 2: 323.

9. Quoted in Terence Emmons, "Russia's Banquet Campaign," *California Slavic Studies* 10 (1977): 47.

10. Quoted in Florinsky, *Russia,* 2: 1169.

11. Quoted in Emmons, "Russia's Banquet Campaign," p. 46.

12. Quoted in Gurko, *Features and Figures of the Past,* p. 299.

13. Galai, *Liberation Movement,* p. 208.

14. Quoted in ibid., p. 213.

15. Quoted in Gurko, *Features and Figures of the Past,* p. 304.

16. Kniaginia E. A. Sviatopolk-Mirskaia, "Dnevnik kn. Ekateriny Alekseevny Sviatopolk-Mirskoi za 1904–1905gg.," *Istoricheskie zapiski,* 77 (1965): 279.

17. Emmons, "Russia's Banquet Campaign," pp. 48–49, 55–58, 81–82; Galai, *Liberation Movement,* pp. 232–37.

18. V. Grinevich, *Professional'noe dvizhenie rabochikh v Rossii* (Moscow, 1923), pp. 45–66.

19. Quoted in Witte, *Vospominaniia,* 2: 615, n. 73.

20. Mehlinger and Thompson, *Count Witte*, pp. 17–19; Galai, *Liberation Movement*, pp. 254–55.

21. P. N. Miliukov, *God bor'by: Publisticheskaia khronika, 1905–1906gg.* (St. Petersburg, 1907), p. 69.

22. Thomas Riha, *A Russian European: Paul Miliukov in Russian Politics* (Notre Dame and London, 1969), pp. 80–91; Galai, *Liberation Movement*, pp. 255–63.

23. Quoted in Vodovozov, *Graf Witte i Imperator Nikolai II*, p. 32.

24. Quoted in ibid., p. 70.

25. Mehlinger and Thompson, *Count Witte*, p. 80.

26. Gurko, *Features and Figures of the Past*, p. 410.

27. S. M. Sidel'nikov, *Obrazovanie i deiatel'nost pervoi gosudarstvennoi dumy* (Moscow, 1962), pp. 76–77.

28. Mehlinger and Thompson, *Count Witte*, p. 123; Sidel'nikov, *Obrazovanie i deiatel'nost'*, p. 74. See also the data in Fedor Dan, "Obshchaia politika pravitel'stva i izmeneniia v gosudarstvennoi organizatsii v periode 1905–1907gg.," in *Obshchestvennoe dvizhenie*, ed. Martov, 4: 368–69.

29. Quoted in Ol'denburg, *Tsarstvovanie Nikolaia II*, 1:343.

30. Nicholas to the Dowager Empress Maria Feodorovna, 12 January 1906, *Letters of Nicholas and Marie*, p. 212.

31. Quotes from Ol'denburg, *Tsarstvovanie Nikolaia II*, 1: 344.

32. *Polnoe sobranoe zakonov Rossiiskoi Imperii*, sobranie 3-oe, 26, pt. 2, no. 27,805.

33. Miliukov, *God bor'by*, pp. 194, 306.

34. Quoted in Florinsky, *Russia*, 2: 1189.

35. Quoted in Ol'denburg, *Tsarstvovanie Nikolaia II*, 1: 355.

36. Count V. N. Kokovtsev, *Iz moego proshlago: Vospominaniia, 1903–1919gg.* (Paris, 1933), 1: 166.

37. Nicholas to the Dowager Empress Maria Feodorovna, November 1906, *Letters of Nicholas and Marie*, p. 221.

38. Mehlinger and Thompson, *Count Witte*, p. 241.

39. Ibid.

40. Sidel'nikov, *Obrazovanie i deiatel'nost' pervoi gosudarstvennoi dumy*, pp. 190–96; E. D. Chermenskii, *Burzhuaziia i tsarizm v pervoi russkoi revoliutsii*, 2nd ed. (Moscow, 1970), pp. 266–68.

41. Judith E. Zimmerman, "The Kadets and the Duma, 1905–1907," in *Essays*, ed. Timberlake, pp. 119–24.

42. Miliukov, *Vospominaniia*, 1: 269.

43. William G. Rosenberg, "Kadets and the Politics of Ambivalence, 1905–1907," in *Essays*, ed. Timberlake, p. 143. See also William G.

Rosenberg, *Liberals in the Russian Revolution: The Constitutional Democratic Party, 1917–1921* (Princeton, 1974), pp. 12–17; V. A. Maklakov, *Vlast' i obshchestvennost' na zakate Staroi Rossii: Vospominaniia* (Paris, 1936), pp. 483–98; Leonard Schapiro, "The *Vekhi* Group and the Mystique of Revolution," *Slavonic and East European Review* 34 (December 1955): 66–68.

44. Miliukov, *God bor'by*, p. 218.

45. Chermenskii, *Burzhuaziia i tsarizm*, pp. 236–43; Sidel'nikov, *Obrazovanie i deiatel'nost' pervoi gosudarstvennoi dumy*, pp. 190–96.

46. Quoted in Sidel'nikov, *Obrazovanie i deiatel'nosti' pervoi gosudarstvennoi dumy*, p. 197.

47. Miliukov, *God bor'by*, p. 247.

48. Quoted in Richard Pipes, *Struve: Liberal on the Right, 1905–1944* (Cambridge, Mass., 1980), pp. 35, 33.

49. Sidel'nikov, *Obrazovanie i deiatel'nost' pervoi gosudarstvennoi dumy*, p. 198.

50. Kokovtsev, *Iz moego proshlago*, 1: 169.

51. Riha, *A Russian European*, p. 113.

52. V. A. Maklakov, *The First State Duma: Contemporary Reminiscences*, trans. Mary Belkin (Bloomington, 1964), p. 235.

53. Ibid., p. 242.

54. Ibid., p. 236.

55. Quoted in Kryzhanovskii, *Vospominaniia*, p. 66.

56. Quoted in Chermenskii, *Burzhuaziia i tsarizm*, p. 265.

57. Kokovtsev, *Iz moego proshlago*, 1: 168.

58. Gurko, *Features and Figures of the Past*, p. 470.

59. A. Martynov, "Konstitutsionno-Demokraticheskaia Partiia," in *Obshchestvennoe dvizhenie*, ed. Martov, 3: 36–37.

60. F. Dan, "Obshchaia politika pravitel'stva i izmeneniia v gosudarstvennoi organizatsii v period 1905–1907gg.," in *Obshchestvennoe dvizhenie*, ed. Martov, 3: pt. 2, pp. 12–14. Cited henceforth as Dan, "Obshchaia politika-2."

61. Quoted in Ol'denburg, *Tsarstvovanie Nikolaia II*, 1: 355.

62. Gurko, *Features and Figures of the Past*, p. 472.

63. Kokovtsev, *Iz moego proshlago*, 1: 186.

64. Miliukov, *Vospominaniia*, 1: 476.

65. Quoted in Pipes, *Struve: Liberal on the Right*, pp. 40–41.

66. Quoted in ibid., p. 41.

67. P. N. Miliukov, "Tri popytki," in *Samoderzhavie i liberaly v revoliutsii 1905–1907 godov*, ed. S. A. Alekseev (Moscow-Leningrad, 1925), especially pp. 72–77; Shipov, *Vospominaniia*, pp. 445–60; Sidel'-

NOTES

nikov, *Obrazovanie i deiatel'nost' pervoi gosudarstvennoi dumy*, pp. 341–62.

68. B. Grave, "Kadety v 1905–1906gg.," *Krasnyi arkhiv* 46 (1931): 64.

69. Quoted in Pipes, *Struve: Liberal on the Right*, p. 43.

70. Grave, "Kadety," p. 131.

71. Riha, *A Russian European*, pp. 139–40; Mary Schaeffer Conroy, *Peter Arkad'evich Stolypin: Practical Politics in Late Tsarist Russia* (Boulder, 1976), p. 179, n. 22.

72. Kryzhanovskii, *Vospominaniia*, p. 104.

73. I. V. Gessen, *V dvukh vekakh. Zhizennyi otchet* (Berlin, 1937), pp. 236–38.

74. V. Levitskii, "Pravye partii," in *Obshchestvennoe dvizhenie*, ed. Martov, 3: 376–80; Hans Rogger, "The Formation of the Russian Right, 1900–1905," *California Slavic Studies* 3 (1964): 66–86.

75. *Soiuz russkogo naroda po materialam sledstvennoi komissii vremennago pravitel'stva 1917g.* (Moscow, 1917), pp. 45–46.

76. Rogger, "Formation of the Russian Right," p. 87; Nicholas to the Dowager Empress Maria Feodorovna, 12 January 1906, in *Letters of Nicholas and Marie*, p. 212.

77. *Materialy k istorii russkoi kontr-revoliutsii* (St. Petersburg, 1908), 1: cxlviii–clxvii.

78. Greenberg, *Jews in Russia*, 2: 77–78; Mehlinger and Thompson, *Count Witte*, p. 357.

79. Levitskii, "Pravye partii," p. 383.

80. Quoted in Mehlinger and Thompson, *Count Witte*, p. 62.

81. Rogger, "Formation of the Russian Right," pp. 90–92.

82. Kryzhanovskii, *Vospominaniia*, p. 153. See also Kryzhanovskii's testimony in P. E. Shchegolev, ed., *Padenie tsarskogo rezhima* (Moscow, 1925), 5: 402–16.

83. S. B. Liubosh, *Russkii fashist Vladimir Purishkevich* (Leningrad, 1925), pp. 28–30; Hans Rogger, "Was There a Russian Fascism? The Union of Russian People," *The Journal of Modern History* 36, no. 4 (December 1964): 404.

84. Alfred Levin, *The Second Duma: A Study of the Social-Democratic Party and the Russian Constitutional Experiment*, 2nd ed. (Hamden, Conn., 1966), p. 67.

85. Rogger, "Was There a Russian Fascism?" p. 407.

86. Levin, *Second Duma*, pp. 67, 70–72.

87. L. Martov, "Sotsialdemokratiia 1905–1907gg.," in *Obshchestvennoe dvizhenie*, ed. Martov, 3: 628–37.

492

88. V. A. Maklakov, *Vtoraia gosudarstvennaia duma. Vospominaniia sovremennika* (Paris, n.d.), pp. 60–63.

89. P. N. Miliukov, *Vtoraia duma. Publitsisticheskaia khronika 1907* (St. Petersburg, 1908), pp. 268–69.

90. Ibid., pp. 21, 17, 24.

91. Quoted in Shipov, *Vospominaniia*, p. 404.

92. V. Ia. Laverychev, *Po tu storonu barrikad. Iz istorii bor'by moskovskoi burzhuazii s revoliutsiei* (Moscow, 1967), pp. 44–47; Menashe, "Alexander Guchkov," pp. 11–14, 56–79.

93. Quoted in Shipov, *Vospominaniia*, p. 413. See also Menashe, "Alexander Guchkov," pp. 121–44.

94. Quoted in Chermenskii, *Burzhuaziia i tsarizm*, p. 236.

95. Ibid.

96. Quoted in Laverychev, *Po tu storonu barrikad*, p. 53.

97. Michael C. Brainerd, "The Octobrists and the Gentry, 1905–1907: Leaders and Followers?" in *The Politics of Rural Russia, 1905–1914*, ed. Leopold Haimson (Bloomington, 1979), p. 81.

98. F. Dan and N. Cherevanin, "Soiuz 17 oktiabria," in *Obshchestvennoe dvizhenie*, ed. Martov, 3: 206–7; Levin, *Second Duma*, p. 67.

99. Brainerd, "Octobrists and the Gentry," pp. 82–83.

100. Miliukov, *Vospominaniia*, 1: 426–27.

101. Quoted in Levin, *Second Duma*, p. 122.

102. Ibid.

103. Nicholas to the Dowager Empress Maria Feodorovna, 1 March 1907, in *Letters of Nicholas and Marie*, p. 224.

104. Quoted in Conroy, *Peter Stolypin*, p. 160. See also pp. 158–61; and Levin, *Second Duma*, pp. 105–82.

105. George Pavlovsky, *Agricultural Russia on the Eve of the Revolution* (New York, 1968), pp. 180–82.

106. P. N. Pershin, *Agrarnaia revoliutsiia v Rossii: Istoriko-ekonomicheskoe issledovanie* (Moscow, 1966), 1: 240–55; V. P. Semennikov, ed., *Revoliutsiia 1905 goda i samoderzhavie* (Moscow-Leningrad, 1928), pp. 10–11, 99–112, 172–94.

107. Quoted in Pershin, *Agrarnaia revoliutsiia*, 1: 270.

108. Ibid., pp. 45–49.

109. Pavlovsky, *Agricultural Russia*, pp. 214–18.

110. Levin, *Second Duma*, p. 163.

111. A. Ia. Avrekh, *Tsarizm i tret'eiunskaia sistema* (Moscow, 1966), pp. 64–80; S. M. Sidel'nikov, *Agrarnaia politika samoderzhaviia v period imperializma* (Moscow, 1980), pp. 75–90; Chermenskii, *Burzhuaziia i tsarizm*, pp. 384–99; Levin, *Second Duma*, pp. 156–99.

112. Nicholas to the Dowager Empress Maria Feodorovna, 29 March 1907, in *Letters of Nicholas and Marie*, p. 229.

113. W. S. Woytinsky, *Stormy Passage: A Personal History Through Two Russian Revolutions to Democracy and Freedom, 1905–1960* (New York, 1961), pp. 133–35; Levin, *Second Duma*, pp. 311–14.

114. Ludwik Bazylow, *Ostatnie Lata Rosji Carskiej. Rządy Stołypina* (Warsaw, 1972), pp. 264–67; Kokovtsev, *Iz moego proshlago*, 1: 271–75; Levin, *Second Duma*, 315–39.

115. Quoted in Geoffrey A. Hosking, *The Russian Constitutional Experiment. Government and Duma, 1907–1914* (Cambridge, 1973), p. 42.

116. Gilbert Doctorow, "The Russian Gentry and the Coup d'État of June 3, 1907," *Cahiers du monde russe et soviétique*, no. 1 (January 1976), pp. 43–51.

117. Leopold Haimson, "The Russian Landed Nobility and the System of the Third of June," in *Politics of Rural Russia*, ed. Haimson, p. 9.

118. Robert Edelman, *Gentry Politics on the Eve of the Russian Revolution: The Nationalist Party, 1907–1917* (New Brunswick, 1980), p. 29.

119. The best modern summary of Stolypin's background and early career is to be found, without doubt, in Bazylow, *Ostatnie Lata Rosji Carskiej*, pp. 53–79. There is an accurate, though less inspired account, in Conroy, *Peter Arkad'evich Stolypin*, pp. 1–18.

120. Gurko, *Features and Figures of the Past*, p. 463.

121. Sir George Buchanan, *My Mission to Russia and Other Diplomatic Memories* (Boston, 1923), 1: 160.

122. Harold Nicolson, *Sir Arthur Nicolson, Bart., First Lord Carnock* (London, 1930), p. 225.

123. Nicholas II, *Dnevnik Imperatora Nikolaia II* (Berlin, 1923), entry for 10 July 1906, p. 244.

124. Nicholas to the Dowager Empress Maria Feodorovna, 11 October 1906, *Letters of Nicholas and Marie*, p. 220.

125. V. I. Gurko, *Tsar i tsaritsa* (Paris, 1927), p. 90; Alexandra Stolypine, *L'Homme du dernier Tzar* (Paris, 1931), pp. 117–18; Alexandre Guerassimov, *Tzarisme et terrorisme* (Paris, 1934), pp. 260–64.

126. Quoted in Salisbury, *Black Night, White Snow*, p. 169.

127. Quoted in *Gosudarstvennaia deiatel'nost' predsedatelia Soveta Ministrov Stats-Sekretaria Petra Arkad'evicha Stolypina* (St. Petersburg, 1911), 1: 2.

128. "Rech' P. A. Stolypina, 10 maia 1907 goda," in M. P. Bok, *Vospominaniia o moem ottse P. A. Stolypina* (New York, 1953), p. 248.

129. Quoted in *Gosudarstvennaia deiatel'nost' Stolypina*, 1: 1.

130. Quoted in Wolfe, *Three Who Made a Revolution*, p. 361.

131. "Rech' P. A. Stolypina, 5-go dekabria 1908g.," in Bok, *Vospominaniia*, pp. 290–92.

132. Quoted in *Gosudarstvennaia deiatel'nost' Stolypina*, 1: 2–4, 8.

133. Gurko, *Features and Figures of the Past*, p. 512.

134. See especially S. M. Dubrovskii, *Stolypinskaia zemel'naia reforma* (Moscow, 1963), pp. 65–230, and Robinson, *Rural Russia*, pp. 208–343. The best summary of Stolypin's agrarian reform program, again, is in Bazylow, *Ostatnie Lata Rosji Carskiej*, pp. 196–228.

135. Crankshaw, *Shadow of the Winter Palace*, p. 369.

136. Gurko, *Features and Figures of the Past*, p. 512.

137. Ibid., pp. 497–98.

138. Conroy, *Peter Arkad'evich Stolypin*, p. 91.

139. Kryzhanovskii, *Vospominaniia*, pp. 115, 117.

140. Edelman, *Gentry Politics*, pp. 35–36.

141. Quoted in Avrekh, *Tsarizm i tret'eiunskaia sistema*, p. 21. See also pp. 19–28; Edelman, *Gentry Politics*, pp. 33–42; Hosking, *Russian Constitutional Experiment*, pp. 45–55.

142. Haimson, "The Russian Landed Nobility," in *Politics of Rural Russia*, ed. Haimson, p. 9; Roberta Thompson Manning, "Zemstvo and Revolution: The Onset of the Gentry Reaction, 1905–1907," in ibid., pp. 36–37.

143. Ruth Delia MacNaughton and Roberta Thompson Manning, "The Crisis of the Third of June System and Political Trends in the Zemstvos, 1907–1914," in ibid., pp. 195–209.

144. Haimson, "Observations on the Politics of the Russian Countryside, 1905–1914," in ibid., pp. 292–94.

145. Quoted in V. S. Diakin, *Samoderzhavie, burzhuaziia, i dvorianstvo v 1907–1911gg.* (Leningrad, 1978), p. 218.

146. Hosking, *Russian Constitutional Experiment*, p. 132.

147. Ibid., pp. 132–46; Diakin, *Samoderzhavie, burzhuaziia, i dvorianstvo*, pp. 212–21.

148. Quoted in Hosking, *Russian Constitutional Experiment*, p. 137.

149. Kokovtsev, *Iz moego proshlago*, 1: 458.

150. Quoted in Hosking, *Russian Constitutional Experiment*, p. 146.

151. Kokovtsev, *Iz moego proshlago*, 1: 463.

152. Kokovtsev, *Iz moego proshlago*, 1: 475–77.

153. Nicholas to the Dowager Empress Maria Feodorovna, 10 September 1911, *Letters of Nicholas and Marie*, pp. 265–66.

154. P. G. Kurler, *Gibel' imperatorskoi Rossii* (Berlin, 1923), pp. 121–34; A. Girs, "Smert' Stolypina. Iz vospominanii byvshago Kievskago

Gubernatora," in A. Stolypin, *P. A. Stolypin, 1862–1911* (Paris, 1927), pp. 86–102.

155. Jacob W. Kipp and W. Bruce Lincoln, "Autocracy and Reform: Bureaucratic Absolutism and Political Modernization in Nineteenth-Century Russia," *Russian History* 6, no. 1 (1979): 19–20.

156. Haimson, "Observations on the Politics of the Russian Countryside, 1905–1914," p. 293.

157. Leopold Haimson, "The Problem of Social Stability in Urban Russia, 1905–1917," in *The Structure of Russian History: Interpretive Essays,* ed. Michael Cherniavsky (New York, 1970), pp. 343–47.

CHAPTER X
"The Children of Russia's Dreadful Years"

1. Lincoln, *Nicholas I,* p. 263.

2. Bernice Glatzer Rosenthal, *Dmitri Sergeevich Merezhkovsky and the Silver Age: The Development of a Revolutionary Mentality* (The Hague, 1975), p. 153.

3. Quoted in Z. Gippius-Merezhkovskaia, *Dmitrii Merezhkovskii* (Paris, 1951), p. 208.

4. James H. Billington, *The Icon and the Axe: An Interpretive History of Russian Culture* (London, 1966), p. 472.

5. Rosenthal, *Merezhkovsky and the Silver Age,* p. 110.

6. James M. Edie, James P. Scanlan, and Mary-Barbara Zeldin, eds., *Russian Philosophy* (Chicago, 1965), 3: 55–56.

7. Marc Slonim, *From Chekhov to the Revolution: Russian Literature, 1900–1917* (New York, 1962), p. 104.

8. Quoted in K. Mochul'skii, *Vladimir Solov'ev: Zhizn' i uchenie,* 2nd ed. (Paris, 1951), p. 127.

9. Ibid., p. 17; Vladimir Solov'ev, *Lectures on Godmanhood* (London, 1948), *passim.*

10. Quoted in Samuel D. Cioran, *Vladimir Solov'ev and the Knighthood of the Divine Sophia* (Waterloo, 1977), p. 21.

11. Vladimir Solov'ev, *The Meaning of Love* (New York, 1947), pp. 17, 82.

12. Rosenthal, *Merezhkovsky and the Silver Age,* p. 82.

13. Kn. Evgenii Trubetskoi, *Mirosozertsanie Vl. S. Solov'eva* (Moscow, 1913), 1: 611–31; 2: 353–65.

14. Quoted from V. V. Zenkovsky, *A History of Russian Philosophy* (London, 1953), 2: 528, 515–17.

15. Mochul'skii, *Vladimir Solov'ev,* pp. 253–61; Cioran, *Vladimir Solov'ev,* pp. 62–67.

16. Billington, *Icon and the Axe*, p. 471.

17. Rosenthal, *Merezhkovsky and the Silver Age*, pp. 82–83.

18. Quoted in Janet Kennedy, *The "Mir Iskusstva" Group and Russian Art, 1898–1912* (New York and London, 1977), p. 1.

19. Quoted in John E. Bowlt, *The Silver Age: Russian Art of the Early Twentieth Century and the "World of Art" Group* (Newtonville, 1979), p. 54.

20. Quoted in Kennedy, *The "Mir Iskusstva" Group*, pp. 2–3.

21. Aleksandr Benua (Benois), *Vozniknovenie "Mira Iskusstva"* (Leningrad, 1928), pp. 5–19.

22. Quoted in John E. Bowlt, "The World of Art," *Russian Literature Triquarterly* (1972), p. 191.

23. Alexandre Benois, *Memoirs*, trans. Moura Budberg (London, 1964), 2: 157.

24. Quoted in Benua (Benois), *Vozniknovenie "Mira Iskusstva,"* p. 42.

25. Charles Spencer, *Leon Bakst* (New York, 1973), pp. 25–28.

26. Quoted in I. N. Prizhan, *Lev Samoilovich Bakst* (Leningrad, 1975), p. 35.

27. Camilla Gray, *The Great Experiment: Russian Art, 1863–1922* (New York, 1962), p. 44; Gippius-Merezhkovskaia, *Dmitrii Merezhkovskii*, pp. 79–81; Bowlt, *The Silver Age*, p. 60.

28. Quoted in Renato Poggioli, *Rozanov* (London, 1962), pp. 34–37, 15.

29. Georgii Florovskii, *Puti russkago bogosloviia* (Paris, 1937), p. 498.

30. Poggioli, *Rozanov*, pp. 18, 73.

31. Quoted in Zenkovsky, *History of Russian Philosophy*, 1: 460.

32. Slonim, *From Chekhov to the Revolution*, p. 110.

33. Ibid.

34. Quoted in ibid.

35. Quoted in Billington, *Icon and the Axe*, p. 508.

36. E. Gollerbakh, *V. V. Rozanov: zhizn' i tvorchestvo* (Petersburg, 1922), pp. 61–62.

37. Quoted in K. Mochul'skii, *Valerii Briusov* (Paris, 1962), p. 78.

38. Quoted in Zenskovsky, *History of Russian Philosophy*, 1: 459.

39. Rosenthal, *Merezhkovsky and the Silver Age*, pp. 106–8.

40. Andrei Belyi, *Nachalo veka* (Moscow-Leningrad, 1933), p. 434.

41. Pachmuss, *Zinaida Gippius*, pp. 86, 89.

42. Quoted in ibid., p. 91.

43. Olga Matich, *Paradox in the Religious Poetry of Zinaida Gip-*

pius (Munich, 1972), pp. 63, 69–71; Rosenthal, *Merezhkovsky and the Silver Age*, p. 109.

44. Rosenthal, *Merezhkovsky and the Silver Age*, p. 108.

45. Quoted in Zenkovsky, *History of Russian Philosophy*, 1: 460.

46. Quoted in Pachmuss, *Zinaida Gippius*, p. 123.

47. Gippius-Merezhkovskaia, *Dmitrii Merezhkovskii*, pp. 90–95; Nicolas Zernov, *The Russian Religious Renaissance of the Twentieth Century* (New York and Evanston, 1963), pp. 90–97.

48. Quoted in Gippius-Merezhkovskaia, *Dmitrii Merezhkovskii*, pp. 92, 107.

49. V. Zlobin, "Z. N. Gippius. Ee sud'ba," *Novyi zhurnal* 31 (1952): 153.

50. Quoted in Rosenthal, *Merezhkovsky and the Silver Age*, p. 142. See also pp. 135–43.

51. A. A. Tyrkova-Williams, *Na putiakh k svobode* (New York, 1952), p. 402.

52. Andrei Belyi, *Nachalo veka*, pp. 189–91; Andrei Belyi, "Vospominaniia o Bloke," *Epopeia*, no. 2 (1922), p. 181; Matich, *Paradox*, pp. 12–17; Rosenthal, *Merezhkovsky and the Silver Age*, pp. 131–32.

53. Quoted in Mochul'skii, *Briusov*, p. 43.

54. Andrei Belyi, *Lug zelenyi* (New York and London, 1967), p. 201.

55. Martin P. Rice, *Valery Briusov and the Rise of Russian Symbolism* (Ann Arbor, 1975), p. 60.

56. Jean Laves Hellie, "Aleksandr Mikhailovich Dobroliubov" (unpublished paper; forthcoming in *The Modern Encyclopedia of Russian and Soviet Literature*, vol. 5), pp. 6–7; Slonim, *From Chekhov to the Revolution*, pp. 89–90.

57. Mochul'skii, *Briusov*, pp. 81–110; Slonim, *From Chekhov to the Revolution*, pp. 91–93.

58. Mochul'skii, *Briusov*, p. 42.

59. Rosenthal, *Merezhkovsky and the Silver Age*, p. 16.

60. Valerii Briusov, *Dnevniki, 1891–1910* (Moscow, 1927), p. 98.

61. Letter of A. Belyi to Aleksandr Blok, 4 January 1903, in *Aleksandr Blok i Andrei Belyi. Perepiska*, ed. V. N. Orlov (Moscow, 1940), p. 7.

62. Quoted in Rice, *Valery Briusov*, p. 59.

63. Belyi, *Nachalo veka*, p. 145.

64. Quoted in Mochul'skii, *Andrei Belyi*, p. 42.

65. Ibid., p. 13.

66. Quoted in K. Mochul'skii, *Andrei Belyi* (Paris, 1955), p. 29.

67. Belyi, *Nachalo veka*, pp. 173–74.

68. Quoted in ibid., pp. 42–43.

69. Rosenthal, *Merezhkovsky and the Silver Age*, p. 133.

70. See A. I. Mendeleeva, "A. A. Blok," in *Aleksandr Blok v vospominaniiakh sovremennikov*, ed. V. N. Orlov (Moscow, 1980), 1: 70–80.

71. Quoted in Avril Pyman, *The Life of Aleksandr Blok: The Distant Thunder, 1880–1908* (Oxford, 1979), p. 149.

72. Quotes from K. Mochul'skii, *Aleksandr Blok* (Paris, 1948), p. 57.

73. Oleg A. Maslenikov, *The Frenzied Poets: Andrey Biely and the Russian Symbolists* (Berkeley, 1952).

74. Quoted in Mochul'skii, *Aleksandr Blok*, p. 64.

75. Pyman, *Distant Thunder*, p. 110. See also pp. 105–11.

76. Quoted in ibid., p. 140.

77. Quoted in ibid., pp. 175–76.

78. Quoted in ibid., p. 155.

79. Quoted in Maslenikov, *Frenzied Poets*, p. 148.

80. Mochul'skii, *Andrei Belyi*, p. 67.

81. Pyman, *Distant Thunder*, p. 149.

82. Belyi, "Vospominaniia," *Epopeia*, no. 2, p. 187.

83. Quoted in Belyi, *Nachalo veka*, p. 295.

84. Quoted in Pyman, *Distant Thunder*, p. 153.

85. Quoted in Belyi, "Vospominaniia," *Epopeia*, no. 2, p. 205.

86. Pyman, *Distant Thunder*, p. 154.

87. Ibid., p. 156.

88. Quoted in Mochul'skii, *Andrei Belyi*, p. 50.

89. Quoted in Slonim, *From Chekhov to the Revolution*, p. 93.

90. Belyi, *Nachalo veka*, p. 272.

91. Quoted in Maslenikov, *Frenzied Poets*, p. 113.

92. Belyi, *Nachalo veka*, p. 286.

93. Gippius-Merezhkovskaia, *Dmitrii Merezhkovskii*, p. 208.

94. Quotes from Pyman, *Distant Thunder*, pp. 156–57.

95. Maslenikov, *Frenzied Poets*, p. 162.

96. Aleksandr Blok, "Neznakomka," *Sobranie sochinenii v shesti tomakh* (Moscow, 1971), 2: 160.

97. Al. Blok, *Dnevnik Al. Bloka, 1917–1922*, ed. P. N. Medvedev (Leningrad, 1928), p. 72.

98. Aleksandr Blok, "Poslednii den'," *Sobranie sochinenii*, 2: 133.

99. Quoted in M. A. Beketova, *Aleksandr Blok* (Petersburg, 1922), p. 102.

100. Quoted in Pyman, *Distant Thunder*, p. 171.

101. Quoted in Mochul'skii, *Andrei Belyi*, p. 73.

102. Belyi, *Nachalo veka*, p. 418.

103. Gippius-Merezhkovskaia, *Dmitrii Merezhkovskii*, p. 131.

104. Ibid., p. 133.

105. Quoted in Maslenikov, *Frenzied Poets*, p. 170.

106. Belyi, *Nachalo veka*, p. 422.

107. Ibid., p. 458.

108. Belyi, *Lug zelenyi*, pp. 8–9.

109. Samuel Cioran has provided a thoughtful discussion about how these two seemingly contradictory images can be reconciled in *The Apocalyptic Symbolism of Andrej Belyj* (The Hague and Paris, 1973), pp. 103–7.

110. Belyi, *Nachalo veka*, p. 459.

111. Belyi, "Vospominaniia," *Epopeia*, no. 2, p. 252.

112. Quoted in Pyman, *Distant Thunder*, p. 205.

113. Quoted in ibid., p. 220.

114. Blok to Belyi, 14 or 15 October 1905, in *Blok i Belyi. Perepiska*, ed. Orlov, p. 159.

115. Maslenikov, *Frenzied Poets*, pp. 166–88.

116. Quoted in Bernice Glatzer Rosenthal, "Eschatology and the Appeal of Revolution: Merezhkovsky, Belyi, Blok," *California Slavic Studies* 11 (1980): 111.

117. Beketova, *Aleksandr Blok*, p. 101.

118. Quoted in Rosenthal, "Eschatology," p. 115.

119. Renato Poggioli, *The Poets of Russia, 1890–1930* (Cambridge, Mass., 1960), p. 161.

120. Maslenikov, *Frenzied Poets*, p. 202.

121. Belyi, *Nachalo veka*, p. 309.

122. Maslenikov, *Frenzied Poets*, p. 203.

123. Belyi, *Nachalo veka*, pp. 321–22, 328.

124. Maslenikov, *Frenzied Poets*, pp. 205, 207.

125. Quoted in Pyman, *Distant Thunder*, p. 229.

126. Quoted in Maslenikov, *Frenzied Poets*, p. 208.

127. Viacheslav Ivanov, *Po zvezdam: stat'i i aforizmy* (St. Petersburg, 1909), p. 372.

128. Quoted in Pyman, *Distant Thunder*, p. 228. See also Andrei Belyi, *Mezhdu dvukh revoliutsii* (Leningrad, 1934), p. 197.

129. A. Blok, *Zapisnye knizhki Al. Bloka*, ed. P. N. Medvedev (Leningrad, 1930), pp. 55–57.

130. Quoted in Pyman, *Distant Thunder*, p. 241.

131. Blok to Belyi, 3 January 1906, in *Blok i Belyi. Perepiska*, ed. Orlov, p. 167.

132. Maslenikov, *Frenzied Poets*, p. 211.

133. *Zolotoe Runo*, 1, no. 1 (January 1906): 142.

134. Quoted in Pyman, *Distant Thunder*, p. 288, n. bb.

135. Belyi, *Mezhdu dvukh revoliutsii*, p. 247; Belyi, *Nachalo veka*, pp. 159–60.

136. Belyi to Blok, 5 or 6 August 1907, in *Belyi i Blok. Perepiska*, ed. Orlov, p. 192.

137. Billington, *Icon and the Axe*, p. 476; Kennedy, *The "Mir Iskusstva" Group*, p. 340.

138. Gray, *The Great Experiment*, pp. 93–94.

139. Quoted in Arnold L. Haskell, *Diaghileff: His Artistic and Private Life* (New York, 1935), p. 137.

140. Quoted in ibid., p. 176.

141. Ibid., p. 185.

142. Quoted in Ellen Terry, *The Russian Ballet* (London, 1913), p. 42.

143. Quoted in Haskell, *Diaghileff*, pp. 187–88.

144. Quoted in ibid., pp. 188, 187. See also pp. 174–203; Sergei Lifar, *Diagilev i s Diagilevym* (Paris, 1939), pp. 213–51; Kennedy, *The "Mir Iskusstva" Group*, pp. 350–69; John Percival, *The World of Diaghilev* (New York, 1971), pp. 15–41.

145. Kennedy, *The "Mir Iskusstva" Group*, pp. 363–64.

146. Gray, *The Great Experiment*, p. 96.

147. Ibid., pp. 63–64.

148. Henri Matisse, "Zametki khudozhnika," *Zolotoe Runo*, no. 6 (1909), p. iv.

149. Gray, *The Great Experiment*, pp. 64–65.

150. D. Filosofov, "Tozhe tendentsiia," *Zolotoe Runo*, no. 1 (1908), p. 74.

151. Quoted in ibid., p. 71.

152. Gray, *The Great Experiment*, p. 97. See also pp. 85–98.

153. Quoted in ibid., pp. 124, 126.

154. Ibid., pp. 85–180.

155. Stites, *Women's Liberation Movement*, p. 183; Belyi, *Mezhdu dvukh stoletii*, p. 198; Kruze and Rutsentov, "Naselenie Peterburga," pp. 115–20, 142–44.

156. M. K. Mukhalov, *Deti ulitsy: Maloletniia prostitutki* (St. Petersburg, 1906), pp. 23–24.

157. Stites, *Women's Liberation Movement*, p. 183.

158. See, for example, Kuprin, *Sobranie sochinenii*, 6: 8.

159. Ibid., p. 311.

160. Stites, *Women's Liberation Movement*, p. 159.

161. Mikhail Kuzmin, *Wings: Prose and Poetry by Mikhail Kuzmin*, trans. and ed. Neil Granoien and Michael Green, with a preface by Vladimir Markov (Ann Arbor, 1972), pp. viii–xi.

162. Lidia Zinov'eva-Annibal, "Thirty-Three Abominations," trans. Samuel Cioran, in *The Silver Age of Russian Culture*, ed. Carl and Ellendea Proffer (Ann Arbor, 1975), p. 325.

163. Belyi, *Mezhdu dvukh stoletii*, p. 197.

164. Mikhail Artsybashev, *Sanine. A Russian Love Novel*, trans. Percy Pinkerton (New York, 1932), pp. 173, 122, 123, 122, 118, 60.

165. Stites, *Women's Liberation Movement*, p. 187.

166. Quoted in ibid.

167. Quoted in Billington, *Icon and the Axe*, p. 501.

168. Beatrice Farnsworth, *Aleksandra Kollontai: Socialism, Feminism, and the Bolshevik Revolution* (Stanford, 1980), pp. 127–211.

169. Quoted in Avril Pyman, *The Life of Aleksandr Blok: The Release of Harmony, 1908–1921* (Oxford, 1980), p. 140.

170. Quoted in ibid., p. 119.

171. Gippius-Merezhkovskaia, *Dmitrii Merezhkovskii*, p. 208.

172. Andrei Belyi, *The Silver Dove*, trans. George Reavy, with a preface by Harrison E. Salisbury (New York, 1974), p. ix.

173. Ibid., p. 214.

174. Ibid., p. 216.

175. Mochul'skii, *Andrei Belyi*, pp. 163–65.

176. Andrei Belyi, *Serebrianyi golub'* (Munich, 1967), p. 42.

177. Quoted in Belyi, *Silver Dove*, p. x.

178. Quoted in Salisbury, *Black Night, White Snow*, p. 176.

179. Georgii Florovskii, *Puti russkago bogosloviia*, p. 498.

180. Quoted in Colin Wilson, *Rasputin and the Fall of the Romanovs* (New York, 1964), p. 33.

181. F. M. Dostoevskii, *Brat'ia Karamazovykh*, in *Polnoe sobranie sochinenii* (Leningrad, 1976), 14: 26.

182. Quoted in René Fülöp-Miller, *Rasputin: The Holy Devil* (New York, 1928), p. 215.

183. Ibid., p. 271; Salisbury, *Black Night, White Snow*, p. 206.

184. Quoted in Salisbury, *Black Night, White Snow*, p. 302.

185. Quoted in Paléologue, *An Ambassador's Memoirs*, 1: 260.

186. Quoted in Deutscher, *The Prophet Armed*, p. 54.

187. *Vekhi: Sbornik statei o russkoi intelligentsii*, 2nd ed. (Moscow, 1909), pp. 70–71.

188. Ibid., pp. 88–89.

189. Ol'denburg, *Tsarstvovanie Imperatora Nikolaia II*, 2: 46.

190. Billington, *Icon and the Axe*, p. 514.

191. Andrei Belyi, "Apokalipsis v russkoi poezii," in *Lug zelenyi*, p. 223.

192. Valerii Briusov, "Griadushchie gunny," in *Sobranie sochinenii v semi tomakh* (Moscow, 1973), 1: 433.

193. Valerii Briusov, "Kon' bled," in ibid., pp. 442–44.

194. Pyman, *The Release of Harmony*, p. 91.

195. Marc Slonim, *Russian Theatre from the Empire to the Soviets* (Cleveland and New York, 1961), p. 193.

196. Aleksandr Blok, introduction to "Vozmezdie," in *Sobranie sochinenii*, 4: 148.

197. Quoted in Pyman, *The Release of Harmony*, p. 135.

198. *Pis'ma Aleksandra Bloka k rodnym*, ed. M. A. Beketova (Leningrad, 1928), 2: 132.

199. Blok, introduction of "Vozmezdie," pp. 187–88.

200. Blok to Belyi, 3 March 1911, in *Blok i Belyi. Perepiska*, ed. Orlov, p. 249.

201. Andrei Belyi, *Petersburg*, translated, annotated, and introduced by Robert A. Maguire and John E. Malmstad (Bloomington and London, 1978), p. 65.

202. Ibid., pp. 186, 29, 9, 22.

203. Mochul'skii, *Andrei Belyi*, p. 169.

204. Belyi, *Petersburg*, pp. 11, 63, 50, 28, 12, 24, 2, 65.

205. Billington, *Icon and the Axe*, p. 507.

CHAPTER XI
The Last Days of Peace

1. Quoted in V. I. Nazanskii, *Krushenie velikoi Rossii i doma Romanovykh* (Paris, 1930), pp. 76–77.

2. Meriel Buchanan, *The Dissolution of an Empire* (London, 1932), p. 35.

3. Viroubova, *Memories*, p. 98.

4. Buchanan, *Dissolution*, p. 35.

5. Ol'denburg, *Tsarstvovanie Nikolaia II*, 2: 99.

6. Buchanan, *Dissolution*, p. 36.

7. This impression permeates the memoirs of Vyrubova and, to a lesser extent, the account of Aleksandra's biographer, the Baroness Sophie Buxhoeveden, *The Life and Tragedy of Alexandra Feodorovna, Empress of Russia* (London, 1928).

8. Kokovtsev, *Iz moego proshlago*, 2: 169.

9. Nazanskii, *Krushenie velikoi Rossii i doma Romanovykh*, pp. 92–115; Ol'denburg, *Tsarstvovanie Nikolaia II*, 2: 99.

10. Ol'denburg, *Tsarstvovanie Nikolaia II*, 2: 99.

11. Viroubova, *Memories*, p. 101.

12. Kokovtsev, *Iz moego proshlago*, 2: 169.

13. Kruze and Kutsentov, "Naselenie Peterburga," p. 143.

14. Quoted in Wolfe, *Three Who Made a Revolution*, p. 361.

15. Stephen F. Cohen, *Bukharin and the Bolshevik Revolution: A Political Biography, 1888–1938* (Oxford, 1971), pp. 43–44; Deutscher, *The Prophet Armed*, pp. 238–41.

16. Quoted in Deutscher, *The Prophet Armed*, p. 188.

17. Kruze and Kutsentov, "Naselenie Peterburga," pp. 115–22.

18. K. Sidorov, ed., "Bor'ba so stachechnym dvizheniem nakanune mirovoi voiny," *Krasnyi arkhiv* 34 (1929): 96–97.

19. Quoted in A. S. Tager, *The Decay of Czarism: The Beiliss Trial* (Philadelphia, 1935), pp. 18–19.

20. Quoted in ibid., p. 21.

21. Ralph T. Fisher, "The Beilis Case," *Modern Encyclopedia of Russian and Soviet History* 3 (1977): 190; Hans Rogger, "The Beilis Case: Anti-Semitism and Politics in the Reign of Nicholas II," *Slavic Review* 25, no. 4 (December 1966): 621–22.

22. A. S. Tager, ed., "Protsess Beilisa v otsenke departamenta politsii," *Krasnyi arkhiv* 44 (1931): 115–16.

23. Quoted in Tager, *Decay of Czarism*, p. 29.

24. Ibid., pp. 60–82; Tager, ed., *Protsess Beilisa*, pp. 87–88; Greenberg, *Jews in Russia*, 2: 90–91.

25. Tager, ed., *Protsess Beilisa*, p. 124.

26. Quoted in Greenberg, *Jews in Russia*, 2: 94.

27. Ibid., pp. 94–97.

28. A. Tiumenev, *Ot revoliutsii do revoliutsii* (Leningrad, 1925), pp. 14–15; Launcelot Owen, *The Russian Peasant Movement, 1906–1917* (New York, 1963), pp. 68–69; Pavlovsky, *Agricultural Russia*, pp. 255–56, 266–74.

29. Ibid., pp. 141–42; Tiumenev, *Ot revoliutsii do revoliutsii*, pp. 50–54; Leopold H. Haimson, "The Problems of Social Stability in Urban Russia, 1905–1917," *Slavic Review* 23, no. 4 (December 1964): 635.

30. Rashin, *Formirovanie rabochego klassa*, pp. 437–40; Haimson, "Problems of Social Stability," pp. 635–36.

31. Quoted in Haimson, "Problems of Social Stability," p. 634.

32. Quoted in ibid., p. 641. See also pp. 640–42.

33. Raymond Poincaré, *Au service de la France: L'Union Sacrée, 1914* (Paris, 1927), 4: 233–79.

34. Ibid., p. 273.

35. Quoted in Baron C. F. von Stockmar, *Memoirs of Baron Stockmar*, trans. G. A. M. and ed. F. Max Muller (London, 1872), 2: 107–8.

36. R. R. Palmer, *A History of the Modern World* (New York, 1957), p. 661.

37. Viscount Edward Grey, *Twenty-Five Years, 1892–1916* (New York, 1925), 1: 48–52; Dwight E. Lee, *Europe's Crucial Years: The Diplomatic Background of World War I, 1902–1914* (Hanover, 1974), pp. 64–78; Sidney B. Fay, *The Origins of the World War* (New York, 1930), 1: 165–68; Bernadotte E. Schmitt, *The Coming of the War, 1914* (New York, 1966), 1: 27–29.

38. Grey, *Twenty-Five Years*, 1: 147–65; Lee, *Europe's Crucial Years*, pp. 152–61; "Anglo-russkoe sopernichestvo v Persii v 1890–1906gg.," *Krasnyi arkhiv* 56 (1933): 59–64; S. Pashukanis, ed., "K istorii anglo-russkago soglasheniia 1907 goda," *Krasnyi arkhiv* 69–70 (1935): 3–39; Harold Nicolson, *Sir Arthur Nicolson, Bart., First Lord Carnock: A Study in the Old Diplomacy* (London, 1937), pp. 232–57; Firuz Kazemzadeh, *Russia and Britain in Persia, 1864–1914: A Study in Imperialism* (New Haven, 1968), pp. 482–509.

39. Grey, *Twenty-Five Years*, 1: 158.

40. Quoted in George M. Trevelyan, *Grey of Fallodon; The Life and Letters of Sir Edward Grey, afterwards Viscount Grey of Fallodon* (Boston, 1937), p. 209; Grey, *Twenty-Five Years*, 1: 154.

41. The preceding quotes are from Tuchman, *Proud Tower*, pp. 272, 280, 277, 278.

42. Quoted in William Manchester, *The Arms of Krupp, 1587–1968* (Boston, 1964), p. 217.

43. Prince Bernhard von Bülow, *The Memoirs of Prince von Bülow* (Boston, 1931), 2: 329.

44. Quoted in Lee, *Europe's Crucial Years*, p. 172.

45. Quoted in Tuchman, *Proud Tower*, p. 278.

46. The preceding quotes are from ibid., pp. 282, 287–88, 284.

47. Luigi Albertini, *Origins of the War of 1914* (Oxford, 1965), 1: 187.

48. Quoted in Barbara Tuchman, *The Guns of August* (New York, 1962), pp. 44, 76.

49. Schmitt, *The Coming of the War*, 1: 8.

50. Stockmar, *Memoirs*, 2: 108.

51. Bülow, *Memoirs*, 2: 324, 371, 325, 435.

52. Ibid., p. 372; Albertini, *Origins of the War*, 1: 190.

53. Bülow, *Memoirs*, 2: 371.

54. Fay, *Origins of the World War*, 1: 369.

55. Quoted in E. A. Adamov, ed., *Konstantinopol' i prolivy po sekretnym dokumentam byvshego ministerstva inostrannykh del* (Moscow, 1925), 1: 9–10.

56. Quoted from Albertini, *Origins of the War*, 1: 191.

57. Bülow, *Memoirs*, 2: 372.

58. Quoted in Bernadotte E. Schmitt, *The Annexation of Bosnia, 1908–1909* (Cambridge, 1937), p. 20.

59. Bülow, *Memoirs*, 2: 400.

60. Grey, *Twenty-Five Years*, 1: 173.

61. Quoted in Albertini, *Origins of the War*, 1: 222.

62. Schmitt, *Annexation of Bosnia*, pp. 46–47.

63. Quoted in Albertini, *Origins of the War*, 1: 223.

64. Quoted in ibid., 1: 233.

65. Schmitt, *Coming of the War*, 1: 122. See also Schmitt, *Annexation of Bosnia*, pp. 19–48; Baron M. de Taube, *La politique russe d'avant-guerre et la fin de l'empire des Tsars (1904–1917). Memoires du Baron M. de Taube* (Paris, 1928); Albertini, *Origins of the War*, 1: 190–256; and Fay, *Origins of the World War*, 1: 369–78; G. P. Gooch, *Before the War: Studies in Diplomacy* (New York, 1967), 1: 331–49, 389–409.

66. Quoted in Albertini, *Origins of the War*, 1: 367.

67. Taube, *La politique russe d'avant-guerre*, pp. 249–51.

68. S. D. Sazonov, *Vospominaniia* (Paris, 1927), pp. 55, 59.

69. Quoted in Gooch, *Before the War*, 2: 312.

70. Sazonov, *Vospominaniia*, p. 63.

71. Quoted in Gooch, *Before the War*, 2: 312.

72. Edward C. Thaden, *Russia and the Balkan Alliance of 1912* (University Park, 1965), pp. 86–108.

73. Quoted in Gooch, *Before the War*, 2: 320.

74. Raymond Poincaré, *The Origins of the War* (London, 1922), p. 117.

75. R. W. Seton-Watson, *The Rise of Nationality in the Balkans* (New York, 1966), pp. 157–61.

76. Thaden, *Russia and the Balkan Alliance*, p. 108.

77. Quoted in Adamov, ed., *Konstantinopol' i prolivy*, 1: 24.

78. Quoted in Thaden, *Russia and the Balkan Alliance*, p. 109.

79. Seton-Watson, *Rise of Nationality*, pp. 166–203.

80. Sir G. Buchanan to Sir Edward Grey, St. Petersburg, 30 October 1912, in G. P. Gooch and Harold Temperley, eds., *British Documents on the Origins of the War, 1898–1914* (London, 1933), 9: pt. 2, p. 65; Sir G. Buchanan to Sir Edward Grey, St. Petersburg, 13 November 1912, in ibid., p. 149.

81. Sazonov, *Vospominaniia*, pp. 83, 87, 88.
82. Quoted in Albertini, *Origins of the War*, 1: 416.
83. Quoted in Adamov, ed., *Konstantinopol' i prolivy*, 1: 25.
84. Quoted in ibid., pp. 34–35.
85. Quoted in Gooch, *Before the War*, 2: 245–46.
86. Grey, *Twenty-Five Years*, 1: 251–52.
87. Sir F. Cartwright to Sir A. Nicolson, private, Vienna, 31 January 1913, in Gooch and Temperley, eds., *British Documents*, 9: pt. 2, p. 467.
88. Quoted in Lee, *Europe's Crucial Years*, p. 321.
89. Ibid., pp. 320–26.
90. Sir G. Buchanan to Sir Edward Grey, St. Petersburg, 4 July 1914, in Gooch and Temperley, eds., *British Documents*, 9: pt. 2, p. 884.
91. Seton-Watson, *Rise of Nationality*, pp. 257–83.
92. Grey, *Twenty-Five Years*, 1: 253.
93. Gooch, *Before the War*, 2: 345.
94. Quoted in Fay, *Origins of the World War*, 1: 445–46.
95. Nicholas to the Dowager Empress Maria Feodorovna, 13 July 1913, *Letters of Nicholas and Marie*, p. 287.
96. Lee, *Europe's Crucial Years*, p. 335.
97. Robert J. Kerner, "The Mission of Liman von Sanders," *Slavonic Review* 6 (1927–28): 12–27, 344–63, 543–60; 7 (1928): 90–112.
98. Fritz Fischer, *Germany's Aims in the First World War* (New York, 1967), pp. 45–46.
99. Taube, *La politique russe*, p. 313.
100. Quoted in Kerner, "Mission of Liman von Sanders," 6: 25.
101. Sazonov, *Vospominaniia*, pp. 149–50.
102. Ibid., p. 150.
103. Quoted in Nicolson, *Sir Arthur Nicolson*, p. 404.
104. Quoted in Lee, *Europe's Crucial Years*, p. 346.
105. Quoted in Nicolson, *Sir Arthur Nicolson*, p. 405.
106. Quoted in Albertini, *Origins of the War*, 1: 549.
107. Sazonov, *Vospominaniia*, p. 148.
108. Quoted in Schmitt, *Coming of the War*, 1: note to p. 100.
109. Quoted in ibid., 1: 99.
110. Quoted in Taube, *La politique russe*, pp. 332–33.
111. Quoted in ibid., pp. 333–34.
112. Quoted in Schmitt, *Coming of the War*, 1: 100.
113. Gooch, *Before the War*, 2: 356.
114. Quoted in Taube, *La politique russe*, p. 334.
115. Quoted in ibid., pp. 338–39.
116. Quoted in Schmitt, *Coming of the War*, 1: 101.

117. Quoted in Albertini, *Origins of the War*, 1: 576–77.
118. Quoted in ibid., p. 577.
119. Quoted in ibid.
120. Quoted in Salisbury, *Black Night, White Snow*, p. 251.
121. Kuropatkin, "Dnevnik," *Krasnyi arkhiv*, 2: 106.
122. Quoted in Albertini, *Origins of the War*, 1: 577.

CHAPTER XII
The Drums of War

1. Quoted in Sir Winston Churchill, *The World Crisis, 1911– 1914* (London, 1923), p. 195.
2. Borivoje Jevtić, *Sarajevski atentat* (Sarajevo, 1923), pp. 3–21; R. W. Seton-Watson, *Sarajevo: A Study in the Origins of the Great War* (London, 1925), pp. 63–79; Stanoje Stanojević, *Die Ermordung des Erzherzogs Franz Ferdinand*, trans. H. Wendel (Frankfurt, 1923), pp. 45–56.
3. Quoted in Schmitt, *Coming of the War*, 1: 179.
4. Quoted in ibid., p. 182.
5. Quoted in Albertini, *Origins of the War*, 1: 297.
6. Stanojević, *Die Ermordung*, p. 50; Miloš Bogičević, *Le Procès de Salonique* (Paris, 1927), p. 64.
7. Quotes from Albertini, *Origins of the War*, 2: 26; Fay, *Origins of the World War*, 2: 88–89.
8. Quoted in Seton-Watson, *Sarajevo*, p. 70.
9. Ibid., pp. 73–75.
10. Albertini, *Origins of the War*, 2: 74–88.
11. Quoted in Albert Mousset, *Un Drame historique. L'Attentat de Sarajevo. Documents inédits et texte intégral des sténogrammes du procès* (Paris, 1930), p. 130.
12. Fay, *Origins of the World War*, 2: 112–21.
13. Quoted in Schmitt, *Coming of the War*, 1: 256.
14. Quoted in Mousset, *L'Attentat de Sarajevo*, p. 130.
15. This account of the assassination has been taken from the following: Mousset, *L'Attentat de Sarajevo*, pp. 128–31; Seton-Watson, *Sarajevo*, pp. 101–5; Fay, *Origins of the World War*, 2: 121–26; Vladimir Dedijer, *The Road to Sarajevo* (New York and London, 1966), pp. 318–23; Albertini, *Origins of the War*, 2: 35–38; and Schmitt, *Coming of the War*, 1: 255–57; Jevtić, *Sarajevski atentat, passim.*
16. Dedijer, *Road to Sarajevo*, p. 323.
17. Max Müller to Sir Edward Grey, Budapest, 14 July 1914, in Gooch and Temperley, eds., *British Documents*, 11: 56.
18. Quoted in Albertini, *Origins of the War*, 2: 27.

19. Quoted in ibid., p. 138.

20. Quoted in ibid., p. 137.

21. Grey, *Twenty-Five Years*, 1: 299.

22. Max Müller to Sir Edward Grey, Budapest, 14 July 1914, in Gooch and Temperley, eds., *British Documents*, 11: 55.

23. Sir Maurice de Bunsen to Sir Edward Grey, Vienna, 5 July 1914, in ibid., p. 32.

24. Quoted in Albertini, *Origins of the War*, 2: 123.

25. Quoted in Lee, *Europe's Crucial Years*, pp. 378–79.

26. Quoted in Albertini, *Origins of the War*, 2: 138–39.

27. Quoted in ibid., p. 138.

28. Quoted in Lee, *Europe's Crucial Years*, p. 386.

29. Quoted in N. P. Poletika, *Vozniknovenie pervoi mirovoi voiny (iul'skii krizis 1914g)* (Moscow, 1964), p. 49.

30. Quoted in Lee, *Europe's Crucial Years*, p. 395.

31. Quoted in Albertini, *Origins of the War*, 2: 291.

32. Sazonov, *Vospominaniia*, p. 210.

33. Sir George Buchanan to Sir Edward Grey, St. Petersburg, 18 July 1914, in Gooch and Temperley, eds., *British Documents*, 11: 47.

34. Sir George Buchanan to Sir Edward Grey, St. Petersburg, 24 July 1914, in ibid., p. 81.

35. Quoted in Albertini, *Origins of the War*, 2: 305.

36. Fay, *Origins of the World War*, 2: 273.

37. Quoted in ibid., p. 337.

38. Quoted in Albertini, *Origins of the War*, 2: 364. See also pp. 361–71.

39. Fay, *Origins of the World War*, 2: 350. See also pp. 348–50.

40. Quoted in Albertini, *Origins of the War*, 2: 305.

41. "Osobyi zhurnal Soveta Ministrov 12 (25) iiulia 1914. O privedenii v deistvii Vysochaishe utverzhdennago 17 fevralia 1913 goda, Polozhenie o podgotovitel'nom k voine periode," reprinted in Fay, *Origins of the World War*, 2: facing p. 314.

42. Paléologue, *Memoirs*, 1: 35.

43. General Iu. N. Danilov, *Rossiia v mirovoi voine, 1914–1915gg.* (Berlin, 1924), p. 14.

44. Quoted in Pierre Renouvin, *The Immediate Origins of the War (28th June–4th August 1914)*, trans. T. C. Hume (New York, 1969), p. 149.

45. Quoted in Renouvin, *Immediate Origins*, pp. 151–52.

46. Quoted in Schmitt, *Coming of the War*, 2: 231.

47. Albertini, *Origins of the War*, 2: 557.

48. Telegram from Kaiser Wilhelm to Nicholas II, Berlin, 29 July 1914, in Max Montgelas and Walther Schücking, eds., *Outbreak of the*

World War: German Documents Collected by Karl Kautsky (New York, 1924), p. 315.

49. Danilov, *Rossiia v mirovoi voine*, pp. 14–19.

50. Quoted in Albertini, *Origins of the War*, 2: 558.

51. Quoted in ibid.

52. Quoted in Renouvin, *Immediate Origins*, p. 158.

53. Sazonov, *Vospominaniia*, pp. 242–43.

54. M. V. Rodzianko, *Khrushenie imperii* (Leningrad, 1929), p. 94.

55. Ibid., p. 93.

56. Sazonov, *Vospominaniia*, p. 242.

57. Quoted in M. F. Shilling, *How the War Began in 1914, being the Diary of the Russian Foreign Office from the 3rd to the 20th (o.s.) of July 1914, published by the "Red Archives" Department of the Russian Soviet Government*, trans. Maj. W. Cyprian Bridge (London, 1925), p. 64.

58. Sazonov, *Vospominaniia*, p. 245.

59. Ibid., pp. 248–49.

60. Ibid., p. 249; Shilling, *How the War Began*, p. 66; S. K. Dobrorolskii, *Die Mobilmachung der russischen Armee 1914* (Berlin, 1922), p. 28.

61. Quoted in Renouvin, *Immediate Origins*, p. 245.

62. Sir Edward Grey, *Twenty-Five Years*, 2: 20. See also Dobrorolskii, *Die Mobilmachung der russischen Armee*, p. 28.

63. Miliukov, *Vospominaniia*, 2: 184. See also Gen. A. A. Brussilov, *A Soldier's Notebook, 1914–1918* (London, 1930), pp. 37–39.

64. Quoted in Florinsky, *Russia*, 2: 1378.

65. N. N. Golovin, *Iz istorii kampanii 1914 goda na russkom fronte. Nachalo voiny i operatsii v vostochnoi Prussii* (Prague, 1926), p. 53; A. M. Zaionchkovskii, *Podgotovka Rossii k imperialisticheskoi voine* (Moscow, 1926), p. 279.

66. Zaionchkovskii, *Podgotovka*, pp. 123–26; B. B. Golovin, *Voennye usiliia Rossii v mirovoi voine* (Paris, 1939), 1: 56–59.

67. Sazonov, *Vospominaniia*, p. 151.

68. Quoted in Albertini, *Origins of the War*, 3: 64.

69. Pares, *Fall of the Russian Monarchy*, p. 186.

70. Aleksandra to Nicholas, 24 September 1914, *Letters of the Tsaritsa to the Tsar*, p. 9.

Afterword

1. Paléologue, *Ambassador's Memoirs*, 1: 52.

2. Danilov, *Rossiia v mirovoi voine*, pp. 111–12.

NOTES

3. Ibid., pp. 110–11; Miliukov, *Vospominaniia*, 2: 190.

4. Shul'gin, *Dni*, p. 60.

5. Golovin, *Voennye usiliia*, 2: 6–7; Nicholas N. Golovine, *The Russian Army in the World War* (New Haven, 1931), pp. 32, 126–27, 131.

6. Nicholas to Aleksandra, 19 November 1914, *Letters of the Tsar to the Tsaritsa*, p. 14.

7. Danilov, *Rossiia v mirovoi voine*, pp. 256–58; Golovin, *Voennye usiliia*, 1: 66; Grand Duke Andrei Vladimirovich, *Dnevnik za 1915g.* (Moscow-Leningrad, 1925), pp. 42–59; E. D. Chermenskii, *Istoriia SSSR. Period Imperializma* (Moscow, 1965), pp. 494–95.

8. Golovin, *Voennye usiliia*, 1: 52.

9. Golovin, *Iz istorii kampanii 1914 goda*, pp. 36–37; Golovin, *Voennye usiliia*, 2: 6–7; Golovine, *Russian Army*, p. 32.

10. Sazonov, *Vospominaniia*, p. 354.

11. Ibid., p. 355.

12. General Basil Gourko, *War and Revolution in Russia, 1914–1917* (New York, 1919), p. 120.

13. Major General Sir Alfred Knox, *With the Russian Army, 1914–1917* (London, 1921), 1: 319.

14. Ibid., p. 348.

15. Michael Cherniavsky, ed., *Prologue to Revolution: Notes of A. N. Iakhontov on the Secret Meetings of the Council of Ministers, 1915* (Englewood Cliffs, 1967), p. 76.

16. Ibid., p. 80.

17. Paléologue, *An Ambassador's Memoirs*, 3: 213.

18. Quoted in Florinsky, *Russia*, 2: 1183.

Works Cited

Adamov, E. A., ed. *Konstantinopol' i prolivy po sekretnym dokumentam byvshego ministerstva inostrannykh del.* 2 vols. Moscow, 1925.

Ainzaft, S. *Zubatovshchina i Gaponovshchina.* Moscow, 1925.

Akselrod, P. B. *Perezhitoe i peredumannoe.* Berlin, 1923.

Albertini, Luigi. *The Origins of the War of 1914.* Translated and edited by Isabella M. Massey. 3 vols. Oxford, 1965.

Aleksandr Il'ich Ul'ianov i delo 1 marta 1887 goda. Sbornik vospominanii i materialov. Moscow-Leningrad, 1927.

Aleksandra Feodorovna, Empress. *Letters of the Tsaritsa to the Tsar, 1914–1916.* Edited by Sir Bernard Pares. Hattiesburg, 1970.

Alekseev, I. V. *Provokator Anna Serebriakova.* Moscow, 1932.

Alekseev, S. A., ed. *Samoderzhavie i liberaly v revoliutsii 1905–1907 godov.* Moscow-Leningrad, 1925.

Alexander, Grand Duke of Russia [Aleksandr Mikhailovich]. *Once a Grand Duke.* New York, 1932

Andrei Vladimirovich, Grand Duke. *Dnevnik za 1915.* Moscow-Leningrad, 1925.

Anfimov, A. M. *Rossiiskaia derevnia v gody pervoi mirovoi voiny.* Moscow, 1962.

"Anglo-Russkoe sopernichestvo v Persii v 1890–1906gg." *Krasnyi arkhiv* 56 (1933): 33–64.

Anushkin, V. A. *Russko-Iaponskaia voina, 1904–1905.* Moscow, 1911.

Aptekman, O. V. *Obshchestvo "Zemlia i Volia" 70-kh gg.* Petrograd, 1924.

Arabazhin, K. I. "Aleksandr Nikolaevich Ostrovskii." In *Istoriia russkoi literatury XIX veka,* edited by D.N. Ovsianiko-Kulikovskii, 3: 425–45. Moscow, 1909.

Artsybashev, Mikhail. *Sanine. A Russian Love Novel.* Translated by Percy Pinckerton. New York, 1932.

Ashmead-Bartlett, Ellis. *Port Arthur: The Siege and Capitulation.* London and Edinburgh, 1906.

Avrekh, A. Ia. *Tsarizm i tret'eiunskaia sistema.* Moscow, 1966.

Baedeker, Karl. *Russia, with Teheran, Port Arthur, and Peking: A Handbook for Travellers.* Leipzig and London, 1914.

Bakh, A. N. *Zapiski narodovol'tsa.* Leningrad, 1931.

Baklanova, I. A. "Formirovanie i polozhenie promyshlennogo proletariata. Rabochee dvizhenie 60-e gody–nachalo 90-kh godov." In *Istoriia rabochikh Leningrada,* edited by Diakin et al., 1: 124–79.

Balabanov, M. *Ocherki po istorii rabochego klassa v Rossii.* 3 vols. Moscow, 1925–26.

Baron, Salo W. *The Russian Jew under Tsars and Soviets.* New York, 1964.

Baron, Samuel H. *Plekhanov: The Father of Russian Marxism.* Stanford, 1963.

Bazilevskii [Iakovlev], B. *Gosudarstvennye prestupleniia v Rossii v XIX veke.* 3 vols. St. Petersburg, 1906.

Bazylow, Ludwik. *Ostatnie Lata Rosji Carskiej. Rządy Stołyina.* Warsaw, 1972.

Beketova, M. A. *Aleksandr Blok.* Peterburg, 1922.

Bel'chikov, N. "S. G. Nechaev v s. Ivanove v 60-e gody." *Katorga i ssylka,* no. 14 (1925), pp. 134–56.

Belinskii, V. G. *Sobranie sochinenii.* Edited by Ivanov-Razumnik. 3 vols. Petersburg, 1919.

Belomor, A. *Port-Arturskaia eskadra nakanune gibeli.* St. Petersburg, 1908.

Belyi [Bugaev], Andrei. "Apokalipsis v russkoi poezii." *Lug zenelyi,* pp. 222–47.

––––––. *Lug zelenyi.* New York and London, 1967.

––––––. *Mezhdu dvukh revoliutsii.* Leningrad, 1934.

––––––. *Nachalo veka.* Moscow-Leningrad, 1933.

––––––. *Petersburg.* Translated, annotated, and introduced by Robert Maguire and John E. Malmstad. Bloomington and London, 1978.

––––––. *Serebrianyi golub'.* Munich, 1967.

––––––. *The Silver Dove.* Translated by George Reavy, with a preface by Harrison E. Salisbury. New York, 1974.

––––––. "Vospominaniia o Bloke." *Epopeia,* no. 1 (1922), pp. 123–273; no. 2 (1922), pp. 105–299; no. 3 (1922), pp. 125–310; no. 4 (1923), pp. 61–305.

Benois, Alexandre. *Memoirs.* Translated by Moura Budberg. 2 vols. London, 1964.

––––––. [Benua]. *Vozniknovenie "Mira Iskusstva."* Leningrad, 1928.

Berlin, P. A. *Russkaia burzhuaziia v staroe i novoe vremia.* Moscow, 1922.

Bill, Valentine T. *The Forgotten Class: The Russian Bourgeoisie from the Earliest Beginnings to 1900.* New York, 1900.

––––––. "The Morozovs." *The Russian Review* 14, no. 2 (April 1955): 109–16.

Billington, James H. *The Icon and the Axe: An Interpretive History of Russian Culture.* London, 1966.

Bing, Edward J., ed. *The Letters of Tsar Nicholas and Empress Marie.* London, 1937.

Blackwell, William L. *The Beginnings of Russian Industrialization, 1800–1860.* Princeton, 1968.

Bliokh, I. S. "Budushchaia voina, eia ekonomicheskie prichiny i posledstvie." *Russkii vestnik* 224, no. 2 (1893): 181–217.

————. *The Future of War in its Technical, Economic, and Political Relations.* Translated by R. C. Long. Boston, 1902.

Blok, A. A. *Dnevnik Al. Bloka, 1917–1922.* Edited by P. N. Medvedev. London, 1928.

————. *Pis'ma Aleksandra Bloka k rodnym.* Edited by M. A. Beketova. 2 vols. Leningrad, 1927–28.

————. *Sobranie sochinenii v shesti tomakh.* 6 vols. Moscow, 1971.

————. *Zapisnye knizhki Al. Bloka.* Edited by P. N. Medvedev. Leningrad, 1930.

Blum, Jerome. *Lord and Peasant in Russia from the Ninth to the Nineteenth Century.* Princeton, 1961.

Bogdanov, I. M. *Gramotnost' i obrazovanie v dorevoliutsionnoi Rossii i v SSSR.* Moscow, 1964.

Bogdanovich, A. V. *Tri poslednykh samoderzhtsa: Dnevnik A. V. Bogdanovicha.* Moscow-Leningrad, 1924.

Bogičević, Miloš. *Le Procès de Salonique.* Paris, 1927.

Bogucharskii [Iakovlev], V. *Aktivnoe narodnichestvo semidesiatykh godov.* Moscow, 1912.

————. *Iz istorii politicheskoi bor'by v 70-kh i 80-kh gg. XIX veka. Partiia "Narodnoi Voli," eia proiskhozhdenie, sud'by, i gibel'.* Moscow, 1912.

Bok, M. P. *Vospominaniia o moem ottse P. A. Stolypina.* New York, 1953.

Borovoi, S. Ia. "Polozhenie rabochego klassa Odessy v XIX i nachale XX v." In *Iz istorii rabochego klassa i revoliutsionnogo dvizheniia,* edited by Nechkina, pp. 308–18.

Borzunov, V. F. *Proletariat Sibiri i dal'nego vostoka nakanune pervoi russkoi revoliutsii.* Moscow, 1965.

Botkina, A. P. *Pavel Mikhailovich Tret'iakov v zhizni i iskusstve.* Moscow, 1960.

Bowlt, John E. *The Silver Age: Russian Art of the Early Twentieth Century and the "World of Art" Group.* Newtonville, 1979.

————. "The World of Art." *Russian Literature Triquarterly,* 1972, pp. 183–218.

Bradley, Joseph C., Jr. "*Muzhik* and Muscovite: Peasants in Late Nineteenth-Century Urban Russia." Ph.D. dissertation, Harvard University, 1977.

———. " 'Once You've Eaten Khitrov Soup You'll Never Leave!': The Slum in Pre-Revolutionary Moscow." Unpublished paper, 1981.

Brainerd, Michael C. "The Octobrists and the Gentry, 1905–1907: Leaders and Followers?" In *Politics of Rural Russia*, edited by Haimson, pp. 67–93.

Briusov, Valerii. *Dnevniki, 1891–1910.* Moscow, 1927.

———. *Sobranie sochinenii v semi tomakh.* 7 vols. Moscow, 1973.

Brower, Daniel R. *Training the Nihilists: Education and Radicalism in Tsarist Russia.* Ithaca and London, 1975.

Brussilov, General A. A. *A Soldier's Notebook, 1914–1918.* London, 1930.

Buchanan, Sir George. *My Mission to Russia and Other Diplomatic Memories.* 2 vols. Boston, 1923.

Buchanan, Meriel. *The Dissolution of an Empire.* London, 1932.

Bukh, N. K. *Vospominaniia.* Moscow, 1928.

Bukhbinder, N. A. "Zubatovshchina v Moskve." *Katorga i ssylka* 14 (1925): 96–133.

Bülow, Prince Bernhard von. *The Memoirs of Prince von Bülow.* Translated from the German by Geoffrey Dunlop. 4 vols. Boston, 1931.

Bunin, I. A. *Sobranie sochinenii v vos'mi tomakh.* 8 vols. Moscow, 1970.

Buryshkin, P. A. *Moskva kupecheskaia.* New York, 1954.

Buxhoeveden, Baroness Sophie. *The Life and Tragedy of Alexandra Feodorovna, Empress of Russia.* London, 1928.

Byrnes, Robert F. *Pobedonostsev: His Life and Thought.* Bloomington and London, 1968.

Carr, E. H. *Michael Bakunin.* New York, 1961.

Caulaincourt, Armand de. *With Napoleon in Russia: The Memoirs of General de Caulaincourt, Duke of Vicenza.* New York, 1935.

Chebarin, A. *Moskva v revoliutsii 1905–1907gg.* Moscow, 1955.

Chekhov, A. P. *Sobranie sochinenii v vos'mi tomakh.* 8 vols. Moscow, 1970.

Chermenskii, E. D. *Burzhuaziia i tsarizm v pervoi russkoi revoliutsii.* 2nd ed. Moscow, 1970.

———. *Istoriia SSSR. Period Imperializma.* 2nd ed. Moscow, 1965.

———. "Zemsko-liberal'noe dvizhenie nakanune revoliutsii 1905–1907gg." *Istoriia SSSR,* no. 5 (1965), pp. 41–60.

Cherniavsky, Michael, ed. *The Structure of Russian History: Interpretive Essays.* New York, 1970.

Chernov, Iu. I. "Tsusima." In *Istoriia Russko-Iaponskoi voiny,* edited by Rostunov, pp. 324–48.

Chernukha, V. G. *Vnutrenniaia politika tsarizma s serediny 50-kh do na-chala 80-kh gg. XIX v.* Leningrad, 1978.

Chernyshevskii, N. G. *What Is To Be Done? Tales about New People.* New York, 1961.

Churchill, Sir Winston S. *The World Crisis, 1911–1914.* London, 1923.

Cioran, Samuel. *The Apocalyptic Symbolism of Andrej Belyj.* The Hague and Paris, 1973.

———. *Vladimir Solov'ev and the Knighthood of the Divine Sophia.* Waterloo, 1977.

Cohen, Stephen F. *Bukharin and the Bolshevik Revolution. A Political Biography, 1888–1938.* Oxford, 1971.

Confino, Michael, ed. *Daughter of a Revolutionary: Natalie Herzen and the Bakunin-Nechaev Circle.* LaSalle, Ill., 1973.

Conroy, Mary Schaeffer. *Peter Arkad'evich Stolypin: Practical Politics in Late Tsarist Russia.* Boulder, 1976.

Crankshaw, Edward. *The Shadow of the Winter Palace: Russia's Drift to Revolution, 1825–1917.* New York, 1976.

Curtiss, John S. *Church and State in Russia: The Last Years of the Empire, 1900–1917.* New York, 1940.

———. *The Russian Army under Nicholas I, 1825–1855.* Durham, 1965.

Dan, F. "Obshchaia politika pravitel'stva i izmeneniia v gosudarstvennoi organizatsii v periode 1905–1906gg." In *Obshchestvennoe dvizhenie,* edited by Martov, 3: pt. 1, pp. 279–392. Cited in the notes as Dan, "Obshchaia politika-1."

———. "Obshchaia politika pravitel'stva i izmeneniia v gosudarstvennoi organizatsii v periode 1905–1907gg. In *Obshchestvennoe dvizhenie,* edited by Martov, 3: pt. 2, pp. 1–148. Cited in the notes as Dan, "Obshchaia politika-2."

———. *The Origins of Bolshevism.* Edited and translated by Joel Carmichael. New York, 1964.

———, and Cherevanin, N. "Soiuz 17 Oktiabria." In *Obshchestvennoe dvizhenie,* edited by Martov, 3: 161–224.

Danilov, General Iu. N. *Rossiia v mirovoi voine, 1914–1915gg.* Berlin, 1924.

———. *Velikii kniaz' Nikolai Nikolaevich.* Paris, 1930.

Davitt, Michael. *Within the Pale.* London, 1903.

Dedijer, Vladimir. *The Road to Sarajevo.* New York and London, 1966.

Dehn, Lili. *The Real Tsaritsa.* Boston, 1922.

Deich, Lev. "Valer'ian Osinskii." *Katorga i ssylka* 14 (1929): 7–43.

Dement'ev, E. M. *Fabrika: chto ona daet naseleniiu i chto ona y nego beret.* Moscow, 1897.

Derzhavin, K. N. "Ostrovskii." In *Istoriia russkoi literatury: Literatura shestidesiatykh godov*, edited by M. P. Alekseev, 8: pt. 2, pp. 407–86. Moscow-Leningrad, 1956.

Deschamps, Philippe. *Livre d'or de l'alliance franco-russe*. Paris, 1898.

Deutscher, Isaac. *The Prophet Armed. Trotsky: 1879–1921*. Oxford, 1954.

———. *Stalin: A Political Biography*. New York, 1967.

Diakin, V. S. et al., eds. *Istoriia rabochikh Leningrada*. 2 vols. Leningrad, 1972.

———. *Samoderzhavie, burzhuaziia, i dvorianstvo v 1907–1911gg*. Leningrad, 1978.

Dobrorolskii, S. K. *Die Mobilmachung der russischen Armee 1914*. Berlin, 1922.

Doctorow, Gilbert. "The Russian Gentry and the Coup d'État of June 3, 1907," *Cahiers du monde russe et soviétique*, no. 1 (January 1976), pp. 43–51.

Dosser, Z. "Na Presne i v Moskovskom komitete bol'shevikov v dekabr'skie dni 1905g." In *Dekabr' 1905 goda na Krasnoi Presne*, edited by Nevskii, pp. 9–20.

Dostoevskii, F. M. *Diary of a Writer*. Translated and annotated by Boris Brasol. New York, 1954.

———. *Polnoe sobranie sochinenii*. 30 vols. Leningrad, 1972–.

Drabkina, Elizaveta. *Chernye sukhari*. Moscow, 1963.

Druzhinin, N. K., ed. *Usloviia byta rabochikh v dorevoliutsionnoi Rossii*. Moscow, 1958.

Druzhinin, N. K., and Rozhkova, M. K., eds. *Istoriia Moskvy: period razlozheniia krepostnogo stroia*. Vol. 3. Moscow, 1954.

Dubnow, S. M. "Anti-Evreiskie dvizhenie v Rossii v 1881–1882gg." *Evreiskaia starina* 1 (1909): 88–110, 265–76.

———. *History of the Jews in Russia and Poland from the Earliest Times until the Present Day*. 3 vols. Philadelphia, 1918.

Dubrovskii, S. *Stolypinskaia reforma*. Leningrad, 1925.

———. *Stolypinskaia zemel'naia reforma*. Moscow, 1963.

Durylin, S. N. "Moskovskie teatry." In *Istoriia Moskvy: Period imperializma*, edited by Pankratova, pp. 543–89.

Edelman, Robert. *Gentry Politics on the Eve of the Russian Revolution: The Nationalist Party, 1907–1917*. New Brunswick, 1980.

Edie, James M., Scanlan, James P., and Zeldin, Mary-Barbara, eds. *Russian Philosophy*. 3 vols. Chicago, 1965.

Ekzempliarskii, P. M. *Istoriia goroda Ivanova*. 2 vols. Ivanovo, 1958.

El'nitskii, A. *Tysiacha deviat'sot piatyi god*. Kursk, 1925.

Emmons, Terence. *The Russian Landed Gentry and the Peasant Emancipation of 1861*. Cambridge, 1968.

————. "Russia's Banquet Campaign." *California Slavic Studies* 10 (1977): 45–86.

Entsiklopedicheskii slovar' Brokgauza-Eifrona. 41 vols. St. Petersburg, 1890–1907.

Erman, L. K. *Intelligentsiia v pervoi russkoi revoliutsii.* Moscow, 1966.

————. "Potemkin." *Sovetskaia istoricheskaia entsiklopediia* 11: cols. 475–77.

Eroshkin, N. P. "Administrativno-politseiskii apparat." In *Istoriia Moskvy: Period imperializma,* edited by Pankratova, pp. 663–75.

"Evrei v Moskve po neopublikovannym dokumentam." *Byloe,* no. 9 (September 1907).

Evreiskaia entsiklopediia: Svod znanii o evreistve i ego kul'ture v proshlom i nastoiashchem. 16 vols. St. Petersburg, 1906–13.

Faleev, N. I. "Rossiia pod Okhranoi. Istoricheskii ocherk." *Byloe,* (October 1907), pp. 1–43.

————. "Shest' mesiatsev voenno-polevoi iustitsii." *Byloe* (2 February 1907), pp. 43–81.

Farnsworth, Beatrice. *Aleksandra Kollontai: Socialism, Feminism, and the Bolshevik Revolution.* Stanford, 1980.

Fay, Sidney B. *The Origins of the World War.* 2 vols. New York, 1930.

Fedorova, M. "Moskovskii Otdel Sviashchennoi Druzhiny po dannym Arkhiva Sekretnago Otdeleniia Kantseliarii Moskovskago General-Gubernatora." *Golos minuvshego* 6, nos. 1–3 (January–March 1918): 139–83.

Figner, Vera. *Zapechatlennyi trud. Vospominaniia.* 2 vols. Moscow, 1964.

Fischer, Fritz. *Germany's Aims in the First World War.* New York, 1967.

Fischer, George. *Russian Liberalism: From Gentry to Intelligentsia.* Cambridge, Mass., 1958.

Fisher, Ralph T. "The Beilis Case." *Modern Encyclopedia of Russian and Soviet History.* Vol. 3 (1977), pp. 189–92.

Florinsky, Michael. *Russia: A History and An Interpretation.* 2 vols. New York, 1968.

Florovskii, Georgii. *Puti russkago bogosloviia.* Paris, 1937.

Fomin, A. A. "Cherty romantizma u A. N. Ostrovksogo." In *Tvorchestvo A. N. Ostrovskogo,* edited by Shambinyi, pp. 92–138.

Footman, David. *Red Prelude, The Life of the Russian Terrorist Zhelyabov.* New Haven, 1945.

Frankel, Jonathan, ed. and trans. *Vladimir Akimov on the Dilemmas of Russian Marxism, 1895–1903.* Cambridge, 1969.

Frederic, Harold. *The New Exodus: A Study of Israel in Russia.* New York and London, 1892.

Frolenko, M. F. "Lipetskii i Voronezhskii s"ezdy." *Byloe*, no. 13 (January 1907), pp. 67–87.

———. *Sobranie sochinenii*. Vol. 2. Moscow, 1932.

Fülöp-Miller, René. *Rasputin: The Holy Devil*. New York, 1928.

Galai, Shmuel. "Early Russian Constitutionalism, 'Vol'noe Slovo' and the 'Zemstvo Union.' A Study in Deception." *Jahrbücher für Geschichte Osteuropas* 22, no. 1 (1974): 35–55.

———. *The Liberation Movement in Russia, 1900–1905*. Cambridge, 1973.

Gapon, G. A. *Zapiski Georgiia Gapona. Ocherki rabochego dvizheniia v Rossii 1900-kh godov*. Moscow, 1918.

Gessen, I. V. *V dvukh vekakh. Zhizennyi otchet*. Berlin, 1937.

Gessen, V. Iu. *Istoriia zakodonatel'stva o trude rabochei molodezhi v Rossii*. Leningrad, 1927.

Getzler, Israel. *Martov: A Political Biography of a Russian Social Democrat*. Cambridge and Melbourne, 1967.

Gil'bert, M. I. "Dvizhenie zarabotkov rabochikh v kontse XIX v." In *Iz istorii rabochego klassa*, edited by Nechkina et al., pp. 319–22.

Giliarovskii, V. A. *Moskva i Moskvichi*. Moscow, 1979.

———. *Trushchobnye liudi*. In *Sochineniia V. A. Giliarovskogo*. 4 vols. Moscow, 1967.

Gilliard, Pierre. *Le tragique destin de Nicolas II et de sa famille*. Paris, 1938.

Gindin, I. F. "Moskovskie banki." In *Istoriia Moskvy*, edited by Kozmin and Iatsunskii, 4: 208–19.

———. "Moskovskie banki v period imperializma, 1900–1917gg." *Istoricheskie zapiski* 58 (1956): 38–106.

Gippius-Merezhkovskaia, Zinaida. *Dmitrii Merezhkovskii*. Paris, 1951.

Girs, A. "Smert' Stolypina. Iz vospominanii byvshago Kievksago Gubernatora." In Stolypin, *P. A. Stolypin*, pp. 86–102.

Giubbenet, V. B. *V osazhdennom Port-Arture. Ocherki voenno-sanitarnago dela*. St. Petersburg, 1910.

Gleason, Abbott. *Young Russia: The Genesis of Russian Radicalism in the 1860s*. New York, 1980.

Glinskii, B. B. "Konstantin Petrovich Pobedonostsev. Materialy dlia biografii." *Istoricheskii vestnik* 108, no. 4 (April 1907): 247–74.

Glukhov, V. A. "Oborona Port-Artura." In *Istoriia Russko-Iaponskoi voiny*, edited by Rostunov, pp. 165–258.

Gogol, N. V. *Sobranie sochinenii*. 6 vols. Moscow, 1959.

Gollerbakh, E. *V. V. Rozanov: zhizn' i tvorchestvo*. Petersburg, 1922.

Golovin, N. N. *Iz istorii kampanii 1914 goda na russkom fronte. Nachalo voiny i operatsii v vostochnoi Prussii*. Prague, 1926.

————. *The Russian Army in the World War*. New Haven, 1931.

————. *Voennye usiliia Rossii v mirovoi voine*. 2 vols. Paris, 1939.

Gooch, G. P. *Before the War: Studies in Diplomacy*. 2 vols. New York, 1967.

————, and Temperley, Harold, eds. *British Documents on the Origins of the War, 1898–1914*. Vol. 9, pts. 1 and 2; vols. 10, 11. London, 1933.

Gorev, B. I., and Koz'min, B. P., eds. *Revoliutsionnoe dvizhenie 1860-kh godov*. Moscow, 1931.

Gor'kii, M. "9-oe ianvaria." In *Pervaia russkaia . . . sbornik vospominanii aktivnykh uchastnikov revoliutsii, 1905–1907gg.*, edited by I. P. Donkov, I. M. Mishakova, and N. V. Senichkina, Moscow, 1975.

Gosudarstvennaia deiatel'nost' predsedatelia Soveta Ministrov Stats-Sekretaria Petra Arkad'evicha Stolypina. 2 vols. St. Petersburg, 1911.

Gots, M. R. "S. V. Zubatov: stranichka iz perezhitago." *Byloe*, no. 9 (September 1906), pp. 63–68.

Govorukhin, O. M. "Vospominaniia O. M. Govorukhina." *Golos minuvshego na chuzhoi storone* 16 (1926): 214–50.

Grave, V. "Kadety v 1905–1906gg." *Krasnyi arkhiv* 46 (1931): 38–68; 47 (1931): 111–39.

Gray, Camilla. *The Great Experiment: Russian Art, 1863–1922*. New York, 1962.

Greenberg, Louis. *The Jews in Russia: The Struggle for Emancipation, 1881–1917*. 2 vols. New Haven, 1951.

Grey, Viscount Edward. *Twenty-Five Years, 1892–1916*. 2 vols. London, 1925.

Grinevich, V. *Professional'noe dvizhenie rabochikh v Rossii*. Moscow, 1923.

Grover, Stuart R. "Savva Mamontov and the Mamontov Circle, 1870–1905. Art Patronage and the Rise of Nationalism in Russian Art." Ph.D. dissertation, University of Wisconsin, 1971.

Grunwald, Constantin de. *Tsar Nicholas I*. Translated from the French by Brigit Patmore. London, 1954.

Guerassimov, Alexandre. *Tsarisme et terrorisme*. Paris, 1934.

Gurevich, L. "Narodnoe dvizhenie v Peterburge 9-go ianvaria 1905 goda." *Byloe* 1, no. 1 (January 1906): 200–229.

Gurko, V. I. *Features and Figures of the Past: Government and Opinion in the Reign of Nicholas II*. Stanford, 1939.

————. *Tsar i tsaritsa*. Paris, 1927.

————. *War and Revolution in Russia, 1914–1917*. New York, 1919.

Gvozdev, S. *Zapiski fabrichnago inspektora. Iz nabliudenii i praktiki v period 1894–1908gg*. Moscow, 1911.

Haimson, Leopold H. "Observations on the Politics of the Russian Countryside, 1905–1914." In *Politics of Rural Russia*, edited by Haimson, pp. 261–300.

———, ed. *The Politics of Rural Russia, 1905–1914*. Bloomington, 1979.

———. "The Problem of Social Stability in Urban Russia, 1905–1917." *Slavic Review* 23, no. 4 (December 1964): 619–42; 24, no. 1 (March 1965): 1–22.

———. "The Problem of Social Stability in Urban Russia, 1905–1917." In *Structure of Russian History*, edited by Cherniavsky, pp. 341–80.

———. "The Russian Landed Nobility and the System of Third of June." In *Politics of Rural Russia*, edited by Haimson, pp. 1–29.

———. *The Russian Marxists and the Origins of Bolshevism*. Cambridge, Mass., 1955.

Hamburg, Gary M. "Russian Noble Families and the Terrorist Movement, 1878–1882." Unpublished scholarly paper, 1981.

Hamilton, General Sir Ian. *A Staff Officer's Scrap-Book during the Russo-Japanese War*. London, 1912.

Harding, Neil. *Lenin's Political Thought*. London, 1977.

Hardy, Deborah. *Peter Tkachev: The Critic as Jacobin*. Seattle and London, 1977.

Haskell, Arnold L. *Diaghileff: His Artistic and Private Life*. New York, 1935.

Hellie, Jean Laves. "Aleksandr Mikhailovich Dobroliubov." Unpublished scholarly essay, forthcoming in *The Modern Encyclopedia of Russian and Soviet Literature*. Vol. 5. Gulf Breeze, Fla., 1977.

Hosking, Geoffrey A. *The Russian Constitutional Experiment. Government and Duma, 1907–1914*. Cambridge, 1973.

Iakovlev, A., and Shorr, Ia. *1905 god v Moskve*. Moscow, 1955.

Iakovlev, N. N. *Vooruzhennye vosstaniia v dekabre 1905 goda*. Moscow, 1957.

Ianzhul, I. I. *Fabrichnyi byt moskovskoi gubernii. Otchet za 1882–1883gg*. St. Petersburg, 1884.

———. *Iz vospominanii i perepiski fabrichnago inspektora pervago prizyva. Materialy dlia istorii russkago rabochego voprosa i fabrichnago zakonodatel'stva*. St. Petersburg, 1907.

———. *Ocherki i izsledovaniia*. 2 vols. Moscow, 1884.

Iaroslavskii, E. *Vooruzhennye vosstaniia v dekabre 1905 goda*. Moscow-Leningrad, 1926.

Ioksimovich, Ch. *Manufakturnaia promyshlennost' v proshlom i nastoiashchem*. Moscow, 1915.

Isaev, G. S. *Rol' tekstil'noi promyshlennosti v genezise i razvitii kapitalizma v Rossii, 1760–1860*. Leningrad, 1970.

Itenberg, B. S. *Dvizhenie revoliutsionnogo narodnichestva. Narodnicheskie kruzhki i "khozhdenie v narod" v 70-kh godakh XIX v.* Moscow, 1965.

——, ed. *Revoliutsionnoe narodnichestvo 70-kh godov XIX veka.* Vol. 1. Moscow, 1964.

——, and Cherniak, A. Ia. *Zhizn' Aleksandra Ul'ianova.* Moscow, 1966.

Ivanov, L. M., ed. *Istoriia rabochego klassa Rossii, 1861–1900.* Moscow, 1972.

——, ed. *Rabochee dvizhenie v Rossii v XIX veke. Sbornik dokumentov i materialov.* Vol. 4, pts. 1 and 2. Moscow-Leningrad, 1961.

——. "Vozniknovenie rabochego klassa." In *Istoriia rabochego klassa Rossii,* edited by L. M. Ivanov, pp. 9–60.

——, ed. *Vserossiiskaia politicheskaia stachka v oktiabre 1905 goda.* 2 vols. Moscow-Leningrad, 1955.

Ivanov, Viacheslav. *Po zvezdam: stat'i i aforizmy.* St. Petersburg, 1909.

Ivanskii, A. I., ed. *Molodye gody V. I. Lenina po vospominaniiam sovremennikov i dokumentam.* 3rd ed. Moscow, 1960.

——, ed. *Zhizn' kak fakel. Istoriia geroicheskoi bor'by i tragicheskoi gibeli Aleksandra Ul'ianova rasskazannaia ego sovremennikami.* Moscow, 1966.

Jevtić, Borivoje. *Sarajevski atentat.* Sarajevo, 1923.

Johnson, Robert E. *Peasant and Proletarian: The Working Class of Moscow in the Late Nineteenth Century.* New Brunswick, 1979.

Joseph, Samuel. *Jewish Immigration to the United States from 1881–1910.* New York, 1914.

Kamenev, S. Iu. "S. Iu. Vitte i K. P. Pobedonostsev o sovremennom polozhenii pravoslavnoi tserkvi." *Vestnik evropy,* no. 2 (1909), pp. 651–91.

Kantor, R. "Aleksandr III o evreiskikh pogromakh, 1881–1883gg. Novye materialy." *Evreiskaia letopis'* 1 (1923): 148–58.

Karamzin, N. M. *Izbrannye sochineniia.* 2 vols. Moscow, 1964.

Karelin, A. E. "Deviatoe ianvaria i Gapon." *Krasnaia letopis',* no. 1 (1922), pp. 106–16.

Karpukhin, N., ed. *1905 god v riazanskoi gubernii.* Riazan, 1925.

Katsnel'son, A. "Iz martirologa Moskovskoi obshchiny. Moskovskaia sinagoga v 1891–1906gg." *Evreiskaia starina* 1 (1909): 175–88.

Kaufman, A. A. *Agrarnyi vopros v Rossii.* Moscow, 1919.

Kazemzadeh, Firuz. *Russia and Britain in Persia, 1864–1917: A Study in Imperialism.* New Haven, 1968.

Keep, J. L. H. *The Rise of Social Democracy in Russia.* Oxford, 1963.

Kennan, George. "Russian 'Mouse-Traps.'" *The Century Illustrated Monthly Magazine* 88 (November 1911–April 1912): 745–52.

————. *Siberia and the Exile System.* 2 vols. New York, 1891.

Kennan, George F. *The Decline of Bismarck's European Order: Franco-Russian Relations, 1875–1890.* Princeton, 1979.

Kennedy, Janet. *The "Mir Iskusstya" Group and Russian Art, 1898–1912.* New York and London, 1977.

Kerner, Robert J. "The Mission of Liman von Sanders." *Slavonic Review* 6 (1927–28): 12–27, 344–63, 543–60; 7 (1928): 90–112.

Khromov, P. A. *Ekonomicheskoe razvitie Rossii v XIX–XX vekakh, 1800–1917.* Moscow, 1950.

Khudiakov, Ivan. *Zapiski Karakozovtsa.* Introduction by M. Klevenskii. Moscow-Leningrad, 1930.

Kipp, Jacob W., and Lincoln, W. Bruce. "Autocracy and Reform: Bureaucratic Absolutism and Political Modernization in Nineteenth-Century Russia." *Russian History* 6, no. 1 (1979): 1–21.

Klimov, P. I. *Revoliutsionnaia deiatel'nost' rabochikh v derevne v 1905–1907gg.* Moscow, 1960.

Kliuchevskii, V. O. *Sochineniia.* 8 vols. Moscow, 1956.

Knox, General Sir Alfred. *With the Russian Army, 1914–1917.* 2 vols. London, 1921.

Kochakov, B. M. et al., eds. *Ocherki istorii Leningrada.* Vols 2–3. Moscow-Leningrad, 1956.

Kogan, D. Z. *Mamontovskii kruzhok.* Moscow, 1970.

Kokovtsev, Count V. N. *Iz moego proshlago: vospominaniia, 1903–1919gg.* 2 vols. Paris, 1933.

Kolokol. Gazeta A. I. Gertsena i N. P. Ogareva. Vol'naia russkaia tipografiia, 1857–1867. 11 vols. Moscow, 1962–64.

Kol'tsov, D. "Rabochie v 1905–1907gg." In *Obshchestvennoe dvizhenie,* edited by Martov et al., 2: 185–338.

Kol'tsov, D. [V. A. Ginzburg], "Rabochee v 1890–1904gg." In *Obshchestvennoe dvizhenie,* edited by Martov et al., 1: 183–229.

Koni, A. F. *Sobranie sochinenii.* 9 vols. Moscow, 1966–69.

————. "Vospominaniia o dele Very Zasulicha." *Sobranie sochinenii,* 2: 24–328.

Konstantin Konstantinovich, Grand Duke. "Iz dnevnika Konstantina Romanova." *Krasnyi arkhiv* 43 (1930): 92–115; 44 (1931): 126–51; 45 (1931): 112–29.

Kopanev, A. I. *Naselenie Peterburga v pervoi polovine XIX veka.* Moscow-Leningrad, 1957.

Korolenko, V. G. *Sobranie sochinenii v desiati tomakh.* Moscow, 1953–55.

Korol'kov, Konstantin. *Zhizn' i tsarstvovanie Imperatora III, 1881–1894gg.* Kiev, 1901.

Kostitsyn, V. "Dekabr'skoe vosstanie 1905g." In *Dekabr' 1905 goda na Krasnoi Presne*, edited by Nevskii, pp. 21–47.

Kovalevskii, M. M. *Obshchinnoe zemlevladenie: prichiny, khod, i posledstviia ego razlozheniia*. Moscow, 1879.

Koz'min, B. P. *Iz istorii revoliutsionnoi mysli v Rossii*. Moscow, 1961.

————. *S. V. Zubatov i ego korrespondenty*. Moscow-Leningrad, 1928.

————, and Iatsunskii, V. K., eds. *Istoriia Moskvy: Period promyshlennogo kapitalizma*. Moscow, 1954.

————, ed. *Nechaev i nechaevtsy: Sbornik materialov*. Moscow-Leningrad, 1931.

————, ed. "Novoe o S. G. Nechaeve." *Krasnyi arkhiv* 14 (1926): 148–58; 15 (1926): 150–63.

Krasnyi-Admonyi, G. Ia., and Dubnov, S. M., eds. *Materialy dlia istorii antievreiskikh pogromov v Rossii*. Vol. I. Petrograd, 1919.

Kropotkin, Prince Peter. *Memoirs of a Revolutionist*. Cambridge, Mass., 1899.

Krupianskaia, V. Iu., and Polishchuk, N. S. *Kul'tura i byt rabochikh gornozavodskogo Urala (konets XIX–nachalo XX v.)*. Moscow, 1971.

Krupskaia, N. *Iz dalekykh vremen*. Moscow-Leningrad, 1930.

Krupskaia, Nadezhda. *Memories of Lenin*. London, 1930.

Kruze, E. E., and Kutsentov, D. C. "Naselenie Peterburga." In *Ocherki istorii Leningrada*, edited by Kochakov et al., 3: 104–46.

Kryzhanovskii, S. E. *Vospominaniia*. Berlin, n. p.

Kuprin, A. I. *Sobranie sochinenii v deviati tomakh*. 9 vols. Moscow, 1964.

Kurler, P. G. *Gibel' imperatorskoi Rossii*. Berlin, 1923.

Kuropatkin, A. N. "Dnevnik A. N. Kuropatkina." *Krasnyi arkhiv* 2 (1922): 5–112; 5 (1924): 82–101; 7 (1924): 55–69; 8 (1925): 70–100; 68 (1935), pp. 65–96; 69–70 (1935): 101–27.

————. *Opisanie boevykh deistvii Man'chzhurskikh armii pod Mukdenom s 4-go fevralia po 4-e marta 1905 goda*. 3 vols. Moscow, 1907.

————. *The Russian Army, and the Japanese War*. Translated by A. B. Lindsay. 2 vols. London, 1909.

————. *Zapiski generala Kuropatkina o Russko-Iaponskoi voine. Itogi voiny*. Berlin, 1911.

Kushner, P. I., ed. *The Village of Viratino*. Translated and edited by Sula Benet. New York, 1970.

Kutsentov, D. G. "Naselenie Peterburga. Polozhenie peterburgskikh rabochikh." In *Ocherki istorii Leningrada*, edited by Kochakov et al., 2: 170–230.

Kuz'min, Dmitrii. "Kazanskaia demonstratsiia 1876g. i G. V. Plekhanov." *Katorga i ssylka* 44 (1928): 7–40.

Kuzmin, Mikhail. *Wings: Prose and Poetry by Mikhail Kuzmin*. Translated and edited by Neil Granoien and Michael Green, with a preface by Vladimir Markov. Ann Arbor, 1972.

Langer, William L. *The Diplomacy of Imperialism*. New York, 1965.

Lapitskaia, S. *Byt rabochikh trekhgornoi manufaktury*. Moscow, 1935.

LaPorte, Maurice. *Histoire de l'Okhrana. La Police secrète des Tsars, 1880–1917*. Paris, 1935.

Larenko, P. *Stradnye dni Port-Artura. Khronika voennykh sobytii i zhizni v osazhdennoi kreposti s 26-go ianvaria 1904g. po 9 ianvaria 1905g.* St. Petersburg, 1904.

Laverychev, V. Ia. *Po tu storonu barrikad. Iz istorii bor'by moskovskoi burzhuazii s revoliutsiei*. Moscow, 1967.

Lavrov, Peter. *Historical Letters*. Translated with an introduction and notes by James P. Scanlan. Berkeley and Los Angeles, 1967.

Lee, Dwight E. *Europe's Crucial Years: The Diplomatic Background of World War I, 1902–1914*. Hanover, 1974.

Lemke, Mikhail. *Politicheskie protsessy M. I. Mikhailova, D. I. Pisareva, i N. G. Chernyshevskago*. St. Petersburg, 1907.

Lenin, V. I. "Chto delat'?" In *Sochineniia*, 5: 319–494.

———. "Iazyk tsifr." In *Sochineniia*. 4th ed., 19: 321–26. Moscow, 1954.

———. "Nasushchennye zadachi nashego dvizheniia," in *Sochineniia*. 4th ed., 4: 341–46.

———. *Razvitiia kapitalizma v Rossii*, in *Sochineniia*, 4th ed. Vol. 3.

Leroy-Beaulieu, Anatole. *The Empire of the Tsars and the Russians*. Translated by Zenaide A. Ragozin. 3 vols. New York and London, 1902–5. Reprint, New York, 1969.

Levin, Alfred. *The Second Duma: A Study of the Social Democratic Party and the Russian Constitutional Experiment*. 2nd ed. Hamden, 1966.

Levitskii, N. A. *Russko-Iaponskaia voina, 1904–1905*. Moscow, 1938.

Levitskii, V. O. [V. O. Tsederbaum]. "Pravye partii." In *Obshchestvennoe dvizhenie*, edited by Martov et al., 3: 347–469.

———. *Za chetvert' veka. Revoliutsionnye vospominaniia*. Vol. I, pts. 1 and 2. Moscow, 1926.

Liashchenko, P. I. *Istoriia narodnogo khoziaistva SSSR*. 2 vols. Moscow, 1956.

———. *Ocherki agrarnoi evoliutsii Rossii*. Moscow-Petrograd, 1923.

Lifar, Sergei. *Diagilev i s Diagilevym*. Paris, 1939.

Lincoln, W. Bruce. *Nicholas I: Emperor and Autocrat of All the Russias*. London and Bloomington, 1978.

———. *Petr Petrovich Semenov-Tian-Shanskii: The Life of a Russian Geographer*. Newtonville, 1980.

————. *The Romanovs: Autocrats of All the Russias.* New York, 1981.

Linkov, Ia. I. *Revoliutsionnaia bor'ba A. I. Gertsena i N. P. Ogareva i Tainoe Obshchestvo "Zemlia i Volia" 1860-kh godov.* Moscow, 1964.

Liubatovich, O. S. "Dalekoe i nedavnee." *Byloe,* no. 6 (June 1906).

Liubimov, D. N. "Gapon i 9 ianvaria." *Voprosy istorii* 40, no. 8 (August 1965): 123–31; 40, no. 9 (September 1965): 114–21.

Liubosh, S. B. *Russkii fashist Vladimir Purishkevich.* Leningrad, 1925.

Livanov, A. I. "Kakoe polozhenie naibolee udobno dlia sblizheniia s narodom?" In *Revoliutsionnoe narodnichestvo,* edited by Itenberg, 1: 145–51.

Lokhtin, Petr. *Bezzemel'nyi proletariat v Rossii.* Moscow, 1905.

Lozovskii, A., ed. *Morozovskaia stachka 1885g.* Moscow, 1925.

Lukashevich, I. "Vospominaniia o dele 1-go marta 1887 goda." *Byloe,* no. 1 (July 1917), pp. 22–49; no. 2 (August 1917), pp. 115–32.

Lukashevich, Stephen. "The Holy Brotherhood, 1881–1883." *The American Slavic and East European Review* 18, no. 4 (December 1959): 491–509.

Lychev, I. *Vospominaniia Potemkintsa.* Moscow-Leningrad, 1925.

McCully, Newton A. *The McCully Report: The Russo-Japanese War, 1904–1905.* Edited by Richard A. von Doenhoff. Annapolis, 1977.

MacNaughton, Ruth Delia, and Manning, Roberta Thompson. "The Crisis of the Third of June System and Political Trends in the Zemstvos, 1907–1914." In *Politics of Rural Russia,* edited by Haimson, pp. 184–218.

Maevskii, E. "Massovoe dvizhenie s 1904 po 1906gg. Obshchaia kartina dvizhenie." In *Obshchestvennoe dvizhenie,* edited by Martov et al., 2: 34–184.

Maklakov, V. A. *The First State Duma: Contemporary Reminiscences.* Translated by Mary Belkin. Bloomington, 1964.

————. *Vlast' i obshchestvennost' na zakate Staroi Rossii: Vospominaniia.* Paris, 1936.

————. *Vtoraia gosudarstvennaia duma. Vospominaniia sovremennika.* Paris, n.d.

Malia, Martin. *Alexander Herzen and the Birth of Russian Socialism, 1812–1855.* Cambridge, Mass., 1961.

Malozemoff, Andrew. *Russian Far Eastern Policy, 1881–1904. With Special Emphasis on the Causes of the Russo-Japanese War.* Berkeley and Los Angeles, 1958.

Mamontov, V. A. *Vospominaniia o russkikh khudozhnikakh (Abramtsevskii khudozhestvennyi kruzhok).* Moscow, 1950.

Manchester, William. *The Arms of Krupp, 1587–1968.* Boston, 1964.

Manning, Roberta Thompson. "Zemstvo and Revolution: The Onset of the Gentry Reaction, 1905–1907." In *Politics of Rural Russia,* edited by Haimson, pp. 30–66.

Mariia Feodorovna, Empress. *Letters of Tsar Nicholas and the Empress Marie.* Edited by Edward J. Bing. London, 1937.

Martov, L. *Zapiski sotsialdemokrata.* Berlin, Petersburg, and Moscow, 1922.

———. "Sotsialdemokratiia 1905–1907gg." In *Obshchestvennoe dvizhenie,* edited by Martov et al., 3: 537–643.

———, Maslov, P., and Potresov, A., eds. *Obshchestvennoe dvizhenie v Rossii v nachale XX-go veka.* 3 vols. St. Petersburg, 1909.

Martynov, A. "Konstitutsionno-Demokraticheskaia Partiia." In *Obshchestvennoe dvizhenie,* edited by Martov et al., 3: 1–85.

Marushevskii, V., and Orlov, P. *Boevaia rabota russkoi armii v voinu 1904–1905gg.* 2 vols. St. Petersburg, 1910.

Maslenikov, Oleg. *The Frenzied Poets: Andrey Biely and the Russian Symbolists.* Berkeley, 1952.

Maslov, P. *Agrarnyi vopros v Rossii.* 2 vols. St. Petersburg, 1905.

———. "Krest'ianskoe dvizhenie." In *Obshchestvennoe dvizhenie,* edited by Martov et al., 2: pt. 2, pp. 202–84.

Massie, Robert K. *Nicholas and Aleksandra.* New York, 1967.

Materialy k istorii russkoi kontr-revoliutsii. Vol. 1. St. Petersburg, 1908.

Matisse, Henri. "Zametki khudozhnika." *Zolotoe runo,* no. 6 (1909), pp. iv–x.

Matossian, Mary. "The Peasant Way of Life." In Vucinich (ed.), *The Peasant in Nineteenth-Century Russia,* edited by Vucinich, pp. 1–40.

Matich, Olga. *Paradox in the Religious Poetry of Zinaida Gippius.* Munich, 1972.

Maxwell, William. *From the Yalu to Port Arthur. A Personal Record.* London, 1906.

Mehlinger, Howard D., and Thompson, John M. *Count Witte and the Tsarist Government in the 1905 Revolution.* Bloomington, 1972.

Menashe, Louis. "Alexander Guchkov and the Origins of the Octobrist Party: The Russian Bourgeoisie in Politics, 1905." Ph.D. dissertation, New York University, 1966.

Mendeleeva, A. I. "A. A. Blok." In *Blok v vospominaniiakh sovremennikov,* edited by Orlov, 1: 70–80.

Men'shchikov, L. F. *Okhrana i revoliutsiia. K istorii tainykh politicheskikh organizatsii v Rossii.* 2 vols. in 3 pts. Moscow, 1925–29.

Mikhailov, M. I. "K molodomu pokoleniiu." In Lemke, *Politicheskie protsessy,* pp. 36–54.

Mikulin, A. A. *Ocherki iz istorii primeneniia zakona 3-go iiulia 1886 goda.* Vladimir, 1893.

Mikulin, P. P. *Nasha bankovaia politika, 1729–1903.* Kharkov, 1904.

Miliukov, P. N. *God Bor'by: publitsisticheskaia khronika, 1905–1906gg.* St. Petersburg, 1907.

———. *Russia and Its Crisis.* Chicago and London, 1906.

———. "Tri popytki." In *Samoderzhavie i liberaly,* edited by Alekseev, pp. 41–96.

———. *Vospominaniia, 1859–1917.* 2 vols. New York, 1955.

———. *Vtoraia duma. Publitsisticheskaia khronika 1907.* St. Petersburg, 1908.

Miliutin, D. A. *Dnevnik D. A. Miliutina.* 4 vols. Moscow, 1947–51.

Miliutin, N. A. "Zapiska po voprosu o preobrazovanii zemskikh uchrezhdeniiakh." 22 maia 1862g. TsGIAL, fond 869, opis' 1, delo no. 397.

Mintslov, S. P. *Peterburg v 1903–1910 godov.* Riga, 1931.

Mirsky, Prince D. S. *Russia: A Social History.* London, 1952.

Mitskevich, S. I. *Revoliutsionnaia Moskva, 1888–1905.* Moscow, 1940.

Mochul'skii, K. *Aleksandr Blok.* Paris, 1948.

———. *Andrei Belyi.* Paris, 1955.

———. *Valerii Briusov.* Paris, 1962.

———. *Vladimir Solov'ev: zhizn' i uchenie.* 2nd ed. Paris, 1951.

Moiseenko, P. A. *Vospominaniia starogo revoliutsionera.* Moscow, 1966.

Montgelas, Max, and Schücking, Walther, eds. *Outbreak of the World War: German Documents Collected by Karl Kautsky.* New York, 1924.

Morekhina, G. G. "Razvitie promyshlennosti i polozhenie proletariata v gody reaktsii i novogo revoliutsionnogo pod"ema." In *Istoriia Moskvy: Period imperializma i burzhuazno-demokraticheskikh revoliutsii,* edited by Pankratova, pp. 207–34.

Mosolov, A. *Pri dvore Imperatora.* Riga, n.d.

Mousset, Albert. *Un drame historique. L'attentat de Sarajevo. Documents inédits et texte intégral des stenogrammes du procès.* Paris, 1930.

Mukhalov, M. K. *Deti ulitsy: Maloletniia prostitutki.* St. Petersburg, 1906.

Nazanskii, V. I. *Krushenie velikoi Rossii i doma Romanovykh.* Paris, 1930.

Nechkina, M. V. et al., eds. *Iz istorii rabochego klassa i revoliutsionnogo dvizheniia. Pamiati akademika Anny Mikhailovny Pankratovoi.* Moscow, 1958.

Nemirovich-Danchenko, Vladimir. *My Life in the Russian Theatre.* Translated by John Cournos. Boston, 1936.

Nesselrode, Count K. V. *Lettres et papiers du Chancelier Comte de Nesselrode.* 11 vols. Paris, 1905–12.

Nevskii, V. I., ed. *Dekabr' 1905 goda na Krasnoi Presne. Sbornik statei i vospominanii.* Moscow, 1925.

———. *Ianvarskie dni v Peterburge v 1905g.* Kharkov, 1925.

———. "Povorotnyi punkt rabochego dvizheniia v Rossii," in *Morozovskaia stachka 1885g.*, edited by Lozovskii, pp. 3–12.

———. *Rabochee dvizhenie v ianvarskie dni 1905 goda.* Moscow, 1930.

———. *Sovety i vooruzhennye vosstanie v 1905 godu.* Moscow, 1931.

Nicholas II. *Dnevnik Imperatora Nikolaia II.* Berlin, 1923.

———. *Letters of Tsar Nicholas and the Empress Marie.* Edited by Edward J. Bing. London, 1937.

———. *Letters of the Tsar to the Tsaritsa, 1914–1917.* Translated by A. L. Hynes. Hattiesburg, 1970.

Nicolson, Harold. *King George the Fifth: His Life and Reign.* New York, 1953.

———. *Sir Arthur Nicolson, Bart., First Lord Carnock: A Study in the Old Diplomacy.* London, 1930, 1937:2nd ed.

Nifontov, A. S. "Naselenie kapitalisticheskoi Moskvy." In *Istoriia Moskvy,* edited by Koz'min and Iatsunskii, 4: 226–61.

———. "Ostrota sotsial'nykh kontrastov v burzhuaznoi Moskve." In *Istoriia Moskvy,* edited by Koz'min and Iatsunskii, 4: 254–62.

Nikitenko, A. V. *Dnevnik.* 3 vols. Moscow, 1955.

Nikolaevskii, Boris. *Aseff the Spy: Russian Terrorist and Police Stool.* New York, 1934.

Nikolai II. Materialy dlia kharakteristiki lichnosti i tsarstvovaniia. Moscow, 1917.

Novorusskii, Mikhail. *Zapiski Shlissel'burzhtsa, 1887–1905.* Moscow, 1933.

Obshchii svod po Imperii rezultatov razrabotki dannykh pervoi vseobshchei perepisi naseleniia, proizvedennoi 28 ianvaria 1897 goda. 2 vols. St. Petersburg, 1905.

The Official History of the Russo-Japanese War. 3 vols. London, 1909.

Okamoto, Shumpei. *The Japanese Oligarchy and the Russo-Japanese War.* New York and London, 1970.

Ol', P. V. *Inostrannye kapitaly v khoziaistve dovoennoi Rossii.* Leningrad, 1925.

Ol'denburg, S. S. *Tsarstvovanie Imperatora Nikolaia II.* 2 vols. Belgrad, 1939.

Orlov, V. I. *Sbornik statisticheskikh svedenii po moskovskoi gubernii: formy krest'ianskago zemlevladeniia v moskovskoi gubernii.* Moscow, 1879.

Orlov, V. N., ed. *Aleksandr Blok i Andrei Belyi. Perepiska.* Moscow, 1940.

———, ed. *Aleksandr Blok v vospominaniiakh sovremennikov.* 2 vols. Moscow, 1980.

Orlovsky, Daniel T. *The Limits of Reform: The Ministry of Internal Affairs in Imperial Russia, 1802–1881.* Cambridge, Mass., 1981.

Ostrovskii, A. N. *Five Plays of Alexander Ostrovsky.* Edited and translated by Eugene K. Bristow. New York, 1969.

Ovsiannikov, N., ed. *Dekabr'skoe vosstanie v Moskve 1905g. Illustrirovannyi sbornik statei, zametok, i vospominanii.* Moscow, 1919.

Owen, Launcelot A. *The Russian Peasant Movement, 1906–1917.* New York, 1963.

Pachmuss, Temira. *Zinaida Hippius: An Intellectual Profile.* Carbondale, 1971.

Paléologue, Maurice. *An Ambassador's Memoirs.* Translated by F. A. Holt. 3 vols. New York, n.d.

Palmer, R. R. *A History of the Modern World.* New York, 1957.

Pankratova, A. M., ed. *Istoriia Moskvy: Period imperializma i burzhuazno-demokraticheskikh revoliutsii.* Vol. 5. Moscow, 1955.

———. *Pervaia russkaia revoliutsiia, 1905–1907gg.* Moscow, 1951.

Parasun'ko, O. A. *Polozhenie i bor'ba rabochego klassa Ukrainy (60-90-e gody XIX v.).* Kiev, 1963.

Pares, Sir Bernard. *The Fall of the Russian Monarchy: A Study of the Evidence.* New York, 1961.

Pashukanis, S., ed. "K istorii Anglo-russkogo soglasheniia 1907 goda." *Krasnyi arkhiv* 69–70 (1935): 3–29.

Pavlov, F. *Za desiat' let praktiki. Otryvki vospominanii, vpechatlenii i nabliudenii iz fabrichnoi zhizni.* Moscow, 1907.

Pavlovich, M. "Vneshniaia politika i russko-iaponskaia voina." In *Obshchestvennoe dvizhenie,* edited by Martov et al., 2: 1–33.

Pavlovsky, George. *Agricultural Russia on the Eve of the Revolution.* New York, 1968.

Pazhitnov, K. A. *Polozhenie rabochego klassa v Rossii.* 2 vols. Leningrad, 1924.

Percival, John. *The World of Diaghilev.* New York, 1971.

Perets, E. A. *Dnevnik.* Moscow, 1927.

Pershin, P. N. *Agrarnaia revoliutsiia v Rossii: Istoriko-ekonomicheskoe issledovanie.* 2 vols. Moscow, 1966.

Peskov, P. A. *Fabrichnyi byt vladimirskoi gubernii. Otchet za 1882–1883gg.* St. Petersburg, 1884.

Petrov, M. N. "Gorodskoe khoziaistvo." In *Istoriia Moskvy: Period imperializma i burzhuazno-demokraticheskikh revoliutsii,* edited by Pankratova, pp. 690–717.

Petrunkevich, I. I. *Iz zapisok obshchestvennago deiatelia: vospominaniia.* Edited by A. A. Kizevetter. Berlin, 1934. Vol. 12, *Arkhiv russkoi revoliutsii,* edited by I. V. Gessen.

Pinson, Koppel S., ed. *Essays on Antisemitism.* New York, 1946.

Piotkovskii, S., ed. "Novoe o Zubatovshchine." *Krasnyi arkhiv* 1 (1922): 289–328.

Pipes, Richard. *Russia under the Old Regime.* New York, 1974.

———. *Struve: Liberal on the Left, 1870–1905.* Cambridge, Mass., 1970.

———. *Struve: Liberal on the Right, 1905–1944.* Cambridge, Mass., 1980.

———. *Social Democracy and the St. Petersburg Labor Movement, 1885–1897.* Cambridge, Mass., 1963.

Pirumova, N. M. *Zemskoe liberal'noe dvizhenie. Sotsial'nye korni i evoliutsiia do nachala XX veka.* Moscow, 1977.

Pisarev, D. I. *Sochineniia.* 4 vols. Moscow, 1955.

Plekhanov, G. V. "Pis'ma G. V. Plekhanova k P. L. Lavrova." *Dela i dni* 2 (1921): 78–103.

———. *Sochineniia.* Edited by D. Riazanov. 24 vols. Moscow-Leningrad, 1923–27.

Pobedonostsev, K. P. "Graf V. N. Panin." *Golosa iz Rossii,* no. 7 (1859), pp. 3–142. Reprint. Moscow, 1974–75.

———. *K. P. Pobedonostsev i ego korrespondenty.* 2 vols. Moscow-Petrograd, 1923.

———. "O reformakh v grazhdanskom sudoproizvodstve." *Russkii vestnik* 21 (1859): 541–80; 22 (1859): 5–34, 153–90.

———. *Pis'ma Pobedonostseva k Aleksandru III.* 2 vols. Moscow, 1925–26.

Poggioli, Renato. *The Poets of Russia, 1890–1930.* Cambridge, Mass., 1960.

———. *Rozanov.* London, 1962.

Pogodin, M. P. *Istoriko-politicheskie pis'ma i zapiski v prodolzhenii krymskoi voiny, 1853–1856gg.* Moscow, 1874.

"Pogromy v Rossii." *Evreiskaia entsiklopediia,* 12: cols. 611–22.

Poincaré, Raymond. *Au service de la France: L'Union Sacrée,* 5 vols. Paris, 1926–27.

———. *The Origins of the War.* London, 1922.

Pokrovskii, M. N., ed. *1905: Materialy i dokumenty.* Moscow, 1927.

Polenova, N. V. *Abramtsevo. Vospominaniia.* Moscow, 1922.

Poletika, N. P. *Vozniknovenie pervoi mirovoi voiny (iiulskii krizis 1914g.).* Moscow, 1964.

Polevoi, Iu. Z. "Na puti soedineniia s sotsializmom." In *Istoriia rabochego klassa Rossii,* edited by Ivanov, pp. 129–211.

———. "Sostav i polozhenie moskovskogo proletariata." In *Istoriia Moskvy: Period imperializma,* edited by Pankratova, pp. 57–67.

———. *Zarozhdenie marksizma v Rossii, 1883–1894gg.* Moscow, 1959.

Poliakova, E. I. *Stanislavskii—akter.* Moscow, 1972.

Polianskii, N. N. *Tsarskie voennye sudy v bor'be s revoliutsiei 1905–1907gg.* Moscow, 1958.

"Politicheskoe polozhenie Rossii nakanune fevral'skoi revoliutsii v zhandarmskom osveshchenii." *Krasnyi arkhiv* 17 (1926): 3–35.

Politovskii, E. S. *Ot Libavy do Tsusimy.* St. Petersburg, 1908.

Polnoe sobranie zakonov Rossiiskoi Imperii. Sobranie 3-oe. St. Petersburg, 1885–1905.

Polovtsov, A. A. "Iz dnevnika A. A. Polovtsova, 1895–1900gg." *Krasnyi arkhiv* 46 (1931): 110–32.

————. *Dnevnik gosudarstvennogo sekretaria A. A. Polovtsova.* 2 vols. Moscow, 1966.

Pomper, Philip. *Peter Lavrov and the Russian Revolutionary Movement.* Chicago, 1972.

————. *Sergei Nechaev.* New Brunswick, 1979.

Ponomarev, I. *Geroi "Potemkina."* Moscow, 1955.

Pososhkov, I. T. *Kniga o skudosti i bogatstve i drugie sochineniia.* Edited by B. B. Kafengauz. Moscow, 1951.

Pospielovsky, Dmitrii. *Russian Police Trade Unionism: Experiment or Provocation?* London, 1971.

Pourtal, Roger. "Industriels moscovites: Le secteur cotonnier (1861–1914)." *Cahiers du monde russe et soviétique* 4, nos. 1–2 (January–June 1963): 5–46.

Prizhan, I. N. *Lev Samoilovich Bakst.* Leningrad, 1975.

Proffer, Carl and Ellendea, eds. *The Silver Age of Russian Culture.* Ann Arbor, 1975.

Prokopovich, S. N. *Krest'ianskoe khoziaistvo.* Berlin, 1924.

"Protsess 17-ti narodovol'tsev v 1883 godu." *Byloe,* no. 10 (October 1906), pp. 193–258.

Pushkareva, I. M. *Zheleznodorozhniki Rossii v burzhuazno-demokraticheskikh revoliutsiiakh.* Moscow, 1975.

Pushkin, A. S. *Polnoe sobranie sochinenii v desiati tomakh.* 10 vols. Moscow, 1962–66.

Pyman, Avril. *The Life of Aleksandr Blok: The Distant Thunder, 1880–1908.* Oxford, 1979.

————. *The Life of Aleksandr Blok: The Release of Harmony, 1908–1921.* Oxford, 1980.

Radishchev, A. N. "Puteshestvie iz Peterburga v Moskvu." *Izbrannye filosofskie i obshchestvenno-politicheskie proizvedeniia,* pp. 49–214. Moscow, 1952.

Radkey, Oliver. *The Agrarian Foes of Bolshevism: Promise and Default of the Russian Socialist Revolutionaries, February to October 1917.* New York, 1958.

Rashin, A. G. *Formirovanie rabochego klassa Rossii: Istoriko-ekonomicheskie ocherki.* Moscow, 1958.

Renouvin, Pierre. *The Immediate Origins of the War (28th June–4th August 1914).* Translated by T. C. Hume. New York, 1969.

Reports of Military Observers attached to the Armies in Manchuria during the Russo-Japanese War. 5 vols. Washington, 1907.

Rice, Martin P. *Valery Briusov and the Rise of Russian Symbolism.* Ann Arbor, 1975.

Rice, Tamara Talbot. *A Concise History of Russian Art.* New York, 1967.

Rieber, Alfred J. "The Moscow Entrepreneurial Group: The Emergence of a New Form of Autocratic Politics." *Jahrbücher für Geschichte Osteuropas* 25, no. 1 (1977): 1–20; 25, no. 2 (1977): 174–99.

Riha, Thomas. *A Russian European: Paul Miliukov in Russian Politics.* Notre Dame and London, 1969.

Robinson, Geroid T. *Rural Russia under the Old Regime.* New York, 1957.

Rodzianko, M. V. *Krushenie imperii.* Leningrad, 1929.

Rogger, Hans. "The Beilis Case: Anti-Semitism and Politics in the Reign of Nicholas II." *Slavic Review* 25, no. 4 (1966): 615–29.

———. "The Formation of the Russian Right, 1900–1905." *California Slavic Studies* 3 (1964): 66–94.

———. "Was there a Russian Fascism? The Union of Russian People." *The Journal of Modern History* 36, no. 4 (December 1964): 398–415.

Romanov, B. A. *Russia in Manchuria, 1892–1906. Essays on the History of the Foreign Policy of Tsarist Russia in the Epoch of Imperialism.* Translated by Susan Wilbur Jones. Ann Arbor, 1952.

Rosenberg, William G. "Kadets and the Politics of Ambivalence, 1905–1917." In *Essays,* edited by Timberlake, pp. 139–63.

———. *Liberals in the Russian Revolution: The Constitutional Democratic Party, 1917–1921.* Princeton, 1974.

Rosenthal, Bernice Glatzer. *Dmitri Sergeevich Merezhkovsky and the Silver Age: The Development of a Revolutionary Mentality.* The Hague, 1975.

———. "Eschatology and the Appeal of Revolution: Merezhkovsky, Bely, Blok." *California Slavic Studies* 11 (1980): 105–40.

Rostunov, I. I., ed. *Istoriia Russko-Iaponskoi voiny, 1904–1905gg.* Moscow, 1977.

———. "Proiskhozhdenie voiny." In *Russko-Iaponskoi voiny,* edited by Rostunov, pp. 22–65.

———, and Chernov, Iu. I. "Nachalo voiny i strategicheskoe razvertyvanie." In *Istoriia Russko-Iaponskoi voiny,* edited by Rostunov, pp. 110–64.

Rozhkova, M. K. "Zarabotnaia plata rabochikh trekhgornoi manufaktury v 1892–1913gg." In *Iz istorii rabochego klassa,* edited by Nechkina et al., pp. 333–41.

Ruckman, JoAnn S. "The Business Elite of Moscow: A Social Inquiry." Ph.D. dissertation, Northern Illinois University, 1975.

Russko-Iaponskaia voina: iz dnevnikov A. N. Kuropatkina i N. P. Linevicha. Leningrad, 1925.

Rutenberg, P. M. "Delo Gapona." *Byloe,* nos. 11–12 (July–August 1909), pp. 29–115.

Ryndziunskii, P. G. "Moskovskaia burzhuaziia." In *Istoriia Moskvy,* edited by Druzhinin and Rozhkova, 3: 292–320.

Sabler, S. V. and Sosnovskii, I. V. *Sibirskaia zheleznaia doroga v eia proshlom i nastoiashchem. Istoricheskii ocherk.* St. Petersburg, 1903.

Sablinsky, Walter. *The Road to Bloody Sunday: Father Gapon and the St. Petersburg Massacre of 1905.* Princeton, 1976.

Sadikov, P. A. "Obshchestvo 'Sviashchennoi Druzhiny.' " *Krasnyi arkhiv* 21 (1927): 200–217.

Salisbury, Harrison. *Black Night, White Snow: Russia's Revolutions, 1905–1917.* New York, 1978.

Sazonov, S. D. *Vospominaniia.* Paris, 1927.

Schapiro, Leonard. "The *Vekhi* Group and the Mystique of Revolution." *Slavonic and East European Review* 34 (December 1955): 56–76.

Schmitt, Bernadotte E. *The Annexation of Bosnia, 1908–1909.* Chicago, 1937.

———. *The Coming of the War, 1914.* 2 vols. New York, 1966.

Schneiderman, Jeremiah. *Sergei Zubatov and Revolutionary Marxism. The Struggle for the Working Class in Tsarist Russia.* Ithaca, 1976.

Semanov, S. N. "Chislennost', sostav, i polozhenie peterburgskikh rabochikh." In *Istoriia rabochikh Leningrada,* edited by Diakin, 1: 179–90.

Semennikov, V. P., ed. *Revoliutsiia 1905 goda i samoderzhavie.* Moscow-Leningrad, 1928.

Semenov, P. P. *Geografichesko-statisticheskii slovar' rossiiskoi imperii.* 5 vols. St. Petersburg, 1863–85.

Semenov, Vladimir. *Rasplata.* London, 1909.

Senchakova, L. T. *Boevaia rat' revoliutsii. Ocherk o boevykh organizatsiiakh RSDRP i rabochikh druzhinakh 1905–1907gg.* Moscow, 1975.

Serebrov, Aleksandr. *Vremia i liudi. Vospominaniia, 1898–1905.* Moscow, 1955.

Seton-Watson, Hugh. *The Russian Empire, 1801–1917.* Oxford, 1967.

Seton-Watson, R. W. *The Rise of Nationality in the Balkans.* New York, 1966.

————. *Sarajevo: A Study in the Origins of the Great War*. London, 1926.

Shambinyi, S. K., ed. *Tvorchestvo A. N. Ostrovskogo: iubileinyi sbornik*. Moscow-Leningrad, 1923.

Shchegolev, P. E., ed. *Padenie tsarskogo rezhima*. 7 vols. Moscow-Leningrad, 1924–27.

Shilling, M. F. *How the War Began in 1914, being the Diary of the Russian Foreign Office from the 3rd to the 20th (old style) of July 1914, published by the "Red Archives" Department of the Russian Soviet Government*. Translated by Major W. Cyprian Bridge. London, 1925.

Shingarev, A. I. *Vymiraiushchaia derevnia*. St. Petersburg, 1907. Republished as an appendix to Shuvaev, *Staraia i novaia derevnia*, pp. 149–347.

Shipov, D. N. *Vospominaniia i dumy o perezhitom*. Moscow, 1918.

Shul'gin, V. V. *Dni*. Belgrade, 1925.

Shuvaev, K. M. *Staraia i novaia derevnia*. Moscow, 1937.

Shvarts, A. fon and Romanovskii, Iu. *Oborona Port-Artura*. 2 vols. St. Petersburg, 1908.

Sidel'nikov, S. M. *Agrarnaia politika samoderzhaviia v period imperializma*. Moscow, 1980.

————. *Obrazovanie i deiatel'nost' pervoi gosudarstvennoi dumy*. Moscow, 1962.

Sidorov, A. L., ed. *Vysshii pod'em revoliutsii 1905–1907gg. Vooruzhennye vosstaniia noiabria–dekabria 1905 goda*. Vol. 4. Moscow, 1957.

Sidorov, K., ed. "Bor'ba so stachechnym dvizheniem nakanune mirovoi voiny." *Krasnyi arkhiv* 34 (1929): 95–125.

Slonim, Marc. *The Epic of Russian Literature: From Its Origins through Tolstoi*. New York, 1964.

————. *From Chekhov to the Revolution: Russian Literature, 1900–1917*. New York, 1962.

————. *Russian Theatre: From the Empire to the Soviets*. Cleveland and New York, 1961.

Smel'skii, V. N. "Sviashchennaia Druzhina (iz dnevnika eia chlena)." *Golos minuvshago* 4, nos. 1–4 (January–April 1916): 222–56, 135–63, 155–76, 95–110.

Smith, Edward Ellis. *"The Okhrana." The Russian Department of Police*. Palo Alto, 1967.

"Sochineniia Karla Marksa v russkoi tsenzure (arkhivnaia spravka)." *Dela i dni. Istoricheskii zhurnal* 1 (1920): 321–45.

Soiuz russkago naroda po materialam sledstvennoi komissii vremennago pravitel'stva 1917g. Moscow, 1917.

Solov'ev, S. M. *Istoriia Rossii s drevneishikh vremen.* Vol. 11. Moscow, 1963.

Solov'ev, V. S. *Lectures on Godmanhood.* London, 1948.

———. *The Meaning of Love.* New York, 1947.

Sonin-M., P. "Vospominaniia o iuzhnorusskikh pogromakh 1881 goda." *Evreiskaia starina* 2 (1909): 207–18.

Spear, Raymond. *Report on the Russian Medical and Sanitary Features of the Russo-Japanese War to the Surgeon-General, U. S. Navy.* Washington, 1906.

Spencer, Charles. *Leon Bakst.* New York, 1973.

Spiridonovich, A. I. "Pri tsarskom rezhime." In *Arkhiv russkoi revoliutsii,* edited by I. V. Gessen, 15 (1924): 85–206.

Stanislavsky, Constantin. *My Life in Art.* Translated by J. J. Robbins. Boston, 1935.

Stanojević, Stanoje. *Die Ermordung des Erzherzogs Franz Ferdinand.* Translated by H. Wendel. Frankfurt, 1923.

Starr, S. F. *Decentralization and Self-Government in Russia, 1830–1870.* Princeton, 1972.

Stieve, Friedrich. *Isvolsky and the World War.* Translated by E. W. Dickes. New York, 1926.

Stites, Richard. *The Women's Liberation Movement in Russia. Feminism, Nihilism, and Bolshevism, 1860–1930.* Princeton, 1978.

Stockmar, Baron C. F. von. *Memoirs of Baron Stockmar.* Translated from the German by G.A.M. and edited by F. Max Müller. 2 vols. London, 1872.

Stolpianskii, P. N. *Zhizn' i byt peterburgskoi fabriki za 210 let ee sushchestvovaniia, 1704–1914.* Leningrad, 1925.

Stolypin, A. *P. A. Stolypin, 1862–1911.* Paris, 1927.

Stolypine, Alexandra. *L'Homme du dernier Tsar.* Paris, 1931.

Storozhev, V. "Dekabr'skoe vooruzhennoe vosstanie po arkhivnym materialam." In *Dekabr'skoe vosstanie v Moskve,* edited by Ovsiannikov, pp. 60–207.

Story, Douglas. *The Campaign with Kuropatkin.* London, 1904.

Struve, P. B. "My Contacts with Rodichev." *Slavonic and East European Review* 12, no. 35 (January 1934): 347–67.

Surh, Gerald D. "Petersburg's First Mass Labor Organization: The Assembly of Russian Workers and Father Gapon." *Russian Review* 40, no. 3 (July 1981): 241–62; 40, no. 4 (October 1981): 412–41.

Suvorin, A. S. *Dnevnik A. S. Suvorina.* Moscow-Petrograd, 1923.

Svechin, A. A. *Evoliutsiia voennago iskusstva.* 2 vols. Moscow, 1928.

———. *Russko-Iaponskaia voina, 1904–1905gg. po dokumental'nym dan-*

nym truda voenno-istoricheskoi komissii i drugim istochnikam. Oranienbaum, 1910.

Sviatopolk-Mirskaia, Kn. E. A. "Dnevnik kn. Ekateriny Alekseevny Sviatopolk-Mirskoi za 1904–1905gg." *Istoricheskie zapiski* 77 (1965): 240–
93.

Svod Zakonov rossiiskoi imperii. 16 vols. in 1. St. Petersburg, 1897.

Sysin, A. N. "Sanitarno-lechebnoe delo." In *Istoriia Moskvy: Period imperializma,* edited by Pankratova, pp. 718–29.

Tager, A. S. *The Decay of Czarism: The Beiliss Trial.* Philadelphia, 1935.

————, ed. "Protsess Beilisa v otsenke departamenta politsii." *Krasnyi
arkhiv* 44 (1931): 85–125.

Takhtarev, K. M. *Rabochee dvizhenie v Peterburge (1893–1901gg.).* Leningrad, 1924.

Tatishchev, S. S. *Imperator Aleksandr II: Ego zhizn' i tsarstvovanie.* 2 vols.
St. Petersburg, 1911.

Taube, Baron M. de. *La politique russe d'avant-guerre et la fin de l'empire
des Tsars (1904–1917). Mémoires du Baron M. de Taube.* Paris,
1928.

Terry, Ellen. *The Russian Ballet.* London, 1913.

Thaden, Edward C. *Russia and the Balkan Alliance of 1912.* University
Park, 1965.

Theen, Rolf H. W. *Lenin. Genesis and Development of a Revolutionary.*
Philadelphia and New York, 1973.

Tikhomirov, Lev. *Vospominaniia L'va Tikhomirova.* Moscow-Leningrad,
1927.

Timberlake, Charles E., ed. *Essays on Russian Liberalism.* Columbia, Mo.,
1972.

Tiumenev, A. *Ot revoliutsii do revoliutsii.* Leningrad, 1925.

Tolstoi, L. N. *Sobranie sochinenii v dvadtsati tomakh.* Moscow, 1960–65.

Trani, Eugene P. *The Treaty of Portsmouth: An Adventure in American
Diplomacy.* Lexington, 1969.

Treadgold, Donald. "The Peasant and Religion." In *The Peasant in Nineteenth-Century Russia,* edited by Vucinich, pp. 41–71.

Trevelyan, George M. *Grey of Fallodon; The Life and Letters of Sir Edward
Grey, afterwards Viscount Grey of Fallodon.* Boston, 1937.

Trotskii, L. *1905.* Translated by Anya Bostock. New York, 1971.

Trubetskoi, kn. Evgenii. *Mirosozertsanie Vl. S. Solov'eva.* 2 vols. Moscow,
1913.

Trusova, N. S., ed. *Revoliutsionnoe dvizhenie v Rossii vesnoi i letom 1905
goda: aprel'–sentiabr'.* 2 vols. Moscow, 1959.

Tuchman, Barbara. *The Guns of August.* New York, 1962.

————. *The Proud Tower: A Portrait of the World Before the War, 1890–1914.* New York, 1966.

Tugan-Baranovskii, M. *Russkaia fabrika v proshlom i nastoiashchem.* Moscow, 1938.

Turgenev, I. S. *Sobranie sochinenii.* 10 vols. Moscow, 1961–62.

Tyrkova-Williams, A. A. *Na putiakh k svobode.* New York, 1952.

Ulam, Adam B. *The Bolsheviks. The Intellectual and Political History of the Triumph of Communism in Russia.* New York, 1965.

————. *In the Name of the People: Prophets and Conspirators in Prerevolutionary Russia.* New York, 1977.

Valentinov, Nikolai [N. V. Volsky]. *Encounters with Lenin.* London, 1968.

Valk, S. N., Volk, S. S., Itenberg, B. S., and Levin, Sh. M., eds. *Revoliutsionnoe narodnichestvo 70-kh godov XIX veka.* 2 vols. Moscow, 1964–65.

Valkenier, Elizabeth. *Russian Realist Art. The State and Society: The Peredvizhniki and Their Tradition.* Ann Arbor, 1977.

Vekhi: Sbornik statei o russkoi intelligentsii. 2nd ed. Moscow, 1909.

Venturi, Franco. *Roots of Revolution: A History of the Populist and Socialist Movements in Nineteenth Century Russia.* New York, 1960.

Veselovskii, Boris. *Istoriia zemstva za sorok let.* 4 vols. St. Petersburg, 1903.

Vilenskaia, E. S. *Khudiakov.* Moscow, 1969.

————. *Revoliutsionnoe podpol'e v Rossii (60-e gody XIX v).* Moscow, 1965.

Vinogradov, V. I., and Sokolov, Iu. F. "Operatsii v Man'chzhurii." In *Istoriia Russko-Iaponskoi voiny,* edited by Rostunov, pp. 259–323.

Viroubova, Anna. *Memories of the Russian Court.* New York, 1923.

Vishniak, Mark. "Antisemitism in Tsarist Russia." In *Essays on Antisemitism,* edited by Pinson, pp. 121–44.

Vodovozov, V. V. *Graf S. Iu. Vitte i Imperator Nikolai II.* Petersburg, 1922.

Voenno-istoricheskaia komissiia po opisaniiu Russko-Iaponskoi voiny. *Russko-Iaponskaia voina 1904–1905: Oborona Kvantuna i Port-Artura.* 8 vols. St. Petersburg, 1910.

Volk, S. S. *Narodnaia volia, 1879–1882.* Moscow-Leningrad, 1966.

————, ed. *Revoliutsionnoe narodnichestvo 70-kh godov XIX veka.* Vol. 2. Moscow-Leningrad, 1965.

Vucinich, Wayne S., ed. *The Peasant in Nineteenth-Century Russia.* Stanford, 1968.

Vysochaishe uchrezhdennaia 16 noiabria 1901g. komissiia po izsledovaniiu voprosa o dvizhenii s 1861g. po 1900g. blagosostoianiia sel'skago naseleniia sredne-zemledel'cheskikh gubernii sravnitel'no s drugimi mestnostiami Evropeiskoi Rossii. Materialy. 3 vols. St. Petersburg, 1903.

Walder, David. *The Short Victorious War: The Russo-Japanese Conflict, 1904–1905.* London, 1973.

Wallace, Sir Donald Mackenzie. *Russia.* London, Paris, New York, and Melbourne, 1905.

Watters, Francis M. "The Peasant and the Village Commune." In *The Peasant in Nineteenth Century Russia,* edited by Vucinich, pp. 133–57.

Westwood, J. N. *Witnesses of Tsushima.* Tokyo and Tallahassee, 1970.

White, John Albert. *The Diplomacy of the Russo-Japanese War.* Princeton, 1964.

Wildman, Allan K. *The Making of a Workers' Revolution: Russian Social Democracy, 1891–1903.* Chicago, 1967.

Wilson, Colin. *Rasputin and the Fall of the Romanovs.* New York, 1964.

Witte, S. Iu. *Samoderzhaviia i zemstvo: konfidential'naia zapiska Ministra Finansov stats-sekretaria S. Iu. Vitte.* 2nd ed. Stuttgart, 1903.

———. "Tsirkuliar Ministra Finansov 'chinam fabrichnoi inspektsii' o merakh bor'by so stachkami rabochikh." In *Rabochee dvizhenie,* edited by Ivanov, 4: pt. 2, pp. 824–25.

———. *Vospominaniia.* 3 vols. Moscow, 1960.

Wolfe, Bertram. *Three Who Made a Revolution: A Biographical History.* New York, 1948.

Wortman, Richard. *The Crisis of Russian Populism.* Cambridge, 1967.

———. *The Development of a Russian Legal Consciousness.* Chicago and London, 1976.

Woytinsky, W. S. *Stormy Passage: A Personal History Through Two Russian Revolutions to Democracy and Freedom, 1905–1960.* New York, 1961.

Zaionchkovskii, A. M. *Podgotovka Rossii k imperialisticheskoi voine.* Moscow, 1926.

Zaionchkovskii, P. A. *Otmena krepostnago prava v Rossii.* 3rd ed. Moscow, 1968.

———. *Krizis samoderzhaviia na rubezhe 1870–1880 godov.* Moscow, 1964.

———. *Rossiiskoe samoderzhavie v kontse XIX stoletiia. Politicheskaia reaktsiia 80-kh–nachala 90-kh godov.* Moscow, 1970.

———. *Voennye reformy 1860–1870 godov v Rossii.* Moscow, 1952.

Zalesskii, A. A. "Rekrutskaia povinnost'." In *Sovetskaia istoricheskaia entsiklopediia,* 11, cols. 1003–4.

Zaslavskii, D. "Evrei v russkoi literature." *Evreiskaia letopis'* 1 (1923): 59–86.

Zavarzin, P. P. *Rabota tainoi politsii*. Paris, 1924.

———. *Souvenirs d'un chef de l'Okhrana, 1900–1917*. Paris, 1930.

Zelnik, Reginald E. "The Peasant and the Factory." In *The Peasant in Nineteenth-Century Russia*, edited by Vucinich, pp. 158–90.

———. "Russian Rebels: An Introduction to the Memoirs of Semen Kanatchikov and Matvei Fisher." *The Russian Review* 35, no. 3 (July 1976): 249–89; 35, no. 4 (October 1976): 417–47.

Zenkovsky, V. V. *A History of Russian Philosophy*. 2 vols. London, 1953.

Zernov, Nicholas. *The Russian Religious Renaissance of the Twentieth Century*. New York and Evanston, 1963.

Zhilinskii, V. "Organizatsiia i zhizn' okhrannago otdeleniia vo vremena tsarskoi vlasti." *Golos minuvshago*, nos. 9–10 (September–October 1917), pp. 247–306.

Ziloti, V. P. *V dome Tret'iakova*. New York, 1954.

Zimmerman, Judith E. "The Kadets and the Duma, 1905–1917." In *Essays*, edited by Timberlake, pp. 119–38.

Zinov'eva-Annibal, Lidia. "Thirty-Three Abominations." Translated by Samuel Cioran. In *Silver Age of Russian Culture*, edited by Proffer, pp. 325–47.

Zlobin, V. "Z. N. Gippius. Ee sud'ba." *Novyi zhurnal* 31 (1952): 139–59.

Zubatov, S. V. et al. "K istorii Zubatovshchiny." *Byloe* 23, no. 1 (July 1917): 86–99.

Index

A

Aberdeen, Lord, 399
About the State Duma, 334
Abramtsevo (Mamantov estate), 94–96
Aehrenthal, Baron Aloys:
  and Balkan Wars, 404–408
Afanasev, Mikhail, 208
Aivazovskii, Ivan, 90
Akimov, Mikhail, 320
Aksakov, Ivan, 94
Aksakov, Sergei, 94
Aksakov, Konstantin, 94
Akselrod, Pavel, 148, 176–78, 180, 185,
  187
Albert (prince consort of England), 228
Aleksandr Mikhailovich (grand duke of
  Russia), 210, 276
Aleksandra (empress of Russia), 237, 260,
  290–91, 292, 437, 441; and
  Russo-Japanese war effort, 242–43;
  influence upon Nicholas, 277–79;
  character of, 390–93
Aleksandrov, Petr, 159
Alekseev, Adm. Evgenii, 235, 236, 238–41,
  244, 255, 267
Alekseev, Konstantin. *See* Stanislavskii,
  Konstantin
Alekseev, Petr, 104, 150
Alekseev family, 86, 97–101
Aleksei (tsarevich of Russia), 331, 341, 393
Aleksei Aleksandrovich (grand duke of
  Russia), 5, 242, 263
Aleksinskii, Grigorii, 332
Alexander I (tsar of Russia), 9, 77, 212,
  390
Alexander II (tsar of Russia), 29, 36, 40,
  105, 140, 179, 182, 313, 347; attempted
  assassination of (1866), 141–43; decree

against radical students abroad, 145–46;
  attempted assassination by Solovev
  (1879); attempted assassination by
  Narodnaia Volia (1880), 163–65;
  assassinated by Hryniewicki (1881),
  167–69
Alexander III (tsar of Russia), 11, 21, 64,
  179, 192, 200, 216, 233, 278, 344, 411;
  entente with France (1891), 4–6; and
  Germany, 6–9; policies in the Far East,
  9–10; and Trans-Siberian Railway,
  12–16; and economic progress, 16–18;
  and famine of 1891, 25–27; character
  of, 27–34; subjects' attitude toward,
  29–30; and father's assassins, 29–30;
  influence of Pobedonostsev, 31–32;
  death of, 32; relationship with son,
  33–34; repressive measures after father's
  death, 169–70; anti-Semitism of, 212–13
Among the Dregs (Gorkii), 101, 123, 351
Andreiushkin, Pakhomii, 170–72
Anti-Semitism:
  in Sacred Guard, 193; Pobedonostsev
  and, 199; history in Russian culture,
  211–12; of Alexander III, 212–13;
  pogroms, 213–16, 222; Elizavetgrad as
  site of first pogrom, 213; mob scene
  in Kiev (1881), 214–15; Balta
  pogrom, 215; "reluctant defenders" of
  Jews, 215–16; "Temporary
  Regulations" (1882), 216; Jews driven
  from Moscow (1891), 217–18; and
  Nicholas II, 218–19; Kishenev
  atrocities, 219–21; Jews blamed for
  October Revolution, 303–304; of
  Union of Russian People, 330–31;
  and Beilis trial (1913), 395–97
Antokolskii, Mark, 95

Apocalypse of Our Time (Rozanov), 355
Apocalyptic literature, 385–88
Aptekman, Osip, 145
Argenteuil Lace (painting), 374
Argunov, Ivan, 37–38
Arshinnik, 71
Art and artists. *See* Cultural life
Artsybashev, Mikhail, 379–80
Assembly, the, 285–86
Austin, Alfred, 402
Avelan, Admiral, 240
Azef, Evno, 287
  as Okhrana double agent, 205–06

B
Babushkin, Ivan, 105, 109, 188–89
Bakst, Lev, 353–54, 373
Bakunin, Mikhail, 144, 152, 154, 155, 158,
  171, 177; participation in foreign
  revolutions, 146–47; and the peasant
  commune, 147–48
Balakirev, Mili Alekseevich, 276
Balashov, Semën, 131
Balkan Wars (1908–14), 403–15
Balmont, Konstantin, 363, 368
Ballet. *See Ballets russe;* Cultural life
Ballets russe, 354
Balta pogrom, 215
Banks, family-established, 87
Bardina, Sofia, 148, 149
Batiushka ("little father"), 64–65
Batu Khan, 321
Beardsley, Aubrey, 359
Beilis, Mendel, 386
  trial of, 396–97
Beliaeva, Elizaveta, 156
Belinskii, Vissarion, 60, 349
Belousov (artist), 174
Belyi, Andrei, 352, 355, 357, 358, 359–68,
  369, 379, 381–82, 384, 385–88; and
  Aleksandr Blok, 366–68
Belyi, General, 252
Benois, Aleksandr, 353–54, 357, 374, 375
Bernstein, Eduard, 185n, 207
Berchtold, Count, 406, 428
Berdiaev, Nikolai, 384
Bessarabets (The Bessarabian), 219, 221
Bezobrazov, Aleksandr, 234
Bieberstein, Baron Marschall von, 8, 402
Bilderling (Russian general), 259
Billington, James, 352, 388

Bismarck (chancellor of German Empire),
  7–8, 403–404, 421
Black Hand, 423
Black Hundreds, 303
Black Soil region, 43
Bliokh, Ivan Stanislavovich, 230–31, 248,
  307, 402; on warfare, 230–31
Blok, Aleksandr, 350, 352, 358, 360–68,
  369, 376, 386–88; and Andrei Belyi,
  366–68
Blok, Liubov, 366–67
Bloody Sunday (January 9, 1905), 268,
  288–91
Bogdanovich, Iurii, 166
Bogrov, Dmitrii, 347–48
Boiarina Morozova (painting), 91
Boisdeffre, General, 9
Bolotnikov, Ivan, 273
Bolsheviki:
  formation of, 189
Boris Godunov (opera), 373
Borodin, Aleksandr, 276
Borovikovskii, Vladimir, 90
Botkin, Mikhail, 374
Boxer Rebellion (1900), 234
Briusov, Valerii, 357–59, 363–65, 368,
  371, 385–88
Bronshtein, Leo Davidovich. *See* Trotskii,
  Leon
Brothers Karamazov, The (Dostoevskii),
  59, 383
Buchanan, Meriel, 390, 391
Buchanan, Sir George, 341, 410, 428, 429
Bugaev, Boris. *See* Belyi, Andrei
Bugaev, Nikolai, 359
Bukharin, Nikolai, 394
Bulavin, Kondratii, 274
Bulgakov, Sergei, 384
Bülow, Prince Bernhard von, 8, 401, 404,
  406, 407
Bulygin, Aleksandr, 317
"Bulygin Duma," 317
Bunge, Nikolai, 33
Burliuk, David, 374
Burliuk, Dmitrii, 376
Burliuk, Vladimir, 376
Byrnes, Robert, 195

Č
Čabrinović, Nedeljko, 424, 425
Campbell-Bannerman, Sir Henry, 401

Carnot, Marie François Sadi, 5
Carr, E. H., 146–47
Cartwright, Sir Fairfax, 411
Catherine the Great (Catherine II,
　empress of Russia), 36, 71, 72, 211
Cézanne, Paul, 374–75
Chaikovskii, Nikolai, 146
Chaliapin, Feodor, 96, 373
Chamberlain, Joseph, 400
Cheberiak, Vera, 396
Chekhov, Anton, 60, 61, 101, 363; and
　The Cherry Orchard, 223–24
Chernyi Peredel (Black Repartition), 162,
　176
Chernyshevskii, Nikolai, 137, 141, 145,
　147, 151, 152, 180, 181; and impact of
　novel What Is To Be Done?, 139–40
Cherry Orchard, The (Chekhov):
　as confrontation of old and new orders,
　223–24, 363
Child labor, 110–11
Children of the Streets, 378
Chukovskii, Kornei, 370
Chulkov, Georgii, 369
Čiurlionis, Mikolojus, 372
Communal Land Tenure: the Reasons, the
　Process, and the Consequences of its
　Disintegration (Kovalevskii), 175
Constitutional Democratic Party. See
　Kadety
Contribution to the Critique of Political
　Economy, A, 176
Cooper, James Fenimore, 131, 133
Crime and Punishment (Dostoevskii), 123
Crimean War, 228–29, 230
Cultural life:
　the Tretiakov Gallery, 89–91; the
　Peredvizhniki, 91–92; artists at
　Abramtsevo, 94–96; characteristics of
　Russian culture, 349–51; and
　Solovev's "free theocracy," 351–52;
　Mir Iskusstva, 352–55; and the cult of
　sex, 354–56, 377–82; and Dom
　Muruzi (salon), 356–68; and Andrei
　Belyi, 359–68; and Novyi put,
　358–60; and Aleksandr Blok, 360–68;
　"Tower" salon of Viacheslav Ivanov,
　368–70; and Zolotoe Runo (The
　Golden Fleece), 370–71; variety in art
　of Silver Age, 372; ballet, 372–73;
　schools of painting, 374–77;

disillusionment with life, 384–88,
　apocalyptic literature, 385–88

D
Dachi (summer houses), 21
d'Alheim, Pierre, 281–82
Dan, Theodore (Feodor), 185n
Danilov, General, 431
Dargomyzhskii, Aleksandr, 96, 237
Das Kapital (Marx), 105, 139n, 180
Davitt, Michael, 220–21
Dead Souls (Gogol), 191
Death of a Hero (Gaćinović), 423
Degas, Hilaire Germain Edgar, 374
Deich, Lev, 158, 177–78
Delbrück, Hans (Russian professor), 417
Delianov, Ivan, 216
Dementev, Dr. E. M., 115
Derain, André, 375
Development of Capitalism in Russia
　(Lenin), 184
Diaghilev, Sergei, 353–54, 372–73
Dimitriević, Col. Dragutin, 422, 423, 424
Djugashvili, Iosif. See Stalin, Iosif
Dmitrii Pavlovich (grand duke of Russia),
　341
Dobroliubov, Aleksandr, 356
Dobroliubov, Nikolai, 71, 137, 151, 170
Dobrorolskii, General, 431, 434, 436
Dontsova, Tamara, 110, 120
Dostoevskii, Feodor, 3, 59, 60, 123, 199,
　216, 351, 383
Double agents (Okhrana agents), 203–11
　repentant revolutionaries as, 204; Anna
　Serebriakova, 204–205; Evno Azef,
　205–206
Dovedenkov, Feodor, 117
Draga (queen of Serbia), 422
Dreadnought (British battleship), 402–403
Drenteln, Gen. Aleksandr, 214
Dubasov, Gen. Fedor:
　governor general during Moscow
　uprisings (1905), 306–309
Dubrovin, Dr. Aleksandr, 330
Duma, defined, 317n
　See also First Duma; Second Duma;
　Third Duma
Duncan, Isadora, 373
Durnovo, Ivan, 22, 23, 217, 346, 348
　on Nicholas I, 318; appointed Minister
　of Internal Affairs, 319–21, 322

INDEX

E

Economic growth, era of. *See* Industrialists
Economism and Revisionism, 185
Edward VII (king of England), 400, 401
Ekaterina Mikhailovna (grand duchess of
   Russia), 168, 203
Elisaveta Feodorovna (grand duchess of
   Russia), 202, 277
Elisaveta Petrovna (empress of Russia),
   165
Elizavetgrad pogrom, 213
Elizabeth (empress of Russia), 10
Emancipation Acts of 1861, 36, 40, 54,
   137
Emancipation of Labor Group, 175–78
Emelianov, Ivan, 158–59, 167
Engels, Friedrich, 104, 111
Era of Counterreforms, 169

F

Fadeev, Rostislav, 193
Famine of 1891:
   warning signs for, 19; frosts of 1890–91,
     19; changing grain traffic, 23–24; ban
     on rye exports, 23–24; feeding the
     peasants, 24–27; lack of railway
     transport, 25; comparison to Indian
     famine of 1899, 27
Fathers and Sons (Turgenev), 138
Felkerzam, Rear Admiral, 265
Figner, Vera, 163, 164, 170, 173
   on peasant life, 40–41; role in
     assassination of Alexander II (1881),
     167–69
Filosofov, Dmitrii, 353, 356, 375–76
First Duma:
   duma defined, 317n; Sergei Witte and,
     317–21; first national election,
     323–30; and the *Kadety*, 328–29;
     dissolved by Nicholas I, 330–31
Fisher, Lord Admiral, 403
Fock (Russian general), 252, 253
Fokin, Mikhail, 373
*Forms of Peasant Land Tenure in Moscow
   Province* (Orlov), 176
Fortachi (child thieves), 127
Franz Ferdinand (archduke of Austria):
   assassination of, 424–26
Franz Joseph (emperor of Austria), 408,
   430
Frederic, Harold, 217

Frederick the Great (Frederick II, king of
   Prussia), 36
Frederiks, Count, 432, 436
Frolenko, Mikhail, 167–68
Frolov (hangman), 169
Fullon, Gen. Ivan, 289–90
Fundamental Laws (1906), 321
Future of War, The (Bliokh), 230, 309

G

Gaćinović, Vladimir, 423–24
Gapon, Father Georgii, 365
   and founding of the Assembly, 285–86;
     and Bloody Sunday, 287–91
Gauguin, Paul, 374–75
Gelfmann, Gesia, 30
Generalov, Vasilii, 170–72
George, Duke of York (George VI, later
   king of England), 249
Gershenzon, Mikhail, 384
Gershuni, Grigorii, 205, 207, 287
Gervais, Admiral, 19–20, 21, 32
   meets Alexander III at Kronstadt, 4–6
Giers, Nikolai, 6, 8
Giesl (Austrian ambassador), 430
Giliarovskii, Vladimir, 124–25, 126, 127
Gippius, Zinaida, 352, 354–61, 365, 381
   Don Muruzi (salon) of, 356–68
Glinka, Fëdor Nikolaevich, 281, 381
Gogol, Nikolai, 60, 191
Golikov, Capt. E. N.:
   captain of the *Potemkin*, 293–94
Golodnyi khleb (famine bread), 19, 22–23
Goluchowski, Count, 406
Goncharova, Natalia, 374, 376–77
Gooch, G. P., 412
Goremykin, Ivan, 322, 324, 327–29, 335,
   341
Gorkii, Maksim, 42, 84, 101, 123, 290,
   291, 351
Grabež, Trifko, 424
Grain traffic, during Famine of 1891,
   23–24
Greenspoon, Mottel, 221
Grey, Sir Edward, 400, 407, 411, 412,
   426, 429, 434
Guchkov, Aleksandr, 347
   as leader of Octobrist party, 333–35
Guchkov family, 86
Guide to the Great Siberian Railway, 11
Gurko, Gen. Vasilii, 442

Gurko, Iosif, 161, 213
Gurko, Vladimir, 326, 327, 341, 343
Gvozdev, Sergei, 116–17, 119

H

Hague Conference (May 1899), 232
Hague Conference (second) (June 1907),
    401–403
Haimson, Leopold, 185, 348
Hamilton, Gen. Ivan, 246, 254
Henry IV (king of England), 6
Herberstein, Sigismund von, 70
Herzen, Aleksandr, 40, 137, 146, 151, 185
Herzen, Natalia, 150
"Historical Letters" (Lavrov), 144–45
History of Russian Pot-Houses, A
    (Pryzhov), 156
Hollweg, Bethmann, 431
Holstein, Friedrich von, 8
Homosexuality in art, 378–79
Hötzendorff, Baron Conrad von, 412, 427
Hryniewicki, Ignacy:
    assassinates Alexander III (1881),
    167–69

I

Iakimova, Anna, 165–66
Iama (Kuprin), 122, 378
Ianushkevich, Gen. Nikolai, 431, 432,
    433–34, 435
Ianzhul, Ivan, 110–11, 112–13, 114, 117
Ignatev, Nikolai, 216
Ignatov, V. I., 178
Ilić, Danilo, 424
Illiteracy:
    among peasants, 63–64, 65; among
    urban proletariat, 131
Industrial development (1880s), 16–18
    economic growth, 16–17; Vyshnegradskii
    and, 17–20
Industrialists:
    as "new lords of Russia," 69–74; origins
    of, 70; population's general ignorance
    about, 70–71; as "Old Believers,"
    71–74; exploitation by, 73; the
    Morozov family, 74–85; Savva
    Vasilevich Morozov, 74–79; "serf
    millionaires," 76–77; and Napoleon's
    Continental System, 77; Timofei
    Morozov, 78–82; strike of 1885 and,
    80–82; Maria Federovna Morozova,

82–85; Savva Timofeivich Morozov,
    83–85; the Riabushinskii family, 86;
    rise of important families, 86–89;
    family-established banks, 87; the new
    work ethic, 87; taxation and, 88;
    scorned by aristocracy, 88; Pavel
    Mikhailovich Tretiakov, 89–93; as
    patrons of the arts, 88–102; Savva
    Ivanovich Mamantov, 93–97;
    Stanislavskii and the Moscow Art
    Theater, 99–101
Infant mortality:
    among the peasants, 52–53; among the
    urban poor, 121–22
Ioann, Father (Kronstadt priest), 222
Irman (Russian colonel), 252
Ishutin, Nikolai:
    and attempted assassination of
    Alexander II, 141–42, 143
Iskra (The Spark), 185
Iushchinskii, Andrei, 396
Ivan VI (emperor of Russia), 17
Ivan the Terrible and His Son Ivan
    Ivanovich (painting), 91, 95
Ivanov, Evgenii, 366
Ivanov, Ivan:
    executed by Nechaev, 157
Ivanov, Luka, 81–82
Ivanov, Mikhail, 95
Ivanov, Viacheslav, 351, 381
    the "Tower" (salon) of, 368–70
Izby (peasant cottages), 36, 44–47
Izvolskii, Aleksandr, 279, 400, 401
    and Balkan Wars, 404–10

J

Jacobi, Valerii, 90
Japan:
    Trans-Siberian Railway and, 15–16; See
    also Russo-Japanese War
Jews. See Anti-Semitism
Journey from St. Petersburg to Moscow
    (Radishchev), 37, 139n
Jovanović, Ljuba, 429
Judicial Reform of 1864, 195

K

Kadety (Constitutional Democratic Party):
    formation of, 303; demands made by,
    326–27; and the Vyborg Manifesto,
    329

Kamenev, Lev, 91

Kaminskii, Aleksandr, 90

Kandinskii, Vasilii, 372, 379

Kanatchikov, Semën, 132

Karakozov, Dmitrii:

   attempted assassination of Alexander II,
   141–43, 151

Karamzin, Nikolai, 38

Karsavina, Tamara, 373

Katkov, Mikhail, 7

Kaufmann, Gen. Konstantin von, 92

Kaulbars (Russian general), 259

Kawamura (Japanese general), 258–59

Keep, J.L.H., 185n

Kennan, George, 9–10, 11

Khalturin, Stepan, 164–65

Khitrovna (Moscow slum), 123–28

Khitrovo, Major-Gen. Nikolai Petrovich,
   124, 125

Khlebnikov, Viktor, 372

Khludov family, 86, 87

Khomiakov, Aleksei, 94

Khudiakov, Ivan, 141, 142, 143

Khudiakov, Vasilii, 89

Kibalchich, Nikolai, 165–67, 169

Kiderlen-Wächter, Alfred von, 411

Kiev:

   anti-Semitic mob scene in (1881),
   214–15

Kireevskii, Ivan, 94

Kishenev pogrom, 219–21

"Kit Kitych," 71

Kliuchevskii, Vasilii, 56, 57

Klodt, Mikhail, 90, 91

Knollys, Lord Francis, 400

Knox, Sir Alfred, 443

Kokovtsev, Count Vladimir, 324, 326, 346,
   348, 392, 393

Kolokol (The Bell), 137, 185

Kollontai, Aleksandra, 357, 380, 394

Kommissarzhevskaia, Vera, 386

Komura, Jutaro, 269–70

Koni, Anatolii, 160

Kononov (silk-factory owner), 75, 76

Konstantin Konstantinovich (grand duke of
   Russia), 289, 302

Korea:

   Russia's conflict with Japan over,
   235–36

Korolenko, Vladimir, 59, 216, 221

Kovalevskii, Maksim, 175

Kozlov, Fedor, 130

Kramskoi, Ivan, 91

Krasivskii, Nikifor, 208

Kravchinskii, Sergei, 148, 149

Krestinskii, Lt. Col. Ivan, 250

Krestovnikov, Grigorii, 333

Krupskaia, Nadezhda, 184

Krushevan, Pavolachi, 219

Kryzhanovskii, Sergei, 344

Kschessinska (ballerina), 33

Kübel (German major), 413

Kuklëv, Ivan, 117, 119, 121, 130

Kupet (merchant), 88

Kuprin, Aleksandr, 122–23, 378

Kurino, Shinichiro, 237

Kuroki, Gen. Tametomo, 254–55, 258–59

Kuropatkin, Gen. Aleksei, 221, 225,
   231–32, 236, 237–48, 240–41, 245, 251,
   254–56, 257–60, 419; command conflict
   with Admiral Alekseev, 255; given full
   command, 257; relieved of duty, 259–60

Kutuzov (Russian field marshal), 390

Kuzmin, Mikhail, 369, 378

Kuzmina-Karavaeva, Elizaveta, 381

Kuznetsov, Aleksei, 156–57

L

Labor exchanges, 129

Laboulaye, Paul de, 4–5, 6–7

Lafargue, Paul, 180

Lake Baikal:

   Trans-Siberian Railway bisected at,
   240

Lampada (ikon lamp), 46

Lamsdorf, Count Vladimir, 6, 238

Landsdowne (British foreign secretary),
   237

Lapti (peasant slippers), 58

Larionov, Mikhail, 374, 376–77

Lassalle, Ferdinand, 144, 176

Lavrov, Petr, 40, 144–45, 147, 148, 149,
   152, 171

Lengerke Meyer, George von, 269

Lenin, Krupskaia, 117

Lenin, Vladimir (Ulianov), 30, 56, 119,
   141, 152, 171, 178, 183–4, 201, 296,
   300, 344, 385, 394; execution of brother
   Aleksandr Ulianov, 174–75; and
   Chernyshevskii's *What Is To Be Done?*,

180–81; conversion to Marxist beliefs, 181–82; and Martov, 182–90; in exile (Siberia, 1896), 184; and Russian Social Democracy, 186–87; split in RSDRP, 187–91
Leroy-Beaulieu, Anatole, 74
Lev Tolstoi and Dostoevskii (Merezhovskii), 359, 361
Levendahl (Okhrana officer), 219
Levitskii, Dmitrii, 90
Liaoyang, battle for, 255–57
Liebermann, Max, 354
Life for the Tsar, A (opera), 281, 391
Liman von Sanders, Gen. Otto, 413, 414
Lincoln, Abraham, 39
Linevich, Gen. Nikolai, 259, 259–60, 269
Literacy. *See* Illiteracy
Liubimov, Dmitrii, 287
Lord of the Manor Claims His Prerogatives, The (painting), 95
Loris-Melikov, Count Mikhail, 161
Lukashevich, Iosif, 174
Lunacharskii, Anatolii, 206
Lynch, Major Charles, 248, 249

M
Maeterlinck, Maurice, 363
Maiakovskii, Vladimir, 372, 377
Makarov, Adm. Stepan, 244
Maklavov, Vasilii, 323, 325, 347
Malevich, Kazimir, 374, 375, 377
Mamantov, Savva Ivanovich, 86, 93–97, 99, 373; commitment to the *narod*, 93–94; and Abramtsevo estate, 94–96; as patron of the arts, 94–97; founds opera company, 96; passion for railroads, 97; collapse of wealth, 97
Mamantova, Elizaveta Saposhnikova, 93
devotion to the peasants, 95–97; establishes "folk-art" workshops, 96–97
Manet, Édouard, 374
Maria Feodorovna (empress of Russia), 5, 21, 277, 291, 301
Martens, Fedor, 401
Martov, Iulii, 184–5, 212, 296
character of, and strikes of 1896, 182–84; and Lenin, 182–90; 178–80; exiled to Siberia, 184; and RSDRP, 187–90

Marx, Karl, 104, 139n, 144, 147, 151, 171, 176–77, 180, 185
Maslenikov, Oleg, 361
Matisse, Henri, 374, 375
Mayerberg, Augustin von, 70
Meinhard (Russian general), 310
Meller-Zakomelskii, Baron Aleksandr, 310
Mendeleeva, Liubov, 360–63
Mensheviki:
formation of, 189
Merezhkovskii, Dmitrii, 351, 352, 354–61, 365, 367–68, 385; *Don Muruzi* (salon) of, 356–68
Meshcherskii, Prince Vladimir, 25, 74, 240
Metallisty (metal workers), 305–306
Mikhail Feodorovich (tsar of Russia), 10
Mikhailov, Aleksandr, 164
Mikhailov, Mikhail, 40
Mikhailov, Timofei, 167, 169
Mikhailovskii, Nikolai, 181
Milanović, Milovan, 422
Miliukov, Pavel, 275, 302–303, 321, 333, 335, 385, 386, 434, 440; as leader of *Kadety*, 323–25, 328–29
Miliutin, Dmitrii, 160
Min, Col. Georgii, 309
Mintslov, Sergei:
impressions of the October Revolution, 298–299, 302
Mir Iskusstva (The World of Art), 352–55
Mitrofanov, Pavel, 417
Mitskevich, Sergei, 205, 295, 304, 306
Mlada Bosna (Young Bosnia), 423
Mochulskii, Konstantin, 358, 362
Moiseenko, Petr, 109
and Morozov Strike of 1885, 80–82
Moltke, Gen. Helmuth von, 402, 411–12, 433
Monet, Claude, 374
Montecuculli, Count Raimund, 231
Morozov, Ivan, 87, 374–75
Morozov, Nikolai, 162
Morozov, Savva Timofeivich:
cultural interests, 83–85; suicide of, 84
Morozov, Savva Vasilevich, 74–79, 87
frees himself from serfdom, 75, 78; escapes from army service, 75–76; wife Uliana as helpmate, 76; starts silk-ribbon factory, 76; escapes burning of Moscow, 77–78; builds

Morozov, Savva Vasilevich (*cont.*)
  woolen mill, 78; and centralization of
  cloth production, 79; death of, 79
Morozov, Sergei, 83
Morozov, Timofei, 78, 89, 93
  replaces father in family business,
  79–82; despotic rule of, 80; and Strike
  of 1885, 80–82; death of, 82
Morozov, Uliana, 76, 77, 78
Morozov Strike of 1885, 80–82, 130
Morozova, Maria Fedorovna, 82–83, 84
Moscow Art Theater, 83, 84–85, 99, 101,
  373
Moscow Merchant Bank, 87
Moscow Merchants' Mutual Credit
  Society, 87
Moscow Trade Bank, 87
Moscow uprisings (1905), 305–11
"Mousetraps" (Okhrana tactics), 203
Mukden, battle of, 258–60
Müller, Max, 238
Muravev, Count Mikhail, 232
Muromtsev, Sergei, 328
Music and musicians. *See* Cultural life
Mussorgskii, Modest, 92, 373

N
Nabat (The Tocsin), 152
Napoleon I, 9, 36, 227, 230, 390
  Alexander I and the Continental
  System, 77; and the burning of
  Moscow, 77–78
Napoleon III, 168
Narodna Odbrana (the People's Defense),
  422–23
Narodnaia Volia (the People's Will):
  attempt to assassinate Alexander II
  (1880), 163–65; and assassination of
  Alexander II (1881), 165–69
Narodniki, 149–51
Naryshkina (Russian princess), 96
Natanson, Mark:
  and the *narodniki,* 149–50
National election (February-April 1906),
  321–22
Nebogatov, Rear Adm. Nikolai, 264, 265,
  266–68, unjustly tried for war crimes,
  267–68
Nechaev, Sergei, 152–57, 192
  character of, 153; execution of Ivan
  Ivanov, 157; death of, 157

Nekliudov, Anatolii, 409
Nekrasov, Nikolai, 139
Nemirovich-Danchenko, Vladimir, 83, 84,
  85, 282, 373; meeting with Stanislavskii,
  99–101
Nesselrode, Count Karl, 228
New Industrialism, era of. *See*
  Industrialists
Nicholas the Miracle-Worker, Saint, 46
Nicholas I (tsar of Russia), 10, 28, 30, 31,
  32, 73, 142, 186, 192, 212, 228
Nicholas II (tsar of Russia), 32, 35, 64, 65,
  66–67, 178, 186, 188, 192, 201, 212,
  224–25, 232, 236, 237, 240, 241–42,
  253, 255, 259, 260, 261, 268, 270, 295,
  297, 299, 301, 309, 310, 316, 318, 322,
  324, 325, 327, 336, 338, 341, 346–48,
  397, 402, 413, 417, 430, 433, 439, 441,
  444; first words as tsar, 32; relationship
  with father, 33; ineptitude as ruler,
  32–34; and anti-Semitism, 218–19;
  biographical sketch of, 275–84; world
  tour of (1890), 276–77; influences upon,
  279–80; reply to *zemstvo* greeting,
  279–80; tragedy at coronation
  celebration, 282–83; open letter from
  Tolstoi, 284; attempted assassination of
  (Epiphany 1905), 287; and Bloody
  Sunday, 288–91; signs October
  Manifesto, 301–304; and Punitive
  Expeditions, 309–10; considers
  renouncing October Manifesto, 320;
  dissolves First Duma, 328–29; and
  Rasputin, 382–84; and Romanov
  tercentenary celebration, 389–94; and
  President Poincaré, 389–99
Nicolson, Sir Arthur, 341, 400–401, 414
Nietzsche, Friedrich, 368
Nikitenko, Aleksandr, 106–107
Nikolaev, Nikolai, 157
Nikolai Aleksandrovich (grand duke of
  Russia), 195–96
Nikolai Nikolaevich (grand duke of
  Russia), 92, 330
Nizhinskii, Waslaw, 373
Nobel, Alfred, 229
Nogi, Gen. Maresuke, 253, 255, 258
  first advance against the Russians by,
  245–47; second advance, 248–50;
  third advance, 250–52
Notes of a Huntsman (Turgenev), 39

Novoselskii (prisoner in Peter and Paul fortress), 174
Novyi put (The New Way), 358, 359–60

O

Obrenović, Alexander, 422
Obruchev, Gen. Nikolai, 9
October Manifesto, 302–304, 320
October Revolution (1905):
  beginning, 296; railway workers' strike, 297–98; general strike, 298–300; October Manifesto and, 302–304; Moscow uprisings, 305–11; general strike in Moscow (December 7), 306; storming of Presnia, 308–309; Punitive Expeditions, 309–10
Octobrist Party, 333–35, 345, 347
Ogarochnyi, 379
Ogarev, Nikolai, 137, 146, 149, 151
Okhrana (security police), 183–85
  effectiveness against revolutionary groups, 201–202; and Imperial mail service, 202; corps of plainclothesmen, 202–203; "mousetraps," 203; use of double agents, 203–206; Zubatov as chief of, 206–11; and Second Duma, 338–39
Oku, Gen. Yasutaka, 255, 258
"Old Believers," 72–74
Oldenburgskii, Prince Petr, 270
Olovennikova, Natalia, 167
Origins of Bolshevism, The (Dan), 185n
Orlov (Russian general), 310
Orlov, Vasilii, 176
Osipanov, Vasilii, 170–73
Ostrovskii, Aleksandr, 71–72
Osvobozhenie (Liberation), 314
Ottepel (spring thaw), 56–57
Oyama, Marshal Iwao, 254, 255–60
Ozol, Ivan, 339

P

Pahlen, Count Konstantin, 320
Painters. *See* Cultural life
"Pale Horse, The" (Briusov), 358, 385–86
Paléologue, Maurice, 408, 430
Pan-Mongolism (Solovev), 352
Pašić, Nikola, 408, 422, 429–30
Pasternak, Boris, 274
Paul I (emperor of Russia), 318
Pavlova, Anna, 373

Peasant life:
  emancipation of serfs, 36, 40; as viewed by educated Russians, 37–39; in fictional works, 37–39; Turgenev on, 39; and radical youth of 1870s, 40–42; and technicians of the 1890s, 42–43; daily life, 43–64; distribution of population, 43; housing, 44–47; fire hazards, 44; furnishings, 45–46; vermin, 46; the "women's corner," 46–47; unsanitary living conditions, 47; and agriculture, 47–51; plows and threshers, 47–48; livestock, 48; migrations to southern Russia, 49; village communes, 49–51; parceling of lands, 50–51; basic foods, 51–52; health and nutrition, 52; infant mortality, 52–53; epidemic diseases, 53; syphilis, 53–55; folk medicine, 55; earnings, 56; seasons of hard labor, 56–57; spinning, weaving, and sewing, 57–58; clothing, 57–58; holiday customs, 59; use of vodka, 59–60; peasant character, 60; and religion, 60–62; superstition, 61–62; illiteracy, 62–63; attitude toward the tsar, 64–65; communication with government, 65; Sergei Witte and peasant prosperity, 65–67
People's Revenge, The, 155
Peredvizhniki (the Itinerants), 91–92, 353
Perov, Vasilii, 91
Perovskaia, Sofia, 164, 165–69
Peskov, Pavel, 110, 112–13, 116
Peter the Great (tsar of Russia), 36, 54, 211, 274, 363
Petersburg (Belyi), 387–88
Petit Bourgeois (Gorkii), 101
Petrovskaia, Nina, 363–64
Petrunkevich, Ivan, 326
Picasso, Pablo, 374, 375, 377
Pikhno, Dmitrii, 303
Pilgrims (painting), 95
Pilot Stars (Ivanov), 368
Pipes, Richard, 64
Pisarev, Dmitrii, 138–39
Pissarro, Camille, 374
"Place of honor" in peasant cottage, 46
Plekhanov, Georgii, 104–105, 139, 171, 184, 187–88; advocates moderation in

Plekhanov, Georgii (*cont.*)
  revolutionary movement, 161–63; forms
  first Russian-Marxist party, 175–78
Plekhanov, Rosalia, 176
Plehve, Viacheslav von, 116, 221–22, 257,
  271, 285, 287, 315; assassination of,
  205–206; and Sergei Zubatov, 210–11
Pobedonostsev, Konstantin, 7, 194, 202,
  276, 279, 284, 356; influence on
  Alexander III, 31–32; and legal reforms,
  195; character, 195; as tutor to
  Alexander III, 195–96; philosophic views
  of, 196; chauvinism of, 197; preference
  for Moscow, 197; and the Russian
  Orthodox Church, 197–99;
  anti-Semitism of, 199, 217; anachronistic
  ideas, 199–200
Poems in Prose (Turgenev), 137
Pogroms. *See* Anti-Semitism
Poincaré, Raymond, 409–10, 411, 428
  meeting with Nicholas II, 398–99
Polenov, Vasilii, 95–96
Polenova, Vera, 96
Politovskii, Sergei, 261–62, 264
Polivanov, Gen. Aleksei, 405, 443
Polovtsov, Aleksandr, 22, 234
Populist movement:
  rejection by peasants, 148–49; "Land
  and Liberty" slogan, 149; the
  narodniki, 149–51
Portrait of a Peasant Girl (painting),
  37–38
Potëmkin mutiny, 270, 292–94
Potiorek, Gen. Oskar, 424, 425, 426
Potresov, Aleksandr, 186
Pourtalès, Count Friedrich, 431
Presnia, storming of (1905), 308–309
Princip, Gavrilo, 426–27, 428
Program of Revolutionary Action, A,
  153–54
Prokhorov, Ivan, 88
Prokhorov family, 86, 87–88
Prostitution:
  among the urban poor, 107; after 1905,
  377–78
Pryzhov, Ivan, 156–57
Pugachev, Emelian, 274
Punitive Expeditions (1905), 309–10,
  336
Purishkevich, Vladimir, 330, 332, 440

Pushkin, Aleksandr, 38, 215, 237
Putilov Works, strike at (1905), 286
Pyman, Avril, 362

R
Radishchev, Aleksandr, 37–38, 139n
Railroads. *See* Trans-Siberian Railway
Railway workers' strike (1905), 297
Rasputin, 330, 341
  and Nicholas II, 382–84
Razin, Stenka, 274
Razumovskii, Kyril, 165
Red Snow, 290
Reid, [Thomas] Mayne, 131
Reinsurance Treaty, 8
Reitern, Count Mikhail, 213
Religious Procession, The (painting),
  95
Remmenkampf, Gen. Pavel, 310
Renoir, Pierre Auguste, 374
Repin, Ilia, 92, 95–96, 353
Rerikh, Nikolai, 353–54, 373
Reuss (Russian colonel), 252, 253
Revolution of 1905:
  history of protests preceding, 273–75;
  character of Nicholas II and, 275–84;
  the founding of the Assembly, 286;
  Putilov Works, strike at, 286;
  attempted assassination of Nicholas
  II, 287; and the *Potemkin* mutiny,
  292–94; strikes preceding the
  revolution, 294–96; October
  Revolution, 296–305
Revolutionary Catechism, 154, 55
Revolutionary movements:
  first appearance in 1860s, 137–40; and
  Turgenev's *Fathers and Sons*, 138;
  and "thinking realists," 138–39; and
  What Is To Be Done?, 139–40;
  women in, 140; Lavrov's "Historical
  Letters," 144–46; Alexander II and
  decree against radical students abroad,
  145–46; and populist movement,
  147–51; terrorism in, 151–74; and
  Sergei Nechaev, 152–57; the trial of
  Vera Zasulich, 159–60; Georgii
  Plekhanov and, 161–63; assassination
  of Alexander II, 167–69; and
  Aleksandr Ulianov, 170–74; first
  Russian Marxist party and, 175–78;

and Martov, 178–80; and Lenin,
180–90; strikes of 1896, 182–84;
founding of Russian Social
Democratic Labor Party, 184–87;
formation of Bolshevik-Menshevik
factions, 187–90
Riabushinskii, Nikolai, 371
Riabushinskii, Pavel, 418
Riabushinskii family, 86, 333
Rimskii-Korsakov, Nikolai, 96, 276, 347
Rise of Social Democracy in Russia, The
(Keep), 185n
Riumin (Russian count), 74, 75, 76, 78
Rodichev, Feodor, 279, 321, 323
Rodzianko, Mikhail, 432–33
Romanov, Mikhail, 392
Romanov tercentenary celebration (1913),
389–94
Romeiko (engineer), 124
Roosevelt, Theodore, 268–69, 401
Root, Elihu, 402
Rozanov, Vasilii, 354–56, 369
Rozhestvenskii, Rear Adm. Zinovii:
as commander of Baltic fleet, 260–67;
fires upon British fishing fleet, 262;
and battle of Tsushima Straits,
265–68, 293
Rubinstein, Ida, 373
Rusalka (opera), 96, 237, 238
Russia (Baedeker), 21
Russian Marxists and the Origin of
Bolshevism, The (Haimson), 185n
Russian Orthodox Church:
Pobedonostsev and, 197–99
Russian Social Democratic Party
(RSDRP):
founding of, 184–87; Second Congress
of, 187–88; split into Bolshevik and
Menshevik factions, 189–90
"Russian steamroller," defined, 9
Russo-Japanese War:
and warfare in Russia generally, 227–32;
Witte and the Far East policy, 235;
conflict with Japan over Korea, 235;
military strength in Japan, 235; sneak
attack on Port Arthur, 238–40;
defense of Port Arthur, 242–53; Port
Arthur surrendered, 252–53; Russian
unpreparedness for, 238–39, 240, 241;
heavy Russian losses, 243–44; first

advance of General Nogi, 245–47;
second advance by Nogi, 248–50;
medical care for Russian troops, 249;
Nogi's third advance, 250–52; 203
Meter Hill, 251; modern
communications and, 253–54; battle
for Liaoyang, 255–56; battle at Sha
River, 256–57; winter "ceasefire,"
257; battle of Mukden, 258–60; the
Baltic fleet, 260–68; battle of
Tsushima Straits, 265–68; Roosevelt's
offer to mediate, 268; peace
conference in United States, 269–70;
terms of settlement, 270
Russo-Turkish War of 1877–78, 231
Rybachenko, Mikhail:
Kishenev anti-Semitism and death of,
219–20
Rye, ban on export of, 23–24
Rysakov, Nikolai, 167–69

S

Sacred Guard, 200, 330
formation and aims of, 192–93;
anti-Semitism in, 193; power of,
193–94; dissolution of, 194–95; as
Union of Russian People, 195
Sadko (opera), 96
St. Petersburg Soviet of Workers'
Deputies, 399–300
Samarin, Iurii, 94
Samoilov, Fedor, 131
Sanin (Artsybashev), 379–80
Sazonov, Sergei, 428–29, 431, 432–33,
436, 442, 444, and Balkan Wars,
408–16
Scanlan, James, 144
Schmitt, Bernadotte, 403
Scythians (Blok), 352
Second Duma:
conservatives form Union of the Russian
People, 330–32; radical left in,
332–33; the Octobrists, 333–35; bitter
confrontations within, 335–40; the
agrarian question and, 336–38; and
"army mutiny" plot, 338–39; and
Petr Stolypin, 340–44
Second Hague Conference, 401–403
Semenov, Commander Vladimir, 266
Serafim (Russian monk), 260

Serebriakova, Anna:
  as Okhrana double agent, 204–05, 210
"Serf millionaires," 76–77
Sergei Aleksandrovich (grand duke of
  Russia), 28, 85, 208, 209, 217, 271,
  291–92, assassination of 205–206
Sex, artists' preoccupation with, 354–58,
  377–82
Sha River, battle at, 256–57
Shcheglovitov, Ivan, 396–97
Shchepkin, Mikhail, 100
Shchi (cabbage soup), 13, 51
Shchukin, Sergei, 374–75
Shemshurian, Andrei, 374
Sheremetev (Russian count), 77
Shevyrev, Petr, 170–73
Shilder, Nikolai, 89
Shingarev, Dr. Andrei, 51–52, 63–64
Shipov, Dmitrii, 319, 325, 328
Shishkin, Ivan, 91
Shornikova, Ekaterina, 338
Shulgin, Vasilii, 303
Siberia, development of, 10–16
  See also Trans-Siberian Railway
Silver Age (era of artistic development),
  349–388
Silver Dove, The (Belyi), 381–82, 384
Šimić, Col. Božin, 426
Sipiagin, Dmitrii, 205, 208, 209, 210,
  287
Skobelev, Gen. Mikhail, 92
Sleeping Beauty (ballet), 276
Smoke (Turgenev), 41
Snow Maiden (opera), 96
Soldatenkov family, 86
Sollogub, Gen. Vladimir, 310
Solovev, Aleksandr:
  attempted assassination of Alexander II
  (1879), 160–61
Solovev, Vladimir, 30, 215, 355, 359, 360,
  361, 363, 367, 384, "free theocracy" of,
  351–52; "Sophia" concept, 351–52
Somov, Konstantin Andreiovich, 372
Sophia Alekseevna (regent of Russia), 363
Sophie (duchess of Hohenberg), 424–26
Stalin, Iosif, 274–75
Stanislavskii, Konstantin, 83, 84–85, 363,
  373, youth of, 98–99; and
  Nemirovich-Danchenko, 99–101
Starets (holy man), 383

Stark, Rear Adm. Oskar, 239
Starskii, Ivan, 180
Stasov, Vladimir, 91
Steed, W. T., 231
Stoessel, Gen. Anatolii, 245–47, 251–53,
  267
  court-martial of, 253
Stolypin, Natalia, 343
Stolypin, Petr, 311, 313, 322, 328, 386,
  392, 393, 395, 405; and the Second
  Duma, 328–48; political portrait of,
  340–43; and agrarian reform, 342–44;
  attempted assassination of, 343; and
  System of June Third, 343–44; and
  Western Zemstvo Bill, 346; assassination
  of, 347–48; effects of reforms, 397–98
Story, Douglas, 243
Stowe, Harriet Beecher, 39
Strike of 1903, 188–89
Struve, Petr, 314, 323, 328, 384
Sukhomlinov, Gen. Vladimir, 416, 418,
  432, 441–42
Superstition among the peasants, 60–62
Surikov, Vasilii, 91
Surorov, Aleksandr, 247, 442
Sviatopolk-Mirskii, Prince Petr, 286
  as Minister of Internal Affairs, 315–16,
  317
Syphilis:
  among the peasants, 53–55; among the
  urban poor, 107
System of June Third (1907), 343–46
Szápáry, Count, 428
Szögyényi, Count, 427

T
Taft, William Howard, 397
Tale of Tsar Saltan (opera), 347
Tatlin, Vladimir, 377
Taube, Baron, 413, 415, 416–17
"Temporary Regulations" (1882), 216
Tennyson, Alfred Lord, 402
Terrorism in the revolutionary movement,
  151–74
Theater. See Cultural life; Moscow Art
  Theater
They Did Not Expect Him (painting),
  92
"Thinking realists," 138–39
Third Duma, 340, 343–47

Thirty-Three Abominations
  (Zinoveva-Annibal), 379
Tiutcheva, Ekaterina, 202
Tkachëv, Peter, 151–54, 163
  revolutionary goals of, 152
"To the Younger Generation" (Mikhailov),
  40
Togo Heihachiro (vice-admiral of Japan),
  243, 244, 260, 263, 265–66; leads attack
  on Port Arthur, 238–40
Tolstoi, Count Dmitrii, 172, 194, 217
Tolstoi, Count Lev, 20, 30, 160, 215, 216,
  285, 356, 384, 386; open letter to
  Nicholas II, 284
Totleben, Count Eduard, 161
"Tower" (salon of Viacheslav Ivanov),
  368–70, 378
Trans-Siberian Railway:
  Alexander III and, 12; labor and
    building conditions, 12–13; increase in
    Siberian population, 14; and relations
    with Japan, 15; economic progress
    resulting from, 16–18; bisected at
    Lake Baikal, 240; strikes along (1905),
    295
Treaty of San Stefano (1878), 403
Treaty of Tilsit, 9
Trepov, Gen. Dmitrii, 208, 209, 301, 304,
  328
Trepov, Gen. Fedor:
  shot by Vera Zasulich, 158–59
Trepov, Sen. Vladimir, 346, 348
Tretiakov, Pavel Mikhailovich, 363; as
  artists' patron, 89; building of gallery,
  90–91; and the *Peredvizniki*, 91–92
Tretiakov Gallery, 90–91, 363
Tretiakova, Vera Mamontova, 90, 91,
  92–93
Trigoni, Mikhail, 167
Triple Alliance, 8, 402
Trotskii, Leon, 275, 300, 304, 310, 384,
  394, 444
Trubetskoi, Prince Sergei, 352
Trushchoba (flophouse), 124
Tryn-travizm, 379
Tsar's Bride (opera), 96
Tschaikovsky, Petr Ilyich, 276
Tschirschky, Heinrich von, 426
Tsederbaum, Iulii. *See* Martov, Iulii
Tsereteli, Iraklii, 332

Tsushima Straits, battle of, 265–68
Turgenev, Ivan, 101, 137, 215–16
  on peasant life, 39, 41; influence of
    novel *Fathers and Sons*, 138
Turgeneva, Asia, 367, 387
203 Meter Hill, 251

U
Ulianov, Aleksandr, 30, 170
  plot to assassinate Alexander III (1887),
    171–72; arrested and executed,
    172–74
Ulianov, Vladimir. *See* Lenin, Vladimir
Ulianova, Anna, 174, 204
Ulianova, Maria, 173, 174, 180, 181
Uncle Tom's Cabin (Stowe), 39
Union of Liberation, 315–16
Union of October 17th, 319
Union of the Russian People:
  as conservative force in Second Duma,
    330–32
Union of Struggle for the Liberation of
  Labor, 182
Urban poor:
  slum conditions, 122–23; and Kuprin's
    Iama, 122; portrait of the Khitrovna
    slum, 122–28
Urban proletariat:
  as potential "soldiers" in the Revolution
    104–105; tenement life, 106, 118;
    unsanitary conditions and disease,
    106; drunkenness among, 106–107;
    and prostitution, 107; and syphilis,
    107; rapid growth of cities, 108;
    peasants in labor force, 108–109;
    family life, 109; women in labor force,
    110, 111–12; child labor, 110–11;
    accidents in factories, 112–13; long
    workdays, 113–14; low wages, 114–16;
    fines on wages, 116; factory-owned
    barracks for workers, 116–17; food,
    118–20; inflation, 119; cooperatives,
    119–20; clothing, 120–21; illness
    among, 121; infant mortality, 121–22;
    and the urban poor, 122–28; layoffs at
    factories, 128–30; labor exchanges,
    129; literacy among, 130–31;
    nonpolitical reading matter, 131–32;
    development of worker intelligentsia,
    132–34

Urusov, Prince Sergei, 333
Ushkov family, 86
Uspenskii, Petr, 156, 158
Ustrugov (Bessarabian deputy governor), 221

V

Valenki (peasants' felt boots), 58
Van Gogh, Vincent, 375
Vasilchikov (Russian prince), 289, 290
Vasilev, Ivan, 290
Vasnetsov, Viktor, 95–96
Vekhi (Signposts), 384–85
Vereshchagin, Vasilii, 92
Verne, Jules, 131, 133
Verses about the Most Beautiful Lady (Blok), 362
Vesy (The Balance), 358, 371
Victoria (princess of Battenberg), 291
Victoria (queen of England), 28, 277
Village communes, 49–51
Vodka:
    in peasant life, 59; zapoi, 59–60, 106–107
Voice of Moscow, The, 334–35
Voitinskii, Vladimir, 338
Volkov, Vasilii, 81–82
Volskii, Nikolai, 181
Vorontsov-Dashov, Count Illarion, 193–94, 234
Vorovskii, Vatslav, 181
Vrubel, Mikhail, 97, 386
Vyborg Manifesto, 331
Vyrubova, Anna, 244, 390, 393
Vyshnegradskii, Ivan, 65, 69, 87; and Russia's industrial growth, 17–20; and famine of 1891, 23–24, 27

W

Warfare:
    army as source of Russia's power, 227–28; modern weaponry, 228–30; the Crimean War, 228–31; prohibitive costs of war, 230–31; Bliokh on, 230–31. See also Russo-Japanese War; World War I
Waterworks Redoubt, 249
Wendrich, Col. Alfred von, 26
Western Zemstvo Bill, 348
What Do the People Need? (Ogarev), 151

What Is To Be Done? (Chernyshevskii), 137, 139, 143–44, 180, 181
What Is To Be Done? (Lenin), 186, 189
"When Will That Day Come?" (Dobroliubov), 137
White slavery, 378
"White Terror," 169–70
Wilhelm II (kaiser of Germany), 7–8, 232, 233, 253, 386, 401, 406, 418–19, 427, 432; role in Russo-Japanese War, 241–42
Wings (Kuzmin), 379
Witheft, Adm. Wilhelm, 244–45
Witte, Sergei, 16, 26, 31, 33, 69, 87, 192–93, 199, 200–201, 209, 210, 218–19, 230, 232, 236, 237, 241, 261, 270, 283, 284–85, 304–305, 310, 313, 315, 322, 325, 330; and peasant prosperity, 65–67; on Pobedonostsev, 199; political philosophy of, 200–201; as defender of autocracy, 200–201; policy in the Far East, 233–35; and October Manifesto, 301–303; role in the First Duma, 317–21
Wolff, Theodor, 402
Women:
    in peasant life, 46–47; in the labor force, 110, 111–12; changing attitudes of, 140
"Women's corner," 46–47
Work ethic, 87
World War I:
    meeting between Poincaré and Nicholas II (1914), 398–99; prewar alliances, 399–401; and Second Hague Conference (1907), 401–403; and Balkan Wars, 403–15; bitterness between Russia and Germany, 415–19; Serbian politics and, 422–26; assassination of Archduke Franz Ferdinand, 424–26; Russia's mobilization for war, 424–26; first year of, 439–44; toll on peasants, 440
Wortman, Richard, 149
Writers. See Cultural life

Y

Yamagata, Field Marshal Marquis Aritomo, 268
"Yellow Shirts," 332

Z

Zapoi (drunken state), 59–60, 106–107
Zaporozhtsy Cossacks, The (painting),
    95
Zasulich (Russian general), 254
Zasulich, Vera, 154, 156, 163, 178, 180,
    184, 187, shoots General Trepov, 159;
    trial of, 159–60
Zavarzin, Gen. Pavel, 202, 203–204
Zemstva (district councils), 42, 55
    role after October Revolution, 313–16
Zerajić, Bogdan, 423
Zheliabov, Andrei, 164–65, 167, 169

Zhilinskii, Gen. Iakov, 436
Zimmermann, Alfred, 426
Zinoveva-Annibal, Lidia, 368, 379
Zinoviev, Gregorii, 201–202
Zolotoe Runo (The Golden Fleece),
    370–71
Zubatov, Sergei, 184, 286
    as chief of Okhrana, 206–16; converts
    revolutionaries, 207; the
    Zubatovshchina program, 208–11;
    organizes workers' march, 209; and
    Viacheslav von Plehve, 210–11;
    suicide of, 211